PowerPoint® 2003
Bible

PowerPoint® 2003
Bible

Faithe Wempen

WILEY

Wiley Publishing, Inc.

PowerPoint® 2003 Bible

Published by
Wiley Publishing, Inc.
10475 Crosspoint Boulevard
Indianapolis, IN 46256
www.wiley.com

Copyright © 2003 by Wiley Publishing, Inc., Indianapolis, Indiana

Library of Congress Control Number: 2003101883

ISBN: 0-7645-3972-8

Manufactured in the United States of America

10 9 8 7 6 5 4 3

1O/RS/QZ/QT

Published by Wiley Publishing, Indianapolis, Indiana
Published simultaneously in Canada

For general information on our other products and services or to obtain technical support, please contact our Customer Care Department within the U.S. at (800) 762-2974, outside the U.S. at (317) 572-3993 or fax (317) 572-4002.

About the Author

Faithe Wempen, M.A., is an A+ Certified hardware guru, Microsoft Office Specialist Master Instructor, and software consultant with over 70 computer books to her credit. When she is not writing, she teaches Microsoft Office classes in the Computer Technology department at Indiana University-Purdue University at Indianapolis (IUPUI), does private computer training and support consulting, and is the business manager of Sycamore Knoll Bed and Breakfast in Noblesville, Indiana (www.sycamoreknoll.com). Faithe is a contributing editor at CertCities.com, and a frequent contributor to CertCities.com, TechProGuild.com, and several magazines. She teaches online classes for the Hewlett-Packard Learning Center, and serves on the advisory board for the Computer Technician program at Training, Inc. in Indianapolis.

Credits

To Margaret, who makes it all possible.

Preface

Some books zoom through a software program so fast it makes your head spin. You'll come out dizzy, but basically able to cobble together some sort of result, even if it doesn't look quite right. This is not one of those books.

The *PowerPoint 2003 Bible* is probably the only PowerPoint book you will ever need. In fact, it might even be the only book on giving presentations you'll ever need. No, seriously! I mean it.

As you probably guessed by the heft of the book, this is not a quick-fix shortcut to PowerPoint expertise. Instead, it's a thoughtful, thorough educational tool that can be your personal trainer now and your reference text for years to come. That's because this book covers PowerPoint from "cradle to grave." No matter what your current expertise level with PowerPoint, this book brings you up to the level of the most experienced and talented PowerPoint users in your office. You might even be able to teach those old pros a thing or two!

But this book doesn't stop with PowerPoint procedures. Creating a good presentation is much more than just clicking a few dialog boxes and typing some text. It requires knowledge and planning—lots of it. That's why this book includes a whole chapter on planning a presentation, and another whole chapter on the practical issues involved in presenting one. You learn things like the following:

✦ How to select the best color schemes for selling and informing

✦ How to gauge the size of the audience and the meeting room when selecting fonts

✦ How to arrange the tables and chairs in the meeting room to encourage (or discourage) audience participation

✦ How to choose what to wear for a live presentation

✦ How to overcome stage fright

And lots more! When you finish this book, you will not only be able to build a presentation with PowerPoint, but you'll also be able to explain why you made the choices you did, and you'll deliver that presentation smoothly and with confidence.

If you are planning a presentation for remote delivery (for example, posting it on a Web site or setting up a kiosk at a trade show), you'll find lots of help for these situations too. In fact, an entire section of the book is devoted to various nontraditional presentation methods, such as live Internet or network delivery, trade show booths, and interactive presentation distribution on a disk or CD.

How This Book Is Organized

This book is organized into parts, which are groups of chapters that deal with a common general theme. Here's what you'll find:

✦ **Part I: The Basics.** Start here if you have never used Windows-based programs before or if you are completely new to PowerPoint. It'll show you how to manage files and how to navigate around the PowerPoint window.

✦ **Part II: Building Your Presentation.** In this part, you start building a robust, content-rich presentation by choosing a template, entering your text, and applying some basic text formatting. If you have created presentations in the past that have not turned out very well, make sure you read Chapter 5, which deals with planning.

✦ **Part III: Improving the Visual Impact.** This part teaches you all about formatting, graphics, backgrounds, and other features that can show off your presentation content to best advantage.

✦ **Part IV: Sound, Movement, and Video.** Here you learn how to include sounds, videos, animation effects, and transitions to jazz up a live presentation.

✦ **Part V: Presenting Speaker-Led Presentations.** If you expect to stand in front of a live audience giving the presentation, this part is for you. You learn about creating support materials and running a live show.

✦ **Part VI: Distributing Self-Serve Presentations.** If the presentation will take place without a live speaker, see this part to learn how to time the transitions between slides, prepare a presentation for Internet distribution, and set up a secure kiosk at a trade show.

✦ **Part VII: Cutting-Edge Solutions.** In this final part, you learn some noncomputer presentation skills that can help make your live shows more professional and compelling. You also find out about advanced features like team collaboration, macros, and add-ins.

✦ **Appendixes.** At the end of the book you'll find information about installing PowerPoint, checking out the new features in PowerPoint 2003, and making the most of the accompanying CD-ROM.

There is no better way to learn a new skill than by actually doing it, so each part concludes with a **Project Lab** chapter containing a real-world project you can complete to practice the skills in the part of the book you just completed.

What's on the companion CD and Web site

Wiley has provided so much add-on value to this book that we couldn't fit it all on the CD! With the purchase of this book, you not only get access to lots of bonus software programs and demos, you also get an entire eBook—free! In addition to all the goodies on the CD, the companion Web site offers access to even more material.

Please take a few minutes to explore the bonus material included on the CD:

✦ **Author-created materials:** The CD that accompanies this book contains all the data files you will need for the Project Lab chapters, but that's just the tip of the iceberg. You'll also find macros and add-ins, sound files, background images, templates, and an amazing assortment of other free and shareware goodies to enhance your PowerPoint presentations. Appendix C describes the CD contents in more detail.

✦ **Bonus software materials:** A plethora of programs (shareware, freeware, GNU software, trials, demos and evaluation software) that work with Office. A ReadMe file on the CD includes complete descriptions of each software item.

✦ *Office 2003 Super Bible* **eBook:** Wiley created this special eBook, consisting of over 500 pages of content about how Microsoft Office components work together and with other products. The content has been pulled from select chapters of the individual Office *Bible* titles. In addition, some original content has been created just for this *Super Bible*.

✦ **PDF version of this title:** If you prefer your text in electronic format, the CD offers a completely searchable, PDF version of the book you hold in your hands.

After you familiarize yourself with all that we have packed onto the CD, be sure to visit the companion Web site at: www.wiley.com/compbooks/officebibles2003/. Here's what you'll find on the Web site:

✦ Links to all the software that wouldn't fit onto the CD

✦ Links to all the software found on the CD

✦ Complete, detailed tables of contents for all the Wiley Office 2003 *Bibles: Access 2003 Bible, Excel 2003 Bible, FrontPage 2003, Office 2003 Bible, Outlook 2003 Bible, PowerPoint Bible,* and *Word 2003 Bible*

✦ Links to other Wiley *Office* titles

Special Features

Every chapter in this book opens with a quick look at what's in the chapter and closes with a summary. Along the way, you also find icons in the margins to draw your attention to specific topics and items of interest.

Here's what the icons mean:

These icons point you to chapters or other sources for more information on the topic under discussion.

Notes provide extra information about a topic, perhaps some technical tidbit or background explanation.

Expert Tips offer ideas for the advanced user who wants to get the most out of PowerPoint.

Cautions point out how to avoid the pitfalls that beginners commonly encounter.

Good luck with PowerPoint 2003! I hope you have as much fun reading this book as I had writing it. If you would like to let me know what you thought of the book, good or bad, you can e-mail me at faithe@wempen.com. I'd like to hear from you!

Acknowledgments

A big thank-you to my wonderful editorial team at Wiley, including Jim Minatel for making the contracting part go smoothly and Sara Shlaer for excellent project management work, often including juggling file replacements and input from all the editors. Thanks also to Kezia Ensley, one of the top veterans of computer book editing, for her copy editing skills.

Special recognition goes to Echo Swinford, this book's technical editor, for one of the best and most thorough tech edits that any of my 70+ books has had. It has been so great to have a real peer on the team to discuss content issues with.

And finally, thanks to the production, layout, and proofreading team at Wiley, who work so hard on these books and who so seldom receive the kudos they deserve.

Contents at a Glance

Contents

Part III: Improving the Visual Impact   305

Part V: Presenting Speaker-Led Presentations 553

The Basics

◆   ◆   ◆   ◆

◆   ◆   ◆   ◆

A First Look at PowerPoint

PowerPoint 2003 is a member of the Microsoft Office 2003 suite of programs. A *suite* is a group of programs designed by a single manufacturer to work well together. Like its siblings Word (the word processor), Excel (the spreadsheet), Outlook (the personal organizer and e-mail manager), and Access (the database), PowerPoint has a well-defined role. It creates materials for presentations.

A *presentation* is any kind of interaction between a speaker and audience, but it usually involves one or more of the following visual aids: 35mm slides, overhead transparencies, computer-based slides (either local or at a Web site or other network location), hard-copy handouts, and speaker notes. PowerPoint can create all of these types of visual aids, plus many other types that you learn about as we go along.

Because PowerPoint is so tightly integrated with the other Microsoft Office 2003 components, you can easily share information among them. For example, if you have created a graph in Excel, you can use that graph on a PowerPoint slide. It goes the other way, too. You can, for example, take the outline from your PowerPoint presentation and copy it into Word, where you can dress it up with Word's powerful document formatting commands. Virtually any piece of data in any Office program can be linked to any other Office program, so you never have to worry about your data being in the wrong format.

In this chapter you'll get a big-picture introduction to PowerPoint 2003, and then we'll fire up the program and poke around a bit to help you get familiar with the interface. You'll find out how to use the menus, dialog boxes, and toolbars, and how to get help and updates from Microsoft.

Who Uses PowerPoint and Why?

PowerPoint is a popular tool for people who give presentations as part of their jobs, and also for their support staff. With PowerPoint you can create visual aids that will help get the message across to an audience, whatever that message may be and whatever format it may be presented in.

The most traditional kind of presentation is a live speech presented at a podium. For live presentations, you can use PowerPoint to create overhead transparencies, 35mm slides, or computer-based shows that can help the lecturer emphasize key points.

Over the last several years, advances in technology have made it possible to give several other kinds of presentations, and PowerPoint has kept pace nicely. You can use PowerPoint to create kiosk shows, for example, which are self-running presentations that provide information in an unattended location. You have probably seen such presentations listing meeting times and rooms in hotel lobbies and giving sales presentations at trade show booths.

The Internet also has made several other presentation formats possible. You can use PowerPoint to create a show that you can present live over a network or the Internet, while each participant watches from his or her own computer. You can even store a self-running or interactive presentation on a Web site and make it available for the public to download and run on the PC.

When you start your first PowerPoint presentation, you may not be sure which delivery method you will use. However, it's best to decide the presentation format before you invest too much work in your materials, because the audience's needs are different for each medium. You learn a lot more about planning your presentation in Chapter 5.

Most people associate PowerPoint with sales presentations, but PowerPoint can be useful for people in many other lines of work as well. The following sections present a sampling of how real people just like you are using PowerPoint in their daily jobs.

Sales

More people use PowerPoint for selling goods and services than for any other reason. Armed with a laptop computer and a PowerPoint presentation, a salesperson can make a good impression on a client anywhere in the world. Figure 1-1 shows a slide from a sample sales presentation.

Why Buy from Value-Tech?

- Top-quality products
- ISO-9000 certified
- 24-hour on-site service
- Free technical consulting for 2 years
- Trade-in allowances for upgrades

Figure 1-1: PowerPoint offers unparalleled flexibility for presenting information to potential customers.

Sales possibilities with PowerPoint include the following:

✦ Live presentations in front of clients with the salesperson present and running the show. This is the traditional kind of sales pitch that most people are familiar with. See Chapter 25 to learn about controlling a live presentation.

✦ Self-running presentations that flip through the slides at specified intervals so that passersby can read them or ignore them as they wish. These types of presentations are great for grabbing people's attention at trade show booths. You create this kind of show in Chapter 28.

✦ User-interactive product information demos distributed on CD or disk that potential customers can view at their leisure on their own PCs. This method is very inexpensive, because you can create a single presentation and distribute it by mail to multiple customers. You learn how to create a user-interactive show in Chapter 29.

Marketing

The distinction between sales and marketing can be rather blurred at times, but marketing generally refers to the positioning of a product in the media rather than its presentation to a particular company or individual. Marketing representatives are often called upon to write advertising copy, generate camera-ready layouts for print advertisements, design marketing flyers and shelf displays, and produce other creative selling materials.

PowerPoint is not a drawing program per se, and it can't substitute for one except in a crude way. However, by combining the Office 2003 clip art collection with some well-chosen fonts and borders, a marketing person can come up with some very usable designs in PowerPoint. Figure 1-2 shows an example. You learn about clip art in Chapter 13.

Figure 1-2: PowerPoint can be used to generate camera-ready marketing materials, although they can't substitute for the tools used by professional advertising companies.

Status reports

You have already seen how PowerPoint can generate presentations that sell goods and services, but it's also a great tool for keeping your internal team informed. For example, perhaps the vice president wants to know how each of the regional sales offices performed over the last fiscal year. You can impress the heck out of the boss with a good-looking informational presentation that conveys all the pertinent details. You can even generate handouts to pass out to the meeting attendees. Figure 1-3 shows a slide from such an informational presentation. As you can see, it contains a graph. PowerPoint can generate its own graphs with its Microsoft Graph module, or you can import graphs from another program, such as Excel. You learn about graphing in PowerPoint in Chapter 16.

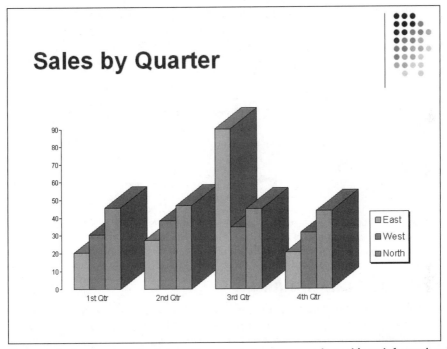

Figure 1-3: Convey your department's progress to your superiors with an informational presentation.

Human resources

Human resources personnel often find themselves giving presentations to new employees to explain the policies and benefits of the company. A well-designed, attractive presentation gives the new folks a positive impression of the company they have signed up with, starting them off on the right foot.

One of the most helpful features in PowerPoint for the human resources professional is the Organization Chart tool. With it, you can easily diagram the structure of the company and make changes whenever necessary with a few mouse clicks. Figure 1-4 shows an organization chart on a PowerPoint slide. You can also create a variety of other diagram types. Organization charts and other diagrams are covered in Chapter 17.

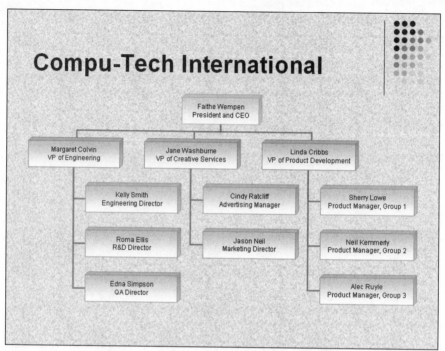

Figure 1-4: Microsoft's Organization Chart lets you easily create organizational diagrams from within PowerPoint.

Education and training

Most training courses include a lecture section in which the instructor outlines the general procedures and policies. This part of the training is usually followed up with individual, hands-on instruction. PowerPoint can't help much with the latter, but it can help make the lecture portion of the class go smoothly.

PowerPoint accepts images directly from a scanner, so you can scan in diagrams and drawings of the objects you are teaching the students to use. You can also use computer-generated images, such as screen captures, to teach people about software.

PowerPoint's interactive controls even let you create quizzes that each student can take on-screen to gauge his or her progress. Depending on the button the student clicks, you can set up the quiz to display a "Yes, You're Right!" or "Sorry, Try Again" slide. See Figure 1-5. I explain this procedure in more detail in Chapter 29.

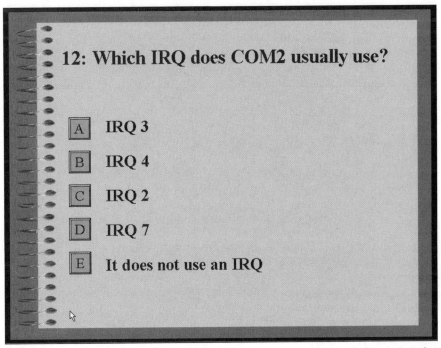

Figure 1-5: Test the student's knowledge with a user-interactive quiz in PowerPoint.

Hotel and restaurant management

Service organizations such as hotels and restaurants often need to inform their customers of various facts, but need to do so unobtrusively so that the information will not be obvious except to those looking for it. For example, a convention center hotel might provide a list of the meetings taking place in its meeting rooms, as shown in Figure 1-6, or a restaurant might show pictures of the day's specials on a video screen in the waiting area.

In such unattended situations, a self-running (kiosk) presentation works best. Typically the computer box and keyboard are hidden from the passersby, and the monitor displays the information. You learn more about such setups in Chapter 28.

Figure 1-6: Information kiosks can point attendees to the right meeting rooms from public lobbies.

Clubs and organizations

Many nonprofit clubs and organizations, such as churches and youth centers, operate much the same way as for-profit businesses and need sales, marketing, and informational materials. But clubs and organizations often have special needs too, such as the need to recognize volunteers for a job well done. PowerPoint provides a Certificate template that's ideal for this purpose. Figure 1-7 shows a certificate generated in PowerPoint. This certificate was generated by an AutoContent Wizard template; you learn how to create new presentations with the AutoContent Wizard in Chapter 6.

Even more ideas

As you learn in Chapter 7, you can create presentations in PowerPoint based on a wide variety of pre-designed templates. Many of these templates include not only design schemes but also sample content structures, into which you can plug your own information for a good-looking, quickly generated result.

With some of these templates, you can create all of the following documents:

✦ Business plans

✦ Company handbooks

✦ Web pages

✦ Employee orientation briefings

✦ Financial overviews

✦ Speaker introductions

✦ Marketing plans

✦ Team motivational sessions

✦ Technical reports

✦ Project post-mortem evaluations

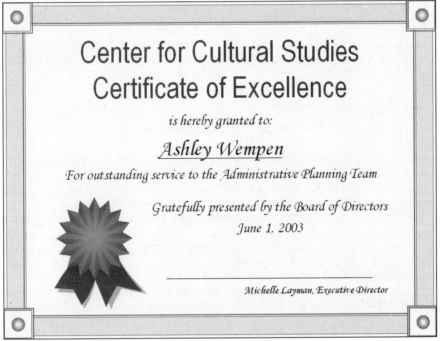

Figure 1-7: With PowerPoint, you can easily create certificates and awards.

Learning Your Way around PowerPoint

Now that you have seen some of the potential uses for PowerPoint, let's get started using the program. PowerPoint is one of the easiest and most powerful presentation programs available. You can knock out a passable presentation in a shockingly short time by skimming through the chapters in Part II of the book, or you can spend some time with PowerPoint's advanced features to make a complex presentation that looks, reads, and works exactly the way you want.

The remainder of this chapter is primarily for those who have not had a lot of experience with other Windows applications. People who know all about menus, dialog boxes, and toolbars may find this material boring. If that description fits you, by all means feel free to skip it. But if you are still a little shaky on using Windows and applications in general, come on in!

Starting PowerPoint

You can start PowerPoint just like any other program in Windows: from the Start menu. Follow these steps:

1. Click the Start button.

2. Click All Programs. A submenu appears. Figure 1-8 shows Windows XP; in earlier Windows versions the menu is called Programs rather than All Programs.

3. Point to Microsoft Office.

4. Click Microsoft PowerPoint. The program starts.

If you are using Windows XP, and you have opened PowerPoint several times before, a shortcut to it might appear on the list directly above the Start button, as pointed out in Figure 1-8. Shortcuts to frequently used applications appear here. If you use other applications more frequently than PowerPoint, PowerPoint may scroll off this list and you therefore have to access it via the All Programs menu.

Expert Tip   If you don't want to worry about PowerPoint scrolling off the list of the most frequently used programs on the Windows XP Start menu, drag its shortcut from the frequently used programs (lower left part of the Start menu) to the top-left area of the Start menu, directly underneath Internet and E-mail. This keeps the shortcut permanently on the top level of the Start menu, as shown in Figure 1-9.

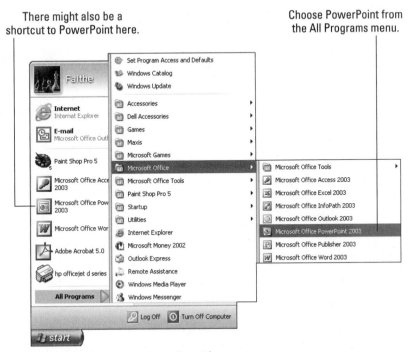

There might also be a shortcut to PowerPoint here.

Choose PowerPoint from the All Programs menu.

Figure 1-8: Starting PowerPoint from the Start menu.

Understanding the screen elements

PowerPoint is a fairly typical Windows-based program in many ways. It contains the same basic elements that you expect to see: a title bar, a menu bar, window controls, and so on. And like all Office 2003 applications, it has a task pane that provides shortcuts for common activities. Figure 1-10 points out these generic controls.

✦ **Title bar:** Identifies the program running. If the window is not maximized, you can move the window by dragging the title bar.

✦ **Menu bar:** Provides drop-down menus containing commands.

✦ **Toolbars:** Provide shortcuts for commonly used commands and features.

✦ **Minimize button:** Shrinks the application window to a bar on the taskbar; you click its button on the taskbar to reopen it.

✦ **Maximize/Restore button:** If the window is maximized (full screen), changes it to windowed (not full screen). If the window is not maximized, clicking here maximizes it.

✦ **Close button:** Closes the application. You may be prompted to save your changes, if you made any.

✦ **Task pane:** Contains shortcuts for activities. May contain different shortcuts depending on the context. In Figure 1-10, it shows shortcuts for starting new presentations and opening existing ones. You can close the task pane at any time to give yourself more room; click its Close (X) button.

✦ **Work area:** Where the PowerPoint slide(s) that you are working on appear.

This list of shortcuts changes based on usage.

Shortcuts above this line are permanent.

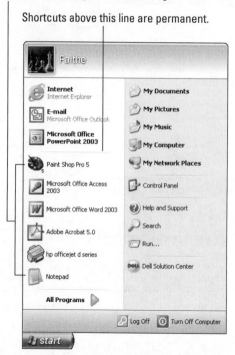

Figure 1-9: You can pin a shortcut to the top of the Start menu to keep it close at hand.

Note   I don't dwell on the Windows controls in detail because this isn't a Windows book, but if you're interested in learning more about Windows-based programs in general, pick up *Windows XP For Dummies* or *The Windows XP Bible*, also published by Wiley.

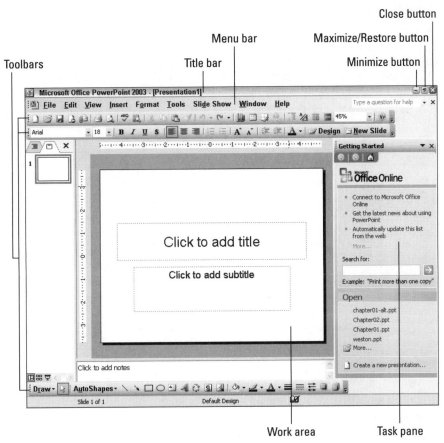

Figure 1-10: The PowerPoint window has all the usual Office 2003 features.

The PowerPoint screen starts out in Normal view, which contains a Slides/Outline list on the left, a Current Slide pane in the middle, and a Notes pane at the bottom. The Slides/Outline list has two tabs; Slides shows miniature versions of the slides in the presentation, whereas Outline shows the text of the slides in an outline. You'll work with these more in Chapter 2, which is devoted entirely to switching among the available views.

The slide and the outline are tied together; you can type text on one, and it appears on the other. To test this function, click the slide where it says *Click to add title* and type your name. Your name appears both on the big slide in the center and in the little slide on the Slides list at the left, as shown in Figure 1-11. If you click the Outline tab, you can see your name on the text outline as well.

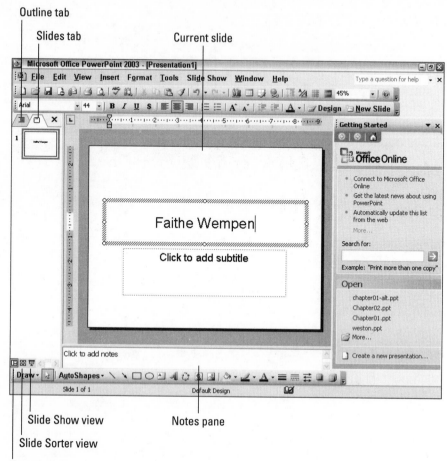

Outline tab

Slides tab

Current slide

Slide Show view

Notes pane

Slide Sorter view

Normal view

Figure 1-11: PowerPoint's Normal view lets you see the slide, the outline, and the notes all at once.

The view buttons in the bottom-left corner of the screen switch among the available views. The default one, shown in Figure 1-11, is Normal, but there are also buttons for Slide Sorter and Slide Show. You learn more about changing views in Chapter 2.

All the panes in the PowerPoint window are resizable so you can control the amount of space that each one takes up on-screen. Just position the mouse pointer on the line between two areas and drag.

Working with menus

Menus are the primary means of selecting commands in PowerPoint. To open a menu, click its name on the menu bar, and then click the command you want to select. In this book, such actions are written in a kind of shorthand. For example, if you are supposed to open the File menu and choose the Save command, it appears in this book like this: Select File ⇨ Save.

Microsoft Office 2003 applications like PowerPoint have the usual drop-down menus that you expect with Windows-based programs, but with a little twist. When you first open a menu, not all the commands appear — only the most commonly used ones. If you click the down arrow at the bottom of the menu, the rest of the commands come into view. Figures 1-12 and 1-13 show the Format menu, for example, when it is first opened and after it has been fully extended.

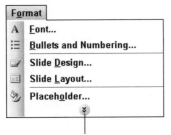

Click here to see the rest of the command

Figure 1-12: When you first open a menu, only certain commands appear; more pop up in a few seconds or when you click the button.

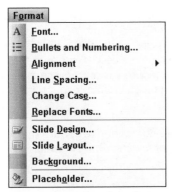

Figure 1-13: The secondary commands appear with a darker bar to their left.

This two-level menu system seems like a great idea, but some people may find it annoying. To turn it off, follow these steps:

1. Select Tools ➪ Customize. The Customize dialog box appears.

2. Click the Options tab.

3. In the Personalized Menus and Toolbars section, mark the Always Show Full Menus check box. See Figure 1-14.

4. Click OK.

Figure 1-14: You can turn off the two-level menu system by selecting the Always Show Full Menus check box.

Expert Tip   The menus always show recently used commands first, but if you are just starting out using PowerPoint, you don't really have any recently used commands yet. Therefore, the program shows a default set of common commands. As you use PowerPoint more, the recently used commands begin to be more meaningful. To reset the calculation of which commands qualify as recent, select Tools ➪ Customize, click the Options tab, and then click the Reset Menu and Toolbar Usage Data button (shown in Figure 1-14). You can also customize each menu to show different commands or delete commands entirely from a menu, covered in Chapter 35.

The figures in the rest of this book always show the full menus to ensure that your screen will look the same as the ones in the book no matter which commands you have recently used.

Some menus have submenus that appear when you point to a certain command. For example, as shown in Figure 1-15, the Alignment command has a submenu.

Some commands have keyboard combinations listed next to them, such as Ctrl+L next to Align Left in Figure 1-15. These are *shortcut keys*. You can use the shortcut key combinations on the keyboard instead of opening the menu and choosing the command. Over time, you can memorize certain shortcuts and might find that it is easier to use them.

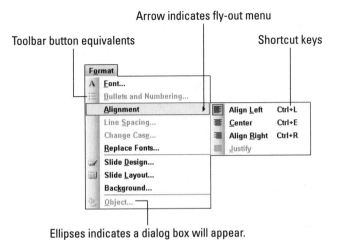

Figure 1-15: This menu has commands with submenus, with shortcut keys, and with ellipses.

Some commands have ellipses (three dots) after them. Such commands open dialog boxes, which are windows that request more information before executing a command. You learn more about dialog boxes in the next section.

Some commands have icons to their left. This points out that there is a toolbar button equivalent for that command. You may not always see the button on one of the displayed toolbars, however, because there are over a dozen toolbars, and some appear only when you are performing certain tasks. You learn more about toolbars later in this chapter.

Sometimes a command appears in gray lettering rather than black; that's called *grayed out*, and it means the command is unavailable at the moment. For example, the Copy command on the Edit menu is grayed out unless you have selected something to copy. (There aren't any grayed-out commands in Figure 1-15.)

Working with dialog boxes

Dialog boxes are PowerPoint's (and Windows') way of prompting you for more information. When you issue a command that can have many possible variations, a dialog box appears so you can specify the particulars.

The Print dialog box (File ⇨ Print) is an excellent example of a dialog box because it has so many kinds of controls. Here are some of the controls you see on the Print dialog box shown in Figure 1-16:

✦ **Check box:** These are individual on/off switches for particular features. Click to toggle them on or off.

✦ **Option buttons:** Each section of the dialog box can have only one option button chosen at once. When you select one, the previously selected one becomes deselected, like on a car radio. Click the one you want.

✦ **Text box:** Click in a text box to place an insertion point (a vertical line) there, and then type.

✦ **Increment buttons:** Placed next to a text box, these buttons allow you to increment the number in the box up or down by one digit per click.

✦ **Drop-down list:** Click the down arrow next to one of these to open the list, and then click your selection from the menu that appears.

✦ **Command button:** Click one of these big rectangular buttons to jump to a different dialog box. OK and Cancel are also command buttons; OK accepts your changes and Cancel rejects them.

When you are finished looking at this dialog box, click Cancel to close it.

You may also sometimes see tabs at the top of a dialog box; this occurs when the dialog box has more controls than will fit on one screen. To move to a tabbed page, click the tab.

Dialog boxes that open or save files have some special controls and icons all their own, but you learn about those in more detail in Chapter 3 when you learn to open and save your files.

Working with toolbars

Toolbars are rows of icons (pictures) that represent common commands. You can click a toolbar button instead of opening a menu and clicking a command. They're purely a convenience; you don't have to use the toolbar buttons if you prefer the menus. Throughout this book, whenever there is a toolbar button equivalent for a command, I try to mention it. To find out what a toolbar button does, point the mouse at it. A ScreenTip pops up explaining it.

Increment button

Text box   Command button

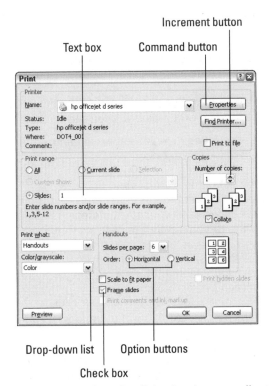

Drop-down list   Option buttons

Check box

Figure 1-16: The Print dialog box is an excellent study in dialog box controls.

All of the toolbar buttons may look more or less equal, but there are several types:

✦ Some buttons are toggle switches that turn on/off a feature. Examples include the Bold and Italic buttons.

✦ Some buttons open drop-down lists that give you a menu of selections, such as the Font and Font Size drop-down lists.

✦ Some buttons open dialog boxes. The Open button does this, for example.

✦ Some buttons perform an action right away, without waiting for a dialog box or confirmation. The New button, for example, starts a new, blank presentation.

✦ Some buttons are actually a set of options, and when you select one, another becomes deselected. Examples are the Left, Centered, and Right alignment buttons.

✦ Some buttons can be clicked normally, but they also have a down arrow that opens a drop-down list for additional controls. A good example is the Undo button. Click it once to undo the last action or open its drop-down list for a list of previous actions to undo.

✦ Some buttons perform a function every time you click them and the effect is cumulative. For example, every time you click the Increase Font Size button, the selected text grows by one size.

I won't go into every single button on these two default toolbars right now, but you learn what most of them are as you go along in this book.

PowerPoint displays three toolbars by default in Normal view: Standard, Formatting, and Drawing. The Standard toolbar contains commands that work with files (save, open, and print) and insert elements in your presentation (slides, graphs, and hyperlinks). The Formatting toolbar applies formatting (font changes, bold, underline, and so on.) The Drawing toolbar, at the bottom of the screen, contains commands that draw and format lines, shapes, and other artwork. You can display or hide toolbars by right-clicking any toolbar to get a pop-up menu that lists them, and then just click a toolbar to toggle it on or off.

Depending on how your copy of PowerPoint is set up, the Standard and Formatting toolbars might be displayed on the same row. This saves space on-screen, but not all the buttons can fit except in the highest display resolutions. The Standard toolbar appears at the left, partially truncated, and the Formatting toolbar appears next to it (to the right), as shown in Figure 1-17. You can change the ratio by dragging the handle (the four vertical dots at the left end) of the Formatting toolbar to the right or left.

A toolbar's "handle" is at its left end.   Drag to the left or right to adjust spacing.

Figure 1-17: When the toolbars share a row, both are truncated, with some buttons showing and some hidden.

If you need to use one of the undisplayed buttons on a toolbar, you must click the down arrow button at the right end of the toolbar to open a list of the remaining buttons, as shown in Figure 1-18. As with the personalized menu system, the application remembers your preferences, and if you use one of the undisplayed buttons, it becomes a displayed one, and something else that you haven't used recently becomes undisplayed.

Click here to open the list

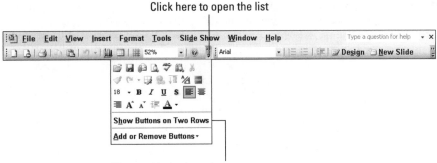

Choose this to place the menus on separate rows

Figure 1-18: To access a toolbar button that does not appear due to screen space limitations, click the down arrow button at the right end of a toolbar.

Many people find this scrunching up of the toolbars inconvenient and prefer to show the toolbars on separate rows. To do so, simply choose the Show Buttons on Two Rows command from Figure 1-18. You can also change this setting from the Customize dialog box (Tools ⇨ Customize).

All the rest of the figures in this book show the toolbars on separate rows so you can more clearly see the buttons that I am pointing out to you along the way.

Exiting PowerPoint

When you are ready to leave PowerPoint, select File ⇨ Exit or click the Close (X) button in the top-right corner of the PowerPoint window. If you have any unsaved work, PowerPoint asks if you want to save your changes. Because you have just been playing around in this chapter, you probably do not have anything to save yet. (If you do have something to save, see Chapter 3 to learn more about saving.) Otherwise, click No to decline to save your changes, and you're outta there.

Getting Help

The PowerPoint Help system is like a huge instruction book in electronic format. You can look up almost any PowerPoint task you can imagine and get step-by-step instructions for performing it.

Expert Tip   Much of the Office 2003 Help system relies on an Internet connection. By default, Office 2003 applications will automatically connect to Microsoft's servers online to gather additional Help information (as well as other materials such as extra clip art and templates) whenever an Internet connection is available. If you don't want this to occur, choose Help ➪ Privacy Options, and click the Online Content category. Then choose the Never option button to prevent Office 2003 applications from going online to get content for any reason. If you turn off the capability to gather online content, however, your options in every area will be greatly restricted. For example, very little clip art will be available, very few help topics, and so on.

Asking a question

There are many ways to get help in PowerPoint. One of the easiest is to type your question in the Ask a Question area in the top-right corner of the screen. This searches the Help system (including the online portion of it if you are connected to the Internet) and produces a list of potential answers, as shown in Figure 1-19.

Type your question here...

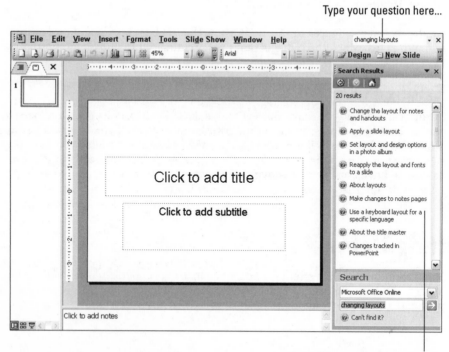

... and possible matches appear here.

Figure 1-19: Type your question in the Ask a Question box, and then click the article that best matches your query.

When you click on the article title you want, the article appears in a window, with the PowerPoint window scrunched up at the left. See Figure 1-20. You can resize these panes as needed to balance your reading of the article with your activity in PowerPoint; this enables you to read step-by-step instructions in a Help article and follow them in PowerPoint at the same time.

Figure 1-20: Read a Help article on-screen; then close it by clicking the X in the top-right corner of the Help window when you are finished with it.

Using the Office Assistant

If you have used earlier versions of Office applications, you might have encountered the Office Assistant, a cartoon character that gives a friendly face to the Help system. It is turned off by default in all Office 2003 applications, but you can use it by choosing Help ➪ Show the Office Assistant. You can then click on it to open a conversation bubble, and enter your question there. This is just the same as working with the Ask a Question feature, but some people might find it more fun. Figure 1-21 shows the Office Assistant. To turn it off again, choose Help ➪ Hide the Office Assistant, or right-click it and choose Hide.

Expert Tip   You can change the cartoon character for the Office Assistant. Right-click the current character and select Choose an Assistant. An Office Assistant dialog box appears, in which you can choose one of eight characters. You can also fine-tune the way the Office Assistant works, including how active it is in suggesting hints, whether it remembers which hints it has already given you once, and so on.

Figure 1-21: The Office Assistant provides a cartoon interface to the Ask a Question feature.

Using the PowerPoint Help pane

More experienced users may prefer to delve into the full Help system in PowerPoint; it's like the difference between having someone else do research in a library for you and actually slogging through the stacks yourself. Some people love slogging through the stacks, and find more information there that they wouldn't have thought to ask an assistant to look for.

To get into the main Help system, choose Help ➪ Microsoft PowerPoint Help, or press F1, or click the Microsoft PowerPoint Help button on the Standard toolbar. The Microsoft PowerPoint Help task pane appears, as shown in Figure 1-22.

From the Help task pane, you can do the following:

✦ Click in the Search box and type a word or phrase to search for, just like with the Ask a Question box or the Office Assistant.

✦ Click the Table of Contents hyperlink to open a full list of topics you can browse, described in the following section.

✦ Click some of the links in the Office Online section to access help content on the Web. The offerings here change periodically.

Browsing Help contents

The Table of Contents section provides a series of books on various broad subjects, such as Startup and Settings, Creating Presentations, Printing, and so on. To enter this system, click the Table of Contents hyperlink in the Help task pane (Figure 1-22). You can browse through these books, narrowing down your interest until you arrive at a particular set of steps or explanation. In Figure 1-23, the items with a question mark next to them are articles, whereas the ones that look like books are topic sections.

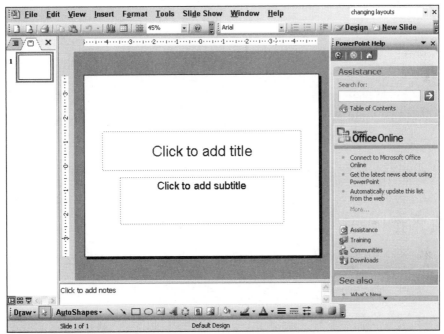

Figure 1-22: The Microsoft PowerPoint Help task pane provides access to the full range of Help features in PowerPoint.

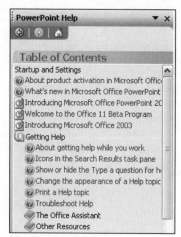

Figure 1-23: The Microsoft PowerPoint Help task pane provides access to the full range of Help features in PowerPoint.

Reading a Help article

No matter which method you use to arrive at a Help article, eventually you will get to the article itself in a separate window, as shown in Figure 1-24. From here you can:

✦ Click the Tile button to toggle between displaying the article on top of the PowerPoint window and displaying the two windows tiled side-by-side.

✦ Click the Print button to print the article.

✦ Click the arrow buttons to move forward and back, just like in a Web browser. Back will take you back to previous Help articles you have viewed during this session.

✦ In the article, click a blue triangle arrow to expand or collapse parts of the article (if it is a long article).

✦ Click a blue term to read its definition.

When you are finished with the Help article window, you can close it, minimize it, or leave it open.

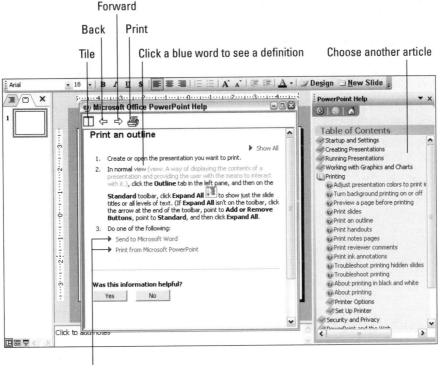

Figure 1-24: Read a Help article in its own Help window.

Getting help from Office Online

Office Online, shown in Figure 1-25, is a Web site that contains lots of helpful information for Office 2003 users. You can access it from the Help task pane by clicking one of the links there under the Office Online heading. You can also get to it from the Help menu (Help ➪ Office Online). You must be connected to the Internet to use this feature.

Some of the sections available at Office Online include:

✦ **Assistance:** Get answers to your questions here that you couldn't find help with in the regular Help system.

✦ **Training:** Get tutorials and explanations here that will make you more proficient with Office applications.

✦ **Templates:** Download additional templates here, not only for PowerPoint, but for other Office applications as well. (You can also get to these through PowerPoint's list of design templates, as you will see in Chapter 12.)

✦ **Clip Art and Media:** Access online clip art collections here. (You can also get to these same clips from the Clip Organizer in PowerPoint, as you will see in Chapter 14.)

✦ **Office Update:** Download any available patches and updates here.

✦ **Office Marketplace:** Browse third-party applications and add-ins that can enhance the features of the core Office products.

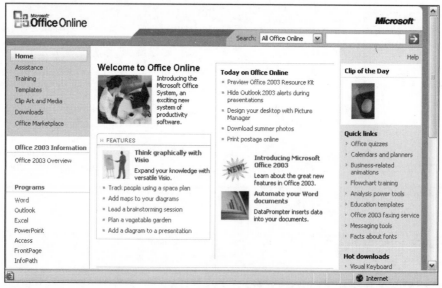

Figure 1-25: Office Online provides additional help with PowerPoint and other Office 2003 applications.

Updating PowerPoint and other Office 2003 applications

As Office 2003 is put to real-world use, problems will undoubtedly be identified with it, and Microsoft will release updates and patches that will correct those problems. You can get these from the Office Online Web site, described in the preceding section. One quick way to get there is to choose Help ➪ Check for Updates. From there, if any updates are available, follow the prompts to download and install them.

Contacting Microsoft

If you run into a problem or issue that none of the available support materials addresses, you might need to contact Microsoft directly. For a list of contact e-mail, phone, and mailing address information, from within PowerPoint choose Help ⇨ Contact Us.

Repairing PowerPoint

If PowerPoint starts having technical problems, such as locking up, terminating unexpectedly, or corrupting your data files, it may need to be repaired.

One way to repair PowerPoint is to uninstall and reinstall it, but in many cases you can shortcut this process by using the Detect and Repair feature. If you can open PowerPoint, choose Help ⇨ Detect and Repair and then follow the prompts.

If you cannot open PowerPoint because of a serious error in the application, try using the Repair feature in the Office 2003 Setup application. To do so, follow these steps:

1. From the Control Panel in Windows, open Add/Remove Programs.
2. Find the Microsoft Office application on the list, and click the Change button for it. This opens the Office Setup maintenance program. See Figure 1-26.
3. Choose Reinstall or Repair and click Next. Then follow the prompts to allow the Setup program to repair your installation.

 Expert Tip If PowerPoint won't open due to a bad add-in, try renaming all files with a .ppa extension.

Activating PowerPoint

All Office 2003 products must be activated after a certain number of days or a certain number of uses. This is a simple matter if you have an Internet connection. Every time you start an Office 2003 application, a reminder to activate appears. Follow the prompts to activate it. You do not have to give any personal information.

If you decline to activate right away, you can do it at any future time by choosing Help ⇨ Activate.

So what is this activation, and why is it required? Activation locks your copy of Office (or PowerPoint, if you bought it separately) to the hardware configuration in your computer, so that it can't be installed on any other PC. It's an anti-copying measure that Microsoft implemented in Office XP and carried over to Office 2003.

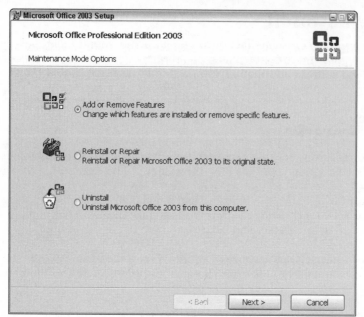

Figure 1-26: You can repair Office from its Setup program if files get corrupted that prevent an Office application from working correctly.

The activation utility surveys a sampling of your PC's hardware (around a dozen different components), and based on their models, serial numbers, and so on, it comes up with a number. Then it combines that number mathematically with the 24-digit installation key code you entered when you installed the software, to produce a unique number that represents that particular copy of Office combined with that particular PC. It then sends that number off to an activation database at Microsoft, along with the original installation key code.

So how does this prevent illegal software copying? Two ways. One is that the installation key code is locked to that hardware ID, so that if you install the same copy on a different PC, it can't be activated there. The other is that it prevents you from radically changing the hardware in the PC without contacting Microsoft for reactivation authorization. For example, you could not take the hard disk out of the PC and put it in another PC without reactivating Office.

It is this second point that has been an issue of conflict between Microsoft and users, because many users like to tinker with their hardware and they do not want to have to contact Microsoft every time they make hardware changes. According to Microsoft documentation, the change of one or two pieces of hardware will not trigger the need for reactivation, but your experience may differ.

There are two situations in which you might not have to activate:

✦ When you buy a new PC with Office pre-installed. Office will already have been activated, so you do not have to go through the process.

✦ If you work for a company that has a licensing agreement with Microsoft for a certain number of copies. You might have a version of Office that does not contain the activation requirement.

When you go through the activation process, you are also asked whether you want to register your copy of the software. Activation by itself sends no identifying information about you or your PC to Microsoft; if you want to be on the Microsoft mailing list for update information, you must go through the additional process of registration.

Privacy settings

In Office 2003 applications, you can elect to be a part of Microsoft's Customer Experience Improvement Program. This gives Microsoft permission to collect anonymous information about your usage habits in Office applications, so they can use the information to develop new features in the future. It does not collect any data that you type—it only pays attention to the features you use. If you want to participate in this, choose Help ⇨ Customer Feedback Options, click the Customer Feedback Options category and click the Yes button. See Figure 1-27. If you ever change your mind, come back to this same spot and choose No instead.

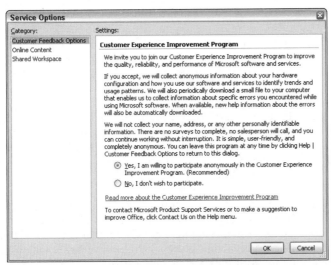

Figure 1-27: You can help Microsoft by allowing the company to gather anonymous data about your usage habits.

Summary

This chapter provided an introduction to PowerPoint for new or inexperienced users of Office applications. You learned how to work with menus and dialog boxes, how to start and exit PowerPoint, how to find your way around the PowerPoint window, and how to get help. In the next chapter, you'll learn how to work with PowerPoint's many viewing options.

✦   ✦   ✦

Controlling the On-Screen Display

It's all in your point of view, as the old saying goes, and
that's true when working in PowerPoint as well. As you create your presentation, there will be times when different on-
screen viewing options will be appropriate. Need to align
something precisely? Turn on the ruler. Need to see a big-
picture view of the presentation? Switch to Slide Sorter view.
Working with the fine details of an item? Zoom in on it. This
chapter explains the many viewing options that users have in
PowerPoint while building and fine-tuning a presentation.

Changing the View

A *view* is a way of displaying your presentation on-screen.
PowerPoint comes with several views because at different
times during the creation process, it is helpful to look at the
presentation in different ways. For example, when you are
adding a graphic to a slide, you want to be able to work
closely with that slide, but when you need to rearrange the
slide order, you need to see the presentation as a whole.

PowerPoint offers the following views:

   ◆ *Normal:* A combination of several resizable panes, so
     you can see the presentation in multiple ways at once.
     Normal is the default view.

   ◆ *Slide Sorter:* A light-table-type overhead view of all the
     slides in your presentation, laid out in rows, suitable for
     big-picture rearranging.

✦ *Slide Show:* The view you use to show the presentation on-screen. Each slide fills the entire screen in its turn.

✦ *Notes Page:* A view with the slide at the top of the page and a text box below it for typed notes. (You can print these notes pages to use during your speech.)

In some earlier versions of PowerPoint, there were also Outline and Slide views, but these have been rolled into the Normal view in PowerPoint 2003.

There are two ways to change a view: open the View menu and select one there, or click one of the view buttons in the bottom-left corner of the screen. See Figure 2-1.

All the views are available in both places except Notes Page; it can be accessed only from the View menu.

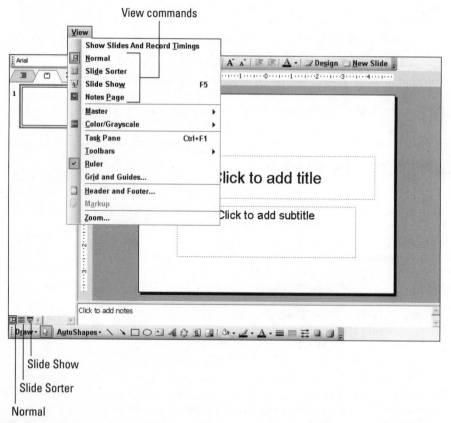

Figure 2-1: You can change the view using the view buttons or the View menu.

Normal view

Normal view, shown in Figure 2-2, is a very flexible view that contains a little of everything. In the center is the active slide, below it is a Notes pane, and to its left is a dual-use pane with two tabs: Outline and Slides. When the Outline tab is selected, the text from the slides appears in an outline form. When Slides is selected, thumbnail images of all the slides appear (somewhat like Slide Sorter view, which you will see later in this chapter).

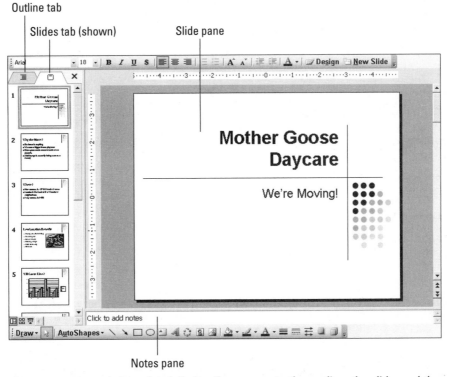

Figure 2-2: Normal view, the default, offers access to the outline, the slide, and the notes all at once.

Each of the panes in Normal view has its own scroll bar, so you can move around in the outline, the slide, and the notes independently of the other panes. You can resize the panes by dragging the dividers between the panes. For example, to give the notes area more room, point the mouse pointer at the divider line between it and the slide area so that the mouse pointer becomes a double-headed arrow, and then hold down the left mouse button as you drag the line up to a new spot. Figure 2-3 also shows Normal view, but with a very different allocation of the space between the panes. (It also shows the Outline tab, rather than the Slides tab as in Figure 2-2.)

The Slides/Outline pane is useful because it lets you jump quickly to a specific slide by clicking on it. For example, in Figure 2-2 you can click on any of the slide thumbnails on the Slides tab to display it in the Slide pane. Or in Figure 2-3 you can click on some text anywhere in the outline to jump to the slide containing that text.

Outline tab (shown)   Slide pane

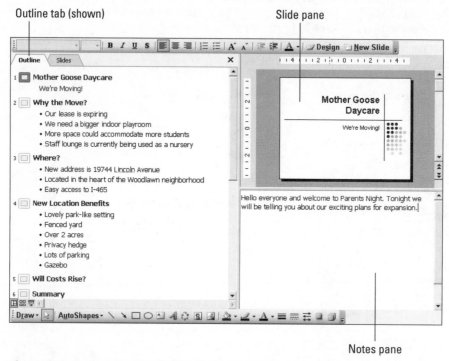

Notes pane

Figure 2-3: By dragging the dividers between the panes in Normal view, you can create a very different work environment for preparing your presentation.

Expert Tip   When working with an outline, you might want to display the Outlining toolbar. It does not automatically appear, but you can display it by right-clicking one of the other toolbars and choosing Outlining. It runs along the left edge of the screen, and includes tools you can use to promote, demote, and move items in your outline. It is covered in more detail in Chapter 8.

The Slides/Outline pane can also be turned off completely, by clicking the X button in its top-right corner. This gives maximum room to the Slides pane, as shown in Figure 2-4. When you turn it off, the Notes pane disappears too; they cannot be turned on/off separately. To get the extra panes back, choose View ➪ Normal (Restore Panes).

Outline/Slide pane is gone

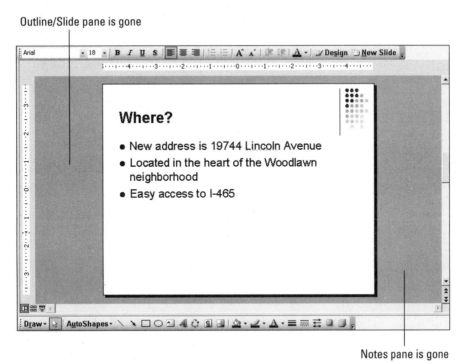

Notes pane is gone

Figure 2-4: The Slides/Outline pane and Notes pane can be turned off entirely if desired.

Slide Sorter view

If you have ever worked with 35mm slides, you know that it can be helpful to lay the slides out on a big table and plan the order in which to show them. You rearrange them, moving this one here, that one there, until the order is perfect. You might even start a pile of backups that you will not show in the main presentation, but will hold back in case someone asks a pertinent question. That's exactly what you can do with Slide Sorter view, shown in Figure 2-5. It lays out the slides in miniature, so you can see the big picture. You can drag the slides around and place them in the perfect order. Chapter 6 covers rearranging slides. You can also return to Normal view to work on a slide by double-clicking the slide.

Slide Show view

When it's time to rehearse the presentation, nothing shows you the finished product quite as clearly as Slide Show view does. In Slide Show view, the slide fills the entire screen (see Figure 2-6). You can move from slide to slide by pressing the PageUp or Page Down keys, or by using one of the other movement methods available. (You learn about these in Chapter 25.)

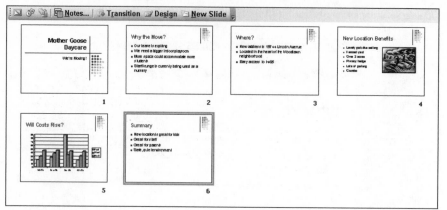

Figure 2-5: Use Slide Sorter view for a birds-eye view of the presentation.

You can right-click in Slide Show view to display a menu that enables you to control the show without leaving it. To leave the slide show, choose End Show from the menu or just press Esc.

Expert Tip   When entering Slide Show view, the method you use determines which slide you start on. If you use the Slide Show View button in the bottom-left corner of the screen, the presentation will start with whatever slide you have selected. If you use the View ⇨ Slide Show or Slide Show ⇨ View Show command, or press F5, it will start at the beginning.

Notes Page view

When you give a presentation, your props usually include more than just your brain and your slides. You typically have all kinds of notes and backup material for each slide—figures on last quarter's sales, sources to cite if someone questions your data, and so on. In the old days of framed overhead transparencies, people used to attach sticky notes to the slide frames for this purpose, and hope that nobody asked any questions that required diving into the four-inch-thick stack of statistics they brought.

Today, you can type your notes and supporting facts directly in PowerPoint. As you saw earlier, you can type them directly into the Notes pane below the slide in Normal view. However, if you have a lot of notes to type, you might find it easier to work with Notes Page view instead.

Notes Page view is accessible only from the View menu. In Notes Page view, you see a single slide with a text area, called the *notes pane*, below it for your notes. See Figure 2-7. You can refer to these notes as you give an on-screen presentation, or you can print notes pages to stack neatly on the lectern next to you during the big event.

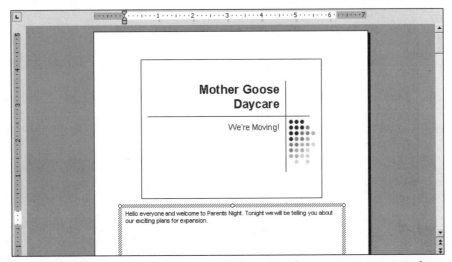

Figure 2-6: Slide Show view lets you practice the presentation in real life.

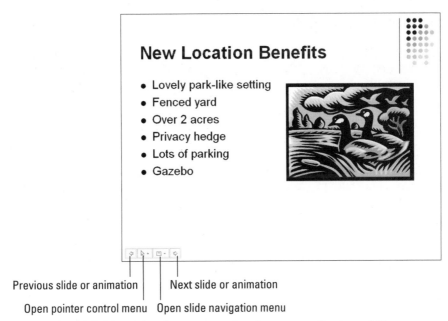

Figure 2-7: Notes Page view offers a special text area for your notes, separate from the slides themselves.

Expert Tip   The Show Formatting tool allows you to see the formatting of the text in the notes area while you're still in normal view.

Zooming In and Out

If you need a closer look at your presentation, you can zoom the view in or out to accommodate almost any situation. For example, if you have trouble placing a graphic exactly at the same vertical level as some text in a box next to it, you might zoom in for more precision. You can view your work at various magnifications on-screen without changing the size of the surrounding tools or the size of the print on the printout.

In Normal view, each of the panes has its own individual zoom. To set the zoom for the Outline/Slides pane only, for example, select it first; then choose a zoom level. Or to zoom only in the Slide pane, click it first. In a single-pane view like Notes Page or Slide Sorter, a single zoom setting affects the entire work area.

 Expert Tip

Instead of clicking a pane in Normal view to switch to it, you can press F6 to move clockwise among the panes, or Shift+F6 to move counterclockwise. You can also use Ctrl+Shift+Tab to switch between the Slides and Outline tabs of the Outline/Slides pane.

The easiest way to set the zoom level is to open the Zoom drop-down list on the Standard toolbar and choose a new level. Figure 2-8 shows the Zoom drop-down list open and the display zoomed to 100%. You can also type a specific zoom percentage into that box. You aren't limited to the choices on the list. (However, some of the panes do limit you to 100% as the highest zoom level.)

Figure 2-8: Choose a specific zoom percentage from the Zoom drop-down list if you need to zoom in or out.

The larger the zoom number, the larger the details on the display. A zoom of 10% would make a slide so tiny that you couldn't read it. A zoom of 400% would make a few letters on a slide so big they would fill the entire pane.

The default zoom setting for the Slide pane (Normal view) is Fit, which means the zoom adjusts so that the entire slide fits in the slide pane and is as large as possible. If you drag the dividers between panes to redistribute the screen space, the size of the slide in the slide pane adjusts too, so that you continue to see the whole slide. You can change the zoom to whatever you like, and then return to the default by choosing Fit as the zoom amount. See Figure 2-9.

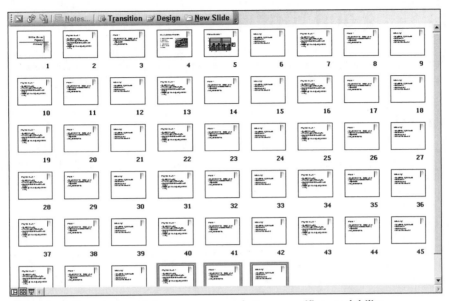

Figure 2-9: Zooming out lets you see more, but you sacrifice readability.

The main advantage to zooming out is to fit more on the screen at once. For example, if you're working with a lot of slides in Slide Sorter view and normally can see three slides on each row, zooming out to 33 percent might let you see eight or more slides on each row, for a total of 40 or more slides per screen. The disadvantage, of course, is that if the slides get too small, as in Figure 2-9, you can't read the text and so you can't tell them apart.

Another way to control the zoom is with the Zoom dialog box. Select View ➪ Zoom to open it. Make your selection, as shown in Figure 2-10, by clicking the appropriate button, and then click OK. Notice that you can type a precise zoom percentage in the Percent text box. This is the same as typing a percentage directly into the Zoom text box on the Standard toolbar.

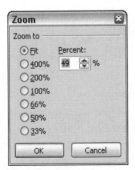

Figure 2-10: You can zoom with this Zoom dialog box rather than the control on the toolbar if you prefer.

Displaying and Hiding Screen Elements

PowerPoint has lots of optional screen elements that you may (or may not) find useful, depending on what you're up to at the moment. In the following sections, I tell you about some of them and explain how to toggle them on and off.

Rulers

Vertical and horizontal rulers around the slide pane can help you place objects more precisely. The rulers aren't displayed by default, however; you have to turn them on. To do so, select View ⇨ Ruler. Do the same thing again to turn them off. Rulers are available only in Normal or Notes Page views.

The rulers help with positioning no matter what content type you are working with, but when you are editing text in a text frame they have an additional purpose as well. The horizontal ruler shows the frame's paragraph indents, and you can drag the indent markers on the ruler just like you can in Word. See Figure 2-11. Text editing on a slide, including tabs and indents, is covered in Chapters 8 and 9.

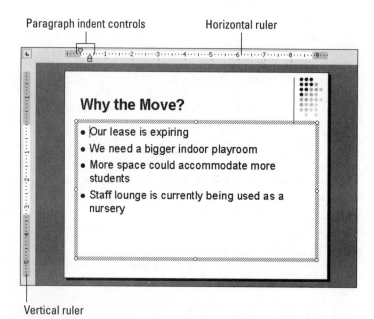

Figure 2-11: Rulers can help you place objects on a slide, and can also help you set and change paragraph indents in a text frame.

Notice in Figure 2-11 that the rulers start with 0 as the spot in the top-left corner of the selected text frame, and run down and to the right from there. When an object other than a text frame is selected, or when no object is selected at all, the ruler's numbering changes. It starts with 0 at the center of the slide vertically and horizontally and runs out in both directions from those midpoints.

You can control the indents more precisely by holding down the Ctrl button while dragging the indent markers on the ruler.

Grid and guides

Guides are on-screen dotted lines that can help you line up objects on a slide. For example, if you want to center some text exactly in the middle of the slide, you can place the object exactly at the intersection of the guidelines. With the ruler alone you would have to eyeball it, but with the guides you can be very precise. Guides are available in the same views as rulers: Normal view and Notes Page view.

To turn Guides on or off, follow these steps:

1. Choose View ➪ Grid and Guides.

2. Mark or clear the Display Drawing Guides On Screen check box.

3. Click OK.

You can also press Alt+F9 to toggle the guides on and off. Once they are on, as in Figure 2-12, you can drag them to reposition them. As you drag, a box pops up telling you the line's exact position..

You can add more guidelines by holding down the Ctrl key while dragging a guide. You can add up to 8 horizontal and vertical guidelines using this method.

The grid is group of evenly spaced lines, like on graph paper. When you drag objects around on a slide, they snap to this grid, to help you get them aligned with one another. It is on by default, although by default it's invisible. To turn it on/off or to change its spacing, do the following:

1. Choose View ➪ Grid and Guides or press Ctrl+G.

2. In the Grid and Guides dialog box (Figure 2-13), choose the grid settings you want:

   • Turn off the usage of the grid by deselecting the Snap Objects to Grid check box.

   • Make objects snap to other objects by selecting the Snap Objects to Other Objects check box.

- Change the grid spacing by setting a different spacing number in the Spacing box.

- Make the grid visible by choosing Display Grid On Screen.

3. *(Optional)* To make these settings the default for all new presentations, click the Set as Default button. Otherwise, these settings will apply only to the current presentation.

4. Click OK.

To toggle the display of the grid on and off, press Shift+F9.

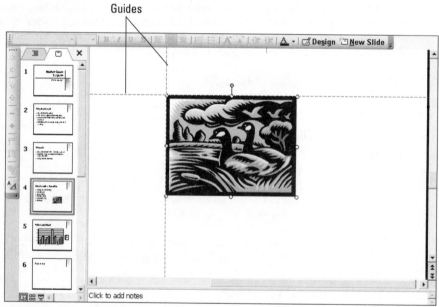

Figure 2-12: Guides help you position objects precisely.

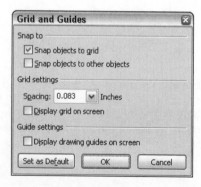

Figure 2-13: Change the grid settings to control how objects snap to the grid or to other objects when you move them with drag-and-drop.

Toolbars

PowerPoint comes with over a dozen toolbars, but only three are displayed by default in Normal view: Standard and Formatting at the top, and Drawing at the bottom.

Note   Your Standard and Formatting toolbars may appear together on the same line. I showed you in Chapter 1 how to fix them so that they appear on separate lines, as they do in the figures in this book. Just click the down arrow at the right end of the toolbar to open a menu, and then choose Show Buttons on Two Rows.

Some of the toolbars appear automatically whenever they are needed. (The Picture, WordArt, and Animation Effects toolbars are like that.) Other toolbars never appear unless you specifically call for them. (Outlining is a good example.) However, you can display other toolbars by right-clicking any displayed toolbar and choosing the one you want from the list. See Figure 2-14. You can also select View ⇨ Toolbars for the same list.

Checkmark means
it's displayed already

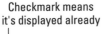

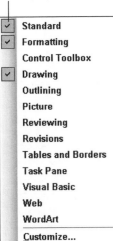

Figure 2-14: Right-click a toolbar to see a list of the other toolbars available.

Toolbar display and availability in Slide Sorter view are a little different from the other views. When you're in Slide Sorter view, you see only the Standard and Slide Sorter toolbars, and the list of available toolbars is decidedly shorter there. (That's because many of the toolbars, such as Picture, apply to individual slides, and you can't edit individual slides in Slide Sorter view.)

The list of toolbars shown in Figure 2-13 is not comprehensive; it excludes some of the special-purpose toolbars that appear only when certain types of content are selected, such as the 3D toolbar (when working with 3D drawn objects) and the Diagram toolbar (when working with diagrams). You would not normally need to turn on those toolbars manually, however, because they appear automatically when they are needed. Should you ever want to manually display one, however, here's how:

1. Choose View ➪ Toolbars ➪ Customize, or choose the Customize command from the right-click menu shown in Figure 2-13. (Or choose Tools ➪ Customize and click the Toolbars tab.)

2. Click to place a checkmark next to each toolbar you want to display, and clear the check box for any toolbars you don't want. See Figure 2-15.

3. Click OK.

Figure 2-15: For a full list of all toolbars available in PowerPoint, open the Customize dialog box and display the Toolbars tab.

You can customize the toolbars as well as turn them on/off, by adding and removing buttons from them. You learn about that in Chapter 35.

Color/Grayscale view

Most of the time you will work with your presentation in color, but if you are eventually going to present the presentation in black and white or grayscale (for example, on overhead transparencies or black-and-white handouts), you might want to check to see what it will look like without color. To do so, choose View ⇨ Color/Grayscale and then choose Color, Grayscale, or Pure Black and White.

Expert Tip   This Color/Grayscale option is especially useful when you are preparing slides that will eventually be faxed, because a fax is pure black and white in most cases. Something that looks great on a color screen could look like a shapeless blob on a black-and-white fax. It doesn't hurt to check.

When you choose Grayscale or Pure Black and White, a Grayscale View toolbar appears. From it you can open a drop-down list of various types of grayscale and black-and-white settings. Choose one that shows the object to best advantage; PowerPoint will remember that setting when printing or outputting the presentation to a grayscale or black-and-white source. See Figure 2-16. When you are finished, click the Close Grayscale View button on the Grayscale View toolbar, or choose View ⇨ Color/Grayscale ⇨ Color. Changing the Black and White or Grayscale settings doesn't affect the colors on the slides; it only affects how the slides will look and print in black and white or grayscale.

Click here for grayscale options

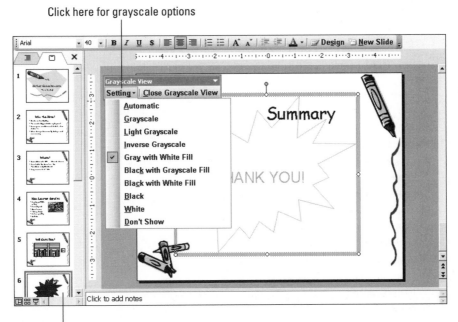

Original was red text on blue background

Figure 2-16: Fine-tune the way PowerPoint converts a colored object to grayscale or black and white.

Task pane

As you learned in Chapter 1, the task pane is a separate pane that sometimes appears to the right of the other PowerPoint window panes. Its content depends on the activity you are performing. Many activities that used to be contained in dialog boxes in earlier versions of PowerPoint are now accessed from the task pane instead, such as changing the design template and the slide layout.

To display the task pane, choose View ➪ Task Pane, or choose a command that requires it to be open (such as Format ➪ Slide Layout). To hide the task pane, click the Close (X) button in its upper-right corner.

Once the task pane is open, you can switch among all the available pages of it by opening its menu. As you can see in Figure 2-17, there are many task pane pages. And just like with any other panes in PowerPoint, you can resize the task pane so it takes up more or less space on-screen; just drag its border.

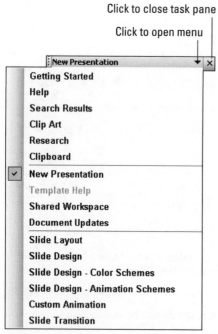

Figure 2-17: Display or hide the task pane as desired, or change to a different page of the task pane by selecting from its menu.

Other viewing options

PowerPoint has a few more elements you can choose to hide or display. Some of them aren't really screen elements, but rather dialog boxes at certain points in the program. To turn these options on/off, follow these steps:

1. Select Tools ➪ Options. The Options dialog box appears.
2. Click the View tab. See Figure 2-18.

Figure 2-18: Set more viewing options for PowerPoint here.

3. Select or deselect the check box for the option you want to display or hide.
4. Click OK.

The View tab is divided into three sections: settings for all the working views (that is, all the views except Slide Show), settings for the Slide Show view itself, and Default View settings.

Here are the options that affect all views except Slide Show:

✦ *Startup Task Pane.* When you opened PowerPoint, recall that the task pane appeared to help you get started. You can turn this off so that it does not appear.

✦ *Slide Layout task pane when inserting new slides.* When you add new slides to a presentation, the Slide Layout task pane appears, prompting you to select the slide layout you want to use. You can turn off this dialog box, signaling PowerPoint to add a standard bulleted slide each time you call for a new slide.

✦ *Status bar.* You can save about half an inch of on-screen space by turning off the status bar. This enables you to make the Zoom setting about three percent larger. Is it worth it? You decide.

✦ *Vertical ruler.* You saw earlier in this chapter that you can turn the rulers on or off; and you can deselect the vertical ruler here so that only a horizontal one appears when you turn the ruler on.

✦ *Windows in Taskbar.* If you don't like the fact that PowerPoint 2003 places a separate bar on the taskbar for each open presentation file, deselect this check box to make PowerPoint display a single bar on the taskbar, just as it did in PowerPoint 97 and earlier.

The following options affect only the Slide Show view:

✦ *Popup menu on right mouse click.* Normally, as you've seen, you can right-click elements in PowerPoint to make shortcut menus appear. You can disable this capability in Slide Show view if you want. Disabling this feature allows you to use the right mouse button to move backwards through your slides when viewing a presentation in Slide Show view.

✦ *Show popup menu button.* When you move your mouse in Slide Show view, an arrow appears in the bottom-left corner. You can click it to open the same menu that you get when right-clicking. You can disable it here to deter tampering.

✦ *End with a black slide.* If you want your presentation to end by displaying a black screen, leave this option selected. (It's a nice touch.)

In the Default View section there is only one option: the Open All Documents Using This View list. This enables you to specify which view will be used when files open. By default, PowerPoint uses whatever view was active when the presentation was last saved, but you can set it up so that all files open in Normal view, for example, or Slide Sorter view, or any other viewing option you want.

Working with Window Controls

If you are familiar with Windows already, you can skip this section. It's all about controlling the windows. I've included it here because without a basic knowledge of how to control a window, your PowerPoint productivity can be severely hampered, especially when you begin working with more than one presentation at a time.

Each window has three control buttons in its top-right corner. They are Minimize, Close, and either Maximize or Restore, depending on the window's current state:

Click the Minimize button to minimize a window. A minimized window is reduced to an icon or a small rectangle.

Click the Maximize button to maximize a window. A maximized window fills the entire screen or the entire space of the window in which it resides, if it's a window within a window.

Click the Restore button to restore a window to the size and shape that it was before it was maximized.

Click the Close button to close a window.

Understanding how PowerPoint uses windows

PowerPoint uses windows within windows, just like most Windows applications do. The outer window is PowerPoint itself. The inner windows include any presentations you have open.

By default, a presentation window is maximized within the PowerPoint window, so you see only one set of window controls. In Figure 2-19, notice that there are two Close (X) buttons — the top one for PowerPoint itself and the bottom one for the current presentation. However, there is only one Maximize/Restore button, for PowerPoint as a whole. That's because the presentation window is maximized.

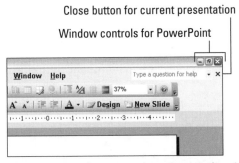

Close button for current presentation

Window controls for PowerPoint

Figure 2-19: When a presentation window is maximized, you see only one set of window controls (plus an extra Close button).

To give the current presentation its own window, with its own set of window controls, choose Window ➪ Arrange All. This arranges all open presentations so that their windows are separately visible. In Figure 2-20, there was only one open presentation, so it continues to fill the entire PowerPoint window, but it now has its own window controls and can be minimized or resized on its own.

Window controls for current presentation

Figure 2-20: Choose Window ➪ Arrange All to place the open presentation file(s) in their own separate windows.

When a presentation sits in its own window, as in Figure 2-20, you can minimize it. When you do so, it becomes a rectangular icon (like a miniature title bar) in the PowerPoint window, as in Figure 2-21. To reopen a minimized presentation, double-click it. If another window is obscuring the icon so you can't get to it, press Alt+Tab until it appears.

Minimized presentation window

Figure 2-21: You can minimize a presentation window to get it out of the way while you work on some other presentation.

Moving and resizing windows

You can move and resize windows that aren't minimized or maximized. You can move and resize the PowerPoint window itself too, or any window for that matter. To move a window, drag its title bar. To resize a window, position the mouse pointer over any border of the window so the pointer changes to a double-headed arrow. Then, drag the border until the window is the size you want it to be.

Opening a new display window

Have you ever wished you could be in two places at once? Well, in PowerPoint, you actually can. PowerPoint provides a way to view two spots in the presentation at the same time by opening a new window.

To display a new window, select Window ➪ New Window. You can use any view with any window, so you can have two slides in Normal view at once, or Slide Sorter and Notes Pages view, or any other combination. Both windows contain the same presentation, so any changes you make in one window are reflected in the other window.

Arranging windows

When you have two or more windows open, whether they are for the same presentation or different ones, you need to arrange them for optimal viewing. You saw earlier in this chapter how to resize a window, but did you know that PowerPoint can do some of the arranging for you?

Almost all Windows-based programs have a Window menu with some commands that help you arrange the windows. These commands also act to restore a presentation window, so that its window controls become available as you saw earlier in the chapter.

When you want to arrange the open windows, do one of the following:

✦ Select Window ➪ Arrange All to tile the open windows so there is no overlap. See Figure 2-22.

✦ Select Window ➪ Cascade to arrange the open windows so the title bars cascade from upper-left to lower-right on the screen. Click a title bar to activate a window. See Figure 2-23.

These commands do not apply to minimized windows. If you want to include a window in the arrangement, make sure you restore it from its minimized state first.

Switching among windows

If you have more than one window open and can see at least a corner of the window you want, click it to bring it to the front. If you have one of the windows maximized, on the other hand, or if another window is obscuring the one you want, open the Window menu and choose the window to display or press Alt+Tab to cycle through.

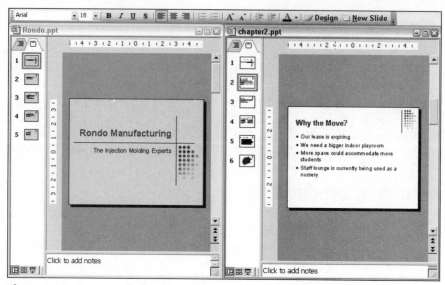

Figure 2-22: Arrange All tiles the windows of the open presentations.

Title bars

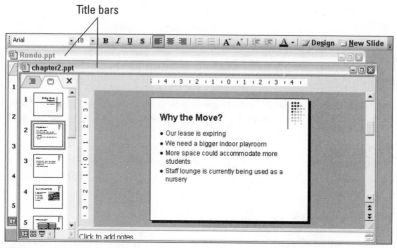

Figure 2-23: Cascade arranges the windows so that you can see all of the title bars.

Summary

In this chapter, you learned about PowerPoint's views, which are somewhat different in PowerPoint 2003 than they were in some previous versions of the program. You also learned how to zoom in and out, display and hide on-screen tools, and control multiple windows. The next chapter covers file management — how to create, save, open, and export PowerPoint presentation files.

✦   ✦   ✦

Managing Presentation Files

If you're an experienced Windows and Office user, file management may be second nature to you. If so — great! You might not need this chapter. On the other hand, if you aren't entirely certain about some of the finer points, like saving in different formats or locations, stick around!

Even people who consider themselves "advanced" users may find something of benefit in this chapter, as it looks at some of the unique advanced saving features of Office applications and explains how to secure files with passwords and use the new Package for CD feature in PowerPoint 2003.

Saving Your Work

PowerPoint is typical of most Windows programs in the way it saves and opens files. The entire PowerPoint presentation is saved in a single file with a .ppt extension; any graphics, charts, or other elements are incorporated into that single file.

The first time you save a presentation, PowerPoint opens the Save As dialog box, prompting you for a name and location. Thereafter, when you save that presentation, PowerPoint uses the same settings and does not prompt you for them again.

Saving for the first time

If you haven't previously saved the presentation you are working on, the File ⇨ Save command and the File ⇨ Save As command both do the same thing: they open the Save As dialog box. From there, you can specify a name, file type, and file location. Follow these steps:

1. Choose File ➪ Save. The Save As dialog box appears.

2. Enter a filename in the File name box. You do not have to type .ppt at the end; the extension is added automatically. The default name is the text in the first text box of the first slide. See Figure 3-1.

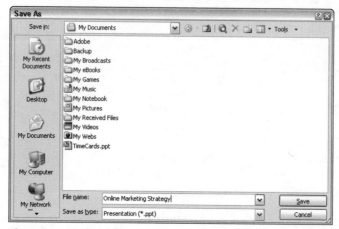

Figure 3-1: Save your work by specifying a name for the presentation file.

3. *(Optional)* If you want to save in a different location, see the "Changing Drives and Folders" section later in this chapter for details. If you want to save in a different format, see "Saving in a Different Format."

4. Click Save. Your work is saved.

Filenames can be up to 255 characters. For practical purposes, however, you should keep the names short. You can include spaces in the filenames and most symbols (although not <, >, ?, *, /, or \). However, if you plan to post the file on a network or the Internet at some point, you should avoid using spaces; use the underscore character instead to simulate a space if needed.

Expert Tip   If you are planning to transfer this presentation file to a different computer and show it from there, and that other computer does not have the same fonts as your PC, you should embed the fonts in your presentation so the fonts needed for the show are available on the other PC. To embed fonts from the Save As dialog box, click the Tools button, choose Save Options, and in the Save Options dialog box mark the Embed TrueType Fonts check box. This makes the saved file much larger than normal, so do it only when necessary. To learn about some other advanced saving features, see "Setting Save Options" later in the chapter.

Saving subsequent times

After you have once saved a presentation, you can resave it with the same settings (same file type, name, and location) in any of the following ways:

✦ Choose File ⇨ Save.

✦ Press Ctrl+S.

✦ Click the Save button on the Standard toolbar.

If you need to save under a different name, as a different type, or in a different location, use the Save As command instead. This reopens the Save As dialog box, as in the preceding steps, so you can save differently. The originally saved copy will remain under the original name, type, and location.

 Expert Tip   If you frequently use Save As, you may want to place a button for it on the toolbar. See Chapter 35 to learn how to do that.

Changing drives and folders

By default, all files in PowerPoint (and all the Office applications) are saved to the My Documents folder. This is convenient for beginners because they never have to worry about changing the drive or folder. More advanced users, however, will sometimes want to save files to other locations. These other locations can include floppy disks, other hard disks in the same PC, hard disks on other PCs in a network, hard disks on Web servers on the Internet, or writeable CDs.

 Caution   Although you can save directly to removable disks such as floppies, CDs, and ZIP disks, it is not a good idea to do so because it can cause file corruption. Save to your hard drive first, and then copy the file to a removable disk.

 Expert Tip   The actual location of My Documents depends on the Windows version. In Windows 95, 98, and Me, the PC has a single My Documents folder, located on the same drive as Windows. For example, if Windows is installed in D:\Windows, My Documents is D:\My Documents. In Windows 2000 and XP, however, each user has a separate My Documents folder, stored on the same drive as Windows in the \Documents and Settings\username folder (where username is the user's name). So, for example, if Windows is D:\Windows, My Documents might be D:\Documents and Settings\Faithe Wempen\My Documents.

To change the save location, follow these steps:

1. Start saving normally in the Save As dialog box.

2. Open the Save In drop-down list and choose the drive to which you want to save. See Figure 3-2.

Places bar   Up one level

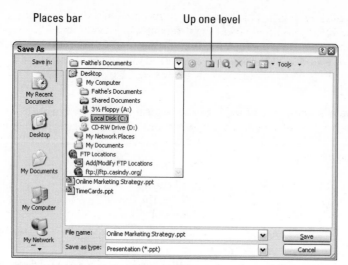

Figure 3-2: Select the drive to which you want to save.

3. All the top-level folders on that drive appear. Double-click the one you want to save in. (If it's a floppy, it may not have any folders. If so, skip this step.)

4. If you need to navigate through additional levels of folders, double-click them as necessary. For example, if you want to save in `C:\Wiley\Books\ PowerPoint Bible`, you would double-click the `Wiley` folder, double-click the `Books` folder, and then double-click the `PowerPoint Bible` folder.

5. Finish saving the file normally.

You've just learned one way to navigate to a different location for file saving, but the Save As dialog box also provides many alternative navigation methods that may sometimes be easier.

One way is to navigate from folder to folder. As you just learned, you can begin your navigation by selecting the drive. This places you at the top level, and you can wade through the folders from there. But if you are already several levels deep in folders, it can sometimes make more sense to go up one level at a time rather than jump all the way to the top. For example, suppose the current Save As folder is `C:\Wiley\Books\PowerPoint Bible` and you want to save something in `C:\Wiley\Books\Office`. You can click the Up One Level button on the Save As toolbar (the icon is a folder with an up arrow on it, shown in Figure 3-2) to change to `C:\Wiley\Books`. From there, you can double-click the `Office` folder.

Along the left side of the Save As dialog box are several folder icons. This area is called the *Places Bar*. You can click one of these folders to jump there immediately to save a file. Here's an explanation of these folders and their functions:

✦ *My Recent Documents.* This folder contains shortcuts to the presentations and folder locations you have used most recently in PowerPoint. This one is primarily for use in the Open dialog box, rather than Save As, although it appears in both. If you want to open a recently used file, you can select its shortcut from the My Recent Documents folder without having to locate it in its real location.

Note Shortcuts are pointers that point to the original files. You probably have several shortcuts on your Windows desktop; when you click one, the program opens. The program itself is not located on your desktop, but the shortcut points to the program's actual location.

✦ *Desktop.* This is a folder containing all the shortcuts that you have on your Windows desktop. If you save a file here, the file is saved on your desktop, rather than in one of the regular folders on your hard disk. This might be useful if you are in a hurry and you want quick access later to the file, but it's not good for long-term storage.

Note The Desktop folder is actually a folder in the Windows folder on your hard disk, but for file-management purposes, it appears on lists as separate from any particular disk drive.

✦ *My Documents.* This is your regular My Documents folder, where files are stored by default. If you navigate elsewhere, you can return to My Documents by clicking this button.

✦ *My Computer.* Choosing this opens a list of all the available drives on the system, so you can choose the one you want. It's similar to looking at the list of drives on the Save In drop-down list, but they're all arrayed in window form.

✦ *My Network Places.* This is a folder containing any shortcuts you have to network drives and folders. If you want to save to another computer on your LAN, or directly to an Internet location, this is the place to do so.

Expert Tip If you consistently want your PowerPoint files saved into a different folder than My Documents, change the default file location. Choose Tools ⇨ Options and click the Save tab. Then type a new file location in the Default File Location text box. You cannot browse for it; you must know the full pathname. For example, if you want to save by default in a folder called PPT, which is in a folder called Books, which is on drive E, the path would be E:\PPT\Books.

Saving in a different format

You can save your PowerPoint work in a variety of other formats for sharing with other people who may not have access to PowerPoint 2003. The available formats are shown in Table 3-1. Simply choose a file format from the Save As Type drop-down list in the Save As dialog box shown in Figure 3-3.

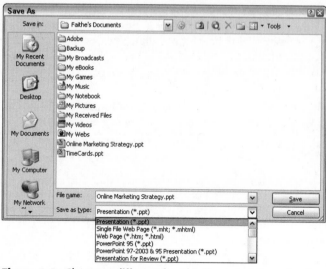

Figure 3-3: Choose a different format, if needed, from the Save As Type drop-down list.

Table 3-1
PowerPoint Save As Formats

Format	Extension	Usage Notes
Presentations:		
Presentation (PowerPoint 2003)	PPT	The default; use in most cases. Can be opened in PowerPoint 97 and higher.
PowerPoint 97-2003 & 95	PPT	For use in a variety of earlier versions of PowerPoint Presentation, including PowerPoint 95. Results in a large file because it contains the uncompressed images needed to support PowerPoint 95. Retains all PowerPoint 2003 features.
Single File Web Page	MHT	Web-based, but all elements in a single file. Suitable for use as an e-mail attachment. Loses all animation.
Web Page	HTM, HTML	Creates a plain text HTM file and pulls out each graphic element in a separate file. Suitable for posting on a Web site. Loses all animation.

Format	Extension	Usage Notes
Presentation for Review	PPT	Creates a normal PowerPoint file but sets it up to track revisions from multiple revisers. Not an option when saving initially.
Design Template	POT	Creates a template that can be used for formatting future PowerPoint presentations you create.
PowerPoint Show	PPS	Just like a normal presentation file except it has a different extension and opens by default in Slide Show view instead of Normal view.
Graphics/Other:		
PowerPoint Add-In	PPA	Stores any Visual Basic for Applications (VBA) code associated with the presentation as an add-in.
GIF Graphics Interchange Format	GIF	Static graphic. GIFs are limited to 256 colors.
PNG Portable Network Graphics Format	PNG	Static graphic. Similar to GIF except without the color depth limitation. Uses lossless compression; takes advantage of the best features of both GIF and JPG.
JPEG File Interchange Format	JPG, JPEG	Static graphic. JPG files can be very small, making them good for Web use. A lossy format, so picture quality may not be as good as with a lossless format.
Tagged Image File Format	TIF, TIFF	Static graphic. TIF is a high-quality file format suitable for slides with high-resolution photos. A lossless compression format.
Device Independent Bitmap	BMP	Static graphic. BMP is the native format for Windows graphics, including Windows background wallpaper.
Windows Metafile	WMF	Static graphic. A vector-based format, so it can later be resized without distortion. Not Mac-compatible.
Enhanced Windows Metafile	EMF	Enhanced version of WMF; not compatible with 16-bit applications. Also vector-based and non-Mac-compatible.
Outline/RTF	RTF	Text and text formatting only; excludes all non-text elements. Only text in slide placeholders will be converted to the outline. Text in the Notes area is not included.

Expert Tip
If you consistently want to save in a different format than PowerPoint 2003, choose Tools ➪ Options and click the Save tab. Then, choose a different format from the Save PowerPoint Files As drop-down list. This makes your choice the default in the Save As Type drop-down list in the Save As dialog box. Not all of the formats are available here; your choices are Presentation (the default), PowerPoint 97-11 Beta & 95 Presentation, Single File Web Page, and Web Page.

Saving in PowerPoint presentation formats

If you decide to save in PowerPoint format, you have three choices:

✦ **PowerPoint 2003** format is very versatile. It is compatible with all PowerPoint versions 97 and above (including 97, 2000, and 2002), and it preserves all features.

✦ **PowerPoint 97-2003 & 95** format adds compatibility for PowerPoint 95 to the mix, but it also greatly increases the file size. That's because in 97 and higher, graphics are compressed, but in 95 they are not. Therefore, presentations saved in this format must support both. All features are preserved, although many of them will not be visible in earlier PowerPoint versions.

✦ **Presentation for Review** format. This one is not an option when you first save the file, but if you use Save As to save it again, you have access to this format. It's almost exactly the same as PowerPoint 2003 format, but it keeps track of changes made to e-mailed copies so you can merge the changes later. Don't use this unless you need to, because the file size grows until you merge the changes each time someone else's revisions are added.

Note that although all of these formats retain all of the presentation whiz-bang of PowerPoint 2003 when you use them to save your work, other people using earlier versions of PowerPoint might not be able to display the presentation exactly as you created it. Table 3-2 lists some of the features of PowerPoint 2003 that earlier versions cannot recognize and support.

Table 3-2 **PowerPoint 2003 Features Not Supported in Previous PowerPoint Versions**	
Feature	*Issues*
PowerPoint 2000 and Below	
Password protection	Presentations with passwords do not open. The user receives an error message, "PowerPoint can't open the type of file represented by <filename>.PPT."
Multiple masters	Editing and re-saving may result in loss of all but the first master of a certain type.

Feature	Issues
Animation effects	Any unsupported effects are either converted to a supported effect format or not used.
Picture rotation	Windows metafiles do not appear rotated. Bitmaps change to nearest 90 degree rotation.
Transparency on a solid fill	May appear less smooth.
Transparency on a fill effect or line	Cannot add transparency to a fill effect or line using the Transparency tool.
Contrast and brightness adjustments on picture fills	Adjustments do not appear on some images.
Fill rotates with shape	Fills do not appear rotated.
Anti-aliasing	Not supported; text and graphics appear less smooth.
Comments	Not visible or editable.
Diagrams	Converted to groups of shapes.
PowerPoint 97 and Below	
Native tables	Converted to a group of shapes.
Voice narration	Sound played with Windows Media Player as a WAV file. Not recognized as narration, and not synchronized to audio.
Automatic numbered list	Appears as a bulleted list.
Picture bullets	Appear as regular bullets.
Animated GIFs	First frame appears as a static image.
PowerPoint 95	
Animated chart elements	Appear as static chart objects that can be edited in Microsoft Graph.
Custom shows	Slides appear in presentation, but Custom Show feature doesn't function.
Native format movies and sounds	Converted to Windows Media Player objects.
Diagrams	Converted to Windows Metafiles (WMF).
Play options for CD tracking and movie looping	Ignored.
Document collaboration	Tracking and merging changes not supported.
3D effects	Converted to pictures.

Continued

Table 3-2 *(continued)*

Feature	Issues
AutoShapes	Converted to freeform shape or picture.
Connectors	Converted to freeform lines; automatic connecting behavior lost.
Curves	Approximated with connected straight line segments.
Transparency on a gradient fill	Appears as a transparent fill without a gradient.
Joins and endcaps of lines	Appear as mitered joins on AutoShapes and round joins and endcaps on freeform shapes.
Linked or embedded objects	Brightness, contrast, and color transformation settings are lost.
WordArt drawing objects	Converted to picture objects.
Picture fills	Converted to picture objects.
Picture fills on shapes	Converted to picture objects with solid fill in which last foreground color is applied to object.
Shadows, engraved	Appears as embossed shadow effect.
Shadows, perspective	Converted to shapes or pictures and grouped with shape casting the shadow.
Shapes or arcs with attached text	Converted to freeform shapes, arcs, or text boxes.
Thick compound lines	Converted to picture objects.
Hyperlinks that combine Play Sound with other Action settings	Play Sound settings are lost.
Hyperlinks embedded within an object	Hyperlinks are lost.
Action settings embedded in an object	Action settings are lost.
Send a copy of a slide in e-mail as the body of the message	Message header information (recipient list, message options) is lost.
Embedded fonts	Not supported.
Embedded Excel charts	Not supported.
Microsoft Graph charts	Editable only if the Convert Charts When Saving As Previous Version check box was selected when saving.
Macros	Not supported.
Unicode characters	Not supported.

Saving for use on the Web

To share the presentation on the Web with people who don't have PowerPoint, you can save in one of the Web Page formats. Selecting either of the Web page formats in the Save As dialog box has the same effect as choosing File ➪ Save as Web Page. It's simply two different ways of getting to the same place.

You have two choices for Web format: Web Page or Single File Web Page. Web Page creates a single HTML document that has links to the slides, and then the slides and their graphics are stored in a separate folder. This would be suitable for posting on a Web site. Single File Web Page creates a single .MHT document that contains all the HTML codes and all the slides. This would be suitable for e-mailing, for example. (In fact, the "M" in the name format is short for "mail," because this format was originally designed for e-mail use.) With either of the Web formats, however, you lose all your animations, transitions, and other special features, so you might prefer to distribute the presentation in a different way on the Web. If keeping the full effect of all the transitions, animations, sounds, and so on is an important consideration, consider saving as a PowerPoint Show (.pps), and then make the PowerPoint Viewer utility available for free download from the same Web page. You'll learn more about this in Chapter 30.

Saving slides in other formats

If you save the presentation in one of the formats shown in the Graphics/Other section of Table 3-1, the file ceases to be a presentation and becomes a series of unrelated graphic files, one per slide. If you choose one of these formats, you're asked whether you want to export the current slide only or all slides. If you choose all slides, PowerPoint creates a new folder in the selected folder with the same name as the original presentation file and places the graphics files in it.

Caution

When you save a file under a different location or name, the original file remains intact, and you create a copy of it. However, if you save as a different format but keep the same name and location, PowerPoint overwrites the original file if the file extensions for both the old and new file types are the same. (For example, all versions of PowerPoint use the extension .ppt.) Be careful not to accidentally overwrite work that you want to keep.

If you want to export the text of the slides to some other application, consider the Outline/RTF format, which creates an outline similar to what you see in the Outline pane in PowerPoint. This file can then be opened in Word or any other application that supports RTF text files.

Specifying advanced save options

The Save Options enable you to fine-tune the saving process for special needs. For example, you can employ Save Options to embed TrueType fonts, to change the interval at which PowerPoint does an AutoSave, and more.

To access the Save Options:

1. Begin to save the file by choosing File ⇨ Save As. The Save As dialog box opens.

2. Choose Tools ⇨ Save Options. The Save Options dialog box opens. See Figure 3-4.

   Most of the options here apply globally to all saving; you do not have to repeat this process for each file you save. An exception is the Embed TrueType fonts option, which applies only to the current presentation being saved.

Figure 3-4: Set Save Options to match the way you want PowerPoint to save your work.

3. Set any of the options desired. They are summarized in Table 3-3.

4. Click OK.

5. Continue saving normally. Or, click Cancel if you do not want to save the current presentation. Your Save Options settings will still be in effect the next time you save.

One of the most important features described in Table 3-3 is AutoRecover, which is turned on by default. That means if a system error or power outage causes PowerPoint to terminate unexpectedly, you do not lose all the work you have done. The next time you start PowerPoint, it opens the recovered file and asks if you want to save it.

Caution

AutoRecover is *not* a substitute for saving your work the regular way. It does not save in the same sense that the Save command does; it only saves a backup version as PowerPoint is running. If you quit PowerPoint normally, that backup version is erased. It is available for recovery only if PowerPoint terminates abnormally (such as due to a system lockup or the power going off).

Table 3-3
Advanced Save Options

Feature	Purpose
Allow fast saves	Speeds up saving a presentation subsequent times by saving only the changes each time. Largely unnecessary on today's PCs with fast CPUs. It's not a good idea to leave this turned on all the time, as some people have found that it is a cause of file corruption.
Prompt for file properties	If your organization uses the File Properties box to record information such as the names of the people who worked on a revision or the notes or keywords involved in it, mark this check box so that the Properties box appears when you save a file. You can also display a file's Properties box from the Save As window by choosing Tools, Properties. In addition, whenever the file is open in PowerPoint you can choose File, Properties to see it.
Save AutoRecover info every ___ minutes	PowerPoint saves your work every few minutes so that if the computer has problems causing PowerPoint to terminate abnormally, you do not lose much work. Lower this number to save more often (for less potential data loss) or raise it to save less often (for less slowdown/delay related to repeated saving).
Convert charts when saving as previous version	Normally when you change the Save As File Type to an earlier version of PowerPoint, it also saves any MS Graph charts in the corresponding earlier format. If you don't want that to happen, clear this check box. Normally you would want the charts to be changed — otherwise they would not be readable in the older version.
Save PowerPoint files as	Choose the file format here that you use most frequently for saving presentations. Usually this would be PowerPoint Presentation (the default), but it might be some earlier version of PowerPoint or it might be Web Page.
Default file location	Specify the location that you want to start from when saving with the Save As dialog box. By default it is your `My Documents` folder.

Continued

Table 3-3 *(continued)*	
Feature	**Purpose**
Embed TrueType fonts	Turn this on if you are saving a presentation for use on a different PC that might not have the fonts installed that the presentation requires. You can choose to embed the characters in use only (which minimizes the file size, but if someone tries to edit the presentation they might not have all the characters out of the font that they need), or to embed all characters in the font set. Unlike the others, this setting applies only to the current presentation file.

Passwords and Privacy Settings

If a presentation contains sensitive or confidential data, you might want to encrypt the file and protect it with a password. Encryption is a type of "scrambling" done to the file so that nobody can see it, either from within PowerPoint or with any other type of file-browsing utility.

Using passwords

There are two separate passwords you can enter for a file: the Open password and the Modify password. Use an Open password to prevent unauthorized people from viewing the file at all. Use a Modify password to prevent people from making changes to it.

You can use one, both, or neither of the password types. For example, suppose you have a personnel presentation that contains salary information. You might use an Open password and distribute that password to a few key people in the Human Resources department who need access to it. But then you might use a Modify password to ensure that none of those people make any changes to the presentation as they are viewing it.

For the Open password, you can specify an encryption method and strength. There are many encryption codes available, and the differences between them are significant mostly to high-end technical users. However, if you do have a preference, you can choose it when you choose the Open password.

To manage a file's passwords and other security settings, do the following:

1. Begin saving the file normally, from the Save As dialog box.

2. Choose Tools ➪ Security Options. The Security Options dialog box opens. See Figure 3-5.

Figure 3-5: Use Security Options to prevent unauthorized access.

3. If you want an Open password, enter it in the Password to Open box. Then if you want to choose an encryption scheme, click the Advanced button and select one. See Figure 3-6. You can choose a type, a key length (the longer it is, the harder it will be to break into), and whether the document properties should be encrypted.

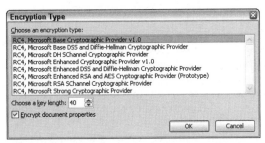

Figure 3-6: Choose an encryption type and length.

4. If you want a Modify password, enter it in the Password to modify box.

5. *(Optional)* If you want your personal information stripped from the file, such as your name removed from the Author field of the Properties box, mark the Remove Personal Information From This File On Save check box.

6. *(Optional)* If desired, adjust the macro security level for PowerPoint (all files, not just this one) by clicking the Macro Security button and making changes to the settings there. See Chapter 35 for more information.

7. Click OK. If you specified a password in step 3, a confirmation box appears for it. Retype the same password and click OK.

8. If you specified a password in step 4, a confirmation box appears for it. Retype the same password and click OK.

9. Continue saving normally.

When you (or someone else) opens the file, a Password prompt appears. The Open password must be entered to open the presentation file. The Modify password will *not* work. After that hurdle, if you have set a separate Modify password, a prompt for that appears. Your choices (shown in Figure 3-7) are to enter the Modify password, to cancel, or to click the Read Only option to open the presentation in Read Only mode.

Figure 3-7: If a Modify password is in use, you can choose to enter it or to open the presentation in Read Only mode.

Restricting distribution with Information Rights Management (IRM)

Office 2003 programs, including PowerPoint, have a new digital rights management feature that enables you to specify what others may do with your data files.

In order to do this, you must have access to a Windows 2003 Server with Information Rights Management (IRM) Services, or contract with a company that provides this. This book will not tackle setting up such a server; if you don't have one available, you may wish to simply skip the following sections. However, if your company does provide such a server, read on to learn how to use it with PowerPoint documents.

Installing the Windows Rights Management Client

In order to use the digital rights management feature, you must first install the Windows Rights Management client on your PC. The first time you attempt to manage a file's rights (for example, by clicking the Permissions button on the PowerPoint toolbar), you will be prompted to allow Windows to install this automatically; click Yes when prompted, and it takes you to a Web site where you can download and install the needed client.

Note What is this Windows Rights Management? Basically it's a system that enables your PC to respond to requests for licenses and keys to the files you distribute. You can use it to specify who shall have what rights.

After installing it, you will be prompted to enter your Passport ID, and to create a Standard or Temporary certificate. Temporary is good for 15 minutes, and useful on a public computer. Standard is good for one year.

Setting permissions with IRM

After you get everything installed for IRM, you can click the Permissions button on the toolbar (the red circle with a white line through it) to open the Permission dialog box for the presentation file, shown in Figure 3-8. From here you can specify users or groups (with Active Directory access only) to have certain permissions for the file. For additional fine-tuning of the permissions, click Advanced.

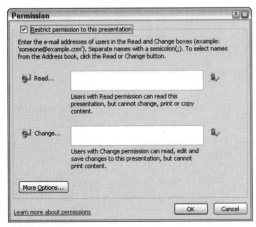

Figure 3-8: Specify permissions for certain users or groups here.

There is much more flexibility and power involved with IRM than is covered in this book, but this should be enough to get you started with it.

Closing and Reopening Presentations

You can have several presentation files open at once and switch freely between them, but this can bog down your computer's performance somewhat. Unless you are doing some cut-and-paste work, it's best to have only one presentation file open—the one you are actively working on. It's easy to close and open presentations as needed.

Closing a presentation

When you exit PowerPoint, the open presentation file automatically closes, and you're prompted to save your changes if you have made any. If you want to close a presentation file without exiting PowerPoint, follow these steps:

1. Choose File ⇨ Close or click the Close (X) button for the presentation. (Note that there are two sets of window controls; the top set is for PowerPoint itself. You want the X in the lower of the two sets. See Figure 3-9.)

   If you have not made any changes to the presentation since the last time you saved, you're done.

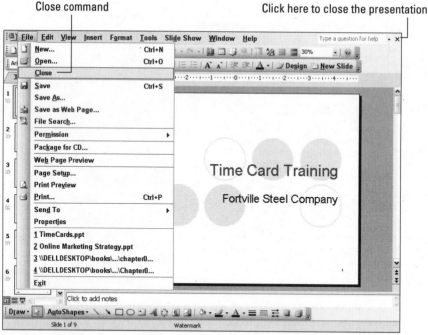

Figure 3-9: Close the presentation with the menu or with its Close button.

2. If you have made any changes to the presentation, you're prompted to save them. If you don't want to save your changes, click No, and you're done.

3. If you want to save your changes, click Yes. If the presentation has already been saved once, you're done.

4. If the presentation has not been saved before, the Save As dialog box appears. Type a name in the File Name text box and click Save.

Opening a presentation

One way to open a presentation is from the task pane that appears when you start PowerPoint or when you click the Home button (it looks like a house) on the task pane. To do so, follow these steps:

1. From the task pane, click one of the names of the last four presentations you have worked with to open it, and you're done. See Figure 3-10.

   OR

   If you want to open some other presentation that doesn't appear, click the More hyperlink in the task pane, or click the Open button on the Standard toolbar, or choose File ➾ Open. Any of those methods displays the Open dialog box, shown in Figure 3-11.

Select from recently used presentations

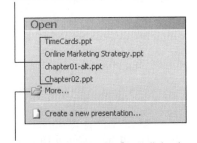

Click here to open the Open dialog box

Figure 3-10: Select the presentation from the list if it appears there. If not, click More . . . to see other files.

2. Choose the file you want from the Open dialog box. Change the location if needed to locate the file. Then click the Open button. The presentation opens.

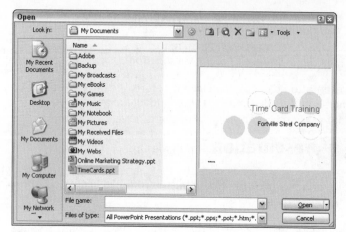

Figure 3-11: Use the Open dialog box to browse for the file you want.

Here are some additional tips for opening files:

✦ The default view in the Open dialog box is Preview, as shown in Figure 3-10. It lets you see a sample of the presentation you have chosen. You can choose a different view by clicking the Views button and selecting a different one (for example, Details, which shows each file's size and date last modified.) Or, you can click the Views button to cycle through the available views without bothering with its drop-down list.

✦ Changing locations works the same for opening as it does for saving. If you need to change to a different location to find the file to open, see the "Changing Drives and Folders" section earlier in this chapter.

✦ If you need help locating the file to open, see "Finding a Presentation File," later in this chapter.

✦ To open more than one presentation at once, hold down the Ctrl key as you click each file you want to open. Then, click the Open button and they all open, each in their own windows. See the "Working with Multiple Presentations" section later in this chapter.

✦ Notice in Figure 3-10 that the Open button in the lower-right corner has its own drop-down list. On that list, you can choose from Open (the default), Open Read-Only (which prevents changes from being saved), and Open as Copy (which creates a copy, leaving the original untouched).

✦ If you want more than four presentations listed in the open task pane, choose Tools ⇨ Options and increase the number on the recently used file list on the General tab. You can have up to nine presentations listed.

Opening a file from a different program

Just as you can save files in various program formats, you can also open files from various programs. This feature is handy, for example, if you are converting from some other presentation program, such as Lotus Freelance Graphics, to PowerPoint.

Caution If you want to include graphics, tables, charts, images, and so on from another program in a PowerPoint presentation, insert them using the Insert Menu command. Do not attempt to open them with the Open dialog box.

PowerPoint can detect the type of file and convert it automatically as you open it. The only problem is that you can't open a file unless you can see it on the list of files in the Open dialog box, and by default only PowerPoint files appear there (that is, files with a .ppt extension).

To change the types of files displayed in the Open dialog box, open the Files of Type drop-down list and choose the format. This filters the file list to show only files that have that particular extension. (This change is valid for only this one use of the Open dialog box; the file type reverts to All PowerPoint Presentations, the default, the next time you open it.)

Finding a presentation file to open

If you have forgotten where you saved a particular presentation file, you're not out of luck. PowerPoint includes a search system that can help you locate it, and you don't even have to know the name of the file. PowerPoint can find files using many criteria. To use the search system, follow these steps:

1. Choose File ➪ Open to display the Open dialog box.

2. Click the Tools button to open its drop-down list and click Search. There are two tabs in the File Search dialog box that appears: Basic and Advanced. Let's look at Basic first.

3. On the Basic tab, enter a text string that you want to search for. This lets you search the entire text of data files, so you don't necessarily need to know the name of the file. For example, maybe you are looking for a presentation that has a slide with the title Regional Sales; you could enter that.

4. By default the search is confined to your local computer. If you want it to also include My Network Places, or if you want to restrict the search to a certain drive, open the Search In list, and make your selections there.

5. By default the search looks at Office files of all types. If you want to confine the search to only PowerPoint files, open the Results Should Be list and deselect the other file types. See Figure 3-12.

6. Click the Search button. The search takes place, and the results appear in the bottom pane.

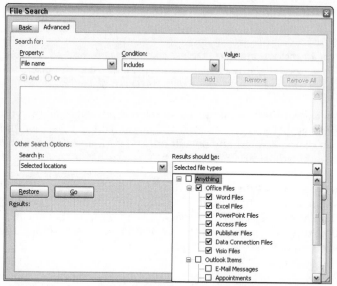

Figure 3-12: Do a simple text search from the Basic tab of the File Search dialog box.

7. Now let's look at the Advanced method. It lets you search by factors other than text contents (although it does allow that too). Click the Advanced tab.

8. Open the Property drop-down list and choose the property that describes what you know about the file. For example, if you know that you created the file on a certain date, choose Creation Date.

9. Open the Condition drop-down list and choose the condition. For example, for creation date you might choose On or Before.

10. In the Value field, enter what you know. For example, to continue with the creation date scenario, you might enter **11/15/02**, knowing that the file was created on or before that date.

11. Click the Add button to add that criterion to the list. See Figure 3-13.

12. If you want an additional criterion in the search, click the And or Or button, and then repeat Steps 8 through 11. Use And if both criteria must match; use Or if either of them can be used.

13. Repeat steps 4 and 5 if needed to change where the search occurs and what types of files are searched.

14. Click the Search button to locate files based on your criteria. The filenames appear at the bottom of the window.

15. Double-click one of the found files to open it.

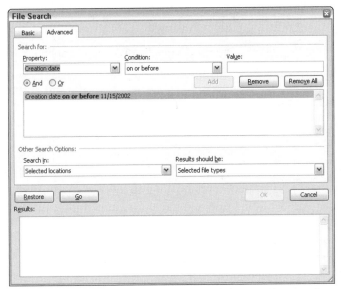

Figure 3-13: Set up criteria and then add them to the search by clicking Add.

Note Windows also offers a good file-finding utility that doesn't have anything to do with PowerPoint. Find it by right-clicking the Windows Start button and choosing Find (or Search, depending on the Windows version). Many people prefer that search method to the one built into PowerPoint.

Managing Files with File Properties

File properties are facts about each file that can help you organize them. If you have a lot of PowerPoint files, using file properties can help you search intelligently for them using the File Search feature you learned about in the preceding section. For example, you can specify an author, a manager, and a company for each file, and perform searches that display the presentations for a certain author, manager, and/or company.

Expert Tip By default, PowerPoint does not prompt for properties when you save a file. If you are planning to use properties to manage your filing system, you can ask PowerPoint to open the Properties dialog box whenever you save a new file. To do so, select Tools ⇨ Options and click the Save tab. Then select the Prompt for File Properties check box.

You can set a file's properties while it is open in PowerPoint by doing the following:

1. Choose File ⇨ Properties. The Properties box for the file opens.

2. On the Summary tab, fill in any information about the presentation that you think can help you maintain your filing system. The Title and Author fields are already filled in for you. See Figure 3-14.

Figure 3-14: Specify values for these properties to help you find a presentation file more easily later.

3. On the Custom tab, choose any additional fields you need and set values for them. For example, click the Checked By field on the Name list, and type a value for it in the Value text box. Repeat this for any of the other custom fields.

4. Review the information on the Statistics and Contents tab if desired. (You can't change that information.)

5. Click OK.

Now you can use the contents of the properties fields when performing a search in the File Search box (Figures 3-12 and 3-13).

Working with Multiple Presentations

You will usually work with only one presentation at a time. But occasionally you may need to have two or more presentations open at once — for example, to make it easier to copy text or slides from one to the other.

To open another presentation, choose File ⇨ Open and select the one you want, the same as usual. When more than one presentation is open, you can switch among them by selecting the one you want to see from the Window menu. Figure 3-15 shows that three presentations are currently open in PowerPoint.

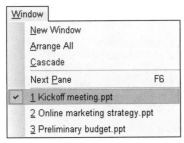

Figure 3-15: Choose from among the open presentations on the Window menu.

When you have multiple presentations open, each one has its own button on the Windows taskbar so you can switch among the presentations by clicking the names on the taskbar. You can also use Alt+Tab to move through presentations.

Note When multiple PowerPoint files are open, depending on your settings in Windows, each of them may appear in a separate horizontal space in the taskbar or they may be "stacked," such that a single taskbar button appears with a number, like "3 Microsoft PowerPoint." Click that button to see a menu of the open individual files. To control this setting, right-click the taskbar and choose Properties, and the mark or clear the Group Similar Taskbar Buttons checkbox.

File Management from the Save As and Open Dialog Boxes

Besides saving and opening files, you can do quite a few other file-management functions from the Save As and Open dialog boxes. To finish off the discussion of these dialog boxes, take a look at these other tasks.

Copying a presentation

Sometimes it is useful to duplicate an existing presentation rather than create a new one from scratch. For example, if you created a presentation last year for your company's annual review, you might want to duplicate that presentation and then modify it for this year's review.

There are several ways to duplicate a presentation. One way, of course, is to copy it using Windows Explorer, which has nothing to do with PowerPoint. Because the PowerPoint presentation is just an ordinary file, and Windows lets you copy files, you can make a copy that way. (For more information about using Windows, check out my book *Windows XP Home Edition Simply Visual*.) You can also duplicate a presentation from within PowerPoint by using File ⇨ Save As to save it under a different name. (You learned to do this earlier in this chapter.)

Here's a way to make a copy from within PowerPoint without opening the file:

1. From the Save As or Open dialog box, select the file you want to copy.
2. Right-click the file and choose Copy from the shortcut menu.
3. If necessary, change to a different drive and/or folder.
4. Right-click an empty area in the list of files.
5. Choose Paste from the shortcut menu. The file appears. If you pasted it into the same folder as the original, the new one has the words *Copy of* at the beginning of its name to differentiate it. You can rename it by pressing F2 and typing a new name. (Don't forget to add the .ppt extension when you rename a file.)
6. Click Cancel to close the dialog box.

Deleting a presentation

Just as you can copy a file, you can delete a presentation file from Windows itself, bypassing PowerPoint altogether. Just select the file in Windows Explorer or My Computer and press the Delete key, or drag it to the Recycle Bin on the Windows desktop.

To delete a file from within PowerPoint, select it from the Save As or Open dialog box and press the Delete key on the keyboard, or click the Delete button at the top of the dialog box, shown in Figure 3-16. You cannot delete a file that is currently open.

Delete

Search the Web   New folder

Up one level   Views

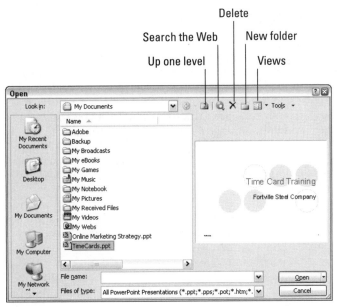

Figure 3-16: You can delete files from the Save As or Open dialog box.

Caution

Be careful when deleting presentations! If you make a mistake in deleting, you can get the file back if you deleted from Windows; just open the Recycle Bin and drag it back out.

Creating a new folder

When saving files, you might want to create a new folder to put them in. You can do this from the Save As box by clicking the New Folder button, pointed out in Figure 3-16. A box appears for the name; type it and click OK, and then save normally.

Renaming a file

To rename a file from within the Save As or Open dialog boxes, click it, and then press F2, or right-click it and choose Rename from the shortcut menu. Then type the new name and press Enter.

Caution

If you have the display of file extensions for known file types turned off in Windows (the default), you do not need to type the .ppt extension when renaming files. In fact, if you do type it, the file may end up with a double extension, like myfile.ppt.ppt. On the other hand, if you have the display of file extensions turned on, you must type the file extension while renaming. To change the setting, from any file management window choose Tools ➪ Folder Options and on the View tab, mark or clear the Hide extensions for known file types checkbox.

Mapping a network drive

This assigns a drive letter to a folder on a remote PC. This might be useful if you save frequently to a network location and you don't want to have to wade through multiple levels of folders each time to find it. (But you can also accomplish the same thing by creating a shortcut in My Network Places.) To map the currently displayed folder as a network drive, open the Tools menu and choose Map Network Drive. This opens a dialog box that lets you associate a drive letter with the location.

Publishing a Presentation to a CD

This feature, new in PowerPoint 2003, enables you to transfer a presentation to a writeable CD and sets up the CD to play the presentation automatically whenever it is inserted in a PC. To use it, obviously, you need a finalized presentation, a write-able CD drive and a blank CD-R or CD-RW disk.

1. Choose File ➪ Package for CD. The Package for CD dialog box opens. See Figure 3-17.

2. Type a name for the CD; this is like a volume label for the disk.

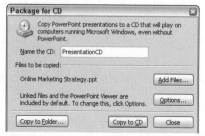

Figure 3-17: When you publish to CD, you generate a CD that will stand alone, running presentations without PowerPoint installed.

3. Edit the list of presentation files to be copied. By default the currently open presentation is on that list, but you might want to add others as well; you might want to put a group of presentations on a single CD.

4. Linked files and the PowerPoint Viewer will be included by default; if you want to fine-tune any other options, click the Options button. (For example, you might do this if you want to embed fonts or specify a password.) Click OK to return to the Package for CD dialog box.

5. If you want to copy directly to a CD, insert a blank CD and then click Copy to CD. Or, if you want to copy the files to CD manually later, click Copy to Folder. These steps assume you have chosen Copy to CD.

6. Wait for the CD to be written. It may take several minutes, depending on the speed of your CD drive's writing capabilities and the size of the presentation files you are placing on it.

7. A message appears when the files are successfully copied to CD, asking whether you want to copy the same files to another CD. Click Yes or No. If you chose No, click Close to close the Package for CD dialog box.

The resulting CD automatically plays the presentation(s) when you insert it in any PC. You can also browse its contents to open the PowerPoint Viewer separately and use it to play specific presentations.

Summary

This chapter made you a master of files. You can now confidently save, open, close, and delete PowerPoint presentation files. You can also save files in different formats, search for missing presentations, and lots more. This is rather utilitarian knowledge and not very much fun to practice, but you will be glad you took the time to learn it later, when you have important files you need to keep safe.

The next chapter is a Project Lab, the first of several in this book. Project Labs are designed to give you hands-on practice with the features you are learning about. Follow the instructions in the Project Lab and use the sample files on the accompanying CD to test and reinforce your skills.

✦   ✦   ✦

Project Lab: Basic PowerPoint Navigation Practice

◆ ◆ ◆ ◆

In This Chapter

Working with
the help system

Practicing file
management
techniques

Practicing
presentation
viewing techniques

◆ ◆ ◆ ◆

Project Labs in this book are designed to give you extra hands-on practice with PowerPoint. Each one includes skills from the chapters that precede it, and may also provide extra practice in the skills from previous sections of the book.

Project Labs use files from the CD that accompanies the book; you'll find the files you need in the Labs folder on the CD.

For each step, the desired goal is first stated and then the specific steps for accomplishing that goal are listed. There are also screenshots along the way to help you see whether you're "on the right page." Notes appear on the figures telling you what part of the instructions each illustration corresponds to. If you are comfortable achieving the goal in some other manner, you are free to do so. However, if you do not know how to achieve the goal, you can use the steps as guidance.

The Scenario

For portions of this lab, you will be working with a presentation file that has already been created for an Addams Publishing company meeting. You will open the file and use it as a training ground for experimenting with PowerPoint features. In future labs you will be working more closely with a scenario.

Lab 1A: Working with the Help System

Level of difficulty: Easy

Time to complete: 5 to 15 minutes

1. Start PowerPoint.

Choose Start ➪ (All) Programs ➪ Microsoft Office ➪ Microsoft PowerPoint 2003.

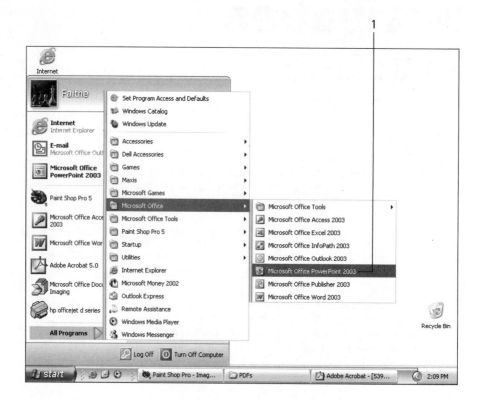

2. Check for available updates to PowerPoint, and install them if found.

a. Make sure you have an Internet connection available.

b. Choose Help ➪ Check for Updates.

c. Follow the prompts at the Web site.

2B

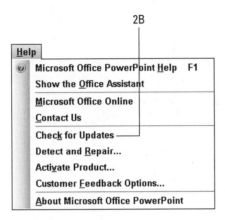

3. Get the product ID number for your copy of PowerPoint, and write it here:

_____

a. Choose Help ⇨ About Microsoft PowerPoint. The About Microsoft PowerPoint window opens.

b. Note the Product ID number and write it on the line provided above.

c. Click OK. The dialog box closes.

3B   3C

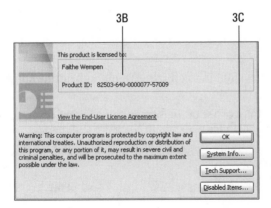

4. Using the Help system, find the steps for printing speaker notes.

a. Type **print speaker notes** in the Help box in the top right corner of the screen and press Enter. The Help task pane opens and displays a list of articles.

b. Click the _Print notes pages_ hyperlink. The article appears in a separate window.

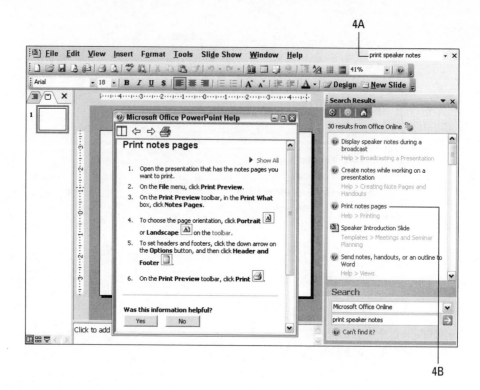

5. **Display an article that describes the steps for inserting comments in a presentation.**

    a. Minimize the window containing the article about printing speaker notes.

    b. In the Help box in the corner of the screen, type **insert comments** and press Enter. A list of articles appears in the Help task pane.

    c. Click the Insert a Comment hyperlink to display the article. The article appears in a window.

6. **Return to the article about printing speaker notes and print it.**

    a. In the article window, click the Back button (left-pointing arrow) to return to the previous article.

    b. Click the Print button on the toolbar. The Print dialog box opens.

    c. Click Print to print the article.

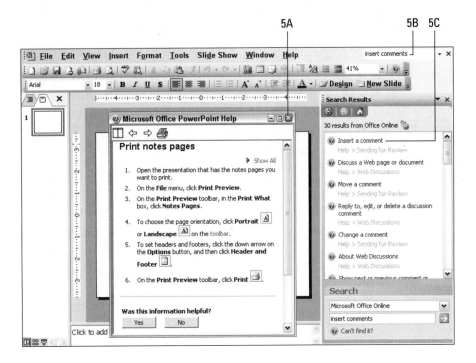

7. Return to the article about inserting comments.

Click the Forward button on the toolbar (right-pointing arrow).

8. Close the article window and the Help task pane.

a. Click the Close (X) button in the article window.

b. Click the Close (X) button on the Help task pane.

9. Using the Office Assistant, display an article that describes how to have two or more slide masters in the same presentation.

a. Choose Help ⇨ Show Office Assistant. The Office Assistant character appears.

b. Click the Office Assistant character. A balloon appears near it.

c. In the text box in the balloon, type **multiple masters,** and then click the Search button. The Help task pane opens with a list of matching articles.

d. In the Help task pane, click the Insert a Slide Master or Title Master hyperlink. The article appears.

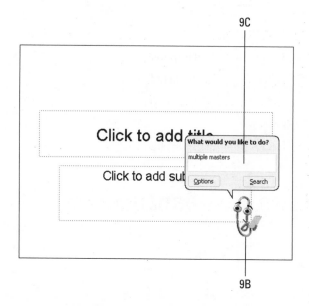

9C

9B

10. Get a definition for the term "Slide Master."

In the article displayed from step 9, click the blue words "Slide Master."

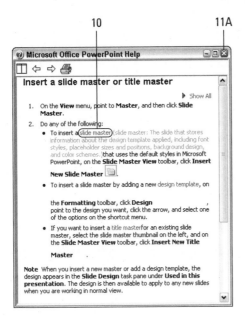

11. **Close the article window and the Help task pane.**

    a. Click the Close (X) button in the article window.

    b. Click the Close (X) button on the Help task pane.

12. **Hide the Office Assistant.**

    Choose Help ➪ Hide the Office Assistant.

Lab 1B: Practicing File Management Techniques

Level of difficulty: Easy

Time to complete: 5 to 15 minutes

1. **Start PowerPoint.**

    Choose Start ➪ (All) Programs ➪ Microsoft PowerPoint.

2. **Open the file Lab01A.ppt from the Labs folder on the CD.**

    a. Insert the CD in your PC's CD drive.

    b. Choose File ➪ Open. The Open dialog box appears.

c. Choose your CD drive from the Look In list. Its content appears.

d. Double-click the Labs folder. The content of the Labs folder appears.

e. Double-click the Lab01A.ppt file. The file opens in PowerPoint.

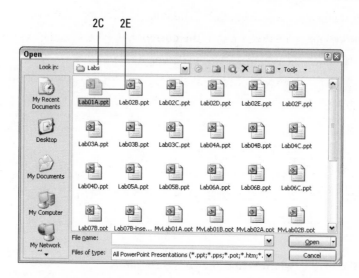

3. Create a new folder in My Documents called Lab01, and save a copy of the Lab01A.ppt file there under the name MyLab01A.ppt.

a. Choose File ➪ Save As. The Save As dialog box appears.

b. Click the My Documents icon. The content of that folder appears.

c. Click the New Folder icon. A New Folder dialog box opens.

d. Type Lab01 and click OK. The new folder is created; it opens automatically.

e. In the File Name box, replace the current text (if any) with MyLab01A.

f. Click Save. The file is saved under the new name in the new location.

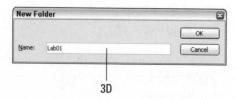

4. Save a copy of the presentation as a PowerPoint Show, and call the copy MyLab01A-show.pps.

   a. Choose File ⇨ Save As. The Save As dialog box appears.

   b. Click the My Documents icon. The content of that folder appears.

   c. Double-click the Lab01 folder. The content of that folder appears.

   d. In the File name box, replace the current text with MyLab01A-show.pps.

   e. In the Save as Type list, choose PowerPoint Show.

   f. Click Save. A warning appears.

   g. Click Yes. The copy is saved.

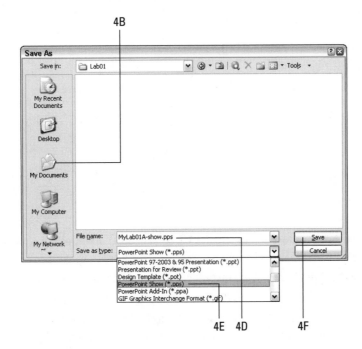

5. Close the PowerPoint Show copy of the presentation.

   Choose File ⇨ Close. The file is closed.

6. Reopen MyLab01A.ppt.

   a. Choose File ⇨ Open. The Open dialog box appears.

   b. Double-click MyLab01A. The file opens.

7. From the Open dialog box, delete MyLab01A-show.pps.

    a. Choose File ➪ Open. The Open dialog box appears.

    b. Click MyLab01A-show.pps. The file name appears highlighted.

    c. Press the Delete key. A confirmation appears.

    d. Click Yes. The file is deleted from the listing.

    e. Click Cancel. The Save As dialog box closes.

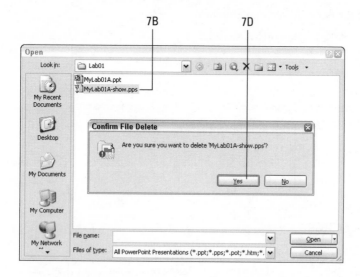

8. Assign an open password of PROTECT to MyLab01A.ppt and a modify password of CHANGE.

    a. Choose File ➪ Save As. The Save As dialog box appears.

    b. Choose Tools ➪ Security Options. The Security Options dialog box opens.

    c. In the Password to Open box, type **PROTECT**. (Passwords are case-sensitive.)

    d. In the Password to Modify box, type **CHANGE**.

    e. Click OK.

    f. When prompted to reenter the password to open, type **PROTECT** and click OK.

    g. When prompted to reenter the password to modify, type **CHANGE** and click OK.

    h. In the Save As dialog box, click Save.

    i. A confirmation box appears; click Yes.

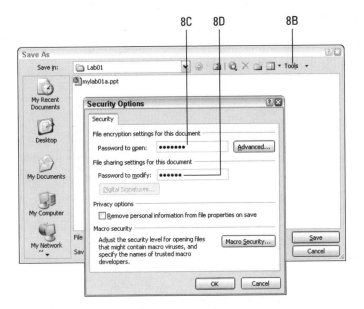

9. Close MyLab01A.ppt.

Choose File ➪ Close.

10. Reopen MyLab01A.ppt.

a. Choose File ➪ Open. The Open dialog box appears.

b. Double-click MyLab01A.ppt. A Password prompt appears.

c. Type **PROTECT** and click OK. Another password prompt appears.

d. Type **CHANGE** and click OK. The file opens.

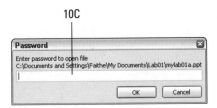

11. Remove all passwords from MyLab01A.ppt.

a. Choose File ➪ Save As. The Save As dialog box appears.

b. Choose Tools ➪ Security Options. The Security Options dialog box opens.

c. Delete the contents of both password boxes, so they are totally empty.

d. Click OK.

e. In the Save As dialog box, click Save.

f. A confirmation box appears; click Yes.

11C   11B

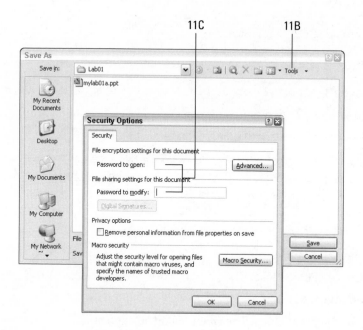

12. Exit PowerPoint.

a. Choose File ➪ Exit.

b. If prompted to save your changes, click Yes.

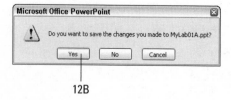

12B

Lab 1C: Practicing Presentation Viewing Techniques

Level of difficulty: Easy

Time to complete: 10 to 15 minutes

Prerequisite: Lab 1B: "Practicing File Management Techniques," steps 1 through 3

1. Open the file MyLab01A.ppt and start PowerPoint at the same time.

a. In Windows, open the My Documents folder.

b. Double-click the Lab01 folder. Its content appears.

c. Double-click the MyLab01A.ppt file. The file opens in PowerPoint.

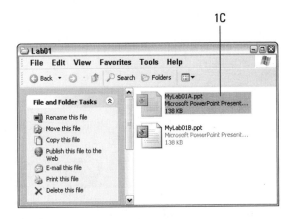

2. Save the file as MyLab01C.ppt.

a. Choose File ⇨ Save As. The Save As dialog box opens.

b. In the File Name box, type MyLab01C.ppt.

c. Click Save. The file is saved under the new name.

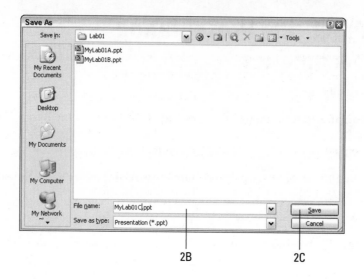

2B   2C

3. View the Outline pane in Normal view.

Click the Outline tab in the left pane. The outline appears there.

3   4B

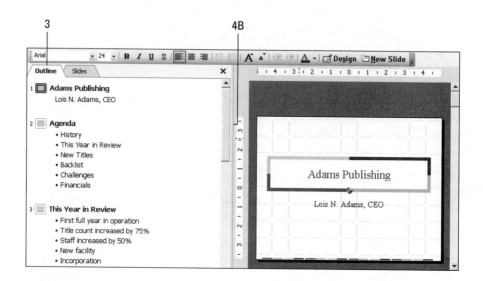

4. **Resize the panes in Normal view so that the Outline pane takes up 50% of the available space.**

   a. Position the mouse pointer between the Outline and Slide panes, so the mouse changes to a double-headed arrow with a vertical line.

   b. Drag to the right until the divider line is in the middle of the screen.

5. **In the Outline pane, change the spelling of the CEO's name from Adams to Addams.**

   a. Click in the Outline pane to move the insertion point there.

   b. Use the arrow keys to position the insertion point between the *A* and the *d* in the name Adams on the title of the first slide.

   c. Type a **d**, changing the name to *Addams*.

   d. Repeat steps b and c for the word *Adams* in body text (the subtitle) on the slide.

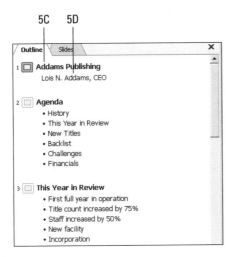

6. **View the Slides pane in Normal view.**

   Click the Slides tab in the left pane. The outline is replaced by a single vertical line of slide thumbnail images.

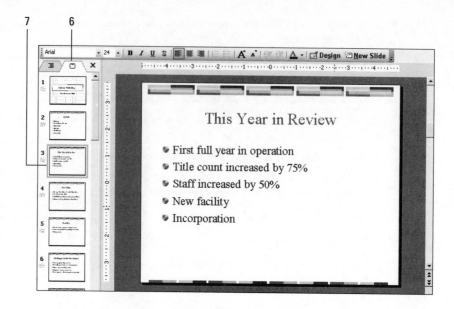

7. **Display the third slide in the presentation.**

    In the Slides pane, click on the third slide from the top. The slide appears in the slide area (center) in Normal view.

8. **Switch to Slide Sorter view, and set the Zoom to 75%.**

    a. Click the Slide Sorter button in the bottom left corner of the screen. The view switches to Slide Sorter.

    b. Click on the arrow at the right of the Zoom to access the drop-down list on the toolbar. Choose 75%.

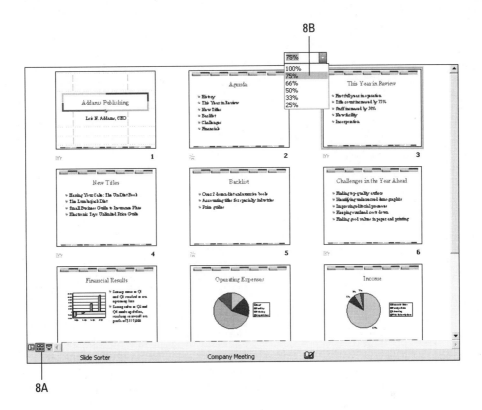

9. Return to Normal view and display slide six.

Double-click the sixth slide in Slide Sorter view. Normal view returns, with the sixth slide selected.

10. Turn off the Drawing toolbar.

Choose View ➪ Toolbars ➪ Drawing. The toolbar disappears and other onscreen panes become slightly larger to use the newfound space.

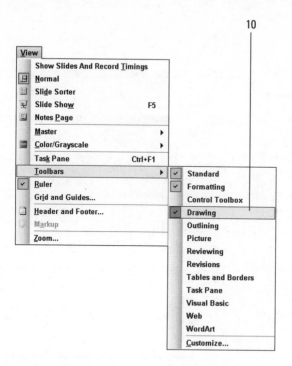

11. Preview the first three slides in Slide Show view, and then return to Normal view.

   a. Choose View ⇨ Slide Show. The first slide appears full-screen.

   b. Move the mouse slightly. Control buttons appear in the lower left corner of the screen.

   c. Click to move to the second slide.

   d. Click to move to the third slide.

   e. Press Esc to return to Normal view.

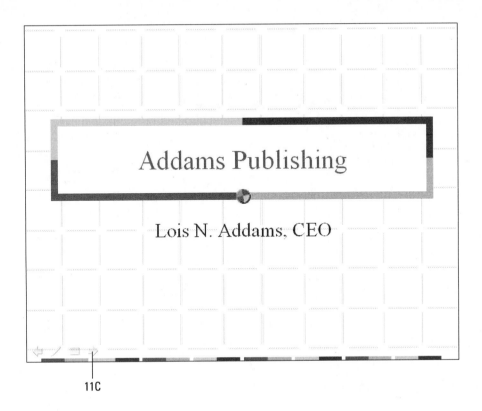

11C

12. **Turn on the task pane.**

   Choose View ➪ Task Pane.

13. **Change the task pane to the New Presentation options, and use the task pane to start a new, blank presentation.**

   a. Open the task pane's drop-down list and choose New Presentation. The New Presentation task pane appears.

   b. Click the Blank Presentation hyperlink.

   c. Close the task pane by clicking the Close (X) button in its top-right corner.

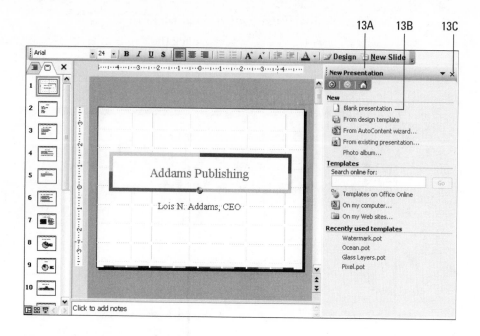

14. Tile the presentation windows.

Choose Window ➪ Arrange All.

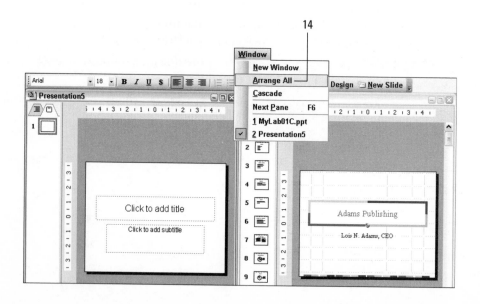

15. Close the Outline/Slides pane in each window.

    a. In the presentation at the left, click the X button in the Outline/Slides pane. If there is no X button, enlarge the pane slightly so that it appears.

    b. In the presentation at the right, click the X button in the Outline/Slides pane.

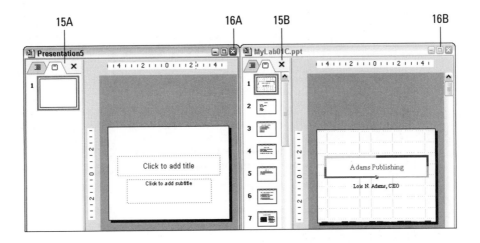

16. Close the new, unnamed presentation without saving your changes to it and maximize the MyLab01C.ppt window.

    a. Click the Close (X) button on the title bar for the unnamed presentation. If prompted to save changes, click No.

    b. Click the Maximize button in the title bar for MyLab01C.ppt.

17. Restore the Outline/Slides pane.

    Choose View ⇨ Normal (Restore Panes).

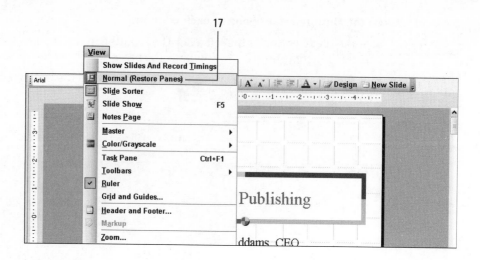

18. **Exit PowerPoint, saving your changes.**

   a. Choose File ➪ Exit.

   b. If prompted to save your changes to MyLab01C.ppt, click Yes.

✦   ✦   ✦

Building Your Presentation

Developing Your Action Plan

◆   ◆   ◆   ◆

In This Chapter

Identifying your audience and purpose

Choosing an appropriate presentation method

Planning the visual image to convey

Deciding whether to use multimedia effects

Deciding whether handouts are appropriate

Planning your rehearsal times and methods

◆   ◆   ◆   ◆

Can you guess what the single biggest problem is when most people use PowerPoint? Here's a hint: It's not a problem with the software at all. It's that they don't think things through carefully before they create their presentation, and then they have to go back and make major modifications later. You've probably heard the saying, "If you don't have time to do it right, how are you going to find time to do it over?" This sentiment is certainly applicable to creating presentations.

In this chapter, I outline an 11-point strategy for creating the appropriate PowerPoint presentation right from the start. By considering the issues addressed here, you can avoid making false assumptions about your audience and their needs and avoid creating a beautiful presentation with some horrible flaw that makes it unusable. Spend a half hour or so in this chapter and you can save yourself literally days in rework later.

Step 1: Identifying Your Audience and Purpose

Before you can think about the presentation you need to create, you must first think of your audience. Different audiences respond to different presentation types, as you probably already know from real-life experience. A sales pitch to a client requires a very different approach than an informational briefing to your coworkers. Ask yourself these questions:

  ◆ **How many people will be attending the presentation?**
    The attendance makes a difference because the larger the group, the larger your screen needs to be so that everyone can see. If you don't have access to a large

screen, you have to make the lettering and charts big and chunky so that everyone can read your presentation.

✦ **What is the average age of the attendees?** Although it's difficult to generalize about people, it's especially important to keep your presentation light and entertaining when you're presenting to a very young audience (teens and children). Generally speaking, the older the audience, the more authoritative you need to be.

✦ **What role will the audience take in relation to the topic?** If you are rolling out a new product or system, the managerial staff will likely want a general overview of it, but the line workers who will actually be operating the product need lots of details. Generally speaking, the higher the level of managers, the more removed they will be from the action, and the fewer details of operation they need.

✦ **How well does the audience already know the topic?** If you are presenting to a group that knows nothing about your topic, you want to keep things basic and make sure that you define all the unfamiliar terms. In contrast, with a group of experts you are likely to have many follow-up questions after the main presentation, so you should plan on having some hidden backup slides ready in anticipation of those questions. See "Hiding Slides for Backup Use" in Chapter 26.

✦ **Does the audience care about the topic?** If the topic is personally important to the attendees (such as information on their insurance benefits or vacation schedule), they will likely pay attention even if your presentation is plain and straightforward. If you must win them over, however, you need to spend more time on the bells and whistles.

✦ **Are the attendees prejudiced either positively or negatively toward the topic?** Keeping in mind the audience's preconceived ideas can make the difference between success and failure in some presentations. For example, knowing that a client hates sales pitches can help you tailor your own to be out of the ordinary.

✦ **Are the attendees in a hurry?** Do your attendees have all afternoon to listen to you, or do they need to get back to their regular jobs? Nothing is more frustrating than sitting through a leisurely presentation when you're watching precious minutes tick away. Know your audience's schedule and their preference for quick versus thorough coverage.

Next, think about what you want the outcome of the presentation to be. You might want more than one outcome, but try to identify the primary one as your main goal. Some outcomes to consider include the following:

✦ **Audience feels good about the topic.** Some presentations are strictly cheerleading sessions, designed to sway the audience's opinion. Don't discount this objective — it's a perfectly legitimate reason to make a presentation! For example, suppose a new management staff has taken over a factory. The new management team might want to reassure the workers that everything is going to be okay. A feel-good, Welcome to the Team presentation, complete with gimmicks like company T-shirts or hats, can go a long way in this regard.

✦ **Audience is informed.** Sometimes you need to convey information to a group of people and no decision is involved on their part. For example, suppose your company has switched insurance carriers and you want to let all the employees know about their new benefits. An informational presentation can cover most of the common questions and save your human resources people lots of time in answering the same questions over and over.

✦ **Audience members make individual decisions.** This presentation is a kind of sales pitch in which you are pitching an idea or product to a group but each person says yes or no individually. For example, suppose you are selling time-share vacation condos. You may give a presentation to a group of 100 in an attempt to sell your package to at least a few of the group.

This presentation type can also have an informational flavor; you are informing people about their choices without pushing one choice or the other. For example, if your employees have a choice of health plans, you might present the pros and cons of each and then leave it to each employee to make a selection.

✦ **Audience makes a group decision.** This is the kind of presentation that scares a lot of people. You face a group of people who will confer and make a single decision based on the information you present. Most sales pitches fall into this category. You might be explaining your product to a group of managers, for example, to try to get their company to buy it.

Think about these factors carefully and try to come up with a single statement that summarizes your audience and purpose. Here are some examples:

✦ *I am presenting to 100 factory workers to explain their new health insurance choices and teach them how to fill out the necessary forms.*

✦ *I am presenting to a group of 6 to 10 midlevel managers, trying to get them to decide as a group to buy my product.*

✦ *I am presenting to a group of 20 professors to convince at least some of them to use my company's textbooks in their classes.*

✦ *I am presenting to individual Internet users to explain how my company's service works.*

Let's take that first example. Figure 5-1 shows some notes that a presenter might take when preparing to explain information about employee benefits enrollment to a group of factory workers. Jot down your own notes before moving to Step 2.

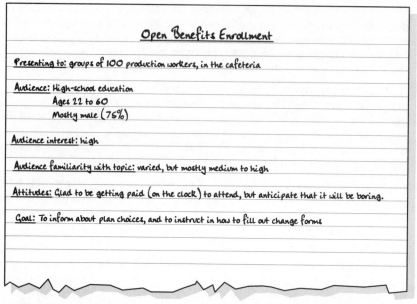

Figure 5-1: Make notes about your presentation's purpose and audience.

Step 2: Choosing Your Presentation Method

You essentially have three ways to present your presentation to your audience, and you need to pick the way you're going to use up front. They include speaker-led, self-running, and user-interactive. Within each of those three broad categories, you have some additional choices. Before you start creating the presentation in PowerPoint, you should know which method you are going to use because it makes a big difference in the text and other objects you put on the slides.

Parts V and VI of this book are broken down by presentation method, because the PowerPoint tools and features for each presentation method are very different. For example, in Part V, "Presenting Speaker-Led Presentations," you will learn about creating support materials like handouts and about setting up hidden slides in your PowerPoint presentation containing support data. In contrast, Part VI covers PowerPoint features pertaining to self-running and interactive presentations, such as recording voice-over narration, setting the timing of a self-running show, and creating presentations that will run from Web sites.

Speaker-led presentations

The speaker-led presentation is the traditional type of presentation: you stand up in front of a live audience (or one connected through teleconferencing) and give a speech. The slides you create in PowerPoint become your support materials. The primary message comes from you; the slides and handouts are just helpers. See Figure 5-2. The special factors involved in this kind of presentation are covered in Part V of the book (Chapters 24 through 27).

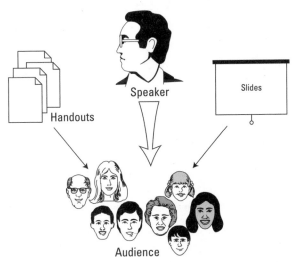

Figure 5-2: In a speaker-led presentation, the speaker is the main attraction; the slides and handouts do not have to carry the burden.

With this kind of presentation, your slides don't have to tell the whole story. Each slide can contain just a few main points, and you can flesh out each point in your discussion. In fact, this kind of presentation works best when your slides don't contain a lot of information, because people pay more attention to you, the speaker, if they're not trying to read at the same time. For example, instead of listing the top five reasons to switch to your service, you might have a slide that just reads: *Why Switch? Five Reasons.* The audience has to listen to you to find out what the reasons are.

This kind of presentation also requires some special planning. For example, do you want to send each audience member home with handouts? If so, you need to prepare them. They may or may not be identical to your PowerPoint slides; that's up to you. Handouts and other support materials (such as speaker notecards) are covered in Chapter 24.

You also need to learn how to handle PowerPoint's presentation controls, which is the subject of Chapter 25. It can be really embarrassing to be fiddling with the computer controls in the middle of a speech, so you should *practice, practice, practice* ahead of time.

Self-running presentations

With a self-running presentation, all the rules change. Instead of using the slides as teasers or support materials, you must make the slides carry the entire show. All the information must be right there, because you won't be looking over the audience's shoulders with helpful narration. See Figure 5-3.

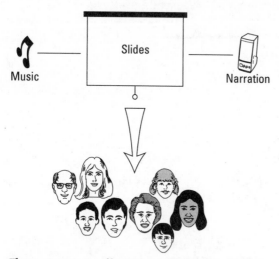

Figure 5-3: In a self-running presentation, the slides carry the entire burden because there are no handouts and no live speaker.

In general, self-running presentations are presented to individuals or very small groups. For example, you might set up a kiosk in a busy lobby or a booth at a trade show and have a brief (say, five slides) presentation constantly running that explains your product or service.

Because there is no dynamic human being keeping the audience's attention, self-running presentations must include attention-getting features. Sounds, video clips, interesting transitions, and prerecorded narratives are all good ways to attract viewers. Part III of this book explains how to use sounds, videos, and other moving objects in a presentation to add interest.

You must also consider the timing with a self-running presentation. Because there is no way for a viewer to tell the presentation, "Okay, I'm done reading this slide; bring on the next one," you must carefully plan how long each slide will remain on-screen. This kind of timing requires some practice! Chapter 28 deals with these timing issues and also explains how to record voice-over narration.

User-interactive presentations

A user-interactive presentation is like a self-running one except the viewer has some input, as in Figure 5-4. Rather than standing by passively as the slides advance, the viewer can tell PowerPoint when to advance a slide. Depending on the presentation's setup, viewers may also be able to skip around in the presentation (perhaps to skip over topics they're not interested in) and request more information. Chapter 29, "Designing User-Interactive Presentations," explains how to place action buttons on slides that let the viewer control the action. This type of presentation is typically addressed to a single user at a time, rather than a group.

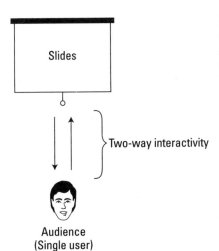

Figure 5-4: In a user-interactive presentation, the audience chooses when to advance slides and what to see next. It typically requires more time to prepare because you must account for all possible user choices.

This kind of presentation is most typically distributed over the Internet, a company intranet, or via CD. The user runs it using either PowerPoint or a free program called PowerPoint Viewer that you can provide for download. You can also translate a PowerPoint presentation to HTML format (the native format for World Wide Web pages), so that anyone with a Web browser can view it. However, presentations lose a lot of their cool features when you do that (such as the sound and video clips), so consider the decision carefully. Chapter 30 contains much more information about online distribution.

Step 3: Choosing Your Delivery Method

Whereas the presentation method is the general conceptual way the audience interacts with the information, the delivery method is the way that you *deliver* that interaction. It's a subtle but important difference. For example, suppose you have decided that speaker-led is your presentation method. That's the big picture, but how will you deliver it? Will you present from a computer, or use 35mm slides, or overhead transparencies, or just plain old handouts? All of those fall under the big umbrella of "speaker-led."

PowerPoint gives you a lot of options for delivery method. Some of these are appropriate mainly for speaker-led shows; others can be used for any presentation method. Here are some of the choices:

✦ **Computer show through PowerPoint.** You can use PowerPoint's View Show feature to play the slides on the computer screen. You can hook up a larger, external monitor to the PC so that the audience can see it better if needed. This requires that PowerPoint (or the PowerPoint Viewer utility) be installed on the computer at the presentation site. This works for speaker-led, self-running, or user-interactive shows. See Chapter 25.

✦ **Computer show through a Web site.** You can save your presentation in Web format and then publish it to a Web site. You can use this for speaker-led, self-running, or user-interactive shows, and no special software is required (just a Web browser. However, you lose some of the cool graphical effects, including some transitions and animation effects. Web delivery is used mostly for user-interactive or self-running shows. See Chapters 29 and 30.

✦ **Computer show on CD.** You can create a CD containing the presentation and the PowerPoint Viewer utility. The presentation starts automatically whenever the CD is inserted into a PC. This would be most useful for user-interactive or self-running shows. See Chapter 31.

✦ **35mm slides.** For a speaker-led presentation, 35mm slides can be created. They look good, but they require a slide projector and viewing screen, and don't show up well in a room with much light. You also, of course, lose all the special effects such as animations and sounds. 35mm slides are for speaker-led shows only, as are the next two options. See Chapter 24.

✦ **Overhead transparencies.** If you don't have a computer or a slide projector available for your speaker-led show, you might be forced to use an old-fashioned overhead projector. You can create overhead transparencies on most printers. (Be careful that the type you buy are designed to work with your type of printer! Transparencies designed for inkjet printers will melt in a laser printer.)

✦ **Paper.** The last resort, if there is no projection media available whatsoever, is to distribute your slides to the audience on paper. You will want to give them handouts, but the handouts should be a supplement to an on-screen show, not the main show themselves, if possible. Chapter 24 covers printing, both on paper and on transparencies.

Step 4: Choosing the Appropriate Template and Design

PowerPoint comes with so many presentation templates and designs that you're sure to find one that's appropriate for your situation. PowerPoint provides three levels of help in this arena, as you learn in Chapter 6. You can use an AutoContent Wizard to work through a series of dialog boxes that help you create a presentation based on a presentation template, you can apply a design template, or you can work from scratch.

PowerPoint includes two kinds of templates: presentation templates and design templates. Presentation templates contain sample text and sample formatting appropriate to certain situations. For example, there are several presentation templates that can help you sell a product or service. The AutoContent Wizard is the best way to choose a presentation template, as you learn in Chapter 6.

If you want to take advantage of the sample text provided by a presentation template, you should make sure you choose one that's appropriate. PowerPoint includes dozens, so you should take some time going through them to understand the full range of options before making your decision. (See "Starting a Presentation Based on a Presentation Template" in Chapter 6.) Remember, once you've started a presentation using one presentation template, you can't change to another without starting over.

A design template, in contrast, is just a combination of fonts, colors, and graphics, and you can apply a different design to any presentation at any time. Therefore, it's not as crucial to select the correct design up front, because you can play with these elements later. You learn a lot more about these design templates in Chapter 12.

Expert Tip You aren't stuck with the color scheme or design that comes with a particular presentation template. If you like the sample text in one presentation template and the design in another, start with the one containing the good sample text. Then borrow the design from the other one later, as explained in "Changing the Presentation Design" in Chapter 12. Each design comes with several alternative color schemes, so pick the design first, and then the color scheme.

Generally speaking, your choice of design should depend on the audience and the way you plan to present. Here are some suggestions:

✦ To make an audience feel good or relaxed about a topic, use blues and greens. To get an audience excited and happy, use reds and yellows. For slides you plan to project on a slide screen or show on a PC, use high contrast, such as dark backgrounds with light lettering or light backgrounds with dark lettering. For slides you plan to print and hand out, dark on white is better. See "Changing the Color Scheme" in Chapter 12.

✦ For readability in print, use serif fonts like Times New Roman. For readability onscreen, or for a casual, modern feel, use sans-serif fonts like Arial. Refer to "Changing the Font" in Chapter 8 for more information.

✦ The farther away from the screen the audience will be, the larger you need to make the lettering.

✦ It's best if all slides use the same design and color scheme, but there may be exceptions when your interests are best served by breaking that rule. For example, you might shake things up midway through a presentation by showing a key slide with a different color background. See "Changing the Background" in Chapter 12.

Step 5: Developing the Content

Only after you have made all the decisions in Steps 1 through 4 can you start developing your content in a real PowerPoint presentation. This is the point at which Chapter 6 picks up, guiding you through creating the file and organizing slides.

Then comes the work of writing the text for each slide, which most people prefer to do in Normal view. (Remember, you learned about Normal view in Chapter 2.) Type the text on the outline or on the text placeholder on the slide itself, reformat it as needed to make certain bits of it special (for example, setting a key phrase in bold or italics), and you're ready to roll.

Developing your content may include more than just typing text. Your content may include charts (created in PowerPoint or imported from another program, such as Excel), pictures, and other elements. You learn about graphics in Chapters 14 and 15, and about various kinds of charts in Chapters 16 and 17. Chapter 18 covers importing content from other programs.

Step 6: Creating the Visual Image

The term *visual image* refers to the overall impression that the audience gets from watching the presentation. You create a polished, professional impression by making small tweaks to your presentation after you have the content down pat.

You can enhance the visual image by making minor adjustments to the slide's design. For example, you can give a dark slide a warmer feel by using bright yellow instead of white for lettering. Repositioning a company logo and making it larger may make the headings look less lonely. WordArt can be used to take the place of regular text, especially on a title slide (as in Figures 5-5 and 5-6). A product picture may be more attractive in a larger size or with a different-colored mat around it. All of these little touches take practice and experience.

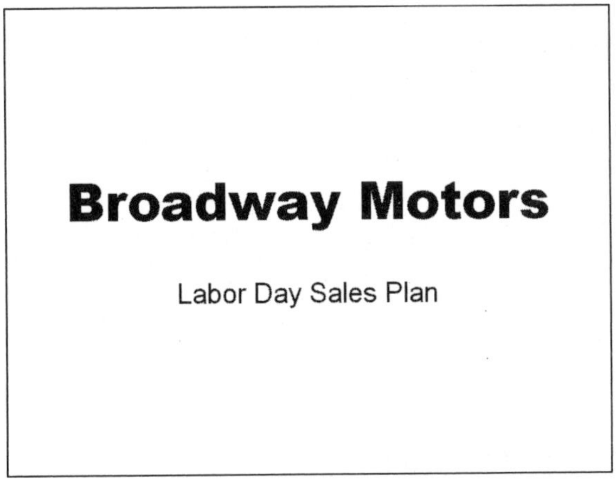

Broadway Motors

Labor Day Sales Plan

Figure 5-5: The look of this sparsely populated page can be easily improved.

Broadway Motors

Labor Day Sales Plan

Figure 5-6: Using WordArt allows this page to make a sharper impact.

Audiences like consistency. They like things they can rely on, like a repeated company logo on every slide, accurate page numbering on handouts, and the title appearing in exactly the same spot on every slide. You can create a consistent visual image by enforcing such rules in your presentation development. It's easier than you might think, because PowerPoint provides a Slide Master specifically for images and text that should repeat on each slide. You see it in action in Chapter 7.

Step 7: Adding Multimedia Effects

If you're creating a self-running presentation, multimedia effects can be extremely important for developing audience interest. Flashy videos and soundtracks can make even the most boring product fun to hear about. How about a trumpet announcing the arrival of your new product on the market, or a video of your CEO explaining the reasoning behind the recent merger? Chapters 20 and 21 deal with the mechanics of placing sound and video clips into a presentation and controlling when and how they play.

Caution   Even if you are going to be speaking live, you still might want to incorporate some multimedia elements in your show. Be careful, however, not to let them outshine you or appear gratuitous. Be aware of your audience (see Step 1), and remember that older and higher-level managers want less flash and more substance.

All kinds of presentations can benefit from animations and transitions on the slides. *Animations* are simple movements of the objects on a slide. For example, you might make the bullet points on a list fly onto the page one at a time so you can discuss each one on its own. When the next one flies in, the previous ones can turn a different color so the current one stands out. Or you might animate a picture of a car so that it appears to "drive onto" the slide, accompanied by the sound of an engine revving. You can also animate charts by making data series appear one at a time, so it looks like the chart is building. You learn about animations in Chapter 22.

Transitions are animated ways of moving from slide to slide. The most basic and boring transition is to simply remove one slide from the screen and replace it with another, but you can use all kinds of alternative effects like zooming the new slide in; sliding it from the top, bottom, left, or right; or creating a fade in transition effect. Transitions are covered in Chapter 22.

Step 8: Creating the Handouts and Notes

This step is applicable only for speaker-led presentations. With a live audience, you may want to provide handouts so they can follow along. The handouts can be verbatim copies of your slides, or they can be abbreviated versions with just the most basic information included as a memory-jogger. Handouts can be either black and white or color.

PowerPoint provides several handout formats. You can print from one to nine slides per printout, with or without lines for the audience to write additional notes. Chapter 24 walks you through selecting the appropriate size and format and working with your printer to get the best results. Figure 5-7 shows a typical page from a set of audience handouts.

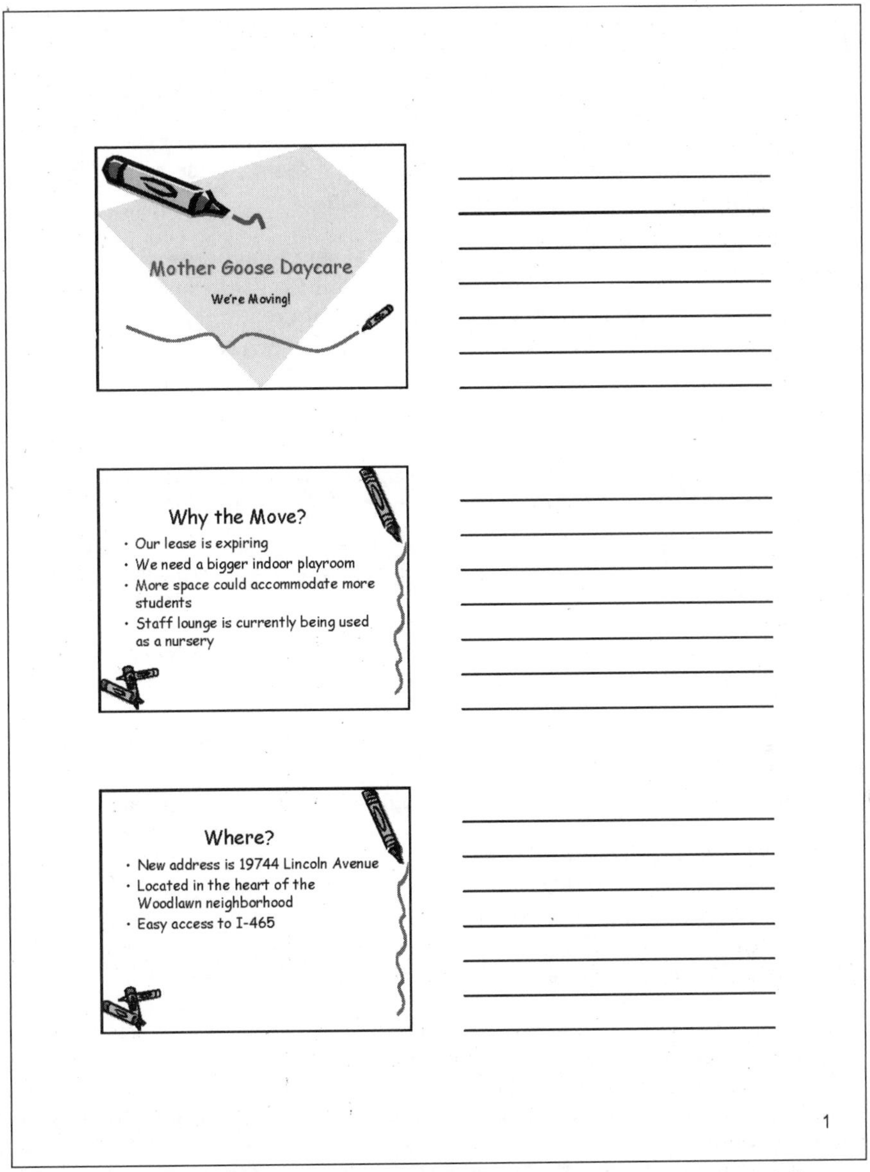

Figure 5-7: A live audience will appreciate having handouts to help them follow along with the presentation and remember the content later.

Expert Tip   A continual debate rages in the professional speakers' community over when to give out handouts. Some people feel that if you distribute handouts before the presentation, people will read them and not listen to the presentation. Others feel that if you wait until after the presentation to distribute the handouts, people will frantically try to take their own notes during the presentation or will not follow the ideas as easily. There's no real right or wrong, it seems, so distribute them whenever it makes the most sense for your situation.

As the speaker, you may need your own special set of handouts with your own notes that the audience should not see. PowerPoint calls these Notes Pages, and as you learned in Chapter 2, there is a special view for creating them. (You can also enter notes directly into the Notes pane in Normal view.) Notes, like handouts, are covered in Chapter 24.

Step 9: Rehearsing the Presentation

No matter which type of presentation you are creating (speaker-led, self-running, or user-interactive), you need to rehearse it. The goals for rehearsing, however, are different for each type.

Rehearsing a live presentation

When you rehearse a live presentation, you check the presentation slides to ensure they are complete, accurate, and in the right order. You may need to rearrange them (see Chapter 6) and hide some of them for backup-only use (see Chapter 26).

You should also rehearse using PowerPoint's presentation controls that display each slide on a monitor and let you move from slide to slide, take notes, assign action items, and even draw directly on a slide. Make sure you know how to back up, how to jump to the beginning or end, and how to display one of your backup slides. These skills are covered in Chapter 25.

Rehearsing a self-running presentation

With a speaker-led presentation, the presenter can fix any glitches that pop up or explain away any errors. With a self-running presentation, you don't have that luxury. The presentation itself is your emissary. Therefore, you must go over and over it, checking it many times to make sure it is perfect before distributing it. Nothing is worse than a self-running presentation that doesn't run, or one that contains an embarrassing error.

The most important feature in a self-running presentation is timing. You must make the presentation pause the correct amount of time for the audience to be able to read the text on each slide. The pause must be long enough so that even slow readers can catch it all, but short enough so that fast readers do not get bored. Can you see how difficult this can be to make perfect?

PowerPoint has a Rehearse Timings feature (Figure 5-8) designed to help you with this task. It lets you show the slides and advance them manually after the correct amount of time has passed. The Rehearse Timings feature records how much time you spend on each slide and gives you a report so you can modify the timing if necessary. For example, suppose you are working on a presentation that is supposed to last 10 minutes, but with your timings, it comes out to only 9 minutes. You can add additional time for each slide to stretch it out to fill the full 10 minutes. Chapter 28 covers timing.

Rehearsal toolbar

Figure 5-8: You can rehearse timings so your audience has enough time to read the slides but doesn't get bored waiting for the next one.

You may also want to record voice-over narration for your presentation. You can rehearse this too, to make sure that the voice matches the slide it is supposed to describe (which is absolutely crucial, as you can imagine!). You learn about voice-overs in Chapter 28, too.

Rehearsing a user-interactive presentation

In a user-interactive presentation, you provide the readers with on-screen buttons they can click to move through the presentation, so timing is not an issue. The crucial factor with a user-interactive presentation is link accuracy. Each button on each slide is a link. When your readers click a button for the next slide, it had better darned well take them to the next slide and not to somewhere else. And if you include a hyperlink to a Web address on the Internet, when the readers click it, the Web browser should open and that page should appear. If the hyperlink contains a typo and the readers see `File Not Found` instead of the Web page, the error reflects poorly on you. Chapter 29 covers creating and inserting these links.

If you are planning to distribute your presentation via the Internet, you have a big decision to make. You can distribute the presentation in its native PowerPoint format and preserve all its whiz-bang features like animations and videos. However, not everyone on the Internet owns a copy of PowerPoint, obviously, so you limit your audience. PowerPoint supplies a free program called the PowerPoint Viewer that you can post for downloading on your Web page, but not everyone will take the time to download and install that, so you may turn off potential viewers before you start.

The other option is to save the presentation in HTML (Web) format. When you save in HTML format, you convert each of the slides to a Web page, and you add links (if you didn't already have them) that move from slide to slide. You lose many of the animations, transitions, sounds, videos, any animated graphics, and some other extras, but you retain your text and most static elements of the presentation. The advantage is that everyone with a Web browser can view your presentation with no special downloads or setup.

You learn more about preparing a presentation for the Internet, no matter which method you choose, in Chapter 30.

Step 10: Giving the Presentation

For a user-interactive or self-running presentation, giving the presentation is somewhat anticlimactic. You just make it available and the users come get it. Yawn.

However, for a speaker-led presentation, giving the speech is the highlight, the pinnacle, of the process. If you've done a good job rehearsing, you are already familiar with PowerPoint's presentation controls, described in Chapter 25. Be prepared to back up, to skip ahead, to answer questions by displaying hidden slides, and to pause the whole thing (and black out the screen) so you can hold a tangential discussion. Chapter 25 covers all these situations in case you need to review them.

What remains then? Nothing except setting up the room and overcoming your stage fright. Chapter 32 provides some hints about using a meeting room most effectively and being a dynamic speaker. Check them out—and then go get 'em, winner!

Step 11: Assessing Your Success and Refining Your Work

If giving a presentation was a one-time thing for you—great. It's over, and you never have to think about it again. But more likely, you will have to give another presentation someday, somewhere, so don't drive the experience out of your mind just yet. Perhaps you learned something that might be useful to you later?

Immediately after the presentation, while it is still fresh in your mind, jot down your responses to these questions. Then keep them on file to refer to later, the next time you have to do a presentation!

- ✦ Did the colors and design of the slides seem appropriate?

- ✦ Could everyone in the audience read the slides easily?

- ✦ Did the audience look mostly at you, at the screen, or at the handouts? Was that what you intended?

- ✦ Did the audience try to take notes as you were speaking? If so, did you give them handouts with note-taking lines to write on?

- ✦ Was the length of the presentation appropriate? Did the audience get bored or restless at any point?

- ✦ Were there any slides that you wished you had prepared but didn't?

- ✦ Were there any slides that you would omit if you were doing it over?

- ✦ Did your speaker notes give you enough help that you could speak with authority?

- ✦ Did the transitions and animations add to the entertainment value, or were they distracting or corny?

- ✦ Did the sound and video clips play with adequate quality? Were they appropriate and useful?

Summary

Creating effective PowerPoint presentations requires more than just knowing the software. It requires careful planning and step-by-step preparation. In this chapter, you learned about the steps you need to take, from start to finish, to assemble the PowerPoint slides for your next great success:

✦ *Step 1: Identify your audience and purpose.* No flip answers are acceptable here; spend some time thinking about the right answers.

✦ *Step 2: Choose your presentation method.* Will you give a live, speaker-led show, distribute it online, or set up a self-running kiosk show?

✦ *Step 3: Choose your delivery method.* Will you deliver with a 35mm projector? With a computer? With overhead transparencies? Over the Internet?

✦ *Step 4: Choose a template and design.* PowerPoint comes with dozens of professional-quality templates, some of which include sample text. Choose the one that matches your answers in Steps 1 and 2.

✦ *Step 5: Develop the content.* Flash is useless without substance. Create the text for your presentation in Outline view in PowerPoint or import an outline from Word.

✦ *Step 6: Create the visual image.* Polish your presentation design by making sure that the slides are attractive and consistent.

✦ *Step 7: Add multimedia effects.* Only after the content and overall image are solid should you add extras like sound, video, transition, and animation.

✦ *Step 8: Create handouts and notes.* If you are giving a live presentation, you may want notes for yourself (speaker notes) and notes for your audience (handouts).

✦ *Step 9: Rehearse.* Run through your presentation several times to make sure it is free from embarrassing mistakes. If necessary, add timing controls and voice-over narratives.

✦ *Step 10: Give the presentation.* Take a deep breath and imagine the audience in their underwear! If you're familiar with PowerPoint's presentation controls, you'll do fine.

✦ *Step 11: Review and revise your work.* There's always room for improvement. Analyze your performance to make the next one even better.

✦   ✦   ✦

Starting a New Presentation

There are several ways to create a new presentation in PowerPoint, ranging from the full-service way (the AutoContent Wizard) to the no-frills way (starting with a blank screen). Each method has its benefits and drawbacks.

✦ **AutoContent Wizard.** You work through a series of dialog boxes to select sample content that matches the presentation you want to give.

- *Pros:* It is very easy, and the sample slides can help you determine how to structure your speech.

- *Cons:* The Wizard chooses the design; you must change the design template later if you don't like it. Also, the sample slides may not fit what you want to say, and the AutoContent Wizard can be time-consuming to go through.

✦ **Presentation template.** You choose a template containing sample content from the same list as the one you see with the AutoContent Wizard, but you do not go through all the AutoContent Wizard dialog boxes.

- *Pros:* It provides sample content more quickly than the AutoContent Wizard.

- *Cons:* Disadvantages are the same as for AutoContent Wizard, but it is less time-consuming.

✦ **Design template.** You choose a template containing a background design, colors, font choices, and other formatting, and then you manually create each slide that goes into the presentation.

- *Pros:* You pick the design to match your message; it is quicker and easier than starting with a blank screen.

- *Cons:* There is no sample content guidance, and it takes some time to create the necessary slides.

✦ **Blank presentation.** You start a new presentation that contains no slides and no formatting, and you add it all from the ground up.

- *Pros:* This method provides maximum flexibility; you do not have to clean up any formatting or content that you didn't want in the first place.

- *Cons:* It can be very time-consuming to build an entire presentation completely from scratch, and it requires you have a greater knowledge of PowerPoint's features than you would otherwise need.

For your first few presentations, I suggest using the AutoContent Wizard. Then, graduate to using either a presentation template or a design template, depending on the situation. You will rarely find a need to start with a blank template, but I include coverage of it in this chapter just in case.

Creating a Presentation with the AutoContent Wizard

As I mentioned earlier, the AutoContent Wizard provides the highest level of automation in creating a new presentation. Beginners find it very useful, as it saves lots of time and forestalls the need to learn about PowerPoint's many formatting features to create a decent-looking show.

Note   You won't be stuck with the choices that the AutoContent Wizard makes when it creates your presentation, by the way. If it assigns a design that you don't like, you can change it. If it creates slides that you don't need, you can delete them and/or add others. You have a full range of customization options at your disposal, as always.

To use the AutoContent Wizard, follow these steps:

1. Choose File ⇨ New. The New Presentation task pane appears.

2. Click the From AutoContent Wizard hyperlink. The Wizard starts.

3. Click Next to bypass the introductory screen.

4. Select the category of presentation you want to give. You can use the category buttons to narrow the list (General, Corporate, Projects, and so on), or click All to see all the presentation templates. See Figure 6-1.

5. Select the template you want to use from the list displayed. Then, click Next.

6. When asked the type of output you need, choose the medium you plan to use to give your show: Onscreen presentation, Web presentation, Black and white overheads, Color overheads, or 35mm slides. Then, click Next.

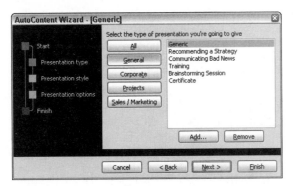

Figure 6-1: Choose a presentation category, and then select an individual presentation template to use.

Note The Wizard wants to know the medium in Step 6 so it can format the slides correctly. For example, 35mm slides need to be a different size and shape than slides shown on a computer screen, and Web presentations need navigation buttons on each slide.

7. When prompted for a presentation title, enter it in the Presentation Title text box. This will appear on the first slide in the presentation (which uses a Title layout). The subtitle will be the name you entered when you installed the application.

Expert Tip If you want your company's name (or some other name) to appear by default as the subtitle of the title slide on all presentations created with the AutoContent Wizard, choose Tools ➪ Options and display the General tab, and put the name in the Name box.

8. In the Items to Include on Each Slide section (see Figure 6-2), enter a footer for the presentation if you want one. This text will repeat at the bottom of each slide. You might use your company name, for example, or *CONFIDENTIAL*.

   If you want a date and/or slide number on each slide, leave those check boxes marked (see Figure 6-2). Otherwise deselect them. The elements you select from this section of the dialog box are added to the Slide Master, which you learn about in Chapter 7.

9. Click Finish. The Wizard creates the presentation. See Figure 6-3.

The one bad thing about using a presentation template is that you don't get to choose the design. However, you can change the design as much as you want after creating the presentation. To change the design template applied to the presentation, choose Format ➪ Slide Design or click the Design button on the toolbar. See Chapter 7 for details.

Figure 6-2: Choose the items to include on each slide.

Sample content

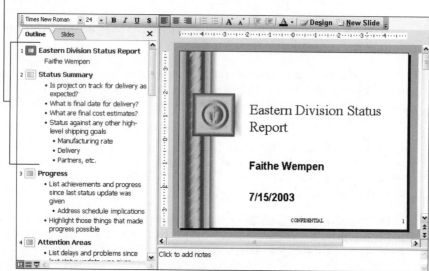

Figure 6-3: The AutoContent Wizard creates a presentation containing slides with sample text and consistent presentation-wide formatting.

Starting a Presentation Based on a Presentation Template

If you want to take advantage of PowerPoint's sample content but you don't want to go through the AutoContent Wizard (which takes some time, doesn't it?), you can create a presentation based on one of the presentation templates. These are the same templates that the AutoContent Wizard draws from; the only difference is that with the following method, they aren't broken down nicely into categories, so you have to know which one you want.

To select an available presentation template, follow these steps:

1. Choose File ⇨ New to open the New Presentation task pane.

2. In the Templates section, click the On My Computer hyperlink. A New Presentation dialog box opens.

3. Click the Presentations tab. A list of the available presentation templates appears, as shown in Figure 6-4. A preview of the selected presentation appears at the right.

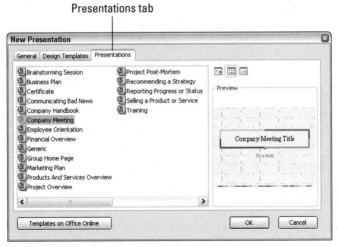

Figure 6-4: Browse the available presentations and choose the one you want.

4. Click the presentation template you want. Don't worry about the formatting and colors; you can change those elements later. Just pick the one that sounds the most like the content you want.

5. Click OK to create a new presentation. Placeholders appear where you must put information, as shown in Figure 6-5 (Company Meeting Title and Presenter). This information would have been inserted by the AutoContent Wizard if you had used it.

6. Replace the text placeholders with the correct information, and then replace the sample text on the other slides with your own content. See Chapters 8 and 9 for more information about editing text.

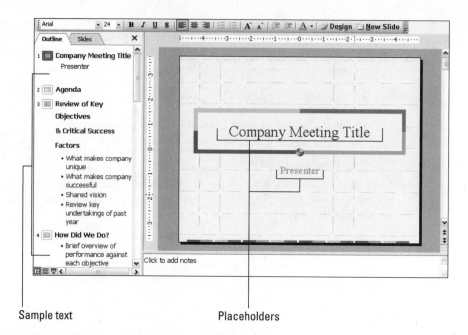

Sample text   Placeholders

Figure 6-5: When you use a presentation template without the Wizard, some placeholders appear for information that the Wizard would have provided.

Starting a Presentation Based on a Design Template

When you start with a design template, you start with all the same formatting advantages as with a presentation template: a background, a color scheme, text styles, and so on. This can save you boatloads of time if you need a professionally formatted presentation right away.

The one thing you *don't* get with a design template, though, is the sample slides. You just get a single title slide, and then you must add the other slides on your own.

To create a new presentation based on a design template, follow these steps:

1. Choose File ➪ New. The New Presentation task pane opens.

2. Click the From Design Template hyperlink. A single blank slide appears in the center of the screen, and the available design templates appear in the task pane.

3. Click one of the designs to apply it to the blank slide; this will show you how it will look. See Figure 6-6. (Keep in mind, however, that with some designs the title slide in the presentation has a different look than subsequent slides, so if you create more slides they might be laid out a little differently.)

Background image   Font scheme   Slide Design task pane

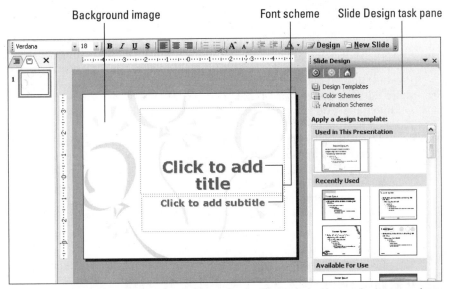

Figure 6-6: Browse the design templates by scrolling, and select a design template by clicking one; close the task pane when you're finished.

4. Close the task pane when you have chosen the design template you want.

5. Create additional slides in the presentation. You can do this in any of several ways, which is covered later in the chapter in the "Adding Slides" section. Briefly, though:

- You can go to the Outline pane and type some text, promoting it with Shift+Tab to new slide status. Slides created this way always have the Title and Text layout.

- You can click the New Slide button on the toolbar to open the New Slide task pane and then click the layout you want for a new slide.

Changing to a different design template at any time is a simple matter — just redisplay the Slide Design task pane and pick a different one. Chapter 7 has more details about design templates.

Starting a Presentation from Scratch

The from-scratch method is for people who know enough about PowerPoint to know exactly what they want — formatting, content, the whole works — and who aren't finding it in any of the presentation templates and design templates. When you create a blank presentation, it's just that — a completely white background on the slides, plain Arial font — no special anything.

To create a blank presentation, click the New button on the toolbar or press Ctrl+N. (Or you can take the long way around by choosing File ➪ New and clicking Blank Presentation.) This starts you off with a single title slide with no formatting. From there you can insert more slides by using layouts, type more slide content in the Outline pane, add formatting, change layouts, and more.

Expert Tip   When starting a show from scratch, you will want to specify your own font choices, background images, colors, and so on. Do this on the Slide Master, covered in Chapter 7, so that you have to make the selections only once instead of individually for every slide. For example, you might want to create a slide design that contains your company logo. You can save your design choices as a design template, and then apply them to future presentations that you create. See Chapter 7 for details.

Starting with a Data File from Another Application

PowerPoint can open files in several formats other than its own, so you can start a new presentation based on some work you have done elsewhere. For example, you could open a Word outline in PowerPoint. The results might not be very attractive — but you can fix that later, with some text editing (Chapters 8 and 9), slide layouts, and design changes (Chapter 7).

To open a file from another application, do the following:

1. Choose File ➪ Open. The Open dialog box appears.

2. Open the Files of Type list and choose the file type. For example, to open a text file, choose All Outlines.

3. Select the desired file and then click Open.

4. Save your work as a PowerPoint file by choosing File ➪ Save As. See Chapter 3 for details.

You can also import a Word outline into an existing presentation, covered later in the "Importing Slides from an Outline" section.

Selecting Slides

PowerPoint has three broad types of commands: those that operate on a single slide, those that operate on a selected group of slides, and those that operate on the entire presentation file. Most of the single-slide commands, such as a command that inserts an object, are executed from Normal or Notes Page views, in which you see only a single slide or notes page, so selecting the slide is not an issue. The selected slide is simply the one that is displayed.

Most of the group-of-slides commands, such as deleting, moving, or applying a transition effect, are best performed in Slide Sorter view. Because you see multiple slides at a time in that view, you must select the slides you want to affect. (You can do this from the Slides pane in Normal view too, but it's a little more awkward.) Here are options for selecting slides in Slide Sorter view:

✦ To select a single slide, click it.

✦ To select multiple slides, hold down the Ctrl key as you click each one. Figure 6-7 shows slides 1, 2, 5, and 6 selected, as indicated by the shaded border around the slides.

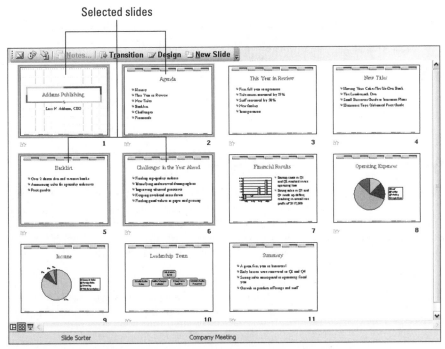

Figure 6-7: Selected slides have a shaded border around them.

✦ To select a contiguous group of slides (for example, slides 1, 2, and 3), click the first one, and then hold down the Shift key as you click the last one. All the ones in between will be selected as well.

To cancel the selection of multiple slides, click anywhere away from the selected slides.

Adding Slides

Now that you have a new presentation and at least one slide, you are ready to start creating your message. You can do this by editing the content of the sample slides, and/or by adding new slides.

Adding slides in the Outline pane

To create plain slides consisting of a heading and a single bulleted list, type the text in the Outline pane, as in Figure 6-8. To make a line of text into a slide title, promote it (press Shift+Tab). To make a line of text into a bullet underneath a slide title, demote it (press Tab). Chapter 8 covers text creation and editing in more detail.

Figure 6-8: Type new text in the Outline pane by typing the title for the new slide and then promote it by pressing Shift+Tab.

Importing slides from an outline

All of the Microsoft Office applications work well together, so it's easy to move content between them. For example, you can create an outline for a presentation in Microsoft Word and then import it into PowerPoint. PowerPoint uses the heading styles assigned in Word to decide which items are slide titles and which items are slide content. The top-level headings (Heading 1) form the slide titles.

If you want to try this out, open Word and switch to Outline view (View ➪ Outline); then type a short outline of a presentation. Press Tab to demote or Shift+Tab to promote a selected line. Then save your work, go back to PowerPoint, and do the following:

1. Choose Insert ➪ Slides from Outline. An Insert Outline dialog box opens. See Figure 6-9.

2. Select the Word file containing the outline, and then click Insert. (You're not limited to Word; you can import from a variety of text formats, including RTF and TXT.)

3. If you see a message about a converter needing to be installed, click Yes to install it. You might need to reinsert your Office CD-ROM.

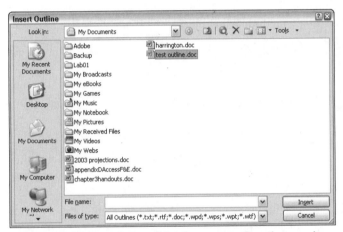

Figure 6-9: You can insert slides from an outline that you have created in a word processing program such as Word.

Expert Tip Text formatted in Normal style in Word will not be included in the outline when imported into PowerPoint. Use Heading 1 style for slide titles, Heading 2 style for top level bulleted text, Heading 3 for secondary bulleted text, and so on. If you are inserting the text in Word while in Outline View, these will be seen as Level 1 for titles, Level 2 for top level bulleted text, Level 3 for secondary bulleted text, and so on.

Creating a new slide with a layout

Slide layouts are very handy. They contain placeholders not only for text, but also for graphics, charts, tables, and other useful elements. Chapter 7 covers them in more detail. After you create a new slide that contains placeholders, you can click a placeholder to open whatever controls are needed to insert that type of object. For example, if you click a placeholder for clip art, the Select Picture window opens. To change to a different slide layout, choose Format ➪ Slide Layout to reopen the task pane. You learn more about the various kinds of slide objects and how to place them on your slides in later chapters.

To create a slide using a slide layout, click the New Slide button or press Ctrl+M to open the Slide Layout task pane. Click the layout you want (Figure 6-10); then close the task pane.

Text box   Clip art placeholder   Selected layout

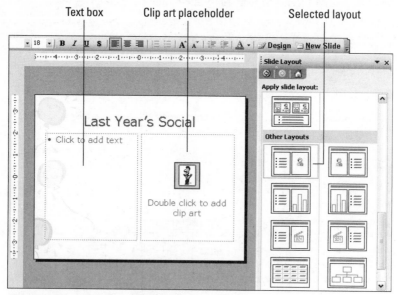

Figure 6-10: Click the New Slide button on the toolbar and then select a slide layout.

Duplicating an existing slide

To make a duplicate of a slide you already have in the same presentation, select it and choose Edit ➪ Duplicate (Ctrl+D). Or, select the slide, choose Edit ➪ Copy (Ctrl+C), and then choose Edit ➪ Paste (Ctrl+V).

Why might you want to duplicate an existing slide? Perhaps it contains several elements that you want to place on several slides in a row. (If you want the same element on all slides, however, you should place it on the Slide Master, described in Chapter 7.) Or perhaps you want to repeat a certain important slide periodically throughout a presentation to reinforce its message.

Copying slides from other presentations

One way to copy an existing presentation is to open the file and then save it under another name. But what if you only want certain slides, not the whole thing?

Or what if you want to include the copied slides in a presentation you are already working on, and not start over? In these cases, it's best to copy the individual slides you want.

To copy slides from an existing presentation into the current one, follow these steps:

1. Choose Insert ➪ Slides from Files. The Slide Finder window opens.

2. Click the Browse button, and locate the presentation file you want to copy from; then click OK. The slides in the selected presentation appear in the Slide Finder window, shown in Figure 6-11.

Mark the presentation as a favorite

Access favorites   Outline view

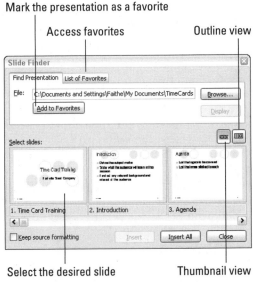

Select the desired slide   Thumbnail view

Figure 6-11: Use the Slide Finder to copy content from other presentations.

Expert Tip   You might want to create a set of presentations that contain boilerplate slides that you use a lot, and then pull slides from them with the Slide Finder as needed. Click the Add to Favorites button in the Slide Finder window to make the selected presentation file easier to find. Notice the List of Favorites tab in the Slide Finder window; click it for quick access to any favorite presentations.

3. *(Optional)* If you want the copied slides to retain their formatting rather than conforming to the design template specified in the current presentation, mark the Keep Source Formatting check box.

4. Select the slide(s) you want. To select more than one slide, hold down Ctrl as you click them. By default you see the slides in thumbnail view in the Slide Finder window, but you can switch to an outline view by clicking the Outline button (indicated in Figure 6-11).

5. After selecting the desired slides, click Insert. The slides are inserted into the presentation. From there you might want to move them around a bit; see "Rearranging Slides" later in this chapter.

Deleting Slides

You may want to get rid of some of the slides, especially if you created your presentation using the AutoContent Wizard or a presentation template. Perhaps the sample presentation is longer than you need, or perhaps you have inserted your own slides instead.

One way to delete a single slide is to display it in Normal view (or Notes Pages view), or select it in Slide Sorter view, and then choose Edit ➪ Delete Slide.

In Slide Sorter view, or in the Slides pane of Normal view, you can delete multiple slides at once. Select the slides to be deleted, and then either choose Edit ➪ Delete Slide or simply press the Delete key on the keyboard.

If you make a mistake with deleting, you can use the Undo command (Edit ➪ Undo or the Undo button on the Standard toolbar) to undo the deletion. See the following section for more information.

Undoing Mistakes

Here's a skill that can help you in almost all of the other chapters in this book: undoing. The Undo command allows you to reverse past multiple actions. You can use it, for example, to reverse all the deletions made to your presentation in the preceding section.

The easiest way to undo a single action is to click the Undo button on the Standard toolbar. You can click it as many times as you like; each time, it undoes one action. (If you don't like using the toolbar button, you can use its equivalent menu command: Edit ➪ Undo.) Ctrl+Z is the keyboard shortcut for this command; you might find that more convenient.

Expert Tip   The maximum number of Undo operations is 20 by default, but can be changed by selecting Tools ➪ Options and changing the value on the Edit tab. However, if you set the number of undos very high, it can cause performance problems in PowerPoint, and has been anecdotally implicated in some cases of file corruption.

You can undo multiple actions all at once by opening the Undo button's drop-down list, as shown in Figure 6-12. Just drag the mouse across the actions to undo (you don't need to hold down the mouse button). Then click when the desired actions are selected, and presto, they are all reversed. You can select multiple actions to undo, but you can't skip around. To undo the fourth item, for example, you must undo the first, second, and third ones, too.

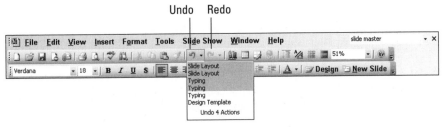

Figure 6-12: Use the Undo button to undo your mistakes.

Redo is the opposite of Undo. If you make a mistake with the Undo button, you can fix the problem by clicking the Redo button. Like the Undo button, it has a drop-down list, so you can redo multiple actions at once. If you haven't used the Undo feature, the Redo button is not available (as in Figure 6-12).

Rearranging Slides

The best way to rearrange slides is to do so in Slide Sorter view. In this view, the slides in your presentation appear in thumbnail view, and you can move them around on the screen to different positions, just like you would manually rearrange pasted-up artwork on a table. You can also do this from the Slides pane of Normal view, but you can see fewer slides at once so it can be more challenging to move a slide from one end of the presentation to another, for example.

To rearrange slides, use the following steps:

1. Switch to Slide Sorter view.

2. Select the slide you want to move. You can move multiple slides at once if you like.

3. Drag the selected slide to the new location. The mouse pointer changes to show a little rectangle next to the pointer arrow as you drag. You also see a vertical line that shows where the slide will go if you release the mouse button at that point. See Figure 6-13.

4. Release the mouse button. The slide moves to the new location.

Slide being dragged   Vertical line shows destination

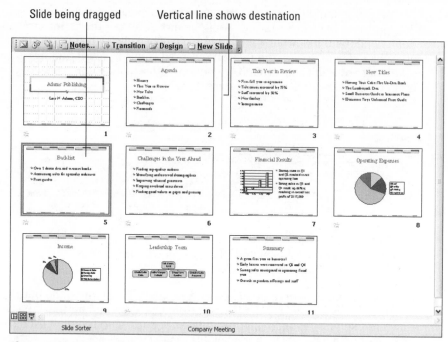

Figure 6-13: As you drag a slide, its new position is indicated by a vertical line.

You can also rearrange slides in the Outline pane of Normal view. This is not quite as easy as Slide Sorter view, but it's more versatile. Not only can you drag entire slides from place to place, but you can also move individual bullets from one slide to another.

> **Note**   You might want to display the Outlining toolbar before rearranging content in the Outline pane. To do so, right-click one of the other toolbars and choose Outlining.

1. Switch to Normal view and display the Outline pane.

2. Position the mouse pointer over the slide's icon. The mouse pointer changes to a four-headed arrow.

3. Click. The entire text of that slide becomes selected.

4. Drag the slide's icon to a new position in the outline. As you drag, you see a horizontal line showing where the slide will go. See Figure 6-14.

5. Release the mouse button when the horizontal line is in the right place. All the slide's text moves with it to its new location.

Line shows destination

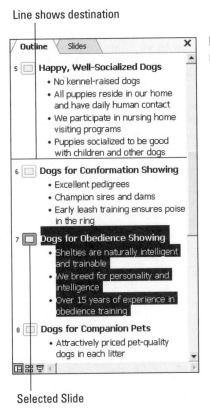

Selected Slide

Figure 6-14: You can drag the slide's icon to move it or use the Outlining toolbar buttons.

If you prefer, instead of Step 4, you can move the slide using the Move Up and Move Down buttons on the Outlining toolbar. Just follow Steps 1 through 3 and then click one of those buttons to move the slide up or down one slide in the outline. Some people prefer to use the toolbar buttons to move a slide if the destination is out of view on-screen. That way, you don't have to try to scroll and drag at the same time to reach the slide's destination.

There are also keyboard shortcuts for moving a slide up or down on the outline. You might find that these are faster than clicking the toolbar buttons. The shortcuts are Alt+Shift+Up arrow key to move up and Alt+Shift+Down arrow key to move down.

All these movement methods work equally well with single bullets from a slide. Just click to the left of a single line to select it, instead of clicking the Slide icon in Step 3.

At this point, you should probably save your work. You don't want anything to happen to it! Choose File ➪ Save to save it, as you learned in Chapter 3.

Summary

In this chapter, you got off to a great start with your new presentation. You learned the four ways of creating a new presentation, and, presumably, used one of them to start your own new project. You also learned about adding, rearranging, and removing slides from your presentation.

The next chapter explains how to change the look of the presentation by changing the design template, slide layouts, and color schemes. So if you aren't happy with the initial choices you made in this chapter, stick around and you will learn how to make changes!

✦   ✦   ✦

Changing the Presentation's Look

Now that you have a basic presentation started, let's make it better. In this chapter, you learn how to apply different formatting to change your presentation's appearance.

Changing an Individual Slide's Layout

Most of the slide formatting you learn about in this chapter affects the entire presentation. But before getting into that, take a moment to review the process for changing a slide's layout.

Recall from earlier chapters that slide layouts control what placeholders appear on a slide. When you insert a new slide into your presentation, you choose which layout to use. There are about two dozen, each suited for a particular combination of slide elements. Figure 7-1 shows an assortment of different layouts of the same material, so you can see the differences.

If you created a presentation with sample content, or if you created slides from the Outline pane, those slides use Title and Text, the default layout.

To change the layout in use for a slide, follow these steps:

1. Select the slide.
2. Choose Format ⇨ Slide Layout. The Slide Layout task pane appears.
3. Click the new layout you want for the slide, and it changes.

Title slide   Title and text   Title, text, and clip art

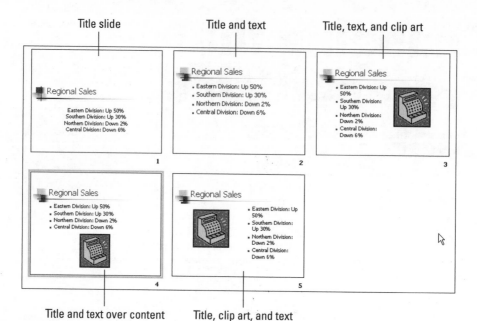

Title and text over content   Title, clip art, and text

Figure 7-1: The same slide content, but with different layouts.

When you click a layout in the Slide Layout task pane, you are actually selecting a default choice from a menu. To see that menu, click the down arrow to the right of the layout. From it you can choose to apply the layout to the current slide, to insert a new slide based on this layout, or to revert an altered slide to the original layout. See Figure 7-2.

When you change a slide's layout, any content that you inserted using a place-holder remains, but new placeholders appear for the new layout too. So, for example, suppose you create a slide with the Title and Text layout, and then you change to a layout for an organization chart. The bullet list remains on the slide, but the placeholder box for the organization chart runs over the top of it, as in Figure 7-3. The two elements can coexist on the slide, but you must resize the boxes so they don't overlap.

The layouts in the Slide Layout task pane are organized by type:

✦ **Text Layouts:** These contain only text.

✦ **Content Layouts:** These contain only non-text content.

✦ **Text and Content Layouts:** These contain placeholders for text as well as placeholders for content.

✦ **Other Layouts:** These contain layouts for text (or at least a title), plus specific types of content.

Selected slide

Slide Layout task pane

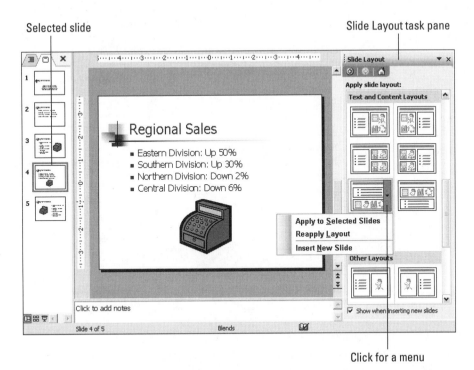

Click for a menu

Figure 7-2: Click a layout to apply it to the current slide, or open its menu for more options.

Expert Tip Sometimes it can make more sense to switch to a Blank AutoLayout or a Title Only layout and then add the objects to the slide manually, as described in Chapter 10. If you don't see an AutoLayout that reflects the slide objects you want to include, consider building your own with a blank slide.

So what is this mysterious item called *content* on all these layouts? PowerPoint defines content here as any graphical element, such as clip art, a chart, or a media clip. The Content placeholders on slides provide an array of six placeholder icons, and you click the one on which you want to insert a particular type of content. Figure 7-4 explains what each icon does.

The Content placeholder can be useful, but if you know exactly what type of item you want, you might find it more straightforward to use one of the layouts with a specific placeholder in it. Most of these are in the Other Layouts section. But it really doesn't matter much which method you use; you get the same result either way.

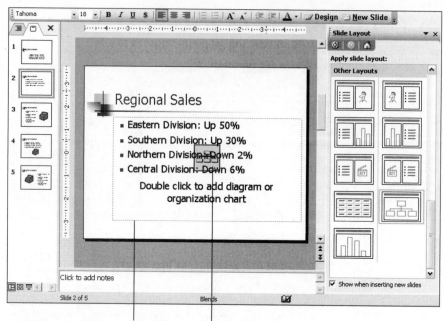

Text frame containing existing text   Placeholder for org chart

Figure 7-3: When you change layouts and the new layout does not have a placeholder for existing content, such as the text here, the existing content becomes a "free agent" that sits on top of the new placeholders.

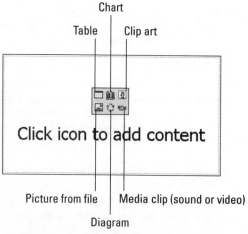

Figure 7-4: In a slide layout that contains a Content placeholder, multiple icons give you a choice of content types.

Using a Different Slide Size and Shape

One of the questions on the AutoContent Wizard (Chapter 6) is what format you plan to use for the presentation. This is an important question because the presentation format determines the appropriate size and shape for the slides. Slides designed for an on-screen display are sized to fit the dimensions of a computer screen; slides destined for a 35mm slide projector are a different size and dimension.

When you display a presentation on-screen, the slides expand to fill the whole screen but they do not change their proportions. Therefore if you show a slide show on-screen that is set up for a 35mm slide size, you will see a black band across the top and bottom of each slide because 35mm slides are wider and shorter than the average computer screen. Therefore when selecting a slide size, it is more a matter of considering the proportions of the target destination rather than its exact size in inches.

If you used the AutoContent Wizard to create your presentation, your slides are probably already the right size and shape. If you created the presentation in another way, however, you might want to check the size and shape to make sure it is what you want. You should do this before getting too far into your final presentation polishing, because changing the size of the slides may throw manually placed content off a little bit. (Perhaps a graphic you have placed is no longer in exactly the same spot, for example.)

Here are the slide sizes and shapes you can choose from:

- ✦ **On-screen show:** 10 x 7.5 inches, resized on the fly as needed to fill the monitor in use. (This is the default size.)
- ✦ **Letter paper:** 10 x 7.5 inches, which is an 8.5 x 11 sheet of paper with a one-half-inch margin on each side.
- ✦ **Ledger paper:** 11 x 17 inches, which is roughly the size of two letter-sized sheets lying side by side.
- ✦ **A3 paper:** 14 x 10.5 inches, an alternative paper size (297 x 420 mm) popular in European countries.
- ✦ **A4 paper:** 10.83 x 7.5 inches (210 x 297mm), another European size.
- ✦ **B4 (ISO) paper:** 11.84 x 8.88 inches (250 x 353 mm).
- ✦ **B5 (ISO) paper:** 7.84 x 5.88 inches (176 x 250 mm).
- ✦ **35mm slides:** 11.25 x 7.5 inches; displayed on a computer screen, this will leave a black band on the top and bottom of the screen, rather like "letter-boxing" on your television set.
- ✦ **Overhead:** 10 x 7.5 inches, the size of most overhead projection screens.

✦ **Banner:** 8 x 1, which is a specialty format good for banner graphics on Web pages.

✦ **Custom:** Enter your own dimensions.

You can also control the orientation of the slides. For on-screen display, the default is Landscape, which is wider than it is tall. The alternative is Portrait, which is taller than it is wide. Almost all presentation formats use Landscape; you will rarely find a projector or presentation medium that requires Portrait. For printing notes, hand-outs, and outlines, the default is Portrait.

To check and change (if needed) the slide dimensions and orientation, do the following:

1. Choose File ➪ Page Setup. The Page Setup dialog box appears, showing the current settings. See Figure 7-5.

2. Open the Slides Sized For drop-down list and choose the format for the presentation.

3. If you choose Custom in Step 2, enter the exact width and height needed.

4. If you want the slide numbering to start at a number other than 1, enter it in the Number slides from box. (You might want this, for example, if a show is a continuation of another show.)

5. In the Slides area, choose Portrait or Landscape. The default is Landscape.

6. In the Notes, handouts & outline area, click Portrait or Landscape. The default is Portrait, because the printed pages are usually printed on regular paper.

7. Click OK.

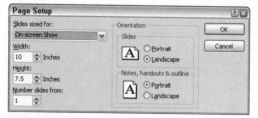

Figure 7-5: Change the file size and orientation in the Page Setup dialog box.

Changing the Design

By now, you are probably quite familiar with design templates and how they work. (If not, refer to Chapter 6.) Design templates give your presentation its backbone of appearance choices: colors, fonts, backgrounds, and so on. You can choose a design template when you create the presentation or you can apply one later.

When you apply a design template to your presentation, all the colors and formatting change, but you do not get any sample content that the template might contain. You get sample content only if you use File ⇨ New and start a new presentation based on the AutoContent Wizard template. (Remember, not all templates even have sample content; only the ones designated presentation templates do. All templates, however, have formatting you can borrow.)

To change the design, follow these steps:

1. Choose Format ⇨ Slide Design. The Slide Design task pane appears.

2. *(Optional)* If you want a different design to apply to certain slides in the presentation, select those slides in Slide Sorter view or in the Slides pane of Normal view.

3. Click a design template to apply it to all slides in the presentation.

   OR

   Click the down arrow next to it and then choose Apply to Selected Slides to apply it only to the slides you selected in Step 2. See Figure 7-6.

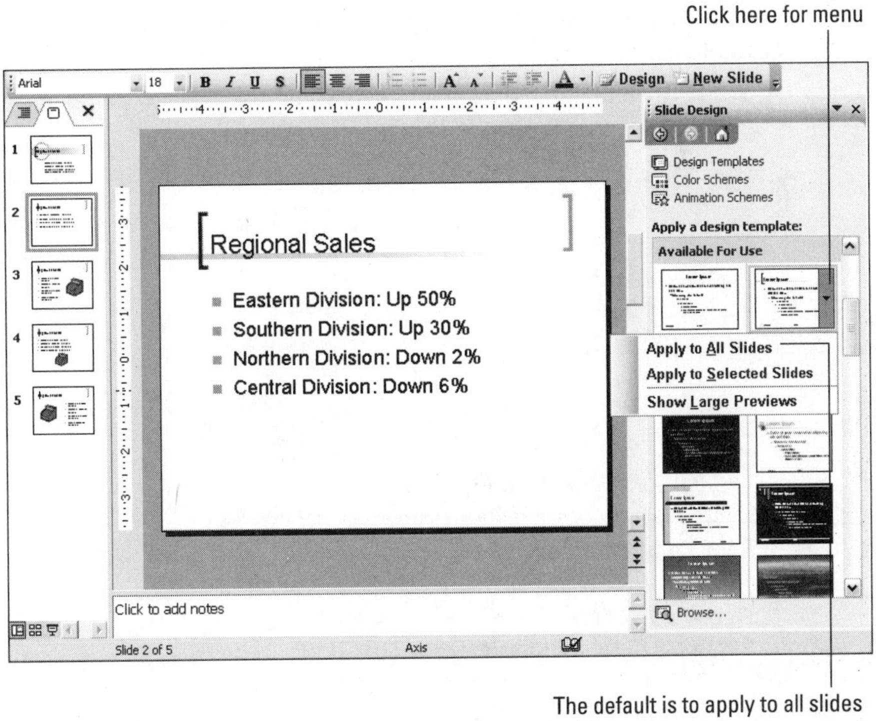

Figure 7-6: Select a design template to change the presentation's overall formatting.

If you have a hard time seeing the thumbnails of the design templates, open the menu for one of the templates and choose Show Large Previews. Repeat to turn the Large Previews feature off again.

The preceding steps show how to apply one of the design templates in PowerPoint's default location for them, but what if the template you want to apply is stored somewhere else? For example, the presentation templates that you learned about in Chapter 6 have their own special designs too, and perhaps you would like to apply a design from one of them. But they don't show up in the Slide Design task pane.

To apply a template that is located in some other location, do the following:

1. Choose Format ⇨ Slide Design to open the Slide Design task pane if it is not already open.

2. At the bottom of the task pane, click the Browse hyperlink. The Apply Design Template dialog box appears. See Figure 7-7.

3. Navigate to the folder containing the template you want to apply. In most installations, for example, the presentation templates are stored in \Program Files\Microsoft Office\Templates\1033. (Note that when you apply designs from presentation templates, you get the design only, not the sample content.)

4. Select the template you want (preview it in the Preview pane) and click Apply.

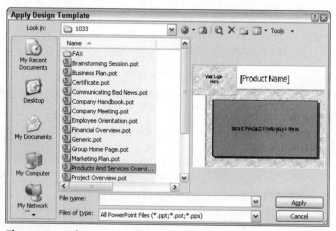

Figure 7-7: Choose a template from another location through this Apply Design Template dialog box.

Changing the Color Scheme

Each design template comes with at least two color schemes. Besides the default colors, you can choose from at least one alternative coloring without abandoning your chosen design. For example, if the default coloring for a template is a dark background, an alternative color scheme might provide a light or white background. There may also be a grayscale color scheme for creating presentations in black and white.

Because different designs have different color scheme choices, it's a good idea to select your design first (see the preceding section); then choose the color scheme. You can change the color scheme for an individual slide or for the entire presentation, and you can use one of the preset color schemes or modify one to suit your exact needs.

 Expert Tip Most experts agree that you should not vary the color scheme from slide to slide; it should remain consistent. Therefore, if you are going to change the color of a single slide, make sure you have a compelling reason to do so. For example, you might want to start a presentation out with a black-and-white color scheme, and then at the height of the drama — the point where you introduce your new product or your most important message — you switch to full color.

Choosing an alternative color scheme

The easiest way to change the color scheme is to choose one of the alternative schemes for your design. To change to one of the existing color schemes, follow these steps:

1. *(Optional)* If you want the change to affect certain individual slides, select them in Slide Sorter view or in the Slides pane of Normal view.

2. If the Slide Design task pane is not already open, open it (by clicking the Design button on the toolbar).

3. At the top of the Slide Design task pane, click the Color Schemes hyperlink. A selection of color schemes available for the current design appears. Depending on the template you used, there may be two, three, four, or even more of them to choose from. See Figure 7-8.

4. To apply the color scheme to the entire presentation, click it. Or, to apply it to only the slides you selected in Step 1, click the down arrow next to it and select Apply to Selected Slides.

Color schemes hyperlink

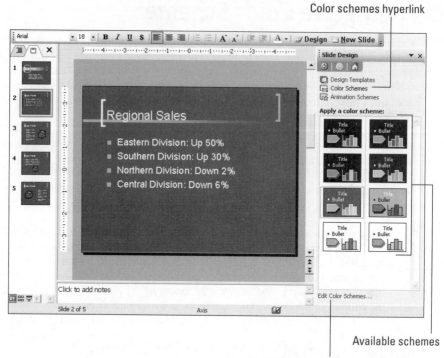

Available schemes

Click here to edit the color schemes

Figure 7-8: Select one of the alternative slide color schemes.

Modifying a color scheme

After you select a color scheme that is as close as possible to what you want, you can make changes to it. For example, you might want to make the text a different color, or make the background color slightly different to accommodate color inconsistencies with your projection equipment or to match your corporate logo.

To modify the chosen color scheme, follow these steps:

1. Start in the Slide Design task pane with the color scheme choices showing.

2. Apply the color scheme that is closest to the one you want, and then click the Edit Color Schemes hyperlink at the very bottom of the task pane (see Figure 7-8). The Edit Color Scheme dialog box opens with the Custom tab on top, as shown in Figure 7-9.

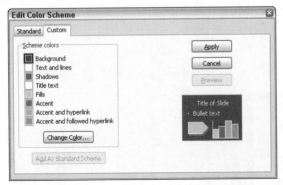

Figure 7-9: You can change any of the individual colors in the scheme from the Custom tab.

3. Click the colored square next to the element you want to change (for example, Background).

4. Click the Change Color button. The Color dialog box appears for the chosen element (for example, Background Color).

5. Select the color you want from either the Standard or Custom tab and then click OK.

Expert Tip If you need very specific colors for the presentation, for example to match your company's exact corporate colors, you can enter the colors by number. There are two color models: RGB (Red Green Blue) and HSL (Hue Saturation Luminance). Select the color model on the Custom tab (Figure 7-10) and then enter the numbers that uniquely describe the color.

6. Repeat Steps 3 through 5 for each color you want to change.

   You can see how your changes are shaping up without closing the dialog box. Just click Preview and then drag the title bar of the dialog box to move it off to the side so you can see the slide underneath.

7. *(Optional)* To save the new colors as a scheme (so it will appear on the Standard tab), click the Add As Standard Scheme button.

8. Click the Apply button to apply the new color scheme.

Click a color

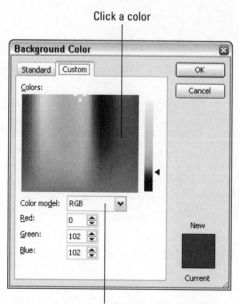

Or choose a color model and enter numeric values

Figure 7-10: Select a color to use for the chosen element of the color scheme.

Changing the Background

One way to change the slide background, as you just saw, is to change its color in the color scheme. But if you are basically happy with the color scheme but just want a different background color — or if you want some special element as the background — you can use the Format ➪ Background command to change it.

A background can be a plain color, but it can also be a gradient pattern, a graphic image, or a texture. Backgrounds can be all kinds of interesting things! In Chapter 12 you will learn about formatting objects, and the same capabilities apply to the background as well. I'll save that detailed discussion for later, but you may want to experiment on your own with the Fill Effects.

To change the background, follow these steps:

1. If you want to change the background only for certain slides, select them in Slide Sorter view. (It's best to keep the background consistent for all slides, though.)

2. Choose Format ➪ Background. The Background dialog box appears.

3. Open the drop-down list (see Figure 7-11) and choose one of the following:

- A colored square from the first row, to select one of the colors from the current color scheme.

- More Colors, to open the Colors dialog box to choose a color as in Figure 7-10.

- Fill Effects, to open the Fill Effects dialog box to choose a pattern, texture, gradient, or picture.

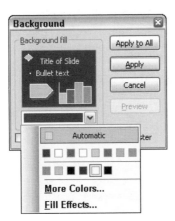

Figure 7-11: Choose a background color or effect.

Note If you have already used a custom color in the presentation, there will be a second row of colored squares in the list in Figure 7-11, showing those custom colors.

4. If you chose More Colors or Fill Effects, use the dialog box that appears to make your selection. (See Chapter 12 for details about fill effects.)

5. In the Background dialog box, click Apply to All to apply the change throughout the presentation, or click Apply to apply it only to the selected slides.

Some templates include background graphics that run over the top of the selected background color or pattern. To omit these from your slide(s), select the Omit Background Graphics from Master check box (obscured by the open menu in Figure 7-11) in the Background dialog box, or remove them manually from the Slide Master, which you learn about later in this chapter.

Ensuring Consistency with Slide and Title Masters

As I mentioned earlier in the book, the Slide Master is a template that affects each slide in the presentation. When you apply a design to a presentation, you are really applying it to the Slide Master, and thereby affecting every slide in the presentation. The Slide Master is shown in Figure 7-12.

There are four kinds of masters you can have in a presentation:

✦ **Slide Master:** Provides a template for the design and layout of all slides in the presentation.

✦ **Title Master:** Provides special settings for any slide that uses the Title Slide layout. It takes some of its settings from the associated Slide Master, and is linked to it.

✦ **Handout Master:** Provides a layout for printing handouts. There are separate settings for each style of handouts (three slides, four slides, six slides, and so on).

✦ **Notes Master:** Provides a layout for printing your speaker notes.

This chapter covers only the first two: Slide Master and Title Master. The other two are covered in Chapter 24, "Creating Support Materials."

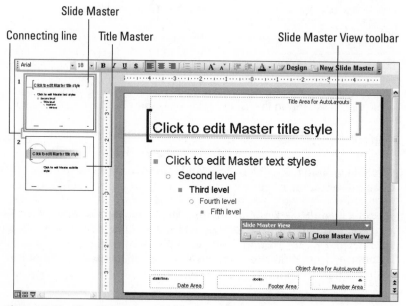

Figure 7-12: The Slide Master holds the elements that appear on each slide.

When you are in Slide Master view, a Slide Master View toolbar is available, shown in Figure 7-13; refer to this figure as you go through the remainder of the chapter for button locations.

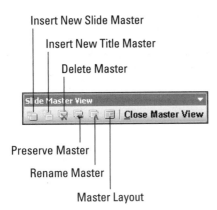

Insert New Slide Master

Insert New Title Master

Delete Master

Preserve Master

Rename Master

Master Layout

Figure 7-13: The Slide Master View toolbar contains buttons for creating, deleting, and editing Slide Masters and Title Masters.

Editing the Slide Master or Title Master

To open the Slide Master or Title Master, choose View ➪ Master ➪ Slide Master. There may be a separate command for Title Master on the menu; if there is, you can use it to jump directly to the Title Master if you prefer. On some design templates, you are taken directly to the Title Master. However you can easily switch between them by clicking the thumbnails on the left once you have entered the Master editing screen (Figure 7-12).

After displaying the Slide Master, you can move things around, change colors and patterns, and a lot more. Anything that you can do to a regular slide, you can do to the Slide Master, and thereby affect all the slides in the presentation at once.

Expert Tip Take a moment to think about what you want to do, and why you think it's best done to the Slide Master. Not all changes are appropriate to make to the Slide Master; some are better made to individual slides. You wouldn't want the same chart to appear on every single slide, for example! However, other additions — such as a company logo — may need to appear on each slide. It is this latter kind of object that you can add to your Slide Master to save yourself the time and trouble of adding it individually to every slide.

For example, with the Slide Master you can make several types of changes:

✦ Change the positioning of the title and the text box on each slide by moving these boxes on the Slide Master.

✦ Change the font used, the text alignment or color, or any other text formatting.

✦ Change the bullet characters used by default for various bullet list levels by selecting a level in the Slide Master's text box and changing its character.

✦ Remove or move the placeholders for the footer, current date, and/or the page number.

Figure 7-14 shows a Slide Master with some changes made to it.

When you are finished working with the Slide Master, click the floating Close button to go back to your normal slides.

Notice in Figure 7-14 that there is a second slide in the Slides pane at the left; that's the Title Master. To make changes to the Title Master, click it to display it and then make your changes.

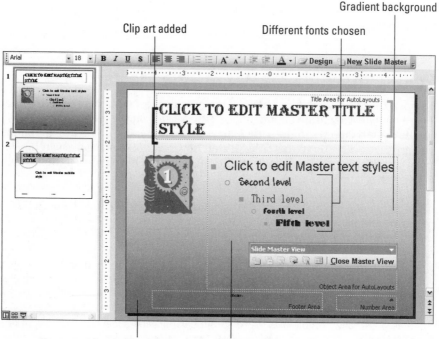

Figure 7-14: Compare this Slide Master to Figure 7-12 to see what changes have been made.

The Title Master has a connecting line to the Slide Master, indicating that it is taking some of its settings from there. If you view the Title Master after making changes to the Slide Master, you can see some of the changes trickling down and others not. Table 7-1 lists some of the changes and whether or not they flow through from the Slide Master to its associated Title Master.

Table 7-1 How Changes to the Slide Master Affect the Title Master	
Change on Slide Master	*Change on Title Master?*
Title font	Yes
Bullet text font	Yes, changes the subtitle
Color scheme	Yes
Design	Yes
Background	No
Clipart or other objects added	No
Placeholders deleted	No

Creating alternative Slide Masters and Title Masters

You can have more than one set of Slide Masters and Title Masters in PowerPoint 2003, which gives you more flexibility in creating long or complex presentations. You might want to have two Title Master layouts, for example—one for the very first slide in the show and one for title slides that indicate sections within the show. Or you might want to have two Slide Master layouts, one for slides with lots of text on them and one for slides with only a few words. It's all up to you.

To create an additional Slide Master, click the Insert New Slide Master button on the Slide Master View toolbar. It appears in the Slides list at the left. Then click it and start customizing it. You can also add new Slide Masters based on other existing design templates by simply clicking one of the other designs while you're in Master view.

After you create the new Slide Master, the Insert New Title Master button becomes available on the Slide Master View toolbar (Figure 7-14); you can click it to associate a new Title Master with the new Slide Master. Slide Masters and Title Masters always have a one-to-one relationship, so if you want an additional Title Master, you must first create a new Slide Master. Figure 7-15 shows an additional Slide Master and Title Master.

Pushpin icons indicate preserved status

Alternate Slide Master

Alternate Title Master   Preserve Master button

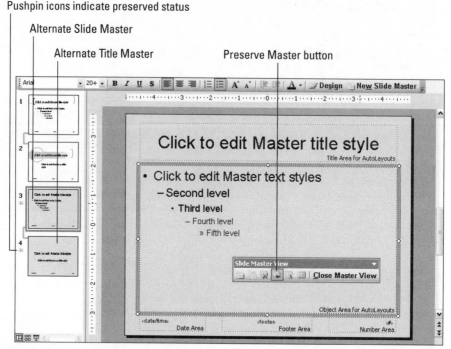

Figure 7-15: Another set of masters has been added; they are blank by default with plain Arial font.

Copying a master

When you create new masters as described previously, they are completely blank and plain. Perhaps you would rather start with a copy of the existing master and modify it. To copy a master, select it and then choose Edit ➪ Copy, and then Edit ➪ Paste.

Renaming a master

The default name for a new master is "Custom Design" but you will probably want to give yours a more descriptive name. For example, you might call your alternative Slide Master something like *Alternative Master for Backup Slides*. To rename a master, select it and click the Rename Master button on the Slide Master View toolbar, and then type the new name.

Deleting a master

To delete a master, select it and press Delete or click the Delete Master button on the Slide Master View toolbar. If you delete a Title Master, its associated Slide Master remains. But if you delete the Slide Master, the Title Master goes too.

When you delete a master, any slides that used it change over to the first remaining master. If you deleted an alternative, the affected slides change to the main master set. If you delete the main master set, the slides change to the first alternative master set in the Slides pane in Slide Master view.

Preserving alternative masters

If a master does not have any slides associated with it, PowerPoint will delete it. Suppose, for example, that you created an alternative master and then applied it to several slides, but then you deleted those slides. The alternative master will go away unless you elect to preserve it.

When a master is preserved, a pushpin symbol appears next to it in the Slides pane at the left. To toggle a master's preservation status, select it and click the Preserve Master button on the Slide Master View toolbar (see Figure 7-15).

Restoring deleted placeholders on masters

If you customize a master by deleting one or more of the placeholders on it, you can get those placeholders back at any time. To do so, click the Master Layout button on the Slide Master toolbar. This opens a dialog box containing check boxes for all the placeholders. Any that have been deleted have open check boxes; mark those check boxes to replace those deleted items.

Using an alternative master for new slides

After you have created the alternative masters you want, and saved them by closing Master View and returning to the presentation, you will probably want to apply the alternative master(s) to some slides.

By default, all slides use the primary set of masters (Slide and Title). To switch to an alternative set for a slide, follow these steps:

1. Open the Slide Design task pane (by clicking the Design button). In the Used in This Presentation section at the top, there should be two designs: your original and your alternative.

2. To apply the alternative to certain slides, select those slides. Then click the down arrow next to the alternative design and choose Apply to Selected Slides. See Figure 7-16.

Select the slides to affect   Apply the alternate master

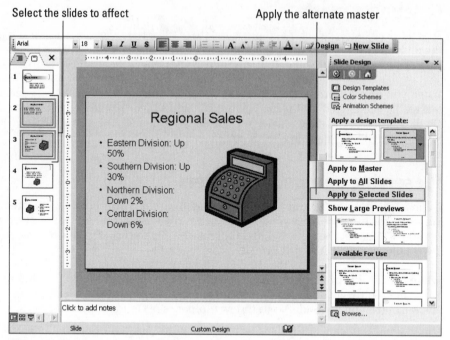

Figure 7-16: Apply an alternative master to selected slides.

The alternative Slide Master will be applied if the slides use any layout except Title Slide; Title slides will receive the alternative Title Master.

Summary

In this chapter, you learned how to change the background, color scheme, and overall design of the slides in your presentation. Now you can modify not only the objects that you place, but also the background on which they appear. You also learned how to modify the global settings for the presentation by displaying and working with the Slide Master.

In the next chapter, you start working on the text in the presentation. You saw in this chapter how to change text globally through designs and masters, but in Chapters 8 and 9 you look at formatting individual text items to make them stand out from the rest, and learn how to create text boxes and other text-based objects.

✦   ✦   ✦

Conveying Your Message with Text and Tables

◆ ◆ ◆ ◆

In This Chapter

Replacing placeholders and sample text

Resizing and moving text boxes

Adding manual text boxes

Finding and replacing text

Exporting a PowerPoint outline

Creating and modifying tables

◆ ◆ ◆ ◆

In most presentations, text is the most important element. Without your textual message, it's all just pretty pictures and flash. That's why the first task you learn to do here, now that you've created your presentation shell, is to enter the text. Then, in later chapters, you learn how to enhance that text with graphic objects and formatting.

Creating New Slides: A Review

Take a moment to review what you learned in Chapter 6 about creating new slides. You can create a slide in any of these ways:

✦ In the Outline pane, type some text and then promote it to the highest outline level by pressing Shift+Tab.

✦ Click the New Slide button on the toolbar (or choose Insert ➪ New Slide or press Ctrl+M) and then use the Slide Layout task pane to select a layout for the new slide.

✦ Copy an existing slide by selecting it and then using Copy (Ctrl+C) and Paste (Ctrl+P).

✦ Import a slide from another presentation with the Insert ➪ Slides from Files command.

This chapter picks up at the point where you have created the slide but it doesn't yet contain the content you want. Maybe you have some slides with some sample content that you need to change, or maybe you need to type some new text.

You might be thinking, "How hard can this be? It's just typing." That's true, it is just typing, but there are a few tricks and quirks in the way PowerPoint handles text. So stick around in this chapter if you're interested in learning about them.

How Text Appears on Slides

If you are familiar with word processing applications like Word, PowerPoint might require you to make a minor adjustment in how you think about text. In most word processing programs you type directly onto the page, but in PowerPoint you can type only in a text box. A *text box* is a frame that holds text. Just like a piece of clip-art or a chart, a text box can be moved, resized, or deleted.

Note Any framed object on a PowerPoint slide is generically referred to as an *object*. In this chapter and the next, you work primarily with text box objects, but keep in mind that there are many different object types. You work with them later in the book.

Because all text must reside in a text box, PowerPoint provides slide layouts that include text box placeholders. You saw these in Chapter 6. Almost all slides have a Title text box, for example, for holding the slide title. A slide may also have a Body text box, containing whatever lines of text are subordinate to the title text on the outline. The layout shown in Figure 8-1 is called Title and Text. You just click in a text box and type, and your typing replaces the placeholder.

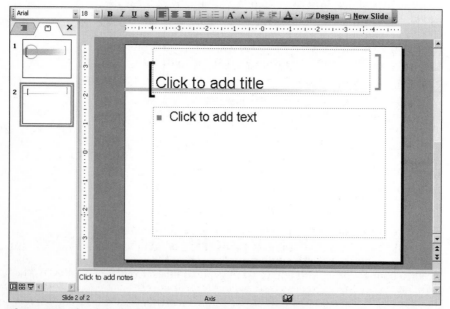

Figure 8-1: The default slide layout contains two text boxes: one for the title and one for the body.

Note The body text appears as a bulleted list by default, but you can turn off the bullet characters if desired by selecting the paragraphs and then clicking the Bullets button on the toolbar.

There are two classes of text boxes. Figure 8-2 shows one of each:

✦ **Automatic text boxes.** These are the text boxes supplied by the slide layout. The initial positioning and formatting of these text boxes are controlled by the Slide Master (Chapter 7) and by the layout that you choose for the slide. Any text that you type in one of these shows up in the Outline pane.

✦ **Manual text boxes.** These are extra text boxes created with the Text Box button on the Drawing toolbar (see the "Adding Text Boxes" section later in this chapter). The text in these boxes is not part of your outline because PowerPoint does not see the box and its content as text—it sees a drawn object that happens to contain some letters.

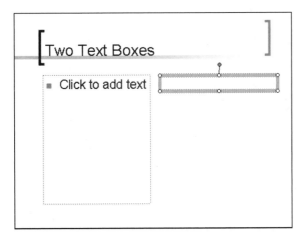

Figure 8-2: The text box on the left is automatic; the one on the right is manual.

The difference between the two may not seem significant right now, but you learn the significance later when you begin changing the formatting and layout of your slides.

Replacing Text Placeholders and Sample Text

If you have inserted a slide using a layout that contains a text box, or started a new slide from the Outline pane, placeholders appear in text boxes on the slide, as shown in Figure 8-2. Click a placeholder to move the insertion point there, and then type your text. Press Enter to start a new paragraph, or click outside the text box to quit.

If you need to place text in a spot where there is no placeholder, you have a choice. You can place a text box manually, or you can change the slide's layout (Format ⇨ Slide Layout), as explained in Chapter 7, so that different placeholders appear.

Expert Tip   If you type text to replace a placeholder (for example, on a Title and Text layout), and then change the slide's layout so that the slide no longer has a placeholder for text, what happens to the text? The text remains on the slide, but it becomes an *orphan*. If you delete the text box, it's simply gone; a placeholder for a text box does not reappear. It does not, however, become a manual text box, because its content still appears on the outline, and a manual text box's content does not.

If there is sample text on your slides (if you start with a presentation template or the AutoContent Wizard, for example), you must delete it and then type your own text in its place. To delete the sample text, highlight it and press Delete, or highlight it and simply begin typing; the new typing replaces it. You can do this either on the Outline pane or the slide.

Editing Text in Outline View

The Outline pane is a great place to edit text, especially when you want to peruse the text from multiple slides at once and move text around. You might want to make the Outline pane larger in Normal view by dragging the line between the panes, so you have more space for the outline. Figure 8-3 shows Normal view adjusted for optimal outline viewing.

You can drag and drop text in the Outline pane, just like in a word processing program. Just select the text and drag it with the mouse to the new location.

If you find yourself spending a lot of time in the Outline pane, you might want to turn on the Outlining toolbar. To do so, choose View ⇨ Toolbars ⇨ Outlining. It contains buttons for promoting and demoting levels, moving slides up or down in the outline, showing and hiding different outline levels, and more. It is displayed in Figure 8-3, and Table 8-1 describes its buttons.

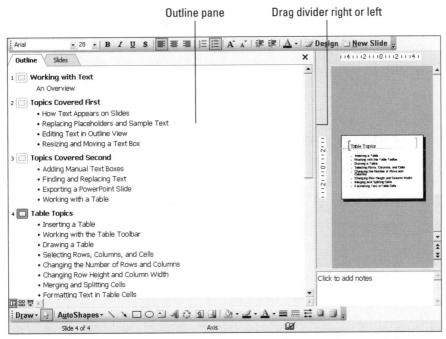

Figure 8-3: For serious outline work, enlarge the Outline pane in Normal view.

| | Table 8-1 |
| | **Outlining Toolbar Buttons** |

Button	Name	Description
	Promote	Promotes the selected paragraph(s) one level.
	Demote	Demotes the selected paragraph(s) one level.
	Move Up	Moves the selected text up in the outline.
	Move Down	Moves the selected text down in the outline.
	Collapse	Collapses (hides) all items subordinate in the outline level to the currently selected paragraph.
	Expand	Expands (displays) all items subordinate in the outline level to the currently selected paragraph.

Continued

Button	Name	Description
Table 8-1 *(continued)*		
	Collapse All	Collapses (hides) all levels of the outline except Level 1 (slide titles).
	Expand All	Expands all levels of the outline completely.
	Summary Slide	Creates a summary slide that contains the titles of the slides that follow it. Useful for creating transition slides in long or complex shows. Selected slides must use a layout containing a title placeholder in order for the Summary Slide feature to be available.
	Show Formatting	Toggles between showing and hiding text formatting in the Outline pane. (It is off by default.)

Working with the Outline pane changes the text on the slides but does not alter its positioning on the slides. To change the location of the text boxes, you must edit on the slide itself, as described in the following section.

Resizing or Moving a Text Box

You can resize a text box to change how much space it takes up on your slide. You might want to do this, for example, to make room to place another object on your slide, such as a graphic. To resize a text box, drag one of its selection handles (white circles) with your mouse, as shown in Figure 8-4. A dotted outline shows where the box is going.

To move a text box (without changing its size), simply drag it by any part of its border other than a selection handle. Position the mouse pointer over a border so the pointer turns into a four-headed arrow. Then drag the text box to a new position.

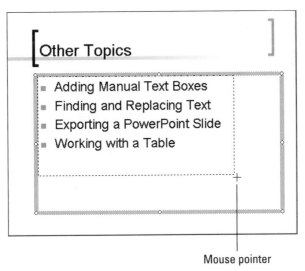

Mouse pointer

Figure 8-4: To resize a text box, drag one of the selection handles.

Adding Manual Text Boxes

If there is room on the slide (or if you can make room by resizing or moving another object), you might want to add your own text box to the slide. For example, suppose you have a bulleted list on the slide, but you want to place a comment next to it in a separate column. You might add a text box to the slide to do this.

Caution

As I mentioned earlier, any text that you type in a manually placed text box does not appear on your outline. It is considered a graphic and is not displayed, even though it is only text. If you need to have two columns of text and want them both to show up on the outline, use the layout that contains two side-by-side bulleted lists.

To place a text box on a slide manually, follow these steps:

1. Click the Text Box button on the Drawing toolbar. The mouse pointer turns into a vertical line.

2. Drag the mouse pointer across the slide to draw a box where you want the text box to be (see Figure 8-5), and then release the mouse button.

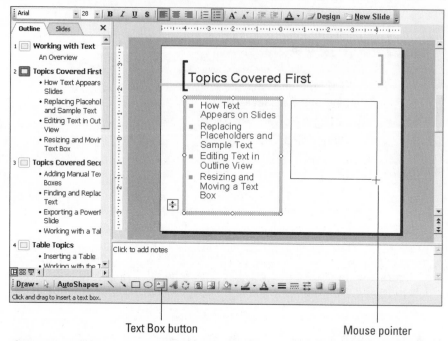

Text Box button   Mouse pointer

Figure 8-5: Click the Text Box button and then draw the text box where you want it to be.

3. Type the text that will appear in the text box.

4. Move or resize the text box as needed.

Finding and Replacing Text

Like all Microsoft applications, PowerPoint has a good built-in Find tool. It enables you to search for (and, optionally, replace) a string of text anywhere in your presentation. The feature works in all views (except Slide Show, in which it isn't applicable). In Slide Sorter view, however, it finds and replaces all instances only.

Take a look at the Find function first because it's simpler than Find and Replace. Say Bob Smith was fired this morning. (Poor Bob.) Now you need to go through your presentation and see whether Bob's name is mentioned so you can take out any lines that refer to him. Follow these steps to find a text string (such as *Bob Smith*):

1. Choose Edit ➪ Find or press Ctrl+F. The Find dialog box appears.

2. Type what you want to find in the Find What text box, as shown in Figure 8-6. If you want to find a text string that you have searched for before, open the Find What drop-down list and select it. That's sometimes faster than retyping.

Figure 8-6: Type what you want to find, and then click the Find Next button.

3. If you want to find only whole words or want to match the case, mark the appropriate check box.

4. Click Find Next. The display jumps to the first instance of the text in your presentation, starting from the insertion point, working downward through the presentation, and then looping back to the top.

5. If the found instance was not the one you were looking for, or if you want to see if there are other instances, click the Find Next button again until you've seen all the instances. (You get a message — The search text was not found — when that happens, and you must click OK to clear the message.)

6. Click Close when you are finished finding text.

You can also perform a replace, which is like a Find plus. The action finds the specified text and then replaces it with other text that you specify. Suppose, for example, that you are preparing a presentation for the Acme Corporation's sales staff. Two days before the presentation, you find out that the Primo Corporation has purchased Acme. So you need to go through the entire presentation and change every instance of Acme to Primo.

Expert Tip   While you are using the Find feature, as explained in the preceding steps, you can switch to the Replace dialog box by clicking the Replace button. When you do so, your Find string transfers over, so you don't have to retype it.

To find and replace a text string, follow these steps:

1. Choose Edit ➪ Replace or press Ctrl+H. The Replace dialog box appears.

2. Type the text you want to find in the Find What text box. If you have previously used Find or Replace, the most recent text you found appears in the text box.

3. Type the new text in the Replace with text box. For example, if you were replacing **layoffs** with **downsizing**, it would look like Figure 8-7.

4. If you want whole words only or a case-sensitive search, select the appropriate check box.

5. Click Find Next to find the first instance.

6. If you want to replace that instance, click the Replace button. The next instance appears automatically. Otherwise, click Find Next to go on.

Figure 8-7: Enter what you want to find and what you want to replace it with.

7. Repeat Step 6 to check and selectively replace each instance, or click the Replace All button to change all instances at once.

8. When you are finished, click Close. (You may have to click OK first to clear a dialog box telling you that the specified text was not found.)

Caution   Find and Replace doesn't work in OLE objects, such as embedded Excel content or MS Graph charts.

Exporting a PowerPoint Outline

After creating a text outline in the Outline pane of PowerPoint, you might decide that you want to use that outline in another application too. For example, perhaps you want to create a Word document to accompany your PowerPoint show, and you want to base the Word document on the slide titles that you have already created in PowerPoint.

To export the entire presentation outline, use the File ⇨ Save As command and choose Outline/RTF as the file format. (See Chapter 3 for help with the Save As command.)

To export only a part of the outline, select the text in the Outline pane and then use the Clipboard (Ctrl+C for Copy and Ctrl+V for Paste) to copy it from PowerPoint and paste it into Word or some other word processing program.

Caution   Saving in Outline/RTF format will save only what appears in the Outline pane in PowerPoint. Any graphics will be omitted — as well as the text in any manually created text boxes and the text in tables (covered in the next section).

Working with Tables

A table is a great way to organize little bits of data into a meaningful picture. For example, you might use a table to show sales results for several salespeople or to contain a multicolumn list of team member names. PowerPoint considers a table a graphical element that contains text — not a text element. Therefore, any text you type in a table will not appear in the Outline pane.

Inserting a table

The best way to insert a table on a slide is to start with a layout that includes a table placeholder. Follow these steps to create a new slide that uses a table:

1. Choose Insert ➪ New Slide or click the New Slide button on the Standard tool-bar. The Slide Layout task pane appears.

2. Click the Title and Table layout (in the Other Layouts section) and click OK. Or you can choose the Title and Content layout, which has an icon for a table among its choices.

3. Click in the Title text box and type a title for the slide.

4. Double-click the table placeholder icon. The Insert Table dialog box appears. See Figure 8-8.

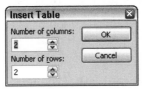

Figure 8-8: Choose the number of columns and rows you want in your table.

5. Enter the number of columns and number of rows, and click OK. A table grid appears on the slide.

6. If the Tables and Borders toolbar does not appear automatically, choose View ➪ Toolbars ➪ Tables and Borders. The toolbar is shown in Figure 8-9.

7. Type your first bit of data in the first cell of the table, and press Tab to move to the next cell. (A *cell* is a block at the intersection of a row and a column.)

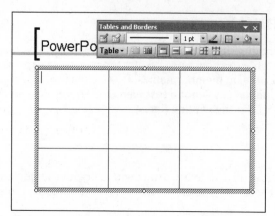

Figure 8-9: Now you are ready to type data into your table.

8. Continue entering text in the cells, pressing Tab to move to the next cell. To move to the previous cell, press Shift+Tab. You can also use the arrow keys on the keyboard to move between cells, or click in the cell you want.

9. When you are finished entering text in the table, click anywhere away from it to deselect it.

You can also insert a table manually, without a table placeholder. To do so, choose Insert ➪ Table and then pick up the preceding steps at step 5.

Working with the Table toolbar

The Table toolbar appears whenever a table is active. It contains a Table menu, from which you can select table-specific commands; it also has a variety of buttons for modifying and formatting the table. Table 8-2 lists the Table toolbar buttons. If you accidentally close the Tables and Borders toolbar, choose View ➪ Toolbars ➪ Tables and Borders to make it reappear. You will work with many of these buttons later in the chapter.

	Table 8-2	
	Tables and Borders Toolbar Buttons	
Button	***Name***	***Description***
	Draw Table	Turns the mouse pointer into a pencil for drawing table lines.
	Eraser	Turns the mouse pointer into an eraser for removing table lines.
	Border Style	Opens a list of line styles for the table borders.
	Border Width	Opens a list of line widths for the table borders.
	Border Color	Opens a list of colors for table borders.
	Borders	Opens a list of border sides, so you can place or remove the border from one or more sides of the table or individual cells.
	Fill Color	Opens a list of colors for filling the insides of the cells.
	Table	Opens a menu of commands for selecting, inserting, and deleting rows.
	Merge Cells	Combines two or more cells into a single cell.
	Split Cell	Splits the current cell into two cells.
	Align Top	Sets the vertical alignment for the selected cells to Top.
	Center Vertically	Sets the vertical alignment for the selected cells to Center.
	Align Bottom	Sets the vertical alignment for the selected cells to Bottom.
	Distribute Rows Evenly	Resizes rows so that they are all the same.
	Distribute Columns Evenly	Resizes columns so that they are all the same.

Drawing a table

When you draw a table, you have precise control over its size and positioning. This can save you some time over modifying a "standard" table if the design that you want is unusual.

If you want to draw a table, start with a Title Only or Blank layout. Then draw the table in the blank "body" area on the slide. To draw a table, follow these steps:

1. Create a new slide with a Title Only or Blank layout.

2. Display the Tables and Borders toolbar (View ⇨ Toolbars ⇨ Tables and Borders).

3. *(Optional)* If you know what line style, width, and color you want, select those settings from the Tables and Borders toolbar. These settings are covered later in the chapter.

4. Click the Draw Table button. The mouse pointer changes to a pencil.

5. Drag to draw a box on the slide that represents the outside of the table you want.

6. Click the Draw Table button again, and then draw inside the table box to create rows and columns as desired. See Figure 8-10.

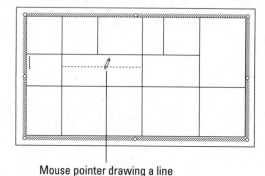

Mouse pointer drawing a line

Figure 8-10: You can create a unique table with the Draw Table tool.

7. If you need to erase any of your lines, click the Eraser button on the toolbar and then click the line(s) to erase.

8. When you are finished drawing, press Esc or click the Draw Table (pencil) button again to turn off the drawing mode.

You can also use the table drawing tools on an existing table to modify it. For example, you can create a standard table and then draw a few extra lines in it or delete a line or two.

Selecting rows, columns, and cells

If you want to apply formatting to one or more cells, or issue a command that acts upon them such as Copy or Delete, you must first select the cells to be affected.

To select a single cell, move the insertion point into it by clicking inside the cell. Any commands you issue at that point will act on that individual cell. Drag across multiple cells to select them.

To select an entire row or column, click any cell in a current row or column and then choose Table ⇨ Select Row or Table ⇨ Select Column. (Remember, the Table menu is accessed from the Tables and Borders toolbar, not the normal menu bar.) You can also select an entire row or column by dragging across it. Figure 8-11 shows a selected column.

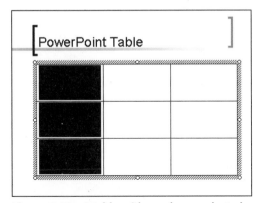

Figure 8-11: A table with a column selected.

Changing the number of rows and columns

The Table menu contains the following important commands that help you insert and remove rows and columns:

✦ **Insert Columns to the Left:** Adds a new column to the left of the column containing the insertion point.

✦ **Insert Columns to the Right:** Same as previous, except inserts to the right.

✦ **Insert Rows Above:** Adds a new row above the one containing the insertion point.

✦ **Insert Rows Below:** Same as previous, except it inserts the row below the current one.

✦ **Delete Columns:** Deletes the column containing the insertion point.

✦ **Delete Rows:** Deletes the row containing the insertion point.

To use any of these commands, position the insertion point in a cell by clicking inside it and then choose the command. The Insert commands refer to left, right, above, or below the active cell; the Delete commands refer to the row or column that contains the active cell (see Figure 8-12).

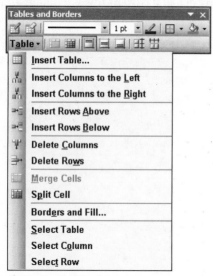

Figure 8-12: The Table menu provides commands that insert and delete rows and columns in the table.

You can use any of the insert or delete commands from the Table menu on more than one row or column at a time. Simply select more than one before issuing the command. When you have more than one row or column selected and you issue an Insert command, PowerPoint inserts the same number of items as you had selected. For example, if you select two columns and then choose Table ➪ Insert Columns to the Right, it inserts two columns to the right of the selected ones.

Caution   Adding and removing rows and columns changes the size of the table, as does resizing rows and columns (covered in the next section). After adding rows or columns, or increasing the size of a row or column, your table could start running off of the slide. PowerPoint does not warn you when your table exceeds the slide's area; you have to watch for that yourself. You can resize the table by dragging the table's outer border.

Changing row height and column width

You might want a row to be a different height or a column a different width than the others in the table. To resize a row or column, follow these steps:

1. Position the mouse pointer on the border below the row or to the right of the column that you want to resize. The mouse pointer turns into a line with arrows on each side of it.

2. Holding down the mouse button, drag the row or column to a new height or width. A dotted line appears as shown in Figure 8-13, showing where it will go.

3. Release the mouse button.

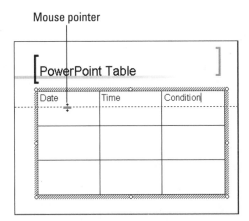

Figure 8-13: Resize the rows or columns of your table as needed to eliminate wasted space or to make more room for longer text strings.

Merging and splitting cells

If you need more rows or columns in some spots than in others, try the Merge Cells and Split Cell commands.

Here are some ways to merge cells:

✦ Select the cells to be merged and choose Table ⇨ Merge Cells.

✦ Select the cells to be merged and click the Merge Cells button on the Tables and Borders toolbar.

✦ Click the Eraser button on the Tables and Borders toolbar and click on the line you want to erase; the cells on either side of the deleted line will be merged.

Here are some ways to split cells:

✦ Select the cell to be split and choose Table ⇨ Split Cell.

✦ Select the cell to be split and click the Split Cell button on the Tables and Borders toolbar.

✦ Click the Draw Table button on the Tables and Borders toolbar and draw a line in the cell you want to split.

The Split Cell command and button both split the cell along its longest dimension. For example, if you have a cell that is 2" by 1", it will create two 1" by 1" cells when it splits. You can't control the way it splits with these methods. If you need to split it the non-standard way, use the Draw Table button method.

Formatting text in table cells

Formatting text in cells is the same as formatting any other text in PowerPoint. Use the Formatting toolbar buttons and the commands on the Format menu. (Turn to Chapter 9 for the full scoop.)

Here are a few table-specific formatting issues for text:

✦ **Table Margins.** You can specify internal margins for the table; this controls how close the text appears to the borders around each cell. To do this, choose Format ⇨ Table, click the Text Box tab, and enter Left, Right, Top, and Bottom margins. See Figure 8-14.

✦ **Rotating Text in the Table.** You can set the text in the table cells to be rotated 90 degrees if desired. Choose Format ⇨ Table, click the Text Box tab, and mark the Rotate Text Within Cell by 90 Degrees check box. This applies to individual cells.

✦ **Text Alignment.** You can set the alignment of the text in cells both vertically and horizontally. Your vertical choices are Top, Center, and Bottom; your horizontal ones are Right, Center, Left, and Justify.

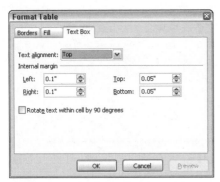

Figure 8-14: Use the Format Table dialog box's Text Box tab to set table margins and text rotation in cells.

Figure 8-15 shows each of the available combinations in a table. I've zoomed in on it a bit so you can see it more clearly. (Of course, it's not much of a look that way, is it? You'd be smarter to stick to a single alignment in your own table.) To set the alignment for a cell, select it (you can select more than one at a time or even the entire table) and then click one of the alignment buttons. The ones for horizontal alignment are on the Formatting toolbar (top of the screen); the ones for vertical alignment are on the Tables and Borders toolbar. You can also set alignment with the Format ⇨ Alignment menu command.

Formatting cell borders

The border lines around each cell are very important because they separate the data in each cell. By default, there is a 1-point (that's ½ of an inch) border around each side of each cell, but you can make some or all borders fatter, a different line style (dashed, for example), a different color, or remove them altogether to create your own effects. Here are some examples:

✦ To make a list of names appear to be floating in multiple columns on the slide (that is, to make it look as if they are not really in a table at all, but just lined up extremely well), remove all table borders. In Figure 8-16, the borders on the top row (Q1, Q2, Q3) have been removed, and the column headings appear to be floating above the grid.

✦ To create a header row at the top, make the border beneath the first row of cells darker or thicker than the others. In Figure 8-16, the line between the column headings and the first row of months has been assigned a 6-point line.

✦ To make it look as if certain items have been crossed off of a list, format those cells with diagonal borders. This creates the effect of an X running through each cell. (These diagonal lines are not really borders in the sense that they don't go around the edge of the cell, but they're treated as borders in PowerPoint.) In Figure 8-16, January and February have both diagonal borders applied.

	Left	Center	Right	Justify
Top	Text Alignment Sample Text Alignment Sample	Text Alignment Sample Text Alignment Sample	Text Alignment Sample Text Alignment Sample	Text Alignment Sample Text Alignment Sample
Center	Text Alignment Sample Text Alignment Sample	Text Alignment Sample Text Alignment Sample	Text Alignment Sample Text Alignment Sample	Text Alignment Sample Text Alignment Sample
Bottom	Text Alignment Sample Text Alignment Sample	Text Alignment Sample Text Alignment Sample	Text Alignment Sample Text Alignment Sample	Text Alignment Sample Text Alignment Sample

Figure 8-15: With three vertical and four horizontal alignment choices, you have twelve potential combinations.

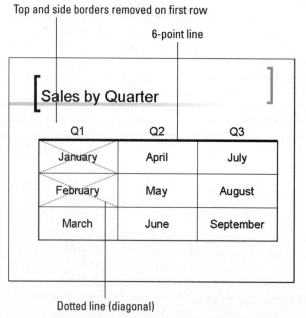

Top and side borders removed on first row

6-point line

Sales by Quarter

Q1	Q2	Q3
January	April	July
February	May	August
March	June	September

Dotted line (diagonal)

Figure 8-16: Here are some things you can do with border formatting.

To format a cell's border, follow these steps:

1. Select the cell(s) that you want to format.

   When you apply top, bottom, left, or right cell borders, they apply to the entire selected block of cells if you have more than one cell selected. For example, suppose you select two adjacent cells in a row and apply a left border. The border applies only to the leftmost of the two cells. If you want the same border applied to the line in between the cells, you must apply an Inside Vertical border.

2. Select a border style from the Border Style drop-down list. The default is solid, but you can choose a variety of dotted or dashed lines.

3. Select a border thickness from the Border Width drop-down list. The default is 1 point.

4. Click the Border Color button and choose a different color for the border if desired. The colors that appear on the palette that opens are the colors from the current color scheme for the presentation. (Learn more about that in Chapter 11.) You can choose a color not shown there by clicking More Border Colors.

Note   Remember, everything on a slide, including a table, is an object. In Chapter 11, when you learn how to format objects, you will see a lot more about color selection tools such as Border Color and Fill Color than you see in passing in this chapter. There you learn how to select custom colors, use fill effects, and more.

5. Click the down arrow next to the Border Sides button to open its drop-down list of borders. See Figure 8-17. Then click the button for the border positioning you want to apply. For example, to place the border on all sides of all selected cells, click the All Borders button, which is the one that looks like a window pane.

Expert Tip   Anytime you see a menu with dots at the top of it, like the Border Sides menu in Figure 8-17, you can drag it off to the side to make it into a floating toolbar.

6. If you need to apply the border to any other sides, repeat Step 5. If you need to turn the border off for any side that currently has a border, click the button for that side to toggle it off.

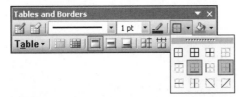

Figure 8-17: Use the controls on the Tables and Borders toolbar to format the border of each cell.

For more control over the borders, choose Format ➪ Table. Then, in the Format Table dialog box, click a Style, Color, and Width and then click the individual lines in the sample to turn the lines on or off (see Figure 8-18).

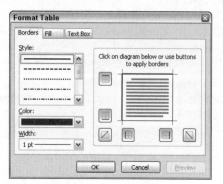

Figure 8-18: The Format Table dialog box lets you specify formatting for the border on each side of each cell.

Changing cell color

By default, table cells have a transparent background so that the color of the slide beneath shows through. Most of the time, this looks very nice, and you should not need to change it. Sometimes, however, you might want a different color background for some or all of the cells in the table.

To change the color of the cells, follow these steps:

1. Select the cell(s) to affect. Or to apply the same color to all the cells, select the table's outer border.

2. Click the down arrow next to the Fill Color button on the Tables and Borders toolbar. A palette of colors opens. See Figure 8-19.

3. Select the color you want. The colors shown are from the current color scheme for the presentation. Most of the time, you will want to stick with these colors.

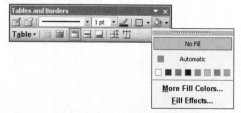

Figure 8-19: Choose a fill color for the selected cell(s).

To remove the background color, repeat the steps but choose No Fill instead of a color.

There is a lot more you can do with fill color. You can choose More Fill Colors to choose a different color, or choose Fill Effects to choose gradients, patterns, or other special effects. But you can find that discussion in Chapter 11, where you learn how to do this for all object types generically. (It's the same for most of them.) Setting the fill color to Background makes it match the background color for the slide.

Expert Tip When you fill a table with a color, picture, texture, or pattern, each cell gets its own individual fill. That means that, for example, if you fill with a picture, each cell has a complete copy of the picture, as in Figure 8-20. If you want a single copy of the picture to fill the entire area behind the table, make the table background transparent (by deselecting the Fill Color check box on the Format Table dialog box's Fill tab) and then place the picture as a separate object on the slide, behind the table. Use the Draw ⇨ Order menu on the Drawing toolbar to change an object's position in a stack. The picture then appears as a background behind the table, as shown in Figure 8-21. See Chapter 11 for more information.

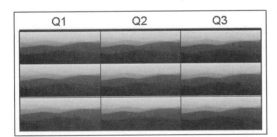

Figure 8-20: When you apply a picture fill to a table in general, each cell gets its own copy of the picture.

Figure 8-21: When you make the table background transparent and then place the picture behind it as a separate object, a single copy of the picture can serve as a background to the table.

Summary

In this chapter, you learned how to enter and edit text in a presentation, and how to create and work with a table. These are important skills, as the average presentation is more than 75 percent text. Graphics, sounds, and other objects usually make up a very small part of a presentation. However, those objects are important attention-getters, and I cover them later in this book in detail.

The next chapter builds on this one by helping you format the text you've just entered. You learn how to change the text's color and attributes, how to modify text box backgrounds and indents, and lots more.

✦   ✦   ✦

Formatting Text and Text Boxes

When you apply a design template to a presentation (as explained in Chapter 7), it assigns fonts to various elements (headings, body text, and so on) that work harmoniously together. Therefore, you don't want to start changing text formatting willy-nilly, or you'll end up with an inconsistent-looking mess. If you want to make a global change to the presentation (for example, format all the slide titles differently), make your change on the Slide Master (see Chapter 7 for details).

But assuming you have a good reason to make changes to your text, what can you do with it? Lots of things. You can dress it up, dress it down, move it, recolor it — the possibilities are endless.

Understanding Fonts

Office 2003 comes with lots of different fonts, and you may have acquired some additional fonts by installing other programs, too. A *font* is a typeface, a style of lettering. For example, compare the lettering of this book's headings to the lettering in this line of text you are reading now. Those are two different fonts.

Note In the past, when most fonts were not scaleable, a distinction was sometimes drawn between the term "typeface" — which referred to a certain style of lettering — and the term "font" — which referred to a specific typeface used at a certain size. Nowadays, however, the terms are synonymous for all practical purposes.

Windows fonts are generic — that is, they work with any program. So a font that came with WordPerfect, for example, works with Microsoft Word and PowerPoint. Within PowerPoint you have access to all installed Windows fonts on your system.

There are several kinds of Windows fonts technologically:

✦ **TrueType:** A scaleable outline font that works with any Windows application and any Windows-compatible printer. These fonts have a TT icon in the Fonts folder. Any Windows fonts that came with earlier versions of Office or that came with Windows versions prior to XP will be of this type.

✦ **OpenType:** An improved, updated version of the TrueType technology. OpenType fonts have all the benefits of TrueType fonts plus they look better on-screen. These fonts have an O icon. These fonts came with Windows XP and Office 2003.

✦ **Fixed:** Fonts that are not scaleable; they come in a few specific sizes only. These fonts have an A icon. A few such fonts came with Windows for display use; there may be others installed by applications that require fixed font usage for their displays. Avoid using these fonts in your presentation if possible.

Look in the Fonts folder in the Control Panel (see Figure 9-1) to see which ones you have. You can also peruse them from the Font drop-down list on the Formatting toolbar in PowerPoint.

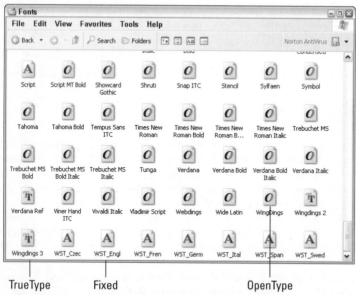

Figure 9-1: Look in the Fonts folder to find out what fonts you have and the types they are.

Appearance-wise there are two basic groups of fonts: *serif* (those with little tails on each letter, like the little horizontal lines on the bottoms of the letters *i* and *t*, for example) and *sans-serif* (those without the tails). The headings in this book are sans-serif and the regular paragraph text is serif.

Your system will likely include some fonts of each type, such as the following:

Courier (serif)

𝕺𝖑𝖉 𝕰𝖓𝖌𝖑𝖎𝖘𝖍 𝕿𝖊𝖝𝖙 𝕸𝕿 (serif)

Times New Roman (serif)

Arial (sans-serif)

Bauhaus 93 (sans-serif)

Broadway (sans-serif)

Impact (sans-serif)

Choosing the Right Fonts

The right font can make a tremendous difference in the readability and appeal of your presentation, so selecting the right one is very important. I discuss the considerations involved in various presentation media in Chapter 32, in the section "Choosing formatting that matches your medium."

One way to ensure harmonious font choices is to apply a design template to the presentation, as you learned in Chapter 7. A design template includes font choices that work well together. You can make manual changes to the font settings on your own, as covered in the next section, but if there's no reason to change, allow the experts who created the templates to be your advisors.

So how do you choose among the hundred or more fonts that are probably installed on your system? Here are some general rules.

✦ Strive for consistency. Very rarely should you change the font on an individual slide. You should generally change it on the Slide Master.

✦ Serif fonts are easier for people to read on paper in long stretches because the tails make letter recognition easier. Use serif fonts for long paragraphs.

✦ Sans-serif fonts are best for headings and short bullet points because they're eye-catching and clean-looking. Use sans-serif fonts for slide titles.

✦ Avoid script fonts in presentations, because they are hard to read.

✦ Avoid novelty fonts, because they take the focus off your message.

✦ When determining what size a font should be, test it by viewing the slide in an environment as close as possible to the actual presentation conditions. Pretend you are an audience member sitting in the back of the room. Can you clearly read each slide? If it's not possible to test your slides under the actual presentation conditions, put the presentation into Show view and step ten to twelve feet away from your monitor. If you cannot read the text on your slides, your audience won't be able to, either.

Another consideration when choosing fonts is whether the PC on which you present the show is likely to have the same fonts installed. If you stick with Windows-supplied fonts like Arial and Times New Roman, this is a non-issue. However if you use a font that came with Office 2003, but you plan on presenting on a PC with an earlier Office version, you might want to embed the fonts in the presentation when saving it. See Chapter 3 for help with that. If you present or edit the show on a PC that does not have the right fonts, and the fonts are not embedded, PowerPoint will use fonts that are as close as possible to a match. Although this is helpful, it can also cause strange, unexpected line breaks in your text.

Expert Tip   If you suspect that PowerPoint is substituting fonts on the presentation machine, you can find out for sure by going to Format ➪ Replace Fonts. If you see a question mark in front of the font name, that means the font you used to create the presentation is not available on the current computer.

Changing the Font, Size, and Text Attributes

To change the font (that is, the typeface), select the one you want from the Font drop-down list on the toolbar. That's the easiest way; you can also select the font from the Font dialog box (Format ➪ Font) shown in Figure 9-2.

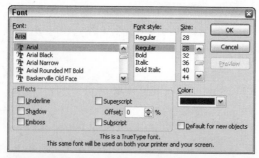

Figure 9-2: You can select a font from the Font dialog box.

Almost all of the fonts that you have on your system are probably TrueType or OpenType fonts, so you can resize them to any size you want, from as small as 6 or 8 points to over 72 points. A *point* is 1/72 of an inch; it's a measurement of how tall the tallest letter in the character set is. To change the font size, choose it from the Font Size drop-down list on the toolbar, or do it from the Font dialog box (Figure 9-2).

To quickly increase or decrease the selected text's font size, click the Increase Font or Decrease Font button on the Formatting toolbar. These look like large and small capital A's, respectively, and they bump the point size on selected text up or down by one place on the size list. This change is not always one point. If you open the Font Size drop-down list, you see that sometimes there is a larger jump between listed sizes.

You can also change the *attributes* of the text. Attributes are special modifiers such as bold, italic, underlined, and shadowed. These attributes are separate from your font and size choices, because any attribute can be applied to any font at any size. Figure 9-3 shows samples of PowerPoint's available text attributes.

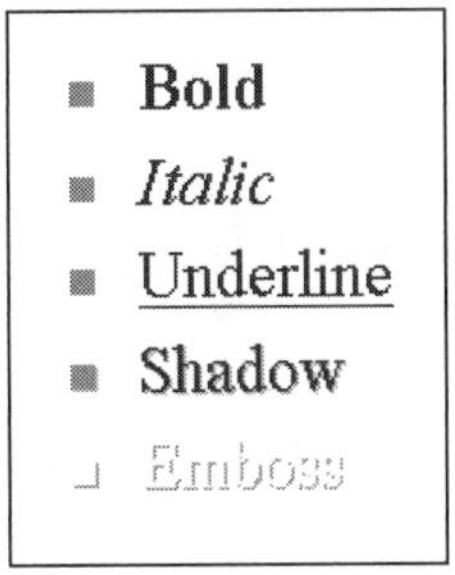

<table>
<tr><td>

■ **Bold**

■ *Italic*

■ <u>Underline</u>

■ Shadow

⅃ Emboss

</td><td>

Figure 9-3: Some attributes that you can apply to your PowerPoint text.

</td></tr>
</table>

To apply bold, italic, underline, or shadow, simply select the text and then click the appropriate button on the Formatting toolbar. To apply embossing, superscript, or subscript, you must open the Font dialog box (Figure 9-2) and mark the appropriate check box there. (Superscript characters appear above the regular text, like X^2. Subscript characters appear below the regular text, like H_2O.)

You can also add the superscript and subscript (but not the emboss) icons to your toolbar by choosing Format ⇨ Tools ⇨ Customize.

Note   Text shadow colors are automatically determined by your background color, not by the shadow color you specified in the slide color scheme.

Here are some ideas for using text attributes:

✦ Apply the shadow attribute to make the text look richer and more 3D.

✦ Apply the italic attribute to new vocabulary words that the audience may not be familiar with and then define those terms in your speech.

✦ Make certain words bold for more emphasis.

✦ Avoid using underlining to emphasize a word in a paragraph; the effect looks too much like typewriter text. Instead, use italics or a different color for that text.

Using AutoFit and Other AutoFormat Features

What happens to the text in a resized box? Nothing, usually. If you make a text box larger than its original size, you simply create more white space. The letters do not get bigger. (To change the size of the letters, see the "Changing the Font, Size, and Text Attributes" section in this chapter.) Similarly, if you make the text box smaller, but all of the text still fits in it, that text will not change size.

However, if you make a text box so small that the text in it no longer fits, PowerPoint resizes the text so that it is all still visible. This is called *AutoFit*. But PowerPoint remembers the original size of the text, and when you make the text box larger again, it returns the text size to its original state.

AutoFit happens automatically in placeholder text boxes. To turn it off for an individual instance, do the following:

1. In a text box that has had the text size changed with AutoFit, an AutoFit Smart Tag icon appears in the lower-left corner. Click on it to display a menu, as shown in Figure 9-4.

2. On the menu, choose the AutoFit setting you want. For example, you might choose Stop Fitting Text to This Placeholder to prevent AutoFit altogether. Or you can choose one of the other alternatives, such as Split Text Between Two Slides, Continue on a New Slide, or Change to a Two-Column Layout.

Note

A Smart Tag is an icon that appears next to an object that has recently been acted upon in a certain way. You can click on the Smart Tag icon to get a list of options for finishing up the operation. You get a Smart Tag when you paste a selection from the Clipboard, for example, letting you choose how you want the pasted text to be formatted. Smart Tags were introduced in Office XP.

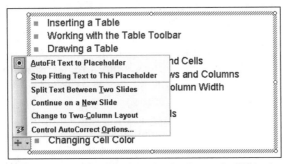

Figure 9-4: Set AutoFit properties for an individual text box.

You can also set general AutoFit properties for all slides in the AutoCorrect options. To do so, follow these steps:

1. Choose Tools ⇨ AutoCorrect Options and click the AutoFormat As You Type tab.

2. In the Apply as You Type section, deselect either or both of the AutoFit check boxes: AutoFit Title Text to Placeholder or AutoFit Body Text to Placeholder. See Figure 9-5.

3. Click OK to accept the new setting.

Figure 9-5: Control overall AutoFit properties for the entire application through the AutoCorrect dialog box.

While you are looking at the AutoFormat As You Type tab (Figure 9-5), take a look at some of the other choices available there too:

✦ **The Replace As You Type list** focuses on replacing ordinary keyboard characters with typeset-looking characters. For example, it replaces fractions that you write like this: 1/2 with fractions that appear as a single character like this: ½.

✦ **The Apply As You Type list** contains not only the AutoFit options described previously, but also one for automatic bulleted and numbered lists. These sense when you are creating a bulleted or numbered list and automatically turn on the Bullets or Numbering attribute. Depending on your work style, this feature can either be wonderful or annoying.

✦ **The Apply as You Work list** has only one item: Automatic Layout for Inserted Objects. This feature attempts to change the slide layout when you manually place an object on it. For example, suppose you have a Title and Text slide, and then you manually place a piece of clip art on it, at the left side. This feature would convert the slide's layout to Title, Clip Art, and Text so that the new clip art would reside in a bona fide placeholder. Beginners will find this helpful, but advanced users will probably want to turn it off because it can impede flexibility.

Changing Text Alignment

You saw earlier how to control text alignment in a table cell; it works the same way with regular text too, except there is no vertical alignment. To align a paragraph to the left, center, or right of its text box, or to justify it within the text box, click one of the alignment buttons on the Formatting toolbar, as shown in Figure 9-6, or pick one from the Format ⇨ Alignment menu.

Note   *Alignment* refers to the text's position in its text box, not on the slide. If you want a text box centered on the slide but the text left-aligned within the box, simply move the text box where you want it.

With Justify alignment, if a paragraph has more than one line, this alignment option aligns all but the last line with both the right and left edges of the text box. It ignores the last line of the paragraph, so if the paragraph has only one line, it is essentially the same as Left alignment. Justify looks good with large paragraphs, but is of limited usefulness for the brief bullet points that are the hallmark of most slides.

Depending on your Windows resolution and toolbar settings, the Justify button might not appear on the toolbar.) To choose it if there is no button, choose Format ⇨ Alignment ⇨ Justify.

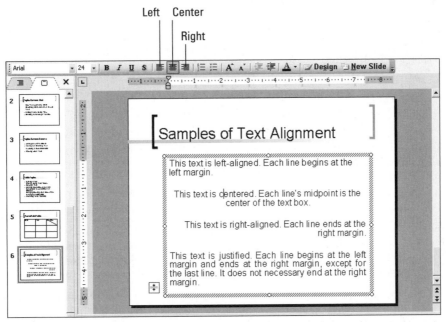

Figure 9-6: Change the alignment of a paragraph with the alignment buttons on the toolbar or with the Format ⇨ Alignment command.

Changing the Text Color

Color really makes your text stand out! When you apply different design templates, the text color changes, but you can also manually change the color of any text by following these steps:

1. Select the text.

2. Open the Font Color drop-down list (on either the Formatting or Drawing toolbar) by clicking the arrow next to the button.

3. Choose a different color for your text, as shown in Figure 9-7. The colors shown are the colors in the color scheme currently in use in your presentation.

4. Click away from the text to deselect it and see your results.

If you don't see the color you want, click the More Colors option in Step 3 and choose a color from the Colors dialog box, and then click OK. You learn more about choosing colors for text and other objects in Chapter 11.

Text Color button

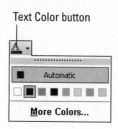

Figure 9-7: Choose a different color for the selected text.

Color is more than just decoration—you can also use it to help convey your message. Here are some ideas:

✦ Different colors connote different emotions. Choose the colors that make your audience feel the way you want. For example, choose red lettering to indicate urgency, or green to say "all is well."

✦ If you are using a dark background, try yellow lettering instead of the usual white. Yellow is a much warmer color and will make the audience feel more positive.

✦ If you are building from one slide to another—for example, if you're showing a list that builds from one slide to the next—make all the bullets on the list that you are not discussing at the moment a neutral color, perhaps a darker or lighter shade of your background color. Then make the one line that you are referring to at the moment a bright, contrasting color.

Expert Tip   Don't forget that attributes such as color and alignment can and should be set on the text placeholder in the Slide Master to ensure consistency in your presentation.

Text Formatting Shortcuts

Now that you know the basics for formatting text, it's time to take a look at some text formatting shortcuts that can save you time.

Changing the type case

If you change your mind about the capitalization in your presentation, you can quickly change the text with the Change Case command in PowerPoint. For example, perhaps you started out thinking that you wanted all the headings to be in all capitals, but you later decided that Title Case is more appropriate (where just the first letters of all the words are capped). To make a change without having to retype, follow these steps:

1. Select the text.

2. Choose Format ➪ Change Case. The Change Case dialog box appears. See Figure 9-8.

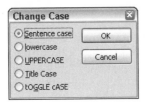

Figure 9-8: Change the case of a lot of text at once, without retyping it, with the Change Case dialog box.

3. Click the case you want to use:

- **Sentence case.** This is like a normal sentence, capped at the beginning and with a period at the end.

- **Lowercase.** This is all lowercase letters.

- **Uppercase.** This is all uppercase letters.

- **Title case.** This capitalizes the first letter of each word.

- **Toggle case.** This reverses the current capitalization and is extremely handy if you accidentally type a few paragraphs with the Caps Lock on and need to correct your error.

4. Click OK.

Changing fonts globally with replace fonts

Say your coworker created a 40-slide presentation in which he used the Carnival font. But now you need to work with the presentation on your own computer, and you don't have that font! You need to change all instances of the Carnival font to a font you have.

Another reason you might want to replace a certain font is simply because you've changed your mind. It seemed like a good idea initially to use a script font for your headings, but now that you see the entire presentation, you realize that plain old Arial Black would have been a better choice. In both cases, the easy way out of the situation is to use the Replace Fonts feature to replace all instances of one font with another instantly.

1. Choose Format ⇨ Replace Fonts. The Replace Font dialog box opens. See Figure 9-9.

2. Open the Replace drop-down list and choose the font to be replaced. Only the fonts currently in use in the presentation appear on this list.

3. Open the With drop-down list and choose the font to substitute for it. This list contains every font installed on your system.

Figure 9-9: Replace all instances of one font with another with the Replace Font dialog box.

4. Click the Replace button. Every instance is replaced.

5. Click Close to close the dialog box.

Copying text formatting with Format Painter

Once you get some text formatted just the way you like it, it's an easy affair to copy that formatting to some other text. This is such a great timesaver! Assume that it takes you six steps to format a particular paragraph the way you want it, with a special font, size, color, and so on. You can then use the Format Painter to transfer that formatting to another paragraph without having to go through those six steps again.

To use Format Painter, follow these steps:

1. Select the paragraph that is already formatted the way you want.

2. Click the Format Painter button on the Standard toolbar.

3. Select the text you want to change by dragging across it with the mouse. The text is immediately "painted" with the formatting.

Expert Tip

Double-clicking the Format Painter makes the tool "sticky," allowing you to paint the formatting to more than one text box. Simply click the Format Painter once to turn it off.

If you select a text box (as opposed to just the text within a text box) and then select the Format Painter, you can apply the formatting to all the text in other text boxes by simply clicking on the other text boxes.

Formatting Text Boxes

Lines and colors (sometimes called borders and shading) can really dress up your text boxes. They provide sort of a pseudo-graphic effect without the hassle of creating a separate rectangle. You can place a line around a text box to make it stand out on its own. Colors (background shading) are useful within text boxes to further make the text stand out. Figure 9-10 shows an example.

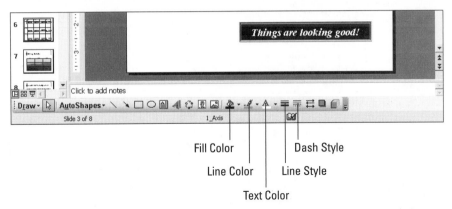

Figure 9-10: Apply borders and shading (color) to a text box to make it stand out.

There are two ways to add lines and background colors to your text box. One is to use the buttons on the Drawing toolbar to control the fill color and the line style and color around the box, as shown in Figure 9-10. Because Chapter 11 goes into those tools in detail, I won't belabor them now.

The other method is to use the Format Text Box dialog box. This method has the advantage of letting you apply both a border color and an inside color at once, whereas if you use the toolbar tools you must apply them separately. Follow these steps to see the dialog box method at work:

1. Select the text box so that selection handles appear around it.

2. Right-click its border and choose Format Text Box (or Format Placeholder) from the shortcut menu.

> **Note** The command name varies depending on whether it is an automatic or manual text box. The dialog box that opens has a different name too; for a placeholder text box it's Format AutoShape, whereas for a manually created text box it's Format Text Box.

3. Click the Colors and Lines tab if it is not already displayed.

4. Open the Color drop-down list in the Fill area and choose a color. See Figure 9-11. (For information about Fill Effects and the other special options listed, see Chapter 11.)

5. Open the Color drop-down list in the Line area and choose a line color for the border around the outside of the text box.

6. Open the Style drop-down list and choose a line style.

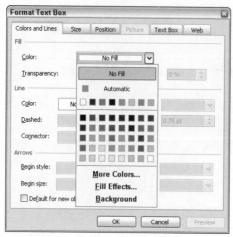

Figure 9-11: Click the color you want to use.

7. Open the Dashed drop-down list and choose a dash style, if you don't want a solid border.

8. Enter a line weight (thickness) in points in the Weight box if you are not satisfied with the line weight shown in the Style box.

9. Click OK.

Adjusting line spacing

You might have noticed as you were typing text into a text box that when you press Enter, you start a new paragraph. By default, PowerPoint leaves some extra space between paragraphs and single-spaces all paragraphs. You can change the spacing if you want. Here are some examples:

✦ Within a bullet list, you might want to eliminate the extra space between paragraphs so your bullet items appear closer together.

✦ If you want to make a large paragraph easier to read, you might add extra space between the lines.

✦ If you need more space between paragraphs, you can add it with the line spacing controls rather than using Enter to insert extra returns between paragraphs.

To adjust line spacing, follow these steps:

1. Select the paragraph(s) to format.

2. Choose Format ➪ Line Spacing. The Line Spacing dialog box appears. See Figure 9-12.

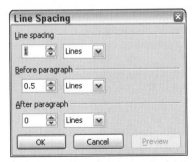

Figure 9-12: Use the Line Spacing dialog box to change the space between lines and paragraphs.

3. To change the spacing between lines, change the number in the Line Spacing text box. (The default is 1.) Leave the drop-down list next to it set to Lines.

Expert Tip For more precise measurement, open the drop-down lists that show Lines in the text box and change the settings to Points. Then you can enter the measurements by points (remember, one point is 1/72 of an inch).

4. To change the spacing between paragraphs, change the number in the Before Paragraph or After Paragraph text boxes.

5. Click OK to close the dialog box.

There is both a Before and After control, as you saw in Step 4; that's so you can specify the extra space between paragraphs as being either before or after each paragraph. In general, you should use one or the other, but not both. If you enter both a Before and After value, you may get more space than you intended. For example, if you set both Before Paragraph and After Paragraph to 1 line, you get one line of space before paragraph number 1, but two lines of space between subsequent paragraphs — one line after the initial paragraph and one line above the paragraph that follows it.

Expert Tip It's recommended that you don't go below .8 lines for text, because doing so might chop off the ascenders and descenders of the letters. If you find the text changing line spacing on its own, check Tools ➪ AutoCorrect (or check the Smart Tag) as described previously to ensure that AutoFit Text To Placeholder has been turned off.

Setting tabs

If you have worked with a typewriter or word processor, you are probably familiar with tabs. You set them, and then press the Tab key to move the insertion point to them quickly. Each text box has its own tab settings in PowerPoint, and you set them (as you do in Microsoft Word) with the Ruler.

Note Unlike in Word, tab settings apply to the text box as a whole in PowerPoint, not to individual paragraphs.

To set tab stops, follow these steps:

1. View the slide containing the text box in Normal or Slide view.

2. If the Ruler does not appear, choose View ➪ Ruler.

3. Click inside the text box you want to set tabs for.

4. Click the Ruler where you want to set the tab. A little L appears, showing that you've just placed a left tab stop.

You can also have centered, right-aligned, or decimal-aligned tab stops. To set one of these, click the Tab Type button at the far left of the Ruler. Each time you click this button, it cycles through the available tab stop types:

Left

Center

Right

Decimal

To get rid of a tab stop, drag and drop it off the Ruler.

Expert Tip Holding down the Ctrl key while dragging a tab stop on the Ruler allows you to place your tab stop more precisely.

Setting indents

You may have noticed the little gray triangles at the left end of the Ruler. These are indent markers; they show how far from the edge of the text box the actual text starts. They're askew in Figure 9-13 because there's a bullet list, and the first line in a bullet paragraph is indented less than subsequent lines (to account for the bullet). In text boxes without bullets or numbered lists, the triangles align with one another by default.

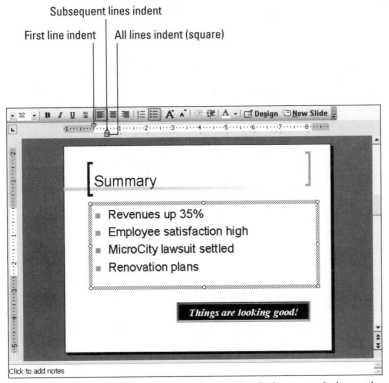

Figure 9-13: The triangles on the Ruler and the little rectangle beneath them control paragraph indentation.

You can drag these triangles to change the indentation:

✦ Drag the top triangle to change where the bullet is placed.

✦ Drag the bottom triangle to change where the paragraph text aligns (minus the bullet).

✦ Drag the rectangle beneath the bottom triangle to change both triangles at once.

The paragraph indents, like the tabs, apply to the entire text box. You can't have two paragraphs with two different indent settings in the same text box. If you want this effect, you have to create a new text box to hold the second bit of text separately.

The exception to this is multilevel bullet lists. These are allowed in a single text box, as you see in the next section.

Formatting bulleted and numbered lists

You have already seen how easy it is to create a bulleted list in PowerPoint. When you create a slide based on a layout that includes a bullet list, or when you type a new slide in the outline pane, you get bullets automatically.

You can turn off the bullets for any paragraph(s) or text placeholder by selecting them and clicking the Bullets button on the Formatting toolbar to toggle the bullet(s) off. In that same way, you can apply bullets to paragraphs or text placeholders that don't currently have them.

You can also format any paragraph(s) as a numbered list. This is just like bullets except numbers replace the bullets. To do so, select the paragraphs or text placeholder and click the Numbering button on the Formatting toolbar.

PowerPoint also lets you have lists embedded within lists, as shown in Figure 9-14. To create one bulleted list within another, go to the Outline pane and select the lines that should be made subordinate. Then, press Tab to demote them in outline level (or use the Increase Indent icon on the Formatting toolbar).

You may notice in Figure 9-14 that the bullet character is different for different outline levels. For the first level, it's a large square; for the second, it's a small circle. PowerPoint does that automatically to help keep you from getting confused. But you can also choose the bullet character yourself for each level.

You can choose from a wide variety of bullet characters, from simple dots and blocks to check marks, happy faces, and more. You can change the bullet for an individual paragraph, for all paragraphs on the slide, or for the entire presentation. It's all in what you select:

  ✦ To change a single paragraph, click in that paragraph before you make the change.

  ✦ To change all the bullets on the slide, select all of the text or the entire text placeholder before you make the change.

  ✦ To change all the bullets in the entire presentation at that outline level, make the change on the Slide Master.

Promote button (or press Shift + Tab)

Demote button (or press Tab)

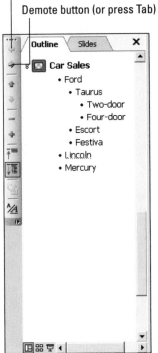

Figure 9-14: To create a multilevel outline, demote the paragraphs in the outline pane or use the Increase Indent icon on the Formatting toolbar.

To change the bullet character, follow these steps:

1. Select the text as appropriate. (See the previous guidelines.)

2. Choose Format ⇨ Bullets and Numbering. The Bullets and Numbering dialog box opens. See Figure 9-15.

3. Make sure the Bulleted tab is displayed. If it isn't, click it.

4. Click one of the other bullet styles shown.

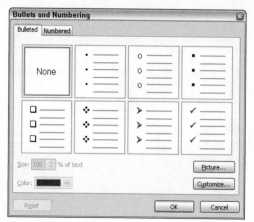

Figure 9-15: Select the bullet style you want.

5. Do any of the following for other bullet modifications:

- To change the size of the bullet in relation to the text, change the number in the Size box.

- To use a different color for the bullet, choose a color from the Color drop-down list.

- To use a picture for a bullet, click the Picture button and select a graphic from the Picture Bullet dialog box that appears, and click OK.

- To use a character from a font (such as a symbol from the Wingdings font), click the Customize button and choose a character from the Bullet dialog box. Then click OK.

6. Click OK to apply your bullet changes.

Summary

In this chapter, you learned how to format both text boxes and the text within them. Combined with what you learned in the preceding chapter, you now have all the skills you need to create text-based presentations in PowerPoint.

Throughout this chapter, I've been promising that you'll learn more about objects. The next chapter explains what objects are (basically, they're everything on a slide) and what they all have in common. Armed with that knowledge, you'll be able to work with almost any of the special object types, such as sounds, movies, graphics, and so on, that you encounter later in the book.

✦   ✦   ✦

Correcting and Improving Presentation Text

PowerPoint contains many tools that can help you avoid embarrassing mistakes in your presentation's text, and this chapter takes a look at some of them. You'll learn how to perform a spelling check, how to check for stylistic consistency, how to set up PowerPoint to correct your most common errors automatically, and how to use the new Research tool in PowerPoint to check your facts.

Correcting Your Spelling

If you think that a spelling check can't improve the look of your presentation, just think for a moment how ugly a blatant spelling error would look in huge type on a five-foot projection screen. Frightening, isn't it? If that image makes you nervous, it should. Spelling mistakes can creep past even the most literate people, and pop up where you least expect them, often at embarrassing moments.

Fortunately, like other Microsoft Office programs, PowerPoint comes with a powerful spelling program that can check your work for you at any time, minimizing the number of embarrassing spelling mistakes. The Office programs all use the same spelling checker, so if you are familiar with it in another Office application, you should be able to breeze through a spell check in PowerPoint with no problem.

When PowerPoint marks a word as misspelled, it really just means that the word is not in its dictionary. Many words, especially proper names, are perfectly okay to use and yet not in PowerPoint's dictionary, so don't believe PowerPoint against your own good judgment.

Checking an individual word

As you work, PowerPoint underlines words that aren't in its dictionary with a red wavy line. Whenever you see a red-underlined word, you can right-click it to see a list of spelling suggestions, as shown in Figure 10-1. Click the correction you want or click one of the other commands:

✦ **Ignore All:** Ignores this and all other instances of the word in this PowerPoint session. If you exit and restart PowerPoint, the list is wiped out.

✦ **Add to Dictionary:** Adds this word to PowerPoint's custom dictionary. (You learn more about this later in the chapter.)

✦ **Spelling:** Opens the full-blown spelling checker, described in the next section.

✦ **Look Up:** Opens the Research tool, discussed later in this chapter.

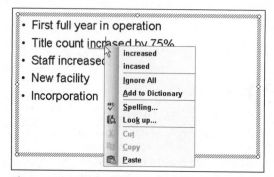

Figure 10-1: Right-click a red-underlined word for quick spelling advice.

If you don't want to see the wavy red underlines on-screen, you can turn off that feature of the spelling checker. To do so, select Tools ⇨ Options and click the Spelling and Style tab. From there, select Hide Spelling Errors in This Document. Then click OK.

Checking the entire presentation

If your document is long, it can get tiresome to individually right-click each wavy-underlined word or phrase. In such cases, it's easier to use the full-blown spell-check feature in PowerPoint to check all the words in the entire presentation.

To begin the spelling check, click the Spelling toolbar button, select Tools ➪ Spelling, or press F7. If there are no misspelled words in your presentation, PowerPoint presents a dialog box telling you that your spell check is complete. Click OK to close that dialog box.

If, on the other hand, PowerPoint finds a misspelled word, you can choose from several dialog box control options (as shown in Figure 10-2):

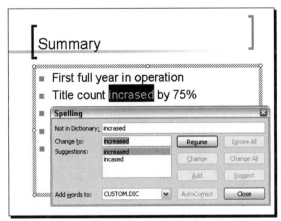

Figure 10-2: When PowerPoint finds a misspelled word with the spelling checker, you can respond to it using these controls.

✦ **Not in dictionary box:** Shows the misspelled word.

✦ **Change to box:** Shows what the spelling will be changed to if you click the Change or Change All buttons. You can choose a word from the Suggestions list or type your own correction here.

✦ **Suggestions box:** Lists words close to the spelling of the word you actually typed. Choose the correct one, moving it to the Change to box, by clicking it.

✦ **Ignore button:** Skips over this occurrence of the word.

✦ **Ignore All button:** Skips over all occurrences of the word in this PowerPoint session only.

✦ **Change button:** Changes the word to the word shown in the Change to text box.

✦ **Change All button:** Changes all occurrences of the word in the entire presentation to the word in the Change to text box.

✦ **Add button:** Adds the word to PowerPoint's custom dictionary so that it will recognize it in the future.

✦ **Suggest button:** Displays the suggestions in the Suggestions box if you have set the spell checker's options so that suggestions do not automatically appear.

✦ **AutoCorrect button:** Adds the word to the AutoCorrect list so that if you mis-spell it the same way in the future, PowerPoint automatically corrects it as you type. See the "Using AutoCorrect to Fix Common Problems" section later in this chapter.

✦ **Close button:** Closes the Spelling dialog box.

When PowerPoint can't find any more misspelled words, it displays a dialog box (or message from the Office Assistant) to that effect; click OK.

Expert Tip   If you have more than one language dictionary available (for example, if you are using PowerPoint in a multilingual office and have purchased multiple language packs from Microsoft), you can specify which language's dictionary to use for which text. To do so, select the text that's in a different language than the rest of the presentation, and then choose Tools ➪ Language. Select the appropriate language from the list and click OK.

Setting spelling options

To control how (and even whether) the spelling checker operates, do the following:

1. Choose Tools ➪ Options.

2. Click the Spelling and Style tab. See Figure 10-3.

3. Mark or clear any of the check boxes as desired in the Spelling section:

- **Check spelling as you type:** This is on by default. Turning it off prevents the spell checker from noticing and red-underlining words it can't find in its dictionary. This can cause a very small improvement in performance on a slow computer; you will not notice anything on a fast computer.

- **Hide all spelling errors:** This is off by default. Marking this check box prevents the red wavy underline from appearing beneath misspelled words. It does not prevent the spell checker from checking them; you can right-click a misspelled word to see suggestions for it, same as always.

- **Always suggest corrections:** This is on by default. It allows suggestions to appear in the Suggestions box in the Spelling window (Figure 10-2). Turn this off for a very small improvement in performance. Then if you want a suggestion as you are checking the spelling, you need to click the Suggest button.

- **Ignore words in uppercase:** This is on by default. It prevents the spell checker from flagging acronyms.

- **Ignore words with numbers:** This is on by default. It prevents the spell checker from noticing words with digits in them, such as license plate numbers or model numbers.

4. Click OK to accept the new settings.

Figure 10-3: Setting spelling options.

Checking Style and Punctuation

As you create your presentation, you are probably focusing on the meaning of the words, not the formatting. Even later, as you begin to apply text formatting, some picky little errors may slip by you. Perhaps you ended each bullet point with a period on one slide but not another, or maybe you capitalized every word in some headings but only the first word of others.

PowerPoint can help with this by applying style and punctuation rules that you specify. It's not pushy about the rules, and it won't make changes automatically without your consent. Instead, it merely suggests ways to make the presentation more consistent and attractive.

Style and punctuation checking happens automatically when the feature is turned on. Whenever PowerPoint sees a problem, a little light bulb appears on the slide. Click it, and you see the Office Assistant appear with a suggestion, as shown in Figure 10-4. Click one of the available options to make the change or ignore the style rule.

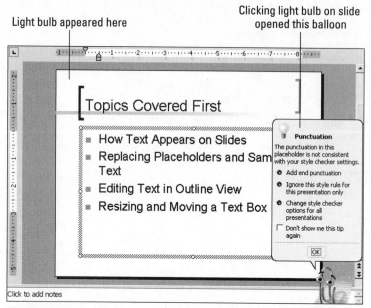

Light bulb appeared here

Clicking light bulb on slide opened this balloon

Figure 10-4: PowerPoint's style checker can identify style errors.

Style checking might be disabled on your PC. To enable it and configure it, do the following:

1. Select Tools ➪ Options. The Options dialog box opens.

2. Click the Spelling and Style tab. See Figure 10-3.

3. Mark the Check Style check box.

4. If you see a message asking whether you want to enable the Office Assistant, click Enable Office Assistant. The style-checking feature requires it.

5. Click the Style Options button to open the Style Options dialog box. See Figure 10-5.

6. If you want to check the case of slide titles and/or body text, make sure to mark the Slide title style and/or Body text style check boxes.

7. For each, choose a style from the drop-down list:

   • **Sentence case:** Checks that the first letter of the first word and nothing else is capitalized, just like in a sentence.

   • **Lowercase:** Checks that all letters of all words are lowercase.

- **Uppercase:** Checks that all letters of all words are uppercase.
- **Title case:** Checks that the first letter of each word begins with a capital letter, just like in a title.

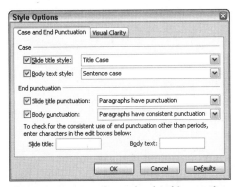

Figure 10-5: Set the style-checking options here.

8. If you want to check end punctuation in the style check, make sure to mark the Slide title punctuation and/or Body punctuation check boxes. (They are not marked by default.)

9. For each, choose Paragraphs Have Punctuation or Paragraphs Do Not Have Punctuation from the drop-down list.

10. If you are using different punctuation than a period at the end of paragraphs, enter the different characters in the Slide title and/or Body text boxes.

11. Click the Visual Clarity tab. See Figure 10-6.

12. In the Fonts section, choose settings for each of the rules you want to apply, or deselect a rule's check box to disable checking for it:

- **Number of fonts should not exceed:** Warns you if you use more than the specified number of different fonts. In general, presentations look nicest when they do not use too many different fonts.
- **Title text size should be at least:** Warns you if the title text on a slide is not at least the specified number of points in size. If a title is too small, it can get lost on the slide.
- **Body text size should be at least:** Warns you if the body text on a slide is not at least the specified number of points in size. If body text is too small, it may be unreadable to the audience members at the back of the room.

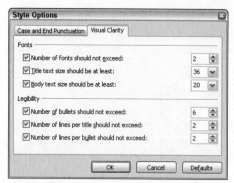

Figure 10-6: Set style-checking options for formatting and legibility.

13. In the Legibility section, choose settings for each of the rules you want to apply, or deselect a rule's check box to disable checking for it:

   - **Number of bullets should not exceed:** Warns you if you have more than a certain number of bullets on a slide. Too many bullets can make a slide confusing.

   - **Number of lines per title should not exceed:** Warns you if a slide's title is longer than two lines. In general, short titles (one line) are best; more than two lines can be confusing.

   - **Number of lines per bullet should not exceed:** Warns you if a bulleted paragraph wraps to more than a certain number of lines. Generally, bullet points should be short so the audience can read them quickly.

14. Click OK to accept your style settings.

15. Click OK to close the Style Options dialog box.

After turning on style checking, if you do not see any style problems identified, you might not have that type of Office Assistant tip turned on. To check, do the following:

1. Right-click the Office Assistant character and choose Options. (If the Office Assistant doesn't appear, choose Help ➪ Show the Office Assistant first.)

2. Make sure that the Using Features More Effectively check box is marked.

3. Click OK.

Using AutoCorrect to Fix Common Problems

With AutoCorrect, PowerPoint can automatically correct certain common mis-spellings and formatting errors as you type. One way to put a word on the AutoCorrect list, as you saw earlier, is to click the AutoCorrect button during a spelling check. Another way is to directly access the AutoCorrect options.

To access AutoCorrect, select Tools ➪ AutoCorrect Options, and then click the AutoCorrect tab. The AutoCorrect settings appear, as shown in Figure 10-7. At the top of the dialog box is a series of check boxes that help you fine-tune some other corrections that AutoCorrect makes besides spelling corrections:

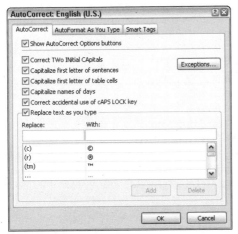

Figure 10-7: Set up the corrections that you want PowerPoint to handle as you type.

✦ **Correct two initial capitals:** If you accidentally hold down the Shift key too long and get two capital letters in a row (such as MIcrosoft), PowerPoint corrects this error if you leave this check box marked.

✦ **Capitalize first letter of sentence:** Leave this check box marked to have PowerPoint capitalize the first letter of the first word after a sentence-ending punctuation mark, such as a period, or to capitalize the first letter of the word that occurs at the beginning of a paragraph.

Expert Tip Click the Exceptions button to open an AutoCorrect Exceptions dialog box. Here, you can enter a list of capitalization exceptions, such as abbreviations that use periods but aren't at the end of a sentence (like approx. and Ave.). You can also set up a list of Two Initial Capitals exceptions.

✦ **Capitalize names of days:** Leave this check box marked to make sure the names of days, such as Sunday, Monday, and so on, are capitalized.

✦ **Correct accidental use of caps lock key:** If you leave the Caps Lock on, PowerPoint can sometimes detect it and fix the problem. For example, if you typed the sentence "hE WAS GLAD TO SEE US," PowerPoint could conclude that the Caps Lock was inappropriately on and would turn it off for you and fix the sentence.

✦ **Replace text as you type:** This check box enables the main portion of AutoCorrect: the word list. You must leave this check box on if you want AutoCorrect to correct spelling as you're typing. For instance, if you type "yoiu," PowerPoint automatically changes it to "you."

On the list in the dialog box, you see a number of word pairs. To the left is the common misspelling, and to the right is the word that PowerPoint substitutes in its place. Scroll through this list to get a feel for the corrections PowerPoint makes.

To add a word pair to the list, type the misspelling in the Replace box and the replacement in the With box. Then click the Add button. You can also add corrections through the Spelling dialog box.

If PowerPoint insists on making a correction that you do not want, you can delete that correction from the list. Simply select it from the list and click Delete. For example, one of my clients likes me to code certain headings with (C) in front of them, so the first thing I do in any Office program is remove the AutoCorrect entry that specifies that (C) must be converted to a copyright symbol (©).

When you are finished, click OK to close the AutoCorrect dialog box.

Caution   Don't use AutoCorrect for misspellings that you may sometimes want to change to some other word or you may introduce embarrassing mistakes into your document. For example, if you often type "pian" instead of "pain," but sometimes you accidentally type "pian" instead of "piano," don't tell PowerPoint to always AutoCorrect to "pain," or you may find that PowerPoint has corrected your attempt at typing *piano* and made it a *pain*!

Using AutoFormat As You Type

The AutoFormat As You Type feature enables PowerPoint to convert certain letter combinations to typographical characters that look nicer on a slide than plain old typed text. For example, one of the AutoFormat As You Type actions is to convert two dashes (–) into a single long dash (—).

Other actions include automatic bulleted and numbered lists. For example, suppose in a manual textbox you type a 1, press Tab, and type a paragraph, and then type 2, press Tab, and type a paragraph. PowerPoint would guess that you want a numbered list, and would apply the Numbering feature to those paragraphs (just as if you had clicked the Numbering button on the toolbar.) Figure 10-8 shows all the AutoFormat As You Type options.

Figure 10-8: Turn on/off the AutoFormat As You Type settings to fit your work style.

To change the AutoFormat As You Type settings, follow these steps:

1. Choose Tools ⇨ Options.

2. Click the AutoFormat As You Type tab.

3. Mark or clear check boxes as desired to select the features you want.

4. Click OK.

Using Smart Tags

Smart Tags is a great time-saving feature in PowerPoint that lets you paste and format information in a presentation. This feature is actually a part of Office 2003 itself, not just PowerPoint, so Smart Tags are common to all Office applications.

You have probably seen a Smart Tag already and not realized it. For example, when you paste something from the Clipboard, a little icon appears in the bottom-left corner of the pasted area. There is a down arrow next to this icon. Click it to open a Smart Tags menu with choices you can apply to the pasted material. In Figure 10-9, some data from Excel is being pasted into PowerPoint.

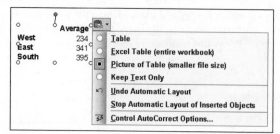

Figure 10-9: Smart Tags make it easier to format inserted data.

There are a wide variety of Smart Tags, not just for Clipboard usage. For example, in Figure 10-10, I have typed a date, and a faint red underline now appears on it, along with a Smart Tag icon to its left. I can click on the icon to display a menu of Smart Tag choices for that date. In this case I could open Outlook by choosing Schedule a Meeting or Show My Calendar.

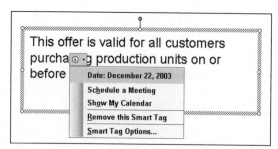

Figure 10-10: Smart Tags make it easier to insert and format certain types of data, such as dates.

Turning Smart Tags on or off

Some Smart Tags are enabled by default; others are not. To see and change the settings:

1. Choose Tools ➪ AutoCorrect Options.

2. Click the Smart Tags tab.

3. *(Optional)* If you want to disable Smart Tags altogether in PowerPoint, clear the Label Text with Smart Tags check box. Then click OK. Otherwise go on to step 4.

4. Mark or clear the check boxes to specify which types of Smart Tags you want to use. See Figure 10-11.

5. *(Optional)* To see more information and choices for a category of Smart Tags, select it and then click the Properties button. This opens a Web page (assuming you are connected to the Internet) where you can download more Smart Tags and find out more about them.

6. *(Optional)* To check the presentation now for text that matches one of the Smart Tags specifications, click the Check Presentation button.

7. Click OK to accept the new settings.

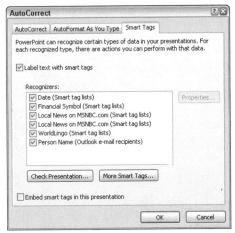

Figure 10-11: Turn certain types of Smart Tags on or off.

Adding more Smart Tags

There are additional Smart Tags available for Microsoft Office via the Web. To find out what other Smart Tags are available, click the More Smart Tags button in the AutoCorrect dialog box (Figure 10-11). This opens a Web browser and a Web site where you can explore other Smart Tag offerings.

Caution When looking for more Smart Tags, pay attention to which applications each tag works with. Some work with Word or Excel only.

For example, MSNBC offers a free download of Smart Tags that can enable you to look up the local news and weather in hundreds of major cities all over the world. After installing it, country, state, and city names become Smart Tag enabled. In Figure 10-12, I am preparing to look up the weather forecast for Bali.

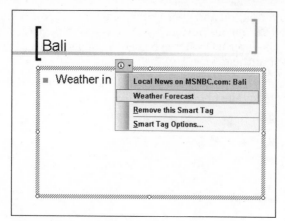

Figure 10-12: Additional Smart Tags can extend the capabilities of the feature to access Web content.

Expert Tip There is also an add-in program called ActiveDocs that enables you to create your own Smart Tags. You can download a 21-day trial version of it at `www.active docs.com/microsoft/eservices.asp`.

Using the Research Tool

The Research feature is available in most of the Office applications, including PowerPoint. It enables you to connect with various online and offline data stores to look up information. This could include online encyclopedias, dictionaries, and news services.

Choosing which tools you want

The first time you attempt to use the feature, a box may appear prompting you to insert the Office CD and install it. Just follow the prompts. At some point during the installation, a box will appear asking you which research tools you want to install. Place a check mark next to the ones you want. If you want to choose additional research tools later, do the following:

1. Choose Tools ⇨ Research. The Research task pane opens. If there is a New Services Are Available hyperlink at the bottom, click it and skip to step 4. Otherwise continue to step 2.

2. Click Research Options at the bottom of the task pane.

3. Click Update/Remove. The Update or Remove Services dialog box appears.

4. Select a service on the list. The ones that you already have installed say (Installed) after their names. See Figure 10-13.

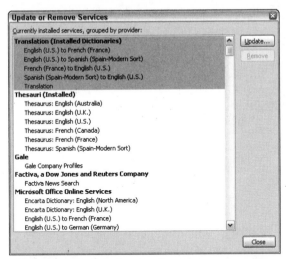

Figure 10-13: Updating the list of Research services that PowerPoint will use.

5. Click the Update button and then follow the prompts to install it, or mark check boxes in a dialog box that appears to configure it. The exact steps vary depending on what you chose.

6. When you are finished updating and removing services, click Close to return to the Research Options dialog box.

Note The Add Services button opens a dialog box where you can specify another service that is not on the Update/Remove list.

7. Click OK to close the Research Options dialog box.

Using reference sites

The available tools are divided into two broad categories of sites: *reference* and *research*. Reference sites include dictionaries, thesauruses, and translation utilities, whereas research sites include encyclopedias and news services.

All the reference sites can be consulted as a group, or you can consult an individual tool. For example, you can look a word up in the dictionary, thesaurus, or translator all at once, or you can just use the thesaurus.

To look a word up in a reference source, follow these steps:

1. Choose Tools ➪ Research or click the Research button on the toolbar.

2. In the Search For box, type the term you want to look up.

3. In the Show Results From box, choose All Reference Sources (or choose a particular source if you prefer).

4. Click the Start Searching (arrow) button. The results of the search appear in the task pane, as in Figure 10-14.

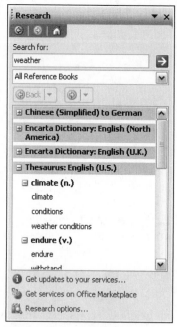

Figure 10-14: Looking up a word in the reference sources.

Let's look at each of these three tools (thesaurus, translation, and dictionary) in more detail.

Using the thesaurus

The thesaurus feature works just like a hardbound thesaurus book. It lets you look up synonyms for a word, so you can make your vocabulary more varied and colorful.

To look up a word in the thesaurus, use the steps in the preceding section. You can also jump directly to the thesaurus for a particular word by doing the following:

1. Select the word.

2. Choose Tools ➪ Thesaurus Dialog. The Research feature looks up the word. The found synonyms appear.

3. To replace the selected word with one of the found words, point to a found word and click the down arrow next to it, then choose Insert. See Figure 10-15. PowerPoint replaces the selected word with the synonym.

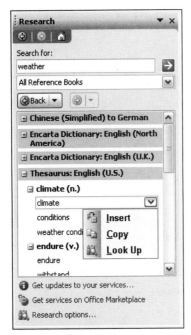

Figure 10-15: Looking up synonyms with the thesaurus.

Using translation

Translation helps you translate text into any of a variety of languages. You can access translation by using the steps in the Using Reference Tools section earlier in the chapter. If you want translation only, do the following:

1. Select the word.

2. Choose Tools ⇨ Research or click the Research button on the toolbar.

3. Open the Show Results From list and choose Translation.

4. Choose the From and To languages. For example, if the word is currently in English and you want it to be in Spanish, choose English for the From and Spanish for the To.

Note   If a dialog box appears saying that the feature is not installed, click Yes to install it. Have your Office CD handy; it might be needed.

5. The translation appears in the task pane, as in Figure 10-16. Read it, and then incorporate the information into your presentation as needed. There is no automatic replacement feature as with the thesaurus, although you can use Ctrl+C to copy and Ctrl+V to paste the information onto your slide if the regular Edit/Copy command isn't available.

Figure 10-16: Translate a word or phrase with translation.

Using the dictionary

The dictionary feature provides a definition of a word, so you can make sure you are using it correctly. You can also use it to verify the spelling of a word (although the Spell Check feature is probably better for that).

Expert Tip   There are multiple dictionaries available; see "Choosing which tools you want" to select the dictionaries to use. It is simplest to select a single dictionary for the country in which your presentation will be presented.

To look up a word in the dictionary, follow these steps:

1. Select the word.

2. Choose Tools ➪ Research or click the Research button on the toolbar.

3. Open the Show Results From list and choose the dictionary you want. For example, in Figure 10-17 I have chosen Encarta World Dictionary: English (U.S.).

4. The definition(s) appear in the task pane. Read them and incorporate the information in your presentation as needed.

Figure 10-17: Getting a definition of a word with the dictionary tool.

Using research sites

The research sites are sources that provide more in-depth information about a particular word or phrase, such as encyclopedias and news services. To look up a term in one of these sources, follow these steps:

1. Select the word.

2. Choose Tools ⇨ Research or click the Research button on the toolbar.

3. Open the Show Results From list and choose All Research Sites. (Or choose a particular site if desired.)

4. In the results that appear, such as in Figure 10-18, click a hyperlink to read its information. Depending on what you select, a separate Web browser window may open.

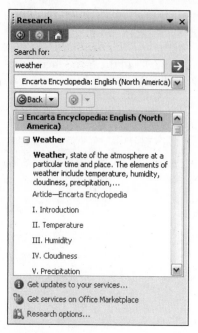

Figure 10-18: Find in-depth information about a term or phrase with the Research Sites' group of sources.

Caution   Remember, proper attribution of sources is a must. If you copy information from an online source such as an encyclopedia or news service, you must cite your source. Further, depending on the source, you might need to get written permission to use the data. This is especially true with photographs. Very few news services permit you to reuse their photos without permission.

Summary

In this chapter you learned how to use the spelling, proofing, and reference tools in PowerPoint to make a good impression on your audience. Now you can present with confidence!

In the next chapter, you'll begin learning how to place and manipulate objects in a presentation. An object can be any element that complements the regular text, such as a drawing, a photo, a graph, or any of many other types of content.

✦   ✦   ✦

Inserting, Positioning, and Sizing Objects

Everything on a slide is an *object*. That means that each object can be moved, sized, and formatted independently. In the last two chapters, you saw that text and tables sit in their own boxes. Here's a fairly exhaustive list of elements that can be objects on slides, and the chapters in which you can find them:

- ✦ Text boxes (Chapters 8 and 9)
- ✦ Imported objects from other programs (this chapter and Chapter 17)
- ✦ Clip art (Chapter 14)
- ✦ Imported pictures (Chapter 14)
- ✦ Scanned artwork (Chapter 14)
- ✦ WordArt (Chapter 15)
- ✦ Lines and shapes you draw with the Drawing toolbar (Chapter 15)
- ✦ Charts that plot data graphically (Chapter 16)
- ✦ Organization charts and diagrams (Chapter 17)
- ✦ Sound files (Chapter 20)
- ✦ CD audio tracks (Chapter 20)
- ✦ Video clips (Chapter 21)
- ✦ Action buttons (Chapter 29)
- ✦ Hyperlinks (Chapter 29)

Most of the manipulation you can do on an object is the same, regardless of the object type. So in this chapter and the next, I teach you those basic object-handling skills so you don't have to go over the process separately for the object types that you look at in individual chapters later. This chapter covers the insertion and placement of objects, and Chapter 12 covers their formatting.

Inserting an Object

As I have pointed out earlier, there are two ways to place an object on a slide. One is to choose a layout that contains a placeholder for that object type, and the other is to place the object manually. A brief review of both of these methods follows. More information about each object type is in the chapter later in the book that pertains to it.

Note   Most of the example figures in this chapter use simple shapes drawn with PowerPoint's shape tools on the Drawing toolbar. You might want to draw some shapes yourself on a blank slide (that is, one formatted with the Blank AutoLayout) if you want something to practice on. See Chapter 15 if you need help drawing these shapes.

Placing an object with a placeholder

When you choose a layout that contains a placeholder, an icon appears in the spot where the object goes, along with a message to double-click it. When you do so, a dialog box or wizard appears to guide you through the process of inserting the object. (See the appropriate chapter later in the book for the specific object type you are interested in.)

Placing an object manually

When you place an object on a slide manually, you don't have a placeholder to call up the appropriate dialog box for you. Instead, you click a toolbar button or choose an object type from the Insert menu (see Figure 11-1) to start the ball rolling. Then, a dialog box appears (the same one that you get with a placeholder, in most cases) and you make your object selection.

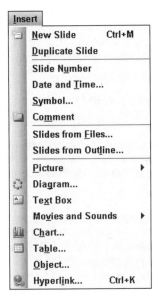

Figure 11-1: You can insert most object types from the Insert menu.

Selecting Objects

No matter which type of object you are dealing with, you select it in the same way: Click it with the mouse. Handles (white circles) appear around it, as shown in Figure 11-2.

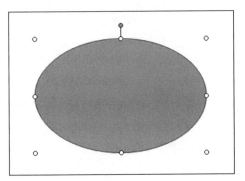

Figure 11-2: Selection handles (handles, for short) appear around a selected object.

You have learned about selecting single objects in earlier chapters, but now it's time to go one step further and select multiple objects. For example, suppose you have drawn several shapes (see Chapter 15) and you want to select them as a group so you can move them. Or, suppose you want to move two text boxes together.

To select more than one object, click the first one to select it, and then hold down the Shift key as you click the other one. They both become selected.

Expert Tip   Holding down Ctrl when you select multiple objects also does the same thing as Shift; however, if you hold down Ctrl and drag, it makes a copy. That's why it's better to use Shift than Ctrl for selecting multiple objects — so you don't accidentally make copies by dragging the item.

If you can't easily click each object (perhaps because they are overlapping one another), an easy way to select a whole group is to drag the cursor around them. For example, suppose you wanted to select all the shapes in Figure 11-3. You would drag the cursor over them, as shown in Figure 11-3, to select them all, as shown in Figure 11-4. To do so, click and hold down the mouse button above and to the left of the objects, and drag down and to the right until you create a box around them. Then, release the mouse button. All objects that were entirely inside the boundary you drew will be selected.

Note   The top-left to bottom-right drag is just one way of selecting the group; you can also drag from lower right to upper left if you prefer.

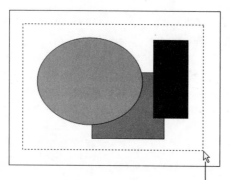

Mouse drags a box around objects

Figure 11-3: Hold down the mouse button and drag a box that includes all the shapes you want to select.

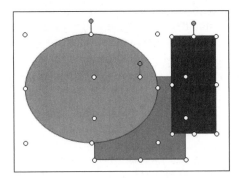

Figure 11-4: Each selected object has its own selection handles.

Moving and Copying Objects

You can move or copy objects anywhere you like: within a single slide, from one slide to another, or from one presentation to another. You can even copy or move an object to a completely different program, such as Microsoft Word or Excel.

Within a slide

To move an object on a slide, drag it with the mouse. Just position the mouse pointer over any part of the object except a handle, so that the mouse pointer changes to a four-headed arrow, and then drag the object to a new location. A dotted outline shows where the object is going. See Figure 11-5.

Holding down Shift as you drag will constrain the movement of the object horizontally or vertically, making it possible to drag *only* horizontally or *only* vertically. Holding down Ctrl as you drag makes a copy.

To copy an object on a slide, use the Copy command. Select the object and press Ctrl+C to copy (or choose Edit ➪ Copy). Then, press Ctrl+V to paste it (or choose Edit ➪ Paste). Then you can drag the copy wherever you want it on the slide.

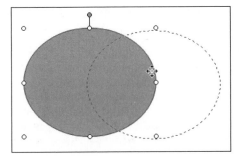

Figure 11-5: Drag an object on the slide to reposition it.

Note Whenever you need to cut, copy, or paste, you have a variety of methods to choose from. There are the Cut, Copy, and Paste toolbar buttons, the Cut, Copy, and Paste commands on the Edit menu, and the shortcut key combinations Cut (Ctrl+X), Copy (Ctrl+C), and Paste (Ctrl+V).

Expert Tip Ctrl+D works as a combination copy/paste command and will automatically duplicate the object(s) you have selected.

From one slide to another

To move an object to a different slide, cut and paste works best. Select the object and press Ctrl+X (or choose Edit ➪ Cut). Then display the slide on which you want the object to appear and press Ctrl+V (or choose Edit ➪ Paste).

To copy an object to a different slide without removing it from the original slide, do the same thing except use Copy (Ctrl+C or Edit ➪ Copy) instead of Cut.

Note Don't forget, if you want an object to appear in the same spot on every slide in the presentation, add the object to the Slide Master rather than trying to copy it onto every slide. See Chapter 7.

Expert Tip When you copy/paste an object onto the same slide, the copy is offset from the original to allow for easy selection. When you copy/paste an object onto a different slide, the copy appears in the same position as the original.

From one presentation to another

The best way to move or copy from one presentation to another is also with the Cut, Copy, and Paste commands. Select the object, and then cut or copy it. Display the destination slide (in normal view) in the other presentation, and then paste.

Another way to move or copy between presentations is using drag and drop. You learned in Chapter 2 how to display multiple presentations at once by opening multiple files, using the Window ➪ Arrange All command, and changing the Zoom in both windows to Fit, so you can see both slides in their entirety. Then you can drag the object from one window to the other to move or copy it. To move an object, simply drag it. To copy an object, hold down the Ctrl key as you drag. See Figure 11-6.

Expert Tip An object moved or copied to a different presentation might change its color. Why? If you chose a color for the object from the initial eight color choices that pop up, you probably chose a color placeholder for the template rather than a particular color. For example, suppose the design template you are using comes with its own color scheme that uses eight colors. Assume that color #3 of those is gray. If your object is formatted as color #3 (gray), and you copy it to a different presentation in which color #3 is blue, the object changes to blue when it gets there. You learn more about this in Chapter 12.

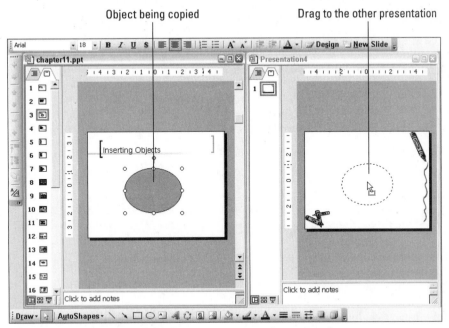

Figure 11-6: To drag an object from one presentation to another, arrange your windows so that both are visible.

To another program

You can also move and copy objects from PowerPoint into other programs. Suppose, for example, you have created a table on a slide (see Chapter 8) and you want to include it in a report in Word. You can move or copy it there with either cut and paste or drag and drop — your choice.

The cut-and-paste method, of course, involves the Cut, Copy, and Paste commands that you saw in the preceding sections. Select the object, cut or copy it, and then paste it. For drag and drop, resize the PowerPoint window so that you can also see the destination window and then drag the object there.

Expert Tip   Depending on the object and the destination application, copy/paste usually results in smaller file sizes than drag and drop.

Using the Office Clipboard

The Microsoft Office Clipboard lets you store more than one object at a time. You can copy or cut many objects to the Clipboard and then paste them all into the same or different locations afterwards.

To use the Clipboard in multi-clip mode, display it in the task pane by choosing View ⇨ Task Pane and then choosing the Clipboard task pane by clicking at the top of the task pane and selecting Clipboard from the menu. See Figure 11-7.

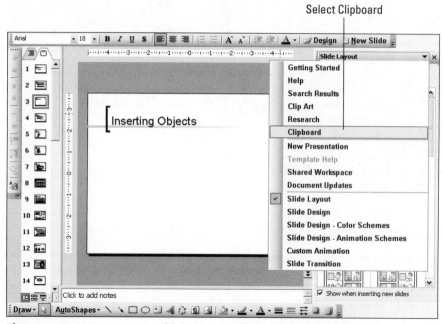

Figure 11-7: Move or copy multiple items with the Clipboard, in the task pane.

As you copy or cut items, they appear on a list in the Clipboard task pane. When you want to paste an item, display the slide on which you want to paste it (and position the insertion point at the desired location if the item is text), and then click on the item in the task pane. The Clipboard can hold up to 24 items. To remove one, point to it, click the arrow next to it, and choose Delete, as in Figure 11-8.

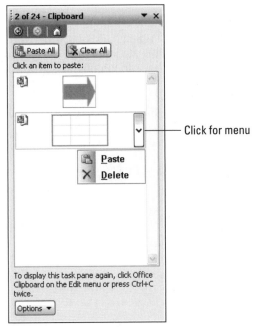

Figure 11-8: Working with individual clips in the Clipboard task pane.

 Expert Tip Click the Options button at the bottom of the Clipboard task pane for a list of on/off toggles you can set for Clipboard operation. For example, you can choose when the Clipboard task pane will appear automatically and whether it will display an icon at the bottom of the screen when it is active.

Repositioning Objects

It's somewhat of an artificial word distinction, but I'm using the terms *move* and *reposition* in this chapter to mean two different things. In the preceding section, you learned how to move objects in large ways — to a totally different spot on a slide, to a different slide, or even to a different program. In this section, I show you how to move — reposition — an object just a tiny bit with the Snap, Nudge, and Align or Distribute commands. These ways of making little movements can make a big difference in your work.

For example, suppose you have three objects on a slide and you want them to all be at the same spot horizontally. It would be very difficult to eyeball the alignment perfectly, but you can easily use the Snap feature to snap the objects to an invisible grid, or use the Align command to align them all neatly.

Snapping

There is an invisible grid on every slide to which all objects snap. In other words, if you move an object and position it so that it doesn't quite align with the gridlines, when you release the object, it moves slightly to snap into alignment with the nearest gridlines. This feature is on by default. To turn it off, click the Draw button on the Drawing toolbar and choose Grid and Guides, or use Ctrl+G. The Grid and Guides dialog box opens (Figure 11-9). Deselect the Snap Objects to Grid check box if desired.

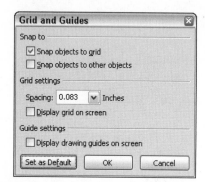

Figure 11-9: Toggle the grid on and off here.

You don't have to turn off the Snap To Grid feature every time you want to temporarily override it. Just hold down the Alt key as you drag or draw an object to suspend this feature.

You can also turn on/off a feature called Snap Objects to Other Objects (also shown in Figure 11-9). This one is off by default. It helps you precisely align shapes (for example, to draw complex pictures where one line must exactly meet another) by snapping shapes into position in relation to one another. You will not want to use this feature all the time because it makes it harder to position objects precisely in those instances where you do not need one shape to align with another.

To display or hide the grid on-screen, mark or clear the Display Grid On Screen check box. To change the grid spacing, enter the desired setting in the Spacing box.

Nudging

If you are one of those people who have a hard time positioning objects precisely by dragging them, you'll appreciate the Nudge command. It moves an object slightly in the chosen dimension without altering its other dimension. For example, suppose you have positioned a text box in exactly the right spot vertically but it is a little bit too far to the right. If you drag it manually, you might accidentally change the vertical position. Instead you can use Nudge Left (Draw ➪ Nudge ➪ Left), as shown in Figure 11-10.

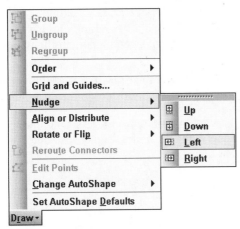

Figure 11-10: The Nudge command lets you move an object slightly in one direction.

 Expert Tip You can also use the arrow keys to nudge. If Snap to Grid is turned on, the arrows will nudge an object by 10 pixels. If Snap to Grid is turned off, the nudge changes to one-pixel increments.

Aligning or distributing

You can align or distribute objects either in relation to the slide itself or in relation to other objects. Here are some examples:

✦ You can align an object to the top, bottom, left, right, or center of a slide.

✦ You can align two objects in relation to one another so they are at the same vertical or horizontal position.

✦ You can distribute three or more objects so that the spacing between them is even.

 Note The commands on the Align or Distribute menu are not always available. They are available if you have selected Relative To from that menu (that is, if that command has a check mark next to it), or if you have selected two or more objects (for aligning) or three or more objects (for distributing).

Aligning an object in relation to the slide

To align a single object in relation to the slide, follow these steps:

1. Choose Draw ⇨ Align or Distribute. If you do not see a check mark next to the Relative To Slide command, click it to place one there.

2. Reopen the menu (Draw ⇨ Align or Distribute), if needed, and choose one of the horizontal align commands: Align Left, Align Center, or Align Right. See Figure 11-11.

3. Reopen the menu (Draw ⇨ Align or Distribute) and choose one of the vertical align commands: Align Top, Align Middle, or Align Bottom.

Expert Tip   Instead of continually reopening the Align or Distribute menu, simply undock it from the Draw menu by clicking the dots at the top of the Align or Distribute menu and dragging them to the workspace.

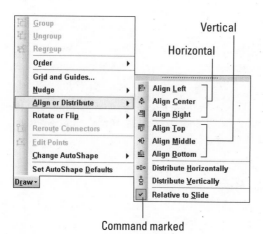

Figure 11-11: Choose an alignment for the object in relation to the slide.

Aligning two or more objects with one another

You can also align two objects in relation to one another. This works by assigning the same setting to both objects. For example, in the first illustration, Figure 11-12, the objects are in their starting positions. The second illustration, Figure 11-13, shows what happened when I used the Draw ⇨ Align or Distribute ⇨ Align Top command to move the lower object to the same vertical position as the higher one. If I had used Align Bottom, the higher object would have been moved to match the lower one. If I had used Align Center, both objects would have moved to split the difference between their two positions.

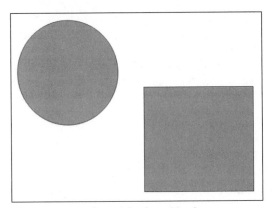

Figure 11-12: The original positioning.

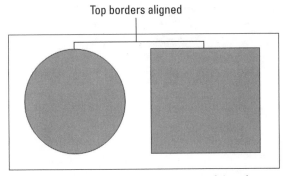

Figure 11-13: The positioning after applying the Align Top command.

To align two or more objects with one another, follow these steps:

1. Choose Draw ➪ Align or Distribute. If the Relative To Slide command has a check mark next to it, click it to turn it off.

2. Select both objects. (To select multiple objects, hold down the Shift key as you click each one.)

3. Choose Draw ➪ Align or Distribute and then choose the alignment command desired.

Note
If you use the Align Top command and the objects move to the very top of the slide, you probably have left the Relative To Slide option on. Undo (Ctrl+Z) the action and then use Choose Draw ➪ Align or Distribute ➪ Relative To Slide to turn it off.

Distributing objects

Distribution works only in relation to the slide or with three or more objects selected. When you distribute objects, you spread them evenly over a given space. For example, suppose you have just aligned three boxes vertically, as shown in Figure 11-14, and now you want to even out the space between each box. You can apply the Distribute Horizontally command to create the uniform spacing shown in Figure 11-15.

To distribute objects, follow these steps:

1. Select the objects. To do so, hold down the Shift key while you click each one or drag an outline that encircles all the objects.

2. Choose Draw ➪ Align or Distribute and then either Distribute Vertically or Distribute Horizontally.

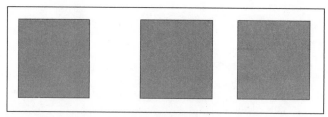

Figure 11-14: The original positioning.

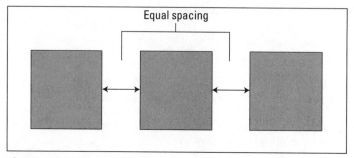

Figure 11-15: The positioning after applying the Distribute Horizontally command.

Rotating and Flipping Objects

Most objects have a green circle at the top when they are selected; this is the *rotation* handle. You can drag it to rotate the object. See Figure 11-16. This is called *free rotation* because there is no precise numeric measurement related to the amount of rotation, although holding down the Shift key while rotating will rotate the object by 15° increments.

You can also rotate an object by exactly 90 degrees. To do so, choose Draw ➪ Rotate or Flip ➪ Rotate Left 90° or Draw ➪ Rotate or Flip ➪ Rotate Right 90°. On this same menu you can also flip an object either vertically or horizontally.

Mouse pointer while dragging

Rotation handle

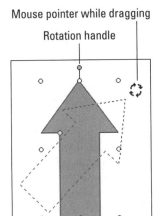

Figure 11-16: Rotate an object by dragging its rotation handle.

Resizing Objects

In Chapter 8, you learned how to resize a text box. All objects can be resized in this same way. Simply drag a corner or side selection handle to change the object's size and shape. The mouse pointer changes to a double-headed arrow when it is over a selection handle, as you may recall from resizing text boxes in Chapter 8. A dotted outline also shows where the resized object will be, as shown in Figure 11-17.

When you resize an object's box, the object inside usually changes its size and shape, too. For example, if the object is a graphic, the graphic gets smaller so the whole thing can still be seen. If you do not want this (for example, perhaps you want to crop off some of the white space around the picture), you can use the Cropping tool, which is explained in Chapter 12.

Expert Tip Some objects maintain their aspect ratio by default when they're resized using a corner handle. Photos are like that, for example. In other words, the ratio of height to width does not change when you resize using the corner selection handles. If you want to purposely distort the object by changing its aspect ratio, drag one of the side selection handles instead of a corner one.

Mouse pointer dragging

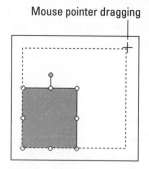

Figure 11-17: Resize an object by dragging a corner selection handle.

Deleting Objects

To delete an object, just select it and press the Delete key on the keyboard. That's the easiest way; other alternatives include choosing Edit ⇨ Clear and right-clicking the object and choosing Cut. (Actually, cutting the object is not the same as deleting it; Cut moves it to the Clipboard, so you can use Paste to place it somewhere else. However, if you cut something, and then never paste it, it's effectively the same as deleting it.)

To delete more than one object at once, select multiple objects before pressing the Delete key.

Layering Objects

You can stack objects on top of each other to create special effects. For example, you might create a logo by stacking a text box on top of an oval or a rectangle, as in Figure 11-18. (See Chapter 8 to learn how to create a text box; see Chapter 15 to learn how to draw an oval.)

Text box in front

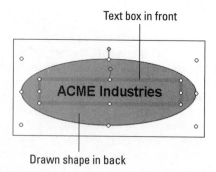

ACME Industries

Figure 11-18: You can create all kinds of logos, artwork, and other special effects by layering objects.

Drawn shape in back

Expert Tip You can also type text directly into a drawn shape without bothering with layering; simply right-click the shape and choose Add Text, or you can just begin typing while the shape is selected. You learn more about this in the discussion of AutoShapes in Chapter 15.

By default, objects stack in the order that you create them. For example, in Figure 11-18, the text box appears over the shape because the shape was created first, so it's on the bottom of the stack. You can move the shape, but it will continue to be on the layer under the text box.

If you need to reorder the objects in a stack, follow these steps:

1. Click the top object in the stack.

2. Click the Draw button on the Drawing toolbar. A menu appears.

3. Point to Order. A submenu appears. See Figure 11-19.

4. Choose the command that reflects what you want to do with the object. Send to Back makes that object the bottom one in the pile; Send Backward sends it back one position (assuming there are more than two objects in the stack).

5. Now a different object is the top one. Repeat the steps to change its position, too, if necessary. Repeat until all objects are in the order you want them in the stack.

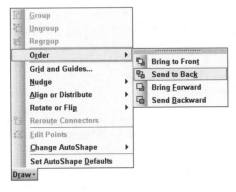

Figure 11-19: Choose a different position in the stack for the top object.

Expert Tip If you stack one object on another, the top object covers up the one underneath unless the top object's background is set to None or its fill color is semitransparent. Text box backgrounds are set to None by default, but if you stack other objects, you may need to know how to do this. Just select the object, right-click it, and choose Format from the menu that appears. (The actual name of the Format command varies with the type of object; it might be Format AutoShape if you are working with a drawn shape, for example.) Then, on the Colors and Lines tab, open the Color drop-down list in the Fill area and choose No Fill. You can also use the transparency slider to set the level of transparency you need. See Chapter 12 for information about setting the color and transparency of an object.

Working with Object Groups

You have already learned how to select multiple objects and work with them as a single unit. For example, you might select several shapes together that collectively form a picture you have drawn. If these objects are always going to be considered a single unit, you can save yourself some time by grouping them. When you group two or more objects, those objects become a single object for the purposes of moving and resizing. You can always ungroup them later if you need to work with the objects separately.

To group two or more objects together, follow these steps:

1. Select all the objects to be grouped.

2. Click the Draw button on the Drawing toolbar. Pause for a moment until the full menu opens.

3. Click the Group command. The objects now form a group.

To ungroup, select the grouped object and choose Ungroup from that same Draw button menu. If you later need to regroup the same items, select one of them and use Draw ⇨ Regroup.

Summary

This chapter taught you how to insert, move, size, and manipulate objects. These skills will come in very handy in later chapters, as you learn to place specific types of objects on your slides, because you will know right away how to work with them once you get them onto the slide. Whether it's a chart, a piece of clip art, or a drawn shape, you'll know just what to do with it.

The next chapter continues this discussion of objects in general by showing you how to format them. You will learn how to change their fill colors, line colors, shadows, and other formatting attributes.

✦   ✦   ✦

Formatting Objects

Chapter 11 introduced the concept of an object and described how to insert, size, and position one. Later chapters will deal with specific object types in more detail, like drawn objects, clip art, and charts. In those chapters, it will be assumed that you have some basic object formatting skills, such as being able to apply a border format, a fill, or a 3-D effect. If you are not confident with those skills at this point, follow along with the information in this chapter to learn.

Formatting an Object's Border

You may want to place a border or frame around an object. Some objects have a border by default; others don't, and you must add one if you want it. A border can draw attention to an item, as well as separate it from surrounding items.

Caution

Many beginners make the mistake of placing a drawn rectangle around an object when they want a border around it. This works, but it is inefficient. Because the rectangle and the object it frames are two separate objects, they move separately, so when you resize or move the object, the rectangle has to be moved and resized separately. (You can group the objects, but that would be another step.) A much easier way to put a frame around an object is to simply turn on the object's border.

Every object has the potential to have a border around it. All you have to do is turn it on. For drawn shapes, the line clings to the shape itself and looks like someone has taken a pencil and outlined the shape. For text and graphic boxes, the line runs around the outer edge of the object frame, in the same area that the selection handles appear. Figure 12-1 shows some examples of lines around various types of objects.

The easiest way to control the border on an object is to use the buttons on the Drawing toolbar, shown in Table 12-1. Each of these buttons opens a pop-up list of choices.

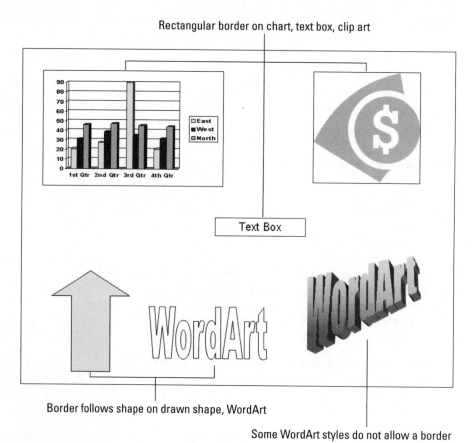

Figure 12-1: Different object types show borders differently.

Table 12-1
Border Buttons on the Drawing Toolbar

Icon	Action
	Choose whether there will be a border and what color it will be.
	Choose how thick the line will be, and whether it will be a single, double, or triple line.
	Choose whether the line will be solid, dashed, or dotted.

When you click the Line Color button, as shown in Figure 12-2, the top eight colored squares that appear are the default colors for the design template that is currently applied. If you choose one of these colors and then change the design template, the colors of the line change, too. If you want a color that will stay put no matter what the template says, click More Line Colors to open a Colors dialog box and choose the color from there. See "Changing an Object's Coloring" later in this chapter for more information about color choices.

Figure 12-2: An easy way to control the border is to use the Line Color button on the Drawing toolbar.

On the Line Color button's menu, you can also choose Patterned Lines to open a Patterned Lines dialog box from which you can choose a pattern. However, unless your line is very thick, your audience won't be able to discern the pattern, and the line will just look broken.

You can also change the line color from the object's Format dialog box. (Its exact name varies depending on the object; for a text box, for example, it's Format Text Box.) Right-click the object and select its Format command to open the dialog box, and then click the Colors and Lines tab, as shown in Figure 12-3. Then, choose a line color, style, weight (thickness), and dashed style from the drop-down lists there.

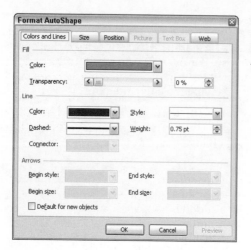

Figure 12-3: You can control an object's border with the controls in the Line section on the Colors and Lines tab of its Format dialog box.

Note The Arrows section in Figure 12-3 doesn't apply to most shapes—only to drawn lines and shapes similar to lines (such as brackets and braces). You will learn more about lines and arrows in Chapter 15.

Changing an Object's Coloring

Almost all objects let you choose a coloring for both their fill (their inside, or background) and their line (their border). I just told you about the line controls; now it's time to look at the fill controls.

To choose a color for an object, you can use the Color drop-down list in the Format dialog box (see Figure 12-3), but it's easier to access the same list from the Fill Color button on the Drawing toolbar, as shown in Figure 12-4.

Figure 12-4: Choose a color or a coloring option from the Fill Color button's menu.

From here, you can make several choices:

✦ Select Automatic to set the object's formatting to the default for that type of object for the design template in use. For example, drawn shapes are, by default, colored with the fifth color in the current color scheme. Refer back to Chapter 7 for information about changing the color scheme.

✦ Click one of the colored squares on the first row to choose any of the colors from the current color scheme. That way, your object will not clash with the rest of the presentation, and if you change templates, the object color changes too.

✦ Click one of the colored squares on the second row (if present) to choose a color that you have previously used for an object in this presentation. Any colors you choose for an object are added here, so you can use them again. If you don't have a second row (for example, there is none in Figure 12-4), it means you haven't chosen any custom colors yet in this presentation.

✦ Click More Fill Colors to open the Colors dialog box and choose a custom color.

✦ Click Fill Effects to open the Fill Effects dialog box and choose a special effect. This is covered in the "Using Special Effect Fills" section later in the chapter.

If you choose More Fill Colors from the Fill Color menu, the Colors dialog box appears, shown in Figure 12-5. You can use this dialog box to choose a color for the object that will not change even if you change the design template in use.

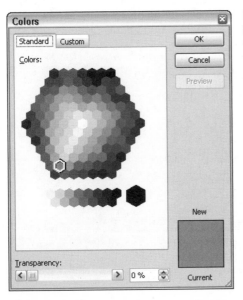

Figure 12-5: Select a color from the Standard palette or use the Custom tab to create your own color.

Most people can find the color they want on the Standard tab in the Colors dialog box. It shows a wide variety of colors. Just click the one you want and click OK.

If you need a specific color, however, you may need to use the Custom tab, shown in Figure 12-6. On this tab, you can enter the precise numbers for a color, to match, for example, the exact color for a company logo.

Colors can be defined numerically using either the HSL (hue, saturation, and luminosity) or RGB (red, green, blue) color models. Choose the color model you want from the Color Model drop-down list

If working with the HSL model, you can type the numbers into the Hue, Sat, and Lum fields on the Custom tab. The hue is the tint (that is, green versus blue versus red). A low number is a color at the red end of the rainbow; a high number is a color at the violet end. Saturation refers to the vividness of the color, and luminosity is the lightness/darkness. A high luminosity mixes the color with white; a low luminosity mixes the color with black.

An alternative way to define colors is by specifying numbers for red, green, and blue. Using this measurement, a 0, 0, 0 is pure black and a 255, 255, 255 is pure white. All other colors are some combination of the three colors. For example, pure blue is 0, 0, 255. A very pale blue would be 200, 200, 255. You can play around with the numbers in the fields on the Custom tab. The new color appears in the New area near the bottom of the dialog box. Click OK to accept your choice.

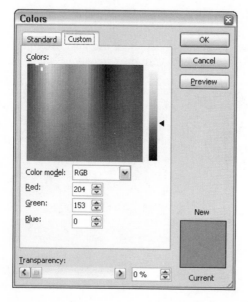

Figure 12-6: You can define a custom color for an object if you need a precise, numerically defined color.

Expert Tip You can create an interesting see-through effect with the color by using the transparency slider. When this slider is used for a color, it creates an effect like a watercolor paint wash over an item, so that whatever is beneath it shows through partially.

Using Special Effect Fills

If you choose Fill Effects for an object's color, a Fill Effects dialog box appears with four tabs: Gradient, Texture, Pattern, and Picture. These are the four kinds of effects you can assign to an object. They are a kind of coloring, but they do not produce solid colors; instead, they produce multicolored or multi-shaded patterns and textures that can create stunning visual effects!

These same special effects can be applied to slide backgrounds as well as objects. You learned about changing a slide background in Chapter 7.

For each of the special effects, you need to open the Fill Effects dialog box:

1. Select the object.

2. Open the Fill Color menu from the Fill Color button on the Drawing toolbar, and then choose Fill Effects.

3. Select the special effect you want, described in the following sections.

Working with gradients

If you've ever watched a sunset (and who hasn't?), you know how the red of the sun slowly fades into the blue/black of the evening sky. You may not have thought of it quite this way before, but that's a gradient. Whenever one color turns gradually into another one, it's a gradient. Gradients are often used on large shapes on logos and on backgrounds. Figure 12-7 shows an oval with a gradient fill.

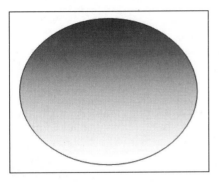

Figure 12-7: This oval has a gradient that fades from dark blue at the top to white at the bottom.

On the Gradient tab in the Fill Effects dialog box, you can choose three kinds of gradients:

✦ **One color:** This gradient uses one color plus either black or white or a shade of gray.

✦ **Two color:** This gradient uses two colors that you choose.

✦ **Preset:** This gradient option lets you select one of the preset color combinations that come with PowerPoint.

One thing that all three gradient types have in common is that you can choose whether the gradient should rotate if you rotate an object. For example, suppose you have an up-pointing arrow you have drawn with the AutoShape tool in PowerPoint (see Chapter 15). You then rotate it to be a left-pointing arrow. Should the gradient rotate too, or stay fixed? Figure 12-8 shows the difference. Mark or clear the Rotate Fill Effect with Shape check box at the bottom of the dialog box to indicate your preference in this matter.

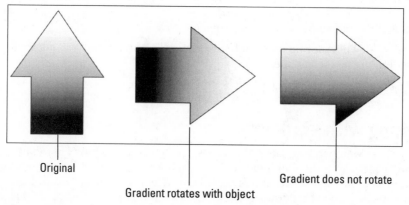

Original

Gradient rotates with object

Gradient does not rotate

Figure 12-8: When a shape is rotated, the gradient will rotate too, or not, depending on your setting in the Fill Effects dialog box.

Setting a one-color gradient

If you click the One Color option button on the Gradient tab, the single-color controls appear. You can use this when you want a single color to gradually fade to either white or black. See Figure 12-9.

Open the Color 1 drop-down list and choose the color you want. As with other color selections, you can choose one of the scheme colors or you can click More Colors to access the Colors dialog box that you saw in Figures 12-5 and 12-6.

After choosing the color, drag the slider below it to change the darkness or light-ness. At the midpoint, there is no gradient at all—both colors are the chosen one. As you slide the slider toward Dark, a second color (black) begins to be used for the gradient in the Sample area. If you slide it toward Light, the second color used becomes white.

You can also make a gradient of the amount of transparency of the fill. For example, in Figure 12-10, the shape gradually becomes more transparent as it goes down the page, revealing the text beneath it. Adjust this in the Transparency section of the Fill Effects dialog box (Figure 12-9).

After setting up your one-color gradient, you need to choose a shading style from the Shading styles area of the dialog box. See "Choosing a shading style" later in this section for details.

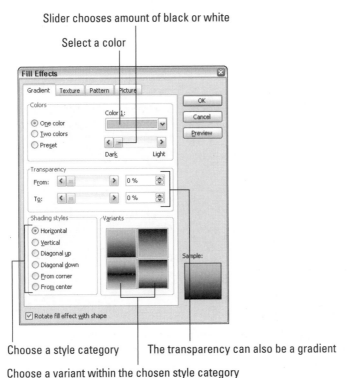

Figure 12-9: A one-color gradient involves one color plus a certain amount of either black or white.

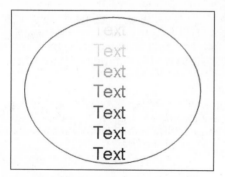

Figure 12-10: A transparency gradient can gradually reveal what is behind an object.

Setting a two-color gradient

When you select the Two Colors option button, the Light/Dark slider goes away and is replaced by a Color 2 drop-down list, shown in Figure 12-11. Choose the second color you want from here. The second color can be black or white if you desire, but it can also be any other color instead. Then select the desired shading style, as explained in "Choosing a Shading Style."

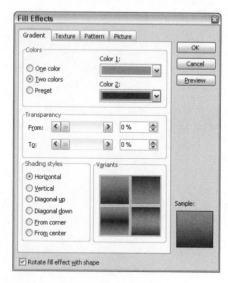

Figure 12-11: With the Two Colors gradient, you select two different colors instead of one color plus black or white.

Using a preset gradient

Preset gradients are nice timesavers. When you click the Preset option button, a Preset colors drop-down list appears. You can select from a variety of preset multi-color gradients with picturesque names like Daybreak and Horizon. Try each of them out, and check the Sample area to see whether any fit your needs. Then choose your shading style, explained next.

Choosing a shading style

The Shading style determines which way the colors run. In a Horizontal shading style, for example, the colors run in bands from left to right, like a sunset. You can also choose Vertical, Diagonal up, or a variety of others, as shown in Figure 12-9.

Each shading style has variants. When you click a Shading style button, the variants appear in the Variants area, and you can click one of the variant examples to select it. There are four variants for every shading style. When you are finished, click OK to accept your choice and apply the formatting to the object.

Applying a texture

On the Texture tab of the Fill Effects dialog box, you can choose from a variety of simulations of textured surfaces, such as marble, straw, sandpaper, and so on. Scroll through the list and find the one you want (see Figure 12-12), click it, and then click OK.

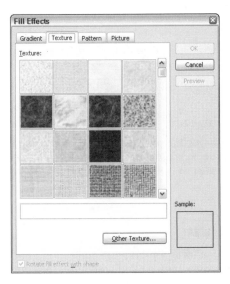

Figure 12-12: Choose a texture that you want to use to fill the object.

You can also specify any image you want to use as a texture. The image will be tiled (repeated) as needed to fill the object. To do so, click Other Texture, select the image file, and click OK.

Applying a pattern

Patterns are not as flashy as gradients or textures, but they have their uses. A *pattern*, simply stated, is an arrangement of lines or shapes of one color over the background of another color. For example, a pinstripe suit has a pattern of gray or white lines over a black, blue, or gray background. You get the idea.

To apply a pattern, click the Pattern tab in the Fill Effects dialog box and then click a pattern that you want to use. See Figure 12-13. You can choose the foreground and background colors from drop-down lists at the bottom of the dialog box.

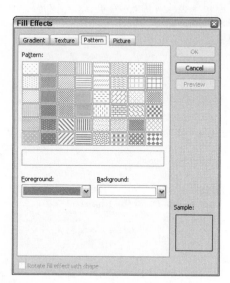

Figure 12-13: Choose the pattern you want, and select a foreground and background color.

Caution   Patterns make text very difficult to read. Don't apply a pattern to a text box unless you have a very compelling reason for doing so. And if you do, make sure the pattern uses subtly contrasting colors and the text is large, bold, and of a strongly contrasting color.

Filling an object with a picture

In rare cases, you might want to fill an object with a picture. It makes for a very interesting effect, but can quickly become overdone if used too often. One good application of this is to place an AutoShape, such as a star (see Chapter 15), and fill it with a picture of a person. This makes the shape into a picture frame for the picture, as shown in Figure 12-14.

Caution   It's seldom a good idea to use a picture for a slide background. It can make the text hard to read, and people may get tired of seeing the same picture over and over on every slide.

Figure 12-14: Filling a shape with a picture can make it into a picture frame.

Here's how to fill with a picture:

1. Click the Picture tab in the Fill Effects dialog box. There won't be any pictures there at first; don't worry.

2. Click the Select Picture button to open the Select Picture dialog box, and browse your hard disk or network to find the picture you want to use.

Note   You can turn on the Preview pane, as shown in Figure 12-15, by opening the View drop-down list in the dialog box and choosing Preview.

3. When you locate the picture you want, double-click it to return to the Fill Effects dialog box.

4. Click OK to place the picture in the object.

Expert Tip   You can apply Background as a fill (for images and AutoShapes). This is somewhat like setting the background fill to "None" so that the background shows through, but it obscures any objects that are between it and the background. Figure 12-16 shows an example. In this figure, the oval has Background as its fill, and it is sitting on top of a text box containing the text. This is better than filling the oval with the same pattern, gradient, or texture as the background because no matter where you move it on the slide, its background will continue to "match" with the slide's background. To apply a Background fill, choose Format ⇨ Autoshape, click on the Fill Color box, and select Background. (This option is not available from the Fill Color button on the Drawing toolbar.)

Click here for Views menu

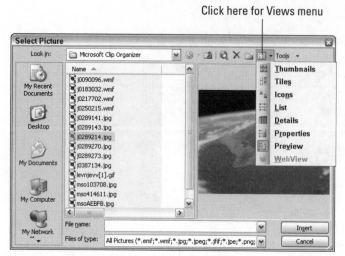

Figure 12-15: Locate the picture you want to use to fill the object.

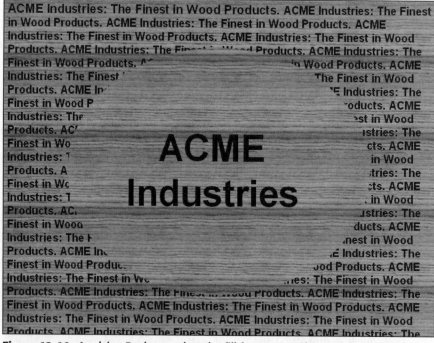

Figure 12-16: Applying Background as the fill for an AutoShape gives it the same coloring as the slide background but does not make it entirely transparent.

Adding Shadows

In Chapter 9, you learned about applying the Shadow attribute to your text. But you can also apply a shadow to any object: a text box, a picture, a chart, a drawn shape, and so on. Further, the shadows you apply to these objects are much more versatile than the shadows that you apply to text. You can control the positioning of the shadow, control how far it appears to be away from the text, and more.

Different objects use shadows differently, and there are other differences within a single object type depending on the background fill. Here are the basic rules, which are exemplified in Figures 12-17 and 12-18.

Figure 12-17: How shadows are applied to WordArt, drawn shapes, and pictures.

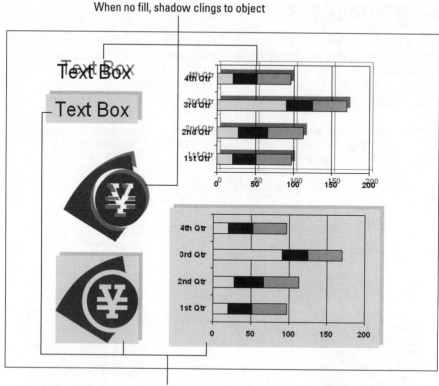

Figure 12-18: How shadows are applied to clip art, text boxes, and charts.

✦ WordArt and drawn shapes always apply the shadow directly to the object, regardless of the background fill.

✦ Inserted pictures (such as scanned photos) always apply the shadow to the frame around the picture.

✦ Clip art, text boxes, and charts with transparent background (no fill) apply the shadow directly to the object, but if there is a background fill, the shadow is then applied to the frame instead.

To apply a shadow to an object, follow these steps:

1. Click the object.

2. Click the Shadow button on the Drawing toolbar. A pop-up menu appears. See Figure 12-19.

3. Click the button for the type of shadow you want. Or, to turn off a shadow, choose No Shadow.

Shadow Settings toolbar

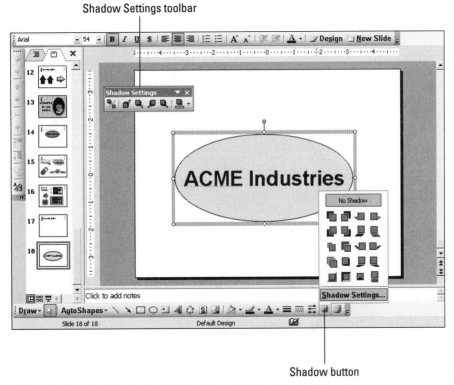

Shadow button

Figure 12-19: Apply a basic shadow from the Drawing toolbar.

Besides the simple buttons on the Shadow shortcut menu shown in Figure 12-19, there are several more sophisticated shadow controls. To see them, choose Shadow Settings from the pop-up menu. A Shadow Settings toolbar appears, containing controls that help you fine-tune the shadow. See Table 12-2 for an explanation of these controls.

| | | Table 12-2 | |
| | | **Shadow Settings Toolbar Buttons** | |
Button	**Name**	**Purpose**
	Shadow On/Off	Toggles the shadow on/off
	Nudge Shadow Up	Moves the shadow up slightly
	Nudge Shadow Down	Moves the shadow down slightly
	Nudge Shadow Left	Moves the shadow to the left slightly
	Nudge Shadow Right	Moves the shadow to the right slightly
	Shadow Color	Opens a drop-down list of colors for the shadow

Once you apply a basic shadow to an object, the Nudge buttons can help you increase or decrease the height and width of the shadow. For example, you might want to make a shadow more prominent, to make it more obvious that the shadow is there. The larger the shadow, the greater the effect of the object floating on the slide.

Caution

If you change the shadow color, make sure you stick with a color that is darker than the object. Lighter-colored shadows do not look realistic. (Exception: for black text, use gray shadow.)

The Shadow Color button opens a drop-down list of colors in the scheme, as well as the More Shadow Colors option. See Figure 12-20. It also contains a Semitransparent Shadow command (an on/off toggle which is On by default), so you can make the shadow less or more opaque.

Figure 12-20: Change the shadow color or turn the shadow's semitransparent state on/off from the Shadow Settings toolbar.

Adding 3-D Effects

Although similar to shadows, 3-D effects make an object look like it has sides, like it's ready to jump off the slide. You can use 3-D effects, for example, to make a circle look like a pillar, or a rectangle look like a box. You can also create some interesting effects with WordArt by applying 3-D. Figure 12-21 shows some examples of objects that have been enhanced with 3-D effects.

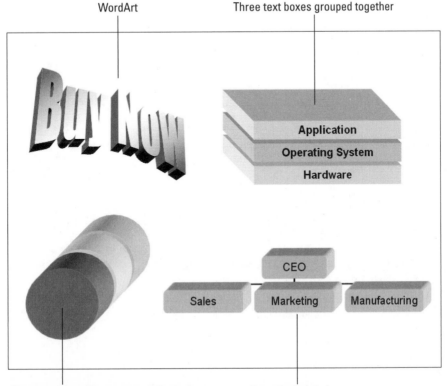

Figure 12-21: Some 3-D effects applied to various types of objects.

Caution   You can use either a shadow or a 3-D effect on an object, but not both. When you apply one, it cancels the other.

To apply a 3-D effect, follow these steps:

1. Select the object.

2. Click the 3-D button on the Drawing toolbar. A pop-up menu of effects appears. See Figure 12-22.

3. Click the button for the type of 3-D effect you want. Or, to turn the 3-D effect off, choose No 3-D.

There is also a special toolbar for 3-D effects, which you can display by choosing 3-D Settings from the menu shown in Figure 12-21. Table 12-3 lists and describes its buttons.

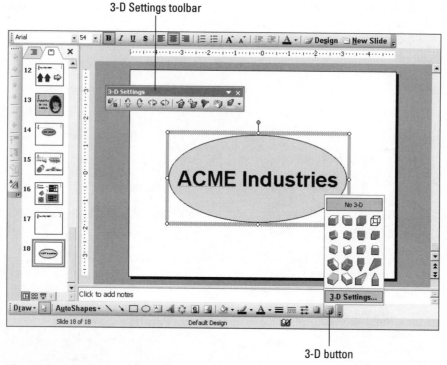

Figure 12-22: Choose a 3-D effect from the menu to apply to your object.

Table 12-3
3-D Settings Toolbar Buttons

Button	Name	Purpose
	3-D On/Off	Toggles the 3-D effect on/off
	Tilt Down	Rotates the shape down slightly
	Tilt Up	Rotates the shape up slightly
	Tilt Left	Rotates the shape left slightly
	Tilt Right	Rotates the shape right slightly
	Depth	Opens a list on which you can select the depth of the 3-D effect
	Direction	Opens a list on which you can select the direction of the 3-D effect
	Lighting	Opens a list on which you can select where the "light" is coming from for the object shading
	Surface	Opens a list of surface types for the object
	3-D Color	Opens a list of colors for the 3-D sides of the object

Summary

This chapter taught you how to apply formatting to objects. Because all objects receive formatting in basically the same way, these skills will serve you well in the upcoming chapters as you learn more about some specific object types.

The next chapter is a Project Lab in which you can practice the text and object skills you have learned in this part of the book by doing some real-world-type PowerPoint work.

✦   ✦   ✦

Project Lab: Building a Simple Presentation with Text and Graphics

Welcome to the second Project Lab in this book! (The first one was in Chapter 4). As in Chapter 4, for each step, this lab first states the goal and then lists the specific steps for accomplishing that goal. If you are comfortable achieving the goal in some other manner, you are free to do so. However, if you do not know how to achieve the goal, you can use the steps as guidance.

The data files for these lab exercises are on the CD that accompanies this book. You can open them from the CD and then save them to your hard disk as you proceed, or you can copy all the data files to your hard disk before you start.

The Scenario

In this lab, you will be working for Spice Meadow Shelties, a kennel that breeds and shows Shetland Sheepdogs (also called Shelties). The owner, Sheri Hineman, is interested in expanding her business to include more dogs, but she needs to find some investors.

She has created an outline in Word, and would like to turn it into a basic presentation about her business that she can show to potential partners. She will be adding to the presentation later, and perhaps creating additional presentations as well, but for now you will start with her simple outline. She would also like you to feature a deep medium green color, because that is the color of her logo and sign, and to create a custom design template that she can reuse in later presentations.

Lab 2A: Starting a New Presentation

In this lab session, you will import the outline that the business owner has provided and do a bit of cleanup and formatting on the imported text, including changing the bullet characters to more attractive, graphical ones.

Level of difficulty: Easy

Time to complete: 5 to 15 minutes

1. **In PowerPoint, start a new presentation based on the Level template.**

    a. Choose File ➪ New. The New Presentation task pane appears.

    b. Click From Design Template. The available design templates appear.

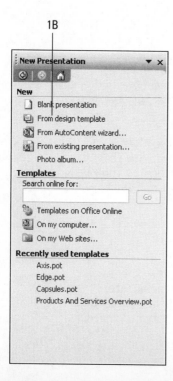

c. Click the Level template (Level.pot).

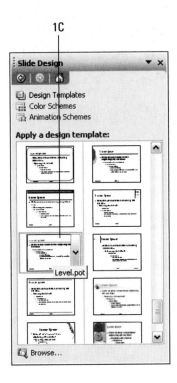

1C

Level.pot

2. **Delete the automatically created slide in the new presentation.**

Select the slide in the Slides pane and press the Delete key.

3. **Import the slides from the file Lab02A.doc.**

    a. Choose Insert ➪ Slides from Outline. The Insert Outline dialog box appears.

    b. Navigate to the drive and folder containing the lab files and select Lab02A.doc.

    c. Click Insert.

4. **Change the layout of the first slide to Title.**

    a. Click the first slide in the Slides pane.

    b. Choose Format ➪ Slide Layout. The Slide Layout task pane appears.

    c. Click the Title Slide layout.

3B

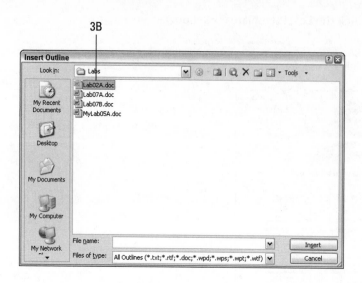

4A   4C   5A

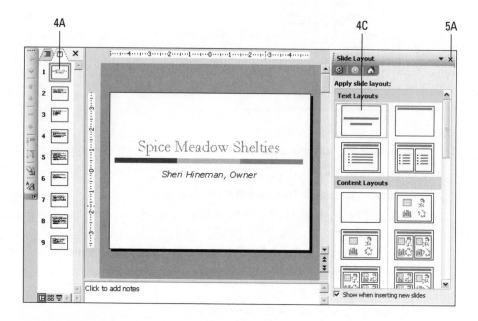

5. Close the Slide Layout task pane.

Click the Close (X) button in the task pane's upper-right corner.

6. Remove all the non-default text formatting from all slides.

   a. Display the Outline by clicking its tab.

   b. Click in the Outline pane to move the insertion point there.

   c. Press Ctrl+A to select all the text.

   d. Press Ctrl+Spacebar to strip off any non-default formatting.

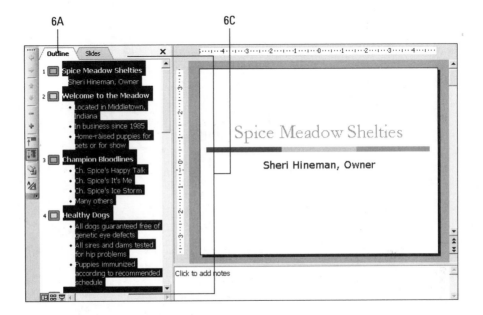

7. Change to a large round gold picture bullet on all slides for the first bullet level.

   a. Choose View ⇨ Master ⇨ Slide Master.

   b. Click in the first-level bullet sample line on the master (the one with the open box square bullet). That line becomes highlighted.

   c. Right-click the selected line and choose Bullets and Numbering.

   d. In the Size box, choose 100%.

   e. Click the Picture button. The Picture Bullet dialog box opens.

   f. Scroll through the pictures and choose a gold-colored circle.

   g. Click OK.

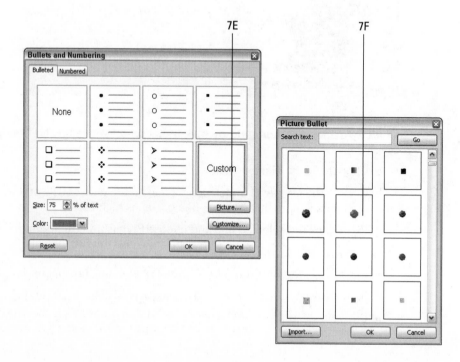

8. **Repeat the process from Step 7 for the remaining bullet levels on the Slide Master so that they are all round and similar in style to the top-level bullet, but different colors:**

   a. Second level: green, 100% of text size

   b. Third level: blue, 110% of text size

   c. Fourth level: purple, 90% of text size

   d. Fifth level: teal, 70% of text size

Tip

If there are too many bullets to look through conveniently, type Network in the Search Text box. The bullets you are looking for come from the Network Blitz scheme.

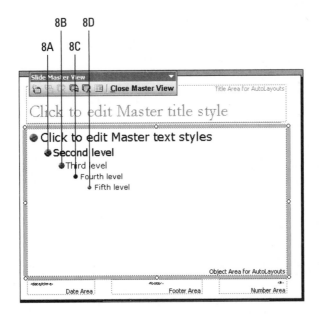

9. **Increase the spacing between the bullet character and its text for each bullet level by about 1/4 of an inch. (If the ruler is not displayed, click on View ⇨ Ruler.)**

   a. Click on any bullet level. Indent markers appear on the ruler at the top.

   b. Drag the bottom triangle (not the square) for each bullet level to the right about 1/4 of an inch. You will need to drag each one individually. Hold down the Ctrl button while you drag to give yourself more control.

10. Exit the Slide Master.

Click the Close Master View button on the Slide Master View toolbar.

11. Save your work as MyLab02A.ppt.

Click File ⇨ Save As and rename the file in the File Name field.

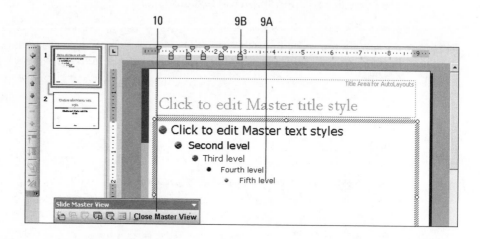

Now you have a decent-looking basic presentation. You could continue working with this presentation now to build up the content, but let's save that for a future lab session. Instead let's next tweak the color and font settings and create a design template that you can reuse when you want to create other presentations for this same client.

Lab 2B: Creating a Custom Design Template

You plan on doing future work for this client, so you will want to save the client's preferences in a template that you can reapply to future work. In this lab session you will start with the presentation you started in Lab 2A, modify its color scheme and title font, and save it as a design template.

Level of difficulty: Moderate

Time to complete: 5 to 15 minutes

1. Open the presentation file if it is not already open.

If you completed Lab 2A, reopen the file MyLab02A.ppt if it is not already open. If you did not complete Lab 2A, open the Lab02B.ppt file from the CD.

2. Switch to the color scheme with the olive green background.

a. Choose Format ⇨ Slide Design. The Slide Design task pane appears.

b. Click the Color Schemes hyperlink in the task pane. Samples of the available color schemes appear.

c. Click on the color scheme with the olive green background (third row, on the left if you've dragged the color scheme task pane to show two columns).

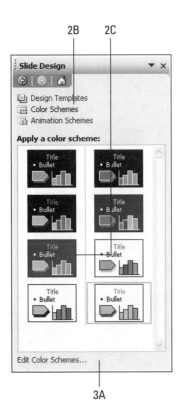

3. **Customize the chosen color scheme so that the background is more of a true green, and save this color scheme as a standard scheme.**

     a. Click Edit Color Schemes on the lower-left side of the task pane. The Edit Color Schemes dialog box opens.

     b. Click the colored square next to Background.

     c. Click Change Color. The Background Color dialog box appears.

     d. Click the Custom tab.

     e. Make sure that RGB is selected as the Color Model.

     f. Enter these numbers: **10** for Red, **116** for Green, and **50** for blue.

     g. Click OK.

     h. In the Edit Color Scheme dialog box, click Add As Standard Scheme.

     i. Click Apply.

     j. Close the task pane.

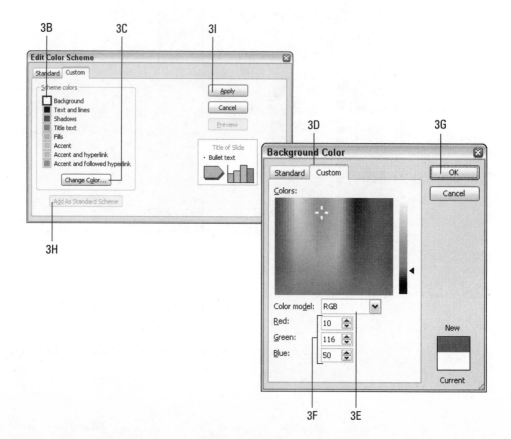

4. **Change the font for all the slide titles to Arial 40-point bold.**

   a. Choose View ⇨ Master ⇨ Slide Master.

   b. Select the slide title on the sample slide, and then choose Format ⇨ Font.

   c. In the Font dialog box, choose Arial from the Font list.

   d. Choose Bold from the Font Style list.

   e. Choose 40 from the Size list.

   f. Click OK.

Caution

If you have a title slide selected when you choose View ⇨ Slide Master, the Title Master appears by default, not the regular Slide Master. Make sure you are working with the Slide Master. This is important because changes to the font on the Slide Master are reflected on the Title Master but not vice-versa.

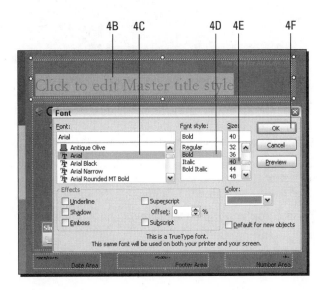

5. **Center the slide titles, and then close the Slide Master.**

   a. Click the slide title to select it if it is not already selected.

   b. Click the Center button on the Formatting toolbar.

   c. Click the Close Master View button on the Slide Master View toolbar.

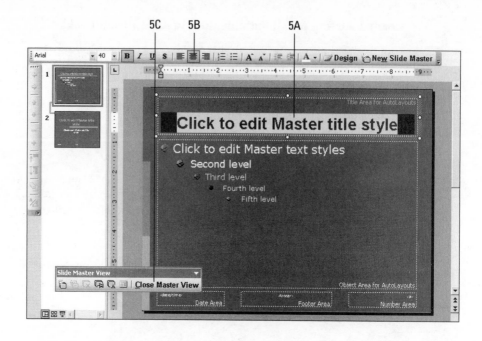

6. **Create a new design template called Spice Meadow based on this presentation.**

    a. Choose File ➪ Save As. The Save As dialog box opens.

    b. In the Save as Type drop-down list, choose Design Template (*.pot). When you do this, the Save In location automatically switches to the default folder for user-created templates.

    c. In the File Name box, type **Spice Meadow**.

    d. Click Save.

6B   6C

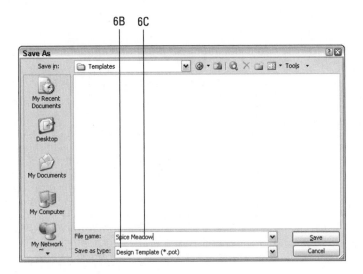

7. **Save it again, this time as a Presentation (.ppt) called MyLab02B, in the Labs folder.**

   a. Choose File ➪ Save As. The Save As dialog box opens.

   b. In the Save as Type drop-down list, choose Presentation (*.ppt).

   c. Change to the folder and drive to the Labs folder where you have been saving your other lab files.

   d. In the File name box, type **MyLab02B**.

   e. Click Save.

7C   7B   7D   7E

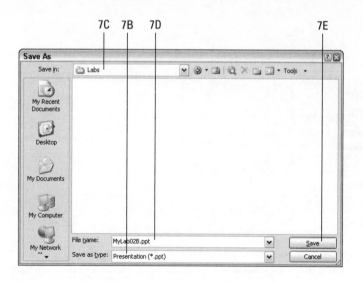

Lab 2C: Creating an Alternate Slide Master Layout

Although the client did not specifically request it, you have decided that it would be a nice touch to have an alternate Slide Master layout with a white background. This layout could be used in long presentations to break up the monotony or draw attention to a certain slide.

Level of difficulty: Moderate

Time to complete: 5 to 15 minutes

1. **Open the presentation file if it is not already open.**

   If you completed Lab 2B, reopen the file MyLab02B.ppt if it is not already open. If you did not complete Lab 2B, open the Lab02C.ppt file from the CD.

2. **Open Slide Master View and create an alternate slide master.**

   a. Choose View ⇨ Master ⇨ Slide Master.

   b. Choose Insert ⇨ Duplicate Slide Master. A copy of the existing slide and title masters appears in the left pane.

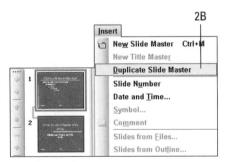

3. Apply a white-background color scheme to the alternate slide master.

    a. Click the alternate Slide Master slide in the left pane to select it.

    b. Choose Format ⇨ Slide Design. The Slide Design task pane appears.

    c. Click the Color Schemes hyperlink. The color scheme choices appear.

    d. Click the white background color scheme where the big arrow is light green (the right one in the fourth row if you've expanded the task pane to show two columns as shown here).

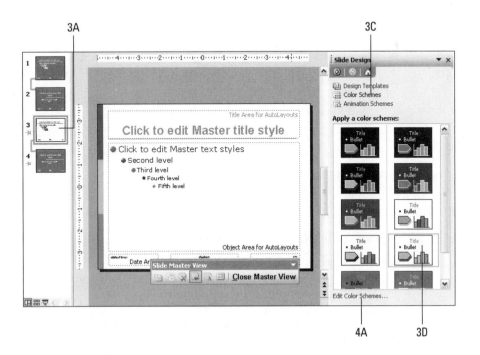

4. **Modify the color scheme of the newly chosen (white background) color scheme so that the Title Text color is Red 10, Green 116, Blue 50.**

   a. Click Edit Color Schemes. The Edit Color Scheme dialog box opens.

   b. Click the colored square next to Title Text.

   c. Click Change Color. The Title Text Color dialog box appears.

   d. On the Custom tab, enter **10** for Red, **116** for Green, and **50** for Blue.

   e. Click OK.

   f. Back in the Edit Color Scheme dialog box, click Add as Standard Scheme if available. (If that button is not available, the scheme is already added.)

   g. Click Apply.

   h. Close the task pane.

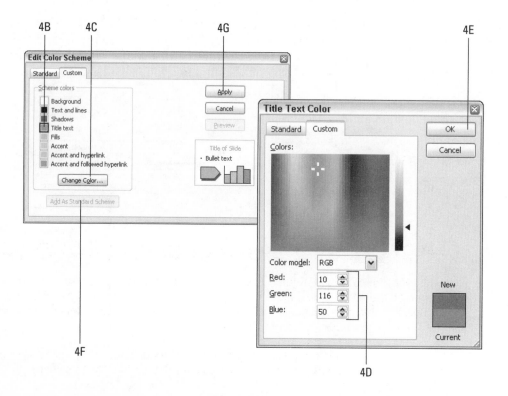

5. **Copy the modified color scheme to the alternate title master associated with the alternate slide master.**

   a. Click the alternate slide layout in the left pane.

   b. Click the Format Painter button on the Formatting toolbar.

   c. Click the associated title master layout. The color scheme is copied.

6. Close Slide Master view.

Click the Close Master View button on the Slide Master View toolbar.

7. Save your work as MyLab02C.ppt.

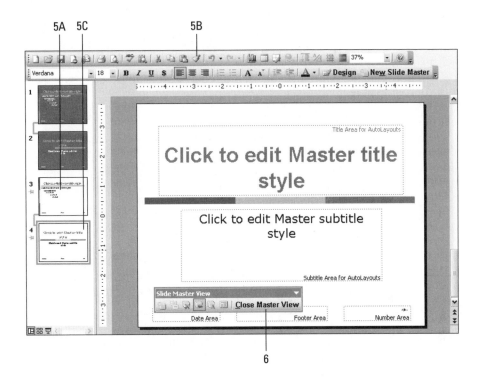

Lab 2D: Adding Graphics to the Slide Master

Along with creating a different color scheme for the alternate Slide Master, you have decided to dress it up a bit more by adding some clip art and other formatting. Because this presentation is for a client who raises and sells Shetland Sheepdogs, you will use some clip art of a Shetland Sheepdog as an accent.

Because the assortment of clip art available through Office may change periodically, the needed clip has been provided with the lab files for this chapter: Sheltie1.png.

Level of difficulty: Challenging

Time to complete: 15 to 30 minutes

1. Open the presentation file if it is not already open.

If you completed Lab 2C, reopen the file MyLab02C.ppt if it is not already open. If you did not complete Lab 2C, open the Lab02D.ppt file from the CD.

2. Display the alternate Slide Master (white background).

a. Choose View ➪ Master ➪ Slide Master.

b. Click the alternate (white background) Slide Master layout to select it.

3. Resize the slide title text box so that there is about 2" of space on each side of it.

a. Click the Title text box to select it. Selection handles appear around it.

b. Drag the left side handle inward until the left side aligns with the 2.5" mark on the ruler.

c. Drag the right side handle inward until the right side aligns with the 2.5" mark on the ruler. Now you have a title text box that is exactly 5" wide.

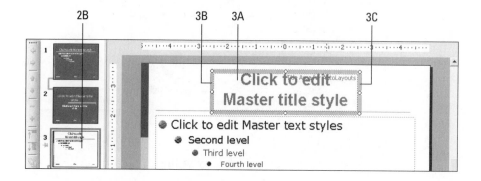

4. Insert the file Sheltie1.png from the Labs folder.

a. Choose Insert ➪ Picture ➪ From File.

b. Change the drive and folder to the Labs folder where you have been keeping your lab files.

c. Select sheltie1.png.

d. Click Insert.

5. Move and resize the image so that it sits to the right of the title text box.

a. Drag the image up to the top-right corner of the slide.

b. Drag a corner selection handle until it fits neatly between the top of the slide and the horizontal line beneath the title text box.

4B   4C

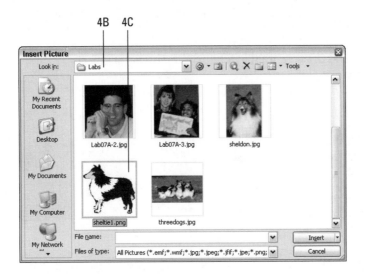

5B   5A

6. Copy the image, and place the copy to the left of the title text box.

   a. Select the image, so selection handles appear around it, if it is not already selected.

   b. Choose Edit ⇨ Copy or press Ctrl+C.

   c. Choose Edit ⇨ Paste or press Ctrl+V.

   d. Drag the copy to the left of the title text box.

6D (copy)   6A (original)

7. Flip the copy so that the dog at the left points toward the title text box.

   a. Select the image to the left of the title text box.

   b. On the Drawing toolbar, choose Draw ➪ Rotate or Flip ➪ Flip Horizontal.

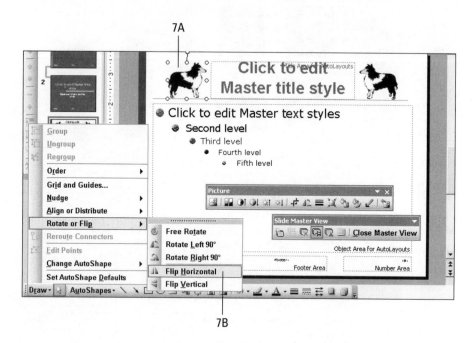

Note   If you are having trouble getting the two pictures to align vertically, use the Draw ➪ Align or Distribute ➪ Align Top command.

8. Place a rectangle behind the title text box and the graphics, and apply a gradient shading to it.

   a. Click the Rectangle button on the Drawing toolbar.

   b. Draw a rectangle that covers the two graphics and the title text box.

   c. With the rectangle still selected, choose Draw ➪ Order ➪ Send to Back.

   d. Open the menu for the Fill Color button on the Drawing toolbar and choose Fill Effects.

8B

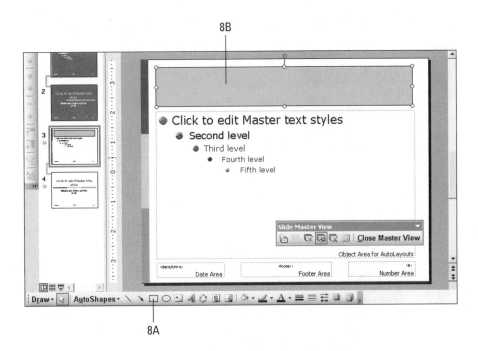

8A

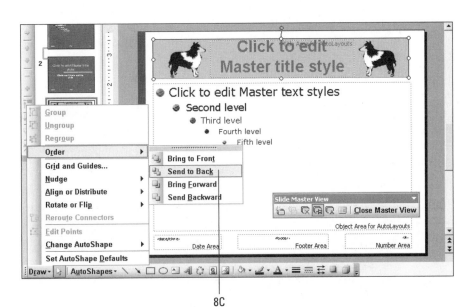

8C

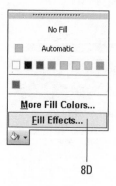

8D

e. In the Fill Effects dialog box, click the Gradient tab.

f. In the Colors section, click the One Color button.

g. Open the Color 1 drop-down list and choose the fifth color from the left (light green).

h. Drag the Dark/Light slider all the way to the Light end.

i. In the Shading Style area, click Horizontal.

j. Click the bottom-right shading variant.

k. Click OK.

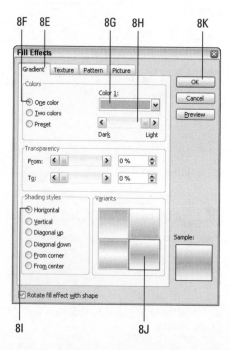

9. Eliminate the border for the rectangle.

    a. Select the rectangle if it is not already selected.

    b. On the Drawing toolbar, open the Line Color button's menu and choose No Line.

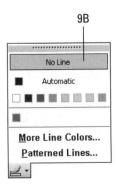

10. Extend the rectangle to the right and left edges of the slide.

    a. Drag the rectangle's left border selection handle to the edge of the slide.

    b. Drag the right border selection handle to the edge of the slide.

11. Group the rectangle and the two images into a single object; then move that grouped object to the back of the Title text box.

    a. Select the rectangle.

    b. Hold down the Ctrl key and click on each of the graphics.

    c. On the Drawing toolbar, choose Draw ➪ Group.

    d. Choose Draw ➪ Order ➪ Send to Back.

12. Exit from Slide Master view.

Note

The slides will not immediately be updated to reflect the new master because you have been working with the alternate master.

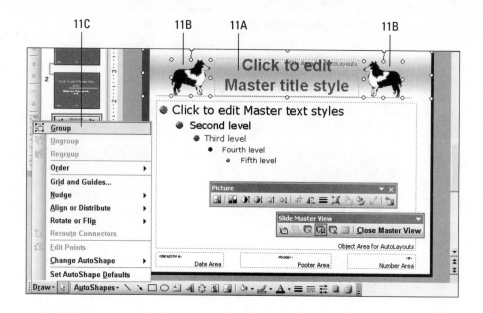

13. **Edit the titles on slides 6 and 7 as follows:**

   a. Click slide 6 in the Slides pane to select it.

   b. Edit the title text to read **Dogs for Conformation**.

   c. Click slide 7 to select it.

   d. Edit the title text to read **Dogs for Obedience**.

14. **Save your work as MyLab02D.ppt.**

Lab 2E: Formatting an Alternate Title Master

You had such success with the alternate Slide Master from Project 2D that you have now decided to create an alternate Title Master as well, and add a gradient background and clip art to it that will make it match your alternate Slide Master.

Level of difficulty: Moderate

Time to complete: 5 to 15 minutes

1. **Open the presentation file if it is not already open.**

   If you completed Lab 2D, reopen the file MyLab02D.ppt if it is not already open. If you did not complete Lab 2D, open the Lab02E.ppt file from the CD.

2. **Open Slide Master view and display the alternate Title Master (white background).**

   a. Choose View ⇨ Master ⇨ Slide Master.

   b. Click the alternate Title Master (white background) in the left pane.

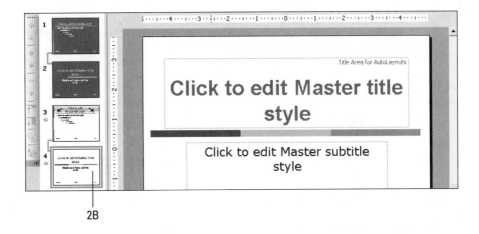

2B

3. **Place a gradient rectangle behind the top half of the slide on the Title Master.**

   a. Click the Rectangle tool on the Drawing toolbar.

   b. Draw a rectangle that completely covers the top half of the Title Master slide, but does not cover the horizontal graphical line in the center.

3B

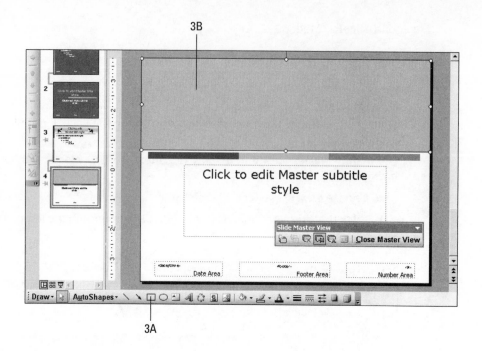

3A

c. Open the Line Color button's menu and choose No Line.

3C

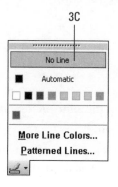

d. Choose Draw ➪ Order ➪ Send to Back.

3D

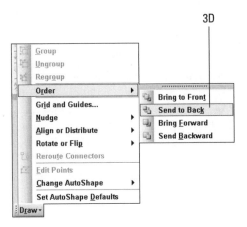

e. Open the Fill Color button's menu and choose Fill Effects.

f. On the Gradient tab, choose One Color.

g. Drag the Light/Dark slider all the way to Light.

h. Under Shading Styles, choose Horizontal.

i. Choose the top-left variant.

j. Click OK.

3F   3G   3J

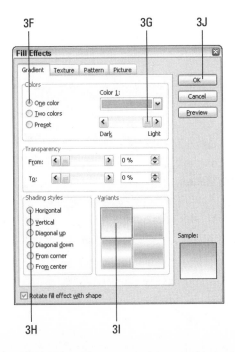

3H   3I

4. Copy one of the sheltie pictures onto the alternate Title Master slide and resize/reposition it attractively.

    a. Click the alternate Slide Master to display it.

    b. Click the grouped object consisting of the gradient rectangle and the two sheltie pictures, and choose Draw ➪ Ungroup. If you skipped Lab D, you can skip this step because the objects are not grouped.

    c. Click away from the group to deselect all items, and then click the dog picture on the left (the dog that faces to the right) to select only that picture.

    d. Click the Copy button on the Standard toolbar, or press Ctrl+C.

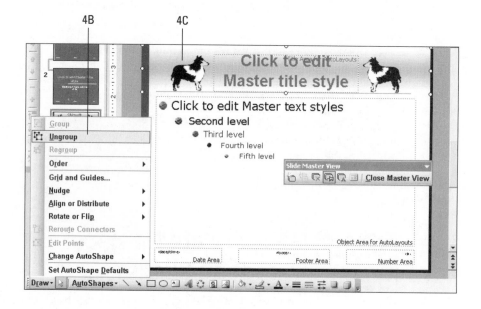

    e. Click the alternate Title Master to display it.

    f. Click the Paste button on the Standard toolbar, or press Ctrl+V. The picture appears on the Title Master.

    g. Drag the left border of the subtitle text box to align with the 1.5" mark on the ruler, so there is some blank space to its left.

    h. Drag the picture into that blank space and enlarge it to fill the available space.

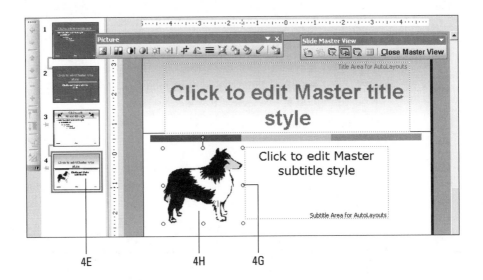

4E   4H   4G

5. Exit from Slide Master view.

Note

Remember, these changes are being made to the alternate slide master, so they do not show up automatically on the existing slides in the presentation. You will apply it to the slides in the next project.

6. Save your work as MyLab02E.ppt.

Lab 2F: Applying Alternate Master Layouts to Presentation Slides

To show your client your new alternate designs, you would like to apply them to all the slides in the presentation. You will keep the original designs too, however, in case the client does not like the new work you have done, and you will apply it to the last slide in the presentation so the client can compare the two designs.

Level of difficulty: Easy

Time to complete: 5 to 10 minutes

1. Open the presentation file if it is not already open.

If you completed Lab 2E, reopen the file MyLab02E.ppt if it is not already open. If you did not complete Lab 2E, open the Lab02F.ppt file from the CD.

2. Preserve the original green background masters.

    a. Choose View ➪ Master ➪ Slide Master.

    b. Click the green background master (either one). Both become selected.

    c. Click the Preserve Master button on the Slide Master View toolbar. A pushpin icon appears next to the set.

    d. Click Close Master View.

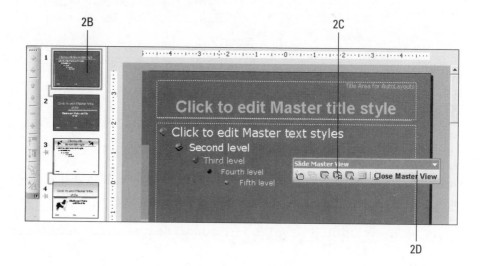

3. Apply the alternate (white-background) masters to all slides in the presentation.

    a. Click the Design button on the Formatting toolbar. The Slide Design task pane appears.

    b. In the Used in This Presentation section of the task pane, click the alternate design. It is immediately applied to all slides.

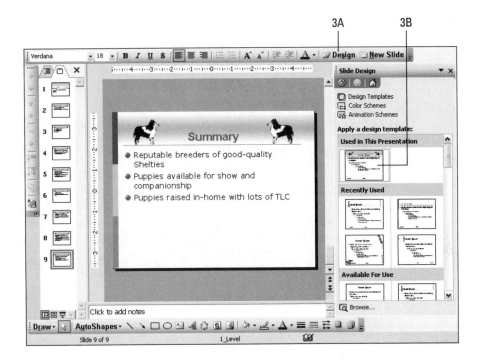

4. **Apply the original (green background) design only to the final slide in the presentation.**

   a. Click the last slide in the Slides list, displaying it.

   b. In the Slide Design task pane, in the Used in This Presentation section, open the drop-down list for the green-background master and choose Apply to Selected Slides.

   c. Close the task pane.

5. **Display the presentation in Slide Show view to check your work.**

   a. Choose View ⇨ Slide Show.

   b. Click to advance the slides until you get to the end; then press Esc to return to PowerPoint.

6. **Save your work as MyLab02F.ppt.**

7. **Exit PowerPoint.**

4C

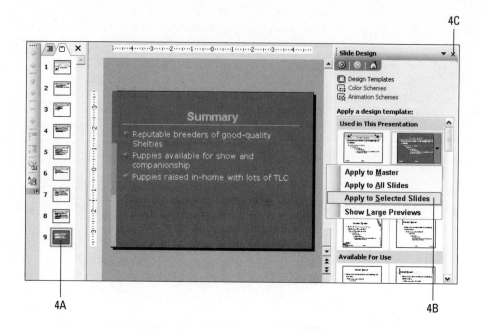

4A   4B

Congratulations! Now you have a basic presentation that you can show to your client, including two different slide designs based on the company's signature color (medium green). You are ready to meet your client and find out what additional work she would like for you to do.

The next project lab will be in Chapter 19, which will cover many other types of graphic objects. But before you can tackle it, you need to learn some additional skills, so proceed to Chapter 14 to find out how to incorporate and organize clip art and other images.

✦   ✦   ✦

Improving the Visual Impact

Adding Clip Art and Other Images

Clip art is pre-drawn art that comes with PowerPoint or that is available from other sources (such as through the Internet). There are hundreds of common images that you can use royalty-free in your work, without having to draw your own. For example, suppose you are creating a presentation about snow skiing equipment. Rather than hiring an artist to draw a picture of a skier, you can use one of PowerPoint's stock drawings of skiers and save yourself a bundle.

Being an owner of a Microsoft Office product entitles you to the use of the huge clipart collection that Microsoft maintains on its Web site, and if you are connected to the Internet while you are using PowerPoint, PowerPoint can automatically pull clips from that collection as easily as it can from your own hard drive. You can also use artwork in a variety of other formats, including photos you scan, photos you take with your digital camera, and drawings and pictures you acquire from the Internet and from other people.

In this chapter you'll learn how to select and insert clip art in your presentations, as well as how to integrate photos and images from other sources and how to organize your clips for easy access.

Choosing Appropriate Clip Art for Your Presentation

Don't just slap down any old image! You must never use clip art simply because you can; it must be a strategically calculated decision. Here are some reasons for using art, and ways to make it look good:

✦ If your message is very serious, or you are conveying bad news, don't use clip art. It looks frivolous in such situations.

✦ Use cartoonish images only if you specifically want to impart a lighthearted, fun feel to your presentation.

✦ The clip art included with Office has many styles of drawings, ranging from simple black-and-white shapes to very complex shaded color drawings. Try to stick with one type of image rather than bouncing among several drawing styles.

✦ Use only one piece of clip art per slide. Don't use clip art on every slide, or it gets overpowering.

✦ Don't repeat the same clip art on more than one slide in the presentation unless you have a specific reason to do so.

✦ If you can't find a clip that's exactly right for the slide, don't use a clip. It is better to have none than to have an inappropriate image.

✦ If clip art is important, and Office doesn't have what you want, buy more. Don't try to struggle along with the clips that come with Office if it isn't meeting your needs; impressive clip art collections are available at reasonable prices at your local computer store, as well as online.

Now, with all that in mind, let's get started working with clip art and other types of art in your presentation.

Inserting Clip Art on a Slide

Let's start out this chapter with something simple: inserting a clip on a slide. You can use a slide with a clip art placeholder or manually place a clip on a slide with some other layout.

 Expert Tip Most clip art in Microsoft Office applications are files with a `.wmf` extension. That stands for Windows Metafile. WMF is a *vector* graphic format, which means it is composed of mathematical formulas rather than individual dots. This makes it resizable without distortion and keeps the file size very small. The Clip Organizer can also organize *bitmap* graphic files (that is, graphics composed of individual dots of color), as you will see later in the chapter, but there are some editing activities through PowerPoint that can be performed only on true clip art, such as re-coloring.

To find and insert a piece of clip art, follow these steps:

1. *(Recommended)* If you want to include Web collections when searching for clips, make sure you are connected to the Internet. Otherwise, you are limited to the clips contained on your local hard disk.

2. Choose Insert ➪ Picture ➪ Clip Art. The Clip Art task pane opens.

Note If you double-click a clip art placeholder instead of going through the menu command, a dialog box may appear instead of the task pane. That works fine too, but these steps cover the task pane search method.

3. Type the subject keyword you want to search for.

4. *(Optional)* Narrow down where you want to search (Search In list) and/or the types of results you want (Results Should Be list). Note that you don't have this option unless you use Insert ⇨ Picture ⇨ Clip Art.

5. Click Go. Matching clips appear, as in Figure 14-1. If desired, you can click the Expand Results button to show more clips at once.

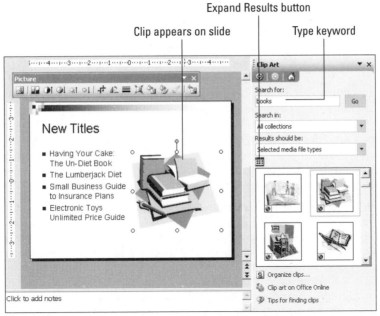

Figure 14-1: The clips that match your search specification appear in the task pane.

6. Click the clip you want to insert. It appears on the slide.

7. Edit the image (resize, move, and so on), as explained later in the chapter.

Expert Tip If you place a clip on a slide that does not have a clip art placeholder, the slide will change to a layout that does have one if the Automatic Layout for Inserted Objects feature is turned on (which it is by default). If you don't want the layout to change when you insert an object, choose Tools ⇨ AutoCorrect Options. On the AutoFormat As You Type tab, clear the Automatic Layout for Inserted Objects check box.

Now you know how to find and insert a piece of clip art. But this "search by keyword" method of finding the art is not your only option. The next section discusses how to manage clip art and other images using the Clip Organizer.

Managing Clip Collections with the Clip Organizer

The Clip Organizer is a utility that manages the clips from various collections. It also manages clips of other types, including bitmap images (such as scanned photos), sounds, and video clips. In the following sections, you will learn how to browse, categorize, and organize clips in it, as well as how to add clips to it.

Understanding clip collections

Clip art is stored in *collections*, which are logical groupings of artwork arranged by subject or location. There are three main collections within the Clip Organizer:

✦ **Office Collections:** These are the clips that came with Microsoft Office 2003.

✦ **My Collections:** This includes any clips you have marked as favorites, plus any uncategorized clips. It also includes any clips that you have added through the Clip Organizer (covered later in the chapter), any downloaded clips, and any clips shared from a network drive.

✦ **Web Collections:** These are clip collections available through Office on the Web (Microsoft). You must be connected to the Internet in order to access this collection. This is by far the largest collection. All the clips from it appear with a little globe icon in the corner when previewed in the task pane.

Within each of these large collections are multiple smaller collections (like subfolders within folders) based on subject. For example, Office Collections has subcollections for Academic, Agriculture, Animals, and so on.

Note   The physical location of the Office Collections clips is `Program Files\ Microsoft Office\MEDIA\CAGCAT10`. However, users don't normally need to know that because PowerPoint manages the locations of the clip art automatically through the application.

Searching for clips only in certain collections

When you search for clips containing certain keywords using the Clip Art task pane, you can optionally specify which collections to look in. If you are working on a PC that uses a dial-up connection, does not have Web access, or has it only sporadically, you might want to exclude the Web Collections from the search to avoid the delay while PowerPoint looks for and fails to find the Internet connection. You might also choose to exclude certain categories to avoid having too many results to wade through.

To narrow the list of collections in which to search, follow these steps:

1. From the Clip Art task pane, open the Search In drop-down list. A list of collections appears.

2. Clear the check box for any collection you want to exclude. Or click the plus sign next to the collection to see its individual subcollections, and then clear the check box for one or more of those. See Figure 14-2.

3. Continue the clip search normally.

Figure 14-2: Narrow the search for a clip to certain collections by deselecting the check boxes for unwanted collections.

Opening the Clip Organizer

To open the Clip Organizer, do the following:

1. From the Clip Art task pane, click Organize Clips.

2. If a dialog box appears asking whether you want to catalog the existing picture, sound, and motion files on your hard disk, as in Figure 14-3, click Now. The process takes anywhere from 1 to 10 minutes depending on the speed of the system and the amount of artwork to be cataloged.

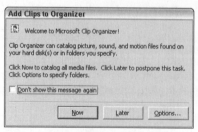

Figure 14-3: Catalog the clips on your entire system.

Expert Tip

In Step 2, you can click Options to see a list of locations to include in the cataloging process. However, the first time you catalog you will probably want to include all possible locations.

After cataloging, several new subcategories may appear under My Collections. The cataloging process creates a category for each location that it finds, and catalogs the artwork within it.

Cataloging clips from other locations

There are probably images elsewhere on your PC that you would like to use in PowerPoint besides the Microsoft Office clip art collection. For example, perhaps you have some scanned photos or some clip art you have downloaded from a Web site that offered free clips. If you need to use this "outside" art only once or twice, you can simply insert it with the Insert ⇨ Picture ⇨ From File command, covered later in this chapter. But if you have a recurring need for the art, you might want to add it to your Clip Organizer.

You can include images of all image formats in the Clip Organizer, not just the default .wmf format that PowerPoint's clip art uses. The image formats that PowerPoint supports include .emf, .wmf, .jpg, .png, .bmp, .pcx, .dib, .rle, .eps, .dxf, .pct, .cgm, .cdr, .drw, .tif, .tga, .pcd, .gif, .wpg, .fpx, and .mix. The Clip Organizer also accepts many sound and video formats as well. The Clip Organizer is not only for clip art, but also for scanned and digital camera photos, video clips, and sound clips. You will work with it further in Chapters 20 and 21, which deal with sound and video.

The first time you open the Clip Organizer it offers to create an automatic catalog; you can perform additional automatic or manual cataloging later. Adding a clip to the Clip Organizer does not physically move the clip; it simply creates a link to it in the organizer so that the clip is included when you search or browse clips.

Note

Any clips you add are placed in the My Collections collection; you cannot add clips to the Office Collections or Web Collections categories. This is true whether you add them automatically or manually.

Adding clips automatically to the Clip Organizer

If in the future the content of the hard disk changes to the point where you want to update the catalog, you can do so. To automatically update the catalog, follow these steps:

1. From the Clip Organizer, choose File ⇨ Add Clips to Organizer ⇨ Automatically.

2. *(Optional)* In the dialog box that appears, click the Options button to open the Auto Import Settings dialog box. You can then mark or clear check boxes for various locations that you want to include in the automatic cataloging. See Figure 14-4.

3. If you performed Step 2, click Catalog to perform the search for clips. If you did not perform Step 2, click OK to perform the search.

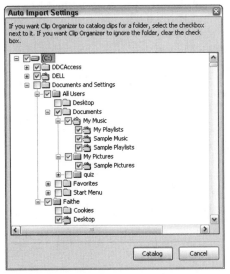

Figure 14-4: You can specify the locations to catalog if desired.

Adding clips manually to the Clip Organizer

Not all clips are picked up automatically during the cataloging process, so you might want to manually add some clips. For example, the automatic cataloging process looks for clips only on your local hard disk(s); you might want to catalog some clips in a network location.

Caution   Earlier versions of Office stored the local collection of clip art in a different place. Office XP, for example, stored it in `Program Files\Common Files\Microsoft Shared\Clipart\Catcat50`. The clip art in this old location does not appear in the collections in Office 2003 applications by default. Neither is it picked up by the automatic cataloging process. The only way to get it into the Clip Organizer is by manually cataloging it, as described here.

To manually add one or more clips, do the following:

1. From the Clip Organizer window, choose File ⇨ Add Clips to Organizer ⇨ On My Own. The Add Clips to Organizer window appears.

2. Navigate to the clip(s) you want to add. This can be a local, network, or Internet location.

3. Select the clips. To select more than one clip, hold down the Shift key to select a contiguous group or the Ctrl key to select a non-contiguous group.

4. Click the Add To button. A list of the existing collections in the Clip Organizer appears. See Figure 14-5.

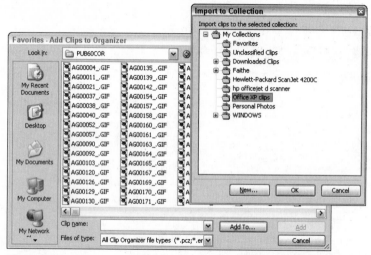

Figure 14-5: You can specify the locations to catalog if desired.

5. Select the collection in which you want to place the new clips and click OK.

   OR

   To create a new clip collection, click My Collections and then click New. Type a name for a new collection and click OK. Then select the new folder on the list and click OK.

6. Click the Add button. The clips are added to the specified collection.

Deleting clips from the Clip Organizer

After the automatic cataloging process (or maybe after the manual one too), you might end up with some subcollections within My Collections that you don't want. The automatic cataloging process sometimes identifies artwork that is not really artwork—that is, little graphics that are part of some other application's operation. To remove these from your Clip Organizer, right-click the graphic and choose Delete. The same goes for entire folders—right-click and choose Delete.

For example, in Figure 14-6, notice that the Clip Organizer has cataloged a clip from the Windows\Help folder. I am right-clicking on the Help folder in the folder tree and choosing Delete Help to get rid of it. This does not delete the picture or its folder from the hard disk; it simply removes its reference from the Clip Organizer.

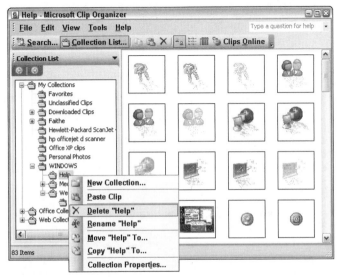

Figure 14-6: Remove a clip from the Clip Organizer by right-clicking and choosing Delete.

Caution The Image Library utility that comes with Office 2003 is another way of browsing graphics on your system. If you delete an image or a folder from that program, it *does* delete it from your hard drive.

Inserting an image in the Clip Organizer from a scanner or digital camera

If you have a scanner or digital camera, you can use it from within the Clip Organizer to scan a picture and store it there. Let's look at a scanner as an example. To scan a picture into the Clip Organizer, do the following:

1. Make sure your scanner is ready. Place the picture to be scanned on the scanner glass.

2. From the Clip Organizer, choose File ⇨ Add Clips to Organizer ⇨ From Scanner or Camera.

3. Select the scanner from the Device list. See Figure 14-7.

4. Choose a quality: Web quality (low) or Print quality (high).

Figure 14-7: Scan a clip into the Clip Organizer.

5. To scan now using default settings, click Insert. Or, to adjust the settings further, click Custom Insert, change the settings, and then click Scan.

The scanned clip appears in the My Collections collection, in a folder with the same name as the device (the scanner's make and model, in this case). From there you can assign keywords to it to make it easier to find, as explained in the next section.

Expert Tip   The scanned file is located in the My Documents\My Pictures\Microsoft Clip Organizer folder on your hard disk, in case you want to use it in some other application that does not support the Clip Organizer. It is assigned a filename beginning with mso (for example, mso414611) and it is saved in JPG format.

Caution   Good-quality scanners can scan at 300 dpi or more, but for use in PowerPoint an image needs to be no higher-resolution than 95 dpi, the resolution of a monitor. Excessive dpi when scanning is one reason that graphics take up so much space. If you want to use an already-scanned image in PowerPoint that has a high dpi, consider opening it in a graphics program and reducing its dpi before importing it into PowerPoint.

Working with clip keywords and information

After creating an automatic catalog, you will probably end up with lots of clips in the Unclassified Clips collection. Some of these you might want to delete, having no use for them, but others you will want to keep. In order for these clips to show up when you do a search, you must assign keywords to them.

Note   Automatically cataloged clips will have several keywords pre-assigned based on the filename and the location. For example, suppose that the clip Blue Hills.jpg has been cataloged from the Documents and Settings\All Users\Documents\ My Pictures\Sample Pictures folder. It will have the following keywords pre-assigned: Blue Hills, Documents and Settings, All Users, Documents, My Pictures, and Sample Pictures. These are not very helpful when trying to locate the clip by subject, however, so you will want to add some content-based keywords too.

Changing the keywords for an individual clip

To modify a clip's keywords and information, do the following:

1. From the Clip Organizer, right-click the clip (or click the down arrow to its right) and choose Edit Keywords.

2. The default caption for the clip is the filename. Change it to a more meaningful caption in the Caption box if desired. This caption will appear in some views and anywhere that an application pulls a caption automatically.

3. To add a keyword for the clip, type the new keywords in the Keyword box and click Add. See Figure 14-8.

4. To remove a keyword, click the keyword on the list and click Delete.

5. When you are finished changing the clip's keywords and caption, click OK to close the dialog box, or click the Previous or Next button to move to a different clip in the same folder.

Figure 14-8: Add, delete, or modify the keywords for a clip.

Changing the keywords for multiple clips at once

You can modify multiple clips at once by selecting multiple clips before you right-click (Step 1 in the preceding steps). When multiple clips are selected, the All Clips at Once tab becomes available in the Keywords dialog box. From there you can add keywords that will apply to all the selected clips. Figure 14-9 shows the Keywords dialog box ready to add a keyword to the selected clips.

Using the Clip Organizer to insert clip art

When you insert clip art from the Clip Art task pane, as you saw at the beginning of this chapter, you can't browse. You can only search based on keyword. If you would rather peruse the available art in a more leisurely fashion, you can open the Clip Organizer to do so.

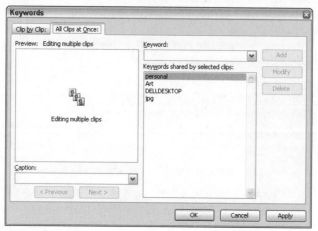

Figure 14-9: Keywords can be added and deleted for multiple clips at once on the All Clips at Once tab.

The Clip Organizer is not really designed for easy insertion of clips into a presentation, but it is possible to do it by using the Clipboard. To select a clip from the Clip Organizer for insertion in your presentation, do the following:

1. From the Clip Art task pane, click Organize Clips. The Clip Organizer window opens.

2. Make sure Collection List is selected on the toolbar (not Search). Click it if needed.

3. Click the collection you want to browse, and then view the available clips there. When you find the clip you want to insert, right-click it and choose Copy.

4. Close or minimize the Clip Organizer. Display the slide in PowerPoint on which you want to place the clip, and then right-click and choose Paste.

Making clips available offline

Most of the clip art that appears in the Clip Organizer is not on your local hard disk; it's online. That means you won't have access to it when you aren't connected to the Internet.

If you find some clip art in the Clip Organizer that you would like to have available offline, here's how to add it to the local hard disk:

1. In the Clip Organizer or the Clip Art task pane, open the menu of the clip you want (the arrow to its right) and choose Make Available Offline. The Copy to Collection dialog box opens.

If the Make Available Offline command is not present, it means that this clip is already on your local hard disk.

2. Select the collection in which you want to place the clip. (Or click New to create a new collection.) Then click OK.

Browsing more clips on the Office Online Web site

When you browse clip art while connected to the Internet, the Office Online clip art automatically appears there. However, you can also visit the Office Online Web site to browse the clip art directly.

To open a Web browser window for the Office Online clip art gallery, do one of the following:

✦ From the Clip Art task pane, click Clip art on Office Online.

✦ From the Clip Organizer window, click the Clips Online toolbar button.

Either way, the same Web page displays (provided you have Internet access). It contains information about clip art, links to art collections, featured clips, and more. It is constantly changing, but Figure 14-10 shows how it looked on the day I visited.

Note Another good source of Microsoft clip art is http://dgl.microsoft.com.

Figure 14-10: Visit the Office Online clip art Web page for more information and more clip art.

If you have a full-time Internet connection, there is little reason to download clips to your hard disk from the Office Online Web site because your clip art search by keyword will always include it. However, if your Internet connection is working now but might not be working later when you need a clip, you might want to snag the clips you need in advance so they will be available.

To copy certain clips from the Office Online Web site to your hard disk for later use, follow these steps:

1. From the Office Online clip art site, scroll down to the Categories list and click a category to display it.

2. At the list of clips, mark the check boxes for the clips you want. See Figure 14-11. There may be multiple pages of clips in that category; click the Next arrow to go to the next page.

3. When you are finished making selections, click the Download hyperlink. For example, in Figure 14-11 the link is <u>Download 5 items</u> because I have five items chosen.

4. If this is the first time you have used the service, a Terms of Use screen will appear. Scroll down to the bottom and click Accept to continue.

5. Click Download Now.

6. A box appears saying it is downloading `Clipart.mpf` and asking whether you want to save or open it. Choose Open.

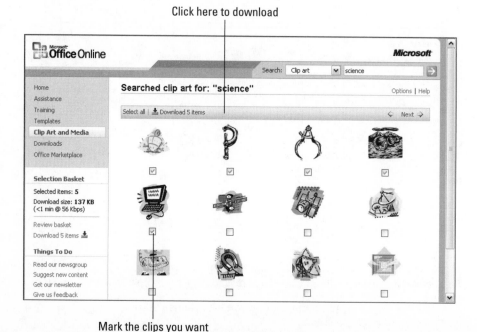

Figure 14-11: Download clips from Office Online for future offline use.

Note MPF stands for Media Package File. When downloading one of these you should nearly always choose to Open it rather than Save it, because opening it integrates its content automatically with the Clip Organizer. Saving it stores the file somewhere on your hard disk without adding the clips to the Clip Organizer. You might need to do that if you were downloading clips that were going to be used on some other PC; then you could transfer the MPF file to that PC before double-clicking to open it.

Caution When an MPF file unpacks, it uses the Temporary Internet File folder. If that folder is too full (that is, not enough space remaining on the drive), the clips may not import into Clip Organizer.

The selected clips appear in the Clip Organizer, in the Downloaded Clips folder under My Collections. They are now ready for you to use.

Inserting a Picture from a File

If you have an image you have already scanned and saved or an image you have acquired from some other source, you can place it into PowerPoint with the Insert ➪ Picture ➪ From File command. This is a quick way to bring in an existing image without fussing with the Clip Art task pane or the Clip Organizer. To place a picture from a file, follow these steps:

1. Display the slide on which you want to place the image.

2. Choose Insert ➪ Picture ➪ From File. The Insert Picture dialog box appears (Figure 14-12).

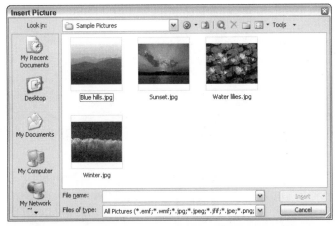

Figure 14-12: Choose the file that you want to use in your PowerPoint presentation.

3. Select the picture you want and click Insert. The image is inserted onto your slide.

4. Edit the image (resize, move, and so on), as explained later in the chapter.

Inserting an Image Directly onto a Slide from a Scanner

If you have a scanner attached to your PC, you can scan a picture directly onto a PowerPoint slide. Scanning directly into PowerPoint saves time because you do not have to run the scanning software and assign a separate filename to the image.

During the scanning process, you can choose to add the image to the Clip Organizer for future use or not. If you choose not to, the image will not exist outside of this presentation, and you will not be able to use it in other presentations or other applications. If you do add it to the Clip Organizer, the image will be placed in a file in the My Documents\My Pictures\Microsoft Clip Organizer folder, in JPG format. You can also drag the image from PowerPoint into the Clip Organizer to store a copy for future use, or copy and paste the image from this presentation into another one.

To scan directly onto a slide, follow these steps:

1. Choose Insert ➪ Picture ➪ From Scanner or Camera. The Insert Picture from Scanner or Camera dialog box appears. See Figure 14-13.

Figure 14-13: Scan an image from PowerPoint using the Windows scanner driver.

2. Choose the scanner from the Device list.

3. Choose a resolution: Web (low) or Print (high). Lower resolution means smaller file size and fewer pixels overall comprising the image. Low resolution is generally the best for presentations.

4. If you don't want to save the scanned picture in the Clip Organizer, clear the Add Pictures to Clip Organizer check box. Otherwise leave it marked.

5. Click Insert to scan with the default settings, or click Custom Insert, make changes to the settings, and then click Scan.

6. Resize, move, or otherwise modify the graphic as needed, as described later in the chapter.

Formatting Pictures for Use in PowerPoint

Besides clip art, you can use many types of images in a PowerPoint presentation. You can acquire or prepare these images outside of PowerPoint and then insert them directly into the presentation or place them in the Clip Organizer, as you have already seen so far in this chapter.

Because there are so many choices, let's review some of the decisions you might need to make.

Resolution

Resolution is the number of pixels that comprise the image. It is measured with two numbers, such as 800 x 600.

When you scan an image, you can set the dots per inch (dpi) setting in the scanner software. Multiply this dpi setting by the sizes of the picture vertically and horizontally to determine how many pixels the image will occupy when scanned. For example, if you scan a 4" by 6" photo at 100 dpi, it results in a 400x600 pixel image. Scanning at higher resolutions result in a larger file size. For example, the same picture scanned at 200 dpi would result in an 800 x 1200 pixel image.

The difference in quality based on the dots per inch of a scan is readily apparent when you zoom in on an image. In Figure 14-14, you can see two copies of an image open in a graphics program. The same photo was scanned at 75 dots per inch (left) and 150 dots per inch (right). However, the difference between them is not significant when the two images are placed on a PowerPoint slide, as shown in Figure 14-15. The lower-resolution image is at the top left, but the observable difference is minimal.

When you acquire an image from some other source, its number of pixels has already been determined. You can change it by resizing the image in a graphics program or you can crop a section of it out, making that section a new graphic file.

An image that is too small for the intended spot in PowerPoint can result in image-quality problems because when you enlarge the picture, it may appear grainy or jagged. For best results with such a picture, re-scan it or re-take the picture with a digital camera if possible.

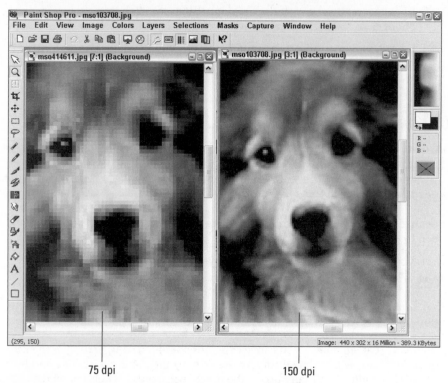

75 dpi   150 dpi

Figure 14-14: At high magnification, the difference in dots per inch for a scan is apparent.

Having an image that is too large is not a problem quality-wise. You can resize it in PowerPoint to make it smaller, as explained later in this chapter, without any loss of quality. However, having a picture that is much larger than needed can increase the overall size of the PowerPoint file, which can become problematic if you plan to distribute the presentation on floppy disk or over the Internet. To avoid this, try placing the file onto the slide using the Insert ➪ Picture ➪ From File command. (Be sure to turn off the autolayout features in Tools ➪ AutoCorrect first.) Notice how much too large it is when first inserted, and then delete it. Then if the image was originally a scan or digital camera picture, re-take it using a lower resolution setting. Or, if the image was originally acquired from some other source, go into a graphics-editing program like Paint Shop Pro or Photoshop and resize the image to make it closer to what you need.

75 dpi   150 dpi

Figure 14-15: When the image is used in a presentation, it is not at a high magnification, and it displays at only 96 ppi (the monitor's resolution), so the difference between a high-dpi and a low-dpi scan is not noticeable.

Expert Tip   On the Picture toolbar in PowerPoint you'll find a Compress Picture button. (See Table 14-2 if you can't find it.) This button opens a dialog box in which you can decrease the resolution of the copy of the picture that has been inserted into PowerPoint, reducing its dpi so the PowerPoint file will be smaller. This is useful if you don't want to reduce the dpi of the original but you need a particular PowerPoint file to be smaller. By the way, even though the feature is called "compress," it doesn't have anything to do with file compression in the same sense as is discussed in the Graphic Format section later in the chapter. It's purely a resolution adjustment.

Color depth

Color depth is the number of bits required to describe the color of each pixel in the image. For example, in one-bit color, a single binary digit represents each pixel. Each pixel is either black (1) or white (0). In four-bit color, there are 16 possible colors because there are 16 possible combinations of 1s and 0s in a four-digit binary number. In 8-bit color there are 256 combinations. The highest number of colors you can have in an image is 16.7 million colors, which is 24-bit color (also called "true color"). The higher the color depth, the larger the file size of the image.

Photos look best when they are used at color depths of 16-bit or higher. Some photos will look all right at 8-bit (256 colors), but will lack realism. Photos at 4-bit (16 colors) are usually unacceptable. Most scanners automatically scan at their maximum available color depth, using the extra bits above 24 for color correction.

Expert Tip

You may have encountered higher color resolutions than 24-bit, such as 32-bit. A 24-bit image uses 8 bits each to describe Red, Green, and Blue. A 32-bit image uses the same 8-bit Red, Green, and Blue, but adds an additional 8 bits for Alpha Channel, which governs transparency.

When shopping for a scanner, you might notice them advertised with even higher bit depths, such as 40 bits. The extra bits are used for image correction; the PC stores only 24 bits per pixel. Having the extra bits makes it possible to discard some of the bits to account for "noise" and still end up with 24 good bits.

You might want to decrease the color depth in a graphic-editing program to create a smaller graphic file if disk space is an issue. Users will normally not be able to detect the difference on-screen between a 24-bit and a 16-bit image, but scaling down the color depth from 24-bit to 16-bit can cut the size of the graphic file considerably.

Graphic format

Many scanners scan in JPG format by default, but most will also support TIF format too, and some support other formats as well. Images you acquire from a digital camera will almost always be JPG. Images from other sources may be any of dozens of graphic formats, including PCX, BMP, GIF, or PNG.

Different graphic formats can vary tremendously in the size and quality of the image they produce. The main differentiators between formats are the color depth they support and the type of compression they use (which determines the file size).

Compression is an algorithm that decreases the amount of space the file takes up on disk by storing the data about its pixels more compactly. A file format will have one of these three states in regard to compression:

✦ **No compression:** The image is not compressed.

✦ **Lossless compression:** The image is compressed, but the algorithm for doing so does not throw out any pixels so there is no loss of image quality when the image is resized.

✦ **Lossy compression:** The image is compressed by recording less data about the pixels, such that when the image is resized there may be a loss of image quality.

Table 14-1 provides a brief guide to some of the most common graphics formats. Generally speaking, for most on-screen presentations, JPG should be your preferred choice for graphics because it is compact and Web-accessible (although PNG is becoming more popular because it uses lossless compression).

Expert Tip If you are not sure what format you will eventually use for an image, scan it in TIF format and keep the TIF copy on your hard disk. You can always save a copy in JPG or other formats later when you need them for specific projects.

Table 14-1
Popular Graphics Formats

Extension	Pronunciation	Compression	Notes
JPG or JPEG	"J-peg"	Yes, built in	Stands for Joint Photographic Experts Group. Very small image size. Uses lossy compression. Common on the Web. Up to 24-bit.
GIF	"gif" or "jif"	Yes, built in	Stands for Graphic Interchange Format. Limited to 8-bit (256 colors). Uses proprietary compression algorithm. Allows animated graphics, useful on the Web. Lossy compression.
PNG	"ping"	Yes	Stands for Portable Network Graphic. An improvement on GIF. Up to 48-bit color depth. Lossless compression, but smaller file sizes than TIF. Public domain format.
BMP	"B-M-P" or "bump"	No	Default bitmap type for Windows. Up to 24-bit. Used for Windows wallpaper and other Windows graphics.
PCX	"P-C-X"	Yes, built in	There are different versions: 0, 2, and 5. Use version 5 for 24-bit support. Originally introduced by ZSoft; sometimes called ZSoft Paintbrush format.
TIF	"tiff"	Yes, optional	An acronym for Tagged Image Format. Supported by most scanners and digital cameras. Up to 24-bit. Uses lossless compression. Large file size.

Modifying Graphics in PowerPoint

When you initially place a picture on a slide, it probably doesn't look exactly the way you want it to. That's because it probably needs to be cropped, resized, recolored, reshaped, or some combination of those alterations. You can perform most of these modifications outside of PowerPoint in a graphics program such as Paint Shop Pro or Photoshop, but it's faster and easier to do them within PowerPoint.

Working with the Picture toolbar

The Picture toolbar is available whenever a picture is selected. If you don't see it, right-click the picture and choose Show Picture Toolbar.

Almost everything you can do to an image can be done in two ways: using the Format Picture dialog box or using the Picture toolbar. In most cases, the Picture toolbar is the easier method, so that's the method I teach you in the following sections. I mention the tools as I go along, but you might want to preview them in Table 14-2 before getting started.

Table 14-2
Buttons on the Picture Toolbar

Button	Button Name	Purpose
	Insert Picture	Opens the Insert Picture from File dialog box again so you can add another picture.
	Color	Switches between grayscale, black and white, color, and washout (watermark) image modes.
	More Contrast	Increases the difference between the lights and darks.
	Less Contrast	Decreases the difference between the lights and darks.
	More Brightness	Makes colors in the picture brighter.
	Less Brightness	Makes colors in the picture darker.
	Crop	Changes the mouse pointer to a cropping tool that you can use to exclude parts of the image.
	Rotate Left 90°	Rotates the image to the left 90 degrees.

Button	Button Name	Purpose
☰	Line Style	Changes the thickness/style of the border surrounding the clip.
⬚	Compress Pictures	Allows you to lower the dpi of the picture to make the file size smaller in PowerPoint.
◳	Recolor Picture	Opens the Recolor Picture dialog box.
◳	Format Picture	Opens the Format Picture dialog box.
✏	Set Transparent Color	Enables you to set one color of the image as see-through (not available for all images).
◳	Reset Picture	Restores the original settings that the picture had when you first imported it.

Moving and resizing

You learned all about moving and resizing objects in Chapter 11, and images are no different from other objects.

To move an image, point at the center of the image (any area except the handles) and drag the image where you want it. To resize an image in one dimension, drag one of the side handles. To resize an image in both dimensions, drag one of the corner handles. Press Shift while you drag the corner handle to maintain the aspect ratio.

Changing the image mode

Most images can be displayed in any of four modes:

✦ **Automatic:** This is usually color if it is a color image. It's the image default appearance and is best for color presentations.

✦ **Grayscale:** This is a gray-shaded version of the original image, with shades of gray substituted for each color. This works well for presentations that you'll give in one color, such as a presentation given with transparencies printed on a black-and-white printer.

✦ **Black and white:** The entire image consists of black and white. There is no shading. Any colors are rounded to either black or white, whichever they are closest to. This results in a loss of image quality in an image that had any shading.

✦ **Washout:** This is a light background image of the original, like a watermark, suitable for placement behind text. Its effect can be subtle.

Figure 14-16 shows an image in each of the four modes. (You can't tell much difference between Automatic and Grayscale since this book is not in color, but you could immediately see the difference on your own screen.) To switch between them, click the Color button on the Picture toolbar and choose from the menu that appears.

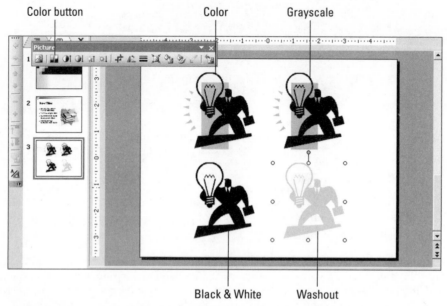

Figure 14-16: Use the Image Control button on the Picture toolbar to switch between image modes.

Changing the colors

To subtly change an image's appearance, you can use the Contrast and Brightness controls on the Picture toolbar. (Refer to Table 14-2 to identify them.) Turn up or down the brightness or contrast as needed, just like you would set the controls on your TV or your computer monitor.

You can also change the coloring more dramatically with the Recolor Picture dialog box. It enables you to choose one or more colors used in the image and change them to some other color(s). Follow these steps to change a picture in that way:

Caution   You cannot recolor a bitmap image (such as a scan) in PowerPoint. Recoloring works only on clip art.

1. Select the image that you want to recolor.

2. On the Picture Toolbar, click the Recolor Picture button. The Recolor Picture dialog box appears showing all the colors used in the image. See Figure 14-17.

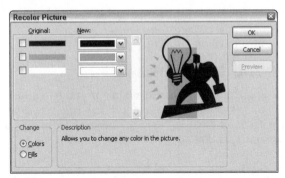

Figure 14-17: Choose the colors you want to change, and choose the colors you want to change them to.

3. Choose Colors or Fills at the bottom of the dialog box. Colors (the default) shows all the colors in the image, both the lines and the fills. The Fills option, on the other hand, shows only the fill colors.

4. Click the check box next to one of the Original colors. Then open the New drop-down list next to it and select a color to change it to.

5. The preview will update automatically. Drag the dialog box out of the way as needed so you can see the change in the image.

6. Repeat Steps 4 and 5 for each of the colors you want to change.

7. Click OK.

Setting a transparent color

The Transparent Color feature can be really neat, but not all pictures support it. It's available for bitmap images (including scans), and for some, but not all, clip art. For example, suppose you have a scanned photo of your CEO and you want to make the background transparent so it looks like his head is sitting right on the slide. This feature could help you out with that.

Caution
Some clip art already has its background set to transparent, which is why it won't work with this Set Transparent Color feature.

First insert the picture into the presentation. Then select the picture. If the Set Transparent Color button is not grayed out on the Picture toolbar, you can set a transparent color by following these steps:

1. Make sure the picture is selected.

2. Click the Set Transparent Color button.

3. On the picture, click on the color that you want to make transparent.

If the results are not what you want, click the Undo button on the Standard toolbar or press Ctrl+Z to undo.

Adding a background to the image

You learned in the preceding chapter how to add a background to a slide. You use the same procedure to add a background to an image. Some images (especially clip art) have a transparent background (that is, No Fill), but you can set any background you want for the image by following these steps:

1. Click the image to select it.

2. Open the Fill Color menu from the Fill Color button on the Formatting toolbar. See Figure 14-18.

3. Choose a color, or choose More Fill Colors or Fill Effects, as you learned in Chapter 12.

Note If you want to apply the color that is already selected (that is, the color of the strip on the Fill Color button), just click the Fill Color button. You don't have to open its menu.

Adding a border to an image

To apply a border to an image, you use the same technique you learned in Chapter 12 for objects. Select the image and then choose a border color, style, and dash style from the Drawing toolbar.

Figure 14-18: Set a fill color for an image by selecting the image and then choosing from the Fill Color button's menu.

Cropping an image

Cropping is for those times when you want only a part of an image and not the whole thing. For example, you might have a great photo of a person or animal, but there is extraneous detail around it, as in Figure 14-19. You can crop out the important object in the image with the cropping tool.

To use the cropping tool, follow these steps:

1. Select the image.
2. Click the Crop tool on the Picture toolbar. Your mouse pointer changes to a cropping tool. See Figure 14-19.

Cropping tool   Mouse pointer when cropping

Figure 14-19: Use the cropping tool for an image like this, where the important object is overshadowed by extraneous material.

3. Position the pointer over a side handle on the image frame, on a side where you want to cut some of the image off.
4. Drag the handle inward toward the center of the image until only the part of the image on that side that you want to keep is in the dotted line.
5. Repeat Steps 3 and 4 for each side.
6. After cropping, move or resize the image as needed. Figure 14-20 shows the result of cropping the image from Figure 14-19.

Figure 14-20: Cropping this image has made a great difference in its appearance.

Working with the Format Picture dialog box

So far in this section, you have done your work from the Picture toolbar. But you can also modify your image from its Format Picture dialog box. To do so, right-click the image and choose Format Picture, or click the Format Picture button on the Picture toolbar.

In the Format Picture dialog box (Figure 14-21) are the same tabs that you saw when you worked with objects in Chapter 12:

✦ **Colors and Lines tab:** Provides an alternative way of changing the fill color and line color, style, and weight.

✦ **Size tab:** Provides an alternative way of resizing a picture.

✦ **Position tab:** Provides an alternative way of moving the image.

✦ **Picture tab:** Provides an alternative way of cropping the image, controlling its brightness and contrast, and changing its image type.

✦ **Web tab:** Enables you to enter alternative text to appear in case the image cannot be displayed. (This is used for presentations designed for Web showing only.)

You may never have occasion to use the Format Picture dialog box, because all the controls you need are available from the Picture toolbar. You might want to use it if you have a lot of different settings you want to adjust for a picture, because you can do them all from a single dialog box.

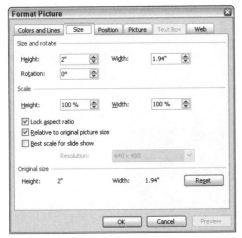

Figure 14-21: Use the Format Picture dialog box to control the picture's placement and appearance.

Working with Photo Albums

Most presentations in PowerPoint are text-based, with accompanying photographs. The default Blank Presentation template is biased in favor of text. Graphics, as you have seen in this chapter, require some extra effort.

The *Photo Albums* feature in PowerPoint creates a new presentation that is specifically designed as a carrier of pictures. It is useful when you need to create a presentation that is very heavy on graphics, with little or no text except picture captions.

Creating a new photo album

When you create a new photo album, it starts a new presentation for you. Any other presentations that you may have open are not disturbed, and you can switch back to them at any time with the Window menu. The new presentation has a title slide, as well as slides for the photos you place in the album.

To start a new photo album, follow these steps:

1. Choose Insert ➪ Picture ➪ New Photo Album. The Photo Album dialog box opens.

2. To add a photo from a file, click the File/Disk button. The Insert New Pictures dialog box opens.

3. Select one or more pictures, and then click Insert. (To select multiple pictures, hold down Ctrl or Shift as you click on the ones you want.) The photos appear in the Photo Album dialog box. See Figure 14-22.

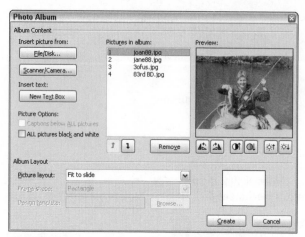

Figure 14-22: Create a picture-based presentation with the Photo Album feature.

4. Repeat Steps 2 and 3 as needed to insert all the photos from disk that you want.

5. *(Optional)* If you have any photos you need to scan or import from a digital camera, click the Scanner/Camera button and then acquire those images as you have learned earlier in this chapter.

6. For each image on the Pictures in Album list, select the picture and then apply any correction needed with the buttons beneath the Preview pane. These are the same as on the Picture toolbar. You can rotate right or left, increase or decrease the contrast, and increase or decrease the brightness.

7. Use the arrows to move an image up or down in the order.

8. In the Album Layout section, open the Picture Layout box and choose the layout for the presentation slides. For example, in Figure 14-22, *1 Picture with Title* has been chosen.

9. If available, choose a frame shape from the Frame Shape list. Some choices from Step 6 do not permit a frame shape to be chosen.

Expert Tip

You can create design templates specifically for photo albums and then use them here by choosing them from the Design Template list or clicking Browse to locate them.

10. *(Optional)* To add caption boxes for each picture, mark the Captions Below ALL Pictures check box.

11. *(Optional)* To show the pictures in black and white, mark the ALL Pictures Black and White check box.

12. Click Create. PowerPoint creates the new presentation containing the photos and the layout you specified.

13. Save the photo album (File ⇨ Save) as a presentation. Or, to save it in Web format, use File ⇨ Save as Web Page.

Figure 14-23 shows a slide from a photo album.

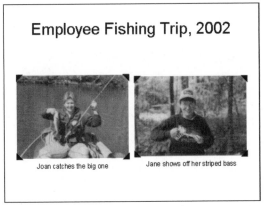

Figure 14-23: Here's a typical photo album slide.

Modifying a photo album

You can modify the photo album later by choosing Format ⇨ Photo Album. This reopens the Photo Album dialog box, the same as in Figure 14-22.

You can also modify the slides in the presentation individually. These are just regular, editable slides, and you can add anything to them that you like, including text boxes, clip art, and so on. Think of it as an on-screen scrapbook!

Summary

In this chapter, you learned how to insert and manage clip art and photos. Now you know how to get images into your presentation, how to organize them in the Clip Organizer, how to select the best resolution, color depth, and graphic format for your presentation. You also learned how to modify graphics using PowerPoint's Picture toolbar. You now know how to use the Photo Album feature to create a presentation that is comprised primarily of graphics.

In the next chapter, you learn how to create your own graphics by drawing them with the Drawing tools in PowerPoint. These are not sophisticated tools, but they can help you create simple, effective drawings consisting of lines and shapes.

✦   ✦   ✦

Using the Drawing Tools

All the Microsoft Office 2003 applications use a common Drawing toolbar, on which you find tools for creating lines and shapes and modifying all kinds of objects. You have already seen in earlier chapters how the Fill Color, Line Color, Line Style, and so on can be controlled with these buttons. In this chapter, I introduce you to the buttons at the *other* end of the Drawing toolbar, the ones that create lines and shapes. This chapter also covers the very popular WordArt feature, which lets you make shaped text for logos, titles, and spot decorations.

Understanding the Drawing Tools

The drawing tools create simple line-based *vector graphics* that are each a separate object on the slide. For example, if you make a drawing consisting of four rectangles, an oval, and six lines, each of those is separately movable or resizable. You can later group them (by choosing Draw ⇨ Group) if you want to create a single object out of them that can be moved or resized as a whole.

> **Note**   A vector graphic is one that is based on a mathematical formula. For example, if you draw a vector graphic line, the application stores the line start point, line end point, and line properties (width, color, and so on) as numeric values, like in geometry. When you move or resize the line, those numbers are updated. Clip art is also of the vector graphic type. In contrast, a scanned image or photo is a bitmap graphic, in which each individual colored dot is represented by a separate numeric value.

The Drawing tools provide for five basic things you can draw: lines, arrows (that is, lines with arrowheads on one or both ends), rectangles, ovals, and AutoShapes. *AutoShapes* are predrawn shapes, usually more complex than the simple ovals and rectangles. There are dozens of them, including all kinds of arrows, sunbursts, brackets, and symbols. By combining these elements you can make a surprising variety of simple drawings.

You might, for example, draw a line to separate two elements on a slide, or draw a line with an arrow to point to an important part of a chart. The rectangles and ovals can be used to draw boxes or frames around important slide objects. Figure 15-1 shows a chart with an oval and a line with an arrow enhancing its main point.

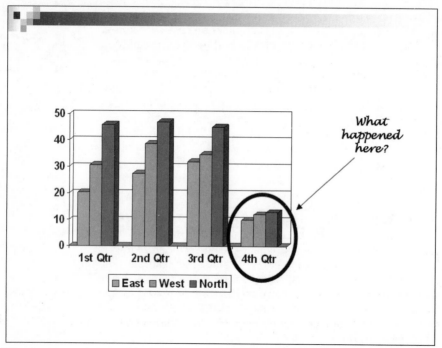

Figure 15-1: You can use simple lines and shapes to accentuate the main point of a slide.

Drawing Lines and Arrows

Let's start with something simple: a line. To draw a line on a slide, do the following:

1. Display the slide you want to draw on.

2. Click the Line button on the Drawing toolbar. The mouse pointer changes to a crosshair.

3. Position the mouse pointer where you want to begin the line and hold down the left mouse button. Drag to the desired end point of the line; then release the mouse button. Figure 15-2 shows a line being drawn.

Expert Tip To draw multiple lines, double-click the Line button on the Drawing toolbar. The mouse pointer will remain charged with the Line feature until you single-click the Line button again to toggle it off.

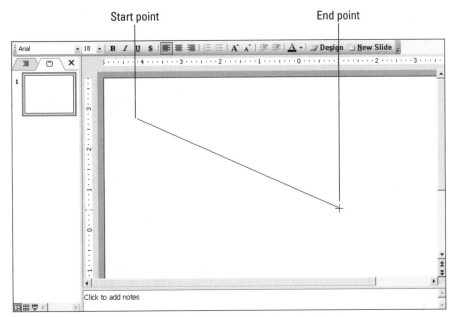

Figure 15-2: A line being drawn.

An *arrow* is the same as a line except there's an arrowhead on one or both ends. You can use the Arrow button instead of the Line button to draw a line with the default arrowhead on one end (the "ending" end), or you can convert a regular line to an arrow by changing its properties.

In earlier chapters you learned about formatting objects, and lines work the same way. A line has no fill — only a border. Therefore, to modify the properties of a line, you modify its border.

A line has the following attributes that you can change:

> ✦ **Line Color:** As with all other objects, you can choose a color placeholder from the color scheme or a specific color.

> ✦ **Line Style:** The number and type of smaller lines that comprise the line. For example, a line might be comprised of three small lines, with the center one slightly thicker than the other two. Or it might be a double or single line.

> ✦ **Dash Style:** The spacing and shape of the dashes in the line (or its quality of being solid, without dashes of any kind).

✦ **Line Weight:** The overall thickness of the line, measured in points. (Each point is 1/72 of an inch.)

✦ **Arrow Style:** The presence or absence of an arrow at one or both ends of the line, and the arrow's size and shape.

You can choose most of these attributes from the Drawing toolbar buttons, pointed out in Figure 15-3.

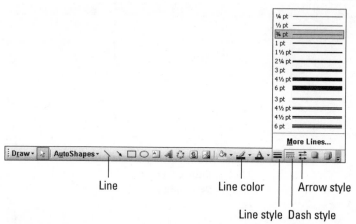

Line   Line color   Arrow style

Line style Dash style

Figure 15-3: You can set some line properties from the Drawing toolbar.

Each of the buttons (Line Style, Line Color, and Dash Style) has a limited array of choices, however. To access the full array of choices, choose Format ➪ AutoShape when the line is selected and make further choices on the Colors and Lines tab, shown in Figure 15-4. Another way to open this dialog box is to select the More command on one of the button's menus. For example, in Figure 15-3, on the Line Style menu, you can choose More Lines.

Note   There is no separate button for Line Weight on the Drawing toolbar. The Line Style list contains both line styles and line weights. However, in the Format AutoShape dialog box, they are separate.

Note   The Format dialog boxes for all drawn objects are titled Format AutoShape, because in a generic sense all drawn objects are AutoShapes.

Fill is not applicable to lines   Line formatting

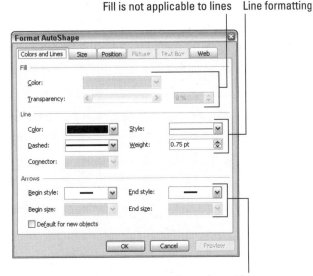

Arrow formatting

Figure 15-4: A fuller array of line formatting choices is available through the Format AutoShape dialog box.

Drawing Rectangles and Ovals

The procedure is the same for each of these tools, although it may take a bit of practice to master them:

1. Display the slide you want to draw on.

2. Click the Oval or Rectangle button on the Drawing toolbar. The mouse pointer changes to a crosshair.

Expert Tip   If you double-click instead of clicking in Step 2, the tool will remain active after drawing the shape so you can draw additional shapes of the same type without re-clicking the button again. Click the tool again to turn it off.

3. *(Optional)* If you want a perfect circle or square, hold down the Shift key.

4. Position the mouse pointer where you want to begin the shape and hold down the left mouse button. Drag to the desired end point; then release the mouse button. Figure 15-5 shows a rectangle being drawn.

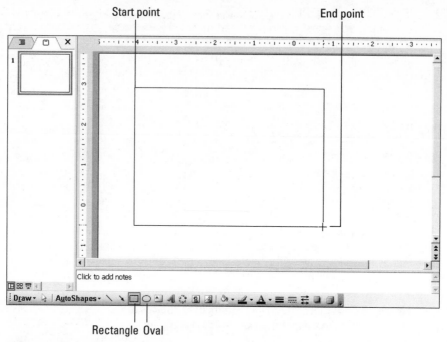

Figure 15-5: Drawing a rectangle.

Drawn shapes are automatically filled with the color designated for Fills in the color scheme (the fifth color in the scheme), and automatically receive a 0.75-point border using the color designed for Text and Lines (the second color in the scheme). See Figure 15-6. You can choose any fill or line color for them, just as you choose colors for lines and other objects. Refer to Chapter 12.

Figure 15-6: Default colors for drawn shapes.

Expert Tip If you have formatted a certain shape the way you want all future shapes to be, you can set the AutoShape defaults to match it. For example, suppose you want all shapes to have a thick green border and be colored yellow. You could format one shape that way and then set that as the default. To set the default, click the Draw button on the Drawing toolbar and choose Set AutoShape Defaults.

Drawing an AutoShape

AutoShapes are pre-drawn shapes that function just like the lines and shapes that you draw with the regular drawing tools. The only difference is their complexity. They're great for people who want shapes like hearts and starbursts but aren't coordinated enough to draw them (or simply don't have the time).

There are several categories of AutoShapes, including Lines, Connectors, Basic Shapes, and so on. Table 15-1 shows each category's menu and explains a bit about how each might be useful.

Table 15-1		
Microsoft Office AutoShapes		
Menu	*Name*	*Description*
	Lines	Freeform shapes or lines, or straight lines, with or without arrows. Use these to draw freehand or to call attention to certain objects.
	Connectors	Flow charting connectors that help create relationship lines between other objects.
	Basic Shapes	A variety of geometric shapes and simple symbols.

Continued

Table 15-1 *(continued)*

Menu	Name	Description
	Block Arrows	Arrows that are thicker than just lines, useful for flow charting or to call attention to another object. These arrows use both fill and border colors, unlike arrows created from lines.
	Flowchart	Standard flowchart symbols.
	Stars and Banners	Lively starbursts and swoops for calling attention. Place text inside them for extra impact.
	Callouts	Thought and speech bubbles for cartoons and explanatory boxes.
	Action Buttons	Buttons useful for moving from slide to slide in a user-interactive presentation.

To place an AutoShape, follow these steps:

1. Display the slide you want to place the AutoShape on.

2. Click the AutoShape button on the Drawing toolbar. A menu of AutoShapes appears.

3. Point to a category that you want to look at (for example, Block Arrows). A menu of shapes appears. See Figure 15-7.

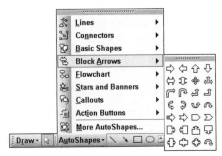

Figure 15-7: Choose an AutoShape from the AutoShapes menu.

4. Click the shape you want. Your mouse pointer turns into a crosshair.

5. Drag on the slide to draw a box where you want the shape to appear. You see the shape as you drag. When you are satisfied with it, release the mouse button.

If you choose the wrong shape, it's easier just to delete the shape and start over if you have not applied any special formatting to it. If you have formatted the shape already, you may find it easier to change the shape rather than re-create it. To do so, open the Draw menu (from the Draw button on the Drawing toolbar), choose Change AutoShape, and then select a new shape from the submenu, just as you chose the original AutoShape.

In addition, don't overlook the More AutoShapes command at the bottom of the AutoShapes menu. This opens the Clip Organizer task pane, with the clip art pieces that are considered AutoShapes. (And speaking of that, see the section "Modifying Clip Art as an AutoShape Drawing" later in this chapter.) Some of the AutoShapes included in the Clip Organizer include those that you can use for office space planning, such as sofas, desks, computers, and so on (see Figure 15-8).

Note There's a fine line between clip art and an AutoShape; both are vector graphics. Therefore you may see them mixed together somewhat in certain areas of Office applications.

Figure 15-8: Choosing More AutoShapes opens the Clip Organizer and displays all clips that are also AutoShapes.

Expert Tip There is also a Freeform AutoShape, which lets you draw your own shapes out of line segments. You'll find it in the Lines category.

Modifying AutoShapes

The following sections describe some formatting options that enable you to change the appearance and positioning of AutoShapes (including lines, rectangles, and ovals).

Rotating an AutoShape

To rotate a shape 90 degrees to the left or right, choose Draw ➪ Rotate or Flip and then Rotate Left or Rotate Right. To flip a shape vertically or horizontally, choose Draw ➪ Rotate or Flip and then Flip Horizontal or Flip Vertical. See Figure 15-9. You can apply these modifications one after the other, so, for example, you could rotate a shape 180 degrees (90 plus 90) and then flip it.

You can also free-rotate a shape if you need a rotation other than 90 degrees or a multiple of 90 degrees. To free-rotate a shape, follow these steps:

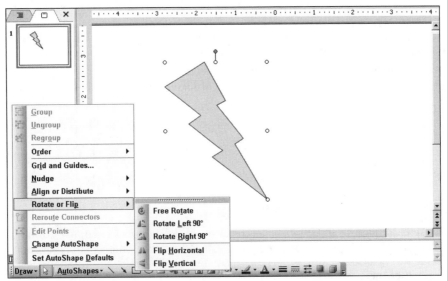

Figure 15-9: Rotate or flip a shape or line with the commands on the Draw menu.

1. Select the object. In addition to the white selection handles, there will also be a green circle at the top. This is the rotation handle.

2. Drag the rotation handle to the right or left to rotate the object as desired. See Figure 15-10. Holding down the Shift key while rotating will constrain the rotation to 15° increments.

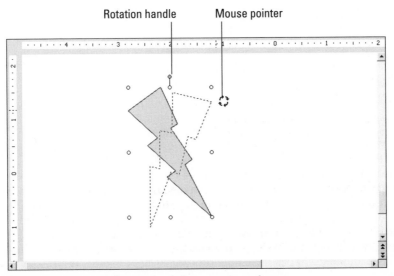

Figure 15-10: Drag the green circle to rotate a shape.

Flipping an AutoShape

Flipping an object changes it into a mirror image of itself, either vertically or horizontally. This can be useful if you need to use the same object twice or more on the same slide at different orientations. For example, you might flip copies of an AutoShape arrow so that each points toward the center of the slide. To flip an object, follow these steps:

1. Select the object.

2. Choose Draw ➪ Rotate or Flip ➪ Flip Horizontal or Flip Vertical. The object is flipped.

Stretching an AutoShape

Most AutoShapes can be twisted, stretched, and otherwise manipulated to meet any special needs you might have for them. Figure 15-11 shows some examples of what you can do to a curved arrow, for instance. The original AutoShape is in the top-left corner.

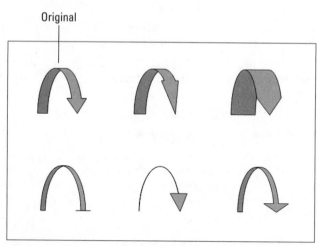

Figure 15-11: Some examples of how stretching an AutoShape can alter its appearance.

The key is in the adjustment handles on the shape. Most AutoShapes have at least one yellow diamond on them. You can drag the yellow diamond to modify the shape. When you drag the diamond, you modify the thickness and size of the shape. For example, on a parallelogram you can change the amount of tilt, or on a block arrow you can change the thickness of the arrow shaft and the height of the arrowhead. Some shapes have only one adjustment handle; others have two or three. It depends on the type of shape and in what ways it can be modified. In Figure 15-12, the shape shown has two diamonds, and one of them is being dragged.

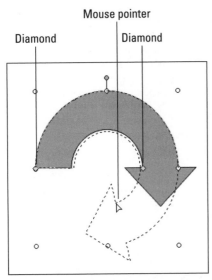

Figure 15-12: To stretch an AutoShape, drag a yellow diamond.

Suggested Uses for AutoShapes

Many times you will want to create multiple drawn objects and then arrange and stack them to create some more complex picture. If you read Chapter 12, and if you have been keeping up in this chapter so far, you already have all of the skills you need to do this kind of artwork. You simply place the basic shapes and then stretch, rotate, resize, recolor, and otherwise modify them to create the drawing. Then group them (as in Chapter 12) to create a single object.

Need a little inspiration to get you started? Try these ideas:

✦ Create a flow chart using the Flowchart AutoShapes. Connect the shapes with Connectors AutoShapes.

✦ Create your own complex math formulas by typing numbers in small text boxes and placing bracket AutoShapes (found on the Basic Shapes submenu) around the parts that should be bracketed.

✦ Create a No sign (no smoking, no cats, no fear, or whatever) by typing text in a text box or placing clip art and then placing the AutoShape that shows a circle with a line through it (one of the Basic Shapes). Then group the text box and the AutoShape so they form a single object. See Figure 15-13.

Figure 15-13: You can place an AutoShape on top of clip art like this.

✦ Fill an AutoShape with a photo so the shape becomes a picture frame, as you saw in Chapter 12. (Use the Fill Effects command on the Fill Color button's menu.)

✦ Place Up or Down block arrows beside bullet points to indicate which are good news and which are bad news.

✦ Use the Callouts AutoShapes option to place thought or speech bubbles over cartoon characters or to label technical drawings.

✦ Place Action Buttons (yes, they're a type of AutoShape) on the Slide Master of a user-interactive presentation to assist with navigation. See Chapter 29 for details.

Placing WordArt

All of the Office 2003 applications have access to a program called WordArt that helps you create stylized, interesting-looking text. You can take a standard bit of text, such as your company name, and bend, squeeze, and tilt it into an unusual form that will catch the audience's attention. Figure 15-14 shows some WordArt samples.

Caution   Use WordArt sparingly. It can add interest to your text in small quantities, but if you use it too frequently it can be annoying and distracting.

Figure 15-14: Here are some examples of what you can do with WordArt.

You can create a piece of WordArt easily using some standard settings and then refine it to be exactly what you want. Follow these steps to create some WordArt:

1. Display the slide you want to place the WordArt on.

2. Click the WordArt button on the Drawing toolbar. The WordArt Gallery dialog box appears. See Figure 15-15.

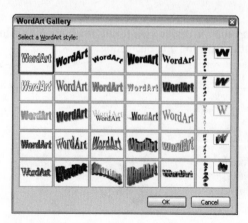

Figure 15-15: Choose an initial design from the WordArt Gallery.

3. Click one of the gallery designs. If there isn't one that matches exactly what you want, pick something similar; you can modify it later.

4. Click OK. The Edit WordArt Text dialog box appears. See Figure 15-16.

Figure 15-16: Type the text you want to use in your WordArt.

5. Type the text you want in the text box.

6. Choose a different Font and Size if needed.

7. If you want the text to be bold or italic, click the Bold and/or Italic button.

 Note   WordArt works best with a simple font like Arial. It creates its own special effect, so you do not need to start with a fancy font.

8. Click OK when you're done. The finished WordArt appears on the slide. See Figure 15-17.

Figure 15-17: The finished WordArt object appears on the slide.

Modifying WordArt

Once you have placed the WordArt, you can perform almost any modification on it that you can imagine. You can change the wording, change the shape, change the color, size, texture, and so on. You have seen many of these modifications before when you've worked with other objects; others are brand new.

First, review some of the modifications you already know how to do:

✦ Drag the yellow diamond(s) to alter the shape.

✦ Drag the green handle to rotate the object.

✦ Use the Fill Color button to change the front surface of the WordArt. You can also use the Fill Effects such as gradients, patterns, textures, and picture fills. See Chapter 12.

✦ Use the Line Color button to choose an outline color for the letters. Use the Line Style and Dash Style buttons, too, if you need to fine-tune the outline.

✦ Click the 3D button and choose a 3D effect. You can also choose 3D Settings to open the 3D toolbar (which you learned about in Chapter 12), and from there you can change the color of the sides of the letters.

✦ Click the Shadow button and choose a Shadow effect. You can also click the Shadow Settings button to open the Shadow Settings toolbar. Again, see Chapter 12 for details.

The WordArt toolbar appears whenever you select a piece of WordArt, and it contains extra buttons for other modifications you can perform. Table 15-2 lists the buttons on the WordArt toolbar.

Table 15-2
WordArt Toolbar Buttons

Icon	Name	Description
4A	Insert WordArt	Opens the WordArt Gallery dialog box so you can create an additional WordArt object.
Edit Text...	WordArt Edit Text	Reopens the Edit WordArt Text dialog box for the current WordArt object.
	WordArt Gallery	Reopens the WordArt Gallery dialog box for the current WordArt object.
	Format WordArt	Opens the Format WordArt dialog box.
A	WordArt Shape	Opens a pop-up array of shapes you can choose for your WordArt.
Aa	WordArt Same Letter Heights	Makes all the letters the same height.
Ab bd	WordArt Vertical Text	Toggles between vertical and horizontal text orientation.
≡	WordArt Alignment	Opens a shortcut menu of alignments (centered, right-aligned, and so on).
AV	WordArt Character Spacing	Changes the spacing between letters (normal, loose, tight, and so on).

One of the most important modifications you can make through the WordArt toolbar is to change the WordArt shape. In Figure 15-18, for example, the shape is being changed to Deflate Bottom. You can find out the names of the various shapes by pointing at them so that a ScreenTip appears showing the name.

Deflate Bottom shape is selected

Figure 15-18: Changing the shape of a piece of WordArt.

Experiment with the WordArt toolbar buttons on your own. You will also have an opportunity to practice them in the Project Lab in Chapter 19.

Summary

In this chapter, you expanded your graphics knowledge by learning how to draw your own lines and shapes and how to place AutoShapes. You also learned how to design your own WordArt.

Graphics can be a lot of fun in PowerPoint, but don't get so carried away with them that you forget the main point of your presentation — to communicate information. In the next chapter, you look at graphs, a type of picture that communicates numeric data very well.

✦   ✦   ✦

Working with Charts

Many times when you include a chart in PowerPoint, that chart already exists in some other application. For example, you might have an Excel workbook that contains some charts you want to use in PowerPoint. This situation is discussed at the end of this chapter and also in Chapter 18.

However, there may be times when you need to whip up a quick chart that has no external source, and PowerPoint's charting tool is perfect for that purpose. It has many of the features of the more sophisticated charting tools of Excel, but you don't have to leave PowerPoint in order to use them. In this chapter, you see how to create, modify, and format charts in PowerPoint.

Note

What's the difference between a chart and a graph? Some purists will tell you that a chart is either a table or a pie chart, whereas a graph is a chart that plots data points on two axes (for example, a bar chart). However, Microsoft Graph does not make this distinction, and neither do I in this book. I use the term "chart" in this book for either kind.

Starting a New Chart

The main difficulty with creating a chart in a non-spreadsheet application like PowerPoint is that there is no data table from which to pull the numbers. Therefore, PowerPoint creates charts in a special chart module that includes a data table. By default it contains sample data, which you can replace with your own data. This Chart module, called Microsoft Graph, is fully integrated with the PowerPoint window, so that when a chart is selected its tools and menus appear in PowerPoint. When you click away from a chart to deselect it, the menus and buttons go back to the normal PowerPoint ones.

You can place a new chart on a slide in two ways: you can use a chart placeholder from an AutoLayout, or you can place one manually.

If you are using a placeholder, just double-click it. If you are placing a chart manually, follow these steps:

1. Display the slide where you want to manually place a chart.

2. Click the Insert Chart button on the Standard toolbar, or select Insert ⇨ Chart.

When you do so, the Chart module opens within PowerPoint. You continue to see your PowerPoint slide, but the Standard toolbar's buttons change, and a sample chart and datasheet appear. See Figure 16-1.

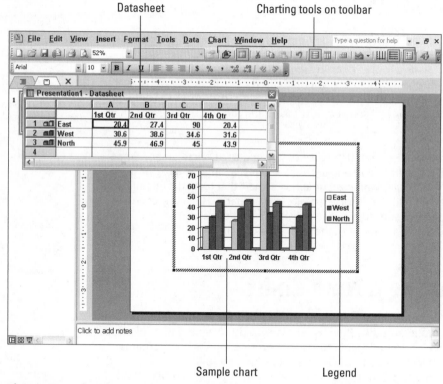

Figure 16-1: The Chart module in PowerPoint changes the buttons and menus to incorporate its features.

Caution When you first start the Chart module, it may move the Formatting toolbar up to the same line as the Standard one, even if you have set them to be on separate lines in PowerPoint. As I mentioned in Chapter 1, this is not the optimal arrangement because you can't see all the tools. To move the Formatting toolbar back below the Standard one, just drag it down there, or click the down arrow at the right end of a toolbar and choose Show Buttons on Two Rows.

The *datasheet* contains the data that comprises the chart. By default are three *data series* of sample data—East, West, and North. Each of them has a separate color code, which is shown in the *legend*. Each series' results are shown over time. The column headings are the times (1st Qtr, 2nd Qtr, and so on).

The first time you create a chart, you may want to make up some dummy data, just for practice, or you may want to stick with the sample data provided until you become comfortable. That way, you can experiment without fear of messing up your real work. There is a lot to learn about creating and modifying charts in PowerPoint!

To create your first chart, just change the data on the datasheet to match what you want to display on your chart. You can make up some sample data, as I've done in Figure 16-2, or you can use data for an actual chart you need in your presentation. Don't forget to change the row and column headings, too. You can add rows or columns as needed by simply typing into new cells, or delete rows or columns by clicking on a cell and then pressing Delete to clear it. You can also resize the Datasheet window if you need to, so you can see all your data at once.

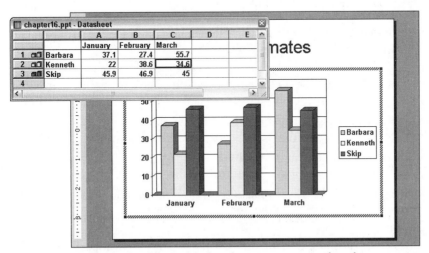

Figure 16-2: Change the data in the datasheet to your own data that you want to plot on a chart.

Note At any point, you can return to your PowerPoint presentation by clicking anywhere outside of the chart on the slide. Your PowerPoint controls reappear. To edit the chart again, double-click it to reopen the Chart controls.

When the Chart module is running, the datasheet is usually displayed. If you need to modify the datasheet later but don't see it, click the View Datasheet button on the Standard toolbar.

Expert Tip If you delete a column or row by selecting individual cells and pressing Delete to clear them, the empty space for them will remain in the chart. To completely remove a row or column from the data range, select the row or column by clicking on its header (letter for column; number for row) and pressing Delete.

Changing the Chart Type

The default chart is a column chart, shown in Figures 16-1 and 16-2. There are lots of alternative chart types to choose from, however. Not all of them will be appropriate for your data, of course, but you may be surprised at the different spin on the message that a different chart type presents.

Caution Many chart types come in both 2D and 3D models. You choose which look is most appropriate for your presentation. Try to be consistent, however. It looks nicer to stick with all 2D or all 3D charts rather than mixing the types in a presentation.

Here are some of the types available:

✦ **Bar and column.** A column chart, shown in Figures 16-1 and 16-2, plots data with vertical columns. A bar chart is the same thing except the bars are horizontal.

✦ **Area and surface.** These charts convey the same information as column charts, but the area between the bars is filled in.

✦ **Line.** Line charts convey the same information as column charts, but instead of the bars, a line or ribbon runs where the tops of the bars would be.

✦ **3D cones, cylinders, and pyramids.** These charts are just like columns except the bars have different, more interesting shapes.

✦ **Pie and doughnut.** These charts show how various parts relate to a whole, rather than showcasing individual number values.

✦ **Bubble and scatter.** These charts show each bit of data as a point (or a bubble) on a grid and are useful for spotting trends among lots of data points.

✦ **Radar.** This is a special-purpose chart that plots points on axes radiating from a center point. Most business presenters never use this type of chart.

Figures 16-3 through 16-5 show some examples of various chart types.

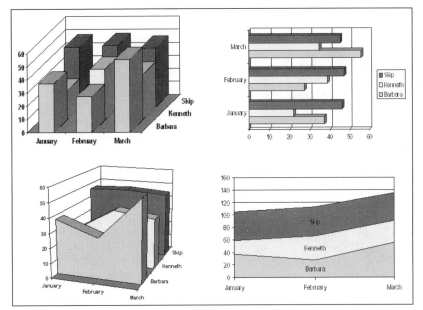

Figure 16-3: Types of charts (clockwise from upper-left): 3D column, 3D clustered bar, 2D area, and 3D area.

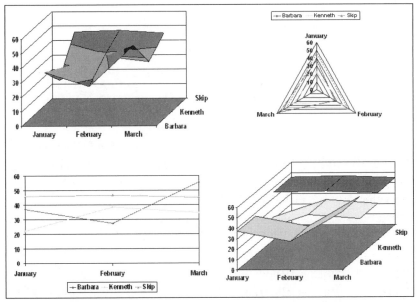

Figure 16-4: Types of charts (clockwise from upper-left): surface, radar, 3D line, and 2D line.

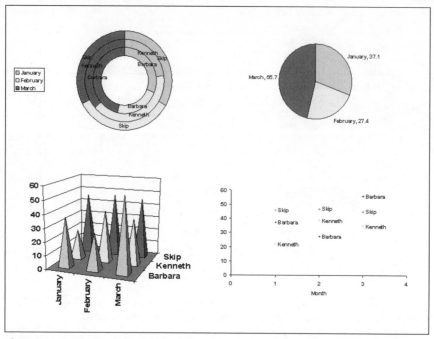

Figure 16-5: Types of charts (clockwise from upper-left): doughnut, pie, scatter, and pyramid.

Choosing a standard chart type

There are several ways to change the chart type. The easiest method is to use the drop-down Chart Type list on the Standard toolbar. Unfortunately, it does not provide access to all of the types, but it can be useful if you want one of the types it provides.

1. Double-click the chart to redisplay the Chart tools and menus, if needed.

2. Click the down-arrow next to the Chart Type button to open its drop-down list. See Figure 16-6.

3. Click the chart type you want.

The more powerful way to change the chart type is with the Chart Type dialog box. Follow these steps:

1. Choose Chart ➪ Chart Type. This opens the Chart Type dialog box, shown in Figure 16-7. (You can also right-click the chart and choose Chart Type.)

2. In the Chart Type dialog box, click one of the chart types on the Chart Type list. The available subtypes appear in the pane to the right. For example, if

you choose Column, as shown in Figure 16-7, you can choose from among seven subtypes.

3. Click the subtype you want.

4. If you want to see how your data will look with that type and subtype, click and hold the Press and Hold to View Sample button.

5. When you are satisfied with the chart type you've selected, click OK.

Expert Tip The default chart type, as you have seen, is Column. If you prefer a different chart type to be the default, make your selection in the Chart Types dialog box and then click the Set as Default Chart button before you click OK in Step 5. This can save you time because you won't have to change the type of each chart that you create. This setting applies to your PC's installed copy of PowerPoint, not to the presentation file.

Figure 16-6: You can change to one of the most common chart types with the toolbar button's list of types.

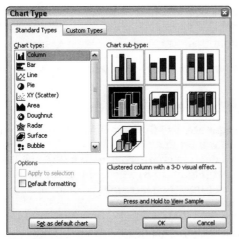

Figure 16-7: You can choose from every available chart type and subtype through this dialog box.

Choosing a custom chart type

You may have noticed that there is a second tab in the Chart Type dialog box: Custom Types. When you click that tab (see Figure 16-8), a list of predesigned chart formats/types appears. You can select one of these custom types as a shortcut for choosing a particular chart type and formatting it in a certain way. For example, Figure 16-8 shows Tubes selected, and you can see an example of it in the Sample area. You could re-create this custom chart type manually with a combination of chart type and chart formatting commands, but it is much easier simply to apply the custom type from this list and then tweak it to create the look you want.

Making a selection on the Custom Types tab overrides any selection you have made on the Standard Types tab, and vice versa. Microsoft Graph goes with whatever you have most recently selected when you click OK.

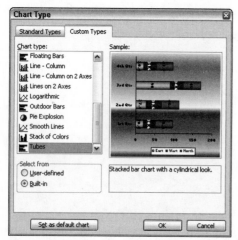

Figure 16-8: You can choose a custom chart type from the Custom Types tab.

Creating your own custom chart types

Here's a great time-saver if you frequently use the same formatting for charts. You can set up a chart just the way you want it in terms of type and formatting, and then define that chart's design as a custom chart. The custom chart will then be available from the Custom Types list (Figure 16-8) when you select the User-Defined option. (You learn more about chart formatting later in this chapter, so you may wish to skip this now and come back to it later.)

To create a custom chart type, follow these steps:

1. Format a chart exactly the way you want the custom chart type to be, and double-click it to select it and to display the Chart tools.

2. Choose Chart ➪ Chart Type, opening the Chart Type dialog box.

3. Click the Custom Types tab, and then click the User-Defined option.

4. Click the Add button. The Add Custom Chart Type dialog box opens. See Figure 16-9.

5. Enter a name and description for the new chart type, and then click OK. The new chart appears on the list of user-defined custom charts.

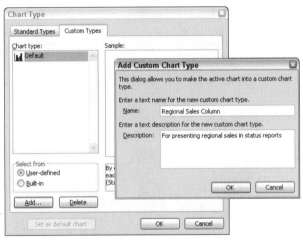

Figure 16-9: Create your own custom chart types using an existing chart as an example.

Plotting by Rows versus by Columns

By default, the rows of the datasheet form the data series. But if you want, you can switch that around so that the columns form the series. Figures 16-10 and 16-11 show the same chart plotted both ways so you can see the difference.

To switch back and forth between plotting by rows and by columns, click the By Row or By Column buttons on the Standard toolbar.

Note What does the term *data series* mean? Take a look at Figures 16-10 and 16-11. Notice that there is a legend next to each chart that shows what each color (or shade of gray) represents. Each of those colors, and the label associated with it, is a series. Depending on the chart, it may be referred to as either the Y or Z axis. The other variable (the one that is not the series) is plotted on the chart's horizontal (X) axis.

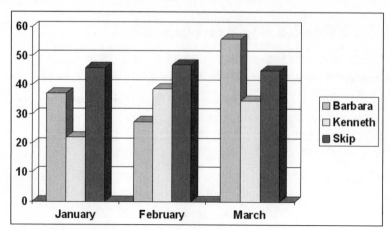

Figure 16-10: The data series are the people's names.

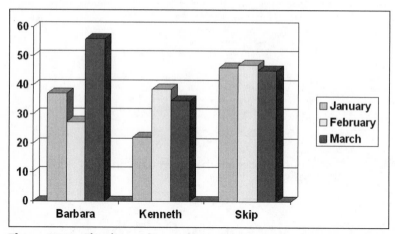

Figure 16-11: The data series are the months.

Expert Tip   A chart can carry a very different message when arranged by rows versus by columns. For example, in Figure 16-10, the chart compares the performance of the people against one another for each month. The message here is competition — which person did the best? Contrast this to Figure 16-11, where the series are the months. Here, you're invited to compare one month to another for each person. The overriding message here is time — which was each person's personal best month? It's easy to see how the same data can convey very different messages; make sure that you pick the arrangement that tells the story you want to tell in your presentation.

Adding and Removing Data Series

You may decide after you have created your chart that you need to use more or less data. Perhaps you want to exclude one of the months or add another salesperson. To add or remove a data series, simply edit the datasheet. To do so, follow these steps:

1. Double-click the chart in PowerPoint to open the Chart tools.

2. If the datasheet does not appear, click the View Datasheet button.

3. On the datasheet, add information in another row and/or another column. Don't forget to include labels in the first cell of the row or column. See Figure 16-12.

4. If you need to delete a row or column, select it by clicking its row number or column letter and then press the Delete key on your keyboard.

5. When you are finished editing the datasheet, click the slide (outside of the chart area) to return to PowerPoint.

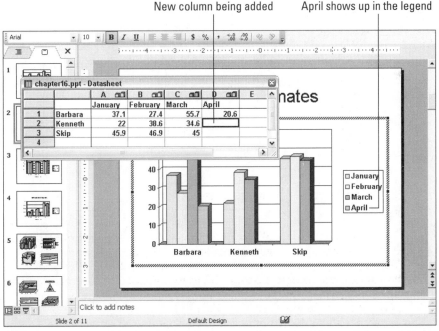

Figure 16-12: Type data into an empty row or column to add more information to the chart.

Displaying, Hiding, and Repositioning the Legend

The legend, as I mentioned before, is the little box that sits to the side of the chart (or above or below it sometimes). It provides the key to what the different colors or patterns mean. Depending on the chart type and the labels in use, you may not find the legend useful. If it is not useful for the chart you are working on, you can turn it off by clicking the Legend button on the Standard toolbar. Turning off the legend makes more room for the chart, and it grows to fill the available space. See Figure 16-13. You simply click the Legend button again to turn it back on, if needed.

Caution   Hiding the legend is not a good idea if you have more than one series in your chart, because the legend is instrumental in helping people decipher which series is which. However, if you have only one series, as in Figure 16-13, a legend might not be useful.

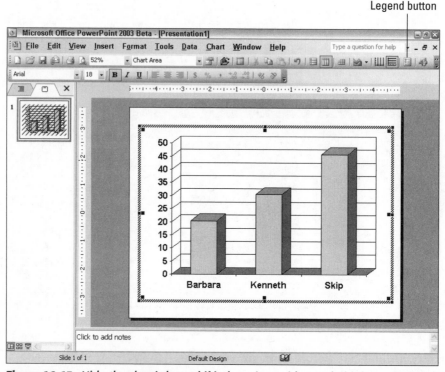

Legend button

Figure 16-13: Hide the chart's legend if it doesn't provide needed information, and allow more room for your chart.

By default, the legend appears to the right of the chart, but you can place it somewhere else if you prefer. To change the legend's position, follow these steps:

1. Choose Chart ⇨ Chart Options.

2. Click the Legend tab. If the Show Legend check box is not already marked, mark it.

3. Select the option representing the desired position (for example, Top, Bottom, Right, and so on). See Figure 16-14.

Note   The controls on the Placement tab refer to the legend's position in relation to the chart, not to the legend text's position within the legend box.

4. Click OK.

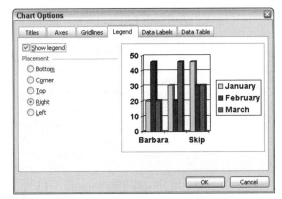

Figure 16-14: Change the legend's position in relation to the chart.

Note   Don't worry if the text looks too big in the sample area or if some text is cut off, as in Figure 16-14. It will straighten itself out when you close the dialog box.

You can also format the legend, just as you can format any other part of the chart. This is covered later in this chapter in detail, but if you want to experiment on your own, try dragging the selection handles for the legend's border to resize it and/or using the Font controls on the toolbar to change its font. You can also right-click it and choose Format Legend from the shortcut menu, or drag the legend where you want it.

Adding a Data Table

Sometimes the chart tells the full story that you want to tell, but other times the audience may benefit from seeing the actual numbers on which the chart is built. In those cases, it's a good idea to include the data table with the chart. (A data table contains the same information that appears on the datasheet.)

To display the data table with a chart, click the Data Table button on the Standard toolbar, as shown in Figure 16-15. (If you don't see the Data Table button, make sure you have double-clicked the chart.) To turn it off, click the Data Table button again.

Note Sometimes PowerPoint's Chart tool doesn't do a very good job of sizing the fonts in the data table appropriately. If the data table's lettering looks too big, you can adjust it. Just right-click the data table and choose Format Data Table. Then, on the Font tab of the dialog box that appears, choose a different font size.

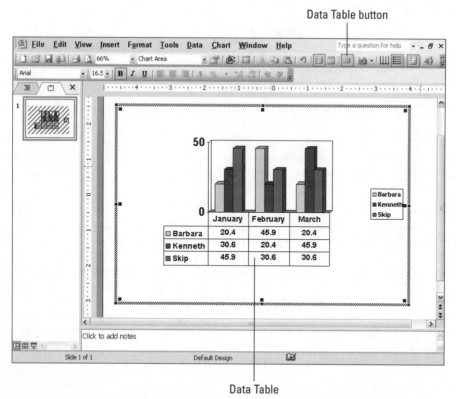

Data Table button

Data Table

Figure 16-15: Use a data table to show the audience the numbers that formed the chart.

Formatting the Chart

In the following sections, you learn about chart formatting. There is so much you can do to a chart that the subject could easily take up its own chapter! You can resize a chart, just like any other object, and you can also change fonts; change the colors and shading of bars, lines, or pie slices; use different background colors; change the 3D angle; and much more.

Understanding chart elements

Before you can learn how to format the parts of a chart, you need to know what those parts are. So far in this chapter, the parts haven't been a big deal — the chart pretty much hung together as a whole. But if you need to change, for example, the Y axis, you had better find out exactly where that is.

Figure 16-16 shows the parts of a typical chart. Most are fairly self-explanatory, but a few require a bit of extra explanation:

✦ The *walls* are the areas behind the chart. They may or may not include gridlines. On a 3D chart, there may be a side wall as well as a back one. You can color the walls or make them transparent.

✦ The *plot area* is the inner frame of the whole chart picture. It contains the chart itself.

✦ The *chart area* is the outer frame. It contains the plot area as well as the legend and data table if either of these elements is used.

✦ The *category axis* is usually the horizontal, or X, axis. It lists the categories that the series are plotted against.

✦ The *value axis* is usually the vertical, or Y, axis. It shows the numbers that the bars (or whatever) reach up to. Depending on the chart, this might be the Z axis instead; some charts have all three, whereas others have X plus either Y or Z.

 Expert Tip   Notice in Figure 16-16 the words Plot Area on the toolbar. This is a drop-down list from which you can select various parts of the chart rather than clicking on them if you prefer.

Another important distinction to be made when formatting is between a data series and a data point. A data series is all the bars, columns, and so on, of a certain color. For example, in Figure 16-16, there are three data series (one for each of the three people listed in the legend), each consisting of three bars. A data point is an individual piece of data (represented by an individual bar in Figure 16-16). You can format either of them. When you click once on a bar, the entire data series becomes selected. You can tell because a small square appears on each bar in the series and if you right-click, a Format Data Series command will appear on the shortcut menu. If you then click again on one of the bars in that data series, that individual bar will become selected, and the right-click menu will issue a Format Data Point command instead. See Figure 16-17.

Side Wall   Back Wall   Plot Area

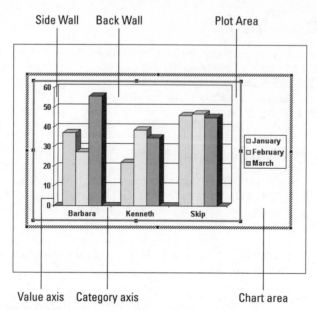

Value axis   Category axis   Chart area

Figure 16-16: You can change the appearance of each part of the chart individually.

All the bars of the same color are a data series.

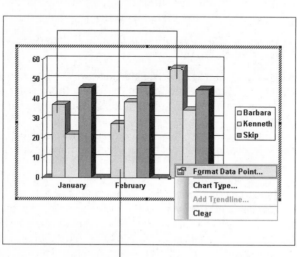

A single bar is a data point.

Figure 16-17: Understand the difference between a data series and a data point.

Adding titles and axis labels

Most of the time, when you place a chart on a slide, that slide has its own title, so the chart itself does not need a separate title. However, if you have more on the slide than just the chart, it might be useful to have some text over the top of the chart indicating why it's there. A title on the chart itself might also be useful if you plan to copy that chart to another application, such as Word.

Besides an overall title for the chart, you can also add labels to each axis to describe the unit of measurement it shows (for example, *Thousands* or *Salespeople*). Figure 16-18 shows a chart with axis labels for both the vertical and horizontal axes.

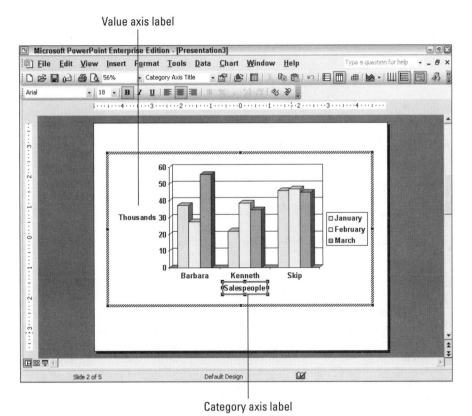

Figure 16-18: Axis labels can help explain a chart's message more clearly.

To work with titles, follow these steps:

1. With the chart selected in Microsoft Graph, select Chart ⇨ Chart Options. Or, you can right-click the Chart area and choose Chart Options from the shortcut menu. The Chart Options dialog box appears.

2. Click the Titles tab if it is not already displayed.

3. Enter a title for the chart in the Chart Title text box. See Figure 16-19.

4. Enter a title for the horizontal axis in the Category (X) Axis field.

5. Enter a title for the vertical axis in the Value (Z) Axis field. (For an explanation of why it's Z rather than Y, see the note at the end of these steps.) Again, don't worry if the sample area doesn't look quite right; the font sizes are sometimes off in the sample, as in Figure 16-19, but are fine on the actual chart.

6. Click OK.

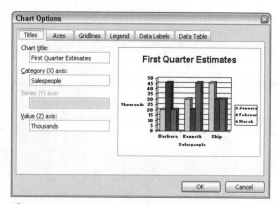

Figure 16-19: Enter the titles and labels you want to use.

Note   If you have taken geometry, you are probably used to calling the horizontal axis of a chart X and the vertical axis Y. That's the terminology I use in this book, too. However, on some 3D charts, the vertical axis is called Z in some dialog boxes, and the axis that runs back to front is called Y. In most charts, there is nothing plotted on the back-to-front axis, so you only deal with vertical and horizontal axes. Don't let the fact that the vertical one is called Z in some dialog boxes confuse you; it's really your old familiar vertical (Y) axis.

When you add titles, you take away from the available space for the plot area in the chart frame. The chart in the plot area appears smaller after you add titles because the Chart tool shrinks it so that it and the added titles and labels all fit in the chart frame. One way to minimize the space taken up by axis labels is to set them in a smaller font or, in the case of the Y-axis label, to rotate the text so it runs parallel to the axis. To learn how to format titles and labels, see the following section.

Formatting titles and labels

Once you have a title or label on your chart, you can change its size, orientation, and font. Just right-click the title you want to format and choose Format Chart Title (or whatever kind of title it is; an axis's label is called Axis Title, for example). The Format Axis Title (or Format Chart Title) dialog box appears.

There are three tabs in this dialog box: Patterns, Font, and Alignment. If you see only one tab (Font) in the dialog box, you have right-clicked the text itself rather than the text box. Close the dialog box and then click beside the text, rather than right on it, to select the text box. Then right-click the text box's frame. If you see three tabs in the dialog box, you know you've done it right.

On the Patterns tab, shown in Figure 16-20, you can set a background color for the area behind the text. (Remember, all text sits in a text box on a slide, and each text box can have background formatting.) To place a border around the text box that contains the label, click the Custom option and then choose a line style, color, and weight. To use a background fill behind the text, click one of the colored squares in the Area part of the dialog box, or click the Fill Effects button to use fill effects, as you learned in Chapter 12.

On the Font tab, you can choose all the usual text effects that you learned about in Chapter 9: font, size, font style, underline, color, and so on. See Figure 16-21. You can also choose a background setting for your text in this box. If you set it to Transparent, whatever is behind the text box will show through as its background. If you choose Opaque, it will use its own color instead. The default (Automatic) is Opaque.

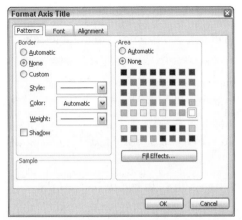

Figure 16-20: The Patterns tab controls the text box in which the title or label sits.

Expert Tip The Auto Scale check box in Figure 16-21 turns on/off the feature that resizes the text when you resize the text box or the chart area. It is on by default. You can turn this off if you want the text in the chart to be a certain size — for example, if you don't want the legend to automatically resize itself when you resize the plot area.

Caution Note that the automatic text boxes that are created when making chart titles as described are not resizable — they resize automatically. It's actually easier just to insert a text box by clicking the Text Box button on the Drawing toolbar; this gives you much better control over the text and the text boxes.

Figure 16-21: Use the Font tab to choose the typeface and its attributes.

Finally, the Alignment tab controls the way the text is aligned in its text box. You can set both vertical and horizontal alignment, just like you did in table cells in Chapter 9.

Note Vertical and horizontal alignments are usually a non-issue in a short label or title text box. The text box is usually exactly the right size to hold the text, so there is no way for the text to be aligned other than the way it is. Therefore, no matter what vertical and horizontal alignment you choose, the text looks pretty much the same. (The only exception might be in a box with a long string of text. The default alignment is centered.)

But the coolest feature on the Alignment tab, shown in Figure 16-22, is the Orientation control. With it, you can rotate the text to any angle. For example, you can rotate the label for the vertical axis to run parallel to that axis.

By default, all text starts out formatted horizontally, at 0 degrees of tilt. (Exception: some Y-axis titles default to vertical.) But it doesn't have to stay that way; you can rotate it to any number of degrees, from 1 to 359. (360 is a full circle, so 360 is the same as 0.) To rotate the text, drag the red diamond up or down. The word *Text* rotates as you drag it. In Figure 16-22, it is dragged all the way to the top, resulting in text that runs straight up. You can also type an angle measurement (for example, 90) in the Degrees text box instead of dragging the red diamond, if you prefer.

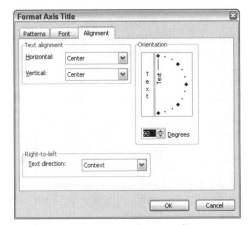

Figure 16-22: Change the text alignment and orientation on the Alignment tab.

Formatting the chart area

Your next task is to format the big picture: the *chart area*. The chart area is the big frame that contains the chart and all its accouterments: the legend, the data series, the data table (if present), the titles, and so on.

The chart area controls two important elements: the background of the chart frame, and the default font in the chart frame. You can override the chart frame's default font by formatting individual elements separately. To change them, follow these steps:

1. Point the mouse pointer at the area outside of the legend (if you have one), or slightly inside the chart frame. A screen tip should pop up reading Chart Area. If you see something different, move the mouse elsewhere until you see the tip.

2. Right-click and choose Format Chart Area from the shortcut menu that appears. The Format Chart Area dialog box appears.

3. Click the Patterns tab if it's not already displayed. Its controls look just like the ones you saw for a text box in Figure 16-20.

4. Change the chart area's border and/or background if desired.

5. Click the Font tab. These controls set the default font for the entire chart. (The controls look just like the ones you saw in Figure 16-21.) If you do not specify otherwise, all text in the chart will have the font you choose here.

6. Make your font selection.

7. Click OK.

Adjusting the axes

No, axes are not the tools that chop down trees. *Axes* is the plural of *axis*, and an axis is the side of the chart containing the measurements that your data is plotted against. For example, in Figure 16-23, the category axis (X, horizontal) contains the names of salespeople, and the value (Y) axis contains thousand dollar amounts (0 through 30).

There are a number of things you can do to an axis. The option with the biggest potential impact on the chart is changing the *scale*. The scale determines which numbers will form the start and end point of the axis line. For example, take a look at the chart in Figure 16-23. The bars are so close to one another in value that it is difficult to see the difference between them. Compare that to the same data shown in Figure 16-24, but with an adjusted scale. Because the scale is smaller, the differences appear more dramatic.

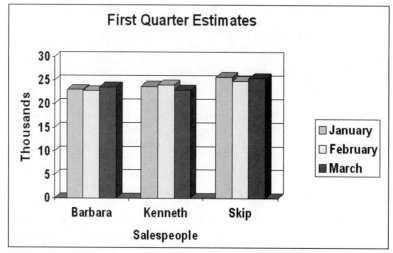

Figure 16-23: This chart doesn't show the differences between the values very well.

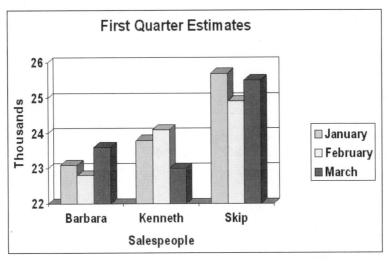

Figure 16-24: A change to the value axis scale makes the differences easier to see.

 Expert Tip You will probably never run into a case as dramatic as the difference between Figures 16-23 and 16-24 because PowerPoint's Chart feature has an auto setting for the scale that's turned on by default. However, you may sometimes want to override it for a special effect, such as to minimize or enhance the difference between data series. This is a good example of "making the data say what you want." If you wanted to make the point that the differences between three months were insignificant, you would use a larger scale. If you wanted to spotlight the importance of the differences, you would use a smaller scale.

To set the scale for an axis, follow these steps:

1. Point your mouse at the axis to be scaled (probably the vertical axis) and wait for a screen tip to pop up telling you you're pointing at the axis. If you don't see it, move the mouse until you do.

2. Right-click and choose Format Axis from the shortcut menu.

3. In the Format Axis dialog box, click the Scale tab. See Figure 16-25.

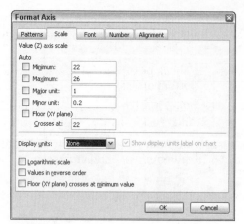

Figure 16-25: Set the scale numbers on the Scale tab.

4. If you do not want the automatic value for one of the measurements, deselect the Auto check box for it and enter a number manually in its text box.

   - **Minimum** is the starting number. The usual setting is 0 (as in Figure 16-23), but in Figure 16-24 it starts at 22.

   - **Maximum** is the top number. This is 30 in Figure 16-23, and 26 in Figure 16-24.

   - **Major unit** determines the axis labels (the numbers on the Y or Z axis). It is also the unit by which gridlines stretch out across the back wall of the chart. In Figure 16-23, gridlines appear by fives; in Figure 16-24, by ones.

   - **Minor unit** is the interval of smaller gridlines between the major ones. Most charts look better without minor units. They can make a chart look cluttered. Leave this set to Auto. This feature can also be used to place tick marks on the axes between the labels of the major units.

Note   If it's a 2D chart, instead of Floor (XY Plane) in the above options you will see Category X instead. And depending on the chart type, you might have a "crosses at maximum value" option, which would run the X axis across the top instead of the bottom.

5. *(Optional)* If you want any of these special features, select their check boxes. Each of these check boxes recalculates the numbers in the Minimum, Maximum, Major Unit, and Minor Unit text boxes. Don't select any of these after you have entered specific values if you want to keep your entered values.

   - **Logarithmic scale.** Rarely used by ordinary folks, this check box recalculates the Minimum, Maximum, Major Unit, and Minor Unit according to a power of 10 for the value axis based on the range of data. (If that explanation doesn't make any sense to you, you're not the target audience for this feature.)

- **Values in reverse order.** This check box turns the scale backwards so the greater values are at the bottom or left.

- **Floor (XY plane) crosses at.** When this is selected, you can enter a value indicating where the axes should cross.

- **Floor (XY plane) crosses at minimum value.** This sets the value of the above setting to the smallest value represented on the axis. In Figure 16-25, this would be 22.

6. If you want a specific number for the X axis other than the number you entered under Minimum, enter it in the Crosses At text box.

7. Click OK and then take a look at the results on your chart.

You may have noticed that the Format Axis dialog box has several other tabs besides Scale. These tabs contain settings you can change for your axis. Many of these controls are like ones you have seen earlier:

✦ **Patterns.** You can set text and background colors and patterns the same as for other parts of the chart. You also use this area to set tick marks on the axis and to place your axis labels (numbers and text).

✦ **Font.** Changing the font used to display the axis labels is the same as changing any other font.

✦ **Number.** You can change the way the numbers on your axis appear, such as making them appear as percentages, currency, dates, or another format.

✦ **Alignment.** You can align the axis text just as you can align the titles and labels on the chart.

Formatting the legend

With a multi-series chart, the value of the legend is obvious — it tells you what colors represent which series. Without it, your audience won't know what the various bars or lines mean.

You can do all the same formatting for a legend that you can for other chart elements you've seen so far. Just right-click the legend, choose Format Legend from the shortcut menu, and then use the tabs in the Format Legend dialog box to make any of these modifications:

✦ **Change the background.** Use the Area controls on the Patterns tab.

✦ **Change the border around the legend.** Use the Border controls on the Patterns tab.

✦ **Change the font, font size, and attributes.** Use the controls on the Font tab or use the drop-down lists and buttons on the Formatting toolbar.

Expert Tip If you select one of the individual keys in the legend and change its color, the color on the data series in the chart itself will change to match. This can be useful with stacked charts, especially where it's sometimes difficult to select the data series you want.

Adding data labels

Data labels announce the value, percentage, series, and so on for a bar, slice, or other value marker. They aren't appropriate for every chart, because they tend to crowd one another on charts with tightly-packed bars or other data representations. The best place to use them is on a pie chart, where there's a fairly large expanse of area for each slide. Series and percentage data labels are shown in Figure 16-26. Notice that this figure doesn't contain a legend. It doesn't need one because the data labels convey the legend information.

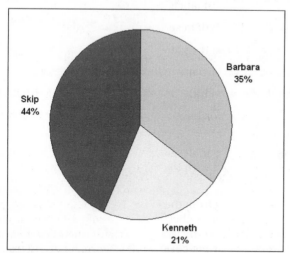

Figure 16-26: For some types of charts, data labels can help make the meaning clearer.

To add data labels, follow these steps:

1. Right-click the chart area and choose Chart Options from the shortcut menu.

2. Click the Data Labels tab. See Figure 16-27.

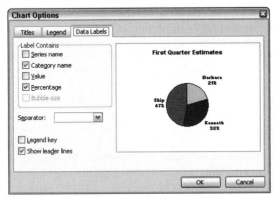

Figure 16-27: Choose the type of labels you want to appear on your chart.

3. Mark the check boxes for the types of labels you want:
   - **Series name.** The names of the data series from the legend.
   - **Category name.** The data from the category (X) axis.
   - **Value.** Shows the actual value from the cell on the datasheet.
   - **Percentage.** Shows what percentage of the whole each slice represents.
   - **Bubble size.** Applicable only for bubble charts. Indicates what each size represents.

4. If you don't want the legend to appear, deselect the Legend Key check box. You might not need it for a pie chart with the Series Name showing, for example.

5. *(Optional)* If you want lines running from the labels to the data points they represent, mark the Show Leader Lines check box. This may be useful if you later move the text frames containing the labels around so that they are farther away from their slice, or if your pie chart contains many small slices. Note that you won't have the option to use Leader Lines on all types of charts.

6. Click OK. Your data labels appear on your chart.

Formatting gridlines and walls

Gridlines help the readers' eyes follow across the chart. Gridlines are related to the axes, which you learned about earlier in the chapter. You have both vertical and horizontal gridlines available, but most people use only horizontal ones. *Walls* are nothing more than the space between the gridlines, formatted in a different color than the plot area. Set the Walls area to None, and good-bye walls. (Don't you wish tearing down walls was always that easy?)

Note   Note that walls are formattable only on 3D charts; 2D charts don't have them. To change the background behind a 2D chart, you must format the plot area itself.

In most cases, the default gridlines that PowerPoint adds work well. However, sometimes you might want to make the lines thicker or a different color, or turn them off altogether.

To change which gridlines are displayed, just click the Category Axis Gridlines or Value Axis Gridlines buttons on the toolbar. These buttons toggle the gridlines on and off. See Figure 16-28. Or, you can follow these steps to set gridlines more precisely:

1. Right-click the chart area and choose Chart Options.

2. In the Chart Options dialog box, click the Gridlines tab. (If you don't have a Gridlines tab, you are not using a chart type that supports them. For example, pie charts do not.)

3. Select or deselect the Major Gridlines and Minor Gridlines check boxes for each of the axes. If you're using a 2D chart, it has two dimensions (X and Y); 3D charts have three (X, Y, and Z, but Y is probably dimmed and unavailable). See Figure 16-28.

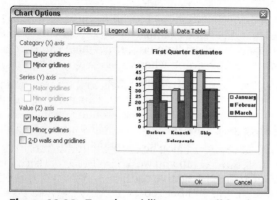

Figure 16-28: Turn the gridlines on or off for the chart as desired.

4. If you are using a 3D chart type, a 2D walls and gridlines check box appears on the Gridlines tab. If you want to make the walls and gridlines 2D, select it. This gets rid of the side wall and floor.

5. Click OK.

You can format gridlines the same way you format other objects on a chart. Just right-click a gridline and choose Format Gridline. Any changes you make affect all the gridlines of that type (for example, all horizontal major ones).

When you open the Format Gridlines dialog box, you see two tabs. One is for Scale, which is the same as the Scale settings for the axis that gridline touches. Any changes made in one place are reflected in the other. The other is Patterns, and the controls there are the same as the controls you saw earlier for changing the other chart parts. The only difference is that the None option is grayed out. That's because you can't turn gridlines off from here. You must use the procedure outlined in the preceding steps or use the toolbar toggle buttons.

Note The gridlines take their spacing from the major and minor units that you have set on the Scale tab. To adjust the gridline spacing, change the units there.

Formatting the data series

Now comes the fun part. You get to change the colors of the bars, lines, or slices, move them around, and otherwise tinker with your charts.

To format a data series, just right-click the bar, slice, or whatever, and choose Format Data Series from the shortcut menu. Then, depending on your chart type, you see different tabs that you can use to modify the series appearance.

You can format either the data series (all bars, lines, or whatever in the series) or the individual data point. When you right-click the data point, if you see and select Format Data Series, the changes you make affect the entire series. If you want to format the individual data point instead (for example, one individual bar), click the data series, and then click again on the individual data point (the bar). You should see selection handles on the one data point; when you do, right-click. The menu option should then read Format Data Point. Most of what you learn in the upcoming sections applies equally to data series and data points.

Controlling series patterns and colors

The first stop in the Format Data Series dialog box is the Patterns tab. This tab operates the same way as the Patterns tab you worked with for backgrounds. There is only one small addition: an Invert If Negative check box. This swaps the foreground and background colors if the number represented by the data point is negative. It applies to bars and columns.

The colors you choose on this tab apply only to the particular series you right-clicked if there is more than one series in your chart. That's because you will want to select the color for each series separately rather than having them all appear in the same color.

Controlling the bar or column shape

On the Shape tab (see Figure 16-29), you can choose which shape you want the bars or columns to be. Why settle for an ordinary bar? Have some fun with these. Don't forget, however, that you don't want to do anything to distract from your message. Don't make each series in the chart a different bar shape, for example.

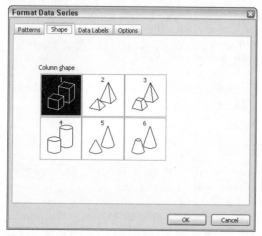

Figure 16-29: On the Shape tab, you can choose from among several bar and column shapes.

One of the coolest shapes is the sawed-off pyramid (number 3 in Figure 16-29). The highest data point is a full pyramid, but the shorter ones look like their tops have been sawed off. Number 6 is the same effect, but with a cone.

Expert Tip   To apply the new shape to all the series in the chart, select the plot area first. To apply it only to a certain series, select that series first. To apply it to only one point, select that point first.

Controlling the data series labels

The Data Labels tab in the Format Data Series dialog box contains the same controls as the Data Labels tab you worked with in the Chart Options dialog box, except that these controls apply only to the one selected series. You can use these, for example, to add data labels only for the series that you wanted to spotlight.

Controlling other series options

The Options tab is different for different chart types. It contains options specific to that type. For example, Figure 16-30 shows the options for a column chart. You can set the gap size between bars and the overall chart depth.

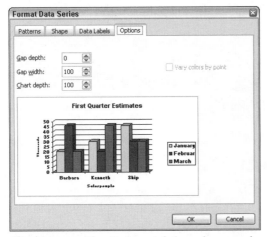

Figure 16-30: The Options tab for column and bar charts enables you to set the gaps between bars.

Figure 16-31 shows the Options tab for a pie chart. Here, you can set the angle of the first slice, effectively rotating the slices so that any slice is at any position you want. This can be very handy if the data labels are all bunched up on a pie chart. By modifying the position of the first slice, you can rotate the pie so that the large slices are at the top or bottom, where there is less room for data labels, and the smaller slices are on the sides, where there is more room.

There is also a Vary Colors by Slice check box on the Options tab for pie charts. Leave this checked. If you deselect it, all the slices will be the same color, and you won't be able to tell them apart without data labels.

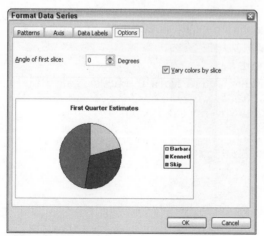

Figure 16-31: The Options tab for pie charts enables you to specify the angle of the first slice.

Changing the 3D effects

This feature is a little bit advanced, but can be a real lifesaver when you have a 3D chart that needs some tweaking.

Not all of PowerPoint's charts turn out perfectly right away. The application can't anticipate how your data is going to look in a chart, so sometimes in a 3D chart some of the data bars or lines are obscured by other, taller ones in front of them. For example, in Figure 16-32, the middle row's values are not visible because the front row is too tall. Modifying the 3D settings makes the chart appear at a different angle and brings the obscured data points into view.

A quick way to tilt a chart differently is to drag a corner of the floor. To do this, point the mouse pointer at a corner of the floor so that a pop-up reads Corner. Then, click and hold down the mouse button. The display turns to a wireframe view of the chart. Drag, continuing to hold down the mouse button, to change the angle (see Figure 16-33). Then release the mouse button to redisplay the chart.

You can also change the 3D view with a dialog box, as shown in these steps:

1. Right-click the chart area and choose 3-D View.

2. In the 3-D View dialog box, shown in Figure 16-34, click the buttons to change the view, then click Apply to try out the settings. (Drag the title bar of the dialog box to move it out of the way as necessary.)

   • Use the Elevation buttons to tilt the chart up and down.

   • Use the Rotation buttons to rotate the chart. When you rotate a chart so much that the walls are in the way, the walls move to the opposite side.

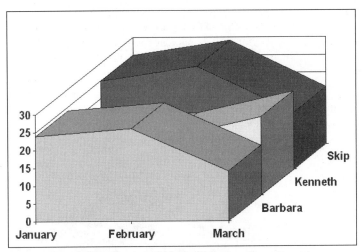

Figure 16-32: This chart could benefit from some 3D setting changes to make the back rows more readable.

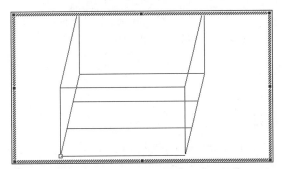

Figure 16-33: Drag a corner of the chart's floor to adjust its 3D tilt and orientation.

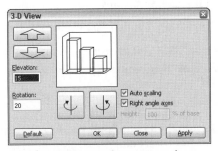

Figure 16-34: Use these 3D tools to adjust the view of the chart.

3. *(Optional)* In the Height text box, enter a percentage of the base width to represent the height of the chart. The default is 100; a setting of less than 100 makes a short, squat chart, whereas a setting of more than 100 makes a taller, thinner chart. This is especially useful for 3D pie charts that appear too "thick."

4. When you are satisfied with your settings and have tested them by clicking Apply, click OK. Figure 16-35 shows the chart from Figure 16-32 adjusted so that all data points are visible.

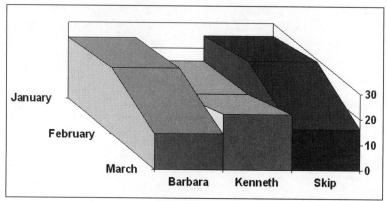

Figure 16-35: Now each series is visible, thanks to some 3D adjustments.

Using Charts from Excel

Using a chart from another application is usually as simple as copy-and-paste. Use the Clipboard to transfer a chart from one application to another.

For example, if you have a chart in Excel, do the following:

1. Select the chart in Excel. Then choose Edit ➪ Copy.

2. Open PowerPoint and display the slide on which you want to paste the chart. Then choose Edit ➪ Paste.

Expert Tip   If you want to create a dynamic link between the two, so that the copy in PowerPoint updates when the Excel copy does, see Chapter 18.

The preceding steps embed an Excel chart into PowerPoint. This opens the full set of Excel charting tools within the PowerPoint window, which some people prefer to the simpler ones in PowerPoint.

Double-click the chart to open it, and an Excel mini-workbook appears in its own frame; the toolbars and menus change to those of Excel. To edit the data on the chart, click the tab where the data is. Then switch back to the Chart tab to see the chart. See Figure 16-36. Edit the chart normally, as you would in Excel. When you are finished, click on the slide outside of the Excel chart's frame to return to PowerPoint.

Caution The entire Excel workbook is embedded in the PowerPoint file, which, depending on the workbook, can dramatically increase the size of your file.

You are not limited to just Excel; you can embed a chart object from any other application that supports OLE linking. See Chapter 18 for more details.

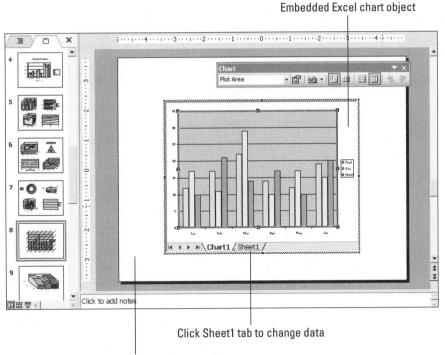

Embedded Excel chart object

Click Sheet1 tab to change data

Click outside Excel object to return to PowerPoint

Figure 16-36: Embed an Excel chart object on a PowerPoint slide to use Excel's charting tools within PowerPoint.

Summary

In this chapter, you learned how to create and format charts using PowerPoint. You covered a lot of ground here, learning not only how to create and modify charts, but also how to format them. In the next chapter, you move on to another kind of object: a *diagram*. PowerPoint includes a utility for making several types of diagrams, including organizational charts.

✦   ✦   ✦

Working with Diagrams

Just as charts and graphs can enliven a boring table of numbers, a diagram can enliven a conceptual discussion. A diagram helps the audience understand the interdependencies of objects or processes in a visual way, so they don't have to juggle that information mentally as you speak. Some potential uses include organizational charts, pyramids, and flow charts.

Understanding Diagram Types and Their Uses

PowerPoint's Diagram tool provides six types of diagrams. Organization chart is the most common one, and also the most complex to use, but you might find uses for the other five as well. The following sections explain each of the six types.

Organization chart

An organization chart shows who reports to whom in a company's employment hierarchy. It's useful when describing how an organization functions and who is responsible for what, as in Figure 17-1. It can also be used to show match-ups for competitions, as in Figure 17-2, so it'll come in handy when you're in charge of the office NCAA pool! They're also good for flow charts for processes.

This chapter covers organization charts last, because they're the most complicated type of chart. (We'll work up to them.)

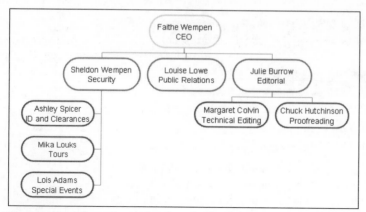

Figure 17-1: Show the chain of command in an organization.

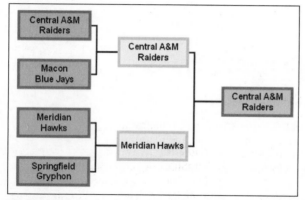

Figure 17-2: Track winners in single- or double-elimination tournaments.

Expert Tip Should you include your company's organization chart in your presentation? That's a question that depends on your main message. If your speech is about the organization, you should. If not, show the organization structure only if it serves a purpose to advance your speech. Many presenters have found that an organization chart makes an excellent backup slide. You can prepare it and have it ready in case a question arises about the organization. Another useful strategy is to include a printed organization chart as part of the handouts you distribute to the audience, without including the slide in your main presentation.

Cycle diagram

A cycle diagram is a flow chart that illustrates a circular process, one with no start or finish. You can have as many different steps in the process as you like. Figure 17-3 provides an example of this type of chart.

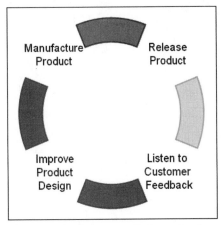

Figure 17-3: Processes that constantly repeat are well illustrated with a cycle diagram.

Expert Tip To change the shapes in a cycle diagram to arrows, select one of the objects in the diagram and choose Draw ➪ Change AutoShape. Choose Block Arrows and then the Circular Arrow. Repeat for each shape. Then on the Diagram toolbar, choose Layout ➪ AutoLayout to turn AutoLayout off. Resize the arrows by dragging the yellow diamonds just as you would any other AutoShape.

Radial diagram

A radial diagram shows relationships such that each item radiates out from the center (hence the name "radial"). It is good for showing how multiple items feed into a center point, or the satellite offices of a central headquarters. In Figure 17-4, for example, it shows the library branches in relationship to the central library.

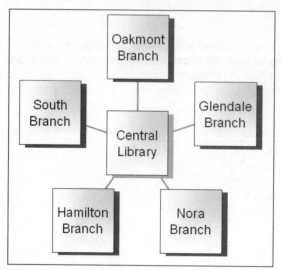

Figure 17-4: A radial diagram is like a simple organization chart that starts from the center rather than from the top.

Pyramid diagram

A pyramid diagram is just what it sounds like. It breaks up a triangle into multiple horizontal slices, and labels each slice. In Figure 17-5 it's used for the classic nutrition pyramid, but you can use it for any hierarchical model.

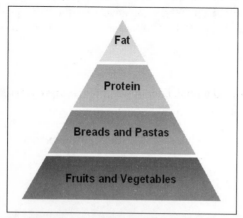

Figure 17-5: A pyramid diagram shows the progression of items from the base level (large) to the top level (small).

Venn diagram

Remember basic math class, when you learned about sets and subsets, and how two sets can intersect? That's the basic idea behind a Venn diagram. It's a series of circles that overlap one another, as in Figure 17-6. It's useful when you need to show conceptually how different groups have some—but not all—members or characteristics in common.

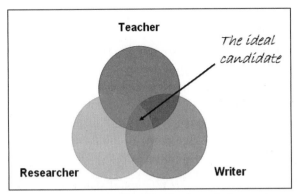

Figure 17-6: A Venn diagram overlaps circles to show groups and their commonalities.

Expert Tip In previous versions of PowerPoint, the colors in Venn diagrams did not blend well, so it was often better to create the diagram in an image-editing program and import it onto the slide. In PowerPoint 2003, however, the colors of the Venn diagrams blend automatically, based on the colors applied to each circle. You can manipulate this somewhat by changing the transparency of the colors in the Format ⇨ AutoShape dialog.

Target diagram

A target diagram shows progress toward a goal. Each layer moves ever closer to the end result at the center, as in Figure 17-7.

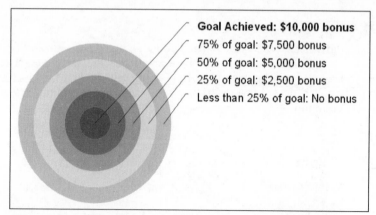

Figure 17-7: A target diagram is like a flow chart but it flows from the outside to the center rather than in a linear fashion.

Inserting a Diagram

All diagrams start out the same way—you insert them on the slide as you can any other slide object. That means you can either use a diagram placeholder on a slide layout or you can insert the diagram manually.

To use a placeholder, start with a slide that contains a layout with a diagram placeholder in it, or change the current slide's layout to one that does (refer to Chapter 7). Then click the Diagram icon in the placeholder.

To insert from scratch, you can use either of these methods:

✦ Click the Diagram button on the Drawing toolbar. (It looks like three colored circles arranged in a ring with arrows between them.)

✦ Choose Insert ⇨ Diagram.

Any way you start it, the Diagram Gallery opens, as in Figure 17-8. Select one of the six diagram types and click OK, and the diagram appears. From there it's just a matter of customizing.

When a diagram is selected, the Diagram toolbar appears. Figure 17-9 shows it. You will learn what each of the buttons does as this chapter progresses. The second and third buttons from the left are different depending on the diagram type, but the others are standard.

Figure 17-8: Select the diagram type you want to insert.

Figure 17-9: The Diagram toolbar.

Editing Diagram Text

All diagrams have text placeholders, which are basically just text boxes. Click in one of them and type. Then use the normal text-formatting controls (Font, Font Size, Bold, Italic, and so on) to change the appearance of the text. See Figure 17-10.

Here are some tips for working with diagram text:

✦ Word wrap doesn't occur automatically, so press Shift+Enter when you want a soft line break or press Enter for a hard return.

✦ If you resize the diagram, its text will resize automatically.

✦ You can't move the text box by default because AutoLayout is turned on for the diagram. To turn it off, click the Layout button on the Diagram toolbar and choose AutoLayout from its menu, turning that feature off. You can then move the text boxes around freely.

✦ To leave a text box empty, just don't type anything in it. The *Click to add text* words do not show up in a printout or in Slide Show view.

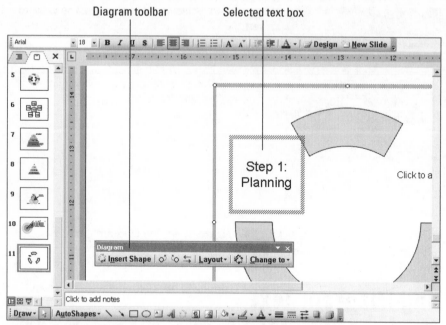

Figure 17-10: Each diagram has at least one text placeholder.

Modifying Diagram Structure

The structure of the diagram includes how many boxes it has and where they are placed. Even though the diagram types are all very different, the way you add, remove, and reposition shapes in them is surprisingly similar across all types.

The exception is the organization chart type; modifying one of these is significantly different from modifying the others. I will address organization charts later in this chapter, and confine the present discussion to non-organization diagrams.

Note   When you add a shape, you add both a graphical element (a circle, a bar, or whatever) and also an associated text box. For example, in the cycle diagram in Figure 17-10, adding a shape to it would add both another graphical piece of circle and another text box. The same goes with deletion; removing a shape also removes its associated text box from the diagram.

Inserting and deleting shapes

To insert a shape, click the Insert Shape button on the Diagram toolbar. Each time you click that button, another shape is added to the diagram.

To delete a shape, click it to select it in the diagram. Gray circles appear around it with Xs in the centers, as in Figure 17-11. Then press the Delete key on the keyboard.

Note   The gray circle selection handles with Xs indicate that the shape is selected but is grouped with other objects such that it cannot be individually moved or resized. However, it can be individually formatted and deleted.

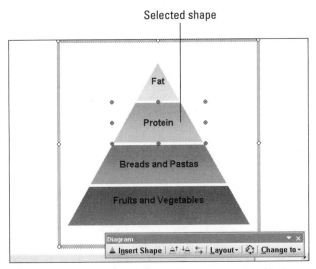

Figure 17-11: A selected shape has gray circle selection handles.

Changing the flow direction

Each diagram flows in a certain direction. A cycle diagram flows either clockwise or counterclockwise. A pyramid flows either up or down. A radial or target diagram flows from the outside in or from the inside out.

If you realize after typing all the text that you should have made the diagram flow in the other direction, you can change it by clicking the Reverse Diagram button on the Diagram toolbar. For example, in Figure 17-12, the diagram from Figure 17-11 has been reversed so that "Fat" is at the bottom of the pyramid. (Not a very healthy diet plan!)

Expert Tip   Notice in Figure 17-12 that the labels do not confine themselves to within the associated shape. Fruits and Vegetables extends outside the top triangle in the pyramid. If this is a problem, you might be able to make the labels fit with a combination of line breaks (Shift+Enter) and font changes.

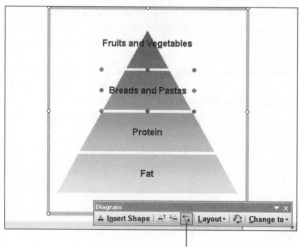

Reverse Diagram button

Figure 17-12: Reversing the diagram flow changes which labels are assigned to which shapes.

Rearranging shapes

Not only can you reverse the overall flow of the diagram, but you can also move around individual shapes. For example, suppose you have a diagram that illustrates five steps in a process and you realize that steps 3 and 4 are out of order. You can move one of them without having to retype all the labels.

To move a shape, select it and then click the Move Shape Forward or Move Shape Backward button on the Diagram toolbar. These buttons look different depending on what kind of diagram you are working with. In Figure 17-13 (for a Target diagram), they are a circle and a dot. Compare these to Figures 17-10 (for a Cycle diagram) and 17-11 (for a Pyramid diagram).

Move Shape Forward

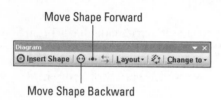

Move Shape Backward

Figure 17-13: Move a shape forward or backward in the diagram structure with the Move Shape Forward and Move Shape Backward buttons.

Changing to a different diagram type

Except for the organization chart, you can change any diagram type to any other diagram type with a simple command. (Organization charts are separate, and I'll discuss them shortly in more detail.)

To change the diagram type, click the Change To button on the Diagram toolbar and choose the desired layout from the menu. See Figure 17-14. (The current diagram type is the unavailable one—Target—in Figure 17-14.)

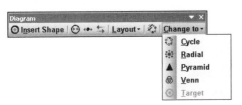

Figure 17-14: Switch to a different diagram type.

To change the diagram type, you must have AutoFormat and AutoLayout turned on. If they're not on, you'll be prompted to allow PowerPoint to turn them on. Note that this will sometimes affect color changes you might have made to the diagram, so it's better to decide on the appropriate diagram type before customizing.

Modifying an Organization Chart Structure

Organization charts are much more complex and customizable than the other diagram types, so they have their own special controls for changing their structure.

Inserting and deleting shapes

The main difference when inserting an organization chart shape (that is, a box into which you will type a name) is that you must specify which existing box the new one is related to and how it is related.

For example, suppose you have a supervisor already in the chart and you want to add some people to the chart who report to him. You would first select his box on the chart, and then insert the new shapes. When inserting a new shape, you can choose one of three types of new shapes in relation to him: Subordinate, Coworker, or Assistant.

Note   An *assistant* is a person whose job is to provide support to a certain person or office. An executive secretary is one example. A *subordinate*, in contrast, is an employee who may report to a manager but whose job does not consist entirely of supporting that manager. Confused? Don't worry about it. You don't have to make a distinction in your organization chart. Everyone can be subordinates (except the person at the top of the heap, of course).

To insert a shape in an organization chart:

1. Click an existing box to which the new one should be related.

2. On the Diagram toolbar, open the Insert Shape button's menu and choose Subordinate, Coworker, or Assistant. See Figure 17-15.

   OR

   To choose Subordinate, simply click the Insert Shape button without opening its menu.

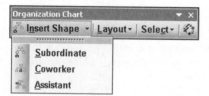

Figure 17-15: Select a type of shape to add based on its relationship to the currently selected one.

As you see in Figure 17-15, the Diagram toolbar is different for organization charts than for other chart types. It lacks the Move Shape Forward, Move Shape Backward, and Change To buttons, and the Insert Shape button has a drop-down list that it didn't have with the other chart types.

Expert Tip   Notice in Figure 17-15 that the Insert Shape menu has a row of small dots across the top, between the button and the menu. That means you can drag that row of dots to make that menu into a separate floating toolbar. This keeps its commands handy so you don't have to keep coming back to the menu.

To delete a shape, select it and press the Delete key, as with all the other diagram types.

Rearranging shapes

As the organization changes, you might need to change your chart so that people report to different supervisors. To do that, simply drag-and-drop a subordinate's box onto a different supervisor.

Changing the organization layout

The subordinates for a supervisor can be arranged in any of several ways on the organization chart. The default is for each one to be shown horizontally beneath the supervisor, as in Figure 17-16.

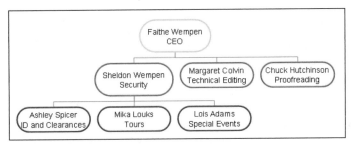

Figure 17-16: This is the standard layout for a branch of an organization chart.

In a large or complex organization chart, however, the diagram can quickly become too wide with the Standard layout. Therefore there are several "hanging" alternatives that make the chart more vertically oriented. The alternatives are Both Hanging, Left Hanging, and Right Hanging. They are just what their names sound like. Figure 17-17 shows examples of Right Hanging (the people reporting to the CEO) and Both Hanging (the Security subordinates).

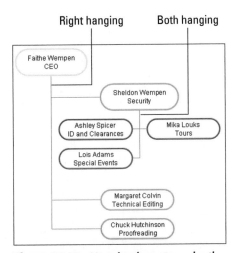

Figure 17-17: Hanging layouts make the chart more vertically oriented.

The layout is chosen for individual branches of the organization chart, so before selecting an alternative layout, you must click on the supervisor box whose subordinates you want to change.

To change a layout, follow these steps:

1. Click the box for the supervisor whose layout should be changed.
2. On the Diagram toolbar, click the Layout button to open a menu.
3. Choose one of the layouts (Standard, Both Hanging, Right Hanging, or Left Hanging).

Selecting multiple shapes of a common type

When working with organization charts, it is often helpful to select all the boxes in a certain branch, or all the boxes at a certain level, before applying formatting. For example, you might want to change the font for all the boxes at a certain managerial level. Or you might want to select all the connecting lines in the diagram so you can make them thinner, thicker, or a different color.

The Diagram toolbar provides an easy way to make the selection:

1. Select a box that belongs in the group you want to select. For example, to select all managers of a certain level, select one such manager.
2. Click the Select button from the Diagram toolbar, opening a menu, and then choose one of these:

     Level: Selects all boxes at the same level as the currently selected one.

     Branch: Selects all boxes in the same branch as this one.

     All Assistants: Selects all boxes with the Assistant type regardless of position.

     All Connecting Lines: Selects all connecting lines regardless of position.

Making such selections will come in handy later in the chapter when I show you how to turn off the automatic controls and do some formatting and restructuring on your own.

Resizing a Diagram

There are two ways to resize a diagram frame. You can resize it so that the diagram itself does not change size—only its frame—or you can resize so that both the frame and the diagram inside change.

To resize the frame only, leaving the diagram at its default size, click Layout on the Diagram toolbar and choose Expand Diagram. (This is the default, so you do not have to choose it explicitly unless some other choice has previously been made.) When this option is on, the corners of the diagram window appear with black lines, and you drag one of those lines to resize. See Figure 17-18.

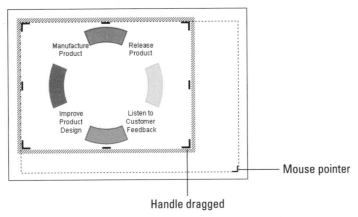

Figure 17-18: Resizing with Expand Diagram turned on resizes only the frame.

To resize the frame and the diagram as a whole, click Layout on the Diagram toolbar and choose Scale Diagram. This makes the selection handles on the diagram frame turn to white circles, and dragging one of them changes the entire object. See Figure 17-19.

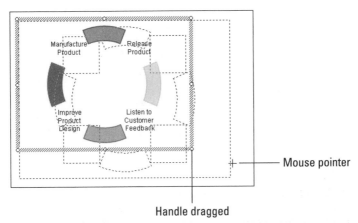

Figure 17-19: Resizing with Scale Diagram turned on resizes everything.

The other option on the Layout menu, Fit Diagram to Contents, shrinks the frame so that it clings closely to the diagram if you have enlarged it previously with Expand Diagram turned on.

Formatting a Diagram

You can format a diagram either automatically or manually. Automatically is the default, and many PowerPoint users don't even realize that manual formatting is a possibility. The following sections cover both.

AutoFormatting a diagram

Each diagram type has a variety of AutoFormat choices you can apply to it. To choose one of these, do the following:

1. From the Diagram toolbar, click the AutoFormat button. (It's the one that looks like a cycle diagram with a lightning bolt on it.) The Diagram Style Gallery dialog box opens.

2. Select a style to apply. See Figure 17-20. A preview of it appears.

3. Click OK to apply it.

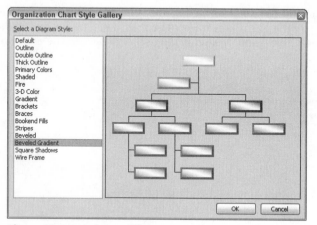

Figure 17-20: Select a different AutoFormat for the diagram.

Turning off AutoFormat

AutoFormat is turned on by default for the chart, and while it is on, you cannot do any manual formatting. To turn off AutoFormat, right-click one of the shapes on the chart and choose Use AutoFormat. (This same command will also toggle it back on again.)

Expert Tip Apply a style to the diagram first, as in the preceding section, and then turn off AutoFormat to fine-tune it.

Manually formatting a diagram

When AutoFormat is off, you can format any shape on the diagram in any of the normal ways you can format an object:

✦ Select a shape and use the Fill Color, Line Color, and/or Text Color buttons on the Drawing toolbar to change any of those colors.

✦ Change the thickness of the shape border with the Line Style button on the Drawing toolbar.

✦ Make the shape border dotted or dashed with the Dash Style button on the Drawing toolbar.

✦ Right-click the shape and choose Format AutoShape to make those same changes in the Format AutoShape dialog box instead if you prefer.

✦ Apply a shadow or 3D effect to the shape with the Shadow or 3D buttons on the Drawing toolbar.

Figure 17-21 shows an example of some manual formatting applied to an organization chart.

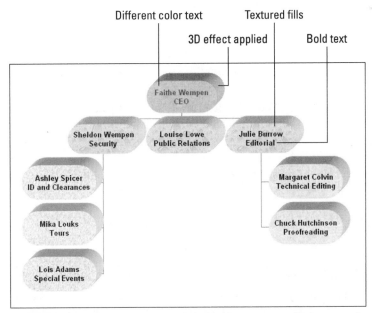

Figure 17-21: This organization chart has been manually formatted.

Manually Restructuring a Diagram

Manually restructuring is different from manually formatting. *Formatting* refers only to the colors, lines, fills, and text formatting of the diagram. The *structure* refers to the placement of the graphical objects and text boxes.

Most of the time you will want to go with the AutoLayout structures for the diagrams. In case an AutoLayout doesn't work for a particular purpose, however, you can turn it off and go your own way.

To turn off AutoLayout, on the Diagram toolbar click Layout and then choose AutoLayout. This turns off AutoLayout, making each box, line, and graphic of the diagram individually editable.

By *editable,* I mean that you can do any of the following:

✦ **Make any item larger or smaller** by dragging its selection handles.

✦ **Reshape a shape,** in some cases, by dragging the yellow diamond on it (as in Chapter 15). For example, you can make the circle segments in a Cycle diagram fatter, thinner, longer, or shorter.

✦ **Reposition a shape** by dragging it to a new location. For example, you can make the circles in a Venn diagram overlap less or more than the default, or make one of them not overlap at all with the others.

✦ **Reposition a text box** by dragging it to a new location. For example, if you have too much text in a text box it might overlap with a shape in the diagram; you can scoot it over so it doesn't anymore. Or you can intentionally place a text box on top of a shape.

✦ **Move the boxes on an organization chart** so that the spacing is different between them. The connecting lines between them will stay connected.

✦ **Connect the connecting lines differently** on an organization chart, or remove individual connecting lines altogether. To disconnect a line, click the line to select it and then drag the circles at the ends. To delete a connector line, click it and then press Delete.

✦ **Add other objects to the diagram.** For example, you can add extra text boxes with explanatory text. To do so, make sure the diagram frame is selected and then use the Text Box tool in the Drawing toolbar to create a new text box. Or alternatively, copy one of the existing text boxes in the diagram by Ctrl+dragging it.

Expert Tip To add more connecting lines to an organization chart, use the Connectors category in the AutoShapes list from the Drawing toolbar. When each end has a red dot, it is connected at both ends. When either end is green, it is unconnected.

You have already seen some examples of manual diagram restructuring in this chapter, perhaps without realizing it. The diagram in Figure 17-2 was restructured from a top-down layout to a left-to-right one, including moving all the connector lines. The connector lines attach to the tops and bottoms of the boxes by default; these were moved to attach to the left and right sides. The diagram in Figure 17-6 was also modified by the addition of the text box that reads *The ideal candidate*.

As a further example, compare Figure 17-22 to the earlier version shown in Figure 17-5. A 3D effect has been applied, and the size and shape of the top and bottom objects in the pyramid have been altered. Two explanatory text boxes have also been added.

Compare Figure 17-23 to the earlier version shown in Figure 17-3. The colored bars have been enlarged and reshaped to form a complete circle, and the text boxes have been placed on top of them. In addition, two block arrows have been added using the AutoShapes on the Drawing toolbar to further clarify the directional flow. The border has also been removed from each shape by setting the Line Color to None.

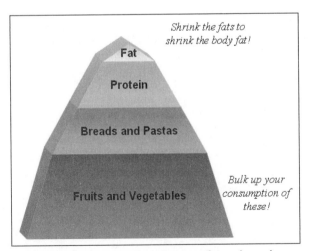

Figure 17-22: This pyramid diagram shows how the top and bottom shapes have been altered.

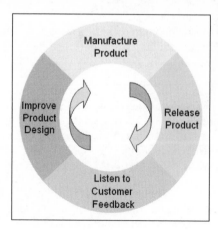

Figure 17-23: In this cycle diagram, the circle segments are enlarged and the text has been moved on top of them.

Adding Hyperlinks to Diagram Shapes

Let's take a look at one final thing you can do with diagrams: you can assign hyperlinks to them. For example, in the diagram in Figure 17-23, wouldn't it be cool if you could click a segment to jump to a slide that further explained that part of the process? It's doable.

To add a hyperlink to a part of a diagram, do the following:

1. Click on the shape or text box in the diagram to which you want to assign a hyperlink.

2. Choose Insert ⇨ Hyperlink. The Insert Hyperlink dialog box opens.

3. If you want to hyperlink to another slide in the presentation, click Place in This Document and then choose the slide you want. See Figure 17-24.

OR

If you want to hyperlink to some other file or Web address, click Existing File or Web Page and then enter the URL or the path to that file. See Chapter 29 for more information about hyperlinks.

4. Click OK.

5. Repeat the process for each shape in the diagram to which you want to assign a hyperlink.

6. Try out your work in Slide Show view if desired. (See Chapter 25 for help with that if needed.)

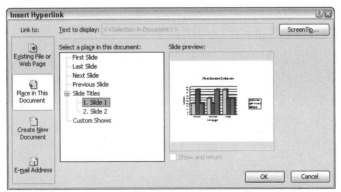

Figure 17-24: Set up hyperlinks so you can click on a part of a diagram to go to a different slide or to a URL or file.

Summary

In this chapter, you learned how to create organization charts and other kinds of diagrams with PowerPoint's Diagram feature. You will probably find lots of creative uses for diagrams now that you know they're available!

In the next chapter, you'll learn how to incorporate content from other applications in PowerPoint. This can include outside diagramming programs such as Microsoft Visio, as well as other art programs, charting programs, or any other program type.

✦   ✦   ✦

Incorporating Data from Other Sources

As you have already seen, PowerPoint contains an assortment of tools for creating various types of objects: charts, WordArt, diagrams, clip art, and so on. You have also learned how to place graphics into PowerPoint from a saved file, a digital camera, or a scanner, how to embed Excel charts on slides, and how to borrow slides from other PowerPoint presentations and outlines from Word or other text editors.

However, there are a lot of other objects that don't fall into any of these categories, so PowerPoint doesn't have a special menu command for bringing in exactly that type of object. Examples include a flow chart from a program like Microsoft Visio, a slide from a different presentation application, some records from a database, or a map from a mapping program.

This chapter looks at the various ways to import and create content from other applications in PowerPoint, as well as how to export PowerPoint objects for use in other programs.

Working with External Content: An Overview

There are several ways of bringing foreign objects into your presentation. The method you choose depends on how you want the object to behave once it arrives. You can make the inserted content a full citizen of the presentation—that is, with no ties to its native application or data file—or you can help it retain a connection to either.

The simplest way to import content into PowerPoint is to use the Copy and Paste commands (or buttons). For text-type data from most applications, this results in the incoming data integrating itself with PowerPoint without retaining any connection to the source. For example, you can select some cells from an Excel worksheet and then choose Edit ⇨ Copy to copy them to the Clipboard. Then in PowerPoint you can paste them with Edit ⇨ Paste onto a slide, and the Excel cells become a PowerPoint table. You can also do the same thing with drag-and-drop from one application to the other.

Caution   Not all data types exhibit the behavior described here. With some source data types, especially types that are more graphical than text-based, copy-and-paste results in an embedded object that will open its native application for editing. For example, when you copy and paste a chart from Excel, it is by default embedded. (See the following paragraphs for an understanding of embedded objects.)

Another choice is to *embed* the data. You can do this for existing or new data. Embedding it maintains the relationship between that data and its native application, so that you can double-click it to edit it with that native application later. To embed existing data, you copy the data to the Clipboard and then use Edit ⇨ Paste Special to choose the appropriate data type from the list. For example, suppose you want to be able to edit the pasted cells in Excel later. You can use Edit ⇨ Paste Special and choose Microsoft Excel Worksheet Object as the type. (More on this shortly.)

To embed new data, you use the Insert ⇨ Object command and then choose to create a new embedded object of the desired type. (More on this shortly too.) For example, suppose you have a favorite program for creating organization charts. You can start a new embedded organization chart on a PowerPoint slide instead of using PowerPoint's own simpler Diagrams feature. That organization chart would then be stored only within your PowerPoint file, not separately.

Yet another choice is to link the data from its original source file. When you do this, PowerPoint maintains information about the name and location of the original, and each time you open the presentation file it re-checks the original to see if any changes have been made to the original data file. If so, PowerPoint updates its copy of the object to the latest version. For example, suppose you want to include data from an Excel workbook that a coworker is creating. He warns you that his data is not final yet, but you want to create the presentation anyway. By creating a link to his data, rather than pasting a static copy of it, you ensure that you will always have the latest data no matter how many times he changes it.

You can create a link to an entire file or to a specific part of a file. For example, you can link to the entire Excel workbook, or just to a certain range of cells on a certain sheet. The procedures are different — for the entire file you use Insert ⇨ Object, but for a portion of the file you use Edit ⇨ Paste Special. Both methods create a link to the entire Excel workbook, but Insert ⇨ Object will automatically display the entire first spreadsheet of the workbook in your PowerPoint file, whereas Edit ⇨ Paste Special will display only the cells that you've selected.

Copying Content from Other Programs

Let's assume for the moment that you don't need any special linking or embedding. You just want the content from some other program to be placed on a PowerPoint slide. You have two choices: use the Clipboard, or use drag-and-drop.

Using the Clipboard

The easiest way to place something into PowerPoint is to use the Windows Clipboard. Because almost all Windows-based programs employ the Clipboard, you can move data from any program to almost any other with a minimum of fuss. Follow these steps:

1. Create the data in its native program or open a file that contains it.

2. Select the data you want, and choose Edit ➪ Copy.

3. Switch to PowerPoint, and display the slide on which you want to place the data.

4. Choose Edit ➪ Paste. The data appears on the slide. PowerPoint makes its best guess as to the correct formatting. For example, if you paste Excel worksheet cells, it attempts to convert them to a table because that's the closest match among the native PowerPoint layouts.

5. Move or resize the new data as necessary on the slide.

Don't forget that there are many alternative methods for using the Copy and Paste commands. The shortcut keys are among the fastest: Ctrl+C for copy and Ctrl+V for paste.

PowerPoint, like all Office 2003 applications, has an enhanced version of the Clipboard that is available when both the source and destination locations are Microsoft Office applications. It enables you to copy more than one item at a time to the Clipboard and then choose among them when pasting. When pasting to a non-Office application, however, only the last item copied to the Clipboard is available.

When you copy twice in a row without pasting while in an Office application, the Clipboard task pane appears, with each copied clip separately listed. You can also open this Clipboard task pane by displaying the task pane and then opening its list and choosing Clipboard.

You can then open the destination and click the clip you want to paste. Or you can click the down arrow next to a clip and choose Delete to delete it. See Figure 18-1.

 Expert Tip Fine-tune the way the Clipboard works in Office 2003 applications by clicking the Options button at the bottom of the Clipboard task pane. This opens a menu from which you can specify when and how the Clipboard task pane appears. For example, you can set it to show a Clipboard icon in the taskbar.

Separate clips on Clipboard   Click to display menu

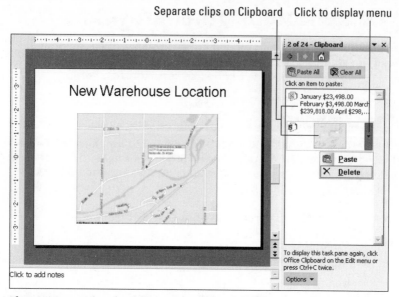

Figure 18-1: Using the Office 2003 Clipboard task pane enables you to copy more than one clip to the Clipboard.

As mentioned earlier, when you are copying and pasting some types of data, especially graphical types, PowerPoint embeds the data by default rather than simply pasting it.

Embedding the data tends to increase the size of the PowerPoint presentation file, so you want avoid doing it unless you think you will need that capability. (More on embedding later in the chapter.) You can tell whether data has been embedded by double-clicking it. If it's embedded, its native application will open within PowerPoint (or in a separate window). If it's not embedded, a PowerPoint dialog box will open for the data.

To avoid embedding data that PowerPoint wants to embed by default, follow these steps:

1. Copy the data to the Clipboard in its native application.

2. In PowerPoint, choose Edit ➪ Paste Special.

3. Choose a different format for the paste, such as Bitmap. Do not choose the format that ends with "Object" or you will get an embedded copy.

4. Click OK.

Using drag-and-drop

In some cases, you can also use drag-and-drop to move an object from some other application to PowerPoint. Not all Windows programs support this feature though. If you're not sure whether a program supports it, try it and see.

Here's how to drag-and-drop something:

1. Create the object in its native program or open the file that contains it. The object can be a single unit such as an entire graphic, or it can be a small piece of a larger document or image such as a few cells selected from a large worksheet.

2. Open PowerPoint and display the slide on which you want to place the data.

3. Resize both applications' windows so that both the data and its destination are visible on-screen.

4. Select the data in its native program.

5. If you want to copy, rather than move, hold down the Ctrl key.

6. Drag the data to the PowerPoint slide. See Figure 18-2. An outline appears on the PowerPoint slide showing where the data will go.

7. Release the mouse button. The data is moved or copied.

As with copying and pasting, not all data gets the "plain paste" treatment when you drag-and-drop. Generally speaking, text-based data will drag without embedding, but graphic-based data will not. (There are exceptions.) Use the Edit ⇨ Paste Special method described earlier rather than drag-and-drop if you run into this situation.

Inserting graphics from a file

When using copy/paste or drag-and-drop to insert content from a graphics-based application, as mentioned in the preceding section, PowerPoint embeds by default. This makes the file size larger than necessary for the PowerPoint presentation, however, so it's better to use Insert ⇨ Picture ⇨ From File when inserting graphics. This inserts a plain old copy of the picture, without embedding, and keeps the PowerPoint file size more manageable. See Chapter 14 to review how to do that.

Introducing OLE

The abbreviation OLE stands for *Object Linking and Embedding*. It enables Windows-based applications that support it to share information dynamically. That means that the object remembers where it came from and has special abilities based on that memory. Even though the name OLE is a little scary (it ranks right up there with SQL in my book!), the concept is very elementary, and anyone can understand and use it.

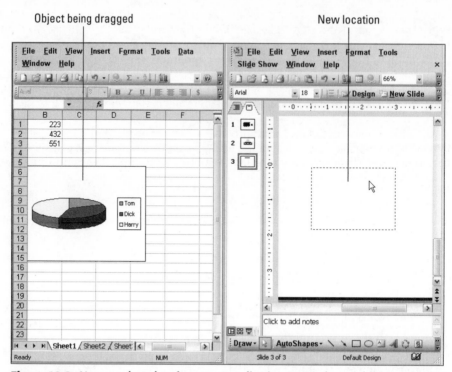

Figure 18-2: You can drag data from one application to another. Hold down the Ctrl key to copy rather than move.

You already understand the term *object* in the PowerPoint sense, and the term is similar to that in the case of OLE. An object is any bit of data (or a whole file) that you want to use in another program. You can paste it in with no connection to its source, or you can link or embed it.

Two actions are involved in OLE: linking and embedding. Here are quick definitions of each:

✦ Linking creates a connection between the original file and the copy in your presentation, so that the copy is always updated.

✦ Embedding creates a connection between the object in the presentation and the application that originally created it, so that the object can be edited in that original application at any time from within PowerPoint.

The key difference is that linking connects to the source *data file*, whereas embedding connects to the source *application*.

For a link to be updatable, linked objects must already exist independently of the PowerPoint presentation. For example, if you want to link an Excel chart, you must first create that chart in Excel and save your work in an Excel file. That way PowerPoint has a filename to refer to when updating the link.

Caution   Links can slow down your presentation's loading and editing performance. Therefore, you should create links last, after you have finished adding content and polishing the formatting.

Linking and embedding are not appropriate for every insertion. If you want to use data (such as cells from an Excel worksheet or a picture from a graphics program) that will not change, it's best to copy it normally. For the Excel data cells or text from a Word document, use regular Copy/Paste; for the graphic image, use Insert ⇨ Picture ⇨ From File. Reserve linking for objects that will change and that you will always need the most recent version of. Reserve embedding for objects that you plan on editing later and require the native applications editing tools to do so.

Here are some ideas of when linking or embedding might be useful:

✦ If you have to give the same presentation every month that shows the monthly sales statistics, *link* to your Excel worksheet where you track them during the month. Your presentation will always contain the most current data.

✦ If you want to draw a picture in Paint (a program that comes with Windows) or some other graphics program, *embed* the picture in PowerPoint. That way, you don't have to open Paint (or the other program) separately every time you want to work on the picture while you're fine-tuning your presentation. You can just double-click the picture in PowerPoint. You can always break the link when you finalize the presentation if you want to cut down on the file size.

✦ If you know that a coworker is still finalizing a chart or drawing, *link* to her working file on the network. Then whenever changes are made to it, your copy will also be updated. (Beware, however, that once you take your presentation away from the computer that has network access, you can no longer update the link.)

Linking and/or embedding part of a file

As I mentioned earlier, you can link or embed either a part of an existing file or the whole file.

If you need only a part of an existing file, such as a few cells from a worksheet, an individual chart, or a few paragraphs of text, you use the following procedure:

1. In its native application, create or open the file containing the data you want to copy.

2. If you have just created the file, save it. The file should have a name before you go any further if you are linking; for embedding this is not necessary but won't hurt anything.

3. Select the data you want.

4. Choose Edit ⇨ Copy.

5. Switch to PowerPoint and display the slide on which you want to paste the data.

6. Choose Edit ⇨ Paste Special. The Paste Special dialog box opens. See Figure 18-3.

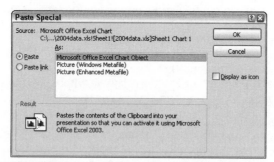

Figure 18-3: Use the Paste Special dialog box to link or embed a piece of a data file from another program.

7. If you want to embed, leave Paste selected. If you want to link, click Paste Link.

8. Choose the format from the As list. Because you want to link or embed, choose a type that ends with the word *object*.

9. If you want the pasted object to appear as an icon instead of as itself, click the Display as Icon check box. This check box might be unavailable if the object type you chose in step 8 does not support it.

10. Click OK. The object is placed in your presentation.

If you linked the object, each time you open your PowerPoint presentation, PowerPoint checks the source file for an updated version.

If you embedded the object, you can double-click it at any time to open it in its native application for editing.

Perhaps you are wondering about the other data types. If you chose Paste in step 7 (rather than Paste Link), you will see other formats on the list. All of these are non-linkable, non-embeddable formats. The choices depend on the type of data, but include some of these:

✦ **Formatted Text (.RTF).** This data type formats text as it is formatted in the original file. For example, if the text is formatted as underlined in the original file, it is pasted as underlined text in PowerPoint.

✦ **Unformatted Text.** This option ignores the formatting from the native file and formats the text as the default PowerPoint font you've specified.

✦ **Picture (Windows Metafile).** The object appears as a 16-bit WMF-format graphic.

✦ **Picture (Enhanced Metafile).** The object appears as a 32-bit EMF-format graphic.

✦ **Device Independent Bitmap.** The object comes in as a bitmap picture, like a Windows Paint image.

Expert Tip

Enhanced Metafile is, as the name implies, an updated and improved file format from Windows Metafile. It is a 32-bit format, whereas Windows Metafile is a 16-bit format. Enhanced metafile graphics cannot be used in MS-DOS or 16-bit Windows applications. If that backward-compatibility is not important to use, use Windows Metafile. You can get more information about Windows metafiles at `http://multivac.fatburen.org/localdoc/libwmf/caolan/ora-wmf.html`.

Embedding an entire file

Sometimes you might want to place an entire file on a PowerPoint slide — for example, if the file is small and contains only the object that you want to display, like a picture. To create this connection, you use the Insert ➪ Object command, which is handier than the procedure you just learned because you do not have to open the other application.

1. In PowerPoint, display the slide on which you want to place the file.

2. Choose Insert ➪ Object. The Insert Object dialog box opens.

3. Click the Create from File button. The controls change to those shown in Figure 18-4.

4. Click Browse, and use the Browse dialog box to locate the file you want. Then click OK to accept the filename.

5. *(Optional)* If you want the file to be linked instead of embedded, click the Link check box.

Caution

Do not link to a file housed on a disk that might not always be available during your presentation. For example, don't link to a floppy unless you are also storing the presentation file itself on the same floppy. And don't link to a network drive unless you know the network will be available at show time from the computer on which you will present.

6. Click OK. The file is inserted on your PowerPoint slide.

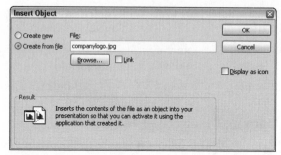

Figure 18-4: Enter the filename or browse for it with the Browse button.

You can tell that the file is embedded, rather than simply copied, because when you double-click it, it opens in its native application. In contrast, when you double-click an item that has been copied without embedding, its Properties box or some other PowerPoint-specific dialog box opens in PowerPoint. If you choose to link the object, you'll need to edit it in the native application.

Essentially, using Insert ➪ Object works the same as Edit ➪ Paste Special.

Embedding a new file

If you want to embed a foreign object but you haven't created that object yet, a really easy way to do so is to embed it on-the-fly. When you do this, the controls for the program open within PowerPoint (or in a separate application window, depending on the application) and you can create your object. Then, your work is saved within PowerPoint rather than as a separate file.

1. Open PowerPoint and display the slide on which you want to put the new object.

2. Choose Insert ➪ Object. The Insert Object dialog box appears.

3. Click Create New. A list of available object types appears. See Figure 18-5.

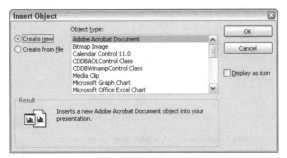

Figure 18-5: Choose the object type you want to create. The object types listed come from the OLE-compliant programs installed on your PC.

4. Click the object type you want and then click OK. The application opens.

5. Depending on the application, additional dialog boxes might appear. For example, if you are creating a new graphic object, a box might appear asking you about the size and color depth. Respond to any dialog boxes that appear for creating the new object.

6. Create the object using the program's controls. The program might be in a separate window from PowerPoint, or it might be contained within the PowerPoint window as in Figure 18-6.

7. When you are finished, if the program was opened within PowerPoint, click anywhere on the slide outside of that object's frame.

   Or, if the application was in a separate window, choose File ➪ Exit and Return to *Filename* (where *Filename* is the name of your PowerPoint file). If prompted to save the file, choose No.

Expert Tip   If you are prompted to save the object in a file and you choose Yes, the application creates a copy of the object that will exist outside of PowerPoint. The copy will not be linked to PowerPoint.

If you are asked whether you want to update the object in *filename* before proceeding, you should choose Yes. This prompt occurs in many of the applications that open in separate windows.

8. Resize and move the object on the slide as necessary.

Because you are creating a file that doesn't have a name or saved location separate from the PowerPoint presentation, there is no need to link it to anything. Embedding is the only option.

Menus from Paint

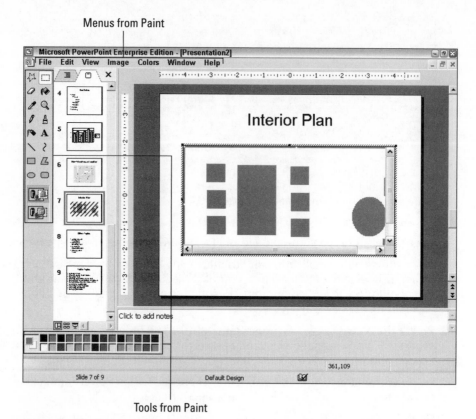

Tools from Paint

Figure 18-6: The embedded program's controls appear, with PowerPoint in the background.

Some interesting types of objects to embed

There are several mini-applications that come with Office 2003 that aren't normally run from outside the "big" applications like PowerPoint. Some of these can insert very useful content into a presentation!

To use one of these object types, choose Insert ⇨ Object, select Create New, and then select the application from the list.

Here are some examples:

✦ **Microsoft Equation:** Opens the Equation Editor, where you can create complex math equations and then embed them into PowerPoint.

✦ **Calendar Control:** Inserts a calendar object. First you insert it (no options), and then you right-click it and choose Calendar Object/Properties to set up the format, date range, and so on.

✦ **Microsoft Clip Gallery:** This one shows up only if you upgraded to Office 2003 from an earlier version of Office. It provides a way of accessing and inserting clip art that came with previous versions of Office.

Working with Linked and Embedded Objects

Now that you have a linked or embedded object, what can you do with it? Lots of things. You can edit an embedded object by double-clicking it, of course. And you can update, change, and even break the links associated with a linked object. The following sections provide some details.

Opening and converting embedded objects

When you select a linked or embedded object in PowerPoint and then open the Edit menu, an *Object* command appears at the bottom. (Its exact name depends on the object type.) You probably won't use this menu very often because there are easier ways to accomplish most of what it offers, but it is worth knowing about for special situations.

✦ **Edit:** Opens the object for editing within PowerPoint if possible. Some applications can work from within PowerPoint, like the Paint example in Figure 18-6. If the object is related to an application that can't do this, the object opens for editing in a separate window for that application.

✦ **Open:** Opens the object for editing in a separate window for the application with which it is associated.

✦ **Convert:** Opens a dialog box that enables you to convert the object to some other type (if possible). This sounds great in theory, but in practice there are usually very few alternatives to choose from.

Expert Tip

Although convert options do appear for linked objects, they cannot be converted; you must break the link first. That's because a linked object must have a certain object type in order to maintain its link. Even after breaking a link, there might not be any viable choices for converting it to other formats.

Editing an embedded object

To edit an embedded object, follow these steps:

1. Display the slide containing the embedded object.
2. Double-click the embedded object, or click once on it to select it and then choose Edit ⇨ Object. The object's program's controls appear. They might be integrated into the PowerPoint window, like the ones for Paint that you saw in Figure 18-6, or they might appear in a separate window.
3. Edit the object as needed.

4. Return to PowerPoint by doing one of these things:

- • If the embedded object is not linked to a saved file, click the slide behind the object to return to PowerPoint.

- • If the object is linked, choose File ➪ Exit. (Remember, the menu system that appears is for the embedded application, not for PowerPoint.) When asked to save your changes, click Yes.

You can also edit a linked object directly in its original application, independently from PowerPoint. Close your PowerPoint presentation and open the original application. Do your editing, and save your work. Then, reopen your PowerPoint presentation and the object will reflect the changes.

Changing how links are updated

OLE links are automatically updated each time you open your PowerPoint file. However, updating these links slows down the file opening considerably, so if you open and close the file frequently, you might want to set the link updating to Manual. That way, the links are updated only when you issue a command to update them.

To set a link to update manually, follow these steps:

1. Open the PowerPoint presentation that contains the linked object(s).

2. Choose Edit ➪ Links. The Links dialog box appears. See Figure 18-7. If the Links command is unavailable on the Edit menu, there are no OLE links in the active presentation.

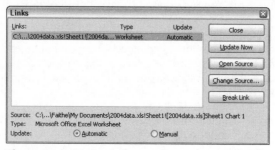

Figure 18-7: You can change the update setting for the links in your presentation here.

3. Click the link that you want to change.

4. Click the Manual button.

5. If you want to change any other links, repeat steps 3 and 4. You can also use the Shift and Control buttons to select more than one link at once.

6. If you want to update a link now, select it and click the Update Now button.

7. Click OK.

8. Choose File ➪ Save to save the presentation changes (including the changes to the link settings).

When you set a link to manual, you have to open the Links dialog box and click Update Now, as in Step 6, each time you want to update it. Or, you can right-click the object and choose Update Link from its shortcut menu.

Breaking a link

When you break a link, the object remains in the presentation, but it becomes an ordinary object, just like any other picture or other object you might have placed there. You can't double-click it to edit it anymore, and it doesn't update when the source changes. To break a link, reopen the Links dialog box (Figure 18-7), click the link to break, and then click Break Link. If a warning box appears, click OK.

When you break a link, embedding information disappears too. So, for example, if you had a linked Excel chart and broke the link, the result is a simple pasted image of the chart with no ties to the Excel application. To reestablish a link, simply recreate it as you did originally.

Changing the referenced location of a link

If you move files around on your hard disk, or move them to other disks, you might need to change the link location reference. For example, perhaps you are moving the presentation file to a floppy disk and you want to place all the linked files needed for the presentation in a separate folder on the floppy disk.

To change a link reference, do the following:

1. Copy or move the files where you want them. For example, if you are going to be transferring the presentation and linked files to a floppy, do that first.

2. Open the PowerPoint presentation that contains the linked object(s) to change. If you copied the presentation to some new location, make sure you are opening the copy that you want to change.

3. Choose Edit ➪ Links. The Links dialog box appears. See Figure 18-7.

4. Click the link you want to change.

5. Click Change Source. A Change Source dialog box opens. It is just like the normal Open dialog boxes you have worked with many times.

6. Select the file to be linked from its new location, and click Open. The link is updated.

7. In the Links dialog box, click Close.

Caution

If you change the location of a link to a different file, the link will refer to the entire file, as if you had inserted it with Insert ⇨ Object. If you used Edit ⇨ Paste Special, Paste Link to insert only a part of the original file, that aspect might be lost and the entire file might appear as the object in the presentation. In such situations it is better to delete the object and recreate the link from scratch.

Exporting PowerPoint Objects to Other Programs

You can copy any object in your PowerPoint presentation to another program, either linked or unlinked. For example, perhaps you created a chart using the PowerPoint charting tools for one of your PowerPoint slides, and now you want to use that chart in a Microsoft Word document.

To use a PowerPoint object in another program, you do the same basic things that you've learned in this chapter, but you start with the other program. Here are some examples:

✦ To copy an object from PowerPoint, select it in PowerPoint and choose Edit ⇨ Copy. Then switch to the other program and choose Edit ⇨ Paste. Just like with other data types, if you're copying text it's a simple process, but if you're copying a graphic element such as a PowerPoint chart, the element is embedded by default so that it can be reactivated within PowerPoint by double-clicking.

✦ To embed (or optionally link) an object from a PowerPoint presentation into another program's document, choose it in PowerPoint and choose Edit ⇨ Copy. Then, switch to the other program and choose Edit ⇨ Paste Special.

✦ To embed or link an entire PowerPoint presentation in another program's document, use the Insert ⇨ Object command in that other program, and choose your PowerPoint file as the source.

You can also save individual slides as various types of graphics with the File ⇨ Save As command, as you learned to do in Chapter 3.

Summary

In this chapter, you learned the mysteries of OLE, a term you have probably heard bandied about but were never quite sure what it meant. You can now use objects freely between PowerPoint and other programs, and include links and embedding for them whenever appropriate.

You have reached the end of this part of the book, so the next chapter is another Project Lab where you have the chance for hands-on practice of your newly acquired skills.

✦   ✦   ✦

Project Lab: Improving the Visual Impact

◆   ◆   ◆   ◆

In This Chapter

Inserting and formatting photographs

Combining WordArt with AutoShapes to produce a custom logo

Inserting and manually formatting a diagram

◆   ◆   ◆   ◆

Welcome to the third Project Lab in this book! Here you will have the opportunity to practice inserting many different kinds of objects into a presentation.

The Scenario

This lab continues your work for Spice Meadow Shelties, which you were introduced to in Chapter 13. The business owner is pleased with the work you did in Project Lab 2 and would like you to continue building her presentation.

The owner, Sheri Hineman, has asked you to incorporate some photos of her dogs into the basic presentation, and also to create a logo for the business using the picture that you worked with in Chapter 13. Finally, she would like you to create a diagram that shows the pedigree of her top-producing stud dog.

Lab 3A: Inserting and Formatting Photographs

In this lab session, you will insert three photographs that the business owner has provided, and resize, move, crop, and adjust them as needed.

Level of difficulty: Moderate

Time to complete: 10 to 20 minutes

1. **Open the file Lab03A.ppt from the Labs folder (from the CD) and save it as MyLab03A.ppt.**

2. **Remove the image from the title slide. (Remember, it is on the Slide Master.)**

   a. Choose View ➪ Master ➪ Slide Master.

   b. On the Slide Master (which is actually the title master), click the image to select it and then press Delete to delete it.

   c. Drag the left border of the subtitle text box to the left so that it is centered beneath the title text box.

   d. Click Close Master View.

3. **Remove the subtitle text box from the title slide, and insert the file fivedogs.jpg from the Labs folder in its place.**

   a. On the title slide, select the subtitle text box and press Delete. The text disappears from the placeholder box but the placeholder remains.

   b. Select the empty placeholder box and press Delete. This time the entire text box disappears.

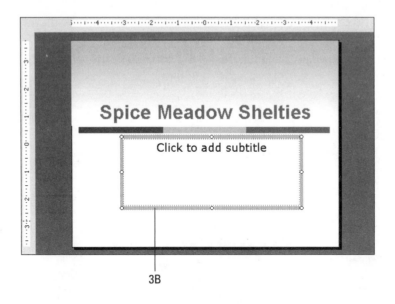

3B

c. Choose Insert ➪ Picture ➪ From File.

d. Navigate to the Labs folder and select fivedogs.jpg.

e. Click Insert.

3D

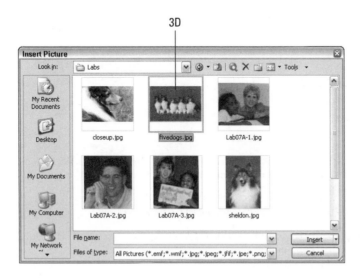

f. Drag the picture into the space previously occupied by the subtitle text box.

g. Drag a corner selection handle inward to make the picture slightly smaller, so it fits more neatly on the slide.

4. Crop the photo to remove the extraneous white border at the right and bottom.

a. Zoom in to 100% by selecting 100% from the Zoom drop-down list on the Standard toolbar.

b. Right-click the picture and choose Show Picture Toolbar if the Picture toolbar is not already displayed.

c. Click the Crop tool on the Picture toolbar.

d. Position the mouse pointer over the bottom-right corner and drag inward until the dotted line aligns with the edge of the picture (the green grass portion). Then release the mouse button to complete the crop.

e. Turn off cropping by clicking the Crop tool again.

f. Zoom out again by selecting Fit from the Zoom drop-down list.

5. Make the picture slightly brighter.

a. Click the picture to select it if it is not already selected.

b. On the Picture toolbar, click the More Brightness button one time.

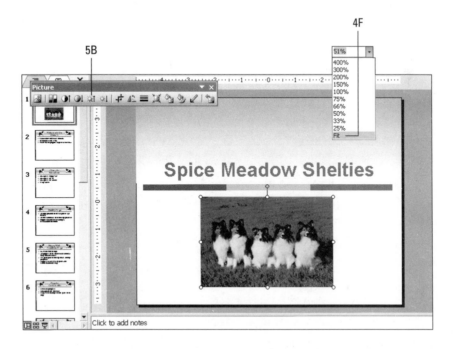

6. Change Slide 3 to a Title, Text, and Content layout.

    a. In the Slides pane, click slide 3 to display it.

    b. Choose Format ⇨ Slide Layout.

    c. Scroll through the available layouts and select Title, Text, and Content (the one with bullets at the left and a content placeholder at the right).

    d. Close the task pane.

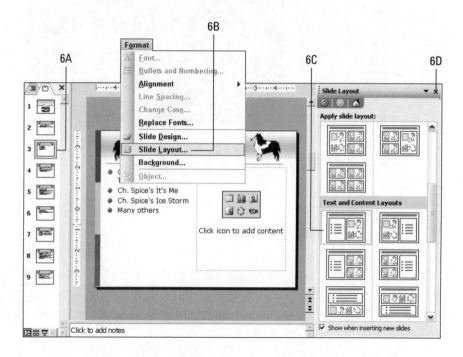

7. On slide 3, insert the file sheldon.jpg in the content placeholder box.

    a. Click the Insert Picture icon in the placeholder on slide 3. The Insert Picture dialog box appears.

    b. Navigate to the Labs folder if needed.

    c. Select sheldon.jpg.

    d. Click Insert.

8. **Increase the font size on slide 3 to 28 points, to match the rest of the presentation.**

   a. Click in the text box containing the bulleted list.

   b. Press Ctrl+A to select all the text.

   c. Open the Font Size drop-down list on the Formatting toolbar and choose 28.

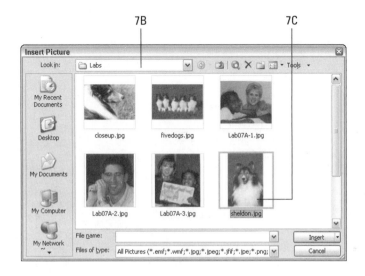

9. Crop the extraneous white border from the bottom and right sides of this image, just as you did in step 4 for the other picture.

    a. Zoom in to 100% by selecting 100% from the Zoom drop-down list on the Standard toolbar.

    b. Right-click the picture and choose Show Picture Toolbar if the Picture toolbar is not already displayed.

    c. Click the Crop tool on the Picture toolbar.

    d. Position the mouse pointer over the bottom-right corner and drag inward until the dotted line aligns with the edge of the picture (the green grass portion). Then release the mouse button to complete the crop.

    e. Turn off cropping by clicking the Crop tool again.

10. Insert the file threedogs.jpg on the last slide.

    a. Display slide 9.

    b. Choose Insert ➪ Picture ➪ From File.

c. Navigate to the Labs folder, select threedogs.jpg, and click Insert. The picture appears on the slide.

If the picture appears in the center of the slide, overlapping the text, go on to step 11. Otherwise continue with step d.

d. Click the down arrow next to the Automatic Layout Options icon at the bottom-right corner of the inserted image. This opens a menu.

e. On that menu, choose Undo Automatic Layout. Now the picture appears in the center of the slide, overlapping the text.

11. Position threedogs.jpg below the text on the slide, and resize as needed.

a. Drag the picture to the bottom of the slide.

b. Click in the bulleted list text box to select it.

c. Drag its bottom-right selection handle up and to the right, so that the text box is wider and shorter and does not overlap the picture.

d. Enlarge the picture by dragging a corner selection handle so that it fills the available space attractively.

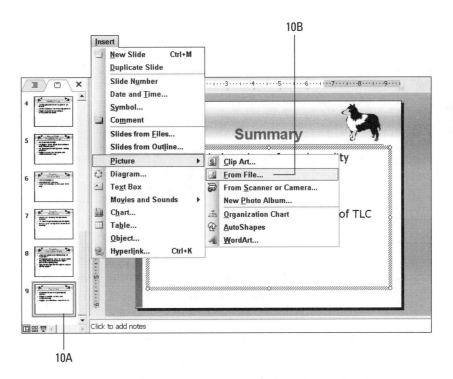

11B   11C

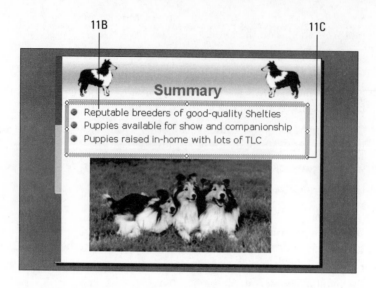

12. Save your work.

You should have saved the file in step 1 as MyLab03A.ppt, so you can simply resave with the Save button.

Lab 3B: Creating a Logo

In Chapter 13 (Lab 2), you created two separate Slide Master and Title Master layouts for this client — one with a green background and one with white. You have been working with the white background so far in this lab, but now it's time to work with the green one.

Your client would like you to create a simple logo with the initials SMS (for Spice Meadow Shelties) and a pawprint, and would like to use this logo on the green-background Slide Master. The following steps show how to do that.

Level of difficulty: Moderate

Time to complete: 10 to 20 minutes

1. **Open the presentation file if it is not already open, and save it as MyLab03B.ppt.**

   a. If you completed Project 3A, use MyLab03A.ppt. If not, open Lab03B.ppt from the Labs folder.

   b. Choose File ⇨ Save As and save the file as MyLab03B.ppt.

2. **Display the green background Slide Master.**

   a. Choose View ⇨ Master ⇨ Slide Master.

   b. Click the green background Slide Master slide.

3. **Draw a 2" pale gold circle with no outside border in the bottom-left corner of the slide.**

   a. Click the Oval tool on the Drawing toolbar.

   b. Hold down the Shift key and drag to draw a circle in the bottom-left corner of the slide.

   c. Double-click the circle to open its Properties box.

   d. Click the Colors and Lines tab.

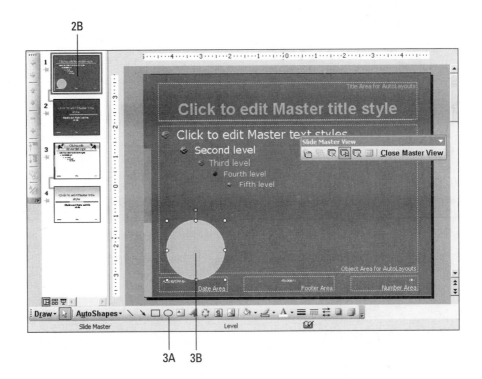

e. Open the Color drop-down list in the Line section and choose No Line.

f. Open the Color drop-down list in the Fill section and choose More Colors. The Colors dialog box opens.

g. Click the Custom tab.

h. Make sure RGB is chosen as the color model.

i. Enter the following values: 255 for Red, 230 for Green, and 125 for Blue.

j. Click OK.

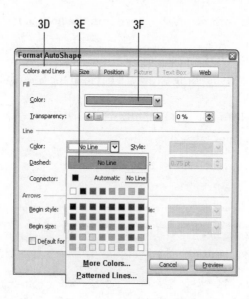

3G 3H 3I   3J

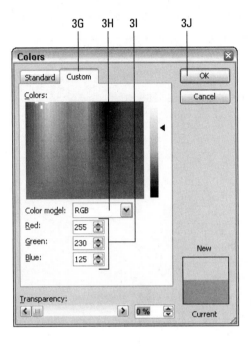

k. Click the Size tab.

l. Enter 1.5" for both the Height and Width measurements in the Size and Rotate section. Click OK.

3K   3L

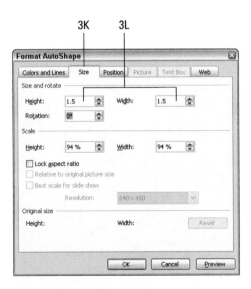

4. Create WordArt with the letters SMS, and place it on the gold circle.

    a. Zoom in to 125% with the gold circle clearly visible on-screen. (Enter 125 manually as the zoom.)

    b. Click the Insert WordArt button on the Drawing toolbar.

    c. In the WordArt Gallery dialog box, select the third style from the left on the top row.

    d. Click OK.

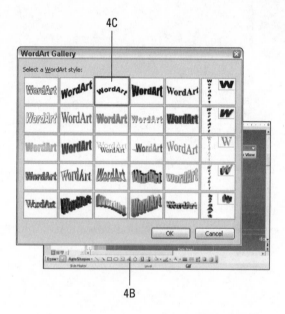

    e. In the Edit WordArt Text box, type **SMS**.

    f. Click OK.

4E

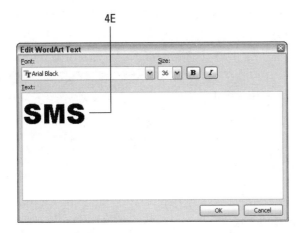

g. Drag the SMS WordArt on top of the gold circle. Hold down the Alt key if you need to fine-tune the positioning without the alignment grid.

h. Resize the WordArt so that it fits neatly in the top half of the circle.

4G   4H

5. Using the Oval tool, draw a black paw print beneath the WordArt on the gold circle.

   a. Zoom in to 200% so the oval is more clearly visible.

   b. Using the Oval tool, draw an oval near the bottom of the gold circle, approximately 1/2" tall and 1/3" wide.

Note

You can check the oval's size by double-clicking it to display its Properties box and then looking on the Size tab.

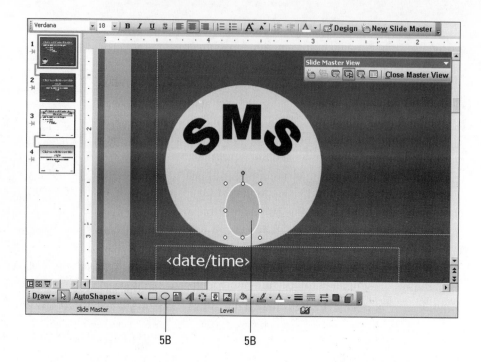

5B   5B

c. Draw a small circle directly above the oval, 0.2" high and 0.2" wide.

d. Select that small circle and copy it by clicking the Copy button on the Formatting toolbar.

e. Paste the copy by clicking the Paste button, and then drag that copy to the left of and slightly below the first one.

f. Click the Paste button again, and drag the next copy to the right of and slightly below the first one.

5D   5E

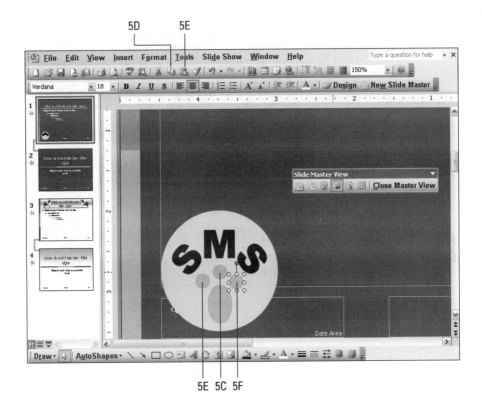

5E 5C 5F

g. Hold down the Shift key and click on the oval and all three of the circles, selecting them all at once.

h. Open the Line Color button's list (Drawing toolbar) and choose No Line.

i. Open the Fill Color button's list (Drawing toolbar) and choose More Fill Colors.

j. In the Colors dialog box, click a black hexagon.

k. Click OK.

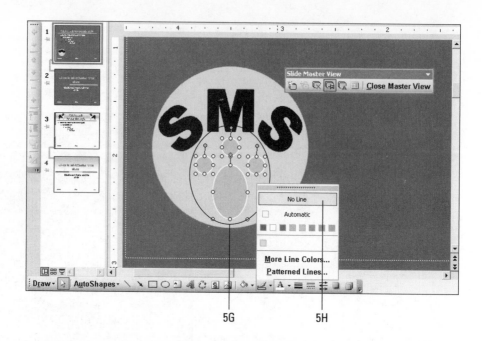

5G   5H

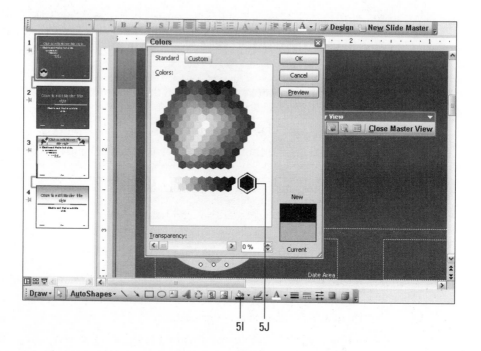

5I   5J

6. Group all parts of the logo into a single object.

    a. Hold down the Shift key and click the WordArt and the gold circle, adding them to the selected items.

    b. Click Draw ⇨ Group to group the items together.

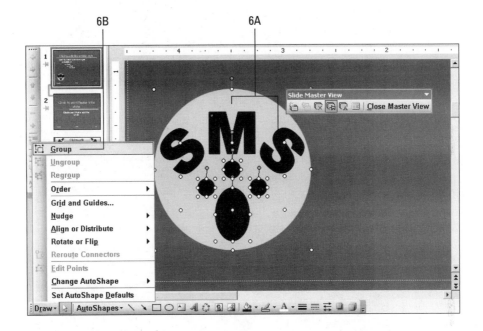

7. Save the logo as a separate graphic for use outside of PowerPoint.

    a. Right-click the logo and choose Save as Picture.

    b. In the Save as Picture dialog box, choose a location in which to save the logo. (For example, choose the folder where you have been saving your other lab files.)

    c. Leave the file type set to Enhanced Windows Metafile (*.emf).

    d. In the Name box, type **SMS**.

    e. Click Save.

8. Zoom out to see the logo position on the slide, and adjust it if needed. Then close Slide Master view.

    a. Open the Zoom list and choose Fit.

    b. Drag the logo so that its bottom and left sides just barely touch the dotted lines for the placeholders in the bottom-left corner of the slide.

    c. Click the Close Master View button on the Slide Master View toolbar.

7B

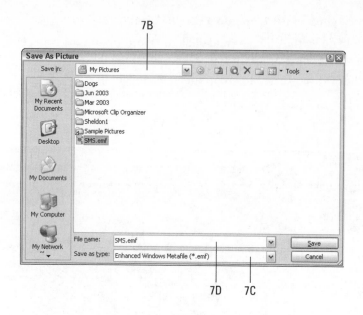

7D   7C

8C

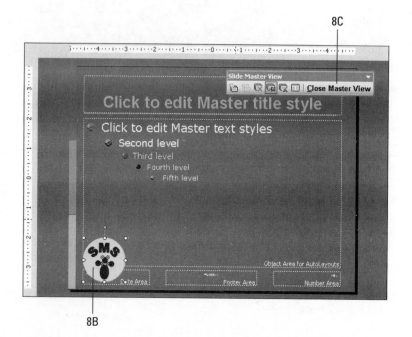

8B

9. **Switch all slides to the green background design, and then check your work in Slide Show view.**

   a. Click the Design button on the Formatting toolbar, opening the Slide Design task pane.

   b. Open the drop-down list for the green background slide master and choose Apply to All Slides.

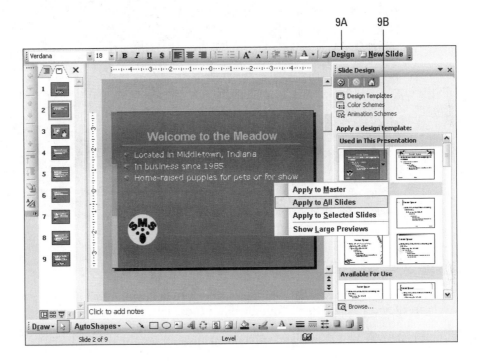

   c. Choose Slide Show ➪ View Show to start the show.

   d. Click to move through the slides, checking to make sure that the logo does not interfere with any text on the slides. When you reach the end of the show, press Esc to return to PowerPoint.

10. **Save your work.**

Happy, Well-Socialized Dogs

- No kennel-raised dogs
- All puppies reside in our home and have daily human contact
- We participate in nursing home visiting programs
- Puppies socialized to be good with children and other dogs

Lab 3C: Using a Diagram to Show Genealogy

One of the many uses for the Diagrams feature in PowerPoint is to illustrate a genealogical progression. Your client for these labs is interested in having a diagram that shows the last two generations in the family tree of her top-producing stud dog; in the following steps you will create that for her.

Level of difficulty: Difficult

Time to complete: 10 to 20 minutes

1. **Open the presentation file if it is not already open, and save it as MyLab03C.ppt.**

   a. If you completed Project 3B, use MyLab03B.ppt. If not, open Lab03C.ppt from the Labs folder.

   b. Choose File ➪ Save As and save the file as MyLab03C.ppt.

2. **Switch the presentation back to the white background design.**

   a. Click the Design button on the Formatting toolbar.

   b. In the Slide Design task pane, click the white background design for this presentation.

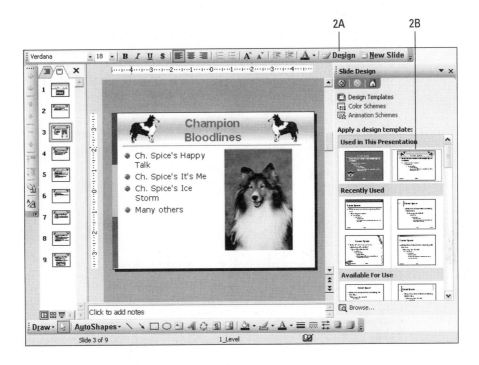

3. Create a new slide with a Title and Diagram or Organization Chart layout following slide 3.

    a. Click slide 3 in the Slides pane to select it.

    b. Click the New Slide button on the Formatting toolbar. A new slide appears with a Title and Text layout. The Slide Layout task pane also appears.

    c. In the task pane, click the Title and Diagram or Organization Chart layout.

    d. Close the task pane.

4. Create an organization chart using the slide placeholder.

    a. Double-click the placeholder on the new slide. The Diagram Gallery dialog box appears.

    b. Click Organization Chart.

    c. Click OK. An organization chart appears.

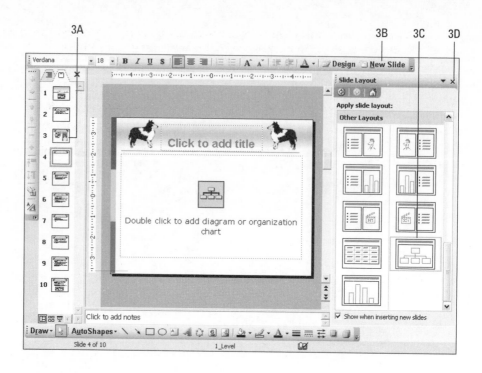

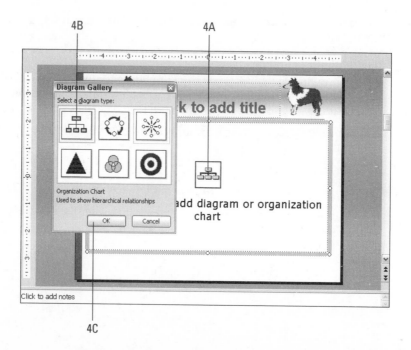

5. **Delete one of the second-level boxes on the chart, and enter the names shown in the following figure in the remaining three boxes.**

   a. Select one of the second-level boxes on the chart and press the Delete key.

   b. Click in the top level box and type **Ch. Spice's Happy Talk.**

   c. Click in the left second-level box and type **Ch. Spice's It's Me.**

   d. Click in the right second-level box and type **Ch. Rainbow Storm.**

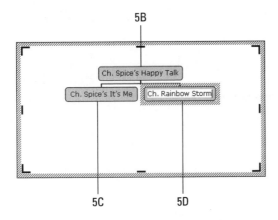

6. **Insert two third-level boxes subordinate to each of the second-level boxes (total of four new boxes).**

   a. Click a second-level box.

   b. Click the Insert Shape button twice (on the Organization Chart toolbar).

   c. Repeat steps a and b for the other second-level box.

6B

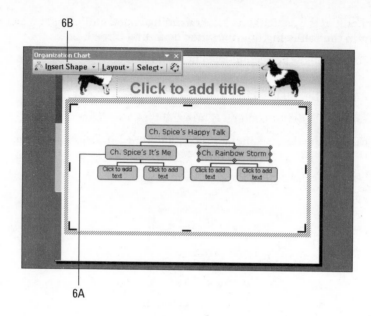

6A

7. **Type the text shown in the following figure into the third-level text boxes.**

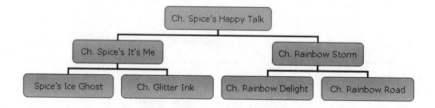

8. **Turn off AutoLayout.**

From the Organization Chart toolbar, choose Layout ➪ AutoLayout.

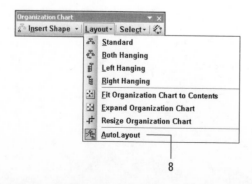

8

9. **Rearrange all the boxes so that they run from right to left rather than from the top down, as shown in the following figure.**

Do not worry about the connecting lines at this point.

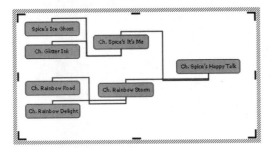

10. **Reposition all the connecting lines so that they connect one side of a box to the opposite side of the next level box.**

    a. Select a connecting line. Red circles appear at each end.

    b. Drag a red circle from its current position to the side of the box nearest to the other box.

    c. Repeat steps a and b for each connecting line, until the connecting lines look like the ones shown in the following figure.

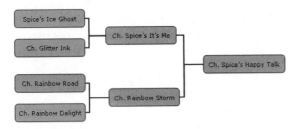

11. **Add a descriptive title to the slide.**

    a. Click in the Title text box for the slide. The organization chart becomes deselected.

    b. Type **Champion Stud Service.**

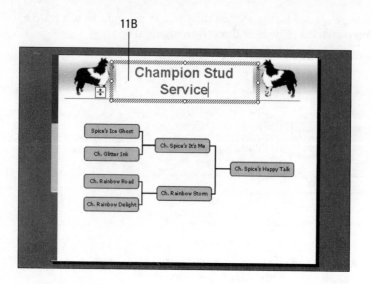

12. Save your work.

Summary

Congratulations, you made it through the lab sessions for this part of the book! You have practiced inserting pictures, and you've learned how to create a logo with simple WordArt and AutoShape components and save it as a graphic. You also practiced your organization chart skills. Your client is sure to be pleased with the work you have done!

The next chapter begins a new part of the book, one on sound and video. In it you will learn how you can pep up a presentation by adding movement and sound to the mix.

✦   ✦   ✦

Sound, Movement, and Video

Adding Sound Effects, Music, and Soundtracks

Whether it's a simple sound effect or a complete musical soundtrack, sounds in a PowerPoint presentation can make a big difference in the audience's perception of your message. In this chapter you'll learn when and how to use sounds, how to place them in the presentation, and how to manage their playback.

When Are Sounds Appropriate?

Sounds should serve the purpose of the presentation. You should never use them simply because you can. If you add lots of sounds purely for the fun of it, your audience may lose respect for the seriousness of your message.

That said, there are many legitimate reasons to use sounds in a presentation. Just make sure you are clear on what your reasons are before you start working with them. Here are some ideas:

✦ You can assign a recognizable sound, such as a beep or a bell, to each slide, so that when your audience hears the sound, they know to look up and read the new slide.

✦ You can record a short voice-over message from a CEO or some other important person who couldn't be there in person.

✦ You can punctuate important points with sounds or use sounds to add occasional humorous touches.

However, if you are trying to pack a lot of information into a short presentation, you should avoid sounds, as they take up time playing. You should also avoid sounds and other whimsical touches if you are delivering very serious news. You may also want to avoid sounds if you will be presenting using a very old and slow computer, because any kind of media clip (sound or video) will slow such a system down even more, both when loading the presentation and when presenting it.

There are several ways to include a sound in a presentation:

✦ **Insert a sound file.** The sound plays during the presentation whenever anyone points to or clicks the sound icon, depending on the settings you specify. This is useful in an interactive presentation because it gives the audience a choice of whether to play the sound.

✦ **Associate a sound with an object** (such as a graphic), so that the sound plays when anyone points to or clicks that object. This is another good one for interactive presentations.

✦ **Associate a sound with an animation effect** (such as a series appearing in a graph), so that the sound plays when the animation effect occurs. For example, you might have some text "drive in" onto a slide and associate the sound of an engine revving with that action.

✦ **Associate a sound with a slide transition** (a move from one slide to the next), so that the sound plays when the next slide appears. For example, you may assign a shutter click sound, like the sound that a slide projector makes when it changes slides, to the transitions between slides.

✦ **Insert a sound that plays automatically in the background.** This is useful for unattended (kiosk-style) presentations.

In this chapter you will learn about the first two of these: inserting files as icons and associating them with objects. In Chapter 22, you will learn about transition and animation sounds as part of the full coverage of those features.

Sound File Formats

Computer sound files come in several formats, but can be broken into two broad categories: wave and MIDI.

The term *wave* can refer to a specific file format that has a .wav extension, but it can also refer generically to any sound file that has an analog origin. For example, when you record sound using a microphone, the resulting file is a wave file in a generic sense of the word because it was originally a "sound wave" in the air that the microphone captured. The tracks on an audio CD can also be considered wave files because at some point, presumably, a person went to a recording studio and made music with voice or instruments that was recorded. Similarly, the very popular MP3 music format is a wave format. Other wave formats include `.rmi`, `.au`, `.aif`, and `.aifc`. Wave files are very realistic sounding because they are basically recordings of real-life sounds. The drawback to wave files is that the file size is typically large. MP3 is a relatively compact format, but even MP3 requires about 1 megabyte per minute of recording.

The other big category of sound file is MIDI. MIDI stands for multi-instrument digital interface, and refers to the interface between a computer and a digital instrument such as an electronic keyboard. When you make a MIDI recording, there is no analog source — it is purely digital. For example, you press a key on an electronic keyboard, and that key press is translated into instruction and written in a computer file. No microphone, no sound waves in the air. What is the sound of one key pressing? It's completely up to the software. It could sound like a piano, a saxophone, a harpsichord — whatever instrument it's set up to "be" at the moment. MIDI files (usually with a `.mid` extension) are smaller in size than wave files. Several minutes of recording typically takes up much less than one megabyte of space. The drawback to MIDI music is that it can sound rather artificial and "computer-ish." A computer emulating a saxophone is not the same thing as a real saxophone, after all.

You need to understand the difference between these sound formats so you can choose the correct format when recording sounds for your presentation or when choosing recorded music. Keep in mind that whenever you use a wave file in a presentation, you are going to be adding considerable bulk to the presentation's file size. But also keep in mind that when you choose MIDI over wave for your music, you get a different type of music, one that is more artificial-sounding.

Caution   The sounds that come with Microsoft Office are royalty-free, which means you can use them freely in your presentation without paying an extra fee. If you download sounds from the Internet or acquire them from other sources, however, you must be careful not to violate any copyright laws. Sounds recorded from television, radio, or compact discs are protected by copyright law, and you or your company might face serious legal action if you use them in a presentation without the permission of the copyright holder.

To hear the difference, do the following exercise as an experiment:

1. In Windows, use the Search (or Find) feature to locate the sample MIDI files that came with Windows. To do so, search for *.MID.

2. Double-click one of the files to play it.

3. Use Search (or Find) to locate some sample wave files that came with Windows. To do so, search for *.WAV.

4. Double-click one of the files to play it.

Hear the difference?

Where to Find Sounds

There are sound collections available all over the Internet, just like there are clip art collections. You can also buy sound collections on CD. If you find yourself putting together lots of presentations, or searching the Internet for hours to find specific sounds for this or that purpose, you might find it more cost effective to simply buy a good collection of sounds.

Here are some Web sites where you can find some sounds:

✦ **A1 Free Sound Effects** (www.a1freesoundeffects.com/noflash.htm) Lots of free sounds for non-commercial use. You can also buy them for commercial use quite cheaply.

✦ **Microsoft** (http://office.microsoft.com/downloads/2002/ Sounds.aspx) Microsoft offers a nice collection of free sounds to work with Office versions 2000 and higher. Also check out http://dgl.microsoft.com.

✦ **Partners in Rhyme** (www.sound-effect.com/) Sound and music collections for sale, plus some free ones for download. Their background music clips are cool because they are set up for perfect looping — that is, continuous play without a noticeable break between the end and the beginning.

✦ **Wav Central** (http://wavcentral.com/) Big repository of all kinds of free sounds in wave format. (Beware of possible copyright violations, though; some of the clips here appear to be from movies, TV shows, and so on.)

A few dozen sounds also come with PowerPoint; you'll see how to access them within the program as you read this chapter.

The Microsoft Clip Organizer can also be a source of sounds from Microsoft's collection of clips. Although the collection of sounds is not as extensive as that of clip art, you may be able to find something of use. This chapter does not specifically address the Clip Organizer, as it was covered pretty thoroughly in Chapter 14; turn back there to learn about it.

Now that you know where to find sounds, and how to make intelligent decisions about their use, let's get into the nitty-gritty of actually using them in your presentation.

Inserting a Sound File as an Icon

The most elementary way to use a sound file in a presentation is to place the sound clip directly on a slide as an object. An icon appears for it, and you can click the icon during the presentation to play the sound. This method works well if you want to be able to play the sound at exactly the right moment in the presentation.

To "hide" the sound icon, drag it off the edge of the slide. The sound will still work but the audience won't see the icon.

You can place a sound file on a slide in either of two ways: by selecting a sound from the Clip Organizer, or by selecting a sound from a file on your computer or network. The following sections cover each method.

You can also assign the sound to another object on the slide instead, as explained in the "Assigning a Sound to an Object" section later in this chapter. When you do that, the object to which you attach the sound serves the same function as an icon; you click the object to play the sound.

Choosing a sound from the Clip Organizer

You learned about the Clip Organizer in Chapter 14. Its primary function is to help you insert clip art (graphics), but it also manages sounds and movie files. The Clip Organizer is a good place to start if you are not sure which sound files are available or what kind of sound you want.

Follow these steps to choose a sound from the Clip Organizer:

1. Establish your Internet connection if possible. This will make a much wider variety of clips available.

2. Choose Insert ➪ Movies and Sounds ➪ Sound from Clip Organizer. The Clip Organizer appears with icons for the available clips.

3. *(Optional)* To narrow down the list of clips to only those with certain keywords, type the keyword in the Search For box and press Enter.

4. *(Optional)* To preview the clip, do the following:

   a. Right-click a clip and choose Preview/Properties from the shortcut menu. A Preview/Properties dialog box opens, and the sound plays.

   b. If you want to play the sound again, click the Play button (right-pointing triangle). See Figure 20-1.

   c. *(Optional)* To preview another clip, click the Next (>) or Previous (<) buttons.

   d. To close the dialog box, click Close.

The Preview/Properties box also enables you to change or add keywords to the clip, as you did with the clip art in Chapter 14. Click the Edit Keywords button to expand the dialog box to include controls for editing the keyword list.

5. Click the clip to insert. A box appears asking how you want it to play: Automatically or When Clicked. Choose one. An icon for the sound appears on the slide, in the center.

Figure 20-1: Preview a clip in the Preview/Properties box.

6. Reposition and/or resize the icon as desired. In Figure 20-2, for example, it has been moved off to the corner where it is less noticeable. You could even drag it completely off the slide and it would still work (but would not appear on-screen).

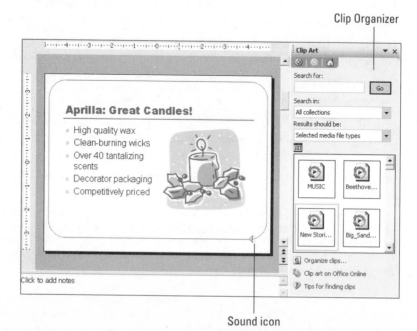

Figure 20-2: The sound clip appears as a small speaker icon on the slide.

Note   The icon shown for sounds in the task pane in Figure 20-2 looks like it does because on my PC, files with a .wav extension are associated with Windows Media Player. If you have sound files associated by default with some other program such as MusicMatch or Real Player, you might have a different graphic for sound icons.

7. If you want to insert another sound clip, repeat Steps 3 through 6. If you are finished with the Clip Organizer for now, close it by clicking its Close (X) button.

Once the Sound icon is on the slide, you can move and resize it like any other object. See Chapter 11 for details. You can also specify when the sound will play: when the mouse pointer moves over it, when you click it, or automatically. See the "Specifying when and how a sound will play" section later in this chapter.

Choosing a sound from a file

If the sound you want is not accessible from the Clip Organizer, you can either add it to the Clip Organizer, as you learned to add a clip in Chapter 14, or you can simply import it from a file. The former is better if you plan on using that clip a lot; the latter makes more sense if you are using the clip only once or expect to use it only infrequently.

Note   There are many sound files in the Windows\Media folder on your hard disk if you installed PowerPoint or Office using the default options. Use one of these if you want to follow along with the following steps as practice but don't have an actual sound clip you want to insert at this point.

Follow these steps to insert a sound from a file:

1. Choose Insert ➪ Movies and Sounds ➪ Sound from File. The Insert Sound dialog box opens.

2. Navigate to the drive and folder that contain the sound you want. If you are not sure which location to use, try Windows\Media on the hard disk where Windows is installed. See Chapter 3 for a refresher on changing the drive and folder.

3. Click the sound file you want to use, as shown in Figure 20-3, and then click OK.

4. A box appears asking how you want it to appear in the slide show. Choose Automatically or When Clicked. A Speaker icon appears on the slide, as you saw in Figure 20-2.

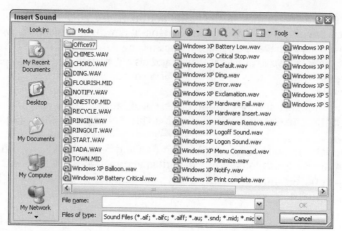

Figure 20-3: Choose a sound file from your hard disk or other location (such as on your company's network).

Expert Tip

Sound (WAV) files smaller than the size specified in PowerPoint's options will be embedded; sounds larger than that specified size will be linked. To adjust the number, choose Tools ⇨ Options, click the General tab, and specify a value in the Link sound files greater than _____ kb box. If you plan on a sound file being linked, place it in the same folder as the PowerPoint presentation file before inserting it. This will ensure a relative reference in the link, so that when you move the files to another location the link will retain its integrity.

Specifying when and how a sound will play

When you insert a sound, as you saw in the preceding sections, you can choose Automatically or When Clicked.

Automatically makes the sound play when the icon appears. If you don't have any animation set up for the slide, the sound icon appears at the same time as everything else on the slide, so basically this means that the sound plays when the slide appears. (See Chapter 22 to learn about animation that can make different items on a slide appear at different times.) When Clicked makes the sound play only when the icon is clicked.

If you want to more precisely define when a sound will play, or change the volume for a sound, try the following method.

Playing on a mouse click or mouseover

If you set up the sound to play when clicked, PowerPoint uses the Action Settings to configure the sound to play whenever it is clicked. You can remove that attribute so that it does not play when clicked, and/or you can set it up to play when the mouse touches it (called a *mouseover*).

Even if you chose Automatically as the initial setting, you can also set it up to play with mouse click and/or mouseover. The two do not preclude one another.

Caution

If you set up a sound to play automatically and also allow it to be played on mouse click or mouseover, you may end up with two copies playing, and not necessarily synchronized.

To play a sound when the mouse either clicks it (mouse click) or touches it (mouseover), or to modify its setting in that regard, do the following:

1. Click the icon to select it. Selection handles appear around it.

2. Choose Slide Show ⇨ Action Settings or right-click the icon and choose Action Settings from the shortcut menu. The Action Settings dialog box appears.

3. Click the Mouse Click or Mouse Over tab. Figure 20-4 shows the Mouse Click tab.

Expert Tip

You can have separate settings for the mouse click and mouseover actions, and one does not preclude the other. For example, you may have also specified that it should play on Mouse Click, and if you set it up to play on Mouse Over, that will not change the Mouse Click setting.

4. To make the sound play on mouse click (or mouseover, depending on the tab you selected), click the Object Action option if it is not already selected. Then make sure that Play is selected from the Object Action drop-down list. Or, to prevent it from playing on mouse click (or mouseover), click the None button.

5. Click OK.

Figure 20-4: To make a sound play when the mouse pointer is over its icon, set it up on the Mouse Over tab. Use the Mouse Click tab to make it play on mouse click.

Accessing a clip's animation settings

When you choose Automatically as the setting when initially placing the sound, it sets it up to play at the exact moment that the sound icon appears on-screen, with no delay. You can change this default so that there is a delay, or you can turn it off so that it does not play automatically.

To access a sound's animation settings, choose Slide Show ⇨ Custom Animation. The Custom Animation task pane appears. A clip that is set up to play automatically appears with an After Previous designation, at the top of the list. It has an icon that looks like a clock. A clip that is set up to play on mouse click or mouseover appears with a mouse icon. See Figure 20-5.

Clips that were inserted from the Clip Organizer will have generic names like "Media 3." Clips that were inserted manually with Insert ⇨ Movies and Sounds ⇨ Sound from File will have names matching the file name, such as TADA.WAV.

Note   The following sections just scratch the surface of the animation settings in PowerPoint; for a fuller discussion see Chapter 22.

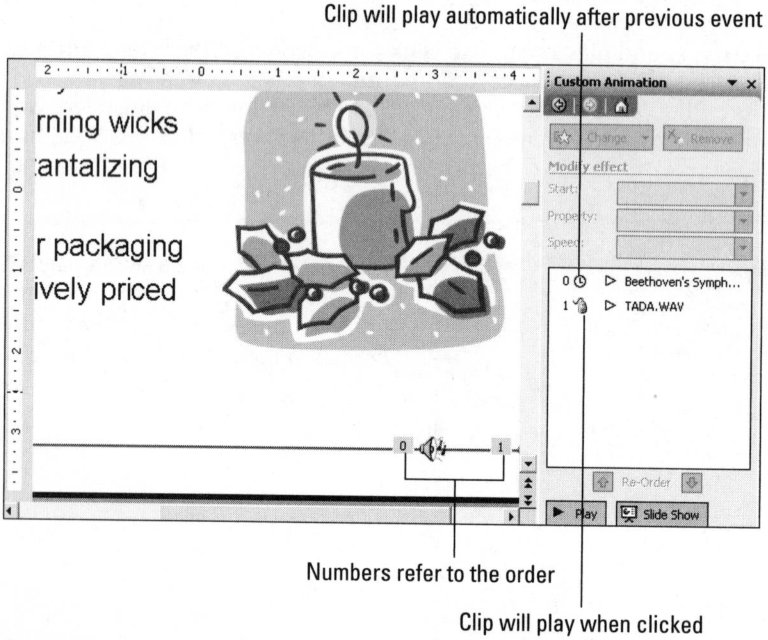

Clip will play automatically after previous event

Numbers refer to the order

Clip will play when clicked

Figure 20-5: Custom animation settings let you fine-tune when a sound will play.

Turning automatic play on/off

To turn on/off the automatic play for a clip, do the following:

1. Choose Slide Show ⇨ Custom Animation to open the Custom Animation task pane if it does not already appear.

2. Select the icon for the sound. A gray box appears around its name in the task pane.

3. Point to the sound on the task pane, so that a down arrow appears to its right. Then click the arrow to open a menu. See Figure 20-6.

4. If you want automatic play, choose Start After Previous. If you don't, choose Start on Click.

Caution   If the clip has been set up not to play on click or on mouseover (through its Action Settings), choosing Start on Click in Step 4 will not turn that option back on. You have to go back to its Action Settings to do that.

Expert Tip   Specifying Start on Click in the Custom Animation task pane will start the sound file when the mouse is clicked anywhere on the slide, even if it's not clicking on the sound icon itself. However, you can mimic the on-mouse-click action settings by clicking on the arrow to the right of the sound name in the Custom Animation task pane to open the Timing tab, clicking the Triggers button, and then selecting the sound in the Start Effect on Click of box.

Figure 20-6: Choose whether the sound should play automatically or only when clicked.

Delaying or repeating a sound

Depending on the situation, it may be useful to have a sound play after a short delay, or to repeat the sound more than once. In Chapter 22 you'll learn more about setting animation options, but here's a quick instruction specifically for sounds:

1. Choose Slide Show ➪ Custom Animation to open the Custom Animation task pane if it does not already appear.

2. Select the icon for the sound. A gray box appears around its name in the task pane.

3. Open the menu for the sound clip, as shown in Figure 20-6, and choose Timing. The Play Sound dialog box opens with the Timing tab displayed. See Figure 20-7.

Delay

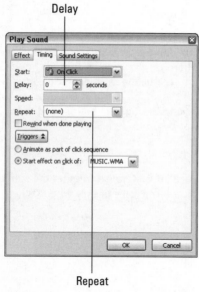

Repeat

Figure 20-7: Use the Timing controls to set a delay for when the sound will play.

4. Enter a number of seconds in the Delay box. The delay will be between the time the previous event happens (in this case, that event is the slide appearing on-screen initially) and the sound beginning.

5. Open the Repeat drop-down list and choose a number of times that the sound should repeat. You can choose 2, 3, 4, 5, or 10 times, Until Next Click, or Until Next Slide. You can also type in a number if you want some other number than the ones shown.

6. Click OK.

Choosing the starting point for a sound clip

There might be times when you'll want to start the clip from some point other than the beginning. For example, maybe you have a really good sound clip except that the first five seconds is garbled or contains something inappropriate for your use, or perhaps you want to play just the first 15 seconds of a clip. All these things are possible in PowerPoint 2003.

To control the point at which a clip starts, do the following:

1. Choose Slide Show ➪ Custom Animation to open the Custom Animation task pane if it does not already appear.

2. Select the icon for the sound. A gray box appears around its name in the task pane.

3. Open the menu for the sound clip and choose Effect Options. The Play Sound dialog box opens with the Effect tab displayed, as in Figure 20-8.

Figure 20-8: You can start a clip playing at other than the beginning, or set it to restart playing wherever it left off if you stop it.

4. In the Start Playing area, choose one of these options:

   From beginning to use the default play mode.

   From last position if you want it to pick up where it left off when you stopped it.

   From time, and then enter the number of seconds into the clip that the clip should begin playing.

5. Click OK.

Choosing when the sound clip will stop

Normally a clip will stop playing after it has played once (or however many times you have set it up to play), or until you click. There may be times when you want it to stop earlier, though. For example, suppose you want a certain song to play while a certain slide is on-screen, but to stop when you move to the next slide. Or maybe you want it to continue for the next two slides, and then stop.

To control when a sound clip stops, use the Effect tab of the Play Sound dialog box, which you saw in Figure 20-8.

1. Perform steps 1–4 of the preceding steps.

2. In the Stop Playing section, choose one of these options:

> **On Click** to use the default play mode.

> **After current slide** to stop the audio when you move to the next slide, or when the clip has finished playing, whichever comes first.

> **After _____ slides,** and then enter a number of slides, to continue the audio until a certain number of additional slides have passed.

3. Click OK.

Expert Tip If you want to play more than one sound back-to-back throughout your presentation (as a background track), enter 999 in the After _____ Slides box. PowerPoint will stop the first sound when it starts the second. If you simply put the number of slides you expect PPT to play the sound, it won't work the way you expect it to. Here's an article with more specifics: www.rdpslides.com/pptfaq/FAQ00047.htm.

Specifying the sound volume

When you give your presentation, you can specify an overall volume for it through the computer's volume controls in Windows. However, sometimes you might want one sound to be more or less loud in comparison to the others.

To set the volume for a specific sound:

1. Right-click the sound icon on the slide and choose Edit Sound Object. The Sound Options dialog box opens.

2. Click the speaker icon button. A volume slider appears. Drag it up or down. See Figure 20-9.

3. Click OK to close the Sound Options dialog box.

Expert Tip The sound will play at a consistent volume throughout the duration of the clip. If you need it to change volume partway through, use a sound editing program on the clip before inserting it.

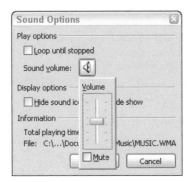

Figure 20-9: Set the volume for an individual sound in comparison to the baseline volume for the entire presentation.

Assigning a Sound to an Object

Many presenters find the Sound icons distracting and unprofessional-looking, and they prefer to assign sound files to clip art or to other objects placed in the presentation. That way, they still have precise control over when a sound plays (for example, when they click the clip art), but the means by which they control the sound is hidden.

Although you can assign a sound to any object, many people assign their sounds to graphics. For example, you might attach a sound file of a greeting from your CEO to the CEO's picture.

Follow these steps to assign a sound to an object:

1. Insert the object that you want associated with the sound. The object can be any graphic, chart, text box, or other object.

2. Right-click the object and choose Action Settings from the shortcut menu. The Action Settings dialog box appears.

3. Click either the Mouse Click tab or the Mouse Over tab, depending on what you want. Mouse Click will play the sound when you click the object; Mouse Over will play the sound when you point to it with the mouse pointer.

4. Select the Play Sound check box. Then open the drop-down list and choose a sound. See Figure 20-10. You can choose from a variety of sounds stored in C:\Windows\Media, or you can choose Other Sound to open the Add Sound dialog box and pick a sound from any location.

Note The first time you select a sound from the Play Sound list, you may be prompted to reinsert your Office or PowerPoint CD-ROM so PowerPoint can install the needed sound files. Just follow the prompts that appear.

Figure 20-10: Choose the sound to assign to the object.

5. Click OK. The object now has the sound associated with it so that when you click it or mouseover during the presentation, the sound plays.

Note   Chapter 22 is devoted entirely to transitions and animation effects, so this chapter won't go into them in detail. When you get to Chapter 22, you will learn how you can assign sounds to the transition between slides, or to the movement (animation) of any object on any slide.

Ten Sound Ideas for Business

Unsure about which sounds to use? Try these ideas on for size:

✦ **Applause:** Use when presenting good news, a success story, or a new product.

✦ **Breaking Glass:** Use to indicate you are "breaking the mold," introducing something bold and innovative, or breaking a sales record.

✦ **Camera or Slide Projector:** These subtle clicking sounds work great as a sound transition from slide to slide.

✦ **Cash Register:** Play this sound when you are talking about making more profits or raising more money.

✦ **Drum Roll:** This sound is great for building suspense before unveiling a new concept, product, or service.

✦ **Explosion:** Use to dramatize how you are "blowing up" the competition, the previous rules, or the old ways of thinking.

✦ **Gunshot:** This sound is reminiscent of the starting gun at the beginning of a race—use it to kick off a sales competition or a new semester.

✦ **Screeching Brakes:** Use this sound when you're talking about stopping the frantic pace to analyze what you're doing or "putting the brakes on" bad behavior.

✦ **Typewriter:** This sound can be really cool when it is combined with the letter-by-letter introduction of text with an animation effect. It looks like the text is being typed!

✦ **Whoosh:** Use this sound with a slide transition that flies or sweeps the next slide onto the screen.

Adding a CD Audio Soundtrack

Lots of great music is available on CD these days, and most computers contain a CD-ROM drive that reads not only computer CDs but also plays audio ones. PowerPoint takes advantage of this fact by letting you play tracks from an audio CD during your presentation.

Adding a CD audio clip to a slide is much like adding a regular sound clip. You place the clip on the slide and a little CD icon appears that lets you activate the clip. Then you can set properties for the clip to make it play exactly the way you want. It's different, however, in that the audio track is not stored with the presentation file. Therefore, the audio CD must be in the CD drive of the computer that you're using to present the show. You can't use CD audio tracks in presentations that you plan to distribute as self-running presentations on a data CD or over the Internet, because the computers on which it will run will not have access to the CD.

 Expert Tip If you need to include audio from a CD in a presentation that will be shown on a PC without access to the original audio CD, you can record a part of the CD track as a .wav file using Windows Sound Recorder program or some other audio-recording utility. Keep in mind, however, that .wav files can be extremely large, taking up many megabytes for less than a minute of sound. To keep the file size smaller, consider using an MP3 or an ASF instead of a WAV. As always, make sure you are not violating any copyright laws.

Placing a CD soundtrack icon on a slide

To play a CD track for a slide, you must place an icon for it on the slide. You can actually place a range of tracks, such as tracks 1 through 4 from a CD, using a single icon. Follow these steps:

1. Choose Insert ➪ Movies and Sounds ➪ Play CD Audio Track. The Insert CD Audio dialog box appears.

2. Enter the starting track number in the Start at Track box under Clip Selection. See Figure 20-11.

Figure 20-11: Specify a starting and ending track, and optionally, a time within those tracks.

3. Enter the ending track number in the End at Track box. If you want to play only a single track, the Start at Track and End at Track numbers should be the same. The start/end time will change only after you click on one of the up or down arrows next to the time. Note that if you want to play tracks 1, 2, and 3, for instance, you should put track 1 as the start track and track 3 as the end track (as opposed to track 4).

4. If you want to begin the starting track at a particular spot (other than the beginning), enter that spot's time in the Time box for that line. For example, to start the track 50 seconds into the song, enter 00:50.

5. If you want to end the ending track at a particular spot, enter that spot's time in the Time box for that line. The default setting is the total playing time for all selected tracks. For example, in Figure 20-11, Track 1 is both the starting and ending track, and the time for that track is 2:10. If I wanted to end it 10 seconds early, I could change the At setting under End to 2:00. You can see the total playing time at the bottom of the dialog box.

6. Click OK. A message appears asking whether you want the sound to play Automatically or When Clicked. Make your selection.

7. The CD icon now appears in the center of the slide. Drag it elsewhere if it is in the way of your slide content. You can also resize it if you want, as you can any other object.

8. Right-click the sound icon and select Custom Animation. Click the downward-pointing arrow next to the clip in the custom animation task pane and select Effect Options. Enter a number in the box for Stop Playing After ___ Slides. Remember that PowerPoint considers each transition (whether backward or forward) a "slide" in this context, so entering **999** in that box will ensure that your soundtrack(s) will play throughout the entire presentation.

Expert Tip You can play any number of tracks from a single CD using a single icon, as long as they are contiguous and you play them in their default order. If you need non-contiguous tracks from the CD, or in a different order, or you just want certain segments of some of the clips, you must place each one individually on the slide, and then control their order in Custom Animation. See Chapter 22 for details. If you don't want the icons to appear on the slide, drag them off the slide's edge.

The CD track is now an animated object on your slide. By animated, I mean that it is an object that has some action associated with it. Depending on your choice in Step 6, the CD track will activate either when the slide appears (Automatically) or when you click its icon during the presentation (When Clicked).

Expert Tip To play CD tracks across multiple slides, you must use custom animation, and you must set the sound to stop playing after 999 slides. Chapter 22 covers custom animation in more detail, but here's how it works: Suppose you have a 30-slide presentation, and you want to play tracks 2, 4, and 6 from your CD, each for 10 slides. On slide 1, you would insert track 2, and set its custom animation to stop playing after 999 slides. Then you would do the same thing for track 4 on slide 11 and track 6 on slide 21.

Editing the CD track start/end times

To change the specification of which track to play and where to start it, do the following:

1. Right-click the CD icon and choose Edit Sound Object. The CD Audio Options dialog box opens. It looks almost exactly like the Insert CD Audio dialog box shown in Figure 20-11.
2. Change the track numbers and/or starting and ending times.
3. Click OK.

Controlling when a CD track plays

You can set many of the same properties for a CD track on a slide that you can set for a sound file icon. For example, you can use the Action Settings command to specify whether the clip should be activated with a mouse click or simply a mouseover.

You can also use the Custom Animation controls to set up precise specifications for when and how a track will play. To get there, do the following:

1. Choose Slide Show ➪ Custom Animation.
2. Select the CD icon on the slide. A gray box appears around its name in the Custom Animation task pane.
3. Open the menu for that clip and choose Effect Options. This opens the Play CD Audio dialog box.

From this point, the options are exactly the same as those for regular sound files that you have learned about earlier in this chapter. Refer back to the "Specifying when and how a sound will play" section earlier in this chapter for details. All the same tabs are available, including Effect, Timing, and Sound Settings.

Using the Advanced Timeline to Fine-Tune Sound Events

The Advanced Timeline is turned off by default. When you turn it on, a timeline appears at the bottom of the Custom Animation task pane, and indicators appear next to each clip that show how long each clip will take to play and at what point each one starts. This can be useful when you are trying to coordinate several sound and/or video clips to play sequentially with a certain amount of space between them. It saves you from having to do a lot of math to calculate their starting and ending times in relation to the initial appearance of the slide.

To turn the Advanced Timeline on, do the following:

1. If the Custom Animation task pane does not already appear, choose Slide Show ➪ Custom Animation.

2. Open the menu for any of the items in the task pane and choose Show Advanced Timeline. The timeline appears.

3. *(Optional)* Widen the task pane by dragging its left border toward the center of the slide, so you have more room to work with it.

4. *(Optional)* Click the word *Seconds* at the bottom of the task pane, opening a menu, and choose Zoom In or Zoom Out from it to change the zoom on the timeline.

5. Click a clip to select it on the Custom Animation list. A red right-pointing arrow appears next to it. The arrow appears at the spot that corresponds to the place on the timeline where the clip is currently set to begin. Figure 20-12 shows several clips, for example, with each beginning at a different point.

6. Open the clip's menu and choose either With Previous or After Previous, depending on how you want it to relate to the earlier clip.

Caution   If there is more than one sound clip set to After Previous, a vertical line appears where the first clip will finish. If a clip is set to After Previous, it cannot start before the clip that precedes it. Therefore, any delay that you set up for a subsequent clip will be in relation to the end of the preceding clip. If the clip is set to With Previous, the two can overlap.

7. *(Optional)* To reorder the clips on the list, click a clip and then click the up or down Reorder arrow at the bottom of the task pane.

ScreenTip shows delay being set

Red arrow

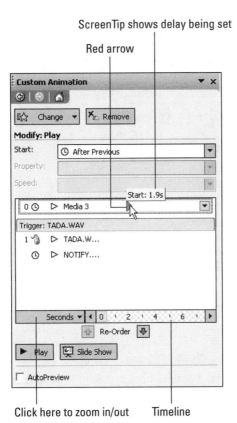

Click here to zoom in/out   Timeline

Figure 20-12: You can use a timeline to set the timing between clips on a slide in a graphical way.

8. To change the amount of delay assigned to a clip, drag the red arrow next to it to the right or left. This is the same as changing the number in the Delay text box in the clip's properties.

Expert Tip   You can use custom animation to create complex systems of sounds that play, pause, and stop in relationship to other animated objects on the slide. See Chapter 22 for full details, but here's a quick explanation of it: add a sound to the Custom Animation task pane by clicking Add Effect and then choosing Sound Actions and then Play, Pause, or Stop. In this way, you can create separate actions for the same clip to start, pause, or stop at various points.

Recording a Sound

Most PCs have a microphone jack on the sound card where you can plug in any of a variety of small microphones. If you have a microphone for your PC, you can record your own sounds to include in the presentation. I'm referring to simple, short sounds right now. If you want to record a full-blown voice-over narration, see Chapter 28.

To record a sound, follow these steps:

1. Display the slide on which you want to place the sound clip.

2. Choose Insert ➪ Movies and Sounds ➪ Record Sound. The Record Sound dialog box appears. See Figure 20-13.

Figure 20-13: Record your own sounds using your PC's microphone.

3. Type a name for the sound in the Name box, replacing the default Recorded Sound label that appears there.

4. Click the Record button (the red circle).

5. Record the sound. When you are finished, click the Stop button (the black square).

6. *(Optional)* To play back the sound to make sure it's okay, click the Play button (the black triangle).

7. Click OK to place the sound on the slide. A sound icon appears on the slide.

8. Use the controls you learned about earlier in this chapter to set when and how the sound plays.

Expert Tip   You can add your recorded sound to the Clip Organizer, described in Chapter 14, for easy reuse.

Summary

In this chapter, you learned about the many ways you can use sound in your presentation. You learned how to place a sound object on a slide, how to associate sounds with other objects, how to use a CD soundtrack, and how to record your own sounds. The next chapter continues in this same multimedia vein by looking at how you can place video clips on slides.

✦   ✦   ✦

Adding Videos

PowerPoint creates fully multimedia presentations, which means that not only can you include pictures and sounds, but movies and animations. In this chapter you'll learn how to select the appropriate video type, how to insert the clips, and how to control when they will play.

Understanding Video Types

Most of this chapter assumes that you have acquired your video clip(s), and that they're ready for insertion into your presentation. But where do those videos come from?

There are two kinds of videos: live-action (recorded video) and cartoons (animated video). PowerPoint can show both kinds. The difference is not that significant once you get them into PowerPoint, but when you are determining how you will acquire the clips you need it's helpful to make the distinction.

Recorded videos have a live origin. You can get them pre-recorded from the Internet, but in most cases you will want to record it yourself to suit your purposes. If you have a digital video camera, you can transfer it directly to PC via a USB or FireWire interface. If you have an analog video camera (that is, one that uses tape for recording), you must have a conversion box or adapter card. (A walk through your local computer store will show many different devices that will do the job.)

You will probably not import the videos directly from the camera into PowerPoint. Instead, you'll want to work with them in a video editing program first, to make them start and end at exactly the right places. A program like Windows Movie Maker will do nicely. It comes with Windows Me and Windows XP. Your digital video camera or video capture device may have software that came with it too. Recorded videos might be useful to:

✦ Present a message from a person who could not attend the presentation in person

✦ Show how a product works

✦ Tour a facility through the eyes of a video camera

Animation does not have a live origin — it is purely digital. There are many applications that can create animation. (PowerPoint isn't one of them, but PowerPoint can accept saved files from most of the popular programs.) You can use an animation clip to achieve the following:

✦ Demonstrate how a planned product will be built or how it will work after it is manufactured

✦ Explain a conceptually difficult subject in a classroom lecture

✦ Add a whimsical touch or lighten the mood

The Clip Organizer in PowerPoint provides many stock animation clips that have simple conceptual plots, like time passing, gears turning, and computers passing data between them. They are more like animated clip art than they are real movies, but they do add an active element to an otherwise static slide. They're just like clip art when it comes to finding and inserting them.

A sub-type of animation clips is the animated GIF. Animated GIFs are not videos in the traditional sense — they are a collection of still graphics stored in a single file. When the file is displayed — on a presentation slide, a Web page, or some other place — it cycles through the still graphics at its own pace, making a very rudimentary animation. The animation cannot be controlled for an animated GIF through PowerPoint, however. The number of times an animated GIF repeats is specified in the header information of the GIF itself; PowerPoint recognizes this information and plays the GIF accordingly.

Note   What's the difference between a movie and a video? There really isn't any. PowerPoint uses the two terms interchangeably, and so will I in this chapter.

Placing a Movie on a Slide

Your first step is to place the movie on the slide. After that, you can worry about position, size, and playing options. Just as with audio clips, you can place a clip on a slide using the Clip Organizer, or do so directly.

Choosing a movie from the Clip Organizer

Just as with sounds and graphics, you can organize movie files with the Clip Organizer. I don't go into it in detail here, because the Clip Organizer is discussed in detail in Chapter 14 and reviewed in Chapter 20. Most of the clips that come with the Clip Organizer are animations rather than recorded videos.

To select a movie from the Clip Organizer, follow these steps:

1. Make sure your Internet connection is established (for the best selection of clips).

2. Display the slide on which you want to place the movie.

3. Choose Insert ➪ Movies and Sounds ➪ Movie from Clip Organizer. The Clip Organizer task pane appears, showing the available movie clips. Thumbnails of each clip appear, showing the first frame of the clip. You can tell that each is an animation or movie rather than a static graphic because of the little star icon in the bottom-right corner of each thumbnail image. See Figure 21-1.

4. *(Optional)* If you want to preview the clip, open its menu (the down arrow to its right) and choose Preview/Properties. The clip plays in a dialog box; when you're done watching, click Close.

5. Click the clip you want to insert. A box may appear asking when you want it to play. (This box won't appear when you insert an animated GIF, as they play automatically.)

6. Click either Automatically or When Clicked. The clip appears on the slide.

7. Close the Clip Organizer, and then move the clip as needed. It won't play in Normal view, but you can switch to Slide Show view to test it if desired.

Caution Be careful resizing, as it can compromise quality; it's usually better to resize the video in your video-editing software.

To test the movie, enter Slide Show view and click it to play it. You can control when and how the clip plays; you learn to do that later in this chapter.

Expert Tip There are lots of interesting clips available through the Clip Organizer if you are connected to the Internet so you can access the Microsoft site. Unlike with artwork, it is not obvious what a clip does just by looking at its name and the first frame (which is what appears as its thumbnail image). Take some time to insert a lot of clips and try them out, to see what you have to choose from.

Remember that you can add your own video clips to the Clip Organizer, as you learned in Chapter 14, and you can categorize them, add keywords, and everything else that you can do to artwork.

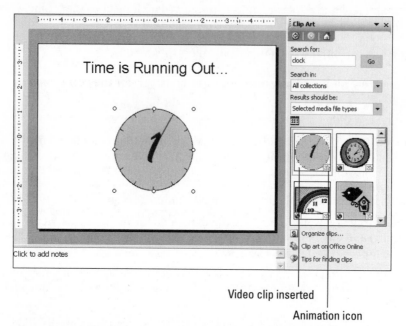

Figure 21-1: Inserting a video clip from the Clip Organizer.

Making Clip Organizer content available offline

If you find some video clips in the Clip Organizer that you would like to have available later, you might want to add them to the local collection of clips on your hard disk. That way if your Internet connection is not available later, you can still access them.

To make a clip available offline, do the following:

1. Make sure your Internet connection is established.

2. Choose Insert ⇨ Movies and Sounds ⇨ Movie from Clip Organizer. The Clip Organizer task pane appears, showing the available movie clips. The clips that are on the Web have a little globe icon in their bottom-left corner.

3. Open the menu of the clip you want (the arrow to its right) and choose Make Available Offline. The Copy to Collection dialog box opens. See Figure 21-2.

   If the Make Available Offline command is not present, it means that this clip is already on your local hard disk.

4. Select the collection in which you want to place the clip. (Or click New to create a new collection.) Then click OK.

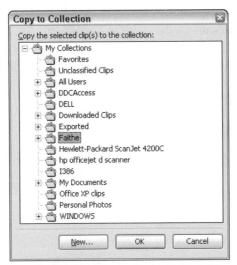

Figure 21-2: Making a clip available offline involves copying it to one of your local clip collections.

Importing a movie from a file

If the movie that you want is not in the Clip Organizer (and you don't want to bother with placing it there), you can place it directly on the slide, just like any other object. For example, you might have video of your CEO's last speech saved to a disk.

Note   Converting video from an analog video camera or videotape requires some sort of video capture device, such as a Snappy or an Iomega Buz. These devices are sold in most computer stores. Basic models start at around $100.

To insert a video clip from a file, follow these steps:

1. Display the slide on which the movie should appear.

2. Choose Insert ⇨ Movies and Sounds ⇨ Movie from File.

3. In the Insert Movie dialog box, change the drive and folder as necessary to locate the clip you want. See Figure 21-3.

4. Select the clip and click OK.

5. A box appears asking when you want it to play. Choose Automatically or When Clicked. The movie clip appears on the slide.

6. Move the clip as desired. Again, be careful when resizing.

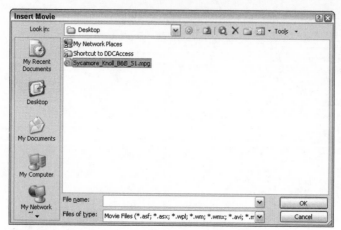

Figure 21-3: Select the movie you want and then insert it by clicking OK.

Setting Movie Options

Video clips are a lot like sounds in terms of what you can do with them. You can specify that they should play when you point at them or click them, or you can make them play automatically at a certain time.

Caution   If you are using an animated GIF, it plays the number of times specified in its header. That could be infinite looping (0), or it could be a specified number of times. You can't set it to do otherwise. (You can, however, delay its appearance with custom animation. See Chapter 22 for details.) Other movies, such as your own recorded video clips (AVI, WMV, and MOV format), have more settings you can control.

Playing on mouse click or mouseover

The default setting for a video clip is to play when you click it with the mouse. To set it to play when you point to it, or not to play in response to the mouse, follow these steps:

1. Right-click the clip and choose Action Settings. The Action Settings dialog box opens. See Figure 21-4.

2. On the Mouse Click and Mouse Over tabs, click the None button if you want no action, or click the Object Action button if you want it to play in either case.

3. Click OK.

Figure 21-4: Set the Object Action to Play on the Mouse Click and Mouse Over tabs.

Controlling the volume and appearance

If you are working with a real video clip (not an animated GIF), you can also edit the Movie object's controls. These controls enable you to specify whether the video plays in a continuous loop or not, and which frame of the movie remains on the screen when it is finished (the first or the last). You can also control whether any clip controls appear on the slide. We looked at these in Chapter 20 for sounds, but they are even more appropriate here for videos because you are more likely to want to pause, rewind, and fast-forward a video clip.

1. Right-click the movie on the slide and choose Edit Movie object. The Movie Options dialog box appears.

2. Set the sound volume for the clip in relation to the overall sound for the presentation by clicking the Sound Volume icon and then dragging the slider. (This works just like it did for sounds in Chapter 20.)

3. If you want the clip to go away when it is not playing, mark the Hide While Not Playing check box. Do this only if you will be playing the clip automatically, because if you set it to On Click and it is hidden, you won't be able to find it.

4. If you want the clip to play in full-screen size, mark the Zoom to Full Screen check box.

5. Click OK.

Expert Tip The same controls in the Movie Options dialog box (Figure 21-5) are also accessible while you are working on Custom Animation (covered in the following section). From the Custom Animation task pane, open the menu for the clip and choose Effect Options; then click the Movie Settings tab.

Figure 21-5: You can control some play options from this dialog box for movie files.

Understanding custom animation play options

When you place a movie clip on a slide, the Custom Animation pane will have two entries for it by default: Play and Pause. For example, in Figure 21-6, it's set to play on click and to pause on click. To view the Custom Animation task pane, choose Slide Show ➪ Custom Animation.

Before setting the custom animation properties for the clip, it's important to select carefully. If you click the clip on the slide, both of the animation triggers become selected at once (gray box around each of them). If you then open the menu for either clip and choose Timing or Effect Options, the Effect Options dialog box appears. These settings refer to all instances of the clip. However, if you select one or the other of the animation triggers, and then choose Timing or Effect Options for it, either a Play Movie or Pause Movie dialog box will appear. These settings refer to only that instance of custom animation.

The two sets of dialog boxes have much in common, but there are some significant differences, especially on the Effect tab. The following sections cover these in more detail.

Play symbol

On click symbol | The clip starts on click...

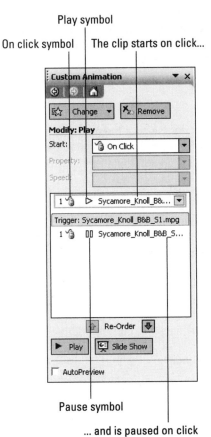

Figure 21-6: These two entries represent a single movie clip. The top one starts it playing, and the second one pauses it.

Pause symbol

... and is paused on click

Controlling when the video will play

You can control the play timing for real video clips (not animated GIFs) through the Custom Animation box. These settings enable you to specify whether the video should play automatically when the slide appears and whether there should be a delay before it.

1. Choose Slide Show ⇨ Custom Animation. The Custom Animation task pane appears.

2. To set the timing for the entire clip, click the clip on the slide. This selects all instances of it in the Custom Animation task pane. Or to set the timing for only one part of the animation, click it on the task pane.

3. Open the menu for the video clip and choose Timing. A dialog box opens, with the Timing tab on top. Depending on what you selected, the dialog box may be called Effect Options, Play Movie, or Pause Movie. Figures 21-7 through 21-9 show the differences.

4. Set the timing options as described in the text following these steps.

5. Click OK.

Note   Instead of opening the menu, you can just double-click the name of the clip in the task pane and the dialog box will open. Then you can click the tab you want (in this case, Timing).

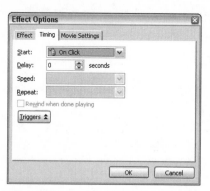

Figure 21-7: Timing for the clip as a whole appears in the Effect Options dialog box.

Figure 21-8: Timing for the clip starting to play appears in the Play Movie dialog box.

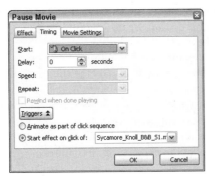

Figure 21-9: Timing for pausing the clip appears in the Pause Movie dialog box.

Here are the settings that they all have in common:

✦ **Start:** Your choices are On Click, With Previous, or After Previous.

✦ **Delay:** This is the delay in seconds between the previous animation event and this one.

In addition, the Play Movie dialog box includes the following items:

✦ **Repeat:** Choose how many times you want the clip to repeat before it stops.

✦ **Rewind when done playing:** If you want the last frame of the movie to remain on-screen after it completes, leave this check box unmarked. If you want the first frame to reappear, mark this check box.

All three dialog boxes have a Triggers button that displays or hides the extra triggers options. Triggers specify when the action should occur. They enable you to trigger an event as a result of clicking on the event object itself or something other than the event object. For example, you can place a sound icon on a slide but then have it triggered when someone clicks on a graphic. In the case of a video, the default setting for the Pause Movie animation event is triggered when you click on the clip itself. See Figure 21-9.

Specifying from what point the video will play

Just like with sounds, you can specify that a video clip should play from some point other than the beginning, and should continue through a certain number of slides and then stop. Because you probably will not want a clip to continue to play after you have moved past its slide, the stopping portion is less useful for videos than for sounds. However, the Start feature can be very helpful in trimming off any portion of the beginning of the clip that you don't want.

To set the start point for the clip, you must have the Play portion of the custom ani-mation selected — not the Pause portion or the clip as a whole.

1. In the Custom Animation task pane, click on the animation event for the clip that represents Play (with the Play triangle to the left of the name), so that only that item is selected.

2. Open the clip's menu and choose Effect Options. The Play Movie dialog box opens with the Effect tab on top. See Figure 21-10.

Caution   If you get the Effect Options dialog box or the Pause Movie dialog box in Step 2, you have selected the wrong option; click Cancel and go back to Step 1 to try again.

Figure 21-10: Specify from what point the clip should begin playing and when it should stop.

3. In the Start Playing section, choose the desired start point:
   - **From beginning:** The default.
   - **From last position:** From whatever point it was paused or stopped ear-lier. If it was not paused or stopped earlier, this is the beginning.
   - **From time:** A certain number of seconds into the clip. (Then specify the number of seconds.)

4. (Optional) In the Stop Playing section, if desired, set up the video to stop either on click, after the current slide, or after a specified number of slides.

5. Click OK.

Choosing the size of the video clip window

You can resize a video clip's window just like any other object. Simply drag its selection handles. Be careful, however, that you do not distort the image by resizing in only one dimension. Make sure you drag a corner selection handle, not one on a single side of the object.

Be aware also that when you enlarge a video clip's window, the quality of the clip suffers. If you make the clip large and are unhappy with its quality, you can reset it to its original size by following these steps:

1. Right-click the clip and choose Format Picture.

2. On the Size tab, click the Reset button.

3. Click OK.

Troubleshooting Problems with Video Play

If a certain video won't play in PowerPoint, try playing it in Windows Media Player in Windows. (Go to www.microsoft.com and download the latest version of the Media Player if you don't have it.) If it plays there, you can insert the clip as an object with the Insert ⇨ Object command, as you learned in Chapter 18. You won't be able to set any of the normal PowerPoint options for the clip; you will play it through Windows Media Player instead during the presentation.

If the clip won't play in Windows Media Player, you might not have the needed codec installed in Windows Media Player. A *codec* is a compression/decompression driver; different video formats use different ones. If you are connected to the Internet when you attempt to play the clip, the Media Player will attempt to connect to Microsoft to get the needed codec.

Still doesn't work? Windows Media Player does not support all video formats, but you might be able to find a different player that will. If you do, you can install it and then embed the movie as an object associated with that program, as you embedded objects in Chapter 18. To do this, you need to set the new program as the default for handling that file extension; choose Tools ⇨ Folder Options ⇨ File Types in a Windows file-management window to change extension associations.

 Expert Tip   For specific issues involving multimedia, you might find this Web site helpful: www.soniacoleman.com/Tutorials/PowerPoint/Multimedia.htm.

Balancing Video Impact with File Size and Performance

When you are recording your own video clips with a video camera or other device, it is easy to overshoot. Video clips take up a huge amount of disk space.

Movie files are linked to the PowerPoint file, rather than embedded, so they do not dramatically increase the size of the PowerPoint file itself. However, since the linked movie file is required when you show the presentation, having a movie does greatly increase the amount of disk space required for storing the whole presentation package.

Depending on the amount of space available on your computer's hard disk, and whether you need to transfer your PowerPoint file to another PC, you may want to keep the number of seconds of recorded video to a minimum to ensure that the file size stays manageable. On the other hand, if you have a powerful computer with plenty of hard disk space and lots of cool video clips to show, go for it!

Be aware, however, that slower, older computers, especially those with less than 64MB of RAM, may not present your video clip to its best advantage. The sound may not match the video, the video may be jerky, and a host of other little annoying performance glitches may occur if your PC is not powerful enough. On such PCs, it is best to limit the live-action video that you use, and rely more on animated GIFs, simple AVI animations, and other less system-taxing video clips.

 Expert Tip Place the movie clip in the same folder as the presentation file before inserting the movie clip. This creates a relative reference to the clip within the PowerPoint link to it, so that when you move both items to another location the link's integrity remains.

Sources of Movie Clips

Not sure where to find video clips? Here are some places to start:

✦ **Your own video camera.** For a few hundred dollars, you can buy a simple video eye that attaches to a board in your PC or an adapter that lets you use input from a regular video camera.

✦ **The Clip Organizer.** When you're connected to the Internet, you get the whole collection as you browse.

✦ **The Internet in general.** There are millions of interesting video clips on every imaginable subject. Use the search term video clips plus a few keywords that describe the type of clips you are looking for. Yahoo! is a good place to start looking (http://www.yahoo.com).

Caution

Whenever you get a video clip from the Internet, make sure you carefully read any restrictions or usage agreements to avoid copyright violations.

✦ **Commercial collections of video clips and animated GIFs.** Many of these companies advertise on the Internet and provide free samples for downloading. Several such companies have included samples on the CD that accompanies this book.

✦ **The Internet Archive.** (`http://www.archive.org`). This site contains links to huge repositories of public domain footage on all subjects, mostly pre-1964 material on which the copyright has expired. Warning—you can easily get sucked in here and waste several days browsing!

Summary

In this chapter, you learned how to place video clips on your slides and how to set them up to play when you want them to.

In the next chapter, you learn about transitions and object animation. With a transition, you can create special effects for the movement from one slide to another. With object animation, you can control the entry and exit of individual objects. You can make them fly in with special effects or build them dramatically one paragraph, bar, or shape at a time.

✦   ✦   ✦

Creating Animation Effects and Transitions

So far in this book, you've been exposed to several kinds of moving objects on a slide. One kind is a movie, or video clip, created in an animation program or recorded with a video camera. Another is an animated GIF, which is essentially a graphic that has some special properties that enable it to play a short animation sequence over and over.

But neither of these is what PowerPoint means by animation. In PowerPoint, *animation* is the way that individual objects enter or exit a slide. On a slide with no animation, all of the objects on it simply appear at the same time when you display the slide. (Boring, eh?) But on a slide with some animation applied to it, the bullet points might fly in from the left, one at a time, and the graphic might drop down from the top afterward.

A *transition* is yet another kind of movement. A transition refers to the entry or exit of the slide, rather than of an individual object on the slide. You learn about transitions at the end of this chapter.

Here are some ideas for using animation effectively in your presentations:

✦ Animate parts of a chart so that the data appears one series at a time. This technique works well if you want to talk about each series separately.

✦ Set up questions and answers on a slide, so that first the question appears, and then, after a mouse click, the answer appears.

✦ Dim each bullet point when the next one comes into view, so you are, in effect, highlighting the current one.

✦ Make an object appear and then disappear. For example, you might have an image of a lightning bolt that flashes on the slide for one second and then disappears, or a picture of a racecar that slides onto the slide from the left and then immediately slides out of sight to the right.

✦ Rearrange the order in which objects make their appearance on the slide. For example, you could make numbered points appear from the bottom up for a Top Ten list.

Using Animation Schemes

PowerPoint includes over 30 animation schemes that you can apply to slides. *Animation schemes* are preset combinations of animation effects for the entry and exit of the slide's content. Most of these schemes involve making one part of the slide appear before another part — the title might appear first, and then the bullets, for example, or each bullet point might appear individually each time you click the mouse. There might also be separate entry and exit animations. Some of the preset animations include sounds. You learned in Chapter 20 how to assign and remove sounds from objects, and you'll review that process later in this chapter too.

If you are new to animation, an animation scheme provides an easy way to get started. You can then customize the animation later as you gain more proficiency with the feature. For example, you could choose a scheme that fades letters in quickly on the slide, and then modify it later so that they fade a little more slowly.

Caution   Be careful not to overuse special effects such as animation. The audience can quickly turn from thinking "what a cool effect!" to thinking "what a silly show-off!" if you use too many different effects or use an effect too frequently.

Animation schemes may be applied either from Normal or Slide Sorter views. It doesn't make much difference; both work equally well. (For custom animation, however, discussed later in this chapter, Normal is better.)

Animation schemes come in three flavors: Subtle, Moderate, and Exciting. These refer to the amount of activity involved in each one, and provide a guide for which one might be appropriate. For example, you might want one of the Exciting schemes on the first or last slide, and one of the Moderate schemes on some of the important slides in-between. A Subtle scheme might work well for an "ordinary" slide.

To apply an animation scheme, follow these steps:

1. Select the slide on which you want to place the scheme.

2. Choose Slide Show ⇨ Animation Schemes. The Slide Design task pane appears showing the animation schemes. See Figure 22-1.

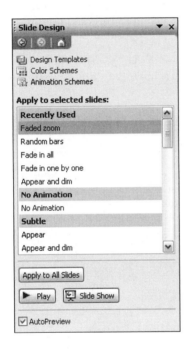

Figure 22-1: Select an animation scheme to quickly and easily apply animation effects to a slide.

3. Click the desired scheme on the list. The list offers you options including Recently Used, Subtle, Moderate, and Exciting.

   When you choose a scheme, it automatically plays on the selected slide, so you can observe its effect. If you don't like it, choose a different one. If it's almost what you want but needs to be changed a little, use Custom Animation to change it (covered later in this chapter).

4. To test the chosen animation scheme, click the Slide Show button in the task bar. The current slide appears in Slide Show view. Press Esc when you're finished watching it.

5. *(Optional)* To apply the same animation scheme to all slides in the presentation, click the Apply to All Slides button in the task pane.

Using Custom Animation

With custom animation, you have full control over the way that the objects on your slides are animated. You can choose not only from the full range of animation effects for each object (including manually placed ones), but you can also specify in what order the objects appear and what sound is associated with their appearance.

Custom animation: A first look

A good way to learn about custom animation is to start with an animation scheme and analyze it in Custom Animation to see how it works. Let's do that now with the Big Title animation scheme:

1. Select a slide that has a title and at least two bullet points on it.

2. Open the Animation Schemes task pane, and click Big Title.

3. Choose Slide Show ➪ Custom Animation to switch to the Custom Animation task pane. The animations appear, as in Figure 22-2.

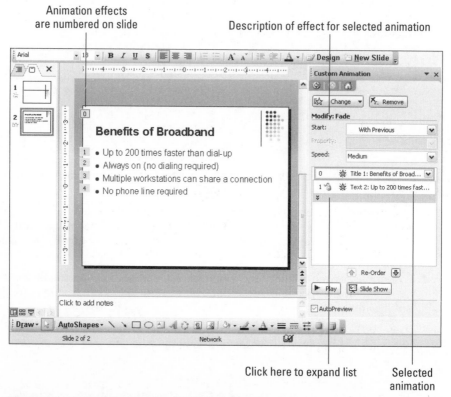

Figure 22-2: Here's one of the animation schemes viewed in Custom Animation.

In Figure 22-2, first look at the slide. Each of the animated items on the slide is numbered in the order in which they will be animated. In this case it's a top-down order, but it doesn't have to be. The Re-Order arrow buttons at the bottom of the task pane can move things around.

Next, look at the task pane. Notice that the 1 animation is selected at the moment; it represents the first bullet point. Here's the information about it that can be gathered from the task pane:

✦ The effect is currently set to Modify: Faded Zoom.

✦ The effect will start when you click (On Click). You can tell this both from the value in the Start box and also from the mouse icon that appears next to it on the list.

✦ The speed will be Very Fast.

✦ There are more identical animations for the additional bullet points beneath it, as evidenced by the double down-pointing arrow in the bar below it.

Clicking the arrow in the bar below the 1 animation expands the list, as shown in Figure 22-3. Notice that each of the other bullet points has identical animation settings to the first one. They can be individually changed if desired, however. If you want to apply a setting for only one of them, expand the list first. If you want to apply a setting that will apply to all of them, collapse the list first.

Click here to collapse list

Figure 22-3: Expanding the animations list shows the animations for items 2 through 4.

The Big Title animation scheme consists of these activities:

✦ When the slide appears, the slide title magnifies and then appears.

✦ When you click, the first bullet appears with a Faded Zoom animation.

✦ Each additional time you click, another bullet appears with a Faded Zoom animation until there are no more bullets. In Figure 22-3, there are a total of four bullets.

Assigning custom animation to an object

Now that you've seen a sample of some custom animation, let's go back and assign some animation "from scratch" to a slide that doesn't have any animation yet.

If you want to follow along, you can create a new slide with a title and a few bullets or you can remove the animation from an existing slide. The easiest way to remove all the animation from a slide is to display the Animation Schemes task pane (Slide Show ⇨ Animation Schemes) and then click No Animation on the list.

Then follow these steps to create a new custom animation:

1. Display a slide that currently has no animation.

2. Choose Slide Show ⇨ Custom Animation to open the Custom Animation task pane.

3. Click the object you want to animate. This can be the title, the bulleted list, a graphic, or any separately selectable object.

4. In the task pane, click Add Effect. A menu appears containing four categories of effects: Entrance, Emphasis, Exit, or Motion Paths. Let's choose Entrance for the example here.

5. A submenu appears containing effects of that category. Select one of them, as in Figure 22-4, and then skip to Step 7.

   OR

   Choose More Effects to open the Add Effect dialog box shown in Figure 22-5. (The exact name of the dialog box depends on the category chosen. In Figure 22-5 it is Add Entrance Effect.)

Note

The menus shown in Figure 22-4 are usage-sensitive; they remember what you chose. If you choose an effect from the dialog box in Figure 22-5, the next time you open the menu in Figure 22-4 that effect will appear on the list.

Figure 22-4: You can apply one of the most popular effects from the Add Effect button's menu system.

Figure 22-5: Choose More Effects from Figure 22-4 to open a dialog box containing additional choices.

6. If you opened the dialog box in Step 5, make your selection and choose OK. As with the animation schemes, the effects are broken down into categories according to how dramatic they are, ranging from Basic to Exciting. If the Preview Effect check box is marked in the dialog box, you will see the effect on the slide behind the dialog box.

7. In the Custom Animation task pane, open the Start box's drop-down list and choose when you want the animation to start. See Figure 22-6.

   • **With Previous:** Runs the animation simultaneously with any previous animations on the slide. For example, you can set up two different objects to animate at the same time by setting the second of the two to With Previous.

Specify when it will happen

Control the animation speed

Preview it full screen

Preview animation

Figure 22-6: Use the task pane's drop-down lists to fine-tune the chosen animation.

- **After Previous:** Runs the animation immediately after the previous animation on the slide. If there is no previous animation, it treats the slide's appearance overall as the previous event and runs immediately after the slide's appearance.

- **On Click:** Runs the animation when the mouse is clicked. This is useful when you want to build a slide item-by-item with each click, or for an exit effect.

8. Some animation effects have extra properties you can set. If the one you chose does, it will appear directly beneath the Start box, and its name will vary. In Figure 22-6 it is Direction. If none is available, that box will be labeled Property and will be grayed out (unavailable). Make a selection here if appropriate.

9. Open the Speed drop-down list and choose a speed for the animation.

That's the basics of custom animation, in a nutshell. Ready to play with it on your own? Go for it. Need some more help and ideas? Keep reading.

Types of custom animation

As mentioned in the preceding steps, there are four categories of custom animation effects. Each has a specific purpose, and each has a different icon color:

✦ **Entrance (green):** The item's appearance on the slide is animated. Either it does not appear right away when the rest of the slide appears, or it appears in some unusual way (like flying or fading), or both.

✦ **Emphasis (yellow):** The item, already on the slide, is modified in some way. For example, perhaps it shrinks, grows, wiggles, or changes color.

✦ **Exit (red):** The item disappears from the slide before the slide itself disappears, and (optionally) it does so in some unusual way.

✦ **Motion Paths (gray):** The item moves on the slide according to a preset path. I'll cover motion paths in a separate section later in the chapter.

Within each of these broad categories are a multitude of animations. The icons' appearances may vary but the colors always match up with the category. Look back at Figure 22-5, for example, to see some of the different icons for Entrance effects.

Other effect categories have other choices. For example, the Emphasis category, in addition to motion effects, also has effects that change the color, background, or other attributes of the object. Look at Figure 22-7 to see some of the choices. Try out some of them on your own to find out what they do.

Figure 22-7: Emphasis effects have some choices that do not involve motion.

Changing to a different animation effect

If you change your mind about an animation for an object, you don't have to remove the animation and reapply it; you can change it.

To change to a different animation for an object, do the following:

1. Start with the Custom Animation task pane displayed (Slide Show ➪ Custom Animation).

2. Select the animation effect from the task pane, and then click the Change button. The same menu system appears as when you originally applied it.

3. Select a different animation. You can choose from the menu system or choose More Effects for the dialog box containing the full assortment of choices.

Besides choosing a different animation effect, you can also fine-tune its settings at any time, such as changing its speed or other properties, the same as when you created the effect.

Removing an animation effect

You can remove the animation for one specific object, or remove all the animation for the entire slide. When an object is not animated, it simply appears when the slide appears with no delay. For example, if the title is not animated, the slide background and the title appear first, and then any animation executes for the remaining objects.

To remove animation for a specific object, do the following:

1. Start with the Custom Animation task pane displayed (Slide Show ➪ Custom Animation).

2. If the object is part of a group, such as a bulleted list, expand or collapse the list depending on what you want. To remove an effect from an entire text box, collapse it first. To remove an effect from only a single paragraph (bulleted item), expand the list first.

3. Select the animation effect from the task pane, and then click the Remove button. The animation is removed, and any remaining animation effects are renumbered as needed.

To remove all animation for the whole slide, do the following:

1. Choose Slide Show ➪ Animation Schemes.

2. Click No Animation in the task pane's list of animation schemes.

Expert Tip   There are actually several ways of displaying the Animation Schemes list besides using the Slide Show menu. You can click the task bar's title to open a list of available task bars, for example, or you can click the Design button on the toolbar and then click the Animation Schemes hyperlink.

Assigning multiple animation effects to a single object

Some objects might need more than one animation effect. For example, perhaps you want an object to have an Entrance and an Exit effect, or perhaps a bulleted list should enter one way and then have each point on it emphasized in turn in a different way.

To assign a new animation effect to an object that already has animation, do the following:

1. On the slide, click the object to receive the animation. The task pane should contain an Add Effect button. If instead it shows a Change button, or if the button is unavailable, you have not clicked on the object on the slide.

2. Click Add Effect, and then create the new effect just as you did earlier in the chapter when you initially added an effect to the object.

Note   Keep in mind that the numbers that appear next to the objects on the slides in Custom Animation do not refer to the objects themselves — they refer to the animations. If an object does not have any animation assigned to it, it does not have a number. Conversely, if an object has more than one animation effect assigned to it, it has two or more numbers.

Reordering animation effects

Animation effects are numbered by default in the order that they were created. To change this order, do the following:

1. On the Custom Animation task pane, click the effect whose position you want to change.

2. Click the Re-Order up/down arrow buttons at the bottom of the task pane to move the animation's position in the list.

You can also drag-and-drop items on the animations list to rearrange them. Position the mouse pointer over an object, so that the pointer turns into a double-headed up/down arrow, and then drag up or down.

Figure 22-8 shows the same slide as before, but now the bullets are set to animate in reverse order—from the bottom up.

Figure 22-8: Rearrange animations on the task pane list by dragging them or by using the Re-Order arrow buttons.

Re-Order arrows

Special animation options for text

When you are animating the text in a text box, you have some extra options available. For example, in the preceding section you saw one way to animate the text in reverse—from the bottom up. There is a special Reverse option you can set for a text box that will do that automatically.

You can also choose the grouping to animate. For example, suppose you have three levels of bullets in the text box, and you want them to be animated with each second-level bullet appearing separately. You can specify the second level as the animation grouping, and all third-level bullets will appear as a whole along with their associated second-level bullet.

To access the text options for an animation effect, do the following:

1. From the Custom Animation task pane, click the animation you want to work with. A down arrow appears to the right of it.

2. Click the down arrow, opening its menu, and choose Effect Options. The title of the dialog box that appears matches the animation name. In Figure 22-9, it is Glide.

3. Click the Text Animation tab. The Text Animation controls appear, as shown in Figure 22-9.

4. Open the Group Text list and choose how you want the animation grouped. The default is By 1st Level Paragraphs.

5. *(Optional)* If you want the next bullet to appear automatically, without having to click again, mark the Automatically check box and then enter a number of seconds of delay for it.

6. *(Optional)* Mark the In Reverse Order check box if you want the list built from the bottom up.

7. Click OK to accept your choices.

Figure 22-9: Control how text in a text box is animated.

Setting animation timing

Now let's look at the settings you can adjust that affect the timing of the animation. Timing refers to the speed of the effect, the delay before it starts, and how many times it should repeat (if any).

To set timing for a custom animation effect, do the following:

1. On the Custom Animation task pane, click the effect whose timing you want to set. A down arrow appears to the right of it.

2. Click the down arrow, opening its menu, and choose Timing. A dialog box appears, with the Timing tab on top. See Figure 22-10.

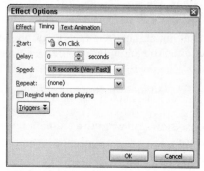

Figure 22-10: Control the timing of the animation effect here.

3. Make your choices on the Timing tab to control the animation timing:

   • **Start** is the same as the Start setting in the task pane.

   • **Delay** refers to the amount of delay between the trigger and the execution of the animation. For example, if the animation effect is set for After Previous, the delay is the number of seconds between the end of the previous event and the beginning of the animation. If the animation effect is set for With Previous, the delay is the number of seconds between the beginning of the previous event and the beginning of the animation. By default, it is set to zero.

   • **Speed** is the overall speed of the animation. This is the same setting as in the Speed drop-down list in the task pane. The choices range from Very Fast (0.5 seconds) to Very Slow (5 seconds). Unlike in the task pane, the number of seconds associated with each choice appears on the Timing tab, as in Figure 22-10.

   • **Repeat** is the number of times the animation should repeat. The default is None. You would rarely set an animation to repeat because it makes it harder for the audience to read (although it can be useful when you want a graphic to flash until the end of the slide).

   • **Rewind when done playing** pertains mostly to video clips; it is available for animation effects, but you will not see much difference between on and off.

- **Triggers** enables you to set up an animation to occur when a particular object is clicked. (It doesn't necessarily have to be the object being animated.) Triggers are covered in the next section.

4. Click OK when you are done selecting animation timing effects. Then try out the new animation settings (by clicking Play or Slide Show in the task pane) to make sure it's the way you want it.

Setting animation event triggers

Animation triggers tell PowerPoint when an animation should execute. The default is to have an animation occur as part of the normal animation sequence, using whatever settings have been assigned to it (On Click, With Previous, or After Previous).

When you set an animation to On Click, the "click" being referred to is *any* click. The mouse does not need to be pointing at anything in particular. Pressing a key on the keyboard will serve the same purpose.

If you want an animation effect to occur only when you click on something in particular, you can use a trigger to set that up.

For example, let's say you have three bullet points on a list, and three photos. You would like each bullet point to appear when you click on its corresponding photo. To set that up, you animate each bullet point with the graphic object as its trigger.

There's a little hitch to the preceding example — you can have only one trigger per object, and in this case "object" means the entire text placeholder. Therefore, if you want to animate bullet points separately with separate triggers, you need to place each of them in a separate text box.

To set up a trigger, do the following:

1. On the Custom Animation task pane, click the effect whose timing you want to set. A down arrow appears to the right of its name.

2. Open the menu for that effect, as you did in the preceding steps, and choose Timing. The Timing tab appears.

3. Click the Triggers button. The controls for setting up a trigger appear on the Timing tab. See Figure 22-11.

4. Click Start Effect on Click Of, and then open the drop-down list and select an object. All objects on the slide appear on this list.

5. Click OK.

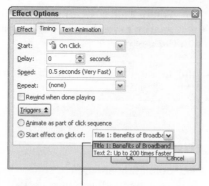

All objects appear on this list

Figure 22-11: Set a trigger for the animation.

Associating sounds with animations

You learned about sounds in Chapter 20, including how to associate one of them with an object. Associating a sound with an animation effect is different, however.

By default, animation effects do not have sounds assigned. To assign a sound, do the following:

1. In the Custom Animation task pane, select the animation effect that should have a sound assigned. Then open its drop-down list and choose Effect Options.

2. On the Effect tab, open the Sound drop-down list and choose a sound. You can choose any of the listed sounds or choose Other Sound to choose from another location. (Refer to Chapter 20 for help with sound selection.)

   OR

   To make the previously playing sound stop when this animation occurs, choose Stop Previous Sound from the drop-down list.

3. *(Optional)* To change the volume for this sound in comparison to the general sound setting for the entire presentation, click the speaker button next to the Sound drop-down list and drag the slider up or down. See Figure 22-12.

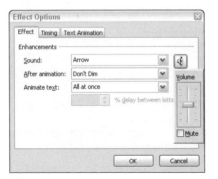

Figure 22-12: Adjust the sound volume in relation to the general sound of the presentation.

4. *(Optional)* If you want the object to change color or be hidden after its animation, open the After Animation drop-down list and choose one of the following options, as in Figure 22-13:

- **A scheme color:** Colored squares for each of the current scheme colors appear; choose one of them.

- **More Colors:** Click here to choose a specific color, just like for any object. You might set text to gray to make it appear dimmed, for example.

- **Don't Dim:** This is the default setting; it specifies that PowerPoint should do nothing to the object after animation.

- **Hide After Animation:** This makes the object disappear immediately after the animation finishes.

- **Hide on Next Mouse Click:** This makes the object disappear when you click the mouse after the animation has completed. This would be useful for showing and then hiding bullet points individually, for example.

Figure 22-13: Choose a color for the object after animation or specify that it should be hidden afterwards.

5. If the object contains text, set the Animate Text setting to indicate how the text should be animated. The default is All at Once, which makes each paragraph appear as a whole. The alternatives are By Letter or By Word.

The Animate Text setting in Step 5 is *not* the setting for specifying which bullet points should appear separately on the slide and which should appear as a group. To do that, use the Text Animation tab, discussed earlier in the chapter.

6. If you chose By Letter or By Word in Step 5, an additional text box appears beneath the box. Enter the percentage delay between letters or words if desired.

7. Click OK to accept the new settings.

Working with motion paths

Motion paths enable you to not only make an object fly onto or off of the slide, but literally make it fly *around* on the slide in a particular motion path!

For example, suppose you are showing a map on a slide, and you want to graphically illustrate the route you took when traveling in that country. You could create a little square, circle, or other AutoShape to represent yourself, and then set up a custom motion path for it that traces the route on the map.

Using a preset motion path

PowerPoint comes with dozens of motion paths, in every shape you can imagine. To choose one of them for an object, follow these steps:

1. Display the Custom Animation task pane.

2. Click on the object you want to animate, and then click the Add Effect button. On the menu that appears, choose Motion Path, and then either click one of the paths on the list or choose More Motion Paths.

3. If you choose More Motion Paths, the Add Motion Path dialog box shown in Figure 22-14 appears. Click the path you want.

   If the Preview Effect check box is marked, the effect previews on the slide behind the dialog box; drag the dialog box to the side to see it better.

4. Click OK. The motion path appears on the slide, to the right of the object. A green arrow shows where the object will begin, and a dotted line shows the path it will take. See Figure 22-15.

5. *(Optional)* To change the starting point for the motion path, drag the green arrow to move the motion path.

Figure 22-14: Select a motion path.

Drag arrow to move motion path

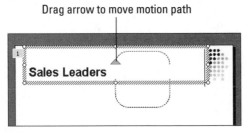

Figure 22-15: The motion path appears on the slide.

6. *(Optional)* Change any of the settings for the motion path as desired, just as you would for any other custom animation:

   • Change the Speed setting. The default is Medium.

   • Change the Start setting. The default is On Click.

   • Change its timing or effects.

7. *(Optional)* Open the Path drop-down list on the task pane and choose any of the following options:

- **Unlocked/Locked:** If the path is unlocked and you move the animated object on the slide, the path repositions itself with the object; if it's locked, the path stays in the same place even when you move the object on the slide. These two options toggle with one another.

- **Edit Points:** This enables you to change the motion path (covered in the next section).

- **Reverse Path Direction:** Just what it sounds like. Makes the animation run in the opposite direction.

8. *(Optional)* Resize or reshape the motion path by dragging its selection handles (the white circles around it). This is just like resizing any other object. See Figure 22-16.

9. *(Optional)* Rotate the motion path by dragging the green circle at the top of it, just like rotating any other object.

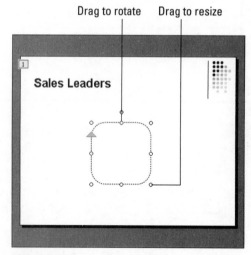

Figure 22-16: A motion path is an object on the slide that can be moved, resized, or rotated.

Editing a motion path

A motion path consists of anchor points with straight lines or curves between them. These points are normally invisible, but you can display them and change them.

To edit a motion path, follow these steps:

1. Select the motion path on the slide.

2. In the Custom Animation task pane, open the Path list and choose Edit Points. Small black squares appear around the path.

3. Click one of the black squares. A slightly larger white square appears near it. This white square is like a handle that you can drag to modify the point. (Or you can drag the black square directly; either way will work, although each affects the path differently. Dragging the black square moves the point itself, whereas dragging the handle repositions the curve while the point remains in place.)

4. Drag the square to change the path. See Figure 22-17.

5. When you are finished editing the path, open the Path list and choose Edit Points again to turn the editing feature off.

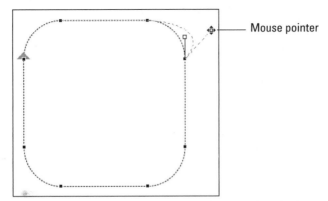

Mouse pointer

Figure 22-17: Edit a motion path by dragging the black squares that represent its anchor points.

Drawing a custom motion path

If none of the motion paths suit your needs, or cannot easily be edited to suit them, you might want to create your own motion path. A motion path can be a straight line, a curve, a closed loop, or a freeform squiggle.

To draw a custom motion path for an object, follow these steps:

1. With the Custom Animation task pane displayed, select the object on the slide.

2. Choose Add Effect ➪ Motion Paths ➪ Draw Custom Path, and then choose the type of path you want: Line, Curve, Freeform, or Scribble.

3. Drag to draw on the slide the path you want. Here are some hints:

   • For a Line, drag from the start point to the end point. The start point will have a green arrow, and the end point will have a red one.

- For a Curve, click at the beginning of the line, and then move the mouse a little and click again to anchor the next point. Keep going like that until you have completely defined the curve. Don't draw the entire curve before you click! You need to create interim anchor points along the way. Double-click when you're finished.

- For a Freeform path, click for each anchor point you want; straight lines will appear between them. Double-click when you're finished.

- For a Scribble, the pointer changes to a pencil. Draw on the slide with the mouse button held down. Double-click when you're finished.

4. After drawing the path, edit and fine-tune it as you would any other motion path.

Animating parts of a chart

If you have a chart created with PowerPoint's charting tool, you can introduce the chart all at once or you can set some other custom animation effects for it. You make the chart appear by series (broken down by legend entries), by category (broken down by X-axis points), or by individual element in a series or category. Figures 22-18 and 22-19 show progressions based on series and category so you can see the difference.

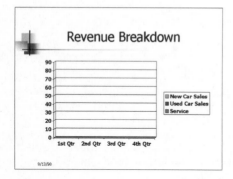
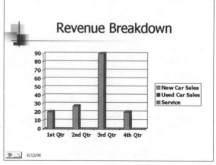
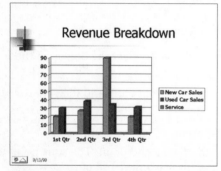
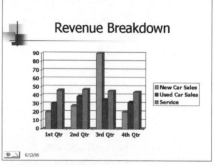

Figure 22-18: In this progression, the chart is appearing by series.

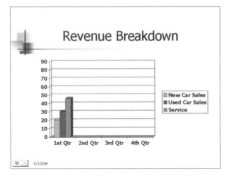

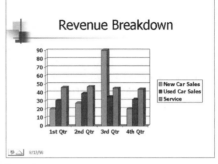

Figure 22-19: Here, the chart is appearing by category.

Along with making various parts of the chart appear at different times, you can also make them appear in any of the animated ways you've already learned, such as flying in, dropping in, fading in, and so on. You can also associate sounds with them, and dim them or change them to various colors when the animation is finished.

First, set the chart up to be animated as a whole, just as you would any other object on a slide.

Note   When you add an animation effect to a chart, you might notice that a new category appears on the Add Effect menu: Object Actions. Ignore it for the moment and choose a normal animation, such as an Entrance effect. I'll explain Object Actions in the next section.

Then, to set up the chart so that different parts of it are animated separately, do the following:

1. In the Custom Animation pane, select the animation for the chart, and open its menu. Choose Effect Options from the menu.

2. Click the Chart Animation tab. Then open the Group Chart drop-down list and choose an animation option: All at Once, By Series, By Category, By Element in Series, or By Element in Category. An *element* is an individual data point such as a bar or slice. See Figure 22-20. You may not have all of these options available, depending on the type of chart you're working with.

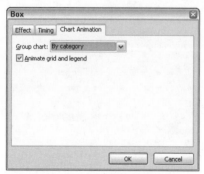

Figure 22-20: Animate the chart by series or category, or by individual data points.

3. *(Optional)* If you want the grid and legend animated too, mark the Animate Grid and Legend check box. If you don't, those items will appear immediately on the slide, and the data bars, slices, or whatever will appear separately from them.

4. Click OK to accept the settings. Then test them if desired.

You don't have to use the same animation effect for each category or each series of the chart. After you set up the chart to animate each piece individually, individual entries appear for each piece on the Custom Animation task pane's list, as shown in Figure 22-21. You can expand the list there and then apply individual settings to each piece. For example, you could have some bars on a chart fly in from one direction and others fly in from another direction. You can also reorder the pieces so that the data points build in a different order from the default.

Controlling animation timing with the advanced timeline

The animation timeline is a graphical representation of the way animated content will appear on the slide. You saw it in Chapter 20 when learning about sounds and soundtracks.

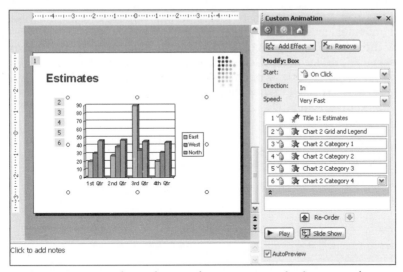

Figure 22-21: On a chart where each category or series is separately animated, each piece has its own number in the custom animation.

To turn on the timeline, open the menu for any animation in the Custom Animation taskbar and choose Show Advanced Timeline. For example, Figure 22-22 shows a timeline for a chart that is animated by category. The timeline is useful because it can give you a feel for the total time involved in all the animations you have set up, including any delays you have built in.

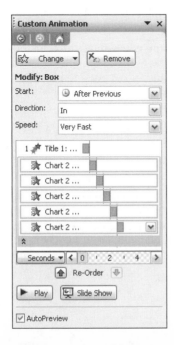

Figure 22-22: The Advanced Timeline helps you see how much time will be devoted to each animated element on the slide.

You can also use the timeline to create delays between animations and increase the duration of individual animations. To increase the duration of an item, drag the right side of the red bar representing its length in the Custom Animation task pane, as shown in Figure 22-23. Drag the left side of the bars to create delays between animations. When you drag the bar for an item that is set to After Previous, the other bars move too. When you drag the bar for an item that is set to With Previous, however, overlap is allowed.

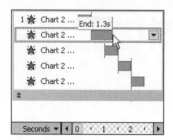

Figure 22-23: Drag a bar on the timeline to increase or decrease its duration.

Animation tips

Here are some tips for using animation in your own work:

✦ Try to use the same preset animation effect for each slide in a related series of slides. If you want to differentiate one section of the presentation from another, use a different animation effect for the text in each different section.

✦ If you want to discuss only one bullet point at a time on a slide, set the others to dim or change to a lighter color after animation.

✦ If there is something you want to obscure but you can't make the animation settings do it the way you want it, consider using an AutoShape that is set to the same color fill as your background color and has no outside border. It will appear "invisible" but will obscure whatever is behind it.

✦ Animate a chart based on the way you want to lead your audience through the data. For example, if each series on your chart shows the sales for a different division and you want to compare one division to another, animate by series. If you want to talk about the results of that chart over time rather than by division, animate by category instead.

✦ If you want to create your own moving graphic but don't have access to a program that creates animated GIFs, you can build a very simple animation on a slide. Simply create the frames of the animation — three or more drawings that you want to progress through in quick succession. Then, lay them one on top of another on the slide and set the timings so they play in order. Adjust the delays and repeats as needed.

Assigning Transitions to Slides

Transitions determine how you get from slide A to slide B. Back in the old slide projector days, there was only one transition: the old slide got pushed out and the new slide plunked into place. But with a computerized presentation, you can choose from all kinds of fun transitions, including wipes, blinds, drives, and much more. These transitions are almost exactly like the animations you saw earlier in the chapter, except they apply to the whole slide (or at least the background—the base part of the slide, if the slide's objects are separately animated).

Note The transition effect for a slide refers to how the slide enters, not how it exits. So if you want to assign a particular transition to occur while moving from slide 1 to slide 2, you would assign the transition effect to slide 2.

The looks of the individual transitions are hard to explain on paper; it's best if you just view them on-screen to understand what each one is. Try out as many of the transitions as you can before making your final selection.

You can apply a transition in either Normal or Slide Sorter view. If you use Slide Sorter view, you can select multiple slides to which the transition should pertain; if you use Normal view you can apply the transition to only one slide at once (unless you apply it to all slides with the Apply to All button).

To apply a transition to a slide, follow these steps:

1. Select/display the slide(s) to affect.

2. Choose Slide Show ➪ Slide Transition. The Slide Transition task pane appears. See Figure 22-24.

3. Select a transition from the Apply to Selected Slides list, or choose No Transition to turn off any existing transition.

4. In the Modify Transition section, fine-tune the effect by choosing a Speed and a Sound. This is the same as for animations.

5. In the Advance Slide section, indicate how you want to signal that it is time to move to the next slide. You can choose either or both of these:

   • **On Mouse Click** advances when you click or press a key. (This is on by default; most people leave it on.)

   • **Automatically After** automatically advances the slide after the number of seconds indicated.

Expert Tip Not sure how many seconds to use for Automatically After? Rehearse your timings (Slide Show ➪ Rehearse Timings), and let PowerPoint automatically set the timing for you. See Chapter 28 for details.

Figure 22-24: Set up transitions for effects that move from one slide to another.

6. *(Optional)* To apply these same transition settings to all slides, click the Apply to All Slides button.

Summary

In this chapter, you learned how to animate the objects on your slides to create some great special effects and how to create animated transitions from slide to slide. Use this newfound knowledge for good, not evil! In other words, don't go nuts applying so many animations that your audience focuses too much on the effects and not enough on your message. The next chapter contains a project lab where you can practice these effects.

✦ ✦ ✦

Project Lab: Adding Sound and Movement to a Presentation

◆ ◆ ◆ ◆

In This Chapter

Applying custom animations

Assigning transitions to slides

Adding a musical soundtrack from a file

◆ ◆ ◆ ◆

Welcome to the fourth Project Lab in this book! This project focuses on improving the pizzazz of a presentation by adding sound and movement to it.

The Scenario

This lab continues your work for Spice Meadow Shelties. The owner is interested in having a presentation that consists only of a set of pictures with a musical soundtrack in the background. She will use this presentation as a backdrop for brief speeches that she gives about her business.

She has already provided you with the basic presentation file containing most of the pictures. It's your job to add animation, transition, and music to this presentation to make it more interesting and appealing.

Lab 4A: Fading Text and Graphics In and Out

In this lab session, you add some text to slide 2 and then animate it and the photos so that first one set fades in and out, and then the other set fades in.

Level of difficulty: Moderate

Time to complete: 15 to 30 minutes

1. **Open the file Lab04A.ppt from the Labs folder (from the CD accompanying the book).**

2. **On slide 2, place a text box over the face of the dog at the left, and in that text box type *Champion Sires*. Format it as center-aligned Arial Rounded MT Bold, 44 points in size and colored black.**

   a. Click the Text Box button on the Drawing toolbar.

   b. Drag to draw the text box where you want it.

   c. Click inside the text box and type **Champion Sires**. Select the text and choose center alignment on the Formatting toolbar.

   d. With the text still selected, choose Arial Rounded MT Bold from the Font drop-down list.

   e. Select 44 from the Font Size drop-down list.

   f. Select black from the Font Color icon on the Drawing toolbar.

3. **Repeat Step 2 over the face of the dog at the right, with the text *Excellent Bloodlines*.**

4. **Set up the Champion Sires text box to appear by fading in when the slide first appears.**

   a. Choose Slide Show ➪ Custom Animation. The Custom Animation task pane appears.

   b. Select the text box on the left (Champion Sires).

   c. Choose Add Effect ➪ Entrance ➪ More Effects.

   d. In the Add Entrance Effect dialog box, choose Fade.

   e. Click OK.

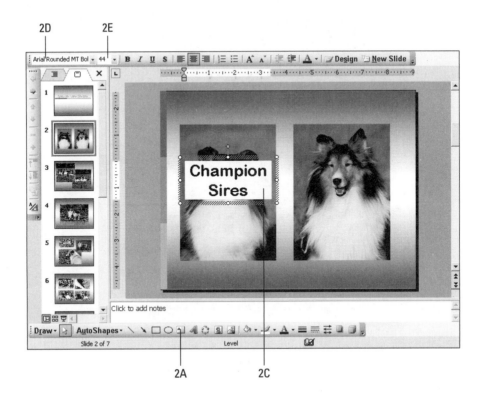

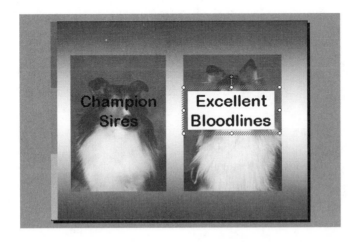

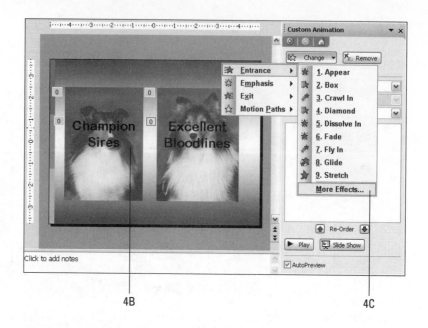

4B   4C

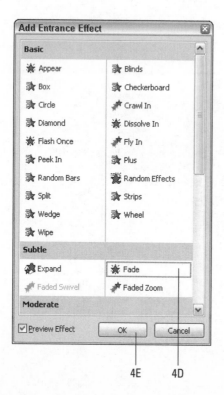

4E   4D

f. In the Custom Animation pane, select the new animation.

g. Open the Start drop-down list and choose After Previous.

5. **Set up the picture on the right to appear by fading in simultaneously with the text you animated in Step 4.**

a. Select the picture on the right.

b. Choose Add Effect ⇨ Entrance ⇨ Fade. (Notice that Fade is on the top-level list because you recently used it.)

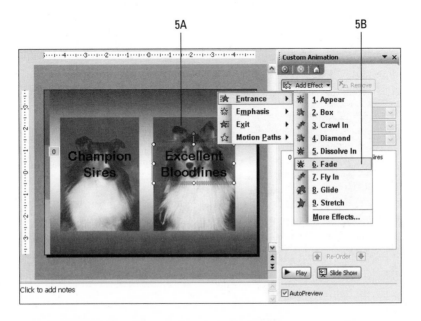

c. Click the new animation in the Custom Animation pane.

d. Open the Start drop-down list and choose With Previous.

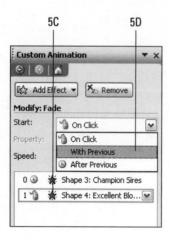

6. Repeat Steps 4 and 5, but this time set up exit effects instead of entrance.

a. Create an exit effect for the left text box set to occur After Previous.

b. Create an exit effect for the right picture set to occur With Previous.

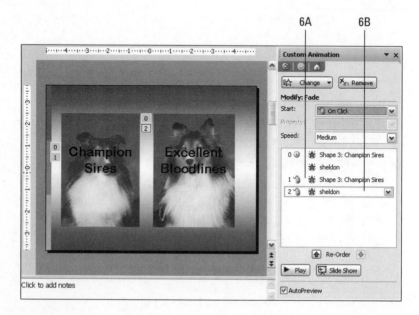

7. Create a delay of five seconds between the text box's entrance and its exit.

    a. Select the exit animation for the text box in the Custom Animation pane.

    b. Open its menu and choose Timing.

    c. Enter 5 in the Delay box.

    d. Click OK.

8. Repeat Step 7 for the exit animation for the right picture.

9. Create a Fade entrance effect for the opposite text box (the one on the right) that occurs After Previous.

    Refer to Step 4.

10. Create a Fade entrance effect for the opposite picture (the one on the left) that occurs With Previous.

    Refer to Step 5.

11. Preview the slide's animation and check your work.

7C

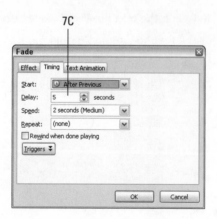

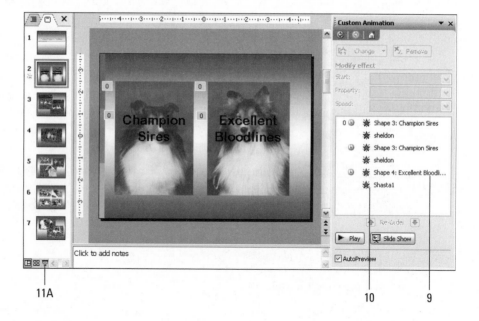

11A   10   9

a. Click the Slide Show View button.

b. If you did the animation correctly, the Champion Sires text and the right photo will appear first, fading in.

c. They will pause for five seconds, and then fade out, and the opposite text and picture will fade in. They will remain on the screen until you click to move to the next slide.

12. Press Esc to exit Slide Show view.

13. Save your work as MyLab04A.ppt.

Lab 4B: Replacing One Picture with Another

In this lab session, you place one photo on top of another and animate the top one so that it disappears, revealing the one underneath, after a delay.

Level of difficulty: Moderate

Time to complete: 10 to 15 minutes

1. **Open the presentation file if it is not already open.**

   Start in your completed file from the previous project (MyLab04A.ppt), or open Lab04B.ppt from the Labs folder if you did not do the previous lab.

2. **Display slide 3, and arrange the pictures so that they are stacked one on top of the other.**

   a. Click slide 3 in the Slides pane.

   b. Drag the pictures so that they are both in the same spot. Only the top one (where all three dogs are sitting up) should be visible.

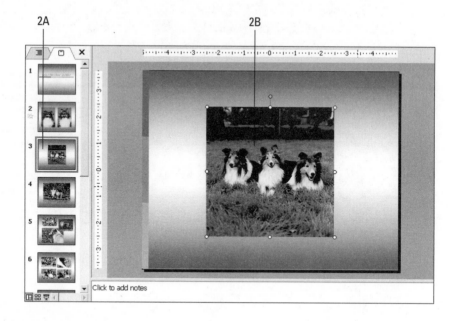

3. Add a Checkerboard exit animation to the top picture so that it goes away after being displayed for six seconds.

    a. Choose Slide Show ⇨ Custom Animation.

    b. Click the top picture to select it.

    c. Choose Add Effect ⇨ Exit ⇨ More Effects.

    d. Choose Checkerboard.

    e. Click OK.

f. Select the animation in the Custom Animation pane and open its menu.

g. Choose Timing.

h. In the Checkerboard dialog box, open the Start drop-down list and choose After Previous.

i. Type **6** in the Delay box.

j. Open the Speed list and choose 2 seconds (Medium).

k. Click OK.

4. Preview the slide's animation and check your work.

a. Click the Slide Show View button. If you did the animation correctly, the top picture will appear, and after six seconds, it will checkerboard into the picture beneath it.

b. Press Esc to return to PowerPoint.

5. Save your work as MyLab04B.ppt.

3F

3G

3I   3H   3J

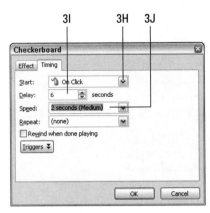

Lab 4C: More Animation Practice

In this lab session, you complete the animations for the rest of the presentation. This project is more challenging, not because of the animations per se, but because less detailed instructions are provided here. You will need to determine how to accomplish each animation on your own.

Level of difficulty: Challenging

Time to complete: 15 to 30 minutes

1. **Open the presentation file if it is not already open.**

   Start in your completed file from the previous project (MyLab04B.ppt), or open Lab04C.ppt from the Labs folder if you did not do the previous lab.

2. **Add a text box to slide 4, near the bottom of the picture, with the following text:** *Puppies raised with adult dogs are better socialized*. **Make the text center-aligned, Arial Rounded Bolt MT font, 24 point, and the default color (white).**

3. **Animate the text box you just added so that it has the Brush-on Color effect turning it to bright yellow after a delay of three seconds.**

   Brush-on color is in the Emphasis effect category.

2

4. **On slide 5, animate each of the pictures to appear using the Dissolve In animation, one after the other, with a two-second delay between them. Set the animation speed for each of them to Fast.**

First   Third

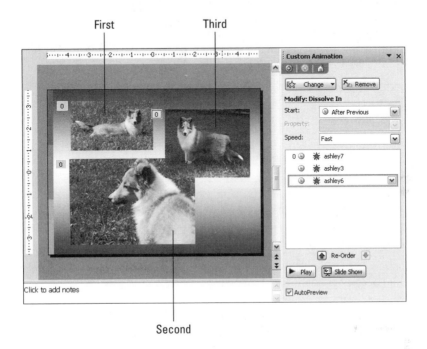

Second

5. **On slide 6, use the Draw ⇨ Align or Distribute commands to more precisely align all four pictures.**

To do this, first align the top two pictures at their tops; then align the two bottom pictures at their tops.

Next align the two left pictures at the left side, and then the two right pictures at the right side.

6. **Animate the pictures on slide 6 so that the top-left and bottom-right pictures appear (simultaneously) first using the Diamond entrance effect, and then a three-second delay, and then the other two pictures appear simultaneously using the same effect.**

5

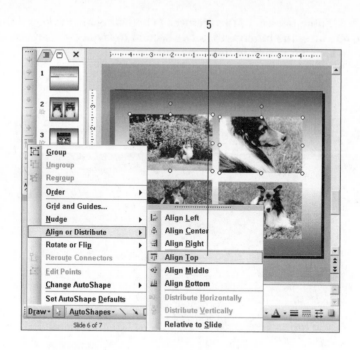

First these two...

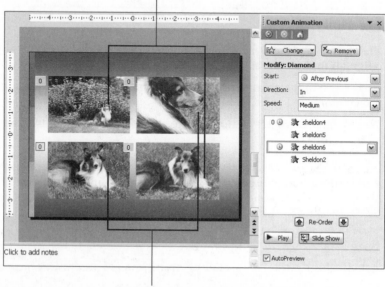

...then these two

7. **On slide 7, make the top-left picture fade out after six seconds, and at the same time as it is fading out, make the bottom-right picture fade in.**

First this one appears, for 6 seconds...

then this one appears as the other fades out

8. **View the entire presentation in Slide Show view to check your work.**

9. **Return to PowerPoint and save your work as MyLab04C.ppt.**

Lab 4D: Using Transitions and Soundtracks

In this project, you set up each slide to automatically advance after 15 seconds, and you specify a transition effect. You also add a MIDI-based soundtrack to the presentation that will loop continuously as long as the presentation is playing.

Level of difficulty: Easy

Time to complete: 5 to 10 minutes

1. **Open the presentation file if it is not already open.**

   Start in your completed file from the previous project (MyLab04C.ppt), or open Lab04D.ppt from the Labs folder if you did not do the previous lab.

2. **Set all slides to the Fade Smoothly transition automatically after 15 seconds.**

   a. Choose Slide Show ➪ Slide Transitions. The Slide Transitions task pane appears.

   b. Choose Fade Smoothly from the list of transitions.

    c. Open the Speed box and choose Slow.

    d. Mark the Automatically after check box and enter **00:15** for the number of seconds.

    e. Click Apply to All Slides.

                       2B   2C

        2D   2E

3. Locate a MIDI, WMA, or MP3 music clip.

There are many sources of free music on the Internet. Use whatever music you think would be appropriate for this presentation. If possible, try to find something without lyrics, so a speaker will be able to speak while the presentation is showing in the background.

If you do not want to take the time to find one for this lab, search your computer for sound files (Start ⇨ Search or Start ⇨ Find).

If you cannot find any suitable music clips, use the sample Beethoven clip in the Labs folder on the CD. This is the same Beethoven clip that comes with some versions of Windows.

4. **Insert the music clip on slide 1, and set it up to play automatically when the slide appears and to continue playing until the presentation is over (or until the clip ends).**

   a. Display slide 1.

   b. Choose Insert ⇨ Movies and Sounds ⇨ Sound From File.

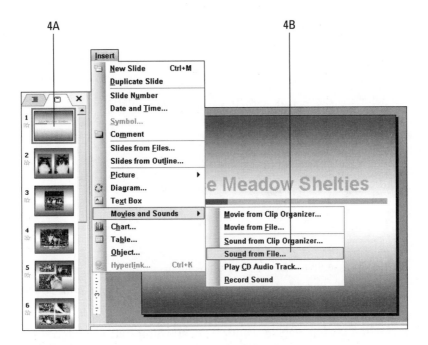

   c. Navigate to the location of the file and select it.

   d. Click OK. The sound appears as an icon on the slide.

4C

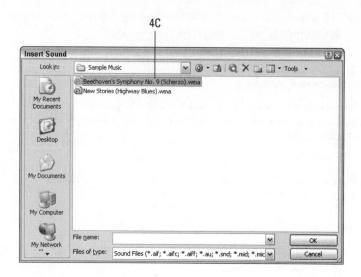

e. In the dialog box that appears, click Automatically.

4E

f. Choose Slide Show ⇨ Custom Animation.

g. Select the sound icon, and then open its menu and choose Timing.

h. Click the Effect tab.

i. In the Stop Playing section, click the After button, and then enter **999** in its text box. This makes it play continuously, looping back through if needed.

j. Click OK.

k. Drag the sound icon off the edge of the slide so it doesn't show in the presentation. (dragsound.jpg).

4G

4H   4I

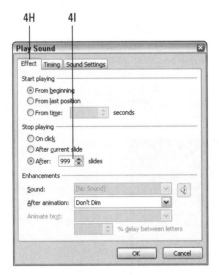

5. On slide 1, insert the picture closeup.jpg and place it in the empty space at the bottom of slide 1.

    a. Display slide 1.

    b. Choose Insert ⇨ Picture ⇨ From File.

    c. Navigate to the folder containing the lab files and select closeup.jpg.

    d. Click Insert.

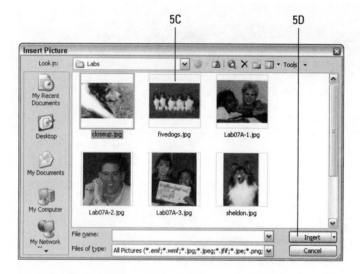

    e. Resize and reposition the picture as needed to make it attractive.

6. **Watch the entire presentation in Slide Show view, without clicking, to check the transitions, animation, and music.**

   a. Choose Slide Show ➪ View Show.

   b. Watch the show and listen, making notes about any changes that need to be made.

   c. When the show is over, press Esc to return to PowerPoint.

   d. Make any changes as needed.

7. **Save your work as MyLab04D.ppt.**

Congratulations, you completed the projects! You now have a presentation that includes transitions, animations, and music — something you can be proud to show to the client for her approval.

✦   ✦   ✦

Presenting Speaker-Led Presentations

Creating Support Materials

I f you are presenting a live show, the centerpiece of your presentation is your slides. Whether you show them using a computer screen, a slide projector, or an overhead projector, the slides — combined with your own dazzling personality — make the biggest impact. But if you rely on your audience to remember everything you say, you may be disappointed. With handouts, the audience members can follow along with you during the show and even take their own notes. They can then take the handouts home with them to review the information again later.

You probably want a different set of support materials for yourself than you want for the audience. Support materials designed for the speaker's use are called speaker notes. They contain, in addition to small printouts of the slides, any extra notes or background information that you think you may need to jog your memory as you speak. Some people get very nervous when they speak in front of a crowd; speaker notes can remind you of the joke you wanted to open with or the exact figures behind a particular pie chart.

The When and How of Handouts

You learned a little bit about handout use in Chapter 5. Presentation professionals are divided as to how and when to use them most effectively. Here are some of the many conflicting viewpoints. I can't say who is right or wrong, but each of these statements brings up issues that you should consider. Each of them, at the bottom line, is an opinion on how much power and credit to give to the audience; your answer may vary depending on the audience you are addressing.

You should give handouts at the beginning of the presentation. The audience can absorb the information better if they can follow along on paper.

This approach makes a lot of sense. Research has proven that people absorb more facts if presented with them in more than one medium. This approach also gives your audience free will; they can listen to you or not, and they still have the information. It's their choice, and this can be extremely scary for less-confident speakers. It's not just a speaker confidence issue in some cases, however. If you are going to give a lot of extra information in your speech that's not on the handouts, people might miss it if you distribute the handouts at the beginning because they're reading ahead.

You shouldn't give the audience handouts because they won't pay as close attention to your speech if they know that the information is already written down for them.

This philosophy falls at the other end of the spectrum. It gives the audience the least power and shows the least confidence in their ability to pay attention to you in the presence of a distraction (handouts). If you truly don't trust your audience to be professional and listen, this approach may be your best option. However, don't let insecurity as a speaker drive you prematurely to this conclusion. The fact is that people won't take away as much knowledge about the topic without handouts as they would if you provide handouts. So, ask yourself if your ultimate goal is to fill the audience with knowledge or to make them pay attention to you.

You should give handouts at the end of the presentation so that people will have the information to take home but not be distracted during the speech.

This approach attempts to solve the dilemma with compromise. The trouble with it, as with all compromises, is that it does an incomplete job from both angles. Because audience members can't follow along on the handouts during the presentation, they miss the opportunity to jot notes on the handouts. And because the audience knows that handouts are coming, they might nod off and miss something important. The other problem is that if you don't clearly tell people that handouts are coming later, some people spend the entire presentation frantically copying down each slide on their own notepaper.

Creating Handouts

To create handouts, you simply decide on a layout (a number of slides per page) and then choose that layout from the Print dialog box as you print. No muss, no fuss! If you want to get more involved, you can edit the layout in Handout Master view before printing.

Choosing a layout

Assuming you have decided that handouts are appropriate for your speech, you must decide on the format for them. You have a choice of one, two, three, four, six, or nine slides per page. The one-slide-per-page layout places a single slide vertically and horizontally "centered" on the page. The two-slide-per-page layout, shown in Figure 24-1, prints two big slides on each page. This layout is good for slides that have a lot of fine print and small details or for situations where you are not confident that the reproduction quality will be good. There is nothing more frustrating for an audience than not being able to read the handouts!

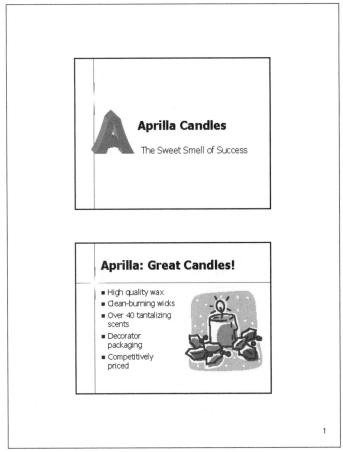

Figure 24-1: The two-slide-per-page layout works well when the slides need to be big.

The three-slides-per-page layout shown in Figure 24-2 makes the slides much smaller — less than one-half the size of the ones shown in Figure 24-1. But you get a nice bonus with this layout: lines to the side of each slide for note-taking. This layout works well for presentations where the slides are big and simple, and the speaker is providing a lot of extra information that isn't on the slides. The audience members can write the extra information in the note-taking space provided.

The four-slides-per-page layout (see Figure 24-3) uses the same size slides as the three-slide model, but they are spaced out two-by-two without note-taking lines. However, there is still plenty of room above and below each slide, so the audience members still have lots of room to take notes.

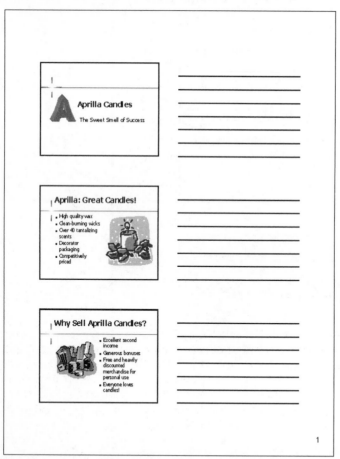

Figure 24-2: The three-slides-per-page format comes with lines for note-taking.

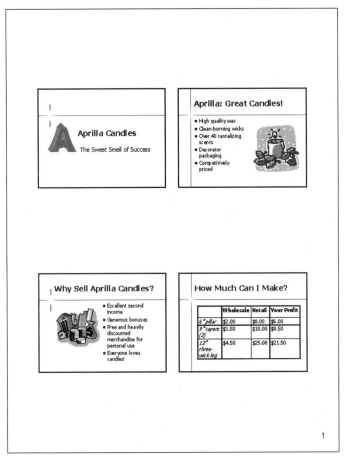

Figure 24-3: The four-slides-per-page format uses the smaller slide size but there are no lines for notes.

The six-slides-per-page layout, shown in Figure 24-4, uses slides the same size as the three-slide and four-slide models, but crams more slides on the page at the expense of note-taking space. This layout is good for presentation with big, simple slides where the audience does not need to take notes. If you are not sure if the audience will benefit at all from handouts being distributed, consider whether this layout would be a good compromise. This format also saves paper, which might be an issue if you need to make hundreds of copies.

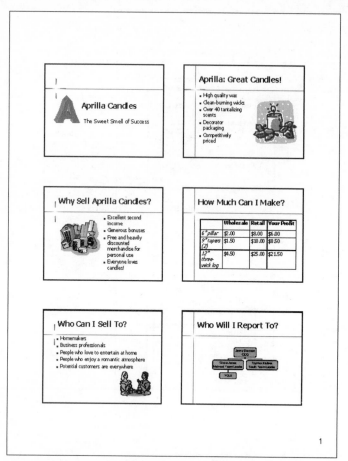

Figure 24-4: Use the six-slides-per-page format to provide handouts on fewer sheets of paper or when the handouts are not critical.

The nine-slides-per-page layout makes the slides very tiny, almost like a Slide Sorter view, so that you can see nine at a time. See Figure 24-5. This layout makes them very hard to read unless the slide text is extremely simple. I don't recommend this layout in most cases, because the audience really won't get much out of such handouts.

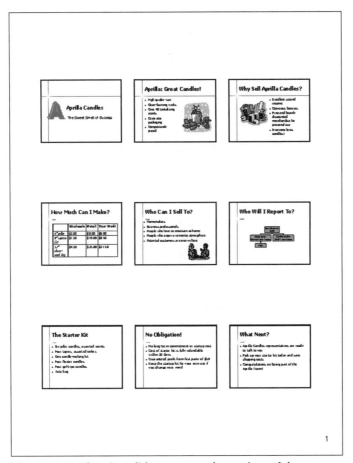

Figure 24-5: The nine-slides-per-page layout is useful as an index or directory, but not as a standalone handout in most cases.

Expert Tip

One good use for the nine-slides model is as an index or table of contents for a large presentation. You can include a nine-slides-per-page version of the handouts at the beginning of the packet you give to the audience members, and then follow it up with a two-slides-per-page version that they can refer to if they want a closer look at one of the slides.

Finally, there is an Outline handout layout, which prints an outline of all the text in your presentation. (That is, all the text that is part of placeholders in slide layouts; any text in extra text boxes you have added manually is excluded.) It is not considered a handout when printing, but it is included with the handout layouts in the Handout Master. More on this type of handout later in the chapter.

Printing handouts

When you have decided which layout is appropriate for your needs, print your handouts as follows:

1. *(Optional)* If you want to print only one particular slide, or a group of slides, select the ones you want in either Slide Sorter view or in the slide thumbnails task pane on the left.

2. Select File ⇨ Print. The Print dialog box appears. See Figure 24-6.

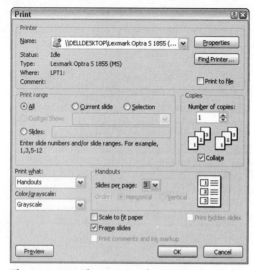

Figure 24-6: Choose Handouts to print and specify which handout layout you want.

3. Set any options for your printer or choose a different printer. See the "Setting Printer Options" section later in this chapter for help with this.

4. In the Print Range area, choose one of the following:

   • **All** to print the entire presentation.

   • **Current Slide** to print whatever slide was selected before you issued the Print command.

   • **Selection** to print multiple slides you selected before you issued the Print command. It is not available if you did not select any slides beforehand.

- **Custom Show** to print a certain custom show you have set up. (See Chapter 26.) It is not available if you do not have any custom shows.

- **Slides** to print the slide numbers that you type in the accompanying text box. Indicate a contiguous range with a dash. For example, to print slides 1 through 9, type **1-9**. Indicate non-contiguous slides with commas. For example, to print slides, 2, 4, and 6, type **2, 4, 6**. Or to print slides 2 plus 6 through 10, type **2, 6-10**. To print them in reverse order, type the order that way, such as **10-6, 2**.

5. Enter a number of copies in the Number of Copies text box. The default is 1. If you want the copies collated (applicable to multi-page printouts only), make sure you mark the Collate check box.

6. Open the Print What drop-down list and choose Handouts. The Handouts section of the box becomes available, as in Figure 24-6.

> **Note**
>
> If you want to print an outline, choose Outline View instead of Handouts in Step 6 and then skip Steps 7-9. An outline can be a useful handout for an audience in certain situations.

7. Open the Slides Per Page drop-down list and choose the number of slides per page you want.

8. If available, choose an Order: Horizontal or Vertical. Not all number-of-slide choices (from Step 6) support an Order choice.

> **Note**
>
> Order in Step 8 refers to the order in which the slides are placed on the page. Horizontal places them by rows, Vertical by columns. This ordering has nothing to do with the orientation of the paper (Portrait or Landscape). You set the paper orientation in the Page Setup dialog box (File ➪ Page Setup).

9. Open the Color/Grayscale drop-down list and select the color setting for the printouts:

- **Color:** Sends the data to the printer assuming that color will be used. This setting used with a black-and-white printer will result in slides with grayscale or black backgrounds. Use this setting if you want the handouts to look as much as possible like the on-screen slides.

- **Grayscale:** Sends the data to the printer assuming that color will not be used. Colored backgrounds are removed, and if text is normally a light color on a dark background, that is reversed. Use this setting if you want PowerPoint to optimize the printout for viewing on white paper, even if it involves changing the slide color scheme.

- **Pure Black and White:** This format hides most shadows and patterns, as described in Table 24-1. It's good for faxes and overhead transparencies.

Table 24-1
Differences Between Grayscale and Pure Black and White

Object	Grayscale	Pure Black and White
Text	Black	Black
Text Shadows	Grayscale	None
Embossing	Grayscale	None
Fill	Grayscale	White
Frame	Black	Black
Pattern Fill	Grayscale	White
Lines	Black	Black
Object Shadows	Grayscale	Black
Bitmaps	Grayscale	Grayscale
Clip art	Grayscale	Grayscale
Slide backgrounds	White	White
Charts	Grayscale	Grayscale

Expert Tip   To see what your presentation will look like when printed to a black and white printer, choose View ➪ Color/Grayscale and choose Grayscale or Pure Black and White. If you see an object that is not displaying the way you want, right-click it and choose Grayscale or Black and White. One of the options there may help you achieve the look you're after.

10. Mark any desired check boxes at the bottom of the dialog box:

   • **Scale to Fit Paper:** Enlarges the slides to the maximum size they can be and still fit on the layout (as defined on the Handout Master, covered later in this chapter).

   • **Frame Slides:** Draws a black border around each slide image. Useful for slides being printed with white backgrounds.

   • **Print Comments:** Prints any comments that have been inserted with the Comments feature in PowerPoint (covered in Chapter 33).

   • **Print Hidden Slides:** Includes hidden slides in the printout. This option is not available if you don't have any hidden slides in your presentation.

11. *(Optional)* Click the Preview button to see a preview of your handouts; then click the Print button to return to the Print dialog box.

12. Click OK. The handouts print, and you're ready to roll!

Caution Beware of the cost of printer supplies. If you are planning to distribute copies of the presentation to a lot of people, it may be tempting to print all the copies on your printer. But especially if you have an inkjet printer, the cost per page of printing is fairly high. You will quickly run out of ink in your ink cartridge and have to spend $20 or more for a replacement. Consider whether it might be cheaper to print one original and take it to a copy shop.

Changing the layout of your handouts

Just as your slide layout is controlled by the Slide Master (see Chapter 7), your handout layout is controlled by the Handout Master. To view the Handout Master, choose View ➪ Master ➪ Handout Master. See Figure 24-7. Unlike the Slide Master and Title Master, you can have only one Handout Master layout per handout type per presentation.

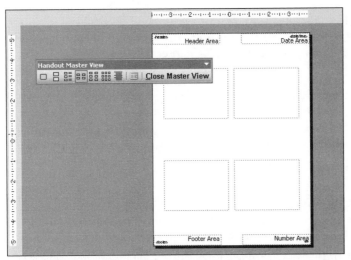

Figure 24-7: The Handout Master lets you define the layout for each type of handout (that is, each number of slides per page).

On the Handout Master, you can set a separate layout for each type of handout (that is, for each number of slides per page), plus for outlines. To choose which layout you want to modify, click the appropriate button on the Handout Master View toolbar. See Figure 24-8.

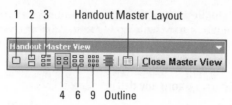

1   2   3   Handout Master Layout

4   6   9   Outline

Figure 24-8: Choose which handout layout you want to alter.

After choosing the layout to work with, you can do any of the following.

✦ **Delete a placeholder:** You can delete the Header Area, Date Area, Footer Area, and/or Number Area placeholders on the layout. Just select one and press the Delete key. This method is useful if you want to delete them for only one particular layout.

✦ **Use (or not use) headers and footers:** Select View ⇨ Header and Footer. This opens the Header and Footer dialog box. See "Turning Note and Handout Header/Footers On or Off" later in this chapter for details. This lets you turn on/off the display of certain header and footer items without actually deleting the placeholders. That way if you ever decide you want them again, they are still there. This method is useful if you want to remove certain elements from the layout of all notes pages and handouts at once.

✦ **Move the header, footer, date, and/or slide number on the handout:** Select the placeholder for the element to move and drag it to a new spot.

✦ **Change fonts:** Select the text in one of the header or footer placeholders and apply a different font, size, color, or attribute to it.

✦ **Change the handout color scheme:** If you have a color printer, right-click the handout area and choose Slide Design; then click Color Schemes in the task pane. Then choose a color scheme, just as you did for slides in Chapter 7.

✦ **Change the handout background:** Right-click the handout area, choose Handout Background, and then choose a background. See Chapter 7 for details. Be aware, however, that a patterned or colored background may distract from the slides' message and use a lot of ink when printed.

Expert Tip   You can't move or resize the slide placeholder boxes on the Handout Master, nor can you change its margins. If you want to change the size of the slide boxes on the handout or change the margins of the page, consider exporting the handouts to Word and working on them there. See the "Sending Your Presentation to Word" section at the end of this chapter.

The Handout Master Layout button, pointed out in Figure 24-8, opens a dialog box containing check boxes for each of the optional elements on the slide. If an element is already displayed, its check box is grayed out. If it has been deleted, however, you can reinstate it by re-marking its check box. For example, suppose you have turned off the header and footer; each of the items involved in it will appear for re-enabling. See Figure 24-9.

Figure 24-9: Restore any deleted placeholders from here.

To leave the Handout Master, click the Close Master View button on the Handout Master View toolbar.

Creating Speaker Notes

Speaker notes are like handouts, but for you. Only one printout format is available for them: the Speaker notes page. It consists of the slide on the top half (the same size as in the two-slides-per-page handout) with the blank space below it for your notes to yourself.

Speaker notes printed in PowerPoint are better than traditional note cards for several reasons. For one thing, you can type your notes right into the computer and print them out on regular paper. There's no need to jam a note card into a typewriter and use messy correction fluid or erasers to make changes. The other benefit is that each note page contains a picture of the slide, so it's not as easy to lose your place while speaking.

Typing speaker notes

You can type your notes for a slide in Normal view (in the notes pane), or in Notes Page view. The latter shows the page more or less as it will look when you print your notes pages; this can help if you need to gauge how much text will fit on the printed page.

To switch to Notes Page view, choose View ➪ Notes Page. See Figure 24-10. Unlike some of the other views, there is no shortcut button for this view. Once you're in Notes Page view, you can zoom and scroll just like in any other view to see more or less of the page at once. You can scroll further to move from slide to slide, or you can move from slide to slide in the traditional ways (the Page Up and Page Down keys on the keyboard or the Next Slide or Previous Slide buttons on-screen).

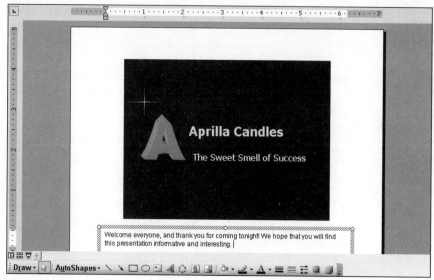

Figure 24-10: Notes Page view is one of the best ways to work with your speaker notes.

Note   Use the Zoom control to zoom in or out until you find the optimal view so that the text you type is large enough to be clear, but small enough so that you can see across the entire width of the note area. I find that 66 to 85 percent works well on my screen at 800x600 resolution, but yours may vary.

Just type your notes in the Notes area, the same as you would type in any text box in PowerPoint. The lines in the paragraph wrap automatically. Press Enter to start a new paragraph. When you're done, move to the next slide.

Expert Tip   If you're typing your notes in the notes area of Normal view, you might want to toggle the Show Formatting button on. This will not show all of the notes formatting (such as colors), but it will reflect any font face and font size changes so that you can tell more realistically what your notes look like. You can change the color of the text in the notes area when you're in Notes Page view.

Changing the notes page layout

Just as you can edit your handout layouts, you can also edit your notes page layout. Just switch to its Master and make your changes. Follow these steps:

   1. Choose View ➪ Master ➪ Notes Master.

2. Edit the layout, as you have learned to edit other masters (Slide Master in Chapter 7, Handout Master earlier in this chapter). See Figure 24-11. This can include:

- Moving placeholders for the slide, the notes, or any of the header or footer elements.
- Changing the font used for the text in any of those areas.
- Resizing the placeholder for the slide graphic.
- Resizing the Notes pane.
- Adding clip art or other graphics to the background.
- Adding a colored, textured, or patterned background to the notes page.

3. When you are finished, click the Close Master View button to return to Normal view.

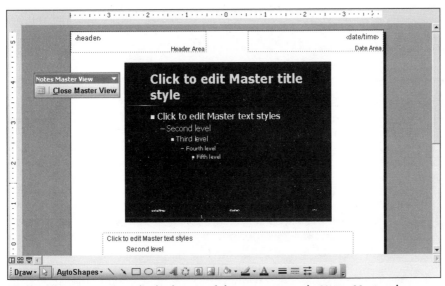

Figure 24-11: You can edit the layout of the notes pages in Notes Master view. For more information specifically about the headers and footers on the masters, see the "Formatting Handout and Notes Page Headers and Footers" section later in this chapter.

Printing notes pages

When you're ready to print your notes pages, follow these steps:

1. Choose File ➪ Print. The Print dialog box opens.

2. Open the Print what drop-down list and choose Notes Pages.

3. Set any other options, just as you did when printing handouts earlier in the chapter. (If you need to choose which printer to use or to set the options for that printer, see the "Setting Printer Options" section later in this chapter.) There are no special options for notes pages.

4. Click OK. The notes pages print.

Caution If you print notes pages for hidden slides, you may want to arrange your stack after they're printed so that the hidden slides are at the bottom. That way you won't get confused when giving the presentation.

Turning Note and Handout Headers/Footers On or Off

You can enable or disable repeated text — date and time, headers, page numbers, and footers — on notes pages and handouts. The process is similar to the one for slides that you learned in Chapter 7.

Follow these steps to control which repeated header and footer elements appear on handouts and notes pages:

Note The following steps set up both notes pages and handouts; you can't set them separately. If you need separate settings for each, set the header and footer settings the way you want them for one, print them, and then set the header and footer settings differently before you print the other.

1. Choose View ➪ Header and Footer. The Header and Footer dialog box opens.

2. Click the Notes and Handouts tab. See Figure 24-12.

3. If you want the date on the printout, make sure the Date and Time check box is marked.

4. Choose Update Automatically or Fixed, depending on the date type you want.

   • If you choose Update Automatically, open the drop-down list and choose a date format. If you use a different language or calendar than English, choose it from the Language and Calendar Type drop-down lists.

   • If you choose Fixed, type the date, in the exact format that you want it to appear, in the Fixed text box.

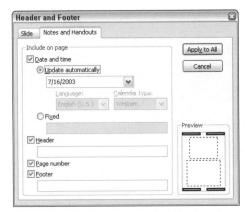

Figure 24-12: You can control the header and footer information for notes pages and handouts here.

5. If you want header text on the slide, make sure the Header check box is marked and then type the text in the Header text box.

6. If you want footer text on the slide, make sure the Footer check box is marked and then type the text in the Footer text box.

7. If you want page numbers on the printouts, make sure the Page number check box is marked.

8. Click Apply to All.

After choosing the repeating elements you want, you can format their placeholders on the appropriate masters.

Setting Printer Options

In addition to the controls in the Print dialog box in PowerPoint, there are controls you can set that affect the printer you have chosen.

In the Printer section of the Print dialog box, you can open the Name drop-down list and choose the printer you want to use to print the job. See Figure 24-13. Most home users have only one printer, but business users may have more than one to choose from, especially on a network.

After choosing a printer, you can click the Properties button to display its Properties dialog box. The properties shown are different for different kinds of printers. Figure 24-14 shows the box for my Lexmark Optra S 1855 printer, a laser printer with PostScript capabilities. Notice that there are two tabs: Layout and Paper/Quality. The tabs may be different for your printer.

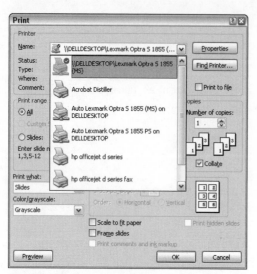

Figure 24-13: You can select among all installed local and network printers, plus any printer-like drivers that may be installed such as for faxing or creating PDF files.

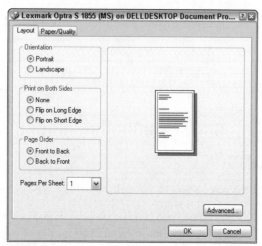

Figure 24-14: Each printer's options are slightly different, but the same types of settings are available on most printers.

These settings affect how the printer behaves in all Windows-based programs, not just in PowerPoint, so you need to be careful not to change anything that you don't want globally changed. Here are some of the settings you may be able to change on your printer:

✦ **Orientation:** You can choose between Portrait and Landscape. I don't recommend changing this setting here, though; make such changes in the Page Setup dialog box in PowerPoint instead. Otherwise, you may get the wrong orientation on a printout in other programs.

✦ **Page Order:** You can choose Front to Back or Back to Front. This determines the order the pages print.

✦ **Pages Per Sheet:** The default is 1, but you can print smaller versions of several pages on a single sheet. This option is usually only available on PostScript printers.

✦ **Paper Size:** The default is Letter, but you can change to Legal, A4, or any of several other sizes.

✦ **Paper Source:** If your printer has more than one paper tray, you may be able to select Upper or Lower.

✦ **Copies:** This sets the default number of copies that should print. Be careful; this number is a multiplier. If you set two copies here, and then set two copies in the Print dialog box in PowerPoint, you end up with four copies.

✦ **Graphics Resolution:** If your printer has a range of resolutions available, you may be able to choose the resolution you want. My printer lets me choose between 300 and 600 dots per inch (dpi); on an inkjet printer, choices are usually 360, 720, and 1,440 dpi. Achieving a resolution of 1,440 on an inkjet printer usually requires special glossy paper.

✦ **Graphic Dithering:** On some printers, you can set the type of dithering that makes up images. *Dithering* is a method of creating shadows (shades of gray) from black ink by using tiny crosshatch patterns. You may be able to choose between Coarse, Fine, and None.

✦ **Image Intensity:** On some printers, you can control the image appearance with a light/dark slide bar.

Some printers, notably inkjets, come with their own print-management software. If that's the case, you may have to run that print-management software separately from outside of PowerPoint for full control over the printer's settings. Such software can usually be accessed from the Windows Start menu.

Printing an Outline

If text is the main part of your presentation, you might prefer to print an outline instead of mini-slides. You can use the outline for speaker notes, audience hand-outs, or both. To print the text from Outline view, follow these steps:

1. View the outline in Normal or Outline view and make sure you click in the Outline pane so it is selected.

2. Choose File ⇨ Print. The Print dialog box opens.

3. Open the Print What drop-down list and choose Outline View.

4. Set any other print options, as you learned in the section "Printing Handouts" earlier in the chapter.

5. Click OK.

Be aware, however, that the outline will not contain text that you've typed in manu-ally placed text boxes or any other non-text information, such as tables, charts, and so on.

Note   New in PowerPoint 2003 is the Print Preview feature, which works just like it does in Microsoft Word. Use it to see how your printouts will appear without actually using the paper to produce them. To access it, click the Print Preview button on the toolbar or choose File ⇨ Print Preview.

Sending Your Presentation to Word

One of the drawbacks to PowerPoint is that the notes and handouts pages are not fully formattable. There's a lot you can't do with them — like set margins, or change the sizes of the slide images for handouts. To get around this, you might want to create your handouts in Microsoft Word.

To send your presentation to Word, follow these steps:

1. Choose File ⇨ Send To ⇨ Microsoft Office Word. The Send to Microsoft Office Word dialog box appears. See Figure 24-15.

2. Choose one of the formats shown in Figure 24-15. You can send to Word in a variety of formats. Some formats are more appropriate for handouts, others for speaker notes. Here are some suggestions:

For Handouts	For Speaker Notes
Blank lines next to slides Blank lines below slides Outline only Notes below slides Outline only	Notes next to slides

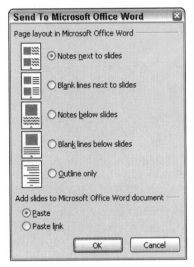

Figure 24-15: Choose a format for sending the presentation to Word.

3. *(Optional)* If you want to maintain a link between the PowerPoint file and the Word file, choose Paste Link. Otherwise, leave Paste selected. If you maintain a link, changes made to the PowerPoint file are reflected in the Word file.

4. Click OK. Word opens and the slides appear in the format you chose. See Figure 24-16.

5. Modify the formatting as desired and then print from Word.

6. *(Optional)* Save your work in Word if you want to be able to print the same pages again later. (You may choose to resend to Word later, after making changes in PowerPoint instead.)

Note

The slides appear in Word in a table. You can resize (or even delete) the columns for each element by dragging the column dividers, just like you do in a table in PowerPoint. (You learned about tables in Chapter 8.) You can also resize the slide thumbnails in Word by clicking the first thumbnail, choosing Format ⇨ Object, and then changing the size on the Size tab. If you have a number of slides to resize, you may want to create a Word macro to do this.

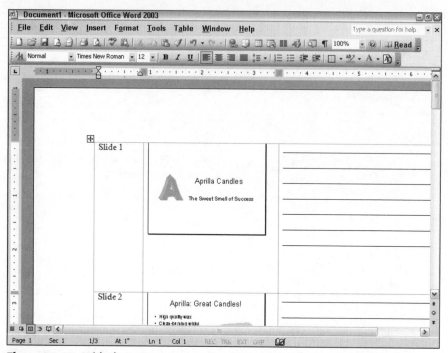

Figure 24-16: With the notes pages or handouts in Word, you can change the margins and other settings.

Summary

In this chapter, you learned how to create hard copy to support your presentation. You can now create a variety of handouts, and write and print out speaker notes for yourself. You also learned how to export handouts, notes pages, and outlines to Word, where you can use the full power of Word's formatting tools to create exactly the look you want.

In the next chapter, you take a look at the controls that PowerPoint offers for showing a presentation on-screen. You learn how to move from slide to slide, take notes, "draw" on the slides, and more.

✦   ✦   ✦

Controlling a Live Presentation

It's show time! Well, actually I hope for your sake that it is *not* time for the show this very instant, because things will go much more smoothly if you can practice using PowerPoint's slide show controls before you have to go live.

Presenting the show can be as simple or as complex as you make it. At the most basic level, you can start the show, move through it slide-by-slide with simple mouse clicks or key presses, and end the show. But to take advantage of PowerPoint's extra show features, you must spend a little time studying the following sections.

Note This first part of the chapter assumes that you are going to be showing your presentation on a PC that has PowerPoint 2003 installed on it; later in the chapter I'll talk about other situations.

Starting and Ending a Show

To start a show, do any of the following:

✦ Click the Slide Show View button in the bottom-left corner of the screen.

✦ Choose View ➪ Slide Show.

✦ Choose Slide Show ➪ View Show.

✦ Press F5.

These methods are not all exactly alike. If you click the Slide Show View button, the first slide to appear is the currently selected one in PowerPoint. If you choose Slide Show ⇨ View Show, View ⇨ Slide Show, or press F5, it starts with the first slide in the presentation, regardless of which slide was selected.

Once the show is underway, you can control the movement from slide to slide as described in "Moving from slide to slide," the next section in this chapter.

To end the show, do any of the following:

✦ Right-click and choose End Show.

✦ Press Esc, - (minus), or Ctrl+Break.

If you want to temporarily pause the show while you have a discussion, you can blank the screen by pressing W or ' (apostrophe) for a white screen or B or . (period) for a black one. To resume the show, press any key.

Expert Tip   If you have the slide transitions set up to occur automatically with a certain timing, you can stop or restart the show by pressing S or + (plus sign). This is more of an issue for self-running shows, however, which are discussed in Chapter 28.

Using the On-Screen Show Controls

As you display a slide show, the mouse pointer and show controls are hidden. To make them appear, move the mouse. Moving the mouse makes three or four buttons appear in the bottom-left corner of the slide show, and also makes the mouse pointer appear. You can toggle the pointer and these buttons on/off by pressing A or = (equals). Ctrl+H hides the pointer and buttons.

Expert Tip   Pressing A or = is not a true toggle; it cycles between three states each time you press one. The three states are On, Off, and Flash, which makes the items appear briefly on-screen.

The leftmost button is Back; it takes you back to the previous slide, or to the previous animation event if you have animation. The next one, with a pen on it, opens a menu for controlling the pointer appearance. (I save its discussion for later in the chapter.) The one with a box on it opens a menu for navigating between slides. See Figure 25–1. And finally, the rightmost button is a forward arrow that advances to the next slide in the presentation.

Note

Because the slide navigation menu is identical whether you click the button or right-click anywhere on the slide, I won't mention both methods each time I ask you to choose something from the menu. I ask you to right-click, because it's simpler. But keep in mind that you can also do a regular click on that button as an alternative anytime you like.

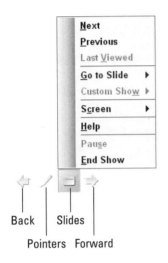

Figure 25-1: Four buttons appear in the corner of a slide in Slide Show view. If they do not appear, move the mouse to display them.

There are a lot of shortcut keys to remember when working in Slide Show view, so PowerPoint provides a handy summary of them. To see it, right-click and choose Help, or press the F1 button. The Slide Show Help dialog box appears, shown in Figure 25-2. Click its OK button to close it when you're finished with it.

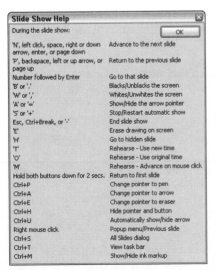

Figure 25-2: The Slide Show Help dialog box provides a quick summary of the shortcut keys available during a presentation.

Moving from slide to slide

The simplest way to move through a presentation is to move to the next slide. To do so, any of these methods works:

✦ Press any of these keys: N, spacebar, right arrow, down arrow, Enter, or Page Down.

✦ Click the left mouse button.

✦ Right-click and then choose Next.

✦ Click the right-pointing arrow button in the bottom-left corner of the slide (present only when the mouse pointer is set to be a pen; discussed later in the chapter).

If you have animated any elements on a slide, the previous methods advance the animation, and do not necessarily move to the next slide. For example, if you have animated your bulleted list so that the bullets appear one at a time, any of the actions on the previous list makes the next bullet appear, rather than making the next slide appear. Only after all the objects on the current slide have been displayed does PowerPoint advance to the next one. If you need to immediately advance to the next slide, use the instructions in "Jumping to specific slides" later in the chapter.

To back up to the previous slide, use any of these methods:

✦ Press any of these keys: P, Backspace, left arrow, up arrow, or Page Up.

✦ Click the left-pointing arrow button on the bottom-left corner of the slide.

✦ Right-click and then choose Previous.

You can also go back to the last slide viewed. To do that, right-click and choose Last Viewed. But wouldn't the last slide viewed be the same as the previous slide? Usually, yes. But if you have been jumping around—for example, jumping to a hidden slide—then it's two different things.

Expert Tip   You can set up your show to move backwards when the right mouse button is clicked. Choose Tools ➪ Options and clear the Popup menu on right mouse click check box.

Jumping to specific slides

There are several ways to jump to a particular slide. One of the easiest is to select the slide by its title. To do so, follow these steps:

1. During the slide show, right-click to display the shortcut menu.

2. Point to Go to Slide. A submenu appears listing the titles of all the slides in the presentation. See Figure 25-3. (Note that parentheses around the slide numbers indicate hidden slides.)

3. Click the slide title that you want to jump to.

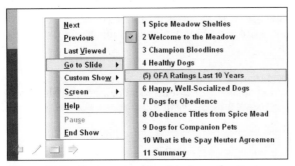

Figure 25-3: Go to a specific slide from the Go to Slide command on the menu.

You can also jump to a certain slide number by typing that number and pressing Enter. For example, to go to the third slide, type **3** and then press Enter.

One more way — you can press Ctrl+S to open an All Slides dialog box listing the titles of all the slides in the presentation, and then make your selection and click OK. See Figure 25-4.

Figure 25-4: The All Slides dialog box lists the titles of all the slides so you can select the one to go to.

Expert Tip If you have custom shows defined, you can choose among them in the All Slides dialog box's Show drop-down list. In Figure 25-3, this list is disabled because there are no custom shows.

To jump back to the first slide in the presentation, hold down both the left and right mouse buttons for two seconds (or type **1** and press Enter).

Viewing hidden slides

Slides that you have marked as hidden do not appear in the main flow of the presentation. (To hide a slide, see the "Hiding Slides for Backup Use" section in Chapter 26.) Therefore, the only way to display a hidden slide is to jump to it using either of the methods explained in the preceding section.

There is not much difference between jumping to a hidden slide and jumping to a visible one. Recall that you can tell at a glance which slides are hidden because hidden slides have parentheses around their slide numbers. For example, in Figure 25-3, slide 3 is hidden.

Viewing Speaker Notes

You have probably printed out any speaker notes that you've created, but Murphy's Law says that when you need your notes, they will be nowhere to be found. Rather than spend long minutes fumbling with your papers, you may want to refer to your notes on-screen.

Not only can you view notes during a presentation, but you can take more notes, too. To access your notes pages during a presentation, follow these steps:

1. Display the slide for which you want to view or type notes.

2. Right-click and choose Screen ⇨ Speaker Notes. A Speaker Notes box appears, showing the current notes for the slide. See Figure 25-5.

3. Read the notes as needed, and add more if appropriate. You might, for example, take notes on audience response to a particular slide.

4. When you are finished with the Speaker Notes box, click its window's Close (X) button to close it.

The disadvantage of this, of course, is that if you have a one-screen setup, the audience reads your notes on-screen along with you. But if you have your presentation set up to display on two screens, as described later in this chapter, the speaker notes appear only on the presenter's screen.

Figure 25-5: View speaker notes on-screen during the presentation.

Using the On-Screen Pen

Have you ever seen a coach in a locker room, drawing out football plays on a chalk-board? Well, you can do the same thing in PowerPoint. You can have impromptu discussions of concepts illustrated on slides and punctuate the discussion with your own circles, arrows, and lines. Perhaps during the discussion portion of your presentation you decide that one point on the slide is not important. You can use the pen to cross it out. Or perhaps a certain point becomes really important during a discussion and you want to emphasize it. You can circle it or underline it with the pen cursor.

Choose your pen color like this:

1. Move the mouse or press A to make the buttons appear.

2. Click the Pointers button (the middle button). A menu appears.

3. Point to Ink Color and then click the color you want. See Figure 25-6.

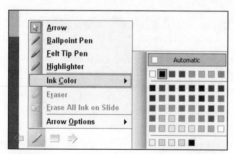

Figure 25-6: Select a pen type and an ink color for it.

Expert Tip

To change the default pen color for the show, so you don't always have to manually select the color you want, choose Slide Show ➪ Set Up Show. Then in the Pen Color drop-down list, choose the desired color.

Turn on the type of pen you want as follows:

1. Click the Pointers button again.

2. Click the type of pen you want:

   • **Ballpoint:** A thin line

   • **Felt Tip Pen:** A thicker line

   • **Highlighter:** A thick, semi-transparent line

Note

The on-screen buttons in the slide show do continue to work while you have a pen enabled, but you have to click on them twice to get them to work—once to tell PowerPoint to switch out of the Pen mode temporarily and then again to open the menu.

You can also turn on the default pen type (Ballpoint) by pressing Ctrl+P, and then go back to the arrow again with Ctrl+A or Esc.

After enabling a pen, just drag-and-draw on the slide to make your mark. Practice drawing lines, arrows, or whatever; it takes a while to get good at it. Figure 25-7 shows an example.

Caution

As you can see from Figure 25-7, the on-screen pen is not all that attractive. If you know in advance that you're going to emphasize certain points, build the emphasis into the presentation by making that point larger, bolder, or a different color. (Or circle the points using a path animation on a line.)

To erase your lines and try again, press E (for Erase), or open the Pointer menu and choose Erase All Ink On Slide. To erase just a part of the ink, open the Pointer menu and choose Erase, and then use the mouse pointer like an eraser tool.

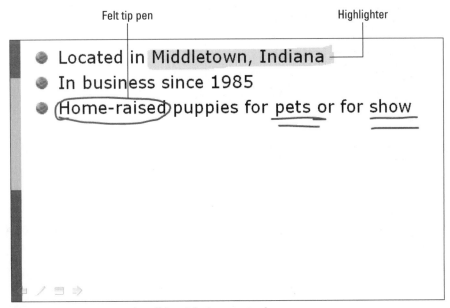

Felt tip pen   Highlighter

- Located in Middletown, Indiana
- In business since 1985
- Home-raised puppies for pets or for show

Figure 25-7: Draw on the slide with the pen tools.

Note   Drawings stay with a slide even when you move away from it (unlike in some earlier versions of PowerPoint).

When you exit Slide Show view after drawing on slides, a dialog box appears asking whether you want to Keep or Discard your annotations. If you choose Keep, the annotations become drawn objects on the slides, which you can then move or delete just like an AutoShape.

Expert Tip   There may be times when you want to draw on a totally blank screen instead of on a slide. To blank out the screen for drawing, press the B key for a black screen or W for a white one. The pen color adjusts to be visible (black on white or white on black).

To change the pen back to a pointer again, open the Pointer menu (click twice on the Pointer button on the slide to open the menu) and choose Arrow, press Ctrl+A, or press Esc. The pen stays a pen when you advance from slide to slide. (In earlier versions of PowerPoint it went back to an arrow automatically when you changed slides.)

Giving a Presentation on a Different Computer

Often the PC on which you create a presentation is not the same PC that you will use to show it. For example, you might be doing the bulk of your work on your desktop PC in your office in Los Angeles, but you need to use your laptop PC to give the presentation in Phoenix.

One way to transfer a presentation to another computer is simply to copy the PowerPoint file (the file with the .ppt extension) using a floppy disk or other removable media. But this method is imperfect because it assumes that the other PC has all the needed fonts, sounds, and other elements needed for every part of the show. This can be a dangerous assumption. For example, suppose your presentation contains a link to some Excel data. If you don't copy that Excel file too, you cannot update the data when you're on the road.

A better way to ensure that you are taking everything you need on the road is to use the Package for CD in PowerPoint. It reads all the linked files and associated objects and makes sure that they are transferred along with the main presentation. You don't actually have to copy it to a writeable CD, and you don't need a CD-R or CD-RW drive to use this feature. You can copy it anywhere you want, such as to a ZIP drive or a network location.

Copying a presentation to CD

If you have a CD-R or CD-RW drive, copying the presentation to CD-R is an attractive choice. It produces a self-running disc that contains a PowerPoint Viewer application, the presentation file, and any linked files.

Expert Tip   You can copy many presentation files onto a single CD, not just the currently active one. The only limit is the size of the disc (usually 650 to 700MB). By default the currently active presentation is included; you'll see in the following steps how to add others too. Further, you can set them up to run automatically one after another, or you can specify that a menu appear so the user can choose.

Here's the basic procedure, which I'll elaborate on in the following sections:

1. Place a blank CD-R disc in your writeable CD drive.

2. Finalize the presentation in PowerPoint. CD-R discs are not rewriteable, so be sure the presentation is exactly as you want it.

3. Choose File ➪ Package for CD. The Package for CD dialog box opens. See Figure 25-8.

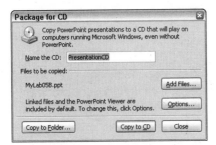

Figure 25-8: Use Package for CD to place all the needed files for the presentation on a CD.

4. Type a name for the CD; this is like a volume label for the disc.

5. *(Optional)* Add more files to the CD layout if desired. See the next section, "Creating a CD containing multiple presentation files," for details.

6. *(Optional)* Set any options as desired. See the "Setting CD options" section later in the chapter for details.

7. Click the Copy to CD button, and wait for the CD to be written. It may take several minutes, depending on the speed of your CD drive's writing capabilities and the size of the presentation files you are placing on it.

8. A message appears when the files are successfully copied to CD, asking whether you want to copy the same files to another CD. Click Yes or No. If you choose No, click Close to close the Package for CD dialog box.

The resulting CD automatically plays the presentation(s) when you insert it in any PC. You can also browse its contents to open the PowerPoint Viewer separately and use it to play specific presentations.

Caution

After burning a CD, test it thoroughly by running the complete presentation from CD before you rely on the CD copy as the version that you take out on the road with you. File corruption has been known to occur on some CD-R drives during the writing process.

Creating a CD containing multiple presentation files

By default, the active presentation is included on the CD, but you can also add others, up to the capacity of your disk. For example, perhaps you have several versions of the same presentation for different audiences; a single CD can contain all of them.

As you are preparing to copy using the Package for CD dialog box (Figure 25-8), do the following to add more files:

1. Click the Add Files button. An Add dialog box opens. (It's just like the Open dialog box you use for opening PowerPoint files.)

2. Select the additional files to include, and click Add to return to the Package for CD dialog box. Now the list of files appears as in Figure 25-9, with extra controls.

Note   You can select multiple files from the same location by holding down Ctrl as you click on the ones you want. To include multiple files from different locations, repeat Steps 1 and 2 for each location.

Reorder the list if desired

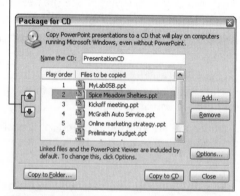

Figure 25-9: When you specify multiple files for a CD, you can specify the order in which they should play.

3. If you set up the CD to play the presentations automatically (see the next section), the order in which they appear on the list becomes significant. Rearrange the list if desired by clicking a presentation and then clicking the Up or Down arrow buttons to the left of the list.

4. If you need to remove a presentation from the list, click it and then click Remove.

5. Continue making the CD normally.

Setting copy options

The default copy options are suitable in most situations, but you will probably want to at least know what they are so you will know how to change them in that occasional odd situation.

To change the copy options, from the Package for CD dialog box, do the following:

1. Click the Options button. The Options dialog box opens. See Figure 25-10.

2. The PowerPoint Viewer is included by default. It is needed if the destination PC does not have PowerPoint or the PowerPoint Viewer installed. Usually it's a good idea to include it, but if you are certain that the destination PC has PowerPoint 2003 and you need the extra space on the CD for more presentation files, omit it by clearing the PowerPoint Viewer check box.

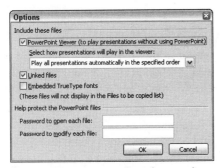

Figure 25-10: Set options for copying the presentation(s) to CD.

3. Open the drop-down list and choose how you want the presentations to play:

   • **Play all presentations automatically in the specified order.** If you choose this, the order in which the presentations appear on the list becomes significant. (That's covered in the preceding section.)

   • **Play only the first presentation automatically.** Again, this makes the order significant. The first presentation by default is the one that was active when you opened the dialog box.

   • **Let the user select which presentation to view.** This shows a menu when the CD is inserted. A nice feature if you want to be able to select a presentation each time.

   • **Do nothing.** This turns off the Autorun for the disc completely.

4. The Linked Files check box is marked by default; it includes the full copies of all linked files. Clear it if desired; a static copy of the linked data will remain in the presentation but the link will not work. This is especially important to leave checked if you have sounds or multimedia files in your presentation, as those are always linked (with the exception of some WAV files).

5. The Embedded TrueType Fonts check box is cleared by default. If you think the destination PC might not contain all the fonts used in the presentation, mark it. This makes the presentation file slightly larger. Remember, not all fonts can be embedded; it depends on the level of embedding allowed by the font's manufacturer.

6. If you want to add passwords for the presentations, do so in the Secure the PowerPoint Files section. There are separate boxes for read and modify passwords.

7. Click OK, and then complete the CD normally.

Copying a presentation to other locations

Although it's not well-advertised, the Package for CD feature can also be used to copy presentation files and their associated support files to any location you want. You can transfer files to another PC on a network, for example, or place them on a floppy or ZIP disk.

To do so, do the following:

1. In the Package for CD dialog box, set up the package exactly the way you want it, including all the presentation files and all the options. See the preceding sections for help.

2. Click the Copy to Folder button. A Copy to Folder dialog box appears.

3. Enter a name for the new folder to be created in the Name the Folder box.

4. Enter a path for the folder in the Choose Location box. See Figure 25-11.

5. Click OK. The files are copied to that location.

6. Click Close to close the Package for CD dialog box.

Figure 25-11: You can copy presentation files and support files anywhere, not just to a CD.

Using a presentation CD with the PowerPoint Viewer

To use a self-running presentation CD, just insert it in the CD drive. The presentation starts automatically. You can then move through it as described later in this chapter.

If you have placed multiple presentations on the CD and specified that a menu should appear for them, a menu like the one shown in Figure 25-12 appears when you insert the CD. Select the presentation you want and click Open to start it. When the presentation has completed, this dialog box will reappear.

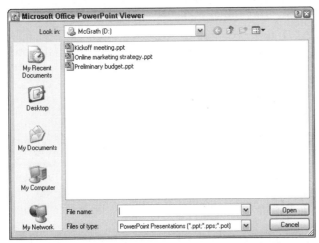

Figure 25-12: The PowerPoint Viewer asks which file you want to open if you configured the options to do so when creating the CD.

Working with Audio Visual Equipment

The first part of this chapter has assumed you were using a computer with a single monitor to show the presentation, but that might not always be true. So let's look at the whole range of AV options you might have to choose from.

There are many models of projection equipment in conference rooms all across the world, but most of them fall into one of these categories:

✦ **Noncomputerized equipment:** This can include an overhead transparency viewer, a 35mm slide projector, or other older technology. You'll have two challenges if you need to work with this category of equipment: one is figuring out how the equipment works (because every model is different), and the other is producing attractive versions of your slides to work with them. There are companies that produce 35mm slides from your PowerPoint files, or you can invest in a slide-making machine yourself. For transparencies, you simply print your slides on transparency film designed for your type of printer.

✦ **Single PC with a single monitor:** If there is a PC with a monitor in the meeting room, you will want to place your presentation files on that PC. You can do this with the Publish to CD feature discussed in the preceding sections, and then run the presentation directly from the CD.

✦ **Single PC with a dual-monitor system:** On systems with dual monitors, one monitor is shown to the audience and the other is for your own use. This is great because you can display your speaker notes on the one that the audience doesn't see. However, you might need to set up multi-monitor support in Windows so that you can have different displays on each monitor.

✦ **Projection system (LCD) or large monitor without a PC:** If the meeting room has a large monitor but no computer, you'll need to bring your own notebook computer and connect it to the monitor. Most such systems have a standard VGA plug and cable.

The following sections look at some of these possibilities in more detail.

Presenting with two screens

If you have two monitors — either your notebook PC screen and an external monitor, or two external monitors hooked up to the same PC — you can display the presentation on one of them and your own notes on the other. This is very handy!

Caution

You need the full version of PowerPoint on your laptop to use two screens, not just the PowerPoint Viewer. Also you need compatible hardware. Your notebook must have an external VGA port and a built-in video card that supports DualView in your version of Windows. Or, if you have a desktop PC, you must have two separate video cards or a video card with two separate VGA ports on it.

Configuring display hardware for multi-screen viewing

First, get your hardware ready. On a notebook PC, that means enabling both the built-in and the external monitor ports and connecting an external monitor. Some notebook PCs toggle between internal, external, and dual monitors with an *Fn* key combination; check your laptop's documentation.

On a desktop PC, install a second video card and monitor, and then do the following to set them up in Windows. (These steps are for Windows XP; other versions are similar.)

1. When Windows restarts after you install the second video card, right-click the desktop and choose Properties; then click the Settings tab. There should be two monitors shown in the sample area, as in Figure 25-13.

Sample area

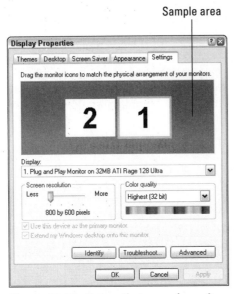

Figure 25-13: Set up the second monitor in Windows before attempting to use it in PowerPoint.

2. The monitor that you use most of the time should be 1, and the other one should be 2. To determine which is which, click the Identify button, and large numbers briefly appear on each screen.

3. If you need to swap the monitors in numbering, click the one that should be the primary monitor and then mark the Use This Device as the Primary Monitor check box. (It will be unavailable, as in Figure 25-13, if the monitor currently selected is already set to be the primary one.)

4. Select the secondary monitor, and then click the Extend my Windows Desktop onto This Monitor check box.

5. *(Optional)* If the monitors are not arranged in the sample area in the way that they are physically positioned on your desk, drag the boxes for the monitors where you want them.

6. *(Optional)* Click a monitor in the sample area and then adjust its display settings if needed. You can change the screen resolution and color quality from the Settings tab.

Expert Tip You can also adjust the refresh rate for each monitor. To do so, make sure you have selected the video card to which the monitor is attached, and then click the Advanced button. On the Monitor tab in the dialog box that appears, change the refresh rate. A higher refresh rate makes the screen more flicker-free, but if you exceed the monitor's maximum supported rate, the display may appear distorted and the monitor may be damaged.

   7. Click OK. You are now ready to work with the two monitors in PowerPoint.

Now you can drag things from your primary monitor to your secondary one! This can be great fun outside of PowerPoint as well as inside. For example, you can have two applications open at once, each in its own monitor window.

Setting up a presentation for two screens

If you have two monitors available, and configured as described in the preceding section, use the following steps to help PowerPoint recognize and take advantage of them:

   1. Open the presentation in PowerPoint.

   2. Choose Slide Show ➪ Set Up Show. The Set Up Show dialog box opens, shown in Figure 25-14.

Figure 25-14: Set up the show for multiple monitors in the Set Up Show box.

   3. In the Multiple Monitors section, open the Display Slide Show On list and choose the monitor that the audience will see.

4. Mark the Show Presenter View check box. This will give you a separate, very useful control panel on the other monitor as the show is progressing. (You learn about it in the next section.)

5. Click OK. Now you are ready to show the presentation using two separate displays — one for you and one for the audience.

Note There are lots of other options in the Set Up Show dialog box; you read about them in more detail in Chapter 28, when you look at self-running shows.

Presenting with two screens using Presenter View

Presenter View is a special view of the presentation that is available only on systems with more than one monitor, and only where the Show Presenter View check box has been marked in the Set Up Show dialog box (see the preceding section). It provides many useful tools for managing the show behind-the-scenes, and is shown in Figure 25-15. It appears automatically on the non-audience monitor when you enter Slide Show view.

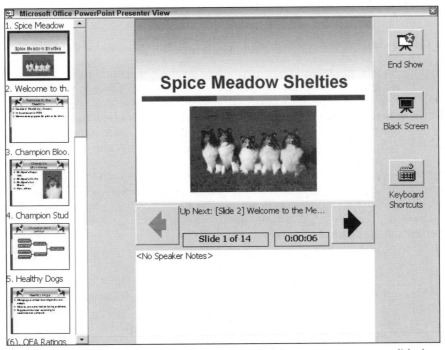

Figure 25-15: Presenter View provides tools for helping you manage your slideshow from a second monitor.

At the left is a pane containing thumbnail images of each slide. You can jump to a slide by selecting it there. You can also move between slides with the large left and right arrow buttons.

The speaker notes for each slide appear in the lower pane. You can edit them from here, or use that area to write notes to yourself about the discussions taking place during the presentation.

The End Show and Black Screen buttons do just what you would think. The Keyboard Shortcuts button opens a dialog box containing a few reminders of the keyboard shortcuts available in Presenter View.

Presenter View doesn't have all of the bells and whistles that you have learned about so far in Slide Show view. For example, it doesn't have a pen, and can only black the screen — not "white" it. However, don't forget that the audience's monitor is still active and available for your use! Because you extended the desktop onto the second monitor, you can simply move the mouse pointer onto the audience's display and then use the buttons in the corner (or the right-click menu) as you normally can.

Summary

In this chapter, you learned how to prepare for the big presentation. You now know how to pack up a presentation and move it to another PC, how to set up single and multiscreen A/V equipment to work with your laptop, and how to control a presentation on-screen using your computer. You also know now how to jump to different slides, how to take notes during a meeting, and how to assign action items. You're all set! All you need now is a nice starched shirt and a shoeshine.

In the next chapter, you learn about some of the special considerations involved in preparing long or complex slide shows. When you're presenting in a situation where there are many contingencies and the show may take one of many different turns depending on the questions asked, you'll appreciate PowerPoint's ability to help you prepare for the unknown.

✦   ✦   ✦

Managing Long or Complex Shows

When you work with a presentation that contains many slides, it is easy to get confused. Fortunately, PowerPoint enables you to organize your show into custom shows, and it enables you to hide certain slides for backup use.

Hiding Slides for Backup Use

You may not always want to show every slide that you have prepared. Sometimes it pays to prepare extra data in anticipation of a question that you think someone might ask, or to hold back certain data unless someone specifically requests it.

By hiding a slide, you keep it filed in reserve, without making it a part of the main slide show. Then, at any time during the presentation when (or if) it becomes appropriate, you can call that slide to the forefront to be displayed. Hiding refers only to whether the slide is a part of the main presentation's flow; it has no effect in any other view.

 Expert Tip　If you have only a handful of slides to hide, go ahead and hide them. But if you have a large group of related slides to hide, consider creating a custom show for them instead.

Hiding and unhiding slides

The best way to hide and unhide slides is in Slide Sorter view because an indicator appears underneath each slide to show whether it is hidden. That way, you can tell easily which slides are part of the main presentation.

Follow these steps to hide a slide:

1. Switch to Slide Sorter view (View ➪ Slide Sorter).

2. Select the slides(s) you want to hide. Remember, to select more than one slide, hold down the Ctrl key as you click the ones you want.

3. Click the Hide Slide button on the Slide Sorter toolbar, or choose Slide Show ➪ Hide Slide. A gray box appears around the slide number and a diagonal line appears through it, indicating that it is hidden. See Figure 26-1.

Hide Slide button   Hidden slides have a line through the number

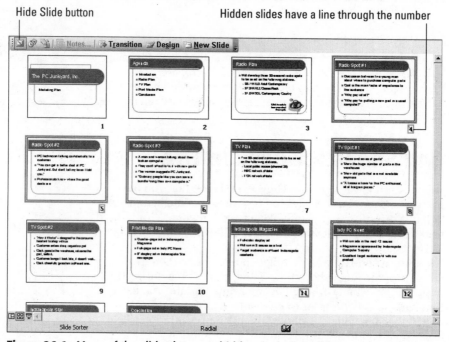

Figure 26-1: Many of the slides here are hidden, including slides 4-6, 8, 9, 11, and 12.

To unhide a slide, select the slide and click the Hide Slide button again or choose Slide Show ➪ Hide Slide again. The slide's number returns to normal.

Expert Tip To quickly unhide all slides, select all the slides (press Ctrl+A) and then click the Hide Slides button twice. The first click hides all remaining slides that were not already hidden, and the second click unhides them all.

Showing a hidden slide during a presentation

When you advance from one slide to the next during a show, hidden slides do not appear. (That's what being hidden is about, after all.) If you need to display one of the hidden slides, follow these steps:

1. In Slide Show view, open the shortcut menu. As you learned in Chapter 25, you can do this by right-clicking or by clicking the button in the bottom left corner of the screen (the one with the rectangle on it, as in Figure 26-2).

2. Choose Go to Slide, and then choose the slide you want to jump to. Hidden slides show their slide numbers in parentheses, but you can access them like any other slide. See Figure 26-2.

Expert Tip   If you already know the number of the hidden slide, you can simply type the number on the keyboard and hit Enter. This will jump to your hidden slide. This also works with slides that aren't hidden.

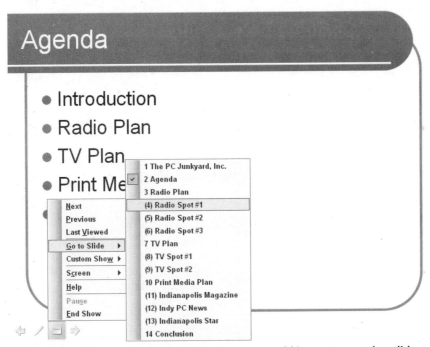

Figure 26-2: Jump to a hidden slide just as you would jump to any other slide.

Once you have displayed a hidden slide, you can easily go back to it later. When you move backwards through the presentation (using Backspace or the left or up arrow key, or the Back button on-screen), any hidden slides that were displayed previously will be included in the slides that it scrolls back through. However, when you move forward through the presentation the hidden slide does not reappear, regardless of its previous viewing. You can always jump back to it again the same as in the preceding steps.

Using Custom Shows

Many slide shows have a linear flow: First you show slide one, and then slide two, and so on, until you have completed the entire presentation. This format is suitable for situations where you are presenting clear-cut information with few variables, such as a presentation about a new insurance plan for a group of employees. However, when the situation becomes more complex, a single-path slide show may not suffice. This is especially true when you are presenting a persuasive message to decision-makers; you want to anticipate their questions and needs for more information and have many backup slides, or even entire backup slide shows, prepared in case certain questions arise. Figure 26-3 shows a flow chart for such a presentation.

Note   If you simply want to hide a few slides for backup use, you do not have to go to the trouble of creating a custom show. Instead, just hide the slides.

Another great use for custom shows is to set aside a group of slides for a specific audience. For example, you might need to present essentially the same information to employees at two different sites. You could create custom shows within the main show that include slides that both shows have in common plus slides that are appropriate for only one audience or the other. Figure 26-4 shows a flow chart for a presentation like that.

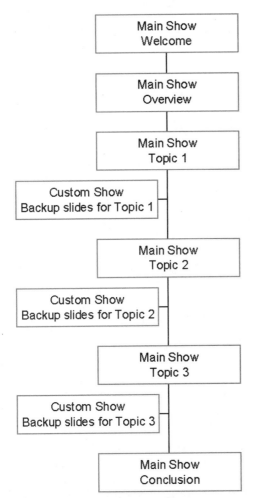

Figure 26-3: You can use custom shows to hide related groups of backup slides.

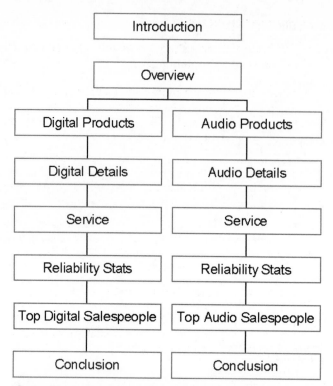

Figure 26-4: You can create custom shows that allow the same presentation to be used for multiple audiences.

Notice in Figure 26-4 that some of the slides in the two custom shows are the same, yet they're repeated in each custom show rather than jumping back to the main presentation. That's because it's much easier to jump to the custom show once and stay there than it is to keep jumping into and out of the show.

Slides in a custom show remain a part of the main presentation. Placing a slide in a custom show does not exclude it from the regular presentation flow. However, you may decide that you don't want to show the main presentation as-is anymore; you may just want to use it as a resource pool from which to select the slides for the various custom shows that you create in it. To learn how to set up PowerPoint so that a custom show starts rather than the main one when you enter Slide Show view, see the "Using a custom show as the main presentation" section later in this chapter.

Ideas for using custom shows

Here are some ideas to get you started thinking about how and why you might want to include some custom shows in your presentation files.

✦ **Avoiding duplication:** If you have several shows that use about 50 percent of the same slides and 50 percent different ones, you can create all of the shows as custom shows within a single presentation file. That way, the presentations can share those 50 percent of the slides that they have in common.

✦ **Managing change:** By creating a single presentation file with custom shows, you make it easy to manage changes. If any changes occur in your company that affect any of the common slides, making the change once in your presentation file makes the change to each of the custom shows immediately.

✦ **Overcoming objections:** You can anticipate client objections to your sales pitch and prepare several custom shows, each of which addresses a particular objection. Then, whatever reason your potential customer gives for not buying your product, you have a counteractive garrison at hand.

✦ **Covering your backside:** If you think you may be asked for specific figures or other information during a speech, you can have that information ready in a custom show (or on a few simple hidden slides, if there is not much of it) to whip out if needed. No more going through the embarrassment of having to say "I'm not sure, but let me get back to you on that."

Creating custom shows

To create a custom show, first create all the slides that should go into it. Start with all the slides in the main presentation. Then follow these steps:

1. Choose Slide Show ➪ Custom Shows. The Custom Shows dialog box opens.

2. Click the New button. The Define Custom Show dialog box appears.

3. Enter a name for your custom show in the Slide Show Name text box.

4. In the Slides in presentation pane, click the first slide that you want to appear in the custom show.

Expert Tip   You can select multiple slides in Step 4 by holding down the Ctrl key as you click each one you want. However, be aware that if you do this, the slides move to the Slides in Custom Show pane in the order that they originally appeared. If you want them in a different order, copy each slide over separately, in the order that you want, or rearrange the order as described in Step 7.

5. Click the Add button to copy it to the Slides in Custom Show pane. See Figure 26-5.

Rearrange order

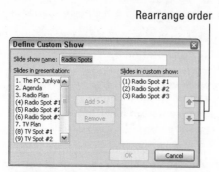

Figure 26-5: Use the Add button to copy slides from the main presentation into the custom show.

6. Repeat Steps 4 and 5 for each slide that you want to include in the custom show.

7. If you need to rearrange the slides in the custom show, click the slide you want to move in the Slides in Custom Show pane and then click the up or down arrow button to change its position.

8. When you are finished building your custom show, click OK. The new show appears in the Custom Shows dialog box.

9. *(Optional)* To test your custom show, click the Show button. Otherwise, click Close to close the Custom Shows dialog box.

Editing custom shows

You can manage your custom shows from the Custom Shows dialog box, the same place in which you created them. This includes editing a show, deleting one, or making a copy of one. To change which slides appear in a custom show, and in what order, follow these steps:

1. Choose Slide Show ➪ Custom Shows. The Custom Shows dialog box appears. See Figure 26-6.

Figure 26-6: Select the custom show to edit, copy, or delete, and then click the appropriate button.

2. Click the custom show you want to edit, if you have more than one.

3. Click the Edit button. The Define Custom Show dialog box reappears. (See Figure 26-5.)

4. Add or remove slides as needed. To add a slide, choose it from the left pane and click Add. To remove a slide, choose it from the right pane and click Remove.

Removing a slide from a custom show does not remove it from the presentation at large.

5. Rearrange slides as needed with the up and down arrow buttons.

6. *(Optional)* Change the custom show's name, if needed, in the Slide Show Name text box.

7. Click OK. Your changes are saved.

8. Click Close to close the Custom Shows dialog box.

Copying custom shows

A good way to create several similar custom shows is to create the first one and then copy it. Then you can make small changes to the copies as necessary. To copy a custom show, follow these steps:

1. Choose Slide Show ➪ Custom Shows to display the Custom Shows dialog box. See Figure 26-6.

2. Select the show you want to copy if you have more than one custom show.

3. Click the Copy button. A copy of it appears. The filename includes the words *Copy of* so you can distinguish it.

4. Edit the copy, as explained in the preceding section, to change its name and its content to differentiate it from the original.

5. When you're finished, click Close to close the Custom Shows dialog box.

Deleting custom shows

It is not necessary to delete a custom show when you do not want it anymore; it does not do any harm lying idle in your presentation. Because custom shows do not display unless you call for them, you can simply choose not to display it. However, if you want to make things a bit more orderly than that, you are free to delete a custom show that no longer serves you. Follow these steps:

1. Choose Slide Show ➪ Custom Shows to display the Custom Shows dialog box. See Figure 26-6.

2. Select the show you want to delete.

3. Click the Remove button. The show is gone.

4. Click Close to close the Custom Shows dialog box.

Displaying a Custom Show

At any time during your main presentation, you can call up the custom show. There are two ways to do it: you can navigate to the custom show with PowerPoint's regular presentation controls, or you can create a hyperlink to the custom show on your slide. (Hyperlinks are covered in detail in Chapter 29, but I touch on them in this chapter as well.)

You can also set the presentation to display one of the custom shows instead of the main presentation. This is useful if you have two complete custom shows, each used for a different audience.

Navigating to a custom show

During a presentation, you can jump to any of your custom shows by following these steps:

1. Open the shortcut menu in Slide Show view.

2. Choose Custom Show and then the custom show you want. See Figure 26-7. The custom show starts.

When you start a custom show, you are no longer in the main presentation. To see this for yourself, open the shortcut menu again, choose Go to Slide, and check out the list of slides. The list shows only the slides from the custom show you're in. In Figure 26-8, for example, the custom show contains three slides, and they're your only choices. (See the next section to get back to the main show.)

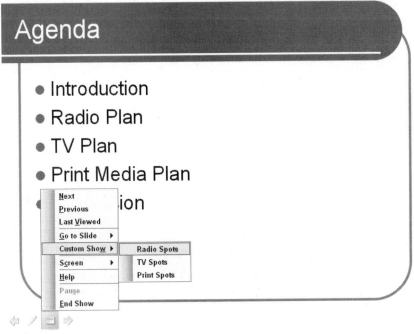

Figure 26-7: Choose the custom show that you want to jump to.

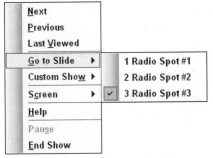

Figure 26-8: Within a custom show, you can jump only to slides within that custom show.

Navigating back to the main show

To get back to the main show, follow these steps:

1. Press Ctrl+S to open the All Slides dialog box.

2. Open the Show drop-down list and choose All Slides.

3. Select the slide that you want to go to. You have all the slides in the entire presentation to choose from, as shown in Figure 26-9.

4. Click Go To.

Expert Tip   To avoid having to click Ctrl+S to go back to the main show, consider creating a hyperlink or action button for a specific slide in your main show.

Figure 26-9: Return to the full presentation from the All Slides dialog box.

Creating a hyperlink to a custom show

You learn a lot about hyperlinks in upcoming chapters, but here's a preview. Hyperlinks are hot links that you place on your slides. When you click a hyperlink, you jump the display to some other location. That's why they're called *hot*. A hyperlink can jump to an Internet location, a different spot in your presentation, an external file (such as a Word document), or just about anywhere else.

One way to give yourself quick access to your custom shows in a presentation is to create hyperlinks for them on certain key jumping-off-point slides.

You can insert a text hyperlink in any text box, and its text is the marker that you click. For example, you can insert a hyperlink for the Radio Spots custom show and the text that appears reads *Radio Spots*. Or, if you want to get fancier, you can select some existing text or an existing graphic object, and then attach the hyperlink to it. For example, in Figure 26-10, I've inserted a clip art image of a radio and set it up to be a hyperlink to the custom show that provides details about the radio spots.

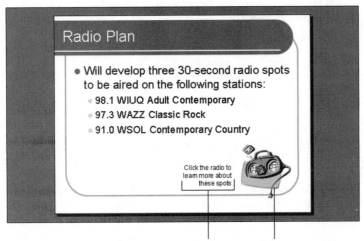

Text box with instructions   Hyperlink to custom show

Figure 26-10: Create hyperlinks on slides that display custom shows.

Follow these steps:

1. If you are attaching the hyperlink to some other object or some text, select the object or text.

2. Choose Insert ⇨ Hyperlink. The Insert Hyperlink dialog box appears.

3. Click the Place in This Document icon along the left side of the screen.

4. In the Select a place in this document pane, scroll down to the Custom Shows list.

5. Click the custom show that you want to jump to with this hyperlink. See Figure 26-11.

6. *(Optional)* If you want to return to the same spot that you left in the main presentation after viewing that custom show, mark the Show and Return check box. If you don't mark this, the presentation will simply end at the end of the custom show.

7. Click OK.

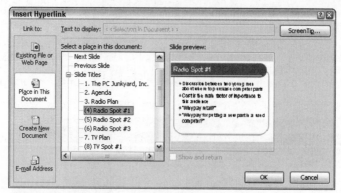

Figure 26-11: Choose one of your custom shows as the place to jump to when the hyperlink is clicked.

If you're using text for the hyperlink, the text now appears underlined and in a different color. This color is controlled by the color scheme of your presentation, specifically the last color swatch—Accent and Followed Hyperlink. If you are using a graphic, it does not appear differently than it did before. However, when you're in Slide Show view, when you move the mouse pointer over the object, the pointer changes into a pointing hand, indicating that the object is a hyperlink. See Figure 26-12.

Expert Tip

If you don't want your linked text to be underlined or change colors upon return, you can put an autoshape rectangle with no line and no fill over the top of the text and link to that instead. Because it's on top of the text, you will click it instead of the text itself. You will probably want to create your link before changing the line and fill to no color!

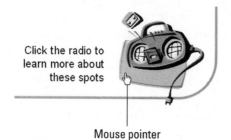

Click the radio to
learn more about
these spots

Mouse pointer

Figure 26-12: A graphic with a hyperlink assigned to it makes the mouse pointer appear as a hand when hovering over it in Slide Show view.

Another way to use hyperlinks for custom shows is to set up the first few slides generically for all audiences and then branch off into one custom show or another based on user input. Take a look at the diagram in Figure 26-4 again; this is one such example. You could set up a "decision" slide after the first two slides, containing two hyperlinks — one for Digital Products and one for Audio Products. Then you would click on one or the other as the situation demanded.

Expert Tip   You can also create hyperlinks to custom shows via action buttons. Action buttons are a special type of AutoShape designed specifically for creating hyperlinks within a presentation. You'll learn about action buttons in Chapter 29 when I discuss hyperlinks.

Using a custom show as the main presentation

If you have a complete show contained in one of your custom shows, you may sometimes wish to present it as such. To do so, you must tell PowerPoint that you want to bypass the main presentation and start with the custom show. Follow these steps:

1. Choose Slide Show ➪ Set Up Show. The Set Up Show dialog box appears.

2. Open the Custom show drop-down list and choose the show you want to use. See Figure 26-13.

3. Click OK. Now when you run the show (with Slide Show ➪ View Show), the custom show will run. See Chapter 25 for more details about running shows.

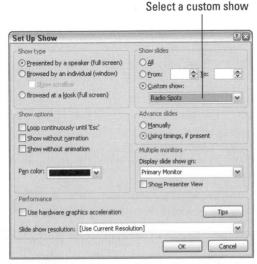

Figure 26-13: Use the Set Up Show dialog box to control which of your custom shows runs when you start the show.

Expert Tip   You do not have to set up a custom show to narrow down the list of slides that appear when you run your presentation. Notice in Figure 26-13 that there are From and To text boxes. To show, for example, slides 5 through 10, you enter **5** in the From box and **10** in the To box.

Merging PowerPoint Files

Another way to create a longer or more complex show is to merge two or more PowerPoint presentation files into a single, long presentation. For example, suppose you have three presentations, one for each of your sales divisions. You realize that they contain many of the same slides, and you want to be able to update those identical slides only one time, rather than in three places. So you decide to merge the three files. You can continue to have separate shows for each division by creating custom shows within the main show, as you have been learning in this chapter.

When you merge shows, all of the slides take on the formatting of the presentation file into which they are coming, unless you specify otherwise. For example, suppose you have a show that uses the Blends design template. If you merge a presentation into it that uses the Network design template, the incoming slides take on the Blends template's settings upon arrival. This ensures that all the slides in your show have a consistent look. However, if you have applied any special formatting to incoming slides, such as a nonstandard background, font choice, or text box placement, that formatting is retained. (An exception is if you mark the Keep Source Formatting check box during the import.)

To merge two presentations, follow these steps:

1. Open the presentation that you want to use for the host.

2. If you want the incoming slides inserted in a certain spot, place your insertion point in the correct spot in the Outline pane, or select the slide after which the new slides should appear.

3. Choose Insert ⇨ Slides from Files. The Slide Finder dialog box appears.

4. Click the Browse button. The Browse dialog box opens.

5. Select the presentation that you want to merge with the open one. Then, click Open. Thumbnails of the slides appear.

6. *(Optional)* If you want the incoming slides to keep their formatting (design template settings), mark the Keep Source Formatting check box.

7. If you want to insert all of the slides, click the Insert All button, and you're done. Otherwise, continue to Step 8.

8. Select the slides you want from the Select Slides area. Use the scroll bar as needed to scroll through the slides. See Figure 26-14. Clicking on a slide selects it; clicking it again deselects it. You do not have to hold down Shift or Ctrl in order to select multiple slides.

Figure 26-14: Insert slides from another presentation one by one or en masse.

9. Click Insert. The slides are inserted.

10. Click Close to close the dialog box.

11. Clean up the presentation by deleting any unneeded slides and rearranging the remaining ones. Slide Sorter view works well for this.

Summary

In this chapter, you learned how to hide and unhide slides and how to create, manage, and run custom slide shows. These skills can be very handy for making you look like the smooth professional who doesn't have to fumble with the presentation controls to display exactly what you want. The next chapter is a Project Lab where you can practice the skills you have learned in the last several chapters.

✦   ✦   ✦

Project Lab: Preparing a Speaker-Led Presentation

◆   ◆   ◆   ◆

In This Chapter

Creating custom
handouts in Word

Creating custom
shows

◆   ◆   ◆   ◆

Welcome to the fifth Project Lab in this book! This project lets you try some of the more advanced PowerPoint features for speaker-controlled presentations, including creating custom handouts and creating a custom show.

The Scenario

This lab continues your work for Spice Meadow Shelties. The owner has added a few new slides to the presentation you created in Project Lab 3, and is almost ready to start showing the presentation to potential customers. Before she does, however, she wants to have some attractive handouts to distribute to the audience. In this project lab, you will create those handouts.

In addition, she is interested in having different versions of the presentation for different types of audiences. You have suggested that she use the Custom Show feature to accomplish this so that she does not need completely separate PowerPoint files, and she agrees.

Project 5A: Creating Custom Handouts in Word

In this project, you will bypass the limited handout formatting capabilities of PowerPoint and export your handouts into Word, where you can really make them shine.

Level of difficulty: Moderate

Time to complete: 10 to 20 minutes

1. **Open the file Lab05A.ppt from the Labs folder (from the CD accompanying the book).**

   (You might want to copy all the lab files to your hard drive before starting the project, or you can open each file from the CD as you proceed.)

2. **Send the presentation to Word as handouts with blank lines next to each slide.**

   a. Choose File ➪ Send To ➪ Microsoft Office Word.

   b. In the Send to Microsoft Office Word dialog box, choose Blank Lines Next to Slides.

   c. Click OK.

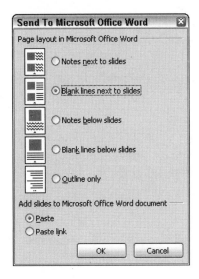

3. **Use Print Preview to get an idea of the current layout of the handouts.**

   a. In Word, choose File ⇨ Print Preview or click the Print Preview button on the Standard toolbar.

   b. In Print Preview, press the Page Down key to go to the next page.

   c. Click the Close button when you are done looking.

4. **Add a title in the header and a page numbering code in the footer.**

   a. Still in Word, choose View ⇨ Header and Footer.

   b. In the Header box that appears, press Tab once.

   c. Type **Spice Meadow Shelties**.

   d. Select the text you just typed and make it 20 point, bold, and in Arial font.

   e. Click the Switch Between Header and Footer button on the Header and Footer toolbar.

   f. In the Footer box, press Tab twice to move the insertion point to the right-aligned tab stop at the footer's right margin.

   g. Click the Page Number button on the Header and Footer toolbar to insert a page numbering code.

   h. Click the Close button on the Header and Footer toolbar.

3C

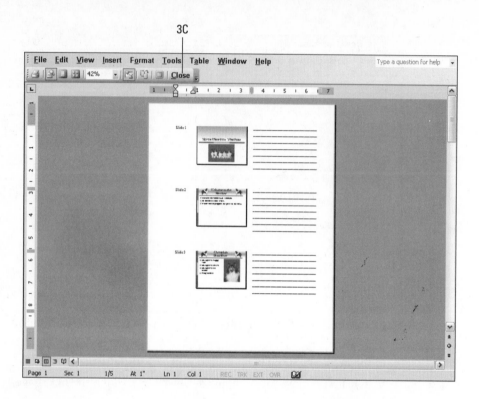

4D   4C   4E

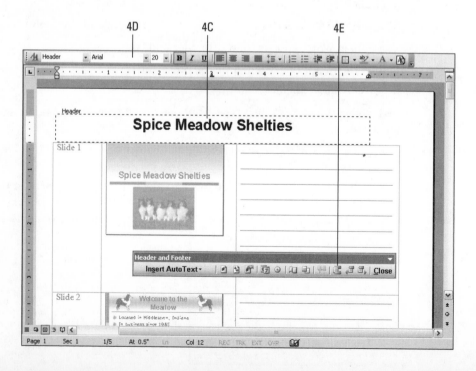

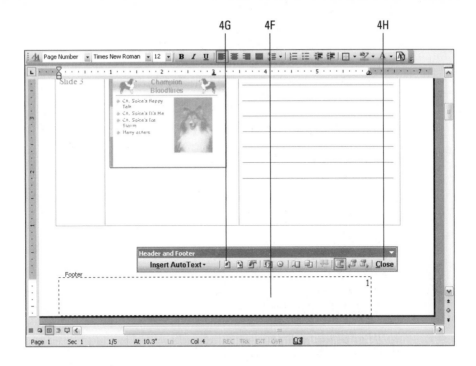

5. Set the vertical alignment for the document to Center and change the document margins to 0.8" on the right and left.

   a. Again in Word, choose File ⇨ Page Setup.

   b. On the Margins tab, enter **0.8** in the Left and Right boxes.

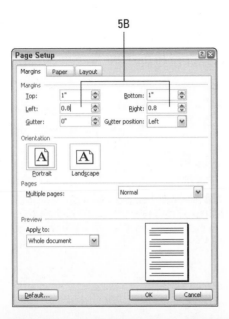

c. Click the Layout tab.

d. Open the Vertical Alignment drop-down list and choose Center.

e. Click OK.

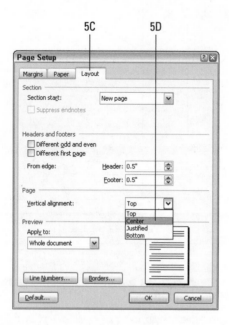

6. Create an extra, blank row in the table at the end of the document.

This is necessary because after setting the vertical alignment to Center, the last page will have the two final slides centered on that page unless an extra placeholder row is inserted.

a. Click in the last cell of the last row in the table.

b. Press Tab to start a new row.

7. Delete the left-most column of the table entirely.

a. Position the mouse pointer over the top of the left column. The mouse pointer turns into a down-pointing black arrow.

b. Click to select the entire column.

c. Choose Edit ➪ Cut or press Ctrl+X.

Note   Why use Cut rather than Delete in Step 7? Delete would remove the text only, leaving the column. You can also use Table ➪ Delete ➪ Columns, but that takes longer.

7A

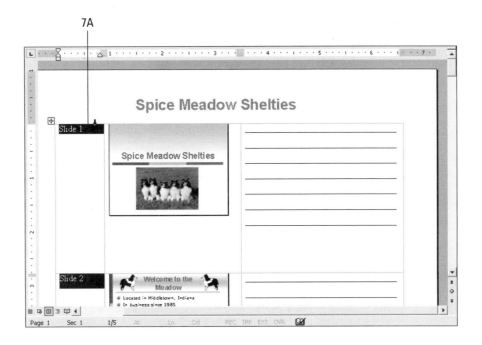

8. **Switch to Print Layout view, and change the zoom so that you can see the entire page width.**

   a. Choose View ⇨ Print Layout or click the Print Layout View button in the bottom-left corner of the screen.

   b. Open the Zoom drop-down list on the Standard toolbar and choose Page Width.

9. **Drag the borders of the table to enlarge it horizontally.**

   a. With nothing selected in the table, position the mouse pointer over the left border of the table. The pointer turns into a double-headed arrow.

   b. Drag it 1/2" to the left. Use the ruler to gauge the distance.

   c. Drag the right border of the table to the 7" mark on the ruler.

   d. Drag the center border to the 4" mark on the ruler.

8B

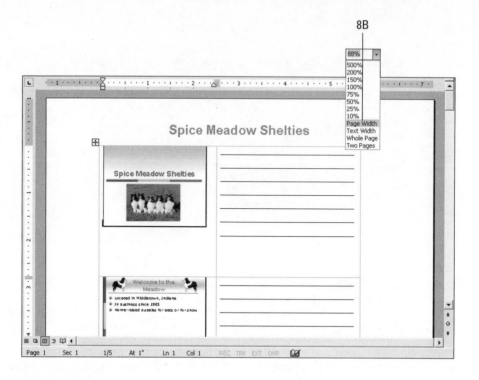

9B   9A

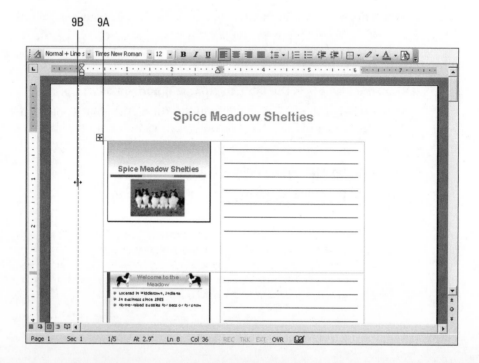

9D   9C

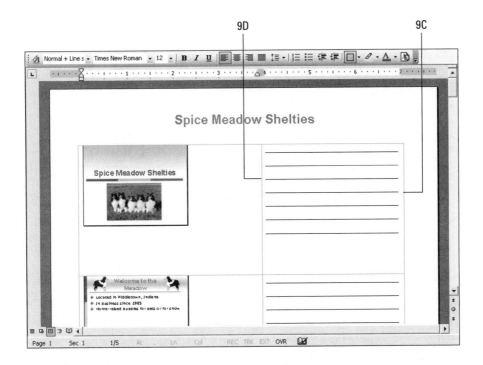

10. Enlarge the first picture to 2.65" in height and 3.52" in width.

   a. Click the first picture to select it.

   b. Choose Format ⇨ Object.

   c. Click the Size tab.

   d. Make sure the Lock Aspect Ratio option is selected. In the Height box, enter **2.65"**. Then press Tab, and the value in the Width box changes automatically.

   e. Click OK.

11. Resize all the other pictures to the same size.

You can use the method from Step 10, or you can drag a picture's corner selection handle to enlarge it.

Expert Tip

Unfortunately you cannot select multiple pictures at once by holding down Ctrl, nor can you use Format Painter to copy the size. But you can use F4 to repeat the action you just did in Step 10. Simply select the next slide image and press the F4 button above the number row on your keyboard. (Changing the view to two pages will help you accomplish this more quickly.)

10 D

10 C

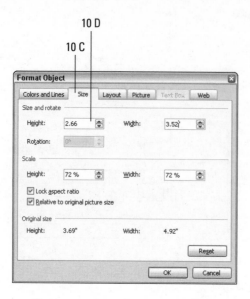

12. Add two extra lines for writing next to each slide.

a. Select one of the existing lines for writing, and press Ctrl+C to copy it.

b. Click at the top of a cell containing lines, moving the insertion point there.

c. Press Ctrl+V twice, pasting two copies of the line.

d. Repeat Steps b and c for each cell that contains writing lines. Or, copy-and-paste the entire cell that you modified in steps a through c.

13. View your work in Print Preview.

a. Choose File ⇨ Print Preview or click the Print Preview button on the Standard toolbar.

b. Scroll through the file using the Page Up and Page Down keys.

c. Click Close to leave Print Preview.

14. Save your work as MyLab05A.doc in the folder where you are storing your lab files, and close the file.

12 B   12 A

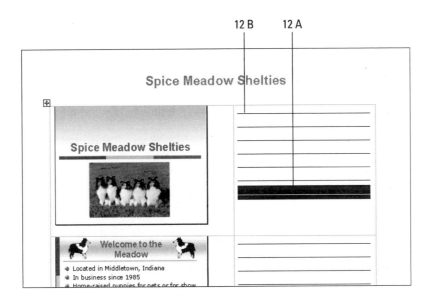

13 C

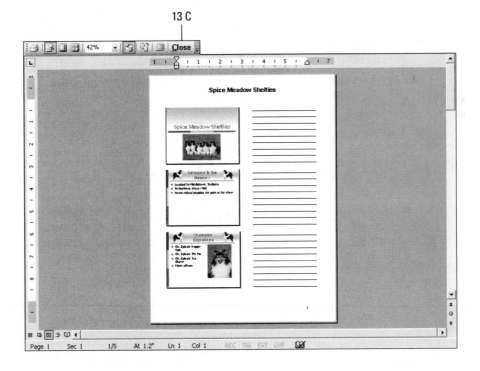

Project 5B: Hidden Slides and Custom Shows

In this project you will set up some slides to be hidden, and save that version as a separate file. Then you will create another version of the presentation that contains two custom shows.

Level of difficulty: Easy

Time to complete: 5 to 10 minutes

1. **Open the file Lab05B.ppt from the Labs folder (from the CD accompanying the book).**

2. **Hide slides 4, 6, 9, and 11.**

   a. Choose View ⇨ Slide Sorter or click the Slide Sorter View button in the bottom-left corner of the screen.

   b. Click slide 4; then hold down Ctrl and click slides 6, 9, and 11.

   c. Click the Hide Slide button on the toolbar.

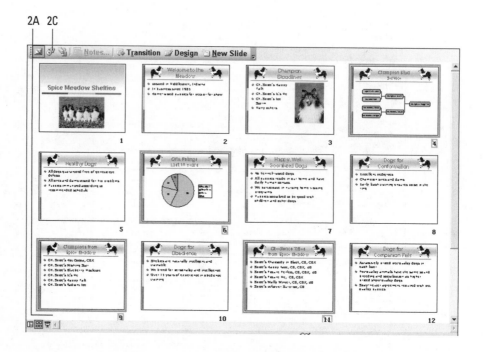

3. **Save this version of the presentation as MyLab0BC-1.ppt.**

4. **Close the presentation file, and reopen Lab05B.ppt.**

5. Create a custom show that contains only slides 1-9 and 14.

    a. Choose Slide Show ➪ Custom Shows.

5A

    b. In the Custom Shows dialog box, click New.

    c. In the Define Custom Show dialog box, type **Conformation** in the Slide Show Name box.

    d. In the Slides In Presentation list, select slides 1-9 (hold down Shift while you click 1, then 9) and then click the Add >> button.

    e. Select slide 14 and click the Add >> button.

    f. Click OK.

5B   5C 5D

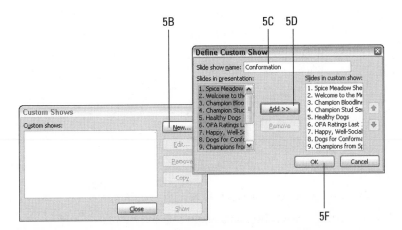

5F

6. Create another custom show that contains slides 1-3, 5-7, and 12-14.

    a. In the Custom Shows dialog box (which should still be open), click New.

    b. Type **Pets** in the Slide Show Name box.

    c. Select slides 1-3 and then click the Add >> button.

    d. Add slides 5-7 and 12-14 to the custom show the same way.

    e. Click OK.

7. Make a copy of the Pets custom show called Obedience, and add slides 10 and 11 to it.

    a. In the Custom Shows dialog box (which should still be open), click the Pets show.

    b. Click Copy. A new show called Copy of Pets appears.

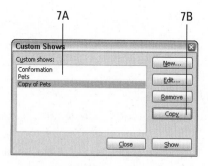

    c. Click Copy of Pets and then click Edit. The Define Custom Show dialog box opens.

    d. Change the show name to Obedience by typing it in the Slide Show Name box.

    e. Click slides 10 and 11 in the original presentation and then click the Add>> button.

    f. On the Slides In Custom Show list, select slide 10 (the first of the newly added slides) and then click the Up arrow button to move it up to position 7.

    g. On the Slides In Custom Show list, select slide 11 (the second of the newly added slides) and then click the Up arrow button to move it up to position 8.

    h. Click OK.

7D

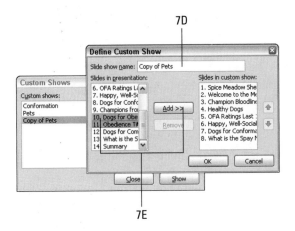

7E

7F

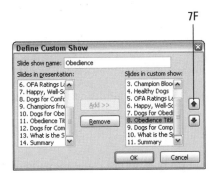

8. Run the Obedience custom show.

a. In the Custom Shows dialog box (which should still be open), click the Obedience show.

b. Click the Show button. The show begins.

c. Move through the slides by clicking. When you are finished, you return to PowerPoint.

9. Set the Obedience show to be the default show for this presentation file.

a. Choose Slide Show ⇨ Set Up Show.

b. In the Show Slides section, choose Custom Show and then select Obedience from the drop-down list.

c. Click OK.

8A

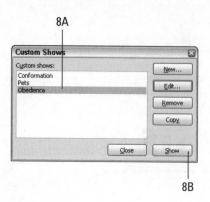

8B

9B

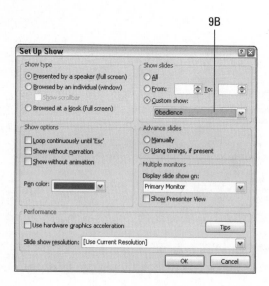

Congratulations, you have completed the project labs for this section! Now you have several presentation options for your client, including some attractive handouts and several custom shows.

In the next chapter, I'll shift gears and start talking about another kind of show — one that has no live speaker. Such shows might be distributed on CD, via the Internet, or at a kiosk.

✦   ✦   ✦

Distributing Self-Serve Presentations

Designing Self-Running Kiosk Presentations

In the last few chapters, you've been learning how to build and present slide shows that support you as you speak to your audience directly. As discussed in Chapter 5, when you build such presentations, you design each slide to *assist* you, not duplicate your efforts. Slides designed for a live presentation typically do not contain a lot of detail; they function as pointers and reminders for the much more detailed live discussion or lecture taking place in the foreground.

When you build a self-running presentation, the focus is exactly the opposite. The slides are going out there all alone and must be capable of projecting the entire message all by themselves. Therefore, you want to create slides that contain much more information.

Another consideration is audience interest. When you are speaking to your audience live, the primary focus is on you and your words. The slides assist you, but the audience watches and listens primarily to you. Therefore, to keep the audience interested, you have to be interesting. If the slides are interesting, that's a nice bonus. With a self-running presentation, on the other hand, each slide must be fascinating. The animations and transitions that you learned about in Chapter 22 come in very handy in creating interest, as do sounds and videos, discussed in Chapters 20 and 21.

In this book, I'm distinguishing between self-running and user-interactive presentations. Both of these show types involve the audience's interaction with a speakerless show; the difference is in the audience's behavior and capability. In a self-running show, the audience is passive; they watch, listen, and wait for the next slide to appear. That's the type of show discussed in this chapter. With a user-interactive show, the audience can control the show's pace and direction through keyboard, mouse, or touch-screen input. You learn about user-interactive shows in Chapter 29.

Note   Another name for a self-running presentation is a *kiosk* presentation. This name comes from the fact that many self-running informational presentations are located in little buildings, or kiosks, in public areas such as malls and convention centers.

Ideas for Using Self-Running Shows

Not sure when you might use a self-running presentation in your daily life? Here are some thought-starters:

✦ **Trade shows:** A self-running presentation outlining your product or service can run continuously in your booth on equipment as simple as a laptop PC and an external monitor. People who might not feel comfortable talking to a salesperson may stop a few moments to watch a colorful, multimedia slide show.

✦ **Conventions:** Trying to inform hundreds of convention-goers of some basic information, like session starting times or cocktail party locations? Set up an information booth in the convention center lobby providing this information. The slide show can loop endlessly through three or four slides that contain meeting room locations, schedules, and other critical data.

✦ **In-store sales:** Retail stores can increase sales by strategically placing PC monitors in areas of the store where customers gather. For example, if there is a line where customers stand waiting for the next available register or clerk, you can show those waiting customers a few slides that describe the benefits of extended warranties or that detail the special sales of the week.

✦ **Waiting areas:** Auto repair shops and other places where customers wait for something to be done provide excellent sales opportunities. The customers don't have anything to do except sit and wait, so they will watch just about anything—including a slide presentation informing them of the other services that your shop provides.

Setting Up a Self-Running Show

The most important aspect of a self-running show is that it loops continuously until you stop it. This is important because there won't be anyone there to restart it each time it ends.

To set up the show to do just that, follow these steps:

1. Choose Slide Show ⇨ Set Up Show. The Set Up Show dialog box opens.

2. Click the Browsed at a Kiosk (Full Screen) option. See Figure 28-1.

3. In the Advance Slides area, make sure the Using Timings, if Present option is selected.

4. Click OK.

Figure 28-1: Tell PowerPoint that this show will be browsed at a kiosk (in other words, self-running).

You haven't set up the timings referenced in Step 3 yet, but don't worry about that; you learn how to set them up in the following section.

Setting Timings

The duration that each slide appears on the screen is very important in a self-running presentation. If the slide disappears too quickly, the audience cannot read all that it contains; if the slide lingers too long, the audience gets bored and walks away.

Expert Tip If you are going to record narration for the slides, skip to the "Recording Narration" section later in this chapter. You can set your timings and your narration at the same time, saving a step.

Setting a single timing for all slides

You might choose to let each slide linger the same amount of time on-screen. This gives a consistent feel to the show and works well when all the slides contain approximately the same amount of information. To set this up, use the Slide Transition feature, as shown in the following steps:

1. Choose Slide Show ➪ Slide Transition. The Slide Transition task pane opens.

2. In the Advance Slide area, mark the Automatically After check box. See Figure 28-2.

Set timing here

Figure 28-2: To set an automatic transition after a certain number of seconds, enter the number of seconds and then click Apply to All Slides.

3. Enter a number of seconds into the text box. For example, to advance each slide after 10 seconds, enter **00:10**. You can use the spin buttons next to the text box to increment the value up or down if you prefer.

4. Click Apply to All Slides to apply the setting to all the slides in the presentation.

As you may have surmised, you can also set the timings for each slide individually through the Slide Transition task pane, by selecting each slide and then entering a timing for it. (You can also apply a transition timing to a group of slides by selecting them in the thumbnail task pane before you set the time as described in Steps 1-3. Or you can do this in Slide Sorter view.) However, if you want to set different timings for different slides, the Rehearse Timings command provides an alternative way to do that. It's described in the following section. Then, afterwards, if you need to adjust the timing of a few slides, you can revisit the Slide Transition task pane for those slides to do so.

Setting custom timings for each slide

If not all slides should receive an equal amount of screen time, you can set up timings individually for each slide. This helps if some slides contain a lot more text to read or numeric information to digest than others. To set custom timings, you use the Rehearse Timings feature. This feature allows you to practice the show with a timer running that records the amount of time you spend on each slide. It then assigns the timings to the slides so you can run the show using the same timings automatically.

Caution   When you set timings with Rehearse Timings, any hidden slide is ignored. If you later unhide that slide, it will not be set to advance automatically. You need to assign it a duration using the Slide Transition task pane, as explained in the preceding section.

Follow these steps to rehearse timings:

1. Choose Slide Show ➪ Rehearse Timings. The slide show begins, with the Rehearsal box floating on it. See Figure 28-3.

Expert Tip   The Rehearsal box can be dragged around on-screen, and can also be docked at any edge of the screen by dragging it there, just like a regular toolbar.

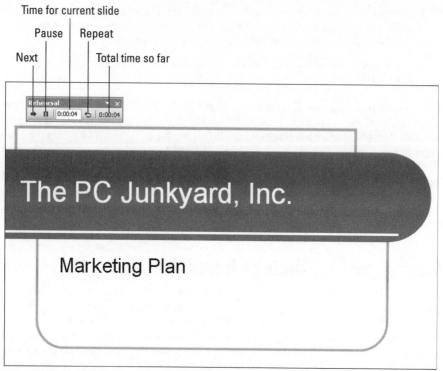

Figure 28-3: The Rehearsal box helps you set timings for moving from slide to slide.

2. Wait until you think it is time for the next slide to appear. Then click the Next button or press Page Down.

   It may help when setting timings to read the text on the slide out loud, rather slowly, to simulate how an audience member who reads slowly would proceed. When you have read all the text on the slide, pause 1 or 2 more seconds and then advance.

   If you need to pause the rehearsal at any time, click the Pause button. When you are ready to resume, click it again.

   If you make a mistake on the timing for a slide, click the Repeat button to begin timing that slide again from 00:00.

3. When you reach the last slide, a dialog box appears telling you the total time for the show. See Figure 28-4. If you want to preserve the timings you have set, click Yes. Otherwise, click No and return to Step 1 to try again.

Figure 28-4: Choose Yes to accept your timings or No to reject them.

4. Test your timings by viewing the show (choose Slide Show ➪ View Show). If any of the timings are off, return to Normal view and adjust them with the Slide Transition task pane, as explained earlier in this chapter.

In Slide Sorter view, the timing for each slide appears beneath it, as shown in Figure 28-5.

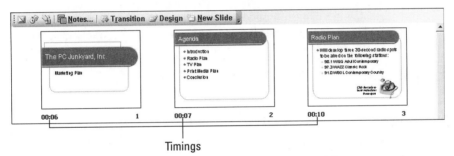

Timings

Figure 28-5: The numbers beneath and to the left of each slide represent the custom timings you set with Rehearse Timings.

Recording Narration

As I mentioned earlier, it's wise to design slides for a self-running presentation to be self-sufficient so that the audience immediately understands them without help. However, sometimes certain slides (or entire shows) can't achieve this for one reason or another. For example, suppose you are creating a self-running show that consists of scanned images of works of art. Almost the entire slide is taken up by each scan, so there is no room for a lengthy text block listing the artist, date, title, and description. In a case like that, recording a voice-over narration might make a lot of sense to relieve the slides from carrying the entire burden of information conveyance.

For a professional-quality show, get the best audio recording equipment you can afford. Get a high-quality microphone (these are relatively inexpensive at your local computer store) and plug it into a high-quality sound card on the recording PC.

Then, set the recording quality to the best quality that you can manage without eating up too much hard disk space. Audio recording uses up an obscene amount of disk space; CD-quality (the highest quality) audio consumes about 10 megabytes per minute of recording. That means for a 20-minute show, you need over 200 megabytes of disk space.

Caution   If you need to transfer the presentation to another PC for the show and you must transfer it using a floppy disk, transfer it first and then record the narration on the show PC (if the show PC has a sound card that you can hook up a microphone to, that is). If you record the narration first, the presentation file will be so large that it won't fit on a floppy disk. You can store the narration separately from the main presentation, as you learn in Step 11 of the following procedure, but even so, the narration file may be too big to fit on a floppy.

If you can't avoid recording the presentation narration before transferring it to the show machine and you don't have any means of transfer besides a floppy disk (such as a network, a Zip drive, or a recordable CD drive), you might try e-mailing the presentation to yourself. Send the e-mail on the machine containing the presentation file, and then receive it using the show machine. (Warning: sending and receiving the e-mail will take a long time, especially with a slow connection.) You could also upload it to a Web site or FTP site if your e-mail account prohibits very large attachments.

Setting narration controls

To set up the narration controls, follow these steps:

1. Make sure your microphone is connected and ready.

2. Choose Slide Show ➪ Record Narration. The Record Narration dialog box appears. See Figure 28-6.

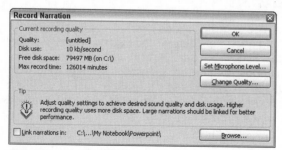

Figure 28-6: Use this dialog box to begin setting up to record narration.

3. Click the Set Microphone Level button. The Microphone Check dialog box appears.

4. Read into the microphone, enabling PowerPoint to set the optimum microphone recording level. See Figure 28-7.

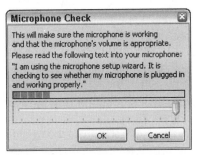

Figure 28-7: Read the text shown on the screen to allow PowerPoint to set the recording level.

Caution

You can also set the recording level by manually dragging the slide bar shown in Figure 28-7, but this is not recommended because you do not know which setting to use without testing the microphone.

5. Click OK to return to the Record Narration dialog box.

6. Click the Change Quality button. The Sound Selection dialog box appears.

7. Open the Name drop-down list and choose a quality. The preset qualities that come with PowerPoint are Telephone Quality (low), Radio Quality (medium), and CD Quality (high). The higher the quality, the more disk space it takes up storing your narration. See Figure 28-8.

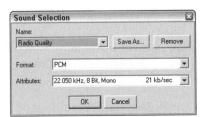

Figure 28-8: Choose a recording quality from the Name box.

If you can afford the disk space, use CD Quality. This results in the best-sounding recording, which is important in most professional situations.

8. If you want the recording in a certain format or with certain attributes, choose them from the Format and/or Attributes drop-down lists. Beginners should leave these settings alone; adjust them only if you know enough about sound recording to know that you need a particular setting.

9. *(Optional)* If you made changes in Step 8, you can save your new quality settings as a new sound quality scheme. To do so, click the Save As button and enter a name for the new setting, as in Figure 28-9. Then click OK to accept the name.

Figure 28-9: You can save your sound quality settings as a reusable scheme if desired.

10. Click OK to close the Sound Selection dialog box.

11. *(Optional)* If you want the narration stored in a separate file linked to the presentation, mark the Link Narrations check box (shown in Figure 28-6). If you don't mark this check box, the narrations are embedded in the presentation file. Linking can be useful if you think you may need to edit a slide's narration later in a sound-editing program.

12. If you marked the check box in Step 11 and you want to change the location of the stored narration file, click the Browse button and choose a different drive or folder. By default, the narration file is stored in the same location as the presentation file.

13. Go on to the steps in the next section.

Recording the narration

Pick up these steps from the preceding ones, or if you are coming here from some other task, choose Slide Show ⇨ Record Narration. Then follow these steps:

1. Click OK to close the Record Narration dialog box. If the first slide of the presentation was not selected initially, the Record Narration dialog box appears. See Figure 28-10.

Figure 28-10: Choose where you want to start recording narration.

2. Click First Slide. The slide show begins.

3. Speak into the microphone, recording narration for the first slide. Then, advance to the next slide with the Page Down key.

4. Continue speaking into the microphone and advancing the slides. When you reach the last slide, the screen goes black and a message appears prompting you to press Esc.

5. Press Esc. A dialog box appears reminding you that the narrations have been saved with each slide, and asking whether you want to save the timings also.

6. Click Yes.

7. Test your show by displaying it in Slide Show view from start to finish and listening to your narration.

Rerecording the narration for a slide

Few people get the narration exactly right for the entire presentation the first time they record it. If you want to rerecord the narration for a particular slide, follow these steps:

1. Select the slide that you want to rerecord the narration for.

2. Choose Slide Show ⇨ Record Narration.

3. Click OK.

4. The Record Narration dialog box appears (Figure 28-10). This time, click Current Slide.

5. When you are finished recording the narration for that slide, press Esc.

6. A dialog box appears asking whether you want to save the timings as well as the narration. Click Yes.

7. Test the new narration by displaying the slide in Slide Show view.

 Expert Tip Keep in mind that good speakers at the show site are as important as a good microphone at the recording site. Make sure you have external speakers that plug into the show PC's sound card. Don't rely on the tinny little speaker built into a laptop PC!

Deleting the narration for a slide

After you add narration to slides, a little speaker icon appears at the bottom of each slide in all views except Slide Show. See Figure 28-11. You can double-click this icon to preview the narration recording at any time. To remove the narration from a slide, delete this icon.

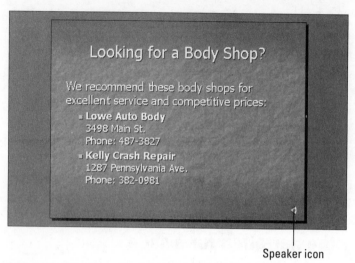

Speaker icon

Figure 28-11: A Speaker icon on each slide holds the narration. Delete it to remove the narration.

Setting Up a Secure System

Security is a definite concern in self-running presentations. Any time you leave a computer unattended with the public, you run the risk of tampering and theft. At the very least, some guru geek will come along and experiment with your PC to see what you've got and whether he or she can do anything clever with it. At the worst, your entire computer setup could disappear entirely.

There are two levels of security involved in unattended presentation situations:

✦ The security of the physical hardware

✦ The security that the presentation will continue to run

Securing your hardware

For the most foolproof hardware security, get it out of sight. Hide everything except the monitor in a locked drawer, cabinet, or panel of the kiosk you are using, if possible. If you are at a trade show or convention where you don't have the luxury of a lockable system, at least put everything except the monitor under a table, and try to make sure that someone is attending the booth at all times.

Caution

Don't drape running computers with cloth or any other material that inhibits the airflow around them; doing so increases the risk of overheating.

In an unattended setting, the best way to protect your monitor from walking off is to place it behind a Plexiglas panel where nobody can touch it. Without such a barrier, you run the risk of some jokester turning off its power or turning down its contrast, and anyone who knows something about computers could walk right up and disconnect it and carry it away.

You can also buy various locking cables at computer stores and office supply centers. These lock down computer equipment to prevent it from being removed. They include steel cables with padlocks, metal locking brackets, and electronically controlled magnetic locks.

Making sure the presentation continues to run

I admit that I am guilty of disrupting other people's presentations. When I walk up to an unattended computer in a store, the first thing I do is abort whatever program is running and restart the system to check out its diagnostics and find out what kind of computer it is. It's a geek thing, but all geeks do it.

You will doubtless encounter such geeks wherever you set up your presentation, but especially at trade shows and conventions. (We geeks love trade shows and conventions.) Your mission must be to prevent them from stopping your presentation.

The best way to prevent someone from tinkering with your presentation is to get the input devices out of sight. Hide the CPU (the main box of the computer), the keyboard, and the mouse. You can't disconnect the keyboard and mouse from the PC, or an error message will appear, but you can hide them. Again, don't cover them with anything that might restrict the airflow, or you might end up with an overheated PC.

You can also set up the following security measures in your presentation file:

✦ Choose Slide Show ⇨ Set Up Show and make sure you have chosen Browsed at a Kiosk. This disables the mouse while the slide show is running. The only way to stop the show will be to use the keyboard. This works best for self-running shows where the slides advance automatically.

Expert Tip

If you make the keyboard available for user navigation, the Esc key will also be available for stopping the program. A utility is available that disables the Esc key at www.mvps.org/skp/noesc.htm.

✦ Show the presentation using the PowerPoint Viewer program rather than PowerPoint itself. That way nobody can access PowerPoint and create a new presentation to show. For further security, remove the PowerPoint application completely from the PC on which the presentation is showing.

✦ Set a startup password for your PC so that if people manage to reboot it, they won't get into your PC to tamper with its settings. This is usually set through the BIOS setup program. If you can't do that, set a Windows startup password (Start ➪ Settings ➪ Control Panel ➪ Passwords).

✦ Assign a password to a PowerPoint file, as you learned in Chapter 3, to prevent it from being opened, modified, or both. Although this will not prevent a running presentation from being stopped, it will at least prevent it from being altered or deleted. However, if it is already open, hackers will have full access to it, and if you set it to have a password only for modifications, a hacker could save it under a different name, make changes, and then run the changed version.

Summary

In this chapter, you learned the ins and outs of preparing a presentation that can run unattended or without user interaction. You can probably think of some uses for such a show, and even more may occur to you later. In the next chapter, I show you how to create user-interactive presentations that allow people to make choices about the presentation content they see.

✦   ✦   ✦

Designing User-Interactive Presentations

In the preceding lesson, you learned how to create a self-running presentation. Self-running presentations do their jobs without any intervention from the audience or from you. If a self-running presentation runs at a trade show and there is no one to hear it, it runs nonetheless.

In contrast, user-interactive shows also lack a human facilitator or speaker, but they rely on an audience's attention. The audience presses buttons, clicks a mouse, or clicks graphics or hyperlinks on-screen to advance the show from one slide to the next, and they might even be able to control which content is displayed. (See the "Interactive Presentation Ideas" section at the end of this chapter for some usage ideas.)

What Is a Hyperlink?

The navigational controls you place in your presentation take various forms, but are all hyperlinks. A *hyperlink* object is a bit of text or a graphic that you (or your audience) can click to jump somewhere else. When you click a hyperlink, you might jump to a different slide in the same presentation, to a different presentation, to another program on your computer, or even to an Internet Web page.

Note   Most people associate the word *hyperlink* with the Internet because of their familiarity with the Web and with hyperlinks on Web pages. However, a hyperlink is simply a link to somewhere else; it does not necessarily refer to an Internet location. Chapter 30 discusses presentation issues specific to Internet delivery.

The most common type of hyperlink is underlined text. Hyperlink text is typically underlined and a different color than the rest of the text on-screen. In addition, followed links may be a different color from ones that you have not yet checked out, depending on the program.

Expert Tip   If you want a hyperlink that never changes its color, place a transparent object over it, such as a rectangle, and apply the hyperlink to that object rather than the text. The user will think he is clicking the text, but he will actually be clicking the rectangle. You can also assign a hyperlink to a whole text box (manual text boxes only, not placeholder text boxes) as opposed to the text within it.

You are not limited to underlined bits of text for your hyperlinks. You can also use graphics or any other objects on your slides as hyperlinks. PowerPoint provides some special-purpose graphics called *action buttons* that serve very well with hyperlinks. For example, you can assign a hyperlink to the next slide to the action button that looks like a right arrow, as you see in Figure 29-1 in the following section.

Navigational Control Choices

Figure 29-1 shows a slide with several types of navigational controls, any of which you can use in your own slides.

✦ **Action buttons:** These graphics come with PowerPoint. You can set them up so that clicking them moves to a different slide in the presentation. The ones in Figure 29-1 move forward (to the next slide) and back (to the previous slide).

✦ **Hyperlink with helper text:** The text "Click here to learn more" in Figure 29-1, for example, provides built-in instructions for less technically sophisticated users. The hyperlink could refer to a Web site, as in Figure 29-1, to a hidden slide in the same presentation, or to any other location.

✦ **Hyperlink without helper text:** The text "Customer Satisfaction Surveys" in Figure 29-1 is a hyperlink, but the audience must know enough about computers to know that clicking those underlined words jumps to the slide containing more information.

✦ **ScreenTip:** Pointing at a hyperlink displays a pop-up note listing the address to which the hyperlink refers. Viewers can jot it down for later exploration if they don't want to visit the page right now.

✦ **Bare Internet hyperlink:** The Internet address in Figure 29-1, `http://www.superiorquality.org`, is also a hyperlink — in this case, to a Web page on the Internet. This kind of hyperlink can be intimidating for beginners who don't recognize Internet syntax, but it is very good for the advanced audience member because it lists the address up front. No clicking or pointing is required to determine the address.

✦ **Instructions:** If you do not build specific navigation controls into the presentation, you may want to add instructions on the slide that tell the reader how to move forward and backward in the presentation. The instruction box at the bottom of Figure 29-1 does just that.

Figure 29-1: Use one or more of the navigational aids shown here.

Choosing Appropriate Controls for Your Audience

Before you dive into building an interactive presentation, you must decide how the audience will navigate from slide to slide. There is no one best way; the right decision depends on your audience's comfort level with computers and with hyperlinks. Consider these points:

✦ Is the audience technically savvy enough to know that they should press a key or click the mouse to advance the slide, or do you need to provide that instruction?

✦ Does your audience understand that the arrow action buttons mean forward and back, or do you need to explain that?

✦ Does your audience understand hyperlinks and Web addresses? If they see underlined text, do they know that they can click it to jump elsewhere?

✦ Is it enough to include some instructions on a slide at the beginning of the show, or do you need to repeat the instructions on every slide?

Think about your intended audience and their needs and come up with a plan. Here are some sample plans:

✦ **For a beginner-level audience:** Begin the presentation with an instructional slide explaining how to navigate. Place action buttons on the same place on each slide (using the Slide Master) to help them move forward and backward, and include a Help action button that they can click to jump to more detailed navigation instructions.

✦ **For an intermediate-level audience:** Place action buttons on the same place on each slide, along with a brief note on the first slide (such as the instruction in Figure 29-1) explaining how to use them.

✦ **For an advanced audience:** Include other action buttons on the slide that allow the users to jump around freely in the presentation — go to the beginning, to the end, to the beginning of certain sections, and so on. Advanced users understand and can take advantage of a more sophisticated system of action buttons.

Understanding Kiosk Mode

Kiosk mode places the keyboard and mouse in limited functionality mode during the presentation, to give you more control over the audience's experience.

Specifically, here's what happens when you use Kiosk mode:

✦ The keyboard does not work, except for the Esc key (which exits the presentation).

✦ The mouse can be used to click on action buttons and hyperlinks, but clicking in general does not do anything.

✦ The control buttons do not appear in the bottom left corner of the display, and you cannot right-click to open their menu. Right-clicking does nothing.

To turn on Kiosk mode, do the following:

1. Choose Slide Show ⇨ Set Up Show. The Set Up Show dialog box opens.

2. Click Browsed at a Kiosk (Full Screen).

3. Click OK.

Caution   If you turn on Kiosk mode, you **must** use action buttons or hyperlinks in your presentation. Otherwise users will not be able to move from slide to slide.

Using Action Buttons

Action buttons, which you saw in Figure 29-1, are the simplest kind of user-interactivity controls. They enable your audience members to move from slide to slide in the presentation with a minimum of fuss. PowerPoint provides many preset action buttons that already have hyperlinks assigned to them, so all you have to do is place them on your slides.

The action buttons that come with PowerPoint are shown in Table 29-1, along with their preset hyperlinks. As you can see, some of them are all ready to go; others require you to specify to where they jump. Most of the buttons have a default action assigned to them, but you can change any of these as needed.

Expert Tip   At first glance, there seems little reason to use action buttons that simply move the slide show forward and backward. After all, isn't it just as easy to use the keyboard's Page Up and Page Down keys, or to click the left mouse button to advance to the next slide? Well, yes, but if you use Kiosk mode, described in the preceding section, you cannot move from slide to slide using any of the conventional keyboard or mouse methods. The only thing the mouse can do is click on action buttons and hyperlinks.

Table 29-1
Action Buttons

Button	Name	Hyperlinks To
□	None	Nothing, by default. You can add text or fills to the button to create custom buttons.
🏠	Home	First slide in the presentation. (Home is where you started, and it's a picture of a house, get it?)
?	Help	Nothing, by default, but you can point it toward a slide containing help.
ⓘ	Information	Nothing, by default, but you can point it to a slide containing information.
◁	Back or Previous	Previous slide in the presentation (not necessarily the last slide viewed; compare to Return).
▷	Forward or Next	Next slide in the presentation.
|◁	Beginning	First slide in the presentation.
▷|	End	Last slide in the presentation.
↵	Return	Last slide viewed, regardless of normal order. This is useful to place on a hidden slide that the audience will jump to with another link (such as Help), to help them return to the main presentation when they are finished.
▯	Document	Nothing, by default, but you can set it to run a program that you specify.
🔊	Sound	Plays a sound that you specify. If you don't choose a sound, it plays the first sound on PowerPoint's list of standard sounds (Applause).
🎞	Movie	Nothing, by default, but you can set it to play a movie that you specify.

Setting up action buttons

To place an action button, follow these steps:

1. If you want to place the button on the Slide Master, display it (View ⇨ Master ⇨ Slide Master).

Some action buttons are best placed on the Slide Master, such as Next and Previous; others, such as Return, are special-use buttons that are best placed on individual slides.

2. Choose Slide Show ➪ Action Buttons. A palette of buttons appears, corresponding to the buttons you saw in Table 29-1. See Figure 29-2.

Drag here to create a floating toolbar

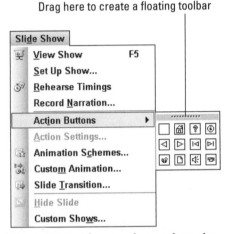

Figure 29-2: Choose a button from the Slide Show menu.

3. Click the button that you want to place. Your mouse pointer turns into a crosshair.

You can drag the Action Buttons palette off the Slide Show menu, making it into a floating toolbar.

4. To create a button of a specific size, drag on the slide (or Slide Master) where you want it to go. Or, to create a button of a default size, simply click once where you want it. You can resize the button at any time later, the same as you can any object.

If you are going to place several buttons, and you want them all to be the same size, place them at the default size to begin with. Then select them all, and resize them as a group. That way they will all be exactly the same size.

5. The Action Settings dialog box appears. Make sure the Mouse Click tab is on top. See Figure 29-3.

Figure 29-3: Specify what should happen when you click the action button.

6. Confirm or change the hyperlink set up there:

   - *If the action button should take the reader to a specific location,* make sure the correct slide appears in the Hyperlink To box. Refer to the right column in Table 29-1 to see the default setting for each action button. Table 29-2 lists the choices you can make and what they do.

   - *If the action button should run a program,* choose Run program and enter the program's name and path, or click Browse to locate it. For example, you could open a Web browser window from an action button. The executable file that runs Internet Explorer is iexplore.exe.

   - *If the action button should play a sound,* click None in the Action on Click section, make sure the Play Sound check box is marked, and choose the correct sound from the Play Sound drop-down list (or pick a different sound file by choosing Other Sound).

Expert Tip   You can also run macros with action buttons. This is not all that common, however, because most of the macros you record in PowerPoint apply to *building* a presentation, not showing one. For example, you might create a macro that formats text a certain way. You would almost never need to format text while a presentation was being shown to an audience. You'll learn about macros in Chapter 36.

7. Click OK. The button has been assigned the action you specified.

8. Add more action buttons as desired by repeating these steps.

9. If you are working in Slide Master view, exit it by clicking the Close button.

10. Test your action buttons in Slide Show view to make sure they jump where you want them to.

To edit a button's action, right-click it and choose Action Settings to reopen this dialog box at any time.

Table 29-2 Hyperlink to Choices in the Action Settings Dialog Box	
Drop-Down Menu Choice	**Result**
Previous Slide Next Slide First Slide Last Slide Last Slide Viewed	These choices all do just what their names say. These are the default actions assigned to certain buttons you learned about in Table 29-1.
End Show	Sets the button to stop the show when clicked.
Custom Show . . .	Opens a Link to Custom Show dialog box, where you can choose a custom show to jump to when the button is clicked.
Slide . . .	Opens a Hyperlink to Slide dialog box, where you can choose any slide in the current presentation to jump to when the button is clicked.
URL . . .	Opens a Hyperlink to URL dialog box, where you can enter a Web address to jump to when the button is clicked.
Other PowerPoint Presentation . . .	Opens a Hyperlink to Other PowerPoint Presentation dialog box, where you can choose another PowerPoint presentation to display when the button is clicked.
Other File . . .	Opens a Hyperlink to Other File dialog box, where you can choose any file to open when the button is clicked. If the file requires a certain application, that application will open when needed. (To run another application without opening a specific file in it, use the Run Program option in the Action Settings dialog box instead of Hyperlink To.)

Adding text to an action button

The blank action button you saw in Table 29-1 can be very useful. You can place several of them on a slide and then type text into them, creating your own set of buttons.

To type text into a blank button, follow these steps:

1. Place a blank action button on the slide.

2. Right-click the action button and choose Add Text. An insertion point appears in it. (You can also select the button and simply start typing.)

3. Type your text. Format it as desired using the normal text formatting commands and buttons.

4. When you are finished, click outside of the button to stop.

5. Resize the button, if needed, to contain the text more neatly. You can drag a button's side selection handles to make it wider.

6. If you need to edit the text later, simply click the text to move the insertion point back into it, just as you do with any text box.

Figure 29-4 shows some examples of custom buttons you can create with your own text.

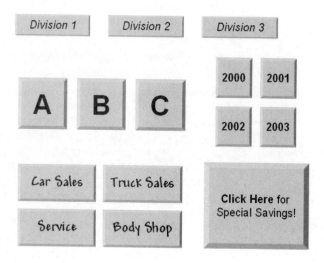

Figure 29-4: You can create any of these sets of action buttons by typing and formatting text on blank buttons.

Creating your own action buttons

You can create an action button out of any object on your slide: a drawn shape, a piece of clip art, a photograph, a text box — anything. To do so, just right-click the object and choose Action Settings. Then, set it to Hyperlink To, Run Program, or Play Sound, just as you did for the action buttons in the preceding sections.

Make sure you clearly label the object that you are using as an action button so that the users will know what they are getting when they click it. You can add text to the object directly (for example, with an AutoShape), or you can add a text box next to the button that explains its function.

Adding Text-Based Hyperlinks to Slides

Now that you know that hyperlinks are the key to user interactivity, you will want to add some to your presentation. You can start with text-based hyperlinks since they're the easiest. You can either add them bare or with explanatory text.

Typing a bare hyperlink

The most basic kind of hyperlink is an Internet address, typed directly into a text box. When you enter text in any of the following formats, PowerPoint automatically converts it to a hyperlink:

✦ **Web addresses:** Anything that begins with `http://`.

✦ **E-mail addresses:** Any string of characters with no spaces and an @ sign in the middle somewhere.

✦ **FTP addresses:** Anything that begins with `ftp://`.

Figure 29-5 shows some examples of these "bare" hyperlinks. I call them bare because you see what's underneath them — the actual address — right there on the surface. There is no friendly "click here" text that the link hides behind. For example, the text support@microsoft.com is a hyperlink that sends e-mail to that address. In contrast, a link that reads "Click here to send e-mail to me" and contains the same hyperlink address is *not* bare, because you do not see the address directly.

Note   If PowerPoint does not automatically create hyperlinks, the feature may be disabled. Choose Tools ➪ AutoCorrect Options. Click the AutoFormat As You Type tab, and make sure the Internet and network paths with hyperlinks checkbox is marked.

You do not have to do anything special to create these hyperlinks; when you type them and press Enter or the space bar, PowerPoint converts them to hyperlinks. You know the conversion has taken place because the text becomes underlined and different-colored. (The exact color depends on the color scheme in use.)

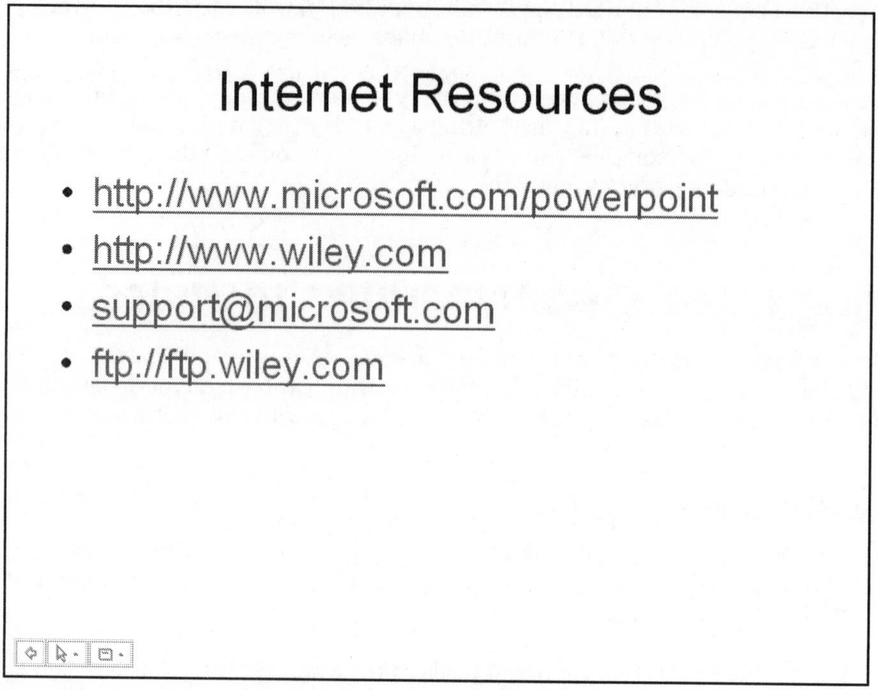

Internet Resources

- http://www.microsoft.com/powerpoint
- http://www.wiley.com
- support@microsoft.com
- ftp://ftp.wiley.com

Figure 29-5: Some examples of bare Internet hyperlinks.

Note   FTP stands for File Transfer Protocol. It's a method of transferring files via the Internet. Up until a few years ago, FTP was a totally separate system from the Web, but nowadays, most Web browsers have FTP download capabilities built in, so anyone who has a Web browser can receive files via FTP. However, to *send* files via FTP, the user must have a separate FTP program.

Creating text hyperlinks

A text hyperlink is a hyperlink comprised of text, but not just the bare address. For example, in Figure 29-1, "Click here to learn more" is a text hyperlink. So is "Customer Satisfaction Surveys."

You can select already-entered text and make it a hyperlink, or you can enter new text. Either way, follow these steps:

Note   These steps take you through the process generically; see the sections in "Choosing the Hyperlink Address" later in the chapter for specific information about various kinds of hyperlinks you can create.

1. To use existing text, select the text or its text box. Otherwise, just position the insertion point where you want the hyperlink.

2. Choose Insert ➪ Hyperlink or press Ctrl+K. The Insert Hyperlink dialog box opens. See Figure 29-6.

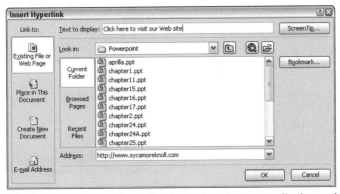

Figure 29-6: Insert a hyperlink by typing the text to display and choosing the address of the slide or other location to jump to.

3. In the Text to Display field, type or edit the hyperlink text. This text is what will appear underlined on the slide. Any text you've selected will appear in this field by default; changing the text here changes it on your slide as well.

4. Enter the hyperlink or select it from one of the available lists. (See the following section, "Choosing the Hyperlink Address," to learn about your options in this regard.)

5. *(Optional)* The default ScreenTip for a hyperlink is its address (URL). If you want the ScreenTip to show something different when the user points the mouse at the hyperlink, click the ScreenTip button and enter the text for the ScreenTip. See Figure 29-7.

Figure 29-7: Enter a custom ScreenTip if desired.

Internet Explorer supports ScreenTips (in version 4.0 and higher), but other browsers may not. This is not an issue if you plan to distribute the presentation in PowerPoint format, but if you plan to convert it to Web pages (see Chapter 30), it might make a difference.

6. Click OK to close the Set Hyperlink ScreenTip dialog box.

7. Click OK to accept the newly created hyperlink.

Choosing the hyperlink address

You can use the Insert Hyperlink dialog box to create a hyperlink to any address that's accessible via the computer where the presentation will run. Although many people think of a hyperlink as an Internet address, it can actually be a link to any file, application, Internet location, or slide.

A hyperlink will not work if the person viewing the presentation does not have access to the needed files and programs or does not have the needed Internet or network connectivity. A hyperlink that works fine on your own PC might not work after the presentation has been transferred to the user's PC.

Possible addresses to hyperlink to include the following:

✦ Other slides in the current presentation

✦ Slides in other presentations (if you provide access to those presentations)

✦ Documents created in other applications (if the user has those applications installed and those document files are available)

✦ Graphic files (if the user has access to an application that can display them)

✦ Internet Web pages (if the user has an Internet connection and a Web browser)

✦ E-mail addresses (if the user has an Internet connection and an e-mail program)

✦ FTP site addresses (if the user has an Internet connection and a Web browser or an FTP program)

Creating a link to a slide in this presentation

The most common kind of link is to another slide in the same presentation. There are lots of uses for this link type; you might, for example, hide several backup slides that contain extra information. You can then create hyperlinks on certain key slides that allow the users to jump to one of those hidden slides to peruse the extra facts.

To create a link to another slide, follow these steps:

1. To use existing text, select the text or its text box. Otherwise, just position the insertion point where you want the hyperlink.

2. Choose Insert ➪ Hyperlink or press Ctrl+K. The Insert Hyperlink dialog box opens.

3. In the Text to Display field, type or edit the hyperlink text. This text is what will appear underlined on the slide. Any text you've selected will appear in this field by default; changing text here changes it on your slide as well.

4. Click the Place in This Document button. The dialog box controls change to show a list of the slides in the presentation. See Figure 29-8.

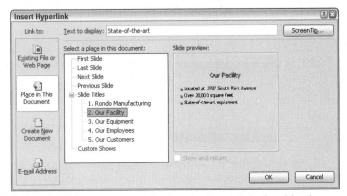

Figure 29-8: Select the slide that the hyperlink should refer to.

5. Select the slide you want.

6. *(Optional)* If you want the presentation to continue from the original spot after showing this slide, mark the Show and Return check box. If you prefer that the presentation continue from the new location forward, leave it unmarked.

7. Click OK.

Creating a link to an existing file

You can also create a hyperlink to any file available on your PC's hard disk or on your local area network. This can be a PowerPoint file or a data file for any other program, such as a Word document or an Excel spreadsheet. Or, if you don't want to open a particular data file, you can hyperlink to the program file itself, so that the other application simply opens.

For example, perhaps you have some detailed documentation for your product in Adobe Acrobat format (PDF). This type of document requires the Adobe Acrobat

Reader. So you could create a hyperlink with the text "Click here to read the documentation" and link to the appropriate PDF file. When your audience member clicks that link, Adobe Acrobat Reader opens and the documentation displays.

To link to a file, follow these steps:

1. To use existing text, select the text or its text box. Otherwise, just position the insertion point where you want the hyperlink.

2. Choose Insert ⇨ Hyperlink or press Ctrl+K. The Insert Hyperlink dialog box opens.

3. In the Text to Display field, type or edit the hyperlink text. This text is what will appear underlined on the slide.

4. In the Insert Hyperlink dialog box, click the Existing File or Web Page button.

5. Do one of the following:

   Click Current Folder to display a file management interface from which you can select any folder or drive on your system. Then navigate to the location containing the file and select the file. See Figure 29-9.

   OR

   Click Recent Files to display a list of the files you have recently opened on this PC (all types). Then click the file you want from the list.

Note   You are not limited to only the folder on your local drives if you choose Current Folder; you can open the Look In list and choose My Network Places to browse the network. However, make sure that the PC on which the presentation will be displayed will also have access to this same location.

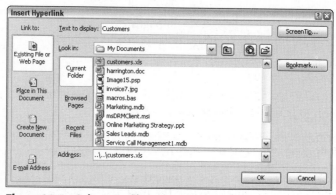

Figure 29-9: Select any file to hyperlink to.

6. Click OK to return to the Insert Hyperlink dialog box.

7. Click OK to insert the hyperlink.

Using a hyperlink to an executable file can result in a warning message each time it is clicked if the file being linked to is executable or is a data file containing macros. To avoid this, first ensure that macro security is set to Low (Tools⇨ Macro⇨Security). Then, instead of using a hyperlink, use an Action Setting and choose Run Program as the action. For the program to run, use the full path to the application, in quotation marks, followed by a space and then the full path to the document, also in quotation marks. Because you must enter the full paths to each of these, the link will probably not work when the presentation is run on a different computer.

Creating a link to a Web or FTP site

If you want to link to a Web or FTP site, as you learned earlier in the chapter, you can simply type the address directly into any text box. Alternatively, you can use the Insert Hyperlink command to create the link, as follows:

1. To use existing text, select the text or its text box. Otherwise, just position the insertion point where you want the hyperlink.

2. Choose Insert ⇨ Hyperlink or press Ctrl+K. The Insert Hyperlink dialog box opens.

3. In the Text to Display field, type or edit the hyperlink text. This text is what will appear underlined on the slide. Any text you've selected will appear in this field by default; changing text here changes it on your slide as well.

4. From the Insert Hyperlink dialog box, click the Existing File or Web Page button.

5. If you know the exact Web or FTP address that you want to link to, type it in the Address box. Then click OK. Otherwise, go to Step 6.

6. Click Browsed Pages to display a list of pages you have visited recently (including pages from PowerPoint's Help system). See Figure 29-10.

7. If the address you want appears as a result of Step 6, click it and click OK. Otherwise, go on to Step 8.

8. Click the Browse the Web button to browse for the page you want. Internet Explorer (or your default Web browser) opens.

If the Dial-Up Connection dialog box appears prompting you to connect to the Internet, enter your username and password, if needed, and then click Connect.

9. In Internet Explorer, navigate to the page that you want to hyperlink to. You can use your Favorites list or look up the page with a search site such as the one found at www.google.com.

Browse the Web button

Figure 29-10: You can select recently viewed or recently linked files from the list, or click Browse the Web to open a Web browser from which to find the desired page.

10. When you have arrived at the page you want, copy the URL from the address bar in your browser, and then jump back to PowerPoint by clicking its button on your Windows task bar. Paste the URL in the Address box of the PowerPoint dialog box using Ctrl+V.

11. Click OK to create the link.

Creating a link to a new document

Perhaps you want the audience to be able to create a new document by clicking a hyperlink. For example, perhaps you would like them to be able to provide information about their experience with your Customer Service department. One way to do this is to let them create a new document using a program that they have on their system, such as a word processor.

Caution

Be careful to set up a new document hyperlink to create a new document using a program that you are sure your audience members will have access to.

To create a link to a new document, follow these steps:

1. To use existing text, select the text or its text box. Otherwise, just position the insertion point where you want the hyperlink.

2. Choose Insert ➪ Hyperlink or press Ctrl+K. The Insert Hyperlink dialog box opens.

3. In the Text to Display field, type or edit the hyperlink text. This text is what will appear underlined on the slide.

4. From the Insert Hyperlink dialog box, click Create New Document. The dialog box controls change, as shown in Figure 29-11.

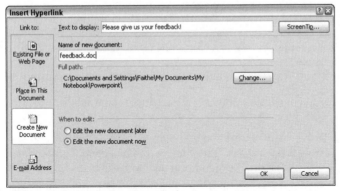

Figure 29-11: PowerPoint prompts you to enter the new document name and location.

5. Enter the name of the new document that you want to create. The type of document created depends on the extension you include. For example, to create a Word document, use the .DOC extension. See Table 29-3 for other extensions.

If you provide this presentation to multiple users, each one will use the same file name for the new document. This can be a problem because one file may overwrite another. It might be easier and less trouble-free to collect information from multiple users using an E-Mail Address hyperlink (discussed later in this chapter).

6. If the path where it should be stored is not correct in the Full Path area, click the Change button. Navigate to the desired location, and click OK to return.

7. Click the Edit the New Document Later option.

8. Click OK.

The most important part about adding a link to create a new file is to make sure that you use an extension that corresponds to a program that users have on the PCs where they will be viewing the presentation. When a program is installed, it registers its extension (the three-character code after the period in a file's name) in the Windows Registry, so that any data files with that extension are associated with that program. For example, when you install Microsoft Word, it registers the extension .DOC for itself, and PowerPoint registers .PPT for its own use. Table 29-3 lists some of the more common file types and their registered extensions on most PCs. Also make sure that the location you specify for the Full Path will always be accessible whenever the presentation is run.

Creating a link to an e-mail address

You can also create a link that opens the user's e-mail program and addresses an e-mail to a certain recipient. For example, perhaps you would like the user to e-mail feedback to you about how he liked your presentation or send you requests for more information about your product.

Table 29-3
Commonly Used Extensions for Popular Programs

Extension	Associated Program
DOC	Microsoft Word, or WordPad if Word is not installed. Use for documents if you are not sure whether your audience has Word, but you are sure they at least have Windows 95.
WRI	Write, the predecessor to WordPad. WordPad and Word also open these if Write is not installed. Safest to use for documents if you do not know which version of Windows your audience will be using.
TXT	Notepad, a plain text editor. Creates text files without any formatting. Not my first choice for documents unless you specifically need them to be without formatting.
WPD	WordPerfect, a competitor to Word.
BMP	Microsoft Paint (which comes free with Windows), or some other more sophisticated graphics program if one is installed.
MDB	Microsoft Access, a database program.
MPP	Microsoft Project, a project management program.
PPT	Microsoft PowerPoint (you know what that is!).
XLS	Microsoft Excel, a spreadsheet program.

Caution For an e-mail hyperlink to work, the person viewing the presentation must have an e-mail application installed on his or her PC and at least one e-mail account configured for sending e-mail. This isn't always a given, but it's probably more likely than betting that they have a certain application installed (as in the preceding section).

To create an e-mail hyperlink, follow these steps:

1. To use existing text, select the text or its text box. Otherwise, just position the insertion point where you want the hyperlink.

2. Choose Insert ➪ Hyperlink or press Ctrl+K. The Insert Hyperlink dialog box opens.

3. In the Text to Display field, type or edit the hyperlink text. This text is what will appear underlined on the slide.

4. From the Insert Hyperlink dialog box, click the E-mail Address button. The dialog box changes to show the controls in Figure 29-12.

Figure 29-12: Fill in the recipient and subject of the mail-to link.

5. In the E-mail Address box, enter the e-mail address. PowerPoint automatically adds `mailto:` in front of it. (You can also select from one of the addresses on the Recently Used E-Mail Addresses list if there are any.)

6. In the Subject field, enter the text that you want to be automatically added to the Subject line of each e-mail.

7. Click OK. The hyperlink appears on the slide.

Editing a Hyperlink

If you need to change the displayed text for the hyperlink, simply edit it just as you do any text on a slide. Move the insertion point into it and press Backspace or Delete to remove characters; then retype new ones.

If you need to change the link to which the hyperlink points, follow these steps:

1. Right-click the hyperlink.

2. On the shortcut menu that appears, choose Edit Hyperlink. The Edit Hyperlink dialog box appears. It is exactly the same as the Insert Hyperlink dialog box except for the name.

3. Make changes to the hyperlink. You can change the displayed text, the address it points to, or the ScreenTip.

4. Click OK.

Removing a Hyperlink

If you decide not to hyperlink in a particular spot, you can delete the displayed text, effectively deleting the hyperlink attached to it. But if you want to leave the displayed text intact and remove the hyperlink only, follow these steps:

1. Right-click the hyperlink.

2. On the shortcut menu that appears, choose Remove Hyperlink.

Creating Graphics-Based Hyperlinks

There are two ways to create a graphics-based hyperlink. Both involve skills that you have already learned in this chapter. Both work equally well, but you may find that you prefer one to the other. The Action Settings method is a little bit simpler, but the Insert Hyperlink method allows you to browse for Web addresses more easily.

Creating a hyperlink with Action Settings

A graphics-based hyperlink is really no more than a graphic with an action setting attached to it. You set it up just as you did with the action buttons earlier in this chapter:

1. Place the graphic that you want to use for a hyperlink.

2. Right-click it and choose Action Settings.

3. Choose Hyperlink To.

4. Open the Hyperlink To drop-down list and choose a URL to enter an Internet address, or choose one of the other options from Table 29-2 to link to some other location or object.

5. Click OK.

Now the graphic functions just like an action button in the presentation; the audience can click on it to jump to the specified location.

Creating a hyperlink with the Insert Hyperlink feature

If you would like to take advantage of the superior address-browsing capabilities of the Insert Hyperlink dialog box when setting up a graphical hyperlink, follow these steps instead of the preceding ones:

1. Place the graphic that you want to use for a hyperlink.

2. Right-click it and choose Hyperlink. The Insert Hyperlink dialog box appears.

3. Choose the location, as you learned earlier in this chapter for text-based hyperlinks. The only difference is that the Text to Display box is unavailable because there is no text.

4. Click OK.

Distributing a User-Interactive Presentation

One of the easiest and best ways to distribute a user-interactive presentation is via CD. In Chapter 25 you learned how to create one of those. You can also distribute the presentation to people within the same company by placing it on a shared network drive and then inviting people to access it. Or you can attach the presentation to an e-mail message and distribute it that way.

Another way is to make the presentation available as a Web page (or series of pages). This is good for information delivery, and it doesn't require the audience to have any special software, but you do lose some of the animation and special effects. I'll discuss this option in more detail in Chapter 30.

You can also place the PowerPoint file on a Web server and then create a link to it from a Web page. This lets people run the presentation in PowerPoint itself (or the PowerPoint Viewer) with all the bells and whistles. Chapter 30 also covers this option.

Interactive Presentation Ideas

You have probably thought of some good ideas for interactive presentations as you worked through this chapter. Here are some more:

✦ **Web resource listings:** Include a slide that lists Web page addresses that the users can visit for more information about various topics covered in your presentation. Or, include Web cross-references throughout the presentation at the bottom of pertinent slides.

✦ **Product information:** Create a basic presentation describing your products, with For More Information buttons for each product. Then, create hidden slides with the detailed information, and hyperlink those hidden slides to the For More Information buttons. Don't forget to put a Return button on each hidden slide so users can easily return to the main presentation.

✦ **Access to custom shows:** If you have created custom shows, as described in Chapter 24, set up action buttons or hyperlinks that jump the users to them on request. Use the Action Settings dialog box's Hyperlink To command and choose Custom Show; then choose the custom show you want to link to.

✦ **Quizzes:** Create a presentation with a series of multiple-choice questions. Create custom action buttons for each answer. Depending on which answer the user clicks, set it up to jump either to a Congratulations, You're Right! slide or a Sorry, Try Again slide. From each of those, include a Return button to go on with the quiz.

✦ **Troubleshooting information:** Ask the users a series of questions and include action buttons or hyperlinks for the answers. Set it up to jump to a slide that further narrows down the problem based on their answers, until they finally arrive at a slide that explains the exact problem and proposes a solution.

✦ **Directories:** Include a company directory with e-mail hyperlinks for various people or departments so that anyone reading the presentation can easily make contact.

Summary

In this chapter, you learned how to create action buttons and hyperlinks in your presentation that can help your audience jump to the information they want in a self-service fashion. Now you can design great-looking presentations that anyone can work their way through on their own, without assistance. In the next chapter, you learn how to distribute these fine user-interactive presentations on the Internet.

✦   ✦   ✦

Preparing a Presentation for Online Distribution

PowerPoint is a rather specialized program. It helps you create presentations very well, but it is not the best choice for creating other business documents such as letters, databases, or spreadsheets. For those needs, you use other tools, such as word processors, database programs, and spreadsheet programs.

Similarly, PowerPoint is probably not the best choice for building your company's main Web site. There are other, better tools for building the traditional newsletter style of Web pages that are a staple of Internet life. Microsoft FrontPage is a good choice if you want to stay all-Microsoft; another good alternative is Macromedia Dreamweaver. You can even use Microsoft Word or Microsoft Publisher to create simple sites. (Both are much better at it than PowerPoint is.)

Even though you probably won't create a lot of standalone Web pages with PowerPoint, you may sometimes want to publish PowerPoint presentations on an existing Web site. You can do this in either of two ways: PowerPoint format and HTML format. This chapter covers both methods.

Special Considerations for Web Publishing

A presentation delivered on the Web has the same overall goal as any other presentation, of course. You want the audience to see it, appreciate it, and buy into it. But the means for accomplishing this over the Web are slightly different.

A successful presentation over the Web is:

+ **Universally accessible to the intended audience.** You must know your audience and their Web browser versions, so you can save your presentation in the best format for their needs. This chapter talks a lot about this issue!

+ **Friendly and user-interactive.** That means you should include directions, hyperlinks, and action buttons to help the users move around, as you learned in Chapter 29.

+ **Quick to download.** That means keep the file size as small as possible without sacrificing the important things. Don't use unnecessary sounds, graphics, videos, or photos, because these items all contribute to the file size.

+ **Quick to view.** Skip the complex animation and transition effects in a Web show. Web users like to get right to the point of each slide. Although long-lasting animation effects may be great for a speaker-led presentation, they are usually just annoying to Web users.

+ **Not heavily reliant on sound.** Don't make sound an integral part of your presentation, because you can't assume that everyone who views it will have a PC with sound support. (Library computers usually don't, for example.) Further, consider making the sounds you do include optional, perhaps by including a button on the slide that they must click to hear the sound. A lot of people object to Web pages that play sounds or music automatically.

You may find that you have to partially sacrifice one of these goals to meet another. For example, there is a way of ensuring compatibility with multiple browsers when saving in Web format, but it results in larger file sizes. I'll tell you about these dilemmas as you go along, and let you come up with your own balance.

Deciding on a File Format

Start out the process by deciding which file format you will use. This can be a rather complex question because of the wide array of choices.

Native PowerPoint format versus Web format

First, will you publish the presentation in Web format, or will you upload it to a Web server in its native PowerPoint format? Both have pros and cons:

✦ **PowerPoint format.** You can make the PowerPoint presentation file available for download from your Web site, just as you can make any other file available like a graphic or an application.

- **Pros:** The audience sees the presentation exactly as you created it, including any embedded sounds, movies, transitions, and animation.

- **Cons:** Only people who own a copy of PowerPoint or who have downloaded the PowerPoint Viewer program can see it.

✦ **Web format.** You can convert your PowerPoint presentation to Web format with an easy-to-use converter included in PowerPoint.

- **Pros:** Anyone with a Web browser can view the presentation without any special preparation. It makes your work widely accessible.

- **Cons:** Certain special effects in your presentation might not be visible to all users, depending on the effects you used and the browsers the audience members use.

If you choose Web format, there are a few PowerPoint features that don't work correctly. It's good to know about these so you can avoid using them in a presentation that is destined for the Web. Here are some examples:

✦ If you set a sound or music clip to continue to play for a certain number of slides, it will stop when you advance past the initial slide.

Expert Tip If you need to make a music clip play through multiple slides, you might be interested in this article: `http://www.powerpointanswers.com/article1018.html`.

You can also doctor the HTML file itself in a text editor. Open fullscreen.html file and add the following line between the `<html>` and the `<head>` tags at the top (where *yoursong* is the name of the music clip and the actual file extension of that clip type is substituted for *wma*):

```
<bgsound src="yoursong.wma" loop=infinite>
```

✦ If you set up the text on an AutoShape to have a different animation than its AutoShape, it will lose the special animation and be animated together with the AutoShape.

✦ If the presentation is set up for automatic transitions between slides, all mouse-click animations behave as automatic animations.

✦ Sounds attached to objects that are hyperlinks (for example, action buttons) don't play.

✦ If a hyperlink on the Slide Master is covered by a placeholder, even if that placeholder is transparent, the hyperlink is unavailable on the individual slides.

✦ Shadow and Embossed text effects are not supported; the text appears as normal text.

You may also find other features that will not work correctly on Web page presentations, such as certain animation effects that don't work properly.

Caution   Do not assume that the presentation will look the same in all browsers. At a minimum, try it in both Internet Explorer and Netscape Navigator, and note any differences.

Traditional HTML versus Single Page Web File

If you decide to go with Web format, you have a second decision: a Single Page Web File or an HTML file. Here's the difference:

✦ **Single Page Web File:** This creates a single file with an .MHT extension that contains everything needed for the entire Web presentation. No support folder is needed.

   • **Pros:** Great convenience. The entire presentation is encapsulated in a single file, so you can e-mail that file, upload it, or do anything else with it as a single unit.

   • **Cons:** The file size is slightly larger than the combined file size of the traditional HTML file plus all its support files. Also, some older Web browsers do not support the use of MHT files, so some audience members may be excluded.

Note   PowerPoint 2000 called the Single Page Web File a Web Archive. It is also known as an MHTML file (which stands for MIME-encapsulated HTML). The most common use for this file format is to e-mail Web pages.

✦ **Traditional HTML:** This creates a single text-based HTML file and a support folder containing all the graphics and helper files needed to turn it into a Web presentation.

   • **Pros:** You can import this page into a larger Web (in FrontPage, for example), and you can edit the HTML file in any application that supports text editing. You don't have to go back to PowerPoint every time you need to make a change.

   • **Cons:** Working with a support folder is somewhat unwieldy. You might forget to copy the folder when you are moving the page to a server, for example.

An HTML presentation consists of many files. PowerPoint creates a home page (an entry point) with the same name as the original presentation. This is the file you name when you save. For example, if the presentation file is named Rondo.ppt, the home page is named Rondo.htm. Then, PowerPoint creates a folder named *presentation name* Files (for example, Rondo Files) that contains all the other HTML, graphics, and other files needed to display the complete presentation.

Caution If you are transferring the HTML presentation to another PC (which is very likely if you are going to make it available on the Internet through your company's server), you must be careful to transfer not only the lone HTML home page but also the entire associated folder.

Browser compatibility file formats

The final format decision is which browsers you will support. This is applicable both to HTML and MHT formats.

The higher the Web browser version you support, the more of PowerPoint's bells and whistles will transfer flawlessly to the Web version, and the better the quality of the multimedia content (sound, video, and so forth). You basically get a nicer show with the higher version support.

However, by choosing higher version support, you potentially exclude a portion of your audience. Anyone who does not have that version or higher will not be able to see the show—either not at all or not as you intended, depending on the version. The lower version means greater compatibility.

The third piece is the file size. The lower the version, the smaller the file size. An exception to this is the option to save for multi-browser compatibility (which you'll see later in the chapter); doing this accomplishes both near-universal support and inclusion of all the features, but at the expense of a much greater file size.

The default browser support is Internet Explorer 4.0 or later, and this works well in most cases. If you decide to support Microsoft Internet Explorer 3.0 and Netscape Navigator 3.0 or later, here are the consequences:

✦ Animation and transitions are not supported.

✦ Animated GIFs do not play if the presentation is saved with a screen size of 640x480 or less.

✦ Sounds and movies are not supported.

✦ Some graphics will appear degraded in quality.

✦ The slide is not scaled to fit the browser window. It runs at a fixed size based on the screen size setting you select when you publish the presentation.

   ✦ You cannot view the presentation full-screen.

   ✦ You cannot open or close frames.

   ✦ The active slide does not appear highlighted in the outline pane.

   ✦ The mouse cannot be used to highlight elements in the outline pane.

If you save the presentation to support IE 4.0 or later but someone tries to view the presentation with an earlier version or with Netscape Navigator, they will still be able to see it, but the following will occur:

   ✦ The presentation outline will appear permanently expanded.

   ✦ No notes or additional frames will appear.

   ✦ Hyperlinks will not work.

   ✦ Clicking a slide title in the outline pane will not jump to that slide.

   ✦ The default browser colors will be used to display the presentation text color and background color. (Exception: The colors do appear correctly in Internet Explorer 3.0.)

   ✦ Sounds and movies will not play.

As you will learn later in this chapter (in the section "Browser options"), you can also further fine-tune the version number by choosing compatibility for Internet Explorer 5.0 or 6.0. If you choose either of these, PowerPoint will use VML (Vector Markup Language) for graphics, to speed up their loading. The graphics are then not viewable with any earlier browser versions.

If you choose Internet Explorer 6.0 compatibility, PowerPoint will allow the use of PNG graphics (a graphic format that is an improved version of GIF) in the presentation. Earlier browser versions will not be able to see those graphics.

Now that you know the pros and cons of your myriad options, let's get down to some of them. We'll start with saving as a Web page.

Saving the Presentation As a Web Page

If you go with the default settings, saving a presentation as a Web page is almost as easy as saving it normally. You simply issue a command and provide a name; PowerPoint does the rest.

Caution

When you save as a Web page, the resulting HTML or MHT presentation remains open and on-screen. If you make additional edits to it, those edits will not apply to the original PowerPoint presentation file (PPT) on which the Web version was based. After saving your work on the Web version, make sure you use File ⇨ Save As to re-save your work in PowerPoint format too if you want all copies to stay updated.

Recall from an earlier discussion that when saving as a Web page, you have a choice of HTML or Single Page Web File (MHT). The latter is the default; if you want HTML, you must change the file type in the Save as Type box when you save.

Follow these steps to perform a basic save in that format without setting any special options.

1. Choose File ⇨ Save As Web Page. The Save As dialog box appears, with Single File Web Page chosen as the Save As type. See Figure 30-1.

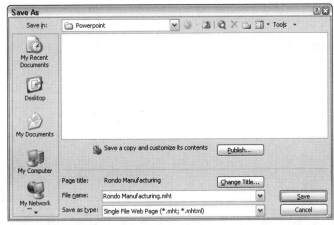

Figure 30-1: When you save as a Web page, the Save As dialog box has a few special options.

2. The default name is the presentation name. If you want a different name, type it in the File Name box.

3. If you want HTML format instead of Single File Web Page, open the Save As Type drop-down list and choose Web Page (*.htm, *.html).

4. PowerPoint takes the default Page title (that is, the words that will appear in the Web browser title bar when the page displays) from the title of the first slide. If you want a different title, click the Change Title button, type a different title, and click OK.

5. If you want to save in a different location, navigate to the drive or folder you want. To save files directly to an FTP site on the Internet, see the "Saving in an FTP Location" section later in this chapter. To save directly to a Web site, see "Saving to a Web Site."

6. Click Save. PowerPoint saves the presentation in the chosen format.

You will probably want to check your work by opening the file in your Web browser and checking to make sure all the slides appear as you intended. To do so, browse to the save location and double-click the file to open it. Figure 30-2 shows an example of how it might look there.

Note   When you view a Web presentation in the default view, shown in Figure 30-2, many of the animations, transitions, and so on do not work. To take full advantage of them, you must switch to Slide Show view by clicking the Slide Show button.

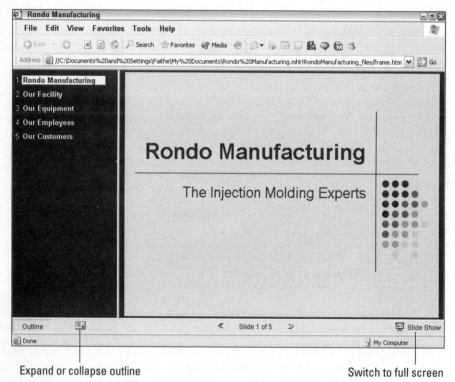

Expand or collapse outline   Switch to full screen

Figure 30-2: Here's a PowerPoint presentation saved in Web page format.

Setting Web Publishing Options

When you save using the steps in the preceding section, you have very little control over how PowerPoint translates the presentation. For more control, click the Publish button in the Save As dialog box. When you do so, the Publish as Web Page dialog box appears. See Figure 30-3.

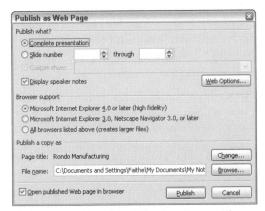

Figure 30-3: Use this dialog box to provide more input on how PowerPoint converts your work to Web format.

Use this dialog box as a replacement for the Save As dialog box and set any of these options:

✦ **Publish What?** The default is Complete Presentation, but you can choose a range of slides or a custom show.

✦ **Display Speaker Notes.** The default is yes (check box marked), so that an icon on each page enables your readers to jump to that page's notes.

✦ **Browser Support.** The default is Microsoft Internet Explorer 4.0 or later. This format takes advantage of these versions' capability to process certain codes and run certain mini-applications. If you think some of your audience may not have this browser, choose one of the other options instead.

• **Microsoft Internet Explorer 3.0, Netscape Navigator 3.0, or Later.** This option results in many of the animated features of the presentation not being saved, but it also makes for a smaller file size and greater compatibility with a wide variety of browsers.

- **All Browsers Listed Above (Creates Larger Files).** This option is for maximum compatibility. It essentially saves two versions of the presentation in the same file — one for Internet Explorer 4.0 and higher, and one for everything else. That way there is no sacrifice of features in order to ensure compatibility.

✦ **Publish a Copy As.** These are the same controls as the ones in the Save As dialog box. You can change the page title with the Change button, or type a different name and/or location in the File Name box.

✦ **Open Published Web Page in Browser.** If you leave this check box marked, PowerPoint opens Internet Explorer and displays your presentation's first page automatically, as shown in Figure 30-2. This is a good way to check your work.

But wait! There's more! Notice the Web Options button in Figure 30-3. You can click it to display the Web Options dialog box, shown in Figure 30-4, where you have even more options to change regarding your presentation's conversion. The following sections cover these options.

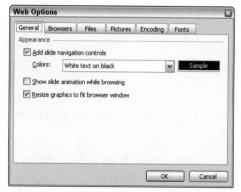

Figure 30-4: You can fine-tune the Web export of your presentation even more precisely with these options.

General options

On the General tab, you can set the following:

✦ **Add Slide Navigation Controls.** This option is turned on by default, and it results in the left pane shown in Figure 30-2 that lists the names of the slides. Users can click a slide's name to jump to it.

✦ **Colors.** Notice in Figure 30-2 that the aforementioned navigation area is black with white lettering. You can choose a different color scheme for that area from this Colors drop-down list. Choices include Browser Colors (whatever default colors are set in the user's Web browser), Presentation Colors (text color or accent color) taken from the presentation, or Black Text on White.

✦ **Show Slide Animation While Browsing.** If you have set any slide animations (see Chapter 20) and you want them to be a part of the Web show, mark this check box. It is unmarked by default because Web users may find animations annoying, rather than clever, because of their Internet connection speed.

✦ **Resize Graphics to Fit Browser Window.** This option is marked by default so that if users are running their browsers at less that full-screen size or using a different screen resolution, your content will not be cut off, but rather resized so that it fits the screen.

Browser options

Have you been wondering what the differences are when saving with compatibility for one browser version versus another? You'll find some answers on the Browsers tab, shown in Figure 30-5.

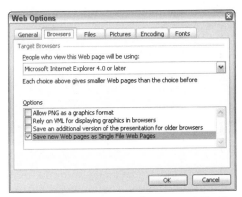

Figure 30-5: Customize the presentation's save for a specific browser version here.

Choose a browser version from the drop-down list, and the check boxes in the Options section are automatically marked or cleared for that version based on its capabilities. You can also manually mark or clear any of these check boxes. The lower the version you choose, the fewer features are used and the smaller the file(s) become.

The four check boxes are:

✦ **Allow PNG as a Graphics Format.** PNG is an improved version of the GIF format. Internet Explorer 6.0 supports that format fully; earlier versions might not. If your presentation contains PNG files and this option is not marked, they will be converted to a supported format when you save.

✦ **Rely on VML for Displaying Graphics in Browsers.** VML stands for Vector Markup Language. It's a way of making graphics appear more quickly in Web pages. You must have at least Internet Explorer 5.0 to see graphics that rely on VML; people with older browsers will not see the graphics.

✦ **Save an Additional Version of the Presentation for Older Browsers.** This check box is turned off by default no matter which version you select. Marking it will insert the needed codes for backward compatibility with older browsers (all the way back to Internet Explorer 3.0) but will increase the file size.

✦ **Save New Web Pages as Single File Web Pages.** This option enables or disables the use of the MHT format discussed earlier in the chapter. To view a Single File Web Page, users must have at least Internet Explorer 4.0.

File options

On the Files tab, shown in Figure 30-6, you can set these options to control how your files are saved, named, organized, and updated:

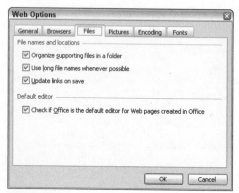

Figure 30-6: All of these file options are enabled by default; deselect any you don't want.

✦ **Organize Supporting Files in a Folder.** This option is the default, as you saw earlier. PowerPoint saves the needed files in a folder with the same name as the presentation home page. If you deselect this option, all the supporting files are saved in the same folder as the home page.

✦ **Use Long File Names Whenever Possible.** This option preserves the Windows 95 and higher long filenames, which are usually more descriptive than the shorter 8-character names in DOS and Windows 3.1. If you need to transfer the presentation to a server that does not support long filenames, deselect this option.

✦ **Update Links on Save.** With this option marked, every time you save your presentation in Web format in PowerPoint, all the links are also updated.

✦ **Default Editor.** Unmark the single check box in this section if you want to use a third-party editing program (non-Office) as the default for editing Web pages and you don't want a warning to appear each time you open the file in the third-party program.

Pictures options

There is only one control on the Pictures tab: Target Monitor. In most cases, the default of 800x600 is the right choice.

The presentation can run at several screen resolutions. The smallest is 640x480. (The numbers refer to the number of pixels, or individual dots, that make up the display.) Most people run Windows at 800x600 or higher, but people with older, smaller monitors may still be using 640x480. If you choose a higher setting for the presentation than users have on their screens, they will have to scroll in Internet Explorer to see the complete slides.

Encoding options

On the Encoding tab are a few settings that only multilingual offices will use:

✦ **Save This Document As.** Choose a language character set here. The default for United States usage is US-ASCII, which is fine in most cases. A more general setting for any English-speaking country or for languages that use the same alphabet as English is Western European (ISO).

✦ **Always Save Web Pages in the Default Encoding.** If you want PowerPoint to always rely on Windows' information about what kind of alphabet you are using, mark this check box, and you never have to worry about the character set again.

Fonts options

The Fonts tab enables you to select a character set to encode with the Web presentation. This is mostly an issue when you are creating a presentation in a non-English language. The default is English/Western European/Other Latin Script, as shown in Figure 30-7.

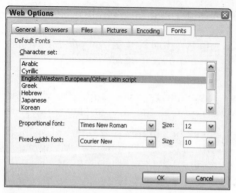

Figure 30-7: Select a character set to use for encoding the fonts in the presentation.

Expert Tip   What's all this about character sets? To see a demonstration, open Microsoft Word and choose Insert ➪ Symbol. Then open the Subset drop-down list. Notice all the different subsets within that font? Each of those is a character set. Each character has a unique 4-digit hexadecimal code — that's over 65,000 possible codes. So there's much more flexibility to a given font than just the few characters you can generate by typing on your keyboard.

You can also select a font for any text in the Web presentation that does not have a specific font assigned to it. Actually you select two fonts: one proportional and the other fixed-width (monospace). Leaving these set at their defaults is a good idea because the defaults (Times New Roman and Courier New) are available on almost every PC.

Transferring a Presentation to a Web Server

Publishing a presentation to the Web means transferring it to a server or other computer that has a direct, full-time Web connection. If you are an individual or small-business user, that server probably belongs to your local Internet service provider (ISP). If you work for a large company that has its own Web site, there may be a server in-house that you should transfer your files to. Consult your company's network administrator or Webmaster to find out what you need to do.

There are several ways of getting your presentation onto a Web server:

✦ You can save it to the server through PowerPoint with a Web address, using the Save As Web Page dialog box.

✦ You can save it directly to the Web site through FTP within PowerPoint, again using Save As Web Page.

✦ You can save it to your hard disk first, check it, and then upload it to the Web server via an FTP utility.

I recommend that you always save first to your hard disk and check your work. After that, however, you can re-save within PowerPoint using either of the first two methods or you can go with a separate FTP utility — it's your choice. This chapter does not cover using a third-party utility because each one is different. One popular utility is WS_FTP, available from most shareware Web sites, such as `http://www.tucows.com`.

 Expert Tip Every Web location has two addresses: its FTP address and its Web address. They both point to the same location; it's just a matter of how you access that location. Some ISPs prefer that you upload your Web pages via the FTP protocol using an FTP address; others allow you to upload them using the HTTP protocol and a Web address.

All of these methods work no matter which format you are using. You can save a file in native PowerPoint format to a Web server just as easily as a presentation in Web format.

Saving directly to a Web server

This is the easiest way of publishing your Web presentation, but it might not work for everyone. The company that owns the server might set up restrictions for security or other reasons that prevent you from using this method. Still, it's worth a try.

To publish directly to the Web, you need a username and password. You can get these from your ISP. (They might not be the same as your logon name and password.)

1. Open the File menu and choose Save As or Save As Web Page, depending on the format in which you are publishing.

2. In the File Name box, type the full Web site address to which you want to publish. For example, if the filename is test.mht, the full address might be `http://www.mysite.com/test.mht`.

3. Click Save. PowerPoint attempts to connect to the Web site, and a Logon box appears prompting you for your username and password.

4. Enter the username and password and click OK. Your presentation is saved to the Web server and the Save As dialog box closes.

Saving to a Web address creates a network shortcut in your My Network Places folder. The next time you save as a Web page, you can click the My Network Places icon and then select the address from the network places stored there.

Saving directly to an FTP location

If you can't save to the Web location directly, you might be able to save to an FTP location. As mentioned earlier, you will need to know the FTP address of the Web server where you want to save, as well as have a username and password for access.

You can save directly whether you are saving as a Web page or just as a regular presentation. Just follow these steps:

Note   The first time you perform the following steps, you must set up the FTP location with Add/Modify FTP Locations, as these steps document. In subsequent sessions, the FTP site you want appears on the Save In list and you can simply select it, skipping the rest of the setup.

1. Open the File menu and choose Save As or Save As Web Page, depending on the format in which you are publishing.

2. Open the Save In drop-down list and choose Add/Modify FTP Locations.

3. The Add/Modify FTP Locations dialog box appears. Enter the server's FTP address in the Name of FTP Site box. See Figure 30-8.

Figure 30-8: Enter a name and address for the FTP location you want to add.

4. You are probably required to log in to the server. If so, click the User button and then type your username in the text box.

5. If you are required to log in, enter your login password in the Password box.

 Note   If you do not have to log in, you can enter anything you want in the Password box, but it is considered courteous to use your e-mail address for it, so the owner of the site you are visiting knows who you are.

6. Click Add, and then click OK. The available FTP locations appear in the Save As dialog box.

7. Double-click the location you just created. If a connection box appears prompting you to connect to the Internet via modem, do so.

8. The top level of folders at the FTP site you specified appear. Double-click the folders to navigate through them to the spot where you are instructed to save your files.

9. When the correct folder appears in the Save In box, click Save.

10. It will take at least a few minutes to transfer the files. While you are waiting, a Transferring File dialog box appears, so you can monitor the progress.

11. When the files have transferred, disconnect your dial-up Internet connection if necessary. Then, check your work by accessing the files using a Web browser. See the "Navigating a Presentation in a Browser" section, next.

Navigating a Presentation in a Browser

Now that your presentation files have been transferred to the Web server, it's time to test them to make sure they work. To do that, you need to use a Web browser. Internet Explorer works very well for this purpose. (It is probably already installed on your PC.) Other Web browsers, such as Netscape Navigator, work fine, too.

To test your work, follow these steps:

1. Open your Web browser, and type the URL of the presentation (that is, the address where you stored it). Then press Enter.

2. The first page appears. Use any of the navigation methods pointed out in the following list to move to each slide, making sure there are no errors.

   • Move to the next slide by clicking the > button at the bottom of the window.

   • Click the Speaker button to pause or play the narration.

   • Click the Slide Show button to switch to a full-screen view of the slide, just like in Slide Show view in PowerPoint. To return to the Web page view, press Esc.

- To jump to a specific slide, click its name in the left pane (the outline). To hide the outline, click the Outline button.

- To expand or collapse the outline, click the Expand/Collapse Outline button.

3. To end the show, close the browser or navigate to a different Web site.

Making Native PowerPoint Presentations Available Online

If you plan to distribute the presentation as a regular PowerPoint presentation, you must do some extra work. You cannot assume that every member of your intended audience owns a copy of PowerPoint, so you should make the PowerPoint Viewer available to them. If you are distributing your presentation internally (that is, only to people in your company), you can make the PowerPoint Viewer program available on your LAN. If, however, the presentation will be available to the entire Internet, you should create a Web page from which the audience can download the viewer and your presentation file.

Expert Tip   If you are providing the presentation in PowerPoint format, you might want to save it as a PowerPoint Show rather than a regular PowerPoint file. A PowerPoint Show is the same thing as a normal PowerPoint file except it opens in Slide Show view instead of normal editing mode.

Making the PowerPoint Viewer available online

Office 2003 comes with a new version of the PowerPoint Viewer, one with greater capabilities than any previous version. The PowerPoint Viewer can show PowerPoint presentation files with almost no loss of features or quality versus PowerPoint itself.

Creating a Viewer distribution package

First, you'll need to package the presentation for distribution. You can do this with the Package for CD feature, except you save it to a folder instead of a CD. You will then make everything in this folder available to users.

1. With the presentation open, choose File ⇨ Package for CD. The Package for CD dialog box opens.

2. Click Copy to Folder. The Copy to Folder dialog box opens. See Figure 30-9.

3. Type the desired name for the new folder in the Name the Folder box.

4. Type the path where you want the folder to be stored in the Choose Location box (or use Browse).

5. Click OK.

6. In the Package for CD dialog box, click Close.

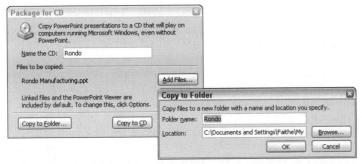

Figure 30-9: Package the presentation for distribution in a folder.

Compressing the distribution package with Windows XP

Next you will need to "zip up" the contents of the packaged-for-CD folder so that you can make that file available for download on the Web. It's easy to do in Windows XP because Windows XP includes built-in support for the Zip format.

1. In Windows, open the folder where you copied the files in the preceding steps.

2. Select all the files (Ctrl+A).

3. *(Optional)* If you want to make the presentation file itself available separately from the PowerPoint Viewer files, deselect it. To do so, hold down the Ctrl key and click it.

4. Right-click the selected files and choose Send To ➪ Compressed (Zipped) Folder. A compressed folder is created with the same name as the first file in the group.

5. Rename the compressed file with a more meaningful name, such as pptviewer.zip. To do so, right-click it and choose Rename, and then type a name and press Enter.

Note Should you type an extension when renaming the Zip file? It depends on whether you have Windows set up to show the file extensions for known file types or not. If the file you are renaming shows up with a .ZIP extension on-screen, type .ZIP at the end when renaming it. If it doesn't, don't type an extension.

Expert Tip   If you want to make many different presentations available online, you might want to zip up only the PowerPoint Viewer and its support files, separate from the presentation file. Then you can make each presentation file a separate download from the viewer. To do so, after selecting all the files in step 2, hold down Ctrl and click the presentation file(s) to deselect.

Compressing the distribution package with a third-party program

If you don't have Windows XP, you will need to use a third-party utility to create the compressed archive of the presentation files.

One of the best-known programs to use for this purpose is WinZip (www.winzip.com). This is a shareware program that works with Windows to compress groups of files into Zip files and to unzip compressed archives.

Expert Tip   One of the advantages of WinZip over the zipping tool in Windows XP is that it can be used to create a self-extracting compressed archive. This is an executable file that unzips its contents when you run it. If you distribute the presentation and the viewer in this format, the users will not need an unzipping utility or Windows XP in order to decompress it.

Copying files to the Web server

You can transfer the presentation file(s) and the PowerPoint Viewer compressed archive file to the server with a third-party FTP utility, or you can use Windows itself (if you have Windows XP) by following these steps:

1. Create a Network Place shortcut to the Web or FTP address. If you saved your file directly to the server using the Web or FTP method explained earlier in the chapter, this has already been done.

2. Open that network location in a Windows file management window. (Hint: Start from My Network Places and double-click the shortcut to that location.) If a prompt appears for your username and password, enter them and click OK.

3. Open the My Computer window and navigate to the folder containing the files you have prepared for uploading to the server. (This probably includes the Zip file for the PowerPoint Viewer and also one or more presentation files.)

4. Drag-and-drop the files to the Web or FTP location to copy them there.

Creating the starting Web page

You can use any Web page creation program to create this simple page. For example, you can use PowerPoint (which has the advantage of being familiar to you already), FrontPage, Publisher, or Microsoft Word. In this chapter, I show you how to do it with PowerPoint.

To create a single Web page in PowerPoint, start a new presentation with a single slide in it. Then, create instructions and hyperlinks on it to access the PowerPoint Viewer and your PowerPoint presentation.

Follow these steps:

1. Start a new presentation. It can either be blank or based on a design template. Do not use the AutoContent Wizard.

2. Change the layout of the slide to Title and Text (see Chapter 7).

3. Add some text to the Title placeholder.

4. Click in the body area, and then click the Bullet List button on the Formatting toolbar to turn off the bullets.

5. Type the instructions. Figure 30-10 shows an example.

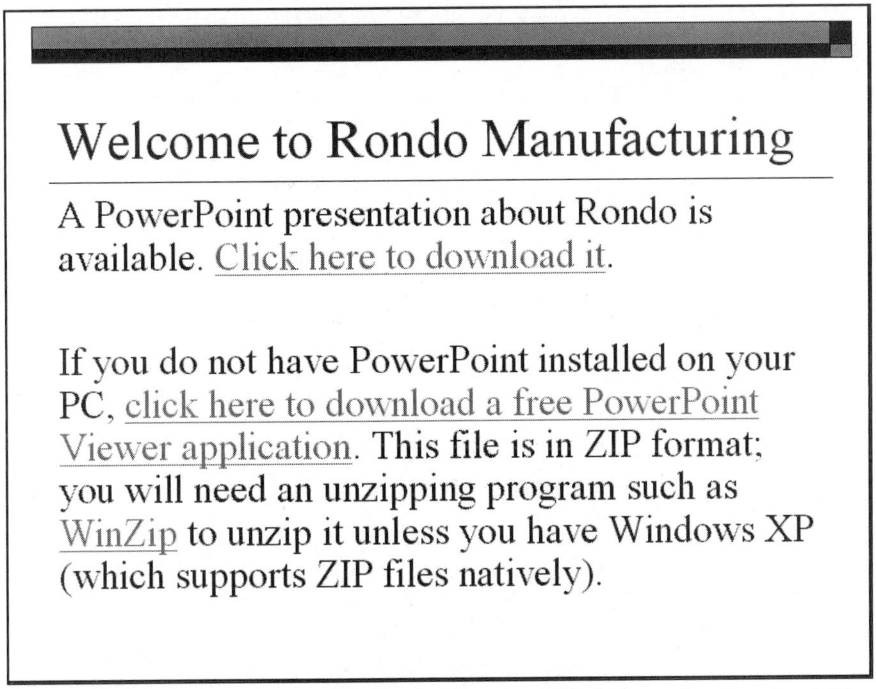

Welcome to Rondo Manufacturing

A PowerPoint presentation about Rondo is available. Click here to download it.

If you do not have PowerPoint installed on your PC, click here to download a free PowerPoint Viewer application. This file is in ZIP format; you will need an unzipping program such as WinZip to unzip it unless you have Windows XP (which supports ZIP files natively).

Figure 30-10: An instruction page like this one provides links to the downloadable PowerPoint file as well as the PowerPoint Viewer program.

6. Create the hyperlinks to the files that you have placed on the server (see Chapter 29).

7. Save the presentation directly to the server as a Web page (using one of the methods you learned earlier in the chapter).

Summary

In this chapter, you learned how to prepare a presentation for Internet distribution. This process involves not only designing the presentation thoughtfully with Internet users in mind, but also saving the file in HTML or MHT format or providing a PowerPoint Viewer for the audience's use. You can now save presentations as Web pages, transfer them to Internet servers online, and prepare introductory Web pages that contain links to presentations.

The next chapter is another Project Lab, where you'll practice the skills you have learned in the last several chapters for preparing a presentation for distribution without a live speaker.

✦   ✦   ✦

Project Lab: Preparing a Presentation for Users to View on Their Own

✦ ✦ ✦ ✦

In This Chapter

Recording narration and timings

Placing action buttons on a slide

Saving a presentation in Web format

✦ ✦ ✦ ✦

Welcome to the sixth Project Lab in this book! This project lets you practice your skills at features designed to make a presentation logical and useful for a self-serve audience. These skills include rehearsing timings, recording narration, adding action buttons, and saving a presentation in Web format.

The Scenario

This lab continues your work for Spice Meadow Shelties. The owner likes the idea of distributing the presentation with narration and automatically advancing slides, and she would like you to set up something like that for her business.

She would also like to save a version of the presentation as a Web site, with hyperlinks in it where users can click to see hidden slides containing more information about certain topics.

In this set of projects, you create two more versions of her presentation. One is a normal PowerPoint presentation with narration and automatic transitions; the other is a Web page presentation with action buttons that hyperlink to hidden slides.

Project 6A: Recording Narration and Timings

In this project, you set up a presentation to include recorded narration and automatically advancing slides.

Level of difficulty: Easy

Time to complete: 10 to 15 minutes

1. **Open the file Lab06A.ppt from the Labs folder (from the CD accompanying the book).**

2. **Print the Speaker Notes pages for the presentation, so you will have a copy of the narration script handy.**

   a. Choose File ⇨ Print.

   b. In the Print What section, choose Notes Pages.

   c. Click OK. Nine pages should print. Keep these pages handy for reading the script later.

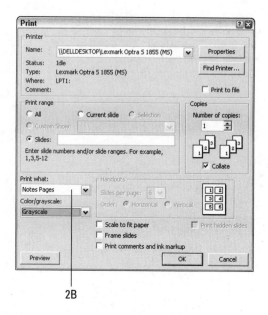

2B

3. **Connect your microphone to your PC if it is not already connected.**

4. Prepare to record narration by checking the microphone level and selecting a recording quality.

    a. Choose Slide Show ➪ Record Narration.

    b. Click the Set Microphone Level button.

    c. Speak into the microphone, and drag the slider to adjust the volume level.

    d. Click OK.

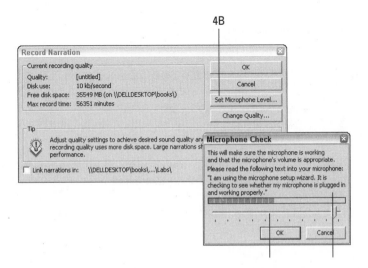

e. Click the Change Quality button.

f. Open the Name list and choose Radio Quality.

g. Click OK.

5. Record the narration.

a. Click the OK button in the Record Narration dialog box.

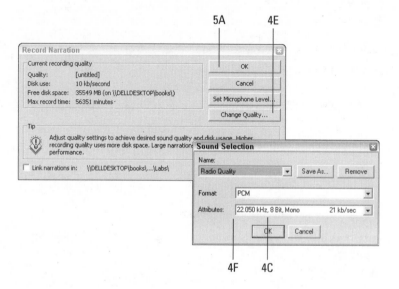

b. If you were not viewing the first slide, a dialog box asks where you want to begin. Click First Slide.

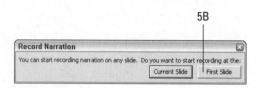

c. When the first slide appears, read the narration for it, and then click to advance.

d. Continue through all the slides, to the end, and then click to return to PowerPoint.

e. A dialog box asks whether you want to save the timings; click Save.

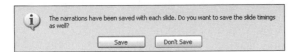

6. **Play back your presentation in Slide Show view to check it.**

a. Choose View ➪ Slide Show.

b. Watch the show and listen to the narration. Make notes about any timings you want to change or any narration you want to re-record.

c. When you are finished, click to return to PowerPoint.

7. **Re-record the narration for slide 4:**

a. Click slide 4 to select it.

b. Choose Slide Show ➪ Record Narration.

c. Click OK to begin the recording.

7C

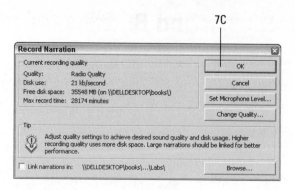

d. Click Current Slide.

7D

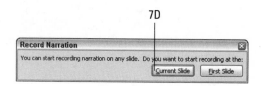

e. The slide appears. Read the following text into the microphone, and then press Esc (do not click).

All our dogs are checked by a vet once a year and receive all recommended immunizations. In addition, any dogs selected for breeding receive hip and eye checks and are certified free of these defects.

f. Click Save to save the timing as well as the narration.

8. **Watch the show again to confirm that the new recording is in place.**

9. **Save your work as MyLab06A.ppt.**

Note

After re-recording narration for a slide, watch the presentation in Slide Show view to make sure that the re-recording integrates smoothly with the previous recordings. You might need to adjust transition timings if the new recording is longer than the old one was.

Project 6B: Creating Action Buttons for Hidden Slides

In this project you create action buttons on certain slides that hyperlink to hidden slides containing more information.

Level of difficulty: Moderate

Time to complete: 15 to 30 minutes

1. **Open the file Lab06B.ppt from the Labs folder (from the CD accompanying the book).**

2. **Add an action button to slide 3 that hyperlinks to slide 4 (which is hidden).**

   a. Display slide 3 in Normal view.

   b. Choose Slide Show ⇨ Action Buttons and select the blank button.

   c. Click in the empty area at the bottom of the slide to place a default-sized blank button there.

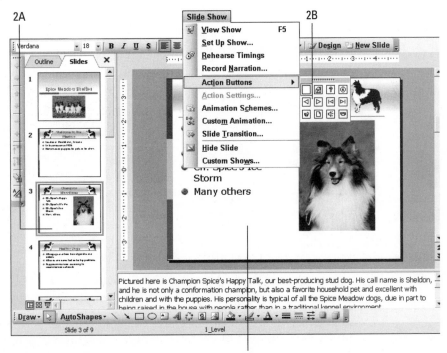

d. The Action Settings dialog box appears. Select the Hyperlink To option button.

e. Open the Hyperlink To drop-down list and choose Slide.

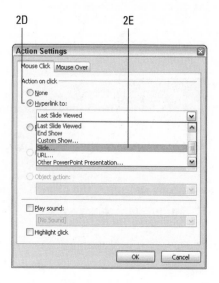

f. In the Hyperlink To Slide dialog box, click slide 4.

g. Click OK.

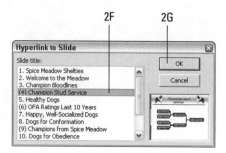

h. Back in the Action Settings dialog box, click OK.

3. Add the text *Pedigree* to the blank action button on slide 3.

a. Right-click the blank action button on slide 3 and choose Add Text.

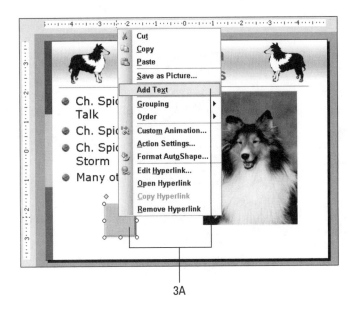

3A

b. The cursor moves into the button. Type **Pedigree**.

c. Select the word you just typed and click the Bold button on the toolbar to make it bold.

d. Drag the right-side selection handle on the button to the right, making the button wider so that the text will fit.

4. Create a Back button on slide 4 that returns to slide 3.

a. Display slide 4 in Normal view.

b. Choose Slide Show ➪ Action Buttons and then choose the button with the left-pointing arrow.

c. Click in the bottom-right corner of the slide to place the action button there.

d. In the Action Settings dialog box, accept the defaults and click OK.

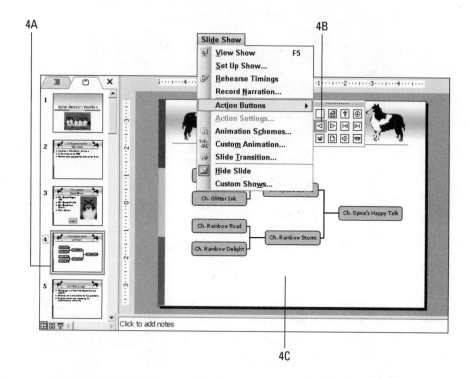

5. Add an action button on slide 5 that hyperlinks to slide 6. Make the button text *OFA Ratings*. Use the same procedures as in Steps 2 and 3.

6. Create a Back button on slide 6 that returns to slide 5. Use the same procedure as in Step 4.

7. Add an action button on slide 8 that hyperlinks to slide 9. Make the button text *List of Champions*.

8. Create a Back button on slide 9 that returns to slide 8.

9. Add an action button on slide 10 that hyperlinks to slide 11. Make the button text *Obedience Titles*.

10. Create a Back button on slide 11 that returns to slide 10.

11. Display the presentation in Slide Show view and try out each of the buttons to make sure it goes where it is supposed to go.

12. Save your work as MyLab06B.ppt.

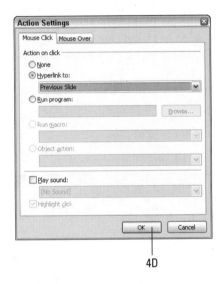

4D

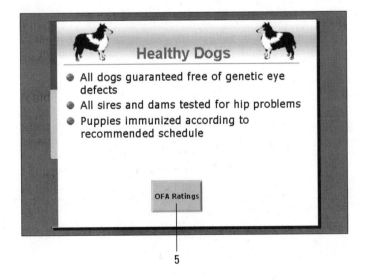

5

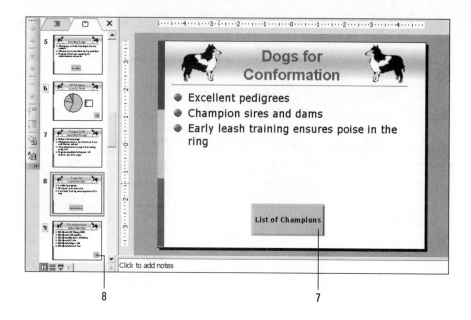

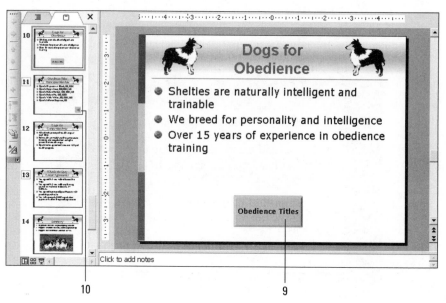

Project 6C: Saving a Presentation for Web Use

In this project, you publish the presentation from Project 6B in Web format.

Level of difficulty: Easy

Time to complete: 5 to 10 minutes

1. **Open the file if needed.**

    If you completed project 6B, start in the file MyLab06B.ppt. If you did not complete that project, open Lab06C.ppt from the Labs folder.

2. **Save the presentation as a single-file Web page suitable for e-mailing to the client.**

    a. Choose File ⇨ Save as Web Page.

    b. In the Save as Web Page dialog box, confirm that Single File Web Page (*.mht, *.mhtml) is selected as the file format.

    c. In the File Name box, type **MyLab06C**.

    d. Click Save.

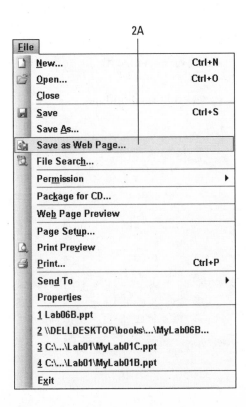

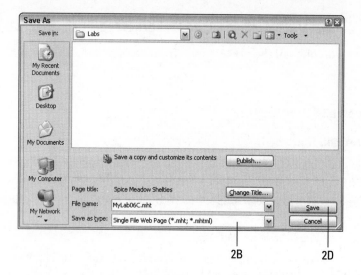

2B   2D

3. **Open Internet Explorer and display MyLab06C.mht to check it. Then return to PowerPoint.**

4. **Save the presentation in HTML format for use in Internet Explorer 5.0 and higher.**

   a. Choose File ➪ Save as Web Page.

   b. In the Save As Web Page dialog box, change the file format to Web Page (*.htm, *.html).

   c. Click the Publish button to set additional options.

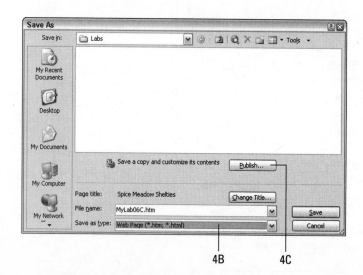

4B   4C

d. Deselect the Display Speaker Notes check box.

e. Click the Web Options button.

4D   4E

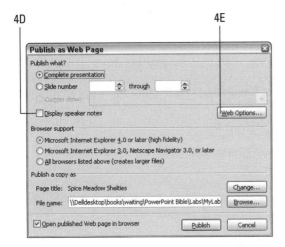

f. Open the Colors list and choose Presentation Colors (Text Color).

4F

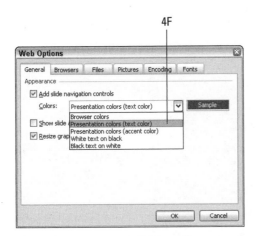

g. Click the Browsers tab.

h. Choose Microsoft Internet Explorer 5.0 or Later.

i. Click OK to close the Web Options box.

4G   4H

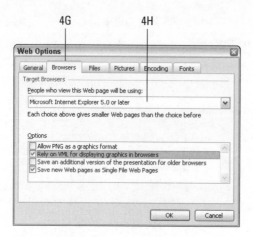

j. In the Publish as Web Page box, mark the Open Published Web page in Browser check box if it is not already marked.

k. Click Publish. The page appears in Internet Explorer.

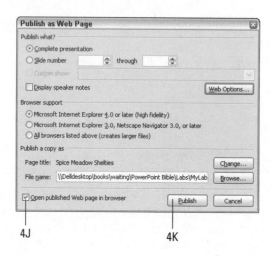

4J   4K

5. Examine the presentation in Internet Explorer to check your work.

   a. Click the names of several slides to jump to them.

   b. Click the first slide to jump back to it.

   c. Click the Slide Show button to watch the entire show full-screen.

5A   5B

5C

6. **Close Internet Explorer and return to PowerPoint.**

7. **Exit PowerPoint, saving your changes if prompted.**

Congratulations, you have completed the lab projects for this section! You now have several versions of self-running and user-interactive presentations you can show to your client for her final approval.

We're coming up on the final part of the book now. In that part, you learn about some ways to be a better public speaker with PowerPoint, some ways to collaborate with teammates on a draft presentation, and some ways to make PowerPoint easier to use.

✦   ✦   ✦

Cutting-Edge Solutions

What Makes a Great Presentation?

Wow! *What a great presentation!* That's what you want your audience to come away thinking, right?

Most people won't be nit-picky enough to pinpoint exactly what they loved about the experience. Nobody is likely to say, "Weren't the colors in that pie chart on slide 43 artfully chosen?" or "Did you see his tie? I wonder where I can buy one just like it." Instead, you'll leave your audience with an overall impression that they gather from a host of little details, from the color scheme on your slides to the anecdotes and jokes you tell.

In this chapter, you take a short break from the details of PowerPoint and learn about some of the little details that, collectively, can work toward making your audience pleased with their experience.

How to Create Great Slides

Because this is a book on PowerPoint, great slides are the top concern. Your slides should say to the audience, "I had you in mind when I created this," and "Relax; I'm a professional, and I know what I'm doing." Good-looking, appropriate slides can give the audience a sense of security, and can lend authority to your message. On the other hand, poorly done or inconsistent slides can tell the audience, "I just slapped this thing together at the last minute," or "I don't really know what I'm doing."

Choosing appropriate designs for the occasion

PowerPoint offers dozens of slide designs, as you've seen throughout this book. They're a diverse bunch because there are many different presentation situations. Table 32-1 reviews some of the presentation design templates that PowerPoint offers and covers what kind of message they send to the audience.

Table 32-1		
Design Templates and Suggested Uses		
Type	**Examples**	**Uses**
White backgrounds	Echo, Eclipse, Pixel, Blends, Quadrant, Watermark	These simple, white-background templates are useful when you want something that's a little more dressed-up than just a plain page, but you don't want the design to be noticed specifically. White backgrounds are especially good for reading on paper or on an overhead transparency projector.
Dark, subtle backgrounds	Textured, Stream, Slit, Ripple	Subtle and elegant when a dark background is required. Great for conservative industries and situations where you don't want a totally plain background but also don't want the background to be noticed. Each of these has a minimal pattern or design.
Motion-oriented backgrounds	Competition, Digital Dots, Teamwork	The designs on these slides imply movement, making them a good choice for a presentation on the subject of taking action.
Nature backgrounds	Clouds, Maple, Mountaintop, Ocean	These are not just for outdoor industries! Something about nature seems to calm people down, so use these to project a peaceful feeling.

Choosing formatting that matches your medium

Are you going to present transparencies on an old-time overhead projector? Or will you use 35mm slides, or a computer screen? Thinking about the size and quality of the image that the audience will see can help you make intelligent formatting choices.

Overhead projector

Using an overhead projector is never anyone's first choice, but sometimes it's all that's available. If that's the case, you just have to be a good sport about it. You can make transparencies by feeding transparency film into your computer's printer.

Caution

Make sure you get the kind of transparencies designed specifically for your printer! The kind for inkjets, for example, melts inside a laser printer and ruins it.

An overhead projector image is medium-sized (probably about 36"x36"), but often of poor quality. You will probably be fighting with room lighting, so your slides may appear washed out. Here are some tips for preparing slides to be shown with overhead projectors:

✦ **Fonts:** For headings, choose chunky block lettering, like Arial Black font, that can stand up to a certain amount of image distortion. For small type, choose clear, easy-to-read fonts like Arial or Times New Roman.

✦ **Text color:** Black letters on a light background stand out well. Avoid semidark lettering, like medium-blue; it can easily wash out under the powerful light of an overhead projector.

✦ **Background color:** Avoid dark backgrounds. You probably will not get each slide perfectly hand-positioned on the overhead projector, and the white space around the edges will be distracting if your transparencies have a dark background. Consider using a simple white background when you know you're going to be using transparencies, and *especially* when you want to be able to write on the transparencies.

✦ **Content:** Keep it simple. Overheads are best when they are text-heavy, without a lot of fancy extras or clipart. The overhead projector is an old technology, and slides that are too dressy seem pretentious.

35mm slides on a slide projector

Although 35mm slides are more expensive to create than overhead transparencies, the extra expense may be justifiable. The image size is generally a bit larger, and the image quality is improved. Slides transport well in carousels, and don't get out of order. You also don't have to fumble with placing them manually on the projector, and they don't have that annoying white space around the edges.

Expert Tip

You can make 35mm slides by sending your PowerPoint file to a slide-making service. Find out from the slide-making service what format they want your slide file to be in. Almost all slide service bureaus accept PowerPoint files. One of the largest services, Genigraphics, provides its own driver for PowerPoint, so you can print to a Genigraphics file. Check out www.genigraphics.com.

Here are some guidelines for formatting slides destined to be 35mm slides:

✦ **Fonts:** You can use almost any readable font on 35mm slides. If your audience is going to be sitting far away from the screen, try to stick with plain fonts like Arial and Times New Roman for the body text.

✦ **Text color:** Go for contrast. Try light text on a dark background. My personal favorite for 35mm slides is bright yellow text on a navy blue background.

✦ **Background color:** Keep it dark; (but not black). Light colors make the screen too bright. Dark blue, dark green, and dark purple are all good choices. Stick with solid backgrounds to compensate for any image distortion on-screen. (Don't attempt patterned, shaded, or clip art backgrounds.)

✦ **Content:** You can use any combination of text and graphics with success, but it has to be static. Animations and transitions don't work with 35mm slides. For example, if you have a bulleted list, don't try to build the bulleted list one bullet at a time from slide to slide, as you learned in Chapter 22. It looks awkward.

Computer-driven presentations

If you are lucky enough to have access to a computer-based presentation system, you can show your slides on a PC monitor or TV screen. Some large meeting facilities even have projection TVs that let you project the image onto very large screens. Presenting from a computer is definitely the way to go if it's available because you have all of PowerPoint's presentation controls at hand, as you learned in Chapter 25. You also don't have to print, convert, or otherwise prepare your slides individually, because you can present from a single PowerPoint file.

Here are some guidelines for formatting for this medium:

✦ **Fonts:** The image on a computer screen is usually nice and sharp, so you can use any fonts you want. Try to test on the computer you'll be presenting from first, though, as some fonts may look more jagged than others. If you are presenting to a large group on a small screen, make sure you keep all the lettering rather large. Also make sure that the font you've chosen will be available on the show computer; if it's not there, your text and bullets may not look the way you anticipated.

✦ **Text color:** As with 35mm slides, go for contrast. Both dark text on a light background and light text on a dark background work well.

✦ **Background color:** Dark backgrounds are good, like dark blue, green, or purple, if the room's not too dark. Light backgrounds can add ambient light to the room, which can sometimes be helpful. You are also free to use gradients, shading, patterns, pictures, and other special backgrounds because all of these show up nicely on most monitors.

✦ **Content:** You can go all out with your content. Not only can you include both text and graphics, but also animations, transitions, sounds, and videos.

Strategies for Avoiding Information Overload

When presenting, you want to give the audience exactly the information they need and no more. You don't want them to leave clutching their heads saying, "Wow, that was too much to absorb!" But neither do you want them to leave saying, "What a waste of time!"

So, suppose you have a great deal of information that you need to convey to the audience in a very short time. You want to make sure they absorb it all without feeling overwhelmed. Here are a few ideas to help you accomplish that goal:

✦ *Analyze your presentation closely before you give it to make sure that only the essential topics are covered.* By trimming some nonessential topics, you make more room to cover the important themes in enough detail.

✦ *Don't try to cram every detail on your slides.* Use the slides for general talking points, and then fill in the discussion with your speech.

✦ *Provide detailed handouts that elaborate on your slides,* and make sure the audience receives them at the beginning of the presentation. Then, refer to the handouts throughout the presentation, letting them know that they can read all the details later. See Chapter 24.

✦ *Summarize at the end of the presentation with a few simple slides* that contain bullet points outlining what the audience should have learned.

Ten Qualities of an Effective Presentation

See how many of these qualities you can incorporate into your own presentation. An effective slide show:

1. Uses the right PowerPoint design, with colors and fonts chosen to reinforce the message of the presentation.

2. Is designed and formatted appropriately for the audience and the medium. Refer to Chapter 5 for planning help.

3. Is tightly focused on its subject, with extraneous facts trimmed away or hidden for backup use. See Chapter 26.

4. Includes the right amount of text on each slide, without overcrowding. See Chapter 7.

5. Uses artwork purposefully to convey information and create an overall visual impression. See Chapters 14 and 15.

6. Uses charts rather than raw columns of numbers to present financial or numeric information. See Chapter 16.

7. Employs sound and video to create interest where needed, but does not allow the effects to dominate the show. See Chapters 20 and 21.

8. Uses animations and transitions if appropriate for the audience and message, but does not allow them to dominate. See Chapter 22.

9. Offers the audience handouts that contain the information they will want to take with them. See Chapter 24.

10. Leaves time at the end for a question-and-answer session so the audience members can clarify any points they were confused about.

How to Be a Dynamic Speaker

No miracle cures here—some people are naturally better, more interesting speakers than others. But there are definite steps that all speakers can take to stack the odds in their favor when it comes to giving a successful live presentation. In the following sections, I tell you about some of them.

Choosing and arranging the room

If you have any say in it, make sure you get an appropriate size room for the presentation. A too-small room makes people feel uncomfortable and crowded, whereas a too-large one can create a false formality and distance that can cause people to lose focus easily. You also don't want to have to shout to be heard.

Caution

Along the lines of not shouting, make sure there is a working sound system, with microphone and amplifier available if necessary. Check this detail a few days ahead of time, if possible, to avoid scrambling for one at the last minute.

Next, make sure tables and chairs are set up appropriately. Figures 32-1 through 32-4 illustrate several setups, each appropriate for a certain kind of presentation:

✦ For a classroom setting where the attendees will take lots of notes, give them something to write on, as in Figure 32-1. This arrangement works well when the audience will be listening to and interacting with you, but not with one another.

✦ If you are giving a speech and the audience is not expected to take notes, consider an auditorium setup, as in Figure 32-2. This arrangement is also good for fitting a lot of people into a small room. (This is also known as theater-style seating.)

✦ If you want the audience to interact in small groups, set up groups where people can see each other and still see you, too. Figure 32-3 shows a small-group arrangement.

✦ To make it easier for the entire group to interact with one another as a whole, use a U-shape, as in Figure 32-4.

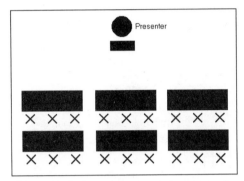

Figure 32-1: In a classroom arrangement, each audience member has plenty of room to write and work.

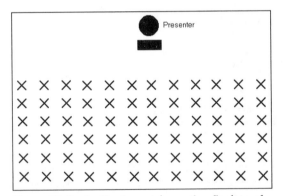

Figure 32-2: Auditorium-style seating fits lots of people into a small space; it's great for large company meetings.

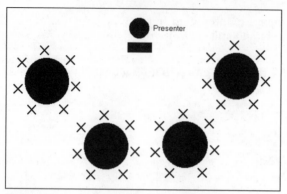

Figure 32-3: Having small groups clustered around tables encourages discussion and works well for presentations incorporating hands-on activities.

Figure 32-4: Arrange the room in a U-shape if you want participants to have discussions as a large group.

What to wear

The outfit you choose for the presentation should depend on the expectations of the audience and the message you want to send to them. Before you decide what to wear, ask yourself, "What will the audience be wearing?" Choose one of these classifications:

✦ **Very informal:** Jeans, shorts, T-shirts

✦ **Informal:** Nice jeans, polo shirts

✦ **Business casual:** Dress slacks and oxfords, with or without a tie, for men; dress slacks or a skirt and a dressy casual shirt (sweater, silk blouse, vest) for women

✦ **Business:** Slacks and a shirt and tie, with or without a jacket for men; dress or skirt (blazer optional) for women

✦ **Business formal:** Suit and tie for men; suit or conservative dress for women

Then, shape your own choice depending on the feeling you want to convey. To convey authority, dress one level above your audience. Use this dress any time your audience does not know who you are and you need to establish yourself as the leader or the expert. (Most teachers fall into this category.) For example, if your audience is dressed informally, you wear a dress shirt and tie (for men) or a skirt and sweater (for women). (If you're female and will be seated on a stage, you might want pants or a very long skirt.) Try not to dress more than two levels above your audience, though; it makes them feel intimidated. For example, if you are presenting to factory workers dressed in very informal clothing, you should not wear a business suit.

To convey teamwork and approachability, dress at the same level as the audience or slightly (no more than one level) above. For example, if you are a CEO visiting a factory that you manage, the workers already know you are authoritative; you don't have to prove this. Instead, you want to appear approachable, so if they are wearing informal clothing, you might wear dress slacks and a dress shirt (but no tie) for a man, or slacks and a sweater for a woman.

Avoid dressing below the audience's level. This is almost never a good idea. If you do not know what the audience will be wearing, err on the side of formality. It is better to look a little stiff than it is to look less professional than your audience.

Keeping the audience interested

This is an age-old question: How do you keep the audience's attention? There is no one sure-fire trick, but this section includes some hints that you can pick and choose as appropriate for your situation.

Public speaking tips

Consider these speech techniques:

✦ *Plant your feet firmly; don't pace.* Pacing looks like nervousness, and people have to work to follow you with their eyes. But keep your upper body mobile; don't be afraid to use arm gestures.

✦ *Use gestures to support your voice.* If you are talking about three points, hold up fingers to illustrate one, two, and three points. If you are talking about bringing things together, bring your hands together in front of you to illustrate. Don't freeze your hands at your sides.

✦ *Don't memorize your speech.* If someone asks a question, it will throw you off and you'll forget where you were.

✦ *Conversely, don't read the speech word for word from your notes.* Notes should contain keywords and facts, but not the actual words that you will say.

✦ *Don't talk with your face in your notes.* Make eye contact with an audience member before you begin speaking.

✦ *Pick a few people in the audience, in different places in the room, and make direct eye contact with each of them, in turn, as you speak.* Talk directly to a single person for the duration of the point you are making and then move on. And don't forget to smile!

✦ *Don't be afraid to pause.* Speaking slowly, with pauses to look at your notes, is much more preferable than rushing through the presentation. Keep in mind that pauses that might seem very long to you really aren't.

✦ *Don't stare at or read your slides.* Focus your attention on your audience, and pay as little attention to the support materials as possible as you speak. You want to engage directly with your audience to deliver your message in your own words.

✦ *Emphasize verbs and action words in your presentation.* Remember that the verb is the most powerful element in the sentence.

Content tips

Consider these content techniques:

✦ If the audience is not in a hurry and you are not rushed for time in your presentation, start with some kind of icebreaker, like an anecdote or joke.

Caution

Be careful with humor. Analyze the joke you plan to tell from all angles, making very sure it will not offend any race, ethnic group, gender, sexual orientation, or class of workers. It is *much* worse to tell a joke that hurts someone's feelings — even one person — than it is to tell none at all.

✦ Include the audience in interactive exercises that help firm up their understanding of the topic.

✦ Ask questions to see whether the audience understood you, and give out small prizes to the people who give correct answers. Nothing energizes an audience into participation more than prizes, even if they are cheap giveaways like key chains and bandannas.

✦ If possible, split the presentation into two or more sessions, with a short break and question-and-answer period between each session.

✦ During the Q&A portion, turn off the slide projector, overhead, or computer screen so people will focus on you and on the question, not on the previous slide. If turning off the equipment isn't practical, consider inserting a simple Q&A Session title slide or a blank slide to be shown during the Q&A.

Managing stage fright

Even if you're comfortable with the PowerPoint slides you've created, you still might be a little nervous about the actual speech you're going to give. And that's normal. A study a few years ago showed that public speaking is the number-one fear among businesspeople. Fear of death came in second. That should tell you something.

It's okay to be a little bit nervous because it gives you extra energy and an edge that can actually make your presentation better. But if you're too nervous, it can make you seem less credible.

One way to overcome stage fright is to stop focusing on yourself, and instead focus on your audience. Ask yourself what the audience needs and how you are going to supply that need. Become their caretaker. Dedicate yourself to making the audience understand you. The more you think of others, the less you think of yourself.

Summary

This chapter had little to do with PowerPoint per se, but lots to do with the successful presentations you will make using your PowerPoint slides as a tool. The information you learned here can help a beginning presenter look more experienced, or help an old pro polish his or her skills to perfection.

In the next chapter, you get back into PowerPoint and learn about one of the most improved features in PowerPoint 2003: team collaboration.

✦   ✦   ✦

Team Collaboration

Few people these days create a presentation with no input or feedback from another living soul. Presentations normally go through review cycle upon review cycle, and everybody gets to add his or her two cents about how to make the presentation slides stronger and more meaningful.

The old way of reviewing was to print out and distribute hard copies of a presentation and let everyone mark them up by hand. Then some poor assistant or junior executive would have to decipher all the handwritten notes (some of them directly conflicting with others!) and make the changes in PowerPoint.

Fortunately, PowerPoint 2003 offers many more appealing options for soliciting and receiving feedback on a presentation, as you learn in this chapter.

Sharing Your Presentation File on a LAN

If your company has a local area network (LAN), you can copy the presentation file to a drive that everyone can access and let whoever is interested in seeing it take a look. Interested people can then either copy the presentation to their own PCs or view it directly from the network.

If not everyone has PowerPoint installed on their PCs, you might also want to place the PowerPoint Viewer program on the network, so people without PowerPoint can review the show. You learned about the PowerPoint Viewer in Chapters 25 and 30.

Caution

Make sure you copy the presentation file to the network, rather than moving it there. That way, if something happens to the networked copy or the whole network server goes down, you still have access to your presentation. You might even want to rename the copy on the server so you can tell, at a glance, which is the original version.

Sharing the presentation locally

In a large company, the network includes one or more servers, which are computers that do nothing except run the network and serve up common files that multiple people need. If your network includes a server, one of its hard disks is probably the best place to copy your presentation file. That's because everyone on the network already has access to the server, so no special setup is necessary. See your network administrator for details.

However, if your company uses peer-to-peer networking, there may not be a server to which you can copy the presentation. In that case, you must make one or more folders on your own hard disk accessible to other network users.

Sharing in Windows 2000 or XP

If you have Windows 2000 or XP (and you probably do, because PowerPoint 2003 won't run on earlier Windows versions), here's what you need to do to share a folder on your PC.

First open the list of network connections:

✦ **In Windows 2000,** choose Start ⇨ Settings ⇨ Network and Dial-Up Connections.

✦ **In Windows XP,** open Network Connections from the Control Panel.

Then right-click the LAN connection and choose Properties, and make sure that File and Printer Sharing for Microsoft Networks is one of the installed services. See Figure 33-1. If it isn't, add it with the Install button. Then close all open dialog boxes.

Next, share the folder:

✦ **In Windows 2000,** right-click the folder and choose Sharing. Select the Share This Folder option button, and enter a Share Name. See Figure 33-2. The default is for others to have full access; if you want to change that, click the Permissions button and clear the Full Control and Change check boxes. Then close all open dialog boxes.

✦ **In Windows XP,** right-click the folder and choose Sharing and Security. Mark the Share This Folder on the Network check box. Enter a Share Name for the folder. See Figure 33-3. If others should be able to make changes, mark the Allow Network Users to Change My Files check box. Then click OK.

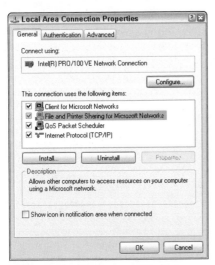

Figure 33-1: Make sure File and Printer Sharing is installed for the LAN connection.

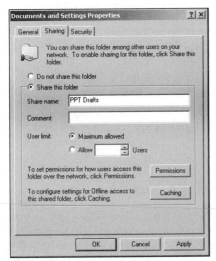

Figure 33-2: Share a folder in Windows 2000.

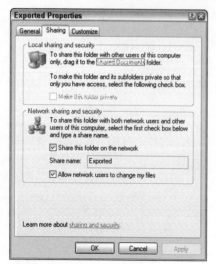

Figure 33-3: Share a folder in Windows XP.

Posting a presentation to an Exchange folder

If your company uses a Microsoft Exchange server to share files, you can easily post a PowerPoint presentation there. (You can ignore this procedure if your company doesn't use Exchange.) To do so, follow these steps:

1. Open the presentation in PowerPoint.

2. Choose File ⇨ Send To ⇨ Exchange Folder. A list of folders appears.

3. Choose the folder you want to post the presentation to.

4. Click OK.

Mailing a Presentation via E-Mail

You can attach a PowerPoint presentation file to an e-mail message, just as you can attach any other file. If you use Outlook, for example, you can click the Insert File button on the toolbar to attach a file to an e-mail message you are creating. See Figure 33-4.

To send a presentation from PowerPoint, choose File ⇨ Send To and then choose Mail Recipient (For Review) or Mail Recipient (As Attachment).

Insert File button   Attached file

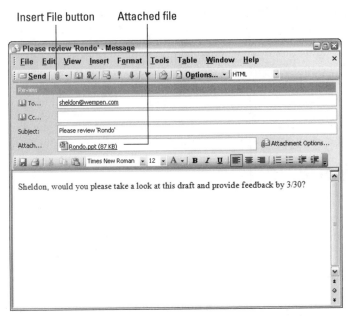

Figure 33-4: Most e-mail programs, including Outlook, let you attach files to send along with e-mail messages.

Both of these commands compose an e-mail message with the presentation file as an attachment. The differences are as follows:

✦ The For Review command begins composing the message in Outlook with "Please Review {presentation name}" as the subject, and with a message already filled into the body. The As Attachment command makes the subject the presentation name by itself and does not fill in a default body message.

✦ The For Review version of the attachment is a slightly larger file, containing instructions for collecting the reviewers' responses for later merging back into the original file.

✦ The For Review command opens a new Outlook message with HTML as the message formatting. The As Attachment command starts the new message in plain text format.

Expert Tip   If you use For Review, you can then click the Attachment Options in the Outlook message composition window and then click Live Attachments. A copy of the attached file is then saved in a team workspace. Recipients of the message are made members of that workspace automatically, and they can either open the attachment as their own copy or they can follow a link in the message to the workspace copy.

Note   You can set up Outlook so that As Attachment works just like For Review. (It's questionable whether you would *want* to do this, however, as it's nice to have the flexibility to choose.) In Outlook, choose Tools ➪ Options, and click the E-mail Options button on the Preferences tab. In the dialog box that appears, click Advanced E-mail Options. Then in the dialog box that appears next, mark the Add properties to attachments to enable Reply with Changes checkbox.

Sharing a Presentation in a Document Workspace

A *document workspace* is a common accessible location where you store files that you want to make available to other people on a team. As a team you can then make edits to the documents, review each other's changes, deal with to-do items, retrieve contact information for one another, and more.

Document workspaces are based on *SharePoint Team Services (STS),* a Microsoft server technology that creates and maintains team spaces. You can log into an STS site from outside of Office applications, and upload, download, and manage shared files that way, but you can also do it from within most Microsoft Office applications.

To create a new workspace for the document, you must have access to an STS server. If you do, choose Tools ➪ Shared Workspace and then enter a name for the document workspace and the address to the server on which you will store it. See Figure 33-5.

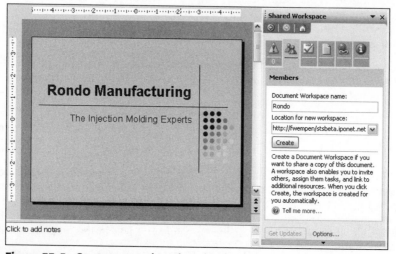

Figure 33-5: Create a new shared workspace for a presentation on a SharePoint Team Services server.

Caution If you get an error about the site being a restricted or non-trusted site, set it up as a trusted site in the Internet Options (from Internet Explorer, choose Tools ➪ Internet Options).

When a document with a shared workspace is open, you can access information about the workspace from the Shared Workspace task pane, shown in Figure 33-6. Click a tab to see the Status, Members, Documents, Links, and so on.

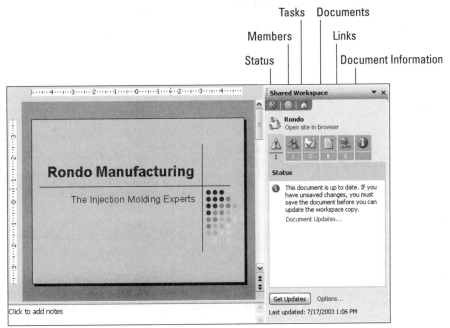

Figure 33-6: Information about the shared workspace is available through the Shared Workspace task pane.

You can also log into a SharePoint Team Services Web site independently of the application, and then locate the file you want and click its hyperlink to open it. Notice in Figure 33-6, the Open Site in Browser hyperlink. This will take you to the site. For example, in Figure 33-7, I'm displaying my SharePoint Team Services list of shared documents, and am ready to open my Rondo Manufacturing presentation from there.

 Expert Tip When you work with a document from a shared workspace, some extra commands become available. For example, you'll find a Check Out command on the File menu that enables you to "check out" the document so that nobody else can edit it until you are finished. This prevents two people from making changes to the same document at the same time. You'll also find a Versions command on the File menu, from which you can select which version of the presentation to open. The latter works only if you enable version support for the document library from within the SharePoint Team Services site administration.

Click to open in PowerPoint

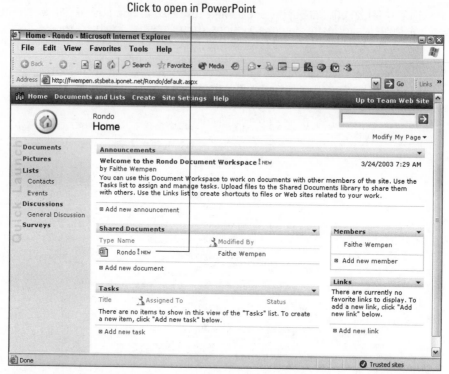

Figure 33-7: Shared documents may be accessed from the Web site as well as from within PowerPoint.

STS is a powerful application for sharing all kinds of files, not just PowerPoint. There is much more to it than can be covered in this chapter's overview of sharing techniques. Explore its features on your own if you have an STS server available.

Working with Comments

As you are soliciting feedback from reviewers, you might not want them to make changes directly to the presentation. Instead, you might request that they use the Comments feature to provide their feedback and leave the actual changes to you.

Comments are like yellow sticky-notes that people reviewing the presentation can add, letting you know what they think about individual slides. You can see them in Normal view, but they don't show up in Slide Show view.

Adding a comment

Here are the steps for adding a comment:

1. Display the slide on which you want to add a comment.

2. Choose Insert ⇨ Comment, or click the New Comment button on the Reviewing toolbar. A yellow box appears with your name in it.

3. Type your comment, as in Figure 33-8. When you are finished typing, click outside the comment box.

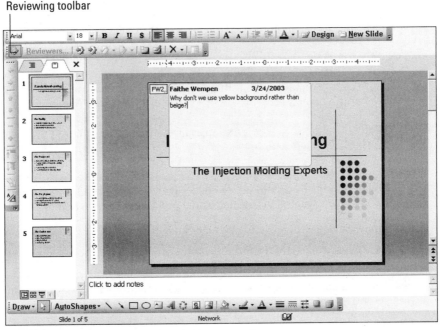

Figure 33-8: Type a comment in the comment box.

The comment floats on the slide, just like any other object. When you click away from it, it disappears except for the small box with your initials and the comment number. For example, in Figure 33-8, it's FW2. To redisplay the full comment, click the little box. (Double-click if you want to re-open it and add text.)

Moving, editing, and deleting comments

Figure 33-8 shows the Reviewing toolbar, which appears whenever you display or work with comments. Figure 33-9 shows it again, with the buttons labeled that pertain to comments. The other buttons, unavailable in Figure 33-9, are used for reviewing changes, as you will see later in this chapter.

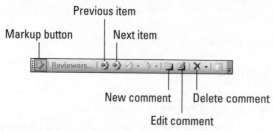

Figure 33-9 labels:
Previous item
Markup button
Next item
New comment
Delete comment
Edit comment

Figure 33-9: The Reviewing toolbar facilitates working with comments.

You can reposition a comment on the slide by dragging its box around. You might want to place a comment next to the item to which it pertains.

To edit a comment, double-click it to open it (or select it and click the Edit Comment button on the Reviewing toolbar) and then make your changes. If you edit someone else's comment, the initials change to your own and you become the "owner" of the comment.

To delete a comment, select it and press Delete (or click the Delete Comment button on the Reviewing toolbar).

You don't have to delete a comment in order to get it off the screen, however. To temporarily hide all comments, choose View ➪ Markup or click the Markup button on the Reviewing toolbar. (Use that same command to turn them back on again.)

Reviewing comments

When you get a presentation back from a reviewer or from multiple reviewers, there will likely be many comments. (Different users' comments show up in different colors so you can more easily distinguish them.)

You can page through the slides one by one, looking for comments, or you can use the Next Comment and Previous Comment buttons on the Reviewing toolbar to move quickly to the next or previous slide that contains a comment.

Incorporating Changes from Reviewers

Suppose you distribute your presentation to several people for review. One way is to use the File ➪ Send To ➪ E-mail Recipient (For Review), as you learned earlier in the chapter. You can also simply send it as a normal e-mail attachment to someone, or even distribute it on a disk.

Now you've received two copies back from two different people. Each has made some changes to the presentation. How do you merge all those changes back into your original and sort them out? You do so using the Reviewing feature.

Merging review revisions

When you receive a revised presentation back via Outlook, and you open it from there, you might see a message asking whether you want to merge the changes with your original. If you get that, click Yes.

If you don't get that message for some reason, you can do the same thing with the Compare and Merge feature within PowerPoint:

1. Start with the original presentation file open in PowerPoint.

2. Choose Tools ⇨ Compare and Merge Presentations. A Choose Files to Merge with Current Presentation dialog box opens. See Figure 33-10.

3. Select the presentation file(s) to merge and then click Merge.

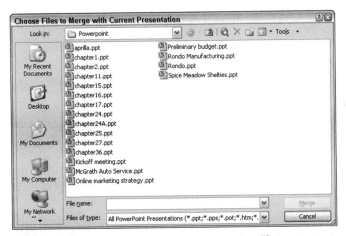

Figure 33-10: Select one or more presentation files to merge with the original.

Note   If all the revised copies still have the same filename, you will not be able to store them in the same folder with one another, so you will not be able to select them all in Step 3. Instead choose one and click Merge, and then repeat Steps 2 and 3 for the next one from a different location.

Accepting or rejecting revisions

The important thing to know about revisions is that they are not accepted automatically. By default they do not appear at all, in fact. Your original presentation remains intact. When you review the revisions, you have the opportunity to individually view and select the revisions you want to apply. Any you do not choose are discarded.

To accept or reject changes:

1. Display a slide that contains revisions. You can tell because information about the revision appears in the Revisions Pane.

2. Click the Revision icon on the slide to see a detailed list of the revisions for that slide.

3. Mark the check boxes for the revisions you want to implement. When you mark one, its change shows on the current slide. See Figure 33-11.

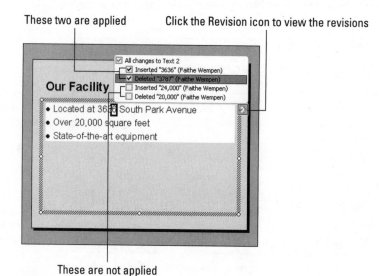

Figure 33-11: Accept or reject changes in the Revisions task pane.

4. To move to the next slide, click the Next button at the bottom of the Revisions pane or simply click a different slide in the Slides pane.

Using the Reviewing toolbar for revisions

As you are reviewing the revisions, the Reviewing toolbar is active. Figure 33-12 shows some of the buttons that come in handy during this phase.

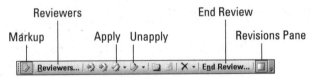

Figure 33-12: Some buttons on the Reviewing toolbar are active only when working with revisions.

- ✦ **Markup:** Toggles all markup on/off, including both revision icons and comments.
- ✦ **Apply:** Applies all revisions to either the current slide or to the entire presentation. (Open its drop-down list to choose which.)
- ✦ **Unapply:** Removes all revisions from either the current slide or from the entire slide. (Again, open its drop-down list to choose which.)
- ✦ **End Review:** Completes the review process, removing all unapplied revisions. Don't do this until you are completely finished reviewing.
- ✦ **Revisions Pane:** Toggles the Revisions Pane on/off.

Finishing a review of revisions

When you have accepted all the revisions that you want, you can exit from the Compare and Merge mode by clicking the End Review button on the Reviewing toolbar. A warning will appear; click Yes. Now you're back to normal, and the Reviewing toolbar disappears.

Live Collaboration with NetMeeting

PowerPoint 2003 supports NetMeeting, an application that you can use to collaborate in real-time with other people online. It includes application sharing, a "whiteboard" for drawing, a chat feature, and other handy activities.

In the past, Microsoft provided Internet Locator Service (ILS) public servers that you could use for this, but nowadays Microsoft is encouraging everyone to move to Windows Messenger instead, so they have discontinued support of public ILS servers. Therefore if you want to use NetMeeting from PowerPoint, you must access your company's own ILS server or a third-party ILS server.

This chapter does not delve into NetMeeting specifics because it's likely that most people will use Windows Messenger instead. However, if you are interested in exploring NetMeeting on your own, choose Tools ➪ Online Collaboration ➪ Meet Now.

Live Collaboration with Windows Messenger

Windows Messenger is a real-time chat program that comes free with Windows XP. You can also download it for free from Microsoft for any older 32-bit version of Windows.

Not only does Windows Messenger provide a means of chatting (that is, typing back and forth in real-time), but it also allows you to share applications over the Internet. That's where its usefulness for PowerPoint comes in. If all the meeting participants are Windows Messenger users, you can employ Windows Messenger to allow everyone to see and work with your copy of PowerPoint. You can then maintain a separate chat window where you and the other participants discuss the draft presentation.

Running Windows Messenger

To run Windows Messenger, choose it from the Start ⇨ All Programs menu. Some earlier versions were called MSN Messenger rather than Windows Messenger; it's the same thing.

To use Windows Messenger, you need a Microsoft .NET Passport. This is simple and free to obtain. The first time you try to log into Windows Messenger, a wizard will walk you through the process.

You also should have all the meeting participants added to your Contacts list. To add a contact, click Add Contact in the Windows Messenger window (see Figure 33-13) and follow the prompts in the wizard.

Figure 33-13: Add the meeting participants to your Contacts list if needed, so you can then invite them to share applications with you.

Expert Tip   Actually having all the participants added to your Contacts list is not an absolute requirement. When selecting people with whom to share applications, you'll find an Other tab; click it and you can enter an e-mail address of a new contact. The new person must be a member of the Microsoft .NET Messenger service.

Inviting someone to share PowerPoint

First, start PowerPoint and open the presentation you want to collaborate on. Then do the following to invite someone else to see it:

1. From Windows Messenger, choose Actions ⇨ Start Application Sharing. A list appears of your contacts who are online. See Figure 33-14.

2. Click the contact with whom you want to share and then click OK.

Figure 33-14: Select the online contact with whom you want to share an application.

A Conversation window appears on your screen. At the same time, a Conversation window appears on the other person's PC, with hyperlinks to Accept or Decline your request. See Figure 33-15. He or she clicks Accept to begin the application sharing.

3. A Sharing box appears on your PC's screen. Click PowerPoint and then click Share. See Figure 33-16.

Also appearing on your screen at this point are the Sharing Session toolbar and the conversation window, both also shown in Figure 33-16. You can click the App Sharing button at any time to reopen the Sharing dialog box. The Close button closes the application sharing session. The Whiteboard button opens the Whiteboard application, discussed later in this chapter.

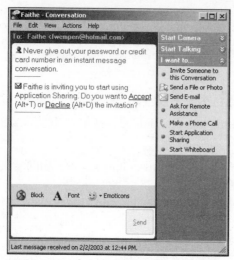

Figure 33-15: This is what the other person sees when you request an application sharing session.

Reopens Sharing dialog box   Opens Whiteboard   Closes Sharing session   Select application to Share

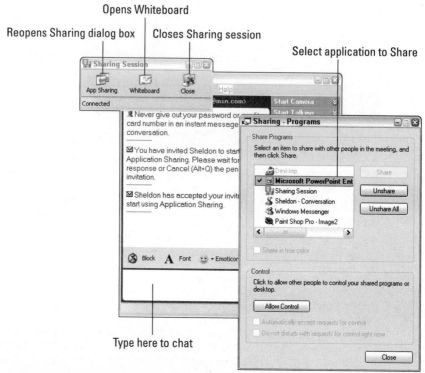

Type here to chat

Figure 33-16: Select the application to share (in this case PowerPoint).

4. Now restore the PowerPoint window and begin working in PowerPoint. The person at the other end of the sharing connection will see everything you do in a Programs window. Figure 33-17 shows what they see. If you share more than one application, they see more than one window.

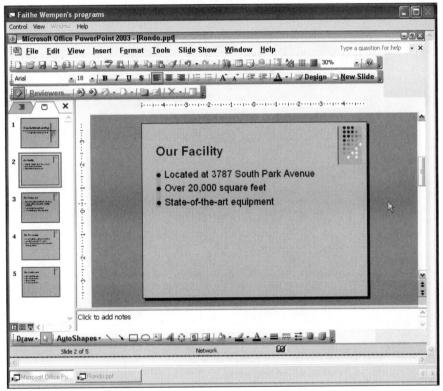

Figure 33-17: This is what the other person sees while you are sharing an application.

5. Use the whiteboard and the Conversation window as needed to communicate. You can also give the other person control of PowerPoint temporarily, as described in the following section.

6. When you are finished, click the Close button on the Sharing Session toolbar to end the application sharing.

Giving another participant control

Only one person can have control of the meeting at a time. By default, this is the person who initiated the meeting. The person who has control can change views, show the presentation in Slide Show view, advance the slides, skip to other slides, and so on. Everyone else can only watch.

If you are holding a collaborative session, you might want to pass control to another meeting participant so he or she can make a point or show an example. You can always take control back later, as the meeting leader.

To let someone else control the presentation (temporarily), follow these steps:

1. On the Sharing Session toolbar, click the App Sharing button to reopen the Sharing dialog box (Figure 33-16).

2. Click the application to select it, and then click the Allow Control button. The Control section changes to the commands shown in Figure 33-18.

Figure 33-18: When you allow control for an application, choices for administering that control appear.

3. Mark either of the two check boxes as desired:

   a. **Automatically Accept Requests for Control:** This bypasses the confirmation message that would normally appear on your screen when a participant requests control.

   b. **Do Not Disturb with Requests for Control Right Now:** This prevents others from requesting control (temporarily).

4. Click Close. Now you are ready to share control of the application.

Note To regain control at any time, the meeting leader can press Esc. This doesn't work for other meeting participants; they must wait until whoever is in control has ceded it before jumping in. If you are eager to gain control, you can make a comment to that effect using the Chat window, described in the following section.

Taking control as a participant

Someone else can take control on his or her own PC by following these steps:

1. Double-click the PowerPoint screen being displayed, or choose Control ⇨ Take Control. Then wait for the person currently in control to respond to a confirmation box that appears on his or her screen.

2. Once you are granted control, your mouse pointer begins working in the shared application box. Make any edits you like.

3. When you are ready to cede control to some other participant, choose Control ⇨ Release Control.

Chatting with other participants

The Conversation window is the main means of communication among participants. It appears initially when you are setting up the application sharing; it is where the Accept and Decline hyperlinks appear when you invite someone to application sharing.

You can chat by typing in this same window at any time during the application sharing. See Figure 33-19. Just type in the bottom box and then press Enter to send your message.

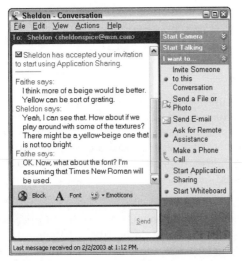

Figure 33-19: Participants communicate through the Chat window.

Caution   Sometimes when you start chatting after sharing applications, Windows Messenger will log you off and you'll have to log back on again.

Using the Whiteboard

The Whiteboard is a simple paint program that participants can use to share conceptual drawings with one another during the meeting.

To use the whiteboard, click the Whiteboard button on the Sharing Session toolbar. A Whiteboard window appears. It looks a lot like the Paint program that comes with Windows, but has some additional features. See Figure 33-20.

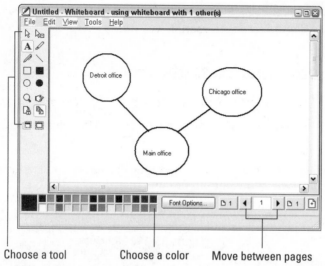

Choose a tool   Choose a color   Move between pages

Figure 33-20: Use the Whiteboard program to draw conceptual diagrams during a meeting.

The Whiteboard is its own application, and there isn't space to cover it fully in this book. However, it is extremely intuitive to use, and you should not have any trouble with it. Select a tool from the palette on the left, and if applicable, select a line thickness from the thicknesses below the tools. Then, select a color from the color palette at the bottom. Finally, drag the mouse on the drawing area to create lines, shapes, text, or whatever.

For example, in Figure 33-20, I have drawn a diagram using three ovals and two straight lines. Then I used the Text tool (A) to type some descriptions of the ovals.

You can have multiple pages of drawings and notes; to move to the next page, click the right arrow button in the bottom-right corner.

Ending an application sharing session

To end a session, you simply click the Close button on the Sharing Session toolbar.

 Expert Tip If you used the Whiteboard during the session, a message appears asking whether you want to save your Whiteboard contents when you close the session. Click Yes or No. If you choose Yes, it'll be saved in Whiteboard (.NMW) format. You can reopen it later through Windows Messenger. From Windows Messenger, choose Actions ⇨ Start Whiteboard, and then within Whiteboard choose File ⇨ Open.

The Conversation window remains open after you terminate the sharing session. You can save the chat text from the Conversation window by choosing File ⇨ Save. It's saved in Text (.TXT) format.

There's a lot more you can do with Windows Messenger than has been covered in this brief overview in this chapter. In addition, Microsoft is always updating that program, so by the time you read this, Windows Messenger may look slightly different and have more features than you saw here.

Summary

In this chapter you learned about many different ways of collaborating with other people on a draft presentation. You learned how to e-mail presentation files, how to incorporate review feedback with Compare and Merge, and how to hold online meetings with Windows Messenger where you share control of a single copy of PowerPoint.

In the next chapter, you will explore the speech and handwriting recognition features of PowerPoint, two alternative ways of inputting data.

✦　　✦　　✦

Using Speech and Handwriting Recognition Tools

PowerPoint, like all Office 2003 applications, supports speech recognition and handwriting recognition as alternative methods of inputting your data. Although for most people this is just a novelty, some people who have a hard time typing might find it very useful! This chapter takes a quick look at those features, including how to set them up and use them within PowerPoint.

What Is Speech Recognition?

Speech recognition occurs when you talk into a microphone and the computer does something because of it. That "something" can be text entry or command issuance. Just like on *Star Trek!*

Caution
Many people approach speech recognition with high hopes, only to give up on it after an hour or so. This happens for several reasons. One is that in order for it to work with maximum accuracy, you must train the software with your own voice. The more you train it, the more accurate it gets. Thorough training can take hours. The second reason is that for maximum accuracy you need a good-quality sound card and microphone (preferably one with a headset), and most people have the cheap kinds that don't work so well. Finally, the sad truth is that speech recognition is never 100% accurate. There will always be a few errors to correct. That's just the way it is. A program that is 99% accurate is still going to mess up one word out of 100.

To make the Speech feature work (or work well!), you need the following:

✦ A good-quality headset microphone with adjustable recording volume. Steer clear of the cheap ones. It really does make a difference. USB interface is recommended.

✦ A good-quality PCI sound card.

✦ At least 128MB of RAM.

✦ At least a 400MHz CPU.

✦ Windows 2000 with Service Pack 3 installed, or Windows XP.

Setting Up Speech Recognition

The first time you use Speech in an Office application, you are prompted to work through a wizard that helps you train it to your voice. This takes about 15 minutes, but you have to do it only once for all Office applications combined.

To start the process, do the following:

1. Connect your microphone to the PC, either through the sound card or via USB interface, depending on the microphone.

2. In PowerPoint, choose Tools ➪ Speech. An introductory box appears explaining that you need to set it up. Click Next.

Note   If you do not have a Speech option on the Tools menu in PowerPoint, set up the speech recognition from inside Microsoft Word instead. Use the same command there: Tools ➪ Speech.

3. Read the information about the Microphone Wizard that appears, and adjust your microphone as needed. Then click Next.

4. Read the on-screen sentence into the microphone. See Figure 34-1. The microphone volume is automatically adjusted as you read. When it is finished, a message appears to that effect. Click Next.

5. Next, adjust the positioning of the microphone in relation to your mouth. Read the on-screen sentence. See Figure 34-2. It will then be played back to you through your speakers. Adjust your microphone in relation to your face and try again until you don't hear any puffs of air in your recording. Then click Finish.

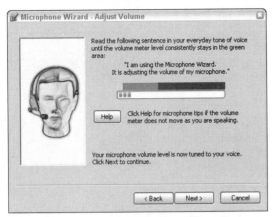

Figure 34-1: Allow the wizard to adjust the microphone volume level.

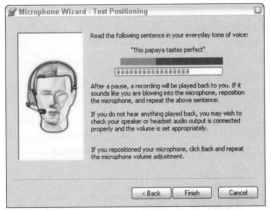

Figure 34-2: Use this sentence recording and playback to determine the optimal physical position for the microphone.

6. An information screen appears about training the voice recognition software. Read the information and then click Next.

7. More information about training appears. Read it and click Next again.

8. Read the text that appears into the microphone. As a word is recognized, it becomes highlighted with gray. See Figure 34-3. Continue through multiple screens of text.

9. When you finish the initial training, a box will report that you are done. Click Finish.

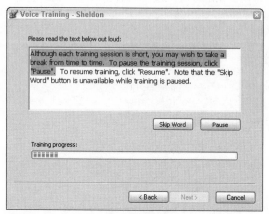

Figure 34-3: Read aloud the text that appears on-screen to help train the voice-recognition software to recognize your voice.

Now you are ready to start using speech recognition in PowerPoint (and in other Office applications too!) If you want to do more training to make it even more accurate, see "Performing additional voice training" later in the chapter.

Managing the Language Bar

The Language bar is a floating toolbar that works across all the Office 2003 applications. Once you enable speech recognition, it's always on-screen unless you turn it off. Figure 34-4 shows it.

Figure 34-4: The Language bar provides a quick entry into the speech recognition feature at any time.

There are two ways to get the Language bar off your screen if it annoys you. One is to minimize it, so that it becomes an icon in the notification area. The other is to close it completely.

To minimize it, right-click it and choose Minimize. When you do so, it becomes an icon in the notification area and an information box appears letting you know how to access it again. (Just double-click its icon in the notification area to get it back.)

To close it, right-click it and choose Close the Language Bar.

When you close the Language bar, an information box appears instructing you how to reopen it. The instructions provided describe the long way around, however. A much easier way to get the Language bar back is to choose Tools ⇨ Speech from within PowerPoint or any other supported Office 2003 application.

Note　You might notice that sometimes the Language bar has more buttons than other times. This is a function of whether the Microphone button is selected (pressed). When Microphone is selected, the microphone is on and it is ready to accept speech input, and you get the full array of buttons on the Language bar. When the Microphone button is not selected, the speech feature is on "idle" and you see only a couple of buttons.

Using Speech Recognition in PowerPoint

There are two modes of speech recognition: Dictation and Voice Command. Dictation records your words as data in the current data file, whereas Voice Commands interprets your words as instructions to the application. For example, in Dictation mode, you might say "file" and the word file would appear on a slide in PowerPoint. In Voice Command mode, you might say "file" and the File menu would open.

Dictating text

To dictate text using the microphone, do the following:

1. On the Language toolbar, make sure Microphone and Dictation are both selected (pressed).

2. In PowerPoint, click to move the insertion point into a text box or into the Outline pane, just as if you were getting ready to type.

3. Speak clearly into the microphone in a normal volume and speed.

   • See Table 34-1 to learn how to dictate punctuation.

   • If you need to spell a word, say "Spelling Mode" and then spell the word.

   • To start a new paragraph, say, "Enter."

4. When you are finished dictating, click the Microphone button on the Language bar or say "Mic Off" to disable its input.

Table 34-1
Punctuation and Special Character Dictation

To Get This:	Say This:
Paragraph break	Enter
Tab	Tab
Backspace	Backspace
Space	Space
&	Ampersand
*	Asterisk
:	Colon
,	Comma
.	Dot or Period
!	Exclamation point
?	Question mark
;	Semicolon
\	Backslash
/	Slash
|	Vertical bar
-	Hyphen
--	Double dash
=	Equal
%	Percent
$	Dollar sign
_	Underscore
~	Tilde
...	Ellipsis
>	Greater Than
<	Less Than
^	Caret
[	Left bracket

To Get This:	Say This:
]	Right bracket
{	Left brace
}	Right brace
(	Left parenthesis
)	Right parenthesis
"	Open quote
"	Close quote
'	Open single quote
'	Close single quote

When you dictate numbers, the program automatically spells out numbers less than 20, and automatically inserts in digit format any numbers 20 or greater. It converts spoken fractions to numbers, so "one-half" becomes ½. If you want a number of less than 20 to appear as numerals, precede its dictation by "Force Num."

Adding words to the speech recognition dictionary

You'll probably get tired of spelling certain proper names and other specialized terms using the Spelling Mode command fairly quickly. A better way: add those words to the speech recognition dictionary. To do so:

1. Click the Tools button on the Language bar, and then click Add/Delete Words.

Note If the Tools button does not appear on the Language bar, click the down arrow at the far right end and choose Speech Tools from that menu to turn on the Tools button. Notice that many of the commands on this menu have check marks beside them, indicating the corresponding button appears on the Language bar. That's how you can turn them on/off there.

2. Type the word in the Word box, and then click the Record Pronunciation button. See Figure 34-5.

3. Say the word in the microphone. If the word does not immediately appear on the Dictionary list, try again — click Record Pronunciation again and then say it again.

4. Repeat Steps 2 and 3 for more words if desired; then click Close.

To delete a word from your custom dictionary, select the word and click Delete.

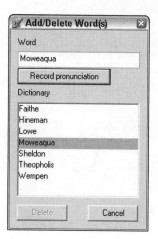

Figure 34-5: Add words to the dictionary to avoid having to re-spell them each time you use them.

Using voice commands in PowerPoint

To switch to Voice Command mode, say "voice command" or click the Voice Command button on the Language toolbar.

When you are in Voice Command mode, you can:

✦ Say the name of a toolbar button to "click" it. Find out a button's name by pointing at it to display a ToolTip.

✦ Say the name of a menu to open it.

✦ Say the name of a command on an open menu to select it. Or say "down arrow" to move the selection down the menu until you come to the command you want, and then say "Enter" to select it.

✦ Say a direction plus "arrow" to use the arrow keys. For example, "up arrow" or "left arrow."

✦ Say "page up" or "page down" to scroll.

✦ Say "right-click" to open the shortcut menu for the current object.

Setting speech recognition properties

To set the properties for speech recognition, click the Tools button on the Language toolbar and select Options. This opens the Speech Properties box, shown in Figure 34-6.

Readjusting the microphone level

To readjust the microphone, click the Configure Microphone button. This re-runs the microphone setup that you went through when you did the initial voice training.

Figure 34-6: Set speech recognition properties here.

The other button in this section, Audio Input, lets you choose between two or more microphones and fine-tune their properties.

Creating additional user profiles

If more than one person wants to use this PC with speech input, you can set up separate profiles for each person. That way, the voice recognition training isn't confused by the two different voices.

To create a new profile from the Speech Properties box, follow these steps:

1. Click New. The Profile Wizard runs.

2. Enter the name for the new profile. It might be the name of the person, for example. Then click Next.

Note After creating a new profile for another person you might want to rename the original profile (Default Speech Profile) to the name of the original user, just for clarity.

3. Follow the instructions to complete the wizard. The steps are identical to those involved in the initial setup and speech training. (See "Setting Up Speech Recognition" earlier in the chapter.)

Once you have more than one user profile, you can switch between them quickly from the Language bar. Just click the Tools button there, choose Current User, and then select the user profile.

Performing additional voice training

The more voice training you do, the more accurate the speech recognition becomes. When you have some extra time and want to work on it, follow these steps:

1. From the Language bar, choose Tools ⇨ Options. Click the Advanced Speech button.

2. Click the profile you want to train (if there is more than one) and then click Train Profile.

3. Follow the prompts that appear to do additional voice training.

Working with Handwriting

Like Speech, handwriting recognition is another data-entry method for use by people who can't (or don't like to) type.

Technically it is possible to use a normal mouse to "write," but it's not practical. Therefore handwriting recognition is really a viable feature only if you have a writing input system with a pen-like stylus. Inexpensive drawing tablets are available for PCs with a USB interface. A company called Wacom makes one for under $100. If you have a Tablet PC, writing capability is already built into the operating system through the touch-sensitive display screen using the OneNote application from Microsoft.

Using the Writing Pad

The Writing Pad lets you use either the mouse or a writing tablet to write text, which is then converted to regular text in PowerPoint (or whatever application you are using with it).

To turn on the Writing Pad, click the Handwriting button on the Language toolbar, and then on the menu that appears, select Writing Pad.

The Writing Pad window floats on top of other applications. To write in it, move the mouse pointer into the window and then hold down the left mouse button as you drag to "write." If you are using a drawing tablet, position your stylus on the pad so that the cursor is in the Writing Pad window onscreen (important!) and then write with the pen. The buttons along the left side of the Writing Pad window enable you to type special characters or enter different modes. Figure 34-7 points out some of these buttons.

Using Write Anywhere

Write Anywhere is very much like the Writing Pad, except that it's not constrained to that little Writing Pad window. This is handy for people with writing tablets because it can be difficult to write and watch the screen at the same time to make sure you are staying within the confines of a small box.

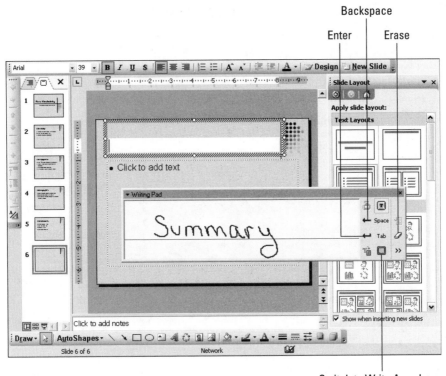

Figure 34-7: Writing some text onto a slide with the Writing Pad.

You can enter Write Anywhere by clicking the Write Anywhere button in the Writing Pad window or by clicking the Handwriting button and choosing Write Anywhere from the menu that appears. The handwriting appears briefly on the screen just as you write it, and then it is converted into typed text. In Figure 34-8, for example, I have already written *Top quality* and those words have been converted. I have just finished writing *parts* and it will be converted momentarily.

Annotating a slide during a presentation

Having a drawing tablet makes it much easier to annotate slides during a presentation. You saw in Chapter 25 how to do this with a regular mouse, and you do it the same way with a tablet:

1. During the presentation, enable one of the Pens.

2. Draw on the tablet with the stylus; whatever you draw appears on the slide as an annotation.

Toolbar   Text already converted   Text just written

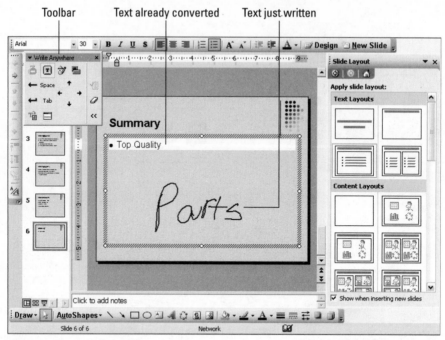

Figure 34-8: Write Anywhere frees you from the need to write within a certain area.

What about OneNote?

OneNote is a separate product from Microsoft Office, designed by Microsoft as an add-on to Windows and Office for people who use a TabletPC or a writing tablet extensively. It has much more sophisticated and flexible features than the simple handwriting tools included with Office. If your version of Office includes it, you can install it (it's on a separate CD) and use it not only in PowerPoint but throughout many different Windows applications.

Summary

This chapter explained the speech and handwriting recognition features in Office 2003 that are applicable to PowerPoint. Now you have two additional ways to enter text in your presentation files, and you can issue voice commands in PowerPoint.

Interested in fine-tuning PowerPoint? Then you'll be interested in the next chapter, which covers the options, settings, menu, and toolbar customization features that make PowerPoint so flexible.

✦   ✦   ✦

Making PowerPoint Easier to Use

This chapter focuses on tweaking PowerPoint to make it work the way you do. If you have ever said to yourself, "I wish PowerPoint would do it this way," this chapter is for you.

Changing PowerPoint's Program Options

PowerPoint contains an amazing array of customizable settings. Some of them make purely cosmetic changes, whereas others enable or disable timesaving or safety features.

In most cases throughout this book, I've been operating with the default options, and assumed that you're doing the same. If you change some of these program options, the steps in this book may not work the same way anymore. You may see more or fewer warning boxes, or the cursor might not behave the same way, or your screen might look different from the ones pictured. That's why I've saved this topic for the end of the book. Now that you understand PowerPoint, these changes won't throw you.

Here's the general procedure for changing an option:

1. Choose Tools ⇨ Options.

2. Click the tab you want to display. (See the descriptions in the following sections.)

3. Select or deselect check boxes, enter text, or choose from drop-down lists to state your preferences for a feature.

4. Click OK to apply your changes.

The program options fall into seven categories, and each has its own tab in the Options dialog box. In the following sections, I tell you about each of the categories and explain your options within each one.

View options

The View tab contains options that affect how PowerPoint appears on-screen. See Figure 35-1. There are three sections:

✦ **Show:** Defines how things appear in all views except Slide Show.

✦ **Slide Show:** Defines how things appear in Slide Show view.

✦ **Default View:** Defines which view is used for opening previously saved and closed files.

Figure 35-1: The View tab of the Options dialog box controls which elements are visible on-screen.

Here are explanations of the Show items:

✦ **Startup Task Pane:** Clear this check box if you do not want the task pane to appear each time you start PowerPoint. Each new presentation you start after clearing this option will by default begin with a blank presentation.

✦ **Slide Layout Task Pane When Inserting New Slides:** Clear this check box if you do not want the Slide Layout task pane to appear each time you create a new slide. If you do so, you won't have to choose a layout for a new slide; all new slides will have the Title and Text layout.

✦ **Status Bar:** Clear this check box to suppress the display of the status bar.

✦ **Vertical Ruler:** Clear this check box to suppress the display of the vertical ruler (when rulers are displayed at all). Remember, you can turn rulers on or off with the View ➪ Ruler command in PowerPoint.

✦ **Windows in Taskbar:** If you want each presentation to appear as a separate taskbar item when multiple presentations are open, leave this marked. If you would prefer that PowerPoint work the old way, with a single taskbar item for PowerPoint, clear this box.

Here are explanations of the Slide Show items:

✦ **Popup Menu on Right Mouse Click:** Clearing this check box allows you to move backwards, instead of accessing the shortcut menu, by right-clicking during a slide show.

✦ **Show Popup Menu Button:** Clear this check box to suppress the shortcut buttons and attached menus that normally appear on the lower-left corner of the slide when you move the mouse during a slide show.

✦ **End with Black Slide:** Deselect this option if you do not want a black slide after the last slide in the show.

The final section, Default View, contains only one setting. The Open All Documents Using this View drop-down list enables you to specify a starting view. The default is to reopen the file in whatever view it was last saved in. You can choose a specific view if you prefer, however. There are actually a lot of different viewing choices — more than just Normal and Slide Sorter. See Figure 35-2.

Figure 35-2: Select the view in which to open presentation files.

General options

Most of the customization I do to PowerPoint comes from the General tab. See Figure 35-3. It contains the features that I most want to tinker with. This may be the case for you too! Take a look at what the General tab offers:

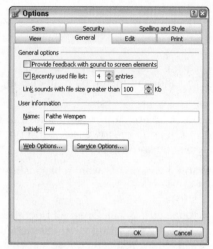

Figure 35-3: General options affect the way PowerPoint operates in general, rather than in a specific area.

✦ **Provide Feedback with Sound to Screen Elements:** When this feature is on, PowerPoint plays the sounds associated with various system events. (You set these up from the Windows Control Panel's Sound feature.) Most people find these annoying after the first ten minutes and turn this feature back off again.

✦ **Recently Used File List:** As you learned in Chapter 3, one way to open a file that you have recently used is to select it from the bottom of the File menu. The File menu, by default, lists the four most recently used files. To increase or decrease this number, change the number in this text box. Or, turn off the feature completely by deselecting the check box.

✦ **Link Sounds with File Size Greater Than:** When you place a WAV sound file in a presentation, PowerPoint creates a link to it, rather than including it in the actual presentation file, if it is larger than the size you list here. This keeps the presentation file from growing too large. For sounds smaller than the listed size, PowerPoint embeds a copy of the sound right in the presentation. You can increase this number up to 50000K, which will embed any WAV file under 50MB. (All other sound files are linked, regardless of size.)

✦ **Name** and **Initials:** Fill in your name and initials in these fields if they don't already appear there. PowerPoint uses this information in several ways, including placing it on the Properties sheet (File ⇨ Properties) and filling it in on certain forms and templates.

✦ **Web Options:** Clicking this button opens the Web Options dialog box, where you can specify how PowerPoint exports presentations to HTML format. I explain this box thoroughly in Chapter 30, so I won't rehash it here. If you find yourself changing certain settings consistently when using File ⇨ Save as Web Page, changing them here instead will save you from having to change them each time.

✦ **Service Options:** This button opens the Service Options dialog box, shown in Figure 35-4, where you can choose settings for shared workspaces, privacy, and online content:

  • **Online Content:** Choose when PowerPoint should connect to Microsoft.com as you work. If you allow it to connect, you get more media clips, more templates, and any other available optional content downloads, as well as more extensive help information. However, if you do not have an always-on Internet connection, there may be delays while it connects to the Internet (or tries to) each time.

  • **Privacy:** Choose whether to participate in Microsoft's Customer Experience Improvement Program by allowing Microsoft to gather non-identifiable data about your work habits.

  • **Shared Workspace:** Set the options for accessing shared workspaces. This is covered in detail in Chapter 33.

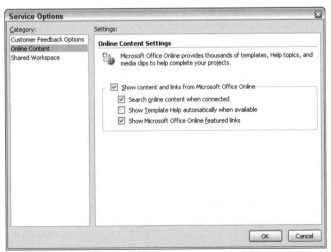

Figure 35-4: Service options govern the way PowerPoint interacts with Microsoft-provided online content and what information is sent to Microsoft.

Edit options

On the Edit tab, you find a variety of options that affect the way PowerPoint works as you create and change objects on slides. See Figure 35-5. Setting these options the way you feel most comfortable can be a big time-saver and frustration-eliminator. Here are some examples:

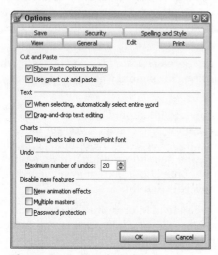

Figure 35-5: Use the Edit tab to set up how PowerPoint behaves when you enter and edit content.

✦ **Show Paste Options Buttons:** When this option is on and you paste text that has manual formatting applied to it, a Smart Tag icon appears next to the pasted material. You can open its drop-down list and choose how you want the item to be pasted. See Figure 35-6.

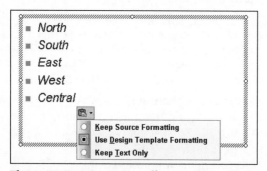

Figure 35-6: A Smart Tag offers pasting options.

✦ **Use Smart Cut and Paste:** When this feature is enabled and you move things around with the Cut, Copy, and Paste commands, PowerPoint automatically removes excess spaces and adds spaces when needed.

✦ **When Selecting, Automatically Select Entire Word:** If this check box is marked and you select part of a word, the entire word becomes selected, along with the white space after it.

✦ **Drag-and-drop Text Editing:** Drag and drop is a great feature that enables you to move text from place to place by dragging with the mouse. Most people leave this feature turned on; however, if you don't use the feature and find yourself accidentally moving things when you didn't mean to, you can turn off the feature.

✦ **New Charts Take on PowerPoint Font:** This option sets the font for inserted charts at 18-point. Clear the check box to use the chart's own fonts.

✦ **Maximum Number of Undos:** This is the number of actions that PowerPoint remembers so you can undo them with the Edit ➪ Undo command or the Undo toolbar button. The higher the number, the more overhead used up by this remembering, so do not increase this number much past 20.

✦ **Disable New Features:** This section contains check boxes for several of the features that are new to PowerPoint 2003. If you share files with someone who uses an earlier version of PowerPoint, you might need to disable some or all of these features.

Print options

PowerPoint can print a variety of handouts, notes, and other items, and the Print tab lets you fine-tune the printing process. See Figure 35-7.

✦ **Background Printing:** If you clear this check box, you won't be able to continue to use PowerPoint after issuing the Print command until the print job has been completely sent to the printer. On the other hand, turning off background printing can actually speed up printing in some cases. Bear in mind that it has nothing to do with printing the background of your slides.

✦ **Print TrueType Fonts as Graphics:** This option sends your presentation's TrueType fonts to the printer as pictures rather than as outline font images. If you are having trouble with your printer running out of memory or misprinting fonts during a print job, experiment with this setting; sometimes changing it can make a difference.

✦ **Print Inserted Objects at Printer Resolution:** If an inserted object has a higher graphic resolution than your printer supports, this option dumbs down the object to match the printer's capabilities, thereby decreasing the size of the print file and making it print faster.

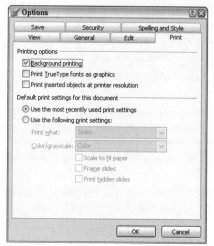

Figure 35-7: The Print tab controls determine how your printouts will print.

✦ **Default Print Settings for this Document:** This option controls what happens when you click the Print button on the Standard toolbar. There are two choices here: Use the most recently used print settings, and Use the following default print settings. If you choose the latter, several additional controls become available at the bottom of the dialog box to enable you to specify your preferences. As the section title implies, these settings are applicable only for the active presentation.

Save options

On the Save tab, you find a number of settings that specify what happens when you save your work in PowerPoint. See Figure 35-8.

✦ **Allow Fast Saves:** Fast saves speed up the saving process by saving only the changes to the presentation each time you save. When you are ready to save the presentation for the final time, if you clear this check box temporarily, you get a full resave of the entire file, which may result in a smaller file size. Although this may have been a useful feature in the early days of computing, with today's computers, you can't really tell a difference in save time with or without Fast Saves. Fast saves has been implicated (albeit anecdotally) in causing document corruption, and it most definitely causes bloated file sizes. It's recommended that you uncheck this option.

✦ **Prompt for File Properties:** If this box is marked, the first time you save a file, the File Properties dialog box appears, prompting you to enter extra information about the file. Some organizations manage their presentation files based on this extra information; most people ignore it.

Figure 35-8: The Save tab controls how your presentation is saved.

✦ **Save AutoRecover Info Every ____ Minutes:** PowerPoint periodically saves your work in an AutoRecover file so that if the power goes out before you have saved your work, all is not lost. You can specify the interval at which this occurs; 10 minutes is the default.

Caution

A lot of people misunderstand the AutoRecover feature. It does not save your work in the same sense that the Save command does. You cannot use it as a substitute for normal saving. Instead, it saves a hidden, temporary copy of your work that is not accessible by normal means. If PowerPoint terminates abnormally, the next time it starts, it reopens any AutoRecover-saved file that it finds. When you exit PowerPoint normally, all AutoRecover-saved files are deleted, as if they never existed.

✦ **Convert Charts When Saving on Previous Version:** When this is enabled and you save the file in an earlier PowerPoint format, any charts are converted to be compatible with that format, even if it means losing chart features.

✦ **Save PowerPoint Files As:** You can save your PowerPoint files by default in any of several PowerPoint formats, including Web page, single file Web page, or previous PowerPoint versions. Unless your recipient uses PowerPoint 95, you will never need to use the previous version format. (See Chapter 3 for details.)

✦ **Default File Location:** By default, PowerPoint saves your work in the My Documents folder. You can change this setting by entering any drive and folder you want.

✦ **Embed TrueType Fonts:** This setting is for the current presentation only. The check box specifies whether TrueType fonts should be embedded when the presentation is saved. It makes the file larger, but it can enable the presentation to be shown on another PC that might not have the same fonts installed. The option buttons below the check box pertain to how the fonts will be embedded. If you embed characters in use only, you might not be able to make changes to text and still have it appear in the same font. However, that option does make the file size slightly smaller. If you're planning to embed your fonts before moving your presentation to another computer, be sure to verify early in the creation process that your font can be embedded, as not all fonts can; it depends on the font manufacturer's specifications.

Spelling and style options

On the Spelling and Style tab, shown in Figure 35-9, you find settings that control the way the Spelling program runs in PowerPoint and that turn on/off and control the Style Checker. (Chapter 10 covers these features in detail.)

Figure 35-9: The Spelling and Style tab lets you fine-tune these two proofreading features.

✦ **Check Spelling as You Type:** This option does just what it says; deselect this box if you do not want PowerPoint to run a spelling check in the background as you work.

✦ **Hide All Spelling Errors:** Marking this check box suppresses the wavy red lines that indicate spelling errors on a slide.

✦ **Always Suggest Corrections:** This option controls whether PowerPoint offers spelling suggestions. If this option is turned off, you must click the Suggest button in the Spelling dialog box to see the suggestions. Turning this off can speed up the spell check somewhat on slower computers.

✦ **Ignore Words in UPPERCASE:** When this check box is marked, all-uppercase words are not spell-checked.

✦ **Ignore Words with Numbers:** When this check box is marked, strings of letters that contain numbers are not spell-checked.

✦ **Check Style:** This check box enables and disables the style checker.

✦ **Style Options:** Click this button to open the Style Options dialog box, described in Chapter 10, where you can configure how the Style Checker works.

Security options

Most of the security options were covered in Chapter 3, where you learned about saving your work. Figure 35-10 shows the Security tab, with these options:

Figure 35-10: The Security Options tab helps you set the appropriate level of security for your presentation.

✦ **Password to Open:** Enter a password here that someone must enter in order to open the file.

✦ **Password to Modify:** Enter a password here that someone must enter in order to save changes to the file.

✦ **Advanced:** Click here to open a box containing choices of encryption methods to use.

✦ **Digital Signatures:** Use this box to manage any digital signatures set up for the document. You can then manage macro security according to the digital signatures.

Expert Tip

You can get digital certificates from companies such as VeriSign (www.verisign. com). You can also generate your own digital signatures with the selfcert.exe tool included with Microsoft Office, although with your own signatures there is no centrally accessible signature authority to verify the integrity. To find out more about using digital signatures, click the Digital Signatures button and then click the Help button.

✦ **Macro Security:** Click this button to open the Security dialog box, shown in Figure 35-11. From there, choose High, Medium, or Low security level for running macros. Macros are covered in Chapter 36. You can also set up certain certificates to be trusted on the Trusted Publishers tab. Note that you have to change your security settings to Medium or Low to install many PowerPoint add-ins.

Figure 35-11: The Security dialog box enables you to set a security level for trusting that macros do not contain harmful content.

Note

Although they are not part of the main Options dialog box, the AutoCorrect options are also an important customization feature to consider. Access them through the Tools ⇨ AutoCorrect Options command. These control PowerPoint's behavior in such areas as SmartTags, AutoFormat As You Type, and AutoFit.

Customizing Toolbars and Menus

The toolbars and menus in PowerPoint change depending on what you're doing. For example, in Slide Sorter view, the Slide Sorter toolbar appears; it goes away when you switch to another view. And when you're working on a picture, the Picture toolbar appears. When a chart is selected, a Chart menu appears; it goes away when you click away from the chart.

In Chapter 2, you learned that you can display and hide toolbars by right-clicking a toolbar and selecting from the pop-up list. You can also customize a toolbar or menu to show the buttons you want it to display. You might remove buttons or commands that you never use, for example, or add buttons for features that you frequently use. You can even add entirely new toolbars and menus of your own, and populate them with any commands you like.

Modifying toolbars with drag-and-drop

Not all PowerPoint users use the program in the same way, and you may find that you frequently use a few commands for which there are no buttons on any of the toolbars. For example, perhaps you often apply the superscript attribute to text. Because there is no toolbar button for superscripting, each time you use it you must choose Format ⇨ Font, click the Superscript check box, and then click OK. You can save yourself a lot of time by adding a Superscript button to the Formatting toolbar that toggles the superscript attribute on/off. (You can also create one for subscript if you also use it often.)

To add a new toolbar button, follow these steps:

1. Choose Tools ⇨ Customize. The Customize dialog box opens.

2. Click the Commands tab.

3. Select a menu or toolbar from the Categories list. All the buttons, commands, and options available from that menu or toolbar appear on the Commands list to the right. See Figure 35-12. For example, many commands on the Format menu open dialog boxes full of options. When you select Format in the Categories list, a complete list of all the options from those dialog boxes appears on the Commands list.

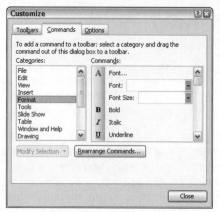

Figure 35-12: Select a category and then select a command within the category.

4. Scroll through the Commands list and select the command that you want to make into a toolbar button. Some of the commands listed have ellipses (. . .) after their names. If you choose one of these, the button you add to the toolbar will open a dialog box or task pane. Others (for example, Font Size in Figure 35-12) have a drop-down list after their names. Choosing one of these places a drop-down list on the toolbar.

Note   Notice in Figure 35-12 that Font appears twice — once with ellipses after it and once with a drop-down list. These are two ways of accessing the list of available fonts. When placing commands on toolbars, make sure that you not only get the right command, but the desired version of it if there is more than one.

5. Drag the command from the Commands list to a toolbar. As you drag onto a toolbar, your pointer becomes a bold vertical line that indicates where the new button will go. When you release the mouse button, the command becomes a button on that toolbar.

6. Repeat Steps 3 through 5 to add more buttons if you want.

7. If you want to remove any buttons from the toolbar, drag them away from the toolbar and release.

8. When you're finished, click Close.

As you saw in Step 7, when the Customize dialog box is open, not only can you add buttons, but you can also remove them. You can also rearrange buttons by dragging them from one toolbar to another or from one spot to another on the same toolbar.

Caution   When the Customize dialog box is open, none of the menu commands and toolbars works normally; instead, they respond to your dragging them around. So don't try to use any of the menus when the Customize dialog box is open (for example, don't try Edit ⇨ Undo to reverse a button-dragging action), or you might accidentally make a change to the menu itself.

Modifying menus with drag-and-drop

Customizing menus is a lot like customizing toolbars, but for some reason many people are more afraid of doing it. It's not complicated, really. When the Customize dialog box is open, the menus become customizable, just like the toolbars. With the Customize dialog box open, you can do the following:

✦ Drag a menu from one spot to another to rearrange the order in which menus appear.

✦ Drag a menu away from the menu bar to remove it (not recommended, because you won't have access to its commands anymore).

✦ Click a menu to open it and then drag a command to a different spot on the menu (or off the menu completely to remove it).

✦ Rename a menu by right-clicking it and typing a new name in the Name text box on the shortcut menu.

Modifying toolbars and menus with the Rearrange Commands dialog box

If you find it difficult to get the right buttons and menu items placed correctly with the drag-and-drop method explained in the preceding sections, try this one instead. It's a new feature of Office 2003. It works for both toolbars and menus.

1. Choose Tools ➪ Customize and click the Commands tab, displaying the screen shown in Figure 35-12.

2. Click the Rearrange Commands button. A Rearrange Commands dialog box opens. See Figure 35-13.

Figure 35-13: Select a menu or toolbar and then move commands around on it, add commands, or delete them.

3. Click the Menu Bar or Toolbar button at the top, indicating what you want to edit.

4. Open the drop-down list for the category you chose in Step 3 and select the desired menu or toolbar name.

5. Do any of the following:

   • To add, click the Add button and then select a command or button to add from the Add Command dialog box. This is the same list of commands as was seen on the Commands tab in Figure 35-12.

   • To delete, click the item to delete on the Controls list and click the Delete button.

   • To rearrange, click the item to move and then click the Move Up or Move Down button.

 Note The Modify Selection button opens a menu of commands that pertain to the chosen menu command or toolbar button. You'll look at these in more detail later in the chapter, but you can play with them on your own now if you like.

6. When you are finished, return to Step 3 and select another menu or toolbar or click Close to close the dialog box.

Resetting a toolbar or menu

If you make mistakes in customizing one of PowerPoint's toolbars, you can undo your changes by selecting the toolbar from the Toolbars tab of the Customize dialog box and clicking the Reset button. This works only with the toolbars that come with PowerPoint, not toolbars and menus you have created.

You can't reset menus that way, however. To reset a menu, open the Rearrange Commands dialog box (Figure 35-13), select the menu, and then click the Reset button. A confirmation box appears; click OK. This method also works for toolbars.

Creating new toolbars and menus

Sometimes a nip and tuck at an existing toolbar just isn't enough. Perhaps you need to add 10 buttons — there won't be enough room for them on an existing toolbar! In cases like that, it's best to create a new toolbar. For example, if you work a lot with multiple presentations, frequently arranging the panes for various purposes, you might want to create a window-arranging toolbar that contains buttons that cascade, arrange all, and so on.

Creating a toolbar

To create a toolbar, follow these steps:

1. Choose Tools ➪ Customize and click the Toolbars tab.

2. Click the New button. The New Toolbar dialog box appears. See Figure 35-14.

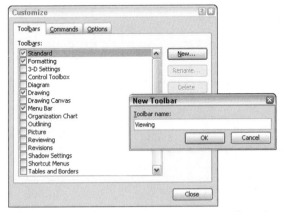

Figure 35-14: You can create your own toolbars from here.

3. Type a name for the new toolbar in the Toolbar Name text box (for example, Viewing in Figure 35-14) and click OK. A little floating window appears alongside the Customize dialog box. This is your new toolbar. See Figure 35-15.

 Note   If you don't see the new toolbar, drag the title bar of the dialog box to move it. The new toolbar might be behind it.

4. *(Optional)* If you want the new toolbar to be anchored at the top of the screen, like the other toolbars, drag its title bar up to the position where you want it. See Figure 35-16.

 Expert Tip   If you plan to use the toolbar in its docked position at the top or bottom of the screen, drag it into place (Step 4) before you add buttons to it (Step 5). That way, you can gauge how many buttons can fit on the toolbar without running off the screen.

5. Add buttons to the new toolbar, as you learned earlier in the chapter. You can either use the drag-and-drop method or the Rearrange Commands method.

6. When you are finished, click Close.

New toolbar

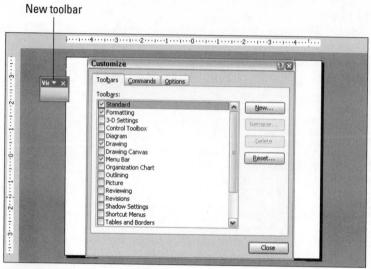

Figure 35-15: Your new toolbar is empty, so it is small. It gets larger as you add buttons.

Drag and drop commands onto the new toolbar

Drag toolbar by its right edge to move it

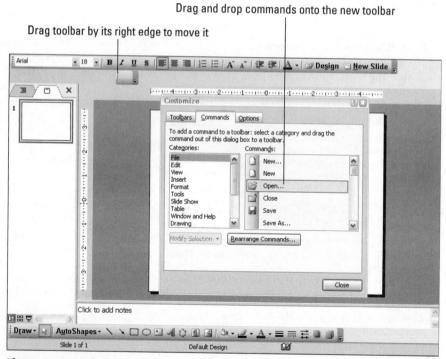

Figure 35-16: When the toolbar is anchored (docked), it no longer has a title bar.

Creating a menu

You can also create your own new menus and add commands to them. To create a new menu, follow these steps:

1. If the Customize dialog box is not open, open it (Tools ⇨ Customize).

2. Click the Commands tab.

3. Choose New Menu at the bottom of the Categories list. See Figure 35-17.

Figure 35-17: Choose New Menu from the Categories list and then drag the words "New Menu" from the Commands list to the menu bar.

4. Drag the words *New Menu* from the Commands list to the spot on the menu bar where you want the new menu. The new menu appears with the name *New Menu*.

5. To change the menu name, right-click it and type a new name in the Name text box. Press Enter when you're finished.

6. To add commands to the menu, locate the command you want to add on the Commands list (after choosing the appropriate category) and drag it up to the new menu. When the mouse pointer touches the new menu, the menu opens, so you can drag the command onto it. Then release the mouse button.

7. Repeat Step 6, filling your new menu with the commands you want.

8. Click Close when you're finished.

Expert Tip   If you right-click one of PowerPoint's default menu's names, you can see that the name of a menu has an ampersand (&) in it. The ampersand precedes the letter that should appear underlined. (Remember, the underlined letter can be pressed along with Alt to open a menu.) For example, F&ormat means the o will appear underlined. When you are naming menus that you create yourself, don't forget to add an ampersand in the name to indicate which letter should be underlined. Make sure you choose a letter that none of the other menu names is currently using as its underlined letter.

Choosing which toolbars to display

You have already learned how to display and hide toolbars — just right-click any toolbar and choose the one you want to display or hide from the shortcut menu. A checkmark means the toolbar is displayed.

Figure 35-15 shows another way to choose which toolbars to display or hide. Each toolbar listed on the Toolbars tab of the Customize dialog box has a check box beside it. Click to place or remove checkmarks to display or hide each toolbar. This method is superior to the other because it gives you the complete list of available toolbars, not the abbreviated list shown in the menu system.

Renaming or deleting your toolbars

You cannot delete the toolbars that come with PowerPoint, but you can delete the custom toolbars you create. To do so, click the check box next to the toolbar's name on the Toolbars tab and then click the Delete button.

Like deleting, renaming works only with toolbars you've created. To rename a toolbar, select it from the Toolbars tab of the Customize dialog box and then click the Rename button. The Rename Toolbar dialog box appears. Type a new name in the Toolbar Name text box and click OK.

Renaming and modifying buttons and commands

Each button, command, drop-down list, or other item on a menu or toolbar has its own properties, which include its name, its icon, the underlined letter in its name, and so on. There are two ways to access these properties:

✦ While the Customize dialog box is open, right-click on a toolbar button or menu command to display its shortcut menu.

✦ From the Rearrange Commands dialog box, select the command and then click the Modify Selection button to open a menu.

Each of these methods results in the same options being displayed, but the latter may be slightly easier to navigate. Figure 35-18 shows a typical menu.

Figure 35-18: Set the properties for an individual button or command through its menu.

Here's a quick look at what you can do with this menu:

✦ **Reset:** Resets the item to its original settings. For example, if you changed its icon, this would reset it to the default icon.

✦ **Delete:** Removes the item from the menu or toolbar on which it currently resides.

✦ **Name:** The text name of the button. This is an issue only if you choose to show the text names of the buttons, or if you put the button on a menu where text display is the default.

✦ **Button Image Commands:** This set of commands enables you to alter the icon associated with the item. You can choose a different icon with Change Button Image, for example, or edit the button in a very simple drawing program with Edit Button Image.

✦ **Style Commands:** This set of commands determines how the item will appear. An item can appear as an icon, as its text name, or with both. For example, most of the buttons on toolbars are set to Text Only (in Menus), which makes them appear as icons only on toolbars. However, the Design and New Slide buttons on the Formatting toolbar are set to Image and Text by default.

✦ **Begin a Group:** When this is selected, a vertical line appears to the left of the button on a toolbar or above the command on a menu. This is used to create groups of buttons on toolbars or groups of commands on menus.

✦ **Assign Hyperlink:** This enables you to create buttons that refer to hyperlinks, which may point to locations outside of PowerPoint.

Setting Toolbar and Menu Options

While the Customize dialog box is open, take a quick look at its Options tab, shown in Figure 35-19. There are a few options here you might find useful:

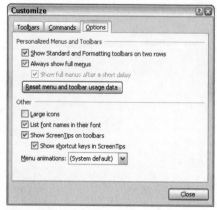

Figure 35-19: The Options tab in the Customize dialog box contains a few miscellaneous settings for menus and toolbars.

✦ **Show Standard and Formatting Toolbars on Two Rows:** You learned about this setting at the beginning of this book. By default, PowerPoint shows these two toolbars on a single row, but you can easily put them on separate rows either by selecting this check box or by manually dragging one of the toolbars to a different row at any time.

✦ **Always Show Full Menus:** When this check box is cleared, PowerPoint displays recently used commands on a menu when you first open it, and then the remaining commands a few seconds later. Mark this check box to display full menus immediately.

✦ **Show Full Menus after a Short Delay:** This option works only in conjunction with the previous one being turned on. If you turn this one off (not recommended), you cannot access the less-used commands from the menu system at all.

✦ **Reset Menu and Toolbar Usage Data:** PowerPoint watches you work to see which commands you use and which toolbar buttons you click. After you use an item, it is placed on a Recently Used list and appears when the menu first opens, or on the toolbar if the display resolution is so low that not all toolbar buttons will fit at once on-screen. To reset the Recently Used list to the default list that comes with PowerPoint, click this button.

✦ **Large Icons:** This option makes the buttons on the toolbars larger. This feature is helpful if you have poor eyesight, but fewer icons fit on the screen at once.

✦ **Show ScreenTips on Toolbars:** Clear this option if you don't want ScreenTips popping up whenever you position your mouse pointer over a toolbar button.

✦ **Show Shortcut Keys in ScreenTips:** Select this check box if you want the ScreenTips to include any shortcut key equivalents for the button.

✦ **Menu Animations:** Open this drop-down list and choose an animation type if you like. This option makes the menus open with more of a flourish, but it may make slower computers run even more slowly.

Summary

In this chapter, you learned how to make PowerPoint your very own by customizing its features, menus, and toolbars. Now there's no excuse for non-productivity because you are free to make PowerPoint work just the way you want it to.

In the next chapter, you learn how to automate your work with macros and how to install and remove add-ins. Macros are sets of recorded steps that you can play back to save time if you do the same lengthy procedures frequently. Add-ins are more complex variants of macros.

✦   ✦   ✦

Extending PowerPoint with Macros and Add-Ins

Macros and add-ins are two ways to improve PowerPoint's functionality.

Macros are recorded sets of steps that you can play back to perform tasks more easily. For example, suppose you frequently need to import your company logo, resize it, and move it to the top-left corner of a slide. You can create a macro that does that, and save yourself several steps.

An *add-in* is a helper file with a .PPA extension that you "add in" to PowerPoint to expand its capabilities. An add-in can do something as simple as adding a new toolbar, or it can be as powerful as adding an entirely new feature set. You probably won't be writing your own add-ins by the end of this chapter, but you will know how to find add-ins and install them.

Recording Macros

Macro recording works a lot like tape recording. You click Record, and PowerPoint records all your actions until you click Stop. The recording is saved under a unique name, and you can play back the recording at any time to re-perform the actions.

You can also write your own macros using the Visual Basic Editor provided in PowerPoint, but this gets a little tricky. To write macros, rather than record them, you must know something about Visual Basic programming, and this book does not assume that you know that. (It's really fascinating stuff, though — take a class!) However, if you need to make a minor change to a recorded macro, such as removing a command that you didn't mean to record, the Visual Basic Editor works well even for non-techies. You learn to work with the Visual Basic Editor later in this chapter.

Here are some ideas for using macros:

✦ Insert boilerplate text, such as disclaimers.

✦ Apply a complex set of formatting, such as text size, paragraph alignment, and line spacing.

✦ Insert the company logo.

✦ Set a default slide transition effect for the presentation.

✦ Create a graph from a selected table and place it on a slide.

Planning your macro

Before you record a macro, *think*. Think about exactly what you want to record, and from what position you want to start. Keep in mind that everything you do after clicking Record will be recorded. For example, suppose you want to create a macro that applies certain formatting to text. You already know that before you can format text, you must select it, but you don't want the text selection to be part of the macro, because you will select different text each time. So select some text first, before you start recording. Along those same lines, if you want to record a macro to format graphics in a certain way, select a graphic before you start recording so that the graphic selection won't be part of the macro.

You also need to think about where you are going to store the macro. If the macro should be used only in the active presentation, record it while that presentation is open. If you want it to be available in every presentation based on a certain template, open that template. (Remember to delete any dummy content that you create in the process of recording the macro in the template so that content does not become part of the template.)

Recording a macro

When you're sure you know what you need to do and you're sure you want to start recording, follow these steps:

1. Choose Tools ⇨ Macro ⇨ Record New Macro. The Record Macro dialog box opens.

2. Enter a name for the macro in the Macro Name box. Be descriptive. For example, if you plan to record a macro that makes text bold, italic, and underlined, you might call it *BoldItalicUnderline*. See Figure 36-1.

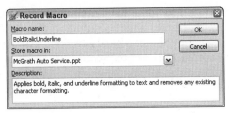

Figure 36-1: Name your macro and enter a description for it if desired.

Macro names must begin with a letter and can contain up to 80 characters. You can't use any spaces, and no symbols are allowed except the underscore character. You also can't use any Visual Basic keywords for the name, such as `Private`, `Public`, `Integer`, or `Sub`.

3. If you have more than one presentation or template open, choose the one in which you want to store the macro from the Store Macro In drop-down list.

4. *(Optional)* Edit the description in the Description box, if desired. This is a good place to put an explanation of what the macro does if the name is not self-explanatory.

5. Click OK. A tiny floating toolbar appears with a square in it, as shown in Figure 36-2. That is the Macro toolbar, and that square is the Stop button. You can click it at any time to stop the recording.

6. Perform the steps that you want to record.

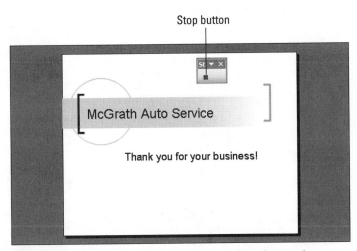

Figure 36-2: The Macro toolbar provides a Stop button for stopping the recording.

Caution When you are recording, you can use the mouse to click commands and options, but any mouse movements involving content selection or navigation are ignored. For example, if you move the insertion point or select an object, that action isn't recorded. You must use the keyboard if you need to record such activities. Certain toolbar buttons' actions aren't recognized, either. For example, the Increase Font Size and Decrease Font Size buttons can't be recorded.

7. When you are finished, click the Stop button to stop recording.

When you finish the previous steps, the Macro toolbar goes away, and it's as if nothing has happened. But don't be fooled; your macro is safely hidden away. Use the steps in the following section to play it back.

Playing a Macro

There are two ways to play a macro. The basic way is to use Tools ⇨ Macro ⇨ Macros, as outlined in the following section, but that's not terribly convenient. The alternative takes more time to set up but is easier in the long run — assigning the macro to a toolbar button or menu.

Playing the macro from the Macro dialog box

Here's the most straightforward way to play a macro. It doesn't require any special setup:

1. Choose Tools ⇨ Macro ⇨ Macros or press Alt+F8. The Macro dialog box opens. See Figure 36-3.

2. If the macro is not in the active presentation, open the Macro In drop-down list and choose All Open Presentations.

Figure 36-3: Choose a macro and then click Run.

3. Select the macro from the Macro Name list if more than one is listed.

4. Click Run. The macro runs.

If you're thinking "That's too much work!" see the following section for steps that make it easier to run that macro.

Expert Tip To play a macro from the Macro dialog box, the presentation or template in which you created it must be open. However, you can use a macro toolbar button regardless of which presentation is open. Therefore, it's a good idea to create a special Macros toolbar and place buttons for all your macros on it. That way, all macros are available in all presentations.

Assigning a toolbar button to a macro

In Chapter 35, you learned how to modify toolbars by adding your own buttons for common commands. But you can add buttons for macros, too, and it's just as easy as adding any other button. Follow these steps:

1. Choose Tools ➪ Customize. The Customize dialog box appears.

2. Click the Commands tab.

3. Scroll down the Categories list and select Macros. A list of all the macros in the active presentation appears. See Figure 36-4.

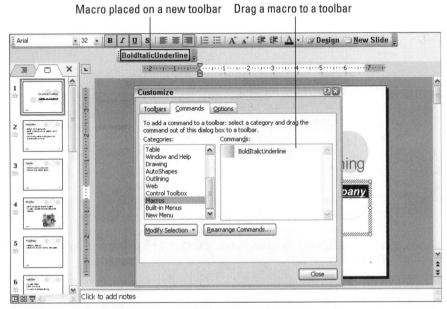

Figure 36-4: Drag a macro to a toolbar to create a button for it.

4. Drag the macro from the Commands box to a toolbar. (Create a new toolbar if you want, as explained in Chapter 35.)

5. *(Optional)* To change the button name, right-click the button and type a new name in the Name box. Or, to add a picture, right-click the button, choose Change Button Image, and then click one of the pictures displayed. See Figure 36-5.

Right click button for menu

Change button text

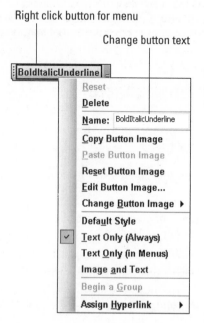

Figure 36-5: Change the button's name or choose a picture to use instead of or in addition to a name.

6. *(Optional)* If you want to use the image alone (without the button text), right-click the button and choose Default Style.

7. When you have finished creating the button, click Close to close the Customize dialog box.

You can also create ActiveX controls in PowerPoint 2003 and then write macros using Visual Basic for Applications for those controls. For example, you might add an ActiveX command button to a slide and then write a script defining what will happen when the user clicks that button. To place ActiveX controls on slides, view the Control Toolbox toolbar (View ➪ Toolbars ➪ Control Toolbox) and use the tools there to place the controls. Then right-click a control and choose View Code to edit the code behind it.

Editing a Macro with Visual Basic

When you're recording a macro, errors inevitably occur. Perhaps you meant to click the Bold button and clicked the Italic button instead, so you had to turn italics back off again. Or maybe you opened the wrong menu.

If the macro performs its function, even with the errors, you might want to leave it alone. For example, it doesn't hurt anything if the macro turns Italics on and then off again, because the end result is that it's off. But if there are a lot of mistakes in a complex macro, it can take a little longer for the macro to run. Some people, too, are sticklers for efficiency and can't stand the thought of their macro being longer and more convoluted than necessary, regardless of the performance issues.

To edit a macro, you use the Visual Basic Editor. This is a complex application that might seem intimidating to the non-programmer, but as long as you stick to editing with it, you should be fine.

Follow these steps to edit a macro:

1. Choose Tools ➪ Macro ➪ Macros or press Alt+F8. The Macro dialog box appears (refer back to Figure 36-3).

2. Click the macro you want to edit.

3. Click Edit. The Visual Basic Editor opens with your macro in it. See Figure 36-6. If you have more than one macro recorded in the same file, both macros appear in the Module1 window, regardless of which one you chose.

4. To remove a line from the macro, highlight it and press Delete. You can figure out what a line does by reading it carefully. For example, the following line turns the Bold attribute on by settings its value to True:

   ```
   ActiveWindow.Selection.TextRange.Font.Bold = msoTrue
   ```

5. When you are finished editing the macro, choose File ➪ Close and Return to Microsoft PowerPoint or press Alt+Q. Your changes are automatically saved.

Visual Basic is a rich programming language, and the version of it that works within Office applications (Visual Basic for Applications, or VBA) enables you to write complex macros and even build mini-applications with dialog boxes that run within PowerPoint. This is way beyond what most business users would ever consider doing, but you may nevertheless be curious about the Visual Basic Editor window that you saw in Figure 36-6.

The Visual Basic Editor is divided into three panes: Project, Properties, and Code. The Project window shows a hierarchy of the modules in the presentation. All of the macros you record are stored in Module1, so you don't have to worry about this much. The Properties panel shows the properties for the module. This pane is FYI only too, as far as beginners are concerned.

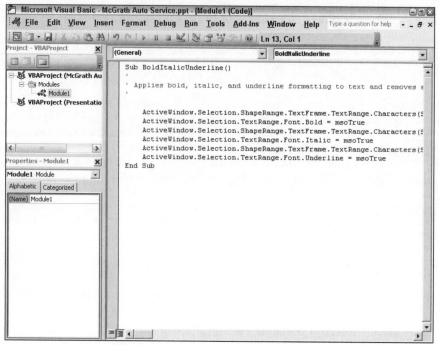

Figure 36-6: The macros in your PowerPoint file open in the Visual Basic Editor.

The main panel that you work with is the Code window, the big one. It contains the lines of programming code that make up your macro.

Here are some things to note about the code:

✦ Each macro begins with the word Sub, followed by the macro name.

✦ Each macro ends with the words End Sub.

✦ Each command of the macro is on its own line.

✦ Some lines begin with | symbols, such as the Macro recorded... line in Figure 36-6. These lines are comments and are ignored when the macro runs.

✦ Each command in the macro narrows down what's being done through a series of words separated by periods. For example, the first line of code in Figure 36-6 starts with ActiveWindow (the active presentation), and then narrows it down to Selection (that is, whatever is selected before you run the macro), then ShapeRange, then TextFrame, then TextRange, and so on.

✦ The indented lines that begin with periods pertain to the path in the unindented line above them. For example, .BOLD=msoFalse means that for the text defined in the string above it, the Bold attribute should be set to False.

If you are interested in learning more about VBA, a good first place to start is the Help system. Don't think, however, that you can teach yourself Visual Basic programming from scratch just by reading the Help system. It's good, but the help there is slanted toward people who already know something about programming. You won't find many easy explanations of how programming works. If you want to write your own Visual Basic macros from scratch, take a Visual Basic class at your local community college.

Deleting a Macro

To delete a macro, follow these steps:

1. Choose Tools ➪ Macro ➪ Macros to open the Macro dialog box.

2. Select the macro you want to delete.

3. Click Delete. A confirmation box appears.

4. Click Yes.

Macro Security

Macros are the primary way that data file viruses spread, so it's good to be cautious about them. For example, a Word macro virus was very common several years ago that forced all documents to be saved as templates rather than as real documents.

Office 2003 offers greatly enhanced security features over earlier versions, especially in the area of macros.

Setting the macro security level in PowerPoint

In PowerPoint you can set three levels of macro security: High, Medium, or Low. These pertain to the types of macros that can be run. The High option runs only signed macros from trusted sources, such as a certificate authority. Medium allows you to choose whether or not to run a macro on an individual basis. Low lets all macros run.

To change the macro security level, follow these steps:

1. Choose Tools ➪ Macros ➪ Security.

2. On the Security Level tab, click High, Medium, or Low. See Figure 36-7.

Figure 36-7: Set the desired security level for running macros.

3. *(Optional)* Click the Trusted Publishers tab to see which macro publishers will be allowed if you chose High. You cannot add to this list from within this window, but you can delete from it.

To add a certificate from a trusted publisher to PowerPoint, see "Adding a Digital Signature to PowerPoint" later in this chapter.

4. Click OK.

Many PowerPoint add-ins that you can download from the Internet will require you to set your macro security to low before they will install. Be sure you trust the author of the add-in before doing so, and don't forget to reset your macro security level to high or medium when finished.

Understanding digital signatures

If you decide to create and distribute macros professionally, the best way to ensure that the macros you write and use have not been tampered with is to get a digital certificate from a certificate authority such as VeriSign and sign all your macro projects with it. A digital certificate is a code that matches up with a code stored with the certificate authority service, to verify that you are a legitimate certificate holder and that your work has not been changed since it was signed.

There are two ways that a digital signature helps in such situations. One is that it identifies the creator of the macro, giving the user a measure of ease in knowing that it has not come from some unknown source. The other is that the certificate authority verifies that it has not been changed.

You can create your own digital signature certificates, but you get only partial bene-fit from them. They do help in telling users who created the macro, but they do not certify that the content of the macro has not been changed. Because they are not connected to any central authority, they do not provide the iron-clad verification of a certificate from a trusted source.

Opening a presentation containing macros

When you open a presentation that contains macros that are signed from trusted sources, the presentation simply opens, even if you have High security set.

For unsigned macros, or macros not from a trusted source, the behavior depends on the Security setting you have chosen. With High, the presentation opens with the macros disabled. With Low, it opens with them disabled. With Medium, the dia-log box shown in Figure 36-8 appears so you can decide what you want to do.

Figure 36-8: When opening a presentation that contains macros, you may be asked about the macros.

Copying Macros between Presentations

A macro usually runs only in the active presentation, or in all open presentations. If you create a macro in one presentation and then close that presentation, the macro is usually not available anymore.

To correct this, you can copy the macro to the other presentation. Macro security must be set to Medium or Low in order to do this.

To copy a macro from one presentation to another, follow these steps:

1. Open both presentations in PowerPoint.
2. Choose Tools ⇨ Macros ⇨ Visual Basic Editor.

3. In the Visual Basic Editor window, in the Project Explorer pane (top-left corner window), drag Module1 from the presentation containing the macros to the presentation that should receive them. See Figure 36-9.

4. Choose File ⇨ Close and Return to Microsoft PowerPoint.

Figure 36-9: Copy macros from one open presentation to another through the VBA Project Explorer pane.

Exporting Macros to a Reusable File

If you want to copy macros into another presentation but the target presentation is not available on the same PC, you can export the macro module into a separate file and then import that file to the target presentation later. When you do this, you save the macros in a Visual Basic file (with a .BAS extension).

To export a macro module, follow these steps:

1. Open the presentation in PowerPoint that contains the macros to export.

2. Choose Tools ⇨ Macros ⇨ Visual Basic Editor.

3. Right-click Module1 in the Project Explorer pane (top left) and choose Export File. An Export File dialog box appears. See Figure 36-10.

4. Choose a name and location for the export and click Save.

5. Choose File ⇨ Close and Return to Microsoft PowerPoint.

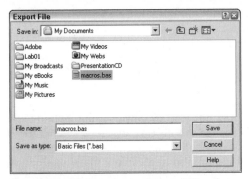

Figure 36-10: Export macros as a Visual Basic module.

To import a macro module into another presentation, follow these steps:

1. Open the presentation in PowerPoint into which the macros should be placed.

2. Choose Tools ➪ Macros ➪ Visual Basic Editor.

3. Right-click the presentation file in the Project Explorer pane and choose Import File. An Import File dialog box appears.

4. Select the exported macro file (.BAS extension) and click Open.

5. Choose File ➪ Close and Return to Microsoft PowerPoint.

Working with Add-Ins

An add-in is a cousin of macros, in that it enables users either to do something more easily that was difficult, or to do something that they couldn't do before without special programming.

Add-ins vary tremendously in terms of their complexity. The high-end add-ins are like full-blown applications; the low-end ones are so subtle you may not even realize they are installed. An add-in typically has a .PPA extension, but some may have .DLL, .EXE, or .PWZ extensions.

Note   One of the coolest high-end add-ins for PowerPoint is Microsoft Producer, which you can get from the Office on the Web Web site (from the Help menu in PowerPoint). It's a utility for creating flashy multimedia presentations that include video and sound. As of this writing, the current version, 1.1, was designed for use with PowerPoint 2000 and 2002; however by the time you read this a new version may be available. It's not just an add-in, but a full standalone application that you can run from outside of PowerPoint.

Finding add-ins

The Web is the best source of PowerPoint add-ins, and one of the best Web sites for listing and categorizing add-ins is Indezine (`www.indezine.com/products/ powerpoint/addin/compatible.html`). You can also find others by typing **PowerPoint add-in** in any search engine.

Expert Tip   If you have an add-in that does not load by default when PowerPoint starts up, but you would like it to do so, see this article at Microsoft's Web site: `http:// support.microsoft.com/?scid=kb;EN-US;q222685`. The article refers to PowerPoint 2000, but the steps are also applicable for later versions. Also check out `www.rdpslides.com/pptfaq/FAQ00031.htm` and `www.mvps.org/skp/ ppafaq.htm` for more information about add-ins.

Installing and removing add-ins

Most add-ins come with their own setup programs, which may or may not automatically install the add-ins in PowerPoint. To check whether a particular add-in is installed, and install it if it isn't yet, follow these steps:

1. Choose Tools ➪ Add-Ins. The Add-Ins dialog box opens. If the add-in is not listed, it is not installed yet. Figure 36-11 shows two add-ins installed.

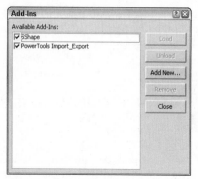

Figure 36-11: The Add-Ins box lists the installed add-ins and enables you to add others.

2. To install another add-in, click Add New. The Add New PowerPoint Add-In dialog box opens. It opens to the `C:\Documents and Settings\{username}\ Application Data\Microsoft\Add-Ins` folder by default, but the add-in might be stored somewhere else.

3. Browse to the folder containing the add-in, select it, and click OK.

Note

If you don't know where the Setup program put the add-in, use the Find or Search feature in Windows to locate files with .PPA extensions.

4. Back in the Add-Ins dialog box, click Close.

You would normally not remove an add-in just to disable it temporarily; for that you would unload it, described in the next section. If you have decided you will not use the add-in anymore, however, you can remove it by clicking it in the Add-Ins box and then clicking Remove.

Loading or unloading an add-in

Notice the check boxes next to the add-ins in Figure 36-12. You can use these to load or unload an add-in. This is useful because you can temporarily remove one without removing it from the handy list in the Add-Ins dialog box. Marking the check box is the same thing as clicking the Load button; clearing it is the same thing as clicking Unload.

Summary

In this chapter, you learned how to automate your work with macros. Macros aren't for everyone — they take some time to set up and may not be worth the trouble if you don't have tasks that you perform over and over the same way. But for those who need them, they can be a real time-saver. You also learned about PowerPoint add-ins, and how to install and remove them.

The next chapter is the final project lab, where you have a chance to practice the full range of PowerPoint skills you have learned from this book.

✦   ✦   ✦

Project Lab: Putting It All Together

This project lab gives you an "extra credit" challenge for practicing many of the skills you learned in this book. Unlike the other project labs in the book, this one doesn't provide the exact steps for accomplishing each task; instead it simply directs you to perform tasks that you should have mastered in earlier chapters. If you don't know how to do something, go back and review. If you can complete this project without looking anything up at all, you have truly mastered PowerPoint.

The Scenario

Literacy for Life, a nonprofit organization, is preparing for a fund-raising event and would like your help in putting together a presentation for it. You will need two copies of the presentation. One copy will be for a speaker-led show during the actual event. The other copy will be a self-running show on a CD that can be distributed to potential donors who were not able to attend the event.

Project 7A: Creating a Speaker-Led Show

Difficulty: Medium

Time to Complete: 30 to 40 minutes

1. Open the Word file **Lab07A.doc** in PowerPoint, and save it as **MyLab07A.ppt**.

2. Apply the **Shimmer.pot** design template.

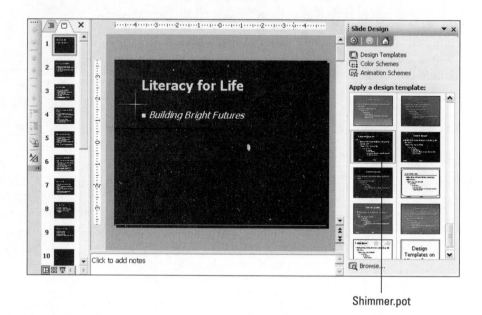

Shimmer.pot

3. Customize the color scheme so that the Background color is a dark green, the Shadow color is a medium green, and the Accent color is bright green.

3

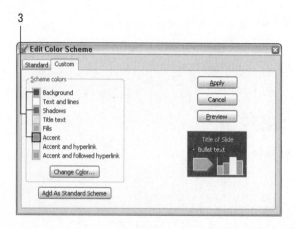

4. Change the layout of the first slide to Title Slide.

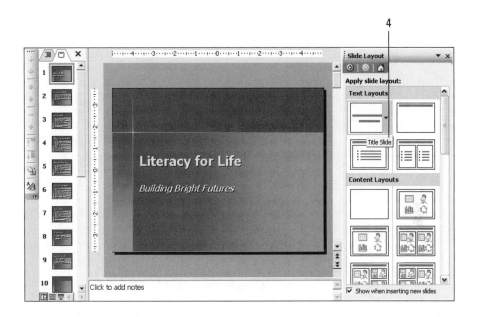

5. Insert a clip art image of a book on the title slide, and arrange the text and picture as needed to make it attractive.

6. Recolor the clip art (if possible) so that it fits in with the color scheme of the presentation attractively.

7. Remove the italic formatting from all the text in the presentation.

8. Insert the picture Lab07A-1.jpg from the Labs folder on slide 2, changing the slide's layout so that the bullet list appears at the left and the picture appears at the right.

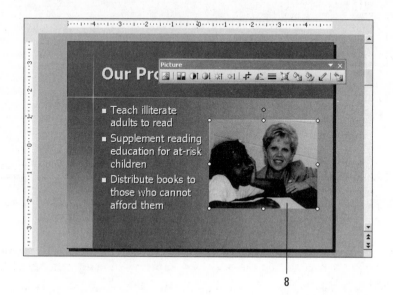

9. Insert the picture Lab07A-2.jpg from the Labs folder on slide 4, changing the slide's layout so that the bullet list appears at the right and the picture appears at the left.

10. Change the size of the text on slide 4 so that it continues to fit on the slide.

    (Hint: use the AutoFit Smart Tag.)

11. Delete the third and fourth bullet points on the slide so that there is more room for the text to be larger. Three bullet points should remain, as shown here.

12. **Insert the picture Lab07A-3.jpg from the Labs folder on slide 5, changing the slide's layout so that the bullet list appears at the left and the picture appears at the right.**

13. **Set the text on slides 5 and 6 to AutoFit to the placeholder.**

14. **Insert a new slide between slides 9 and 10 with a Title and Chart layout. For the new slide's title, type *Current Expenses*. Then for the chart, create a 3D pie with the following data.**

    Staff Salaries $78,000

    Facility Rental $10,400

    Supplies $22,000

    Other $5,000

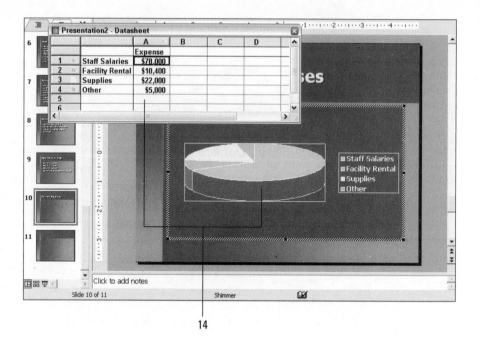

14

15. **Set the 3D rotation for the chart so that the Facility Rental slice is at the bottom, and then explode it out of the pie.**

    (Hint: select the slice and drag it.)

16. **Set the Plot Area border to None, removing the rectangular box around the pie.**

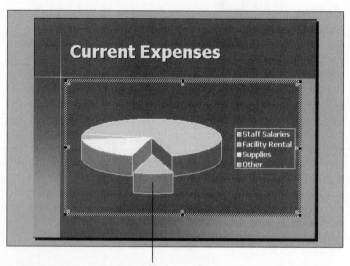

15

17. **Add Category and Value labels to the pie, and remove the legend.**

17

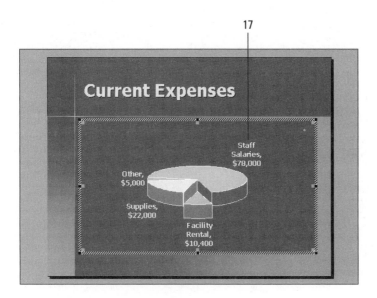

18. **Apply a Fade In custom animation to the chart, so that each of the slices fades in separately on a mouse click.**

18

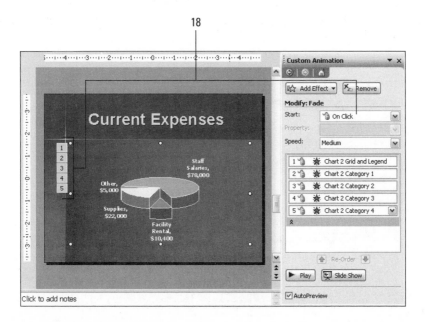

19. **Apply the Push Down transition, Medium speed, to all the slides in the presentation.**

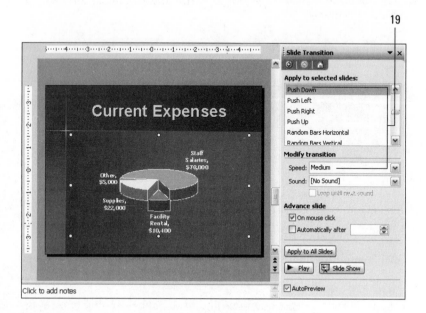

20. **Replace all instances of Tahoma font in the presentation with Arial font.**

21. **Add a CD soundtrack to the entire presentation, using a track from your favorite audio CD.**

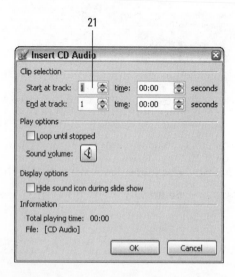

22. On the Slide Master and Title Master, change the title text color to the palest bright green.

23. On the Slide Master only (*not* the Title Master), make the slide title place-holder centered.

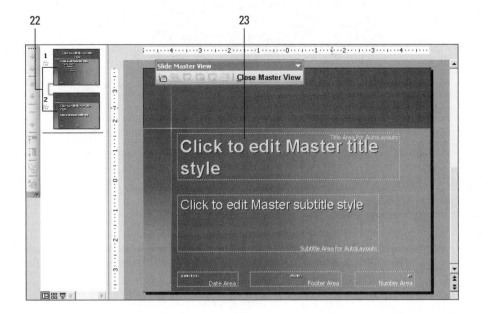

24. Watch the entire presentation to make sure it is okay, and then save your work.

Project 7B: Creating a Self-Running Show on CD

Difficulty: Medium

Time to Complete: 10 to 20 minutes

1. Open the file Lab07B.ppt from the Labs folder and save it as MyLab07B.ppt.

2. Set the transition effect to occur automatically after 30 seconds for all slides.

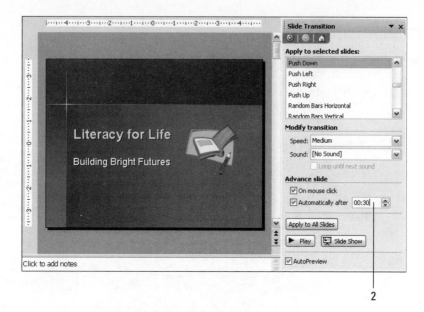

2

3. Set the custom animation on the chart (slide 8) to begin automatically when the slide appears (no mouse click required). Each of the individual slices should still require a mouse click.

3

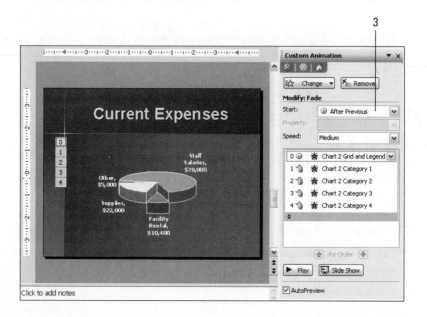

4. In Word, open the file Lab07B.doc, which contains the script for the presentation. Print this out for your reference. Then, using your microphone, record this script as narration for the presentation.

5. After slide 8, insert the four slides from Lab07B-insert.ppt.

5

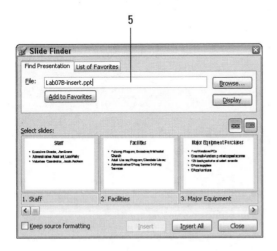

6. Make all of the inserted slides hidden.

7. On slide 8, edit the chart text to change *Supplies* to *Equipment*.

8. Create hot-spot hyperlinks from the labels on the pie chart to each of the hidden slides. To do this, draw a rectangle over the top of a label, set it as a hyperlink to the slide, and then change its border and fill to None.

8

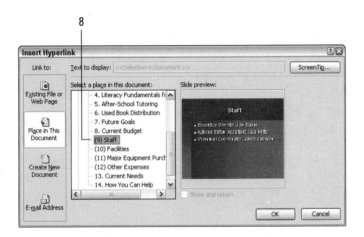

Note

Alternatively, you can draw text boxes over the tops of the labels. You will need to put hard returns in to make the text boxes the right size, but you will not need to set the border and fill to None because it is set that way automatically for text boxes.

9. Near the bottom of slide 8 create a text box that reads *Click a label on the chart for more detail.*

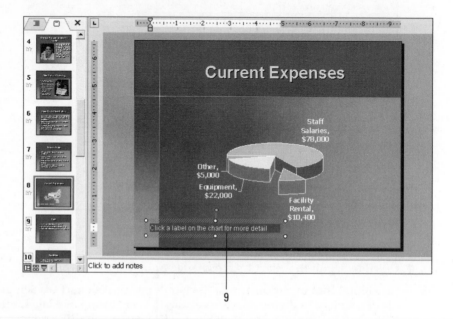

9

10. On each of the hidden slides, create a Return action button that takes the users back to slide 8. Make the button bright yellow with black text.

(Tip: Create the button on one slide, and then copy it to the others.)

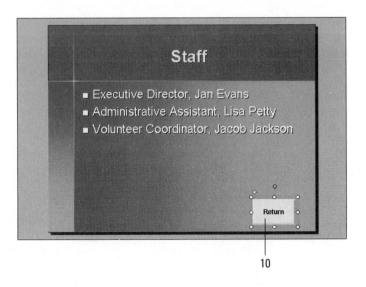

10

11. **Save your work.**

12. **Print a set of 6-per-page handouts for your own reference.**

13. **Publish the presentation to a CD-R.**

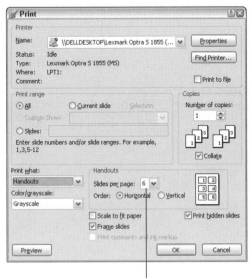

12

13

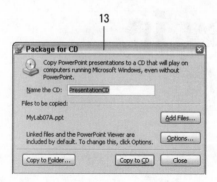

Congratulations, you have completed your final PowerPoint project! You have mastered many of the most useful features of the program, and are ready to create presentations of your own for all occasions and uses.

In the Appendixes section of the book that follows, you will find information about new features in PowerPoint, about installing the application, and about using the CD that is included with this book.

✦   ✦   ✦

What's New in PowerPoint 2003?

Trying to decide whether to upgrade from PowerPoint 2002 or 2000 to PowerPoint 2003? In this appendix you will learn about the differences between these versions to help you make the call.

New Features in PowerPoint 2003

In terms of new features, PowerPoint 2003 is a rather minor update to PowerPoint 2002 (XP), the previous version. However, there are a few really great new features to enjoy!

The PowerPoint Viewer

One of the biggest benefits of PowerPoint 2003 over all earlier versions is its vastly improved version of the PowerPoint Viewer. The PowerPoint Viewer is an external program that you can distribute freely to anyone in your potential audience who might not have a full version of PowerPoint installed on his or her PC. It enables people to watch PowerPoint shows without having to shell out the money to buy PowerPoint. The new viewer is covered in Chapter 25.

The PowerPoint Viewer has not been updated in a long, long time. The last version of it came with PowerPoint 97, and that same old, tired version has been circulating ever since. Because that software was designed to display presentations created in PowerPoint 97, it does not support any of the new features that have been introduced in PowerPoint 2000, 2002, or 2003. That's why this new update is so cool! At last you have a Viewer that can display almost all of the whiz-bang new features that PowerPoint itself can display.

Package for CD

Here's my personal favorite of the new features in PowerPoint 2003. Remember the old Pack and Go feature in earlier PowerPoint versions? You could use it to package a presentation and all its support files in one location so you could transfer it to some other location. That was all well and good, but the Package for CD feature lets you package the presentation—along with the PowerPoint Viewer—directly onto a writeable CD. Nothing has to be installed on the recipient's computer in order for it to run. See Chapter 4 for details.

Windows Media Player support

PowerPoint 2003 lets you play media clips using the same controls as the Windows Media Player, rather than through a separate media player interface. This makes clip-playing faster, easier, and less buggy.

Research pane

All Office 2003 applications now include a Research pane, which is connected to research sites on the Internet. The Thesaurus and Dictionary work as part of this pane now, and you can also look things up in online encyclopedias and news services with just a few clicks. This feature is covered in Chapter 10.

SharePoint team services

Here's another cool new Office-in-general feature for Office 2003 that also works with PowerPoint. With a server application called Windows SharePoint Services, users can set up Web-based SharePoint team sites that enable groups of people to share files and have discussions. This makes it much easier for groups of people to collaborate on draft presentations when they are not physically located in the same place! This is covered in Chapter 33.

Internet faxing

PowerPoint 2003 comes with a Send to Fax Service capability that enables you to fax things without having to actually have a fax machine. It works through the Internet and is a subscription-based service. This is not just for PowerPoint, but for all Office applications.

OneNote and Tablet PC integration

In all Office 2003 applications you can interact with a Tablet PC. For example, in PowerPoint you can use the writing capabilities of a Tablet PC to mark up a presentation and save your marked-up annotations. Handwriting integration is accomplished through a utility called OneNote, which can be used with any PC, not just the Tablet PC. Chapter 34 discusses the OneNote feature.

Saving annotations

And speaking of annotations, with PowerPoint 2003 you can save all those marks, scribbles, notes, or whatever that you jotted down using the Pen feature in Slide Show view. They are called annotations, and you can preserve them after leaving Slide Show view now. See Chapter 25.

More options for pens in Slide Show view

In earlier versions of PowerPoint, you had just one pen type to choose from; in PowerPoint 2003 you have several pen types, each one with a different shape or thickness of "tip." You also can choose from a rainbow of pen colors. Chapter 25 covers this.

Upgrading from PowerPoint 2000?

If the last version of PowerPoint you used was 2000, you'll notice some big changes in PowerPoint 2003. Here's a short list of the most important differences:

✦ **More animations.** There are at least twice as many custom animation choices, and you can use them for entry, emphasis, and exit effects. You can even create path animations now.

✦ **Multiple masters.** Each presentation can have more than one slide and title master, and you can switch easily between them for individual slides via the task pane.

✦ **Task panes.** Many of the activities previously performed in dialog boxes, such as choosing a slide layout, now happen through a task pane.

✦ **Diagrams.** Microsoft Organization Chart has gone away as of Office XP, replaced by a Diagrams tool that is kind of like an extended AutoShape utility.

✦ **Print preview.** Other applications in the Office Suite have always had Print Preview; now PowerPoint has it too.

✦ **Password protection.** In PowerPoint 2002 and higher, you can password-protect the presentation files.

✦ **Save as MHT.** The Single File Web Page format, also known as MHT or MHTML, was new to PowerPoint 2002.

✦   ✦   ✦

Installing PowerPoint

You can purchase PowerPoint by itself or as part of the Office 2003 suite. The latter is the more common way of acquiring it; Microsoft Office is the best-selling business application suite in the world.

Either way, it comes on a CD-ROM, and you must install it on your PC in order to use it. Installation involves several processes:

+ Copying files from the CD to your hard disk.

+ Decompressing files that have been compressed for shipping.

+ Adding information in your Windows configuration files to help Windows recognize PowerPoint.

All of this happens behind the scenes, however; all you do is issue the installation command, and the setup program does the rest.

Caution Microsoft Office 2003 products will not run on Windows 95, 98, or Me. You must have Windows 2000 or Windows XP installed as the operating system.

Using the Setup Program

To start the Setup program, place the Office or PowerPoint CD in your CD-ROM drive. Open the My Computer window and double-click the CD-ROM drive icon, and then double-click Setup.exe.

The Setup program is fairly self-explanatory, except for a few areas. Rather than walk you through the many steps that are easy, I'll save my breath here for the hard stuff. In most cases, you simply follow the prompts, clicking Next to move to the next screen and entering the data requested.

Product key and user information

The very first thing the Setup program asks for is the product key. See Figure B-1. The product key is the 25-character combination of numbers and letters on a sticker on the Office or PowerPoint package you purchased. Enter it and click Next.

Figure B-1: Enter the product key for your copy of Office (or PowerPoint).

Next, it asks for your name, initials, and organization. Of these, only the name is mandatory. Enter the information and click Next.

End user license agreement (EULA)

You must accept the license agreement before you can install. It's a contract that specifies how you can and can't use the software. This is boring legalese, but the crux of it is that you must not use the software on more than one PC or share it on a network without buying a multi-user license. Mark the *I accept the terms in the License Agreement* check box and then click Next to move on.

Expert Tip Different versions of Office or PowerPoint may have different wording in the EULA. Some of them may allow you to install the software on a second PC; others may not. If you think you might want to install it on a second PC, check the wording carefully. On copies that don't allow this, you would be able to install it on other PCs but not activate it there.

Installation type

After the user info and the EULA, you choose the type of installation you want:

✦ **Typical Install:** Installs the most popular portions of all of the Office applications. You can add more of the optional components later if needed.

✦ **Complete Install:** Installs everything, down to the last obscure feature. Use this if you want to never have to locate your Office.NET CD to install another feature, and if you have plenty of hard disk space available.

✦ **Minimal Install:** Installs only the essential files for each application. You may be prompted to insert the Office CD to install features frequently as you work. This is suitable for a system that is running out of hard disk space, but on which you need to install all of the Office applications.

✦ **Custom Install:** Lets you choose which applications and features to install. This is useful for a system where you don't need certain applications. For example, perhaps your company has its own e-mail program and you don't need Outlook, or perhaps you know you are never going to use Access.

In addition, at the bottom of this window is an Install To box. If you want to change the location where Office will be installed, do it here. For example, you might want to install it on a different hard disk if your default hard disk is getting full but you still have plenty of room elsewhere. See Figure B-2.

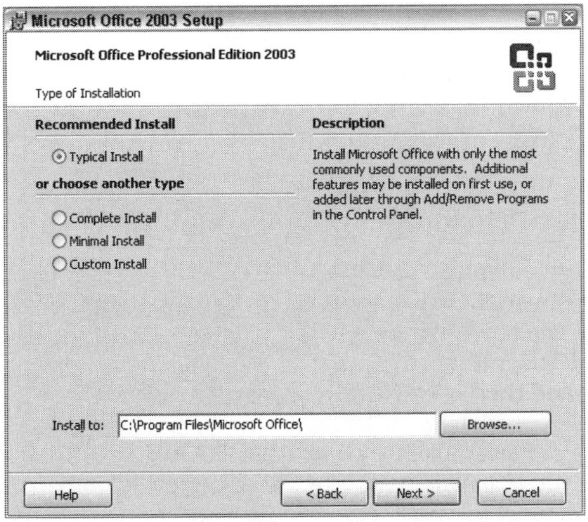

Figure B-2: Choose the type of installation and specify the Install To path.

If you choose Typical, Complete, or Minimal, you can set the book down now and follow along with whatever pops up on your screen, because nothing else will be difficult for you. See "Activating Your Software" later in the chapter for information about your next hurdle.

If you chose Custom Install, however, keep reading.

Selecting applications

If you chose Custom Install, the next thing you see is a list of the applications in Office 2003 with checkmarks next to each one. To choose not to install an application, clear its check box. See Figure B-3.

If you are done customizing at this point, just click Next and then follow the prompts to the completion. The hard part is over for you.

If you want to fine-tune what gets installed even further, however, mark the Choose Advanced Customization of Applications check box, click Next, and then go on to the next section.

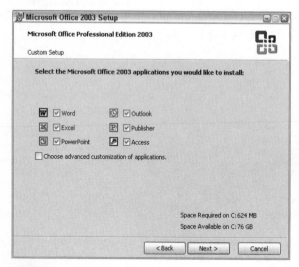

Figure B-3: Clear the check box for any of the applications you don't want.

Customizing application installation

If you chose advanced customization, and you are installing Office rather than just PowerPoint, a tree appears with each of the Office applications as a "branch." You can expand a branch by clicking the plus sign next to it, just like in Windows file management. If you are installing a PowerPoint-only version, only PowerPoint options appear on the tree.

The icons are defined as follows:

✦ **Drive icon with white background:** All features of the component will be installed.

✦ **Drive icon with gray background:** Some features of the component will be installed.

✦ **Red X with white background:** The component will not be installed.

✦ **Drive icon with yellow 1:** The feature will be installed upon first use of it (and you may be prompted for the CD at that time).

Figure B-4 shows examples of each.

For each icon, you can click it to open a menu and then choose a different status. Here are the choices on each menu:

✦ **Run from My Computer:** This means install it. Leave this chosen for the programs you want to be installed.

✦ **Run All from My Computer:** This option sets not only the chosen item to run from your local PC, but also every item subordinate to it on the tree.

✦ **Installed on First Use:** This sets up a link to the program on your hard disk, but does not install the program itself until you activate the link. That way the program is not installed until the last possible moment, so if you end up never needing it, it never takes up the space.

✦ **Not Available:** Choose this option if you don't want to install the application. This is the same as deselecting the application's check box back in Figure B-3.

You may have noticed that besides the Office applications (or PowerPoint features), there are two other big categories: Office Tools and Office Shared Features. Office Tools contains an assortment of add-in programs that work with more than one of the Office programs. It includes the Equation Editor, Microsoft Graph, Microsoft Office Picture Manager, HTML Source Editing, and more. Office Shared Features are utilities and features such as Fonts, the Clip Organizer, Microsoft Handwriting Component, the Office Assistant, and Proofing Tools.

When you are finished making your feature selections, click Next to see a summary of the features you have chosen, and then click Install to start copying the files.

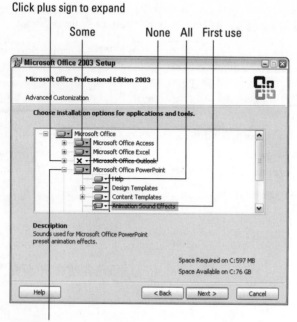

Click plus sign to expand

Some   None All First use

Click minus sign to collapse

Figure B-4: Examples of the various statuses that features can have in a custom install.

Copying the files

While the file copying is taking place, there's nothing to do but be patient. This takes a long time (a half-hour or more on some systems, depending on what you are installing and the speed of the PC). You may not see any progress, and it may even seem like your PC has locked up. It hasn't. Just wait it out.

Finishing the setup and getting Web updates

At the end of the process, you will see a Setup Completed screen containing a check box: Check the Web for updates and additional downloads. Establish your Internet connection if needed, mark this check box, and click Finish. This takes you to the

Product Updates page at Microsoft's Web site. Click Check for Office Updates and allow it to check your PC for any updates or patches you may need.

Activating Your Software

The first time you run any of the Office applications, you will be prompted to activate the software. Activating locks the product key you entered during Setup to this PC's hardware configuration, so it cannot be used on any other PC.

If you are not sure you want to keep Office, let this go the first few times. You can use Office applications up to 50 times before you are forced to activate the software.

 Expert Tip If you are trying to put off activation as long as possible, don't close and reopen the applications. Open an application and then leave it open—indefinitely. Leave your computer on, and leave the application running. The "uses" counter increments each time you start an Office application, and you have 50 uses before you must activate.

If you do decide to activate, make sure your Internet connection is established and then just follow the prompts. It is quick and you don't have to enter any information. After activation, you will be prompted for registration, but this is optional.

If you install or remove hardware from the PC, the activation should hold—unless you install or remove a significant amount of hardware. If that happens you might need to contact Microsoft for help re-activating. The same goes if you get a new PC and want to install the software on your new PC (and your Office license isn't tied to an OEM computer). In those cases, just use the telephone activation instead of the Internet activation when you get to that screen. It's quick and should be painless.

 Expert Tip Maybe you are wondering "isn't there any way to foil this activation thing?" Not really, no. Unlike copy protection schemes of old, this one is pretty hack-proof. If you are a member of an organization that has a site license, though, such as a school system or a large corporation, your copy of Office might not have the activation feature in it. For details about how it works, check out www.microsoft.com/piracy/basics/activation/mpafaq.asp.

Repairing or Reinstalling Microsoft Office or PowerPoint

Should PowerPoint fail to start, or crash frequently, you might need to repair it. This is a fairly simple process. You can repair it directly from within PowerPoint by choosing Help ➪ Detect and Repair.

You can also repair the entire Office installation by doing the following:

1. Insert the Office 2003 CD (or PowerPoint 2003 CD) in your CD drive. Display a listing of the files there, and double-click Setup.exe.

2. On the options list that appears, choose Reinstall or Repair. Then click Next.

3. Choose either Reinstall Office or Detect and Repair Errors in my Office Installation. The latter takes less time, so may be preferable; if you try it and it doesn't help, try again with Reinstall Office.

4. Click Install, and then just wait for the repairs or reinstallation to take place.

Removing Microsoft Office or PowerPoint

Should you ever need to remove Office or PowerPoint from your PC, do the following:

1. Open the Control Panel, and double-click Add or Remove Programs.

2. Find Microsoft Office 2003 (or PowerPoint 2003) on the list, and click it. Two buttons appear: Change and Remove.

3. Click the Remove button, and follow the prompts to remove Office from your PC.

Another way to do it is to insert the Office 2003 or PowerPoint 2003 CD and double-click the Setup.exe file. In the Microsoft Office Setup dialog box that appears, choose Uninstall Microsoft Office and then follow the prompts.

Caution If you bought your PC with Office preinstalled, you might not have a CD that can reinstall it. Check your CDs before you remove Office, lest you end up not being able to get it back. Contact your PC's manufacturer and ask if you are not sure.

✦   ✦   ✦

What's on the CD-ROM?

This appendix provides you with information on the contents of the CD that accompanies this book. For the latest and greatest information, please refer to the ReadMe file located at the root of the CD.

This appendix provides information on the following topics:

✦ System requirements

✦ Using the CD

✦ Files and software on the CD

✦ Troubleshooting

System Requirements

Make sure that your computer meets the minimum system requirements listed in this section. If your computer doesn't match up to most of these requirements, you might have a problem using the contents of the CD.

For Windows 9x, Me, XP, Windows 2000, Windows NT4 (with SP 4 or later):

✦ PC with a Pentium processor running at 120 MHz or faster

✦ At least 32MB of total RAM installed on your computer; for best performance, we recommend at least 64MB

✦ Ethernet network interface card (NIC) or modem with a speed of at least 28,800 bps

✦ A CD-ROM drive

Office 2003 specific requirements:

✦ PC with Pentium 133 MHz or higher processor; Pentium III recommended

✦ Microsoft Windows 2000 with Service Pack 3 or Windows XP or later operating system

  • Minimum of 245MB of hard disk space

  • Minimum of 64MB RAM (128MB RAM recommended)

Using the CD

To install the items from the CD to your hard drive, follow these steps:

1. Insert the CD into your computer's CD-ROM drive.

2. A window appears displaying the License Agreement. Press Accept to continue. Another window appears with the following buttons (which are explained in greater detail in the next section):

   PowerPoint 2003 Bible: Click this button to view an eBook version of the book as well as any author-created content specific to the book, such as the Project Lab files.

   Super Bible: Click this button to view an electronic version of the *Office 2003 Super Bible,* along with any author-created materials from the Super Bible, such as templates and sample files.

   Bonus Software: Click this button to view the list and install the supplied third-party software.

   Related Links: Click this button to open a hyperlinked page of Web sites.

   Other Resources: Click this button to access other Office-related products that you might find useful.

Files and Software on the CD

The following sections provide a summary of the software and other materials available on the CD.

eBook version of *Office 2003 Super Bible*

The *Super Bible* is an eBook PDF file made up of select chapters pulled from the individual Office 2003 *Bible* titles. This eBook also includes some original and exclusive content found only in this *Super Bible.* The products that make up the Microsoft Office 2003 suite have been created to work hand-in-hand. Consequently,

Wiley has created this *Super Bible* to help you master some of the most common features of each of the component products and to learn about some of their inter-operability features as well. This *Super Bible* consists of over 500 pages of content to showcase how Microsoft Office 2003 components work together.

eBook version of *PowerPoint 2003 Bible*

The complete text of the book you hold in your hands is provided on the CD as a PDF file. This searchable file lets you find just the information you need quickly and painlessly.

Lab files

The Project Lab chapters in this book require certain Office data files, and those files are contained in a folder called **Labs**. You can copy this folder to your hard disk or access the files directly from the CD.

Bonus software materials

The CD contains software distributed in various forms: shareware, freeware, GNU software, trials, demos, and evaluation versions. The following list explains how these software versions differ:

✦ **Shareware programs:** Fully functional, trial versions of copyrighted programs. If you like particular programs, you can register with their authors for a nominal fee and receive licenses, enhanced versions, and technical support.

✦ **Freeware programs:** Copyrighted games, applications, and utilities that are free for personal use. Unlike shareware, these programs do not require a fee or provide technical support.

✦ **GNU software:** Software governed by its own license, which is included inside the folder of the GNU product. See the GNU license for more details.

✦ **Trial, demo, or evaluation versions:** Software usually limited either by time or functionality, such as not permitting you to save projects. Some trial versions are very sensitive to system date changes. If you alter your computer's date, the programs may "time out" and will no longer be functional.

Software highlights

Here are descriptions of just a few of the programs available on the CD specifically for PowerPoint users:

✦ **Shyam's Toolbox:** A collection of useful VBA code from Shyam Pillai that allows you to more easily perform specific tasks such as inserting Flash animation, converting OLE objects to graphics, and toggling OLE link updating between manual and automatic.

✦ **Presentation Librarian:** Maintains a searchable database of your presentation files, making it easier to quickly locate a presentation with specific content within a large collection of PowerPoint files. From Accent Technologies.

✦ **Digital Juice:** A collection of royalty-free high quality presentation graphics from Digital Juice, Inc. On the CD, you will find free samples from the much larger collection.

✦ **RnR PPTools Starter Set, Version 2:** A great collection of PowerPoint add-ins from RDP that perform various useful functions. Some of these include prepping a file for PDF conversion, fixing links, and exporting images.

✦ **PowerFinish samples:** A collection of templates and backgrounds for PowerPoint from Studio F.

Comprehensive list of software on the CD

Here is a list of all the products available on the CD. For more information and a description of each product, see the CD Interface Software section of the CD.

A1 "Bible Sounds"	Acc Compact	Access Form Resizer
Access Image Albums	Access Property Editor	Access to VB Object Converter
AccessViewer	ACDSee	Acrobat Reader
ActiveConverter Component	Advanced Disk Catalog	Advanced Office Password Recovery
Analyse-It	Attach for Outlook	Attachment Options
AutoSpell for Microsoft Office	BadBlue Prsnl Ed	Barcode ActiveX Control & DLL
Business Card Creator	c:JAM	Capture Express
CD Case & Label Creator	CD Player	Charset Decoding
Classify for Outlook	ClipMate	Code 128 Fonts demo with VBA
Code Critter	Collage Complete	Colored Toolbar Icons
COM Explorer	CompareDataWiz 2002	CompareWiz 2002
CONTACT Sage	CSE HTML Validator	CSE HTML Validator Pro
Database Password Sniffer	Datahouse	DataMoxie
DataWiz 2002	DeskTop.VBA	Digital Juice
DinkIT Listbar AX	El Scripto	Eliminate Spam!
eNavigator Suite	Excel Import Assistant	EZ-ROM Presentation Pro Edition

Fax4Outlook	FileBox eXtender	Filter Builder
Fort Knox	Fundraising Mentor	Gantt Chart Builder (Access)
Gantt Chart Builder (Excel)	Gif Movie Gear	GraphicsButton
GuruNet	Handout Wizard	HiddenFileDetector_addin
HtmlIndex	HyperCam	HyperSnap-DX
IdiomaX Office Translator	Image Importer Wizard	IT Commander
Judy's TenKey	JustAddCommerce	Lark
Macro Express	Macro Magic	MailWasher Pro
Math Easy for Excel	Mathematical Summary Utility	Mouse Over Effects
MultiNetwork Manager	OfficeBalloonX	OfficeRecovery Enterprise
OfficeSpy	Outcome XP	OutlookSpy
Paint Shop Pro	PhotoSpin Image Sampler	PlanMagic Business
PlanMagic Finance Pro	PlanMagic Marketing	PlanMagic WebQuest
PocketKnife	Polar Spellchecker Component	Power Utility Pak
PowerFinish sample templates	PowerPak	PowerPoint Backgrounds
PowerPoint template samples	Powerpointed	POWERSEARCH Plug-In
Presentation Librarian Persl Ed	Presenters University Templates	PROMODAG StoreLog
QDocs	Recover My Files	Registry Crawler
ReplaceWiz 2002	Responsive Time Logger	RFFlow
RnR PPTools Starter Set	Scan to Outlook	Screen Capture
ScreenTime for Flash	Secrets Keeper	Secure Pack
ShrinkerStretcher	Shyam's Toolbox	Signature995
SimpleRegistry Control	Smart Login	Smart Online templates
SmartBoardXP	SmartDraw	Soft Graphics Buttons
Splitter for Access	StoreBot 2002 Stnd Ed	Style Builder
Style XP	Summary Wizard	SuperFax
TelePort Pro	TeraPod File Transfer for Messenger	Toolbar Doubler

TPH Office Batch Printer	Turbo Browser	TX Text Control
Ulead Gif Animator	UltraPdf	VBAcodePrint
WebCompiler	WebMerge	WebSpice Animation sampler
WebSpice Objects	WinACE	WinFax Pro Automator
WinRAR	WinZIP	Wordware 2002
Wordware PIM	WS_FTP Pro	WS_Ping Propack
X2Net WebCompiler	ZIP Disk Jewel Case and Label Creator	Zip Express
Zip Repair		

ReadMe file

The ReadMe contains the complete descriptions of every piece of bonus software on the CD, as well as other important information about the CD.

Troubleshooting the CD

If you have difficulty installing or using any of the materials on the companion CD, try the following solutions:

✦ **Turn off any anti-virus software that you have running.** Installers sometimes mimic virus activity and can make your computer incorrectly believe that a virus is infecting it. (Be sure to turn the anti-virus software back on later.)

✦ **Close all running programs.** The more programs you're running, the less memory is available to other programs. Installers also typically update files and programs; if you keep other programs running, installation might not work properly.

✦ **Set macro security to low.** This will be necessary when installing PowerPoint add-ins such as RnRPPTools, Shyam's Toolbox, and so on. The macro security settings can be found under Tools ➪ Macro ➪ Security. Be sure to reset the macro security level to high when you've finished installing the add-ins.

✦ **Reference the ReadMe.** Please refer to the ReadMe file located at the root of the CD-ROM for the latest product information at the time of publication.

If you still have trouble with the CD, please call the Wiley Product Technical Support phone number: 1 (800) 762-2974. Outside the United States, call 1 (317) 572-3994. You can also visit www.wiley.com/techsupport. Wiley Publishing, Inc. will provide technical support only for installation and other general quality control items; for technical support on the applications themselves, consult the program's vendor or author. To place additional orders or to request information about other Wiley products, please call (800) 225-5945.

✦   ✦   ✦

Index

Wiley Publishing, Inc.
End-User License Agreement

5. Limited Warranty.

    (a) WPI warrants that the Software and Software Media are free from defects in materials and workmanship under normal use for a period of sixty (60) days from the date of purchase of this Book. If WPI receives notification within the warranty period of defects in materials or workmanship, WPI will replace the defective Software Media.

    (b) WPI AND THE AUTHOR(S) OF THE BOOK DISCLAIM ALL OTHER WARRANTIES, EXPRESS OR IMPLIED, INCLUDING WITHOUT LIMITATION IMPLIED WARRANTIES OF MERCHANTABILITY AND FITNESS FOR A PARTICULAR PURPOSE, WITH RESPECT TO THE SOFTWARE, THE PROGRAMS, THE SOURCE CODE CONTAINED THEREIN, AND/OR THE TECHNIQUES DESCRIBED IN THIS BOOK. WPI DOES NOT WARRANT THAT THE FUNCTIONS CONTAINED IN THE SOFTWARE WILL MEET YOUR REQUIREMENTS OR THAT THE OPERATION OF THE SOFTWARE WILL BE ERROR FREE.

    (c) This limited warranty gives you specific legal rights, and you may have other rights that vary from jurisdiction to jurisdiction.

6. Remedies.

    (a) WPI's entire liability and your exclusive remedy for defects in materials and workmanship shall be limited to replacement of the Software Media, which may be returned to WPI with a copy of your receipt at the following address: Software Media Fulfillment Department, Attn.: *PowerPoint 2003 Bible*, Wiley Publishing, Inc., 10475 Crosspoint Blvd., Indianapolis, IN 46256, or call 1-800-762-2974. Please allow four to six weeks for delivery. This Limited Warranty is void if failure of the Software Media has resulted from accident, abuse, or misapplication. Any replacement Software Media will be warranted for the remainder of the original warranty period or thirty (30) days, whichever is longer.

    (b) In no event shall WPI or the author be liable for any damages whatsoever (including without limitation damages for loss of business profits, business interruption, loss of business information, or any other pecuniary loss) arising from the use of or inability to use the Book or the Software, even if WPI has been advised of the possibility of such damages.

    (c) Because some jurisdictions do not allow the exclusion or limitation of liability for consequential or incidental damages, the above limitation or exclusion may not apply to you.

7. U.S. Government Restricted Rights. Use, duplication, or disclosure of the Software for or on behalf of the United States of America, its agencies and/or instrumentalities "U.S. Government" is subject to restrictions as stated in paragraph (c)(1)(ii) of the Rights in Technical Data and Computer Software clause of DFARS 252.227-7013, or subparagraphs (c) (1) and (2) of the Commercial Computer Software - Restricted Rights clause at FAR 52.227-19, and in similar clauses in the NASA FAR supplement, as applicable.

8. General. This Agreement constitutes the entire understanding of the parties and revokes and supersedes all prior agreements, oral or written, between them and may not be modified or amended except in a writing signed by both parties hereto that specifically refers to this Agreement. This Agreement shall take precedence over any other documents that may be in conflict herewith. If any one or more provisions contained in this Agreement are held by any court or tribunal to be invalid, illegal, or otherwise unenforceable, each and every other provision shall remain in full force and effect.

Where can you find the best information on Microsoft Office 2003?

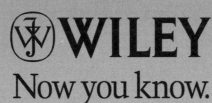

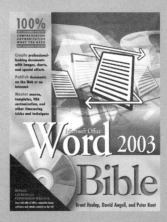
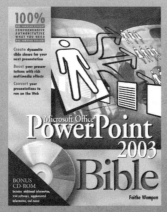
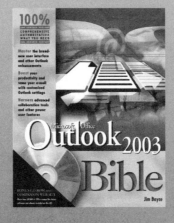